BUSINESS ENGLISH BASICS

A Programmed Approach

BUSINESS ENGLISH BASICS

A Programmed Approach

Ruth Moyer
Colorado State University

John Wiley & Sons
New York   Chichester   Brisbane   Toronto

Editorial and Production Services by
Cobb/Dunlop Publisher Services, Inc.

Library of Congress Cataloging in Publication Data:

Moyer, Ruth, 1924–
  Business English basics.

  Includes index.
  1. English language—Business English.   2. English
language—Programmed instruction.   3. English language—
Grammar—1950–   I. Title.
PE1115.M6   428.2   80-64
ISBN 0-471-04337-0

Printed in the United States of America

10 9 8 7 6 5 4 3 2 1

PREFACE

Business English Basics, a one-volume programmed book, provides an intensive study of English fundamentals within the context of a business environment. The lessons are designed to help a student understand why English fundamentals are important and how to apply the principles in typical, realistic communications (letters, memoranda, reports).

This book can be used under any circumstances in which a self-paced instructional method is feasible to learn or to review English. Students in universities, junior colleges, community colleges, and proprietary schools can improve their background and receive an orientation to the vocabulary in various areas of business before they take a business communications class. Employees in training programs or by self-study can assimilate the content rapidly and apply it to their jobs immediately.

Business English Basics has these features:

1. Comprehensive Coverage
    In addition to grammar and punctuation, format, spelling, vocabulary building, dictionary usage, and number usage are included. All examples and exercises contain business vocabulary and concepts. More practice and exercises are provided for difficult principles (pronoun cases, possessives, sentence structure) than for those which are easier (certain punctuation usages).
2. Business Vocabulary Section (in 24 lessons)
    In this section, a few important words from the vocabulary of a business area or function (direct mail advertising or the production department, for example) are explained. Each section includes questions that require the student to recall or write about the vocabulary.
3. Applying Your Knowledge Section (all lessons)
    Here the student is expected to locate and correct grammatical errors in a letter, memorandum, or report by applying the knowledge gained from the lesson. Because the error and the correct usage are not shown within parentheses, the location and correction of an error are true tests of understanding.
4. Pretest (all lessons)
    Each lesson contains a Pretest to test knowledge of a topic before the lesson is studied. All pretest answers, with the exception of Lesson 1, are in the Appendix and all answers are coded with the number of the frame where the principle is explained. Therefore, the student can identify the parts of the lesson that may need to be emphasized.
5. Frequently Misused Words (5 lessons)
    Each lesson contains explanations, examples, and exercises for approximately 15 pairs of words that are frequently misused (for example, principal/principle). The pretests are in the form of an Applying Your Knowledge section (see item 3 above). The student is requested to write sentences, each correctly using one of the words crossed out in completing the exercise.
6. Teacher's Manual
    A course pretest and postest, each containing 100 items on grammar and punctuation, are included in the Teacher's Manual. Also provided are test keys, answer sheets, a diagnostic sheet, and a diagnostic sheet key.

Without careful, meaningful reviews, any book is a project prepared in isolation and reflects only the author's ideas. Helpful reviews, along with examples and suggestions, were provided by these instructors: Jill Mellick (Golden Gate University), Betty van Meter (Laney College), Marcia Shallcross (Palomar College), Mary Jane Yarborough (Central Carolina Technical Institute), Doris Fleming (Eastern New Mexico University) and Edward Goodin (University of Nevada). Linda H. Yee and Deborah A. Schmidt (Golden Gate University) class-tested the book, providing additional feedback for the final revision.

In addition, Lois Meyer, my colleague and co-author (*Machine Transcription in Modern Business*) agreed to the inclusion of many examples from the Language Skills section of that book. These class-tested examples provide for rapid assimilation of certain principles in specific language skills (capitalization, punctuation, abbreviation, and number usage).

Finally, I sincerely appreciate the time, effort, and interest of Ms. Elizabeth Young, who typed and edited most of the preliminary and all the final manuscript.

Ruth Moyer

CONTENTS

Lesson 1
What Is Business English?

Introduction

Business English is a study of English fundamentals (grammar, punctuation, spelling, word usage, capitalization, and so on) applied to sentences containing the vocabulary and concepts of business. In courses labeled "English," the study of the fundamentals is applied to sentences containing a general vocabulary.

In this book you will study the English fundamentals in the context in which you will use them on the job. In addition, you will apply them to typical internal and external communications (letters, memoranda, and reports) prepared in a business organization.

Oral and written communication skills are needed in nearly every job today. Through the study of business English, you prepare yourself to communicate in a written and oral manner that is acceptable to the business community. Employees who can write and speak well reflect a favorable image of themselves and of the organization for which they work. The image that customers, other business organizations, and the public have of an organization can negatively or positively affect the sales of its goods or services—the lifeblood of any profit-making organization.

A person who writes business communications should be able to achieve these criteria of effective writing:

Criterion	Purpose
1. Correctness	To present the content accurately and without errors in the fundamentals (grammar, spelling, punctuation, word usage, capitalization, number usage, and so on).
2. Clarity	To prepare a communication that can be easily understood on the first reading.
3. Conciseness	To prepare a brief, but complete, communication that includes essential information and excludes nonessential information.
4. Concreteness	To use specific, exact words that are meaningful to the reader.

This course emphasizes these four criteria. With sufficient skill in using them, you will become confident of your ability to communicate on the job. In addition, your ability to apply these criteria will provide you with an excellent background for a course in business communications or report writing.

How to Use This Book

The first seven lessons in this book provide you with the tools of English usage: spelling, dictionary usage, vocabulary building, overview of grammar and sentence construction, and word division. The remaining lessons provide an intensive study of the parts of speech and use of punctuation.

Each lesson contains a *Pretest* to test your knowledge of a topic before you study the lesson. By taking this pretest, you can identify the parts of the lesson that you may need to emphasize. (The pretest in this lesson covers letter format and also includes a proofreading exercise.) With the exception of Lesson 1, all pretest answers are in the Appendix.

This book is prepared in a programmed format, meaning that each part of a lesson is presented to you in a frame (designated by horizontal lines). Each frame contains only the amount of information you need to complete the exercises within the frame. Each frame contains three parts:

1. *Explanation.* Here you are given the rule or guideline that introduces the topic of that frame (see Frame 1, "Letter from an Individual to a Business").
2. *Example.* In this section, the rule or guideline is illustrated for you. Occasionally, you will be asked to answer questions or react to the information. The example in Frame 1 shows an application letter with the parts keyed to an explanation that follows the letter.
3. *Exercise.* Each exercise contains questions that you should be able to answer after having completed the frame (see Frame 1, Exercise).

The answers to each exercise are shown at the end of the frame. The advantage of programmed instruction is that you can discover immediately after completing an exercise if your answers are correct. If you have answered all questions correctly, then you proceed to the next frame; if you have made an error, you should review the information in the frame to determine why you made the error. After satisfying yourself that you know the reason for the error, you can proceed to the next frame.

All lessons contain a frame with the title, *Applying Your Knowledge.* You are given the background of a situation and told to find the errors in the following letter, memo, or report. This frame provides the realism of an actual business situation: the employee is responsible for verifying the accuracy of the content and fundamentals of a communication.

Posttest

There is a *Posttest* for each lesson in the *Teacher's Manual* for this book. After a lesson is completed, your instructor may wish to assign the posttest so that you can demonstrate your retention and understanding of the information in the lesson.

Pretest

Part I

This pretest has two parts. The first is a multiple-choice test. The second is a proofreading exercise. The answers to the pretest follow the proofreading exercise.

Directions

In the blank provided, write the letter that represents the correct answer to each question. The following example illustrates this.

Example

What is the error in the sender's address? _____c_____

> 168 Yale Boulevard
> Nebraska City, Nebraska

a. The sender's name should be shown above the street address.
b. The last word in the street address should be spelled <u>Bolevard</u>.
c. The ZIP code has been omitted.
d. The address is presented correctly.

Now take the pretest.

1. What is the error in this inside address? _____

> Mr. Robert Kastens, Personal Director
> Carbonite Corporation
> 1333 Second Avenue
> Milford, Connecticut 06460

a. The state should be spelled <u>Conecticut</u>.
b. <u>Mr.</u> should be omitted before the name of the addressee.
c. <u>Personal</u> should be <u>Personnel</u>.
d. The inside address is accurate.

2. Given the inside address below, how should the salutation be shown? _____

> Ms. Yvette Carlson, Account Supervisor
> Haley-Richardson Company
> One Perry Park Plaza
> Detroit, MI 12345
>
> Dear Haley-Richardson Company:

a. The salutation should be <u>Dear Ms. Carlson:</u>
b. The salutation should be <u>Dear Account Supervisor:</u>
c. The salutation should be <u>Dear Ms. Yvette Carlson:</u>
d. The salutation is correct.

3. The writer of an application letter presents the date as shown below. What is the error in this presentation? _____

> March 27, 19____

a. The date should precede the year: 27 March 19____.
b. The date should be written in figures: 3/27/____.
c. The comma should be omitted.
d. The date is correct.

4. The writer of an application letter presents the salutation as <u>Dear Ms. Sala:</u> and the complimentary closing in the following manner. What is the error in the presentation of the closing?

         Sincerely

   a. The closing should be spelled <u>Sincerly</u>.
   b. The complimentary closing should be followed by a comma.
   c. The complimentary closing should be followed by a semicolon.
   d. The complimentary closing is correct.

5. An employee of a business organization originated this letter to a customer and presented the signature element in the following manner. What is the error in the presentation?

         Ann Redding, Coordinator
         Talent Division

   a. The name should not be separated from the title by a comma.
   b. The name, title, and unit (division) should be on the same line.
   c. The title should be hyphenated (<u>Co-ordinator</u>)
   d. The presentation is correct.

6. An employee of a business organization originated this letter to a customer and presented the signature element in the following manner. What is the error in the presentation?

         Mr. Cornwall Harding, Manager
         Training Division

   a. The name of the department should be spelled <u>Trainning</u>.
   b. <u>Mr.</u> should not be followed by a period.
   c. The courtesy title should not be used.
   d. The signature element is correct.

Part II

Directions

The paragraph below the heading CASE tells you why the following letter was written. Make corrections in the format and body of the letter as follows:

1. Underscore an incorrect item (word or punctuation mark) and write the correction below it.
2. Draw a line through an item (word or punctuation mark) that should be omitted.
3. Add an item (word or punctuation mark) that should be inserted directly below that item.
4. The corrected letter is shown in the Answers to the Pretest.

    CASE

As sales manager at the Rocky Mountain High Country Realty, you have just drafted this letter to an attorney. The letter contains five errors in format and five in fundamentals—grammar, spelling, punctuation, capitalization, hyphenation, and so on.

Rocky Mountain High Country Realty
Mile High Building
One Denver Plaza
Denver, Colorado 80200

Ms. Kim, Jameston Attorney
2009 West Prospect Street
Pueblo, CO. 81001

Dear Ms. Jameston:

We appreciate your April 23 letter concerning the failure of one

of our Sales representatives to inform your client of the possible

zoning of the Blake property.

Please accept my sincere apology for not having coresponded with

you sooner. The sales associate, who showed this property, Pete

Fargo, is no longer with our firm; he is presently operating his

own business in Greeley. Therefore Jack Dodge, branch manager

of our office at 2165 South Adams Avenue, where Mr. Fargo was

employed, interviewed Mr. Fargo at Greeley. Yesterday Jack and

me reviewed the transaction and the commitments made by Mr. Fargo.

I'm sure, Kim, that you can expect a detailed report from Mr.

Dodge within the next day or so.

Cordially,
ROCKY MOUNTAIN HIGH COUNTRY REALTY*

Joe Crossman, Sales Manager
Residential property

ANSWERS TO PRETEST

Frame numbers, in parentheses following each answer, indicate where a topic is discussed in the lesson. They are for easy reference so you can review.

Part I

1. c (Frame 1)	3. d (Frame1)	5. d (Frame 2)
2. a (Frame 1)	4. b (Frame 1)	6. c (Frame 2)

Part II

Corrected letter appears on p. 6.

* By permission. Lois Meyer and Ruth Moyer, *Machine Transcription in Modern Business: Instructor's Resource Package* (New York: John Wiley & Sons, 1978), p. 16.

Rocky Mountain High Country Realty
Mile High Building
One Denver Plaza
Denver, Colorado 80200

Ms. Kim Jameston, Attorney
2009 West Prospect Street
Pueblo, CO 81001

Dear Ms. Jameston:

We appreciate your April 23 letter concerning the failure of one of our

Sales representatives to inform your client of the possible zoning of the
s

Blake property.

Please accept my sincere apology for not having corresponded with you
corresponded

sooner. The sales associate who showed this property, Pete Fargo,

is no longer with our firm; he is presently operating his own business

in Greeley. Therefore, Jack Dodge, branch manager of our office at

2165 South Adams Avenue, where Mr. Fargo was employed,

interviewed Mr. Fargo at Greeley. Yesterday Jack and me reviewed
I

the transaction and the commitments made by Mr. Fargo. I'm sure,

Kim, that you can expect a detailed report from Mr. Dodge within the

next day or so.

Cordially,
ROCKY MOUNTAIN HIGH COUNTRY REALTY

Joe Crossman, Sales Manager
Residential property
Property

Lesson 1
What Is Business English?

Formats and Proofreading

This lesson illustrates the most frequently used arrangements (formats) of business letters. Learning the formats of communications to a business or used by a business puts you a step ahead of many young people who enter the business world without this background.

A proofreading procedure is demonstrated in this lesson for this reason: In this era of inflated costs, usually only top managers and administrators have the privilege of assistance from a private secretary. Until you reach a sufficiently high level in an organization, you are likely to dictate your letters, memos, and reports into a telephone or desk dictating set. They will be recorded on tape in the word processing center, where they will be transcribed by a correspondence secretary. This person may be remote from you in distance: on a different floor or even in a different building. Furthermore, this correspondence secretary handles the internal and external communications for many people in the organization. Although this secretary is expected to proofread all transcripts, knowledge of each person's job and special projects would be an impossible requirement to make. Therefore, when a communication is returned to you from this word processing center, your duty is to proofread it for accuracy of content and fundamentals before signing it.

WORK THROUGH THE FOLLOWING THREE FRAMES.

Frame 1   Letter from an Individual to a Business

All the knowledge you obtain from this textbook can be applied to business letters that you write and that you approve.

Explanation

This frame pertains to the format of the most important business letter you will ever write—the application letter. The letter has these parts:

1. The sender's address
2. Date of the letter
3. Inside address—the recipient's address
4. Salutation
5. Body
6. Complimentary closing
7. Signature element
8. Enclosure

The application letter may be solicited (a response to an organization that is seeking applicants) or unsolicited (a prospecting letter sent by a person who is interested in working for a specific organization).

Example

This example shows a typical solicited application letter. The style of the letter is full block, meaning that each line begins at the left margin. Read each numbered part and then read the correspondingly numbered explanation of this part that follows the letter.

7

(1)   620 South Shields Street
      Fort Collins, Colorado 80521

(2)   August 13, 1980

(3)   Ms. Jane Irwin, Personnel Director
      The Global Life Insurance Company
      615 Third Avenue
      New York, New York 10016

(4)   Dear Ms. Irwin:

(5)   Having a bachelor of science in business administration with a major in general business and having worked part time as a trainee in the regional Global office, I meet the basic qualifications you requested for applicants to the Global management trainee program. This letter and résumé have been prepared in response to your advertisement in the August 12 issue of The Wall Street Journal.

In a business writing class, I wrote an analytical report comparing three life insurance policies taken out from three companies by a hypothetical twenty-one-year-old male. My criteria—rate of return as an annuity, variety of clauses under which the matured policy could be paid, and cash value of the matured policy—revealed that Global is Number 1 in each criterion!

Because I am interested in working for an insurance company, I performed case studies, special projects, and computer analyses that pertained to insurance. For example, I wrote and tested a computer program that would forecast regional life insurance sales according to monthly gross national product indices.

Since my junior year, I have worked part time as a trainee under Mr. Neil Gregory in the Global regional office. I wrote local advertisements for radio and newspapers, prepared brief lectures on insurance for junior high school and high school students, and assisted Mr. Gregory in making presentations on group life insurance.

As president of the Administrative Management Society, publicity chairman of the Data Processing Club, and student council treasurer, I learned how to work with business people, the faculty, and other students. This year, the Administrative Management Society, in collaboration with the other clubs and the student council, developed a careers day program that was attended by over 1,000 students and 200 business people from the region.

The enclosed résumé lists courses, honors, awards, activities, and references. Will you please evaluate my résumé and contact my references to determine how my qualifications meet your requirements for a trainee. I can come to New York for an interview any time before September 15; therefore, I would appreciate hearing from you before that date.

(6)   Sincerely,

(7)   Michael Sudduth
(8)   Enclosure

Letter Parts

The following is an explanation of the parts of the letter.

(1) *Return Address*

The return address contains sufficient information for the recipient to respond to the sender. At the minimum, this section contains the street address, the city, the state, and the ZIP code. An apartment number follows the street address and is separated from it with a comma.

> 790 Washington Street, #405
> or
> 790 Washington Street, Apt. 405

The number sign is customarily used to replace the abbreviation.

The return address begins flush with the left margin (full block style) or at the center (modified block style).

(2) *Date*

The current date is presented in this order: month, day, and year (January 11, 1980), unless the employing organization prefers a different order.

The date begins flush with the left margin or at the center; it is aligned under the return address.

(3) *Inside Address*

Each line of the inside address begins flush with the left margin. The recipient's address contains sufficient information so that the letter reaches the addressee rapidly once it arrives at its destination. In a letter to a company, the sender should use both the addressee's name and business title. Notice that a courtesy title (Ms.) also precedes the given name of the addressee. If the name is not known, the business title may be sufficient; however, the name alone is not sufficient, except in a very small organization. Mail-room searches for the recipient's location delay the letter's delivery to the desk of the appropriate addressee.

(4) *Salutation*

The salutation begins at the left margin and is followed by a colon. An individual is addressed by courtesy title and surname preceded by the word Dear (Dear Mr. [or Mrs.] Jones). The writer may use Ms. preceding a woman's surname (Dear Ms. Jones), regardless of her marital status. The salutation for a letter addressed to a firm (first line of the inside address) is usually Gentlemen. However, if the writer believes that the addressees may consist of men and women or may be either a man or a woman, the writer may solve the problem by using Dear Personnel Director or To Whom It May Concern or by omitting the salutation altogether. If the salutation is omitted, a subject line is usually used to identify the subject of the letter and is placed in the position of the salutation.

When the salutation is omitted, the complimentary closing is also omitted. This style is called a "Simplified Letter" and was recommended many years ago by the National Office Management Association (now the Administrative Management Society).

(5) *Body*

The lines within a paragraph are single-spaced, and the paragraphs are separated by a double space. The paragraphs may either be indented or begin flush with the left margin if the date begins at the center of the paper. If the date begins flush with the left margin, the paragraphs are not indented.

(6)   Complimentary Closing

The complimentary closing begins in the same position as the date. When a colon follows the salutation, a comma is used after the close. From the variety of common complimentary closings, the writer usually selects a more formal one for a letter destined to an individual with whom he or she is not acquainted. For example, Very truly yours, Yours truly, Sincerely, and Sincerely yours are appropriate for application letters. If the writer is acquainted with the recipient, a less formal closing is acceptable: Cordially, Cordially yours. Note that only the first letter of the first word is capitalized.

(7)   Signature Element

The writer signs his or her name above the typed signature. The courtesy title Mr. is not used before the written or typed signature in a letter signed by a man.

A married woman usually does not use the courtesy title Mrs. or her husband's first name in signing business correspondence. The trend for both married and single women is to sign one's own first name along with the surname in an application letter, without a courtesy title. The accompanying résumé, or data sheet, carries the information regarding her marital status, if a woman wishes to include it.

(8)   Enclosure

Because an application letter is usually accompanied by a résumé, the word enclosure appears below the signature element and flush with the left margin.

>   Mary Aire
>   Enclosure

In an application letter, only one enclosure is likely to be presented; however, if additional enclosures are included, they may be shown any one of several ways. Here are two examples:

>   Enclosures: Résumé
>   Report prepared for Heyder Industries
>   Enclosures 2

Exercise

In questions 1, 2, and 3, fill in each blank with the appropriate answer.
In questions 4–10, write the letter of the correct choice in the blank provided.

1.   List (in order) the parts of a letter from an individual to a company.

   (1) _____   (5) _____
   (2) _____   (6) _____
   (3) _____   (7) _____
   (4) _____

2.   The sender's name is typed in only one place in the letter—in the
   _____ .

3. Why should the sender try never to send a business letter to a person without that person's title?

    _____

    _____

4. Presenting the date in this manner—9/13/80—is acceptable in a business letter.
    a. Yes
    b. No   _____

5. Which of the following presentations is more acceptable to use in identifying a recipient in an inside address?
    a. Ms. Jane Irwin
    b. Jane Irwin   _____

6. If the letter is addressed to Mr. Harold Goff, which of the following is the best salutation?
    a. Dear Sir:
    b. Dear Mr. Goff:
    c. Dear Mr. Harold Goff: _____

7. The body of the letter is usually:
    a. single-spaced.
    b. double-spaced.   _____

8. Although the full-block style is the most frequently used because of the ease and speed of preparation, other styles may be used. If the date begins at the center of the paper, the:
    a. paragraphs are indented five spaces.
    b. paragraphs are started at the left margin.   _____

9. A man's typed and written signatures are:
    a. never preceded by a courtesy title (<u>Mr.</u>).
    b. always preceded by a courtesy title.   _____

10. The trend is for both single and married women to:
    a. write the appropriate courtesy title preceding the name and show it in the typed signature line.
    b. omit the courtesy title in both the written and typed signatures.   _____

ANSWERS TO FRAME 1

1. (1) sender's address   (5) body
    (2) date   (6) complimentary closing
    (3) inside address   (7) signature element
    (4) salutation
2. signature element
3. The letter is delayed because the mail-room personnel need to locate the department in which the recipient is employed.
4. b   6. b   8. a or b   10. b
5. a   7. a   9. a

Frame 2   *Letter from a Business*

Explanation

As an employee in a business organization, you may be responsible for writing to customers, other businesses, the government, applicants, and so on. The letters you prepare will be typed on company letterhead, which contains, at the minimum, the company name, address, and telephone number.

   The remainder of this type of business letter is similar to one written by an individual.

Example

Read a numbered part and then read the correspondingly numbered explanation of this part that follows the letter.

(1)   POTOMAC NATIONAL BANK*
                  1825 Pennsylvania Avenue, N.W.
                  Washington, D.C. 20420
                  (212)476-8204

(2) August 18, 1980

(3) Mr. George Noble
     800 Connecticut Avenue, N.W.
     Washington, D.C. 20428

(4) Dear Mr. Noble:

(5) You are to be congratulated on the satisfactory manner in
     which you handled your Money Plus Account at Potomac
     National. We value customers like you.

     Your Money Plus Account will expire within sixty days. To
     avoid any lapse in this service, will you please fill out
     the enclosed application and return it in the envelope
     provided.

     Should you decide not to renew your Money Plus Account, the
     total balance outstanding will be due and payable on your
     renewal date.

     Thank you for banking at Potomac National, Mr. Noble.

(6) Sincerely,

(7) Larry Lawton, Manager
     Money Plus Department
(8) LL
(9) Enclosures 2

Letter Parts

(1) Letterhead

At the minimum, the name, address, and phone number of the company are shown in the printed letterhead.

(2) Date

The date is usually presented in this order: month, day, year, as in <u>January 7, 1980</u>, unless the company requires a different arrangement. The date may begin flush with the left margin or at the center of the page.

(3) Inside Address

The complete address is shown. Notice the use of the courtesy title preceding the addressee's name. The arrangement and placement of the inside address are the same as in Letter 1.

---

* *Ibid.,* p. 21.

(4) *Salutation*

The salutation is appropriate for the name given in the inside address. The kind of salutation used in a letter is determined by the name(s) shown on the first line of the inside address, as explained for Letter 1.

(5) *Body*

The body is single-spaced with a double space between paragraphs. The paragraph indentation follows the same rules as given in the explanation for Letter 1.

(6) *Complimentary Closing*

The complimentary closing is appropriate for a formal letter from a business to an individual. The selection and placement of the closing follow the same rules as given in the explanation for Letter 1.

(7) *Signature Element*

The writer's name, title, and department are shown. If the customer needs to respond to a letter, the information in the signature element will be used in the inside address of the customer's letter.

(8) *Initials*

The initials of the transcriber are shown. The purpose of showing these initials is to fix the responsibility for the transcription. The transcriber can be located and complimented or requested to make corrections. The dictator's initials may also appear in the Initials section. When the dictator's (writer's) initials are used, they precede those of the transcriber. Various styles may be used:

RCM/ev   RCM:EV   RCM:ev

(9) *Enclosure*

Often enclosures accompany a business letter. The number of enclosures may be shown, or the enclosures may be listed. A variety of styles may be used to identify the enclosures. Examples are given in the explanation for Letter 1.

Exercise

Fill in each blank with the appropriate answer.

Example

At the minimum, what information is shown in a company's printed letterhead? <u>The company's name, address, and phone number are shown</u>.

1. If a letter were written today, how should the date be presented? _June 20, 1982_

2. If the letter were intended for Mary Noble, and you did not know whether she was single or married, what might the first line on the inside address be?
    Ms Mary Noble

3. What should the salutation be? _Dear Ms Noble_
4. How many paragraphs does the body of the letter in the example contain?
    _4_

5. Name three other complimentary closings that are appropriate for a letter of this type.

   _____   _____   _____

6. Name the three items in the signature element that identify the writer and provide the information the recipient needs to know in order to respond.

   _____   _____   _____

7. If the dictator's initials are used, where are they located in relation to the transcriber's initials?

   _____

8. Two items are enclosed within the example letter. What are they?

   _____   _____

9. If the letter had been signed by Elizabeth Lawton, would you expect to see a courtesy title preceding her name? _____

ANSWERS TO FRAME 2

1. Give in this order: month, day, year.
2. Ms. Mary Noble
3. Dear Ms. Noble:
4. four
5. Very truly yours, Yours truly, Sincerely, Sincerely yours,
6. Name, title, and department
7. The dictator's initials precede the transcriber's initials.
8. An application and an envelope are enclosed.
9. No; the trend is to omit a courtesy title preceding a woman's name in business correspondence.

Frame 3 Applying Your Knowledge

Many, many employees (and students!) believe that when the last word is written or dictated, the job is done. You will learn two additional steps: (1) how to proofread to detect errors in the fundamentals and the content and (2) how to revise the communication.

Proofreading is a careful reading of the prepared copy in an effort to discover errors in content and fundamentals. Revising is the action of correcting these errors.*

Proofreading is a two-way operation. The originator of the communication is responsible for proofreading and revising the rough draft or dictation outline before it is submitted or dictated. When the finished transcript is returned to the originator, this person is again responsible for proofreading and revising it, if necessary, despite the fact that the proofreading procedure was also performed by the transcriber. Many people who originate communications omit the first or second step, or both, mistakenly believing that a communication that has been typed must be correct. The person who is guilty of this omission may send letters, memos, and reports that contain errors in content or fundamentals. Such inaccurate communications reflect unfavorably upon the sender, the sender's department, and the company.

* The Proofreading Procedure on the opposite page is used by permission. Lois Meyer and Ruth Moyer, *Machine Transcription in Modern Business* (New York: John Wiley & Sons, 1978) pp. 158–159.

Proofreading Procedure

Task	Purpose	Method	Action	
1. Proofread heading	Confirm accuracy: Dates Names Titles Addresses Special parts: Attention Subject line Salutation	Read word by word	(a) (b)	Make corrections Go to Step 2
2. Proofread paragraphs	Confirm accuracy (mechanics): Omissions Additions Spelling Capitalization Number usage Punctuation Grammar Typing	Verify with reference book	(a) (b)	Make corrections Go to Step 3
3. Proofread transcript, overall	Confirm accuracy: Logical ideas Facts Dates Names Places Agreement of ideas and facts Omission of data	Read entire communication rapidly	(a) (b)	Make corrections Go to Step 4
4. Proofread closing	Confirm accuracy: Complimentary closing Names Titles Reference initials Enclosures Carbon copy notations Other elements	Read line-by-line	(a) (b) (c)	Make corrections Acceptable? Sign the communication Not acceptable? Submit for correction

CASE

Michael Sudduth has typed the first draft of this letter and plans to proof-read and revise it before having it and his résumé typed professionally. The letter contains ten errors.

Directions

Follow the steps outlined in the proofreading procedure and make corrections in the following manner:

1. Underscore an incorrect item (word or punctuation mark) and write the correction below it.
2. Draw a line through an item (word or punctuation mark) that should be omitted.
3. Add an item (word or punctuation mark) that should be inserted.

The corrected letter is shown in the Appendix.

620 South Shields Street
Fort Collins, Colorado 80521
August 13, 19____

Ms. Jane Irwin, Personnel Director
The Global Insurance Company
615 Third Avenue
New York, New York 10016

Dear Ms. Jane Irwin:
        (1)

Having a bachelor of science degree in business administration
with a major in general business and having worked parttime as
a trainee in the regional Global office. I meet the basic
qualifications you requested for applicants to the Global
management training program. This letter and résumé have been
prepared in response to your advertisement in the August 12
issue of The Wall Street Journal.

In a business writing class, I wrote an analytical report
comparing three life insurance policies taken out by a hypothetical twenty one year old male. My criteria—rate of return
as an annuity, variety of clauses under which the matured policy could be paid, and cash value of the matured policy—revealed that Global is Number 1 in each criterion!

Because I am interested in working for an insurance company
I performed case studies, special reports, and computer analyses
that pertained to insurance. For example, I wrote and tested
a computer program that would forecast regional life insurance
sales according to monthly gross national product indices.
The program showed no less than a 97 percent accuracy rate for
each month during the past five years'.

Since my junior year I have worked part time as a trainee under
Mr. Neil Gregory (a million-dollar sales representative) in
the Global regional office. I wrote local advertisements for
radio and newspapers, prepared brief lectures on insurance
for junior high school and high school students, and assisted
Mr. Gregory in making presentations on group life insurance.

As president of the Administrative Management Society, publicity chairman of the Data Processing Club, and student council treasurer, I learned how to work with business people, the faculty, and other students. This year the Administrative Management Society, in collaberation with the other clubs and the student council, developed a careers day program that was attended by over 1,000 students and 200 business people from the region.

The enclosed résumé lists courses, honors, awards, activities, and references. Will you please evaluate my résumé and contact my references to determine how my qualifications meet your requirements for a trainee. I can come to New YORK for an interview at any time before August 13; therefore, I would appreciate hearing from you before that date.

Sincerly,

Mike Sudduth
Enclosure

ANSWERS TO FRAME 3

620 South Shields Street
Fort Collins, Colorado 80521
August 13, 19____

Ms. Jane Irwin, Personnel Director
The Global Insurance Company
615 Third Avenue
New York, New York 10016

Dear Mrs. Jane Irwin:
　　　　(1)

Having a bachelor of science degree in business administration

with a major in general business and having worked parttime

as a trainee in the regional Global office, I meet the basic
　　　Use a comma to set off an introductory participial phrase.
qualifications you requested for applicants to the Global

management training program. This letter and résumé have been

prepared in response to your advertisement in the August 12

issue of The Wall Street Journal.
　　　Underscore newspaper titles.

In a business writing class, I wrote an analytical report com-

paring three life insurance policies taken out by a hypothetical

twenty-one-year-old male. My criteria—rate of return as an
  Hyphenate compound adjectives before a noun.
annuity, variety of clauses under which the matured policy

could be paid, and cash value of the matured policy—revealed

that Global is Number 1 in each criterion!

Because I am interested in working for an insurance company,
  Set off an introductory dependent clause with a comma.
I performed case studies, special reports, and computer analyses

that pertained to insurance. For example, I wrote and tested

a computer program that would forecast regional life insurance

sales according to monthly gross national product indices.

The program showed no less than a 97 percent accuracy rate for

each month during the past years.
  Years is not possessive.
Since my junior year I have worked parttime as a trainee under

Mr. Neil Gregory (a million-dollar sales representative) in

the Global regional office. I wrote local advertisements for

radio and newspapers, prepared brief lectures on insurance for

junior high school and high school students, and assisted Mr.

Gregory in making presentations on group life insurance.

As president of the Administrative Management Society, publicity

chairman of the Data Processing Club, and student council

treasurer, I learned how to work with business people, the

faculty, and other students. This year the Administrative

Management Society, in collaboration with the other clubs and
  The word is now spelled correctly.
the student council, developed a careers day program that was

attended by over 1,000 students and 200 business people from

the region.

The enclosed résumé lists courses, honors, awards, activities,

and references. Will you please evaluate my résumé and contact

my references to determine how my qualifications meet your

requirements for a trainee. I can come to New York for an interview
  Typographical error is corrected.
at any time before September 13; therefore, I would appreciate
  The original date cannot be accurate, as it is the date of the letter
  (lack of agreement in facts).
hearing from you before that date.

Sincerely,
The spelling error is now corrected.

Mike Sudduth
Enclosure

Remember this slogan: SIGN YOUR NAME, TAKE THE BLAME!

Lesson 2
Spelling

Pretest

Directions

One of the words within parentheses is spelled correctly. Select the correctly spelled word in each sentence, and write it in the blank provided.

Example

She (believes, beleives) that too much money has been withheld from her paycheck this month.   believes

1. The cost-of-(liveing, living) index has risen this month.   _____
2. Have you had a course in (managment, management)?   _____
3. The error is (noticable, noticeable).   _____
4. You are not (truely, truly) independent until you have obtained a job.   _____
5. How much (mileage, milage) is shown on the odometer of your car?   _____
6. New employees are often given in-service (trainning, training).   _____
7. The managers (conferred, confered) about the employee ratings.   _____
8. The dictionary should be your primary (reference, referrence) book.   _____
9. Many people (benefitted, benefited) from the recent tax break.   _____
10. A copy of the (reciept, receipt) must be given to the customer.   _____
11. When you are not busy at your desk, you will (relieve, releive) other employees for break periods.   _____
12. For only 10 cents you will (receive, recieve) a copy of the book *Making Money Grow*.   _____
13. The (hieght, height) of the door is 6 feet 4 inches.   _____
14. The teller (admitted, admited) that she had been embezzling money.   _____
15. This fluid does not remove the errors (effectively, effectivly).

Lesson 2
Spelling

America is often called a "melting pot" because its population consists of every nationality and ethnic group in the world. English, the language of Americans, also represents a melting pot—a melting pot of words.

The three most widely used languages in the world are Mandarin Chinese, spoken by 610 million people; English, spoken by 275 million; and Spanish, spoken by 210 million.* Most of the world's business, trade, politics, and scholarly pursuits are communicated in oral or written English.

Introduction

All languages are dynamic. They are continually, though slowly, changing for the following reasons:†

1. *Words are borrowed.* The English language that we speak today is almost the same as that spoken by the first English settlers in America. Their vocabulary had undergone many changes over the centuries due to invasion and conquests of the British Isles by Romans, French, Germans, and Danes. The English people borrowed or adapted many words from their invaders and conquerors. Today we also borrow words from other languages. Some words we spell differently from the originals, and others we spell and pronounce the same as in the original language.

> ACCOUCHEUR—from the French. It means someone who assists at a birth. We spell and pronounce this word the same as the French do.

2. *Words are compounded.* We often combine two already accepted words to form a new word.

> HANDY and MAN combine to form HANDYMAN.

3. *Derivatives are added.* To the root word we affix beginnings (prefixes) or endings (suffixes).

> Root—SPELL; prefix—*MIS*SPELL; suffix—MISSPELL*ING*

4. *Meanings are added or changed.* As a result of new technology, scientific advancements, and cultural changes, we often give accepted words new or additional meanings.

> The original meaning of PAD was a thin mat or cushion; the new meaning which has been added is PAD as living quarters.

5. *Words are clipped.*

> DISCOTHEQUE to DISCO

6. *Words are blended.*

> BREAKFAST and LUNCH into BRUNCH

7. *Acronyms are made.* The first letter of two or more words is combined into a word that can be spoken.

> HOUSING and URBAN DEVELOPMENT to HUD

---

* *Webster's New Collegiate Dictionary,* 8th edition, G. & C. Merriam Company, Springfield, Mass., 1977, p. 20a.

† *Ibid.,* pp. 20a–25a.

8. *Words are abbreviated according to sound.* The first letters of two or more words may be combined to form a word that can be spoken.

DISC JOCKEY to DEEJAY

Explanation

Borrowed words, combined words, added derivatives, added meanings, and so on—is it any wonder that the English language is a complex system of communication! However, we can make order from what appears to be a complex and even confusing language system by breaking it down into recognizable parts and studying these parts.

Example

1. VOCABULARY: words that comprise the language (the words in a dictionary).
2. GRAMMAR: framework in which we arrange the words to convey a thought (a phrase, clause, or sentence).
3. SEMANTICS: meaning attributed to words (dictionary meanings).
4. PHONETICS: speech sounds given to the letters of a word ("c" as in "cat" or "ceiling").*

Our first attack on the English language will be to learn how commonly used words are spelled. We can spell over 80 percent of these words correctly if we learn some prespelling aids and only three easy rules.

You are now ready to begin on orthography (the study of spelling).

Frame 1   Prespelling Aids

Vowels, Consonants, Syllables

Before we can follow the directions in a spelling rule, we must be able to identify the sounds of letters within a word.

Explanation

1. The alphabet consists of these letters:
   a. Vowels: A, E, I, O, U, and sometimes Y (when sounded as I or E).
   b. Consonants: all other letters.
2. A SYLLABLE is a single speech sound:
   a. It may consist of one or more letters.
   b. Each syllable must have one or more vowels.

Example

1. Say each syllable.
2. "V" identifies the vowels; look at each vowel.

EAT   ←one syllable
VV

---

* *Ibid.*

A BOUT   ←two syllables
V   VV

PER SON NEL   ←three syllables
V   V   V

RE CIP I ENT   ←four syllables
V   V   V   V

Exercise .

Underscore the vowels in the following sentences.

1.   The Receiving Department is on the fifth floor of our building.
2.   The personnel manager interviewed Roger Sampson.

ANSWERS TO FRAME 1
1.   The Receiving Department is on the fifth floor of our building.
2.   The personnel manager interviewed Roger Sampson.

Frame 2   Prespelling Aids

Roots, Prefixes, Suffixes

Explanation

1.   The basic word is called a ROOT: SPELL
2.   The syllable(s) joined to the beginning of a root is (are) called a prefix: *MIS*-SPELL
3.   The syllable(s) joined to the end of a root is (are) called a suffix: MISSPELL-*ING*
4.   The addition of a prefix rarely, if ever, changes the spelling: USE, *MIS*USE
5.   The addition of a suffix often changes the spelling: USE, US*AGE*

Example

Study the following lists. Read each root word, the root word with its prefix, and the root word with its suffix.

Root	*Prefix*		*Suffix*		
mount	dis	mount	dis	mount	ed
correct	in	correct	in	correct	ly
form	con	form	con	form	ation
view	pre	view	pre	view	er
circle	semi	circle	semi	circl	ing
verb	ad	verb	ad	verb	ial
date	post	date	post	dat	ing
continue	dis	continue	dis	continu	ing

Exercise

1.   Underscore the prefixes and suffixes in the following sentences.
2.   Label the prefixes with a P and the suffixes with an S.

Example

The Data Processing Unit misplaced Mary's social security number.
<u>S</u>   <u>P</u>

  a. A new connecting wire has been found.
  b. The unnecessary records should be sent to the storage area.
  c. Good management often requires superhuman effort.

ANSWERS TO FRAME 2

  a. connect<u>ing</u>
          S

  b. <u>un</u>necessary; stor<u>age</u>
      P   S

  c. manage<u>ment</u>; <u>super</u>human
           S   P

Frame 3   Spelling Rules

Rule 1: Final Silent E

Explanation

Drop the final silent E of the root word before adding a suffix beginning with a vowel.

Example

  1. Read the root word in the first column.
  2. Notice that the final silent E is dropped before adding a suffix beginning with a vowel.

Root	*Root + Suffix*
delegate	delegat ing
arrive	arriv al
active	activ ity
retrieve	retriev able

Exercise

One of the two words in parentheses is spelled correctly. Write the correctly spelled word in the blank provided.

Example

Ms. Davis devised the information (retrieveal, retrieval) system for the Accounting Department.   <u>retrieval</u>

  1. (Managing, Managcing) a department requires leadership ability.   ————
  2. The (exciteable, excitable) young man was hired.   ————
  3. Ann spent an hour (analyzeing, analyzing) the data on the computer printout.   ————
  4. Students who want to succeed in business should take a course in (management, managment).   ————
  5. A quick (movment, movement) of the steering wheel will make a car spin on the icy road.   ————
  6. It is (inconceivable, inconceiveable) that the fire extinguisher had not been checked for two years.   ————
  7. Mrs. Adams has an (incureable, incurable) illness; therefore, Ms. Blake is (replacing, replaceing) her.   ————

8. We cannot (adequatly, adequately) cope with the (increaseing, increasing) paper work. _____

9. Correct grammar and punctuation (usage, useage) is important to anyone who writes letters, memos, and reports. _____

10. The counterfeit dollar bill has a good (likeness, likness) of George Washington. _____

11. The machines are not (compareable, comparable) in cost. _____

ANSWERS TO FRAME 3

1. Managing (*i* is a vowel)
2. excitable (*a* is a vowel)
3. analyzing (*i* is a vowel)
4. management (*m* is a consonant; did you notice that?)
5. movement (*m* is a consonant; did you notice this one?)
6. inconceivable (*a* is a vowel)

7. incurable (*a* is a vowel)
   replacing (*i* is a vowel)
8. adequately (*l* is a consonant)
   increasing (*i* is a vowel)
9. usage (*a* is a vowel)
10. likeness (*n* is a consonant)
11. comparable (*a* is a vowel)

Frame 4   Spelling Rules

Rule 1a: -OUS, -ABLE

Explanation

Some words ending in -CE or -GE retain the E before the suffixes -OUS and -ABLE. The following list is not complete; however, it does contain words common to the business vocabulary.

Example

1. Read the root word.
2. Notice that the final E is retained before adding -OUS or -ABLE.

Root	*Root + Suffix*
advantage	advantage ous
change	change able
outrage	outrage ous
notice	notice able
service	service able
manage	manage able
courage	courage ous

Exercise

Select the correctly spelled word and write it in the blank provided.

Example

The damaged washing machine is so old that it is no longer (servicable, serviceable).   serviceable

1. The (courageous, couragous) man spoke against the unsafe conditions in the factory. _____

2. (Changable, Changeable) market conditions prohibit our having a sale in January. _____

3. The guard dog at Gate 2 is (unmanagable, unmanageable). _____

4. A (noticable, noticeable) correction of a legal document is not acceptable. _____
5. The reduced property taxes are (advantagous, advantageous) to new businesses located in the industrial park. _____

ANSWERS TO FRAME 4

1. courageous
2. Changeable
3. unmanageable
4. noticeable
5. advantageous

Frame 5   Spelling Rules

Rule 1b: Only Two Exceptions

Explanation

Life is full of surprises, and so is orthography! The rules you will learn apply to most of the words in the category defined by that particular rule; however, there are exceptions to all rules. You can cope with these exceptions by memorizing the most common ones.

Example

1. Rule: Drop the final E before adding a suffix beginning with a vowel. EXCEPTION: mile, mileage.
2. Rule: Keep the final E before adding a suffix beginning with a consonant. EXCEPTION: true, truly.

Exercise

These sentences cover Rule 1, Rule 1a, and Rule 1b. Select the correct word and write it in the blank provided.

Example

The company is (acquireing, acquiring) a new word processing machine to replace the one which broke down last month.

<u>acquiring</u>
(Rule 1)

1. Company policy requires that letters to customers be signed "Yours (truly, truely)." _____
2. The dishonest car salesman changed the odometer to show less (milage, mileage). _____
3. You cannot write (effectively, effectivly) if you do not prepare an outline first. _____
4. The most (valueable, valuable) real estate in the world is located on Wall Street. _____
5. Some (distastful, distasteful) tasks seem to be a part of every job. _____
6. A new position has been created in the Accounts (Receiveable, Receivable) Department. _____
7. Her supervisor has noticed some (improvment, improvement) in Carol's work. _____
8. Della has been (evaluateing, evaluating) the employees in her department. _____
9. A programmer must give (carful, careful) attention to detail. _____
10. The (changable, changeable) weather has caused many absences this month. _____
11. (Forcible, Forceible) entry into the property of another person without that person's permission is a misdemeanor. _____
12. Frank is (hopeful, hopful) that he will receive a raise. _____
13. The average monthly (milage, mileage) for our nine delivery trucks has increased. _____

14. The judge has taken the case under (advisment, advisement).
15. Prices at the Emporium are (outrageous, outragous).
16. Using vulgar language is (inexcuseable, inexcusable).
17. By adding a prefix or suffix to a root word, you can create a (deriveative, derivative).
18. That point is not (relative, relateive) to our disagreement.
19. Eric is not considered (promoteable, promotable) because he cannot get along with his co-workers.
20. Observe the employee's (movements, movments) (closely, closly) when you perform a time and motion study.

ANSWERS TO FRAME 5

1. truly (Rule 1b)
2. mileage (Rule 1b)
3. effectively (Rule 1)
4. valuable (Rule 1)
5. distasteful (Rule 1)
6. Receivable (Rule 1)
7. improvement (Rule 1)
8. evaluating (Rule 1)
9. careful (Rule 1)
10. changeable (Rule 1a)
11. Forcible (Rule 1)
12. hopeful (Rule 1)
13. mileage (Rule 1b)
14. advisement (Rule 1)
15. outrageous (Rule 1a)
16. inexcusable (Rule 1)
17. derivative (Rule 1)
18. relative (Rule 1)
19. promotable (Rule 1)
20. movements (Rule 1) closely (Rule 1)

Frame 6   Spelling Rules

Rule 2: Doubling the Final Consonant
Rule 2a: One-syllable Words

Explanation

For a one-syllable word	HIT
Ending in one pronounced consonant	HI*T*
Preceded by one vowel	H*I*T
Double the final consonant	HIT T
Before adding a suffix beginning with a vowel	HIT T *ING*

Example

Study the examples below.

1. Notice that the *root* word ends in a pronounced consonant preceded by one vowel.
2. Notice that the consonant is doubled before adding a suffix beginning with a vowel.

Root	Doubled	Suffix	New Word
sit	t	er	sitter
got	t	en	gotten
crab	b	y	crabby (Y sounds like E)
lug	g	age	luggage
drag	g	ing	dragging

Exercise

Select the correct word in the parentheses and write it in the blank provided.

Example

Ms. Axelrod's promotion is apt reward for her (doged, dogged) determination.   <u>dogged</u>

1. George Zack was the first (bater, batter) to make a home run in the preliminary game.   _____
2. He was ticketed for not (stoping, stopping) at the red light.   _____
3. Hand (bagage, baggage) must be placed in the rack above the passenger's head.   _____
4. Stewardesses will be (fitted, fited) for uniforms after they successfully complete the orientation period.   _____
5. Clemencia has (gotten, goten) four awards in speed typing contests.   _____

ANSWERS TO FRAME 6

1. batter   3. baggage   5. gotten
2. stopping   4. fitted

Frame 7   Spelling Rules

Rule 2b: Two-syllable Words

Explanation

For a two-syllable word	RE	FER
Accented on the second syllable (if you are in doubt about the location of the accent mark, check your dictionary)	RE	<u>FER</u>
Ending in one consonant	RE	FE<u>R</u>
Preceded by one vowel	RE	FER
Double the final consonant	RE	FER R
Before adding a suffix beginning with a vowel.	RE	FER R ED

Example

Study the examples below.

1. Notice that the word is accented on the second syllable.
2. It ends in a single consonant preceded by a single vowel.
3. The final consonant is doubled before adding a suffix beginning with a vowel.

First Syllable	Second Syllable	Doubled	Suffix	New Word
pre	fer	r	ing	preferring
oc	cur	r	ence	occurrence

Exercise

Select the correct word in the parentheses and write it in the blank provided.

Example

Personal data, such as marital status and birthdate, may be (omited, omitted) from your résumé.   <u>omitted</u>

1. The department heads (concurred, concured) on the choice of the person to be promoted.   _____

2. The cost-of-living increase is (benefitting, benefiting) the hourly employee.
3. The company is (profitting, profiting) from the addition of the new product line.
4. One of the watchmen reported that the attempted theft (occurred, occured) between midnight and 4 A.M. on February 7.
5. The employees (prefered, preferred) to work overtime during the week rather than to work on Saturdays.
6. A person cannot be held (accounttable, accountable) for a job if he has not been given the authority to perform the activities.
7. The correction fluid (congealed, congealled) because the bottle cap was not replaced.

ANSWERS TO FRAME 7
1. concurred
2. benefiting (Rule does not apply; *benefit* has three syllables: ben-e-fit.)
3. profiting (Rule does not apply; *profit* is accented on the first syllable.)
4. occurred
5. preferred
6. accountable (Rule does not apply; *account* ends in two consonants, not one.)
7. congealed (Rule does not apply; the final consonant in *congeal* is preceded by two vowels.)

Frame 8   Spelling Rules

Rule 2c: Exception

Explanation

This exception does not apply to many words, but we should note it particularly for those words common to the business vocabulary.

Exception

If the accent shifts to the first syllable when the suffix is added, do not double the final consonant.

Example

Study the examples given below.

1. Notice the root word; the accent is underscored.
2. Notice the suffix to be added.
3. Notice that the accent falls on the first syllable in the new word.

Root (verbs)	*Suffix*	*New Word*
prefer	able	preferable
refer	ence	reference
defer	ence	deference

Exercise

This exercise includes (1) Rule 2a: one-syllable words; (2) Rule 2b: two-syllable words; and (3) Rule 2c: exceptions. Select the correct word in the parentheses and write it in the blank provided.

Example

The (recurrence, recurence) of absenteeism and employee turnover may indicate low morale within the company.   recurrence

1. At the graduation exercises, a bachelor of science in business administration was (confered, conferred) upon Jack Saring. _____
2. As a short-term income investment, common stock is (preferrable, preferable) to bonds. _____
3. Kelley (shunned, shuned) tasks involving equipment because he was not mechanically inclined. _____
4. The enclosure should be (attachhed, attached) to the letter. _____
5. The cafeteria serves coffee that has been (reheated, reheatted) from the previous day. _____
6. Imogene has a (recurring, recuring) illness. _____
7. (Begining, Beginning) March 1, all employees below Grade 4 will punch time cards upon arrival and departure. _____
8. The letter was (returnned, returned) because it was incorrectly addressed. _____
9. The new employee was (conceited, conceitted) and caused hard feelings in his work group. _____
10. The customers (defered, deferred) their payments while the Food and Drug Administration was investigating the inherent dangers of the product. _____
11. Older employees (benefited, benefitted) from the raised social security tax rate. _____
12. Lana (braged, bragged) about her new job. _____
13. The (flopy, floppy) magnetic disc is a new recording medium. _____
14. The foreman (steped, stepped) on a wrench and injured his foot. _____
15. Our account will be (creditted, credited) when we return the damaged merchandise. _____

ANSWERS TO FRAME 8

1. conferred (Rule 2b)
2. preferable (Rule 2c)
3. shunned (Rule 2a)
4. attached (Rule 2b does not apply; final consonant is not preceded by a vowel.)
5. reheated (Rule 2b does not apply; final consonant is preceded by two vowels.)
6. recurring (Rule 2b)
7. Beginning (Rule 2b)
8. returned (Rule 2b does not apply; final consonant is not preceded by a vowel.)
9. conceited (Rule 2b does not apply; final consonant is preceded by two vowels.)
10. deferred (Rule 2b)
11. benefited (Rule 2b does not apply; *benefit* has three syllables.)
12. bragged (Rule 2a)
13. floppy (Rule 2a; Y has the sound of E, a vowel.)
14. stepped (Rule 2a)
15. credited (Rule 2b does not apply; accent is on first syllable.)

Frame 9   Spelling Rules

Rule 3: IE or EI?

Explanation

Learn this four-line verse, and you will be able to spell 99 percent of the words requiring the ie–ei decision:

> Use I before E
> Except after C
> Or when sounded like A
> As in n<u>ei</u>ghbor or w<u>ei</u>gh.

Example

In the following examples, notice the combination in the usual order, the combination after C, and the combination sounded like A.

USUAL	bel<u>ie</u>ve	rel<u>ie</u>f
AFTER C	conc<u>ei</u>t	rec<u>ei</u>ve
A SOUND	fr<u>ei</u>ght	r<u>ei</u>gn

Exercise

Select the correctly spelled word in the parentheses and write it in the blank provided.

Example

David's scholastic (achievements, acheivements) earned him a graduate fellowship from a national foundation. <u>achievements</u>

1. The Sports Department sold 184 (sleighs, slieghs) during the pre-Christmas sale. _____
2. Save your tax (receipt, reciept) as proof of payment. _____
3. The applicant (decieved, deceived) the (interviewer, interveiwer) by giving the incorrect age. _____
4. The student nurses learned how to inject the flu vaccine into the (patients', pateints') (viens, veins). _____
5. The contents were damaged when the box was dropped on the (recieving, receiving) platform. _____
6. (Mischeivous, Mischievous) children wrote on the walls of the local plant. _____
7. Mary (riegned, reigned) as queen of the freshman festival. _____
8. Employees who live in the same (neighborhood, nieghborhood) can form a carpool to save gas. _____
9. Some students (perceive, percieve) themselves as potential managers. _____
10. The DC 4 Model truck (wieghs, weighs) two tons. _____
11. You may list your heirs, other relatives, or (freinds, friends) as your beneficiaries. _____
12. You may (acheive, achieve) success if you will continue to try, even though failure seems likely. _____

ANSWERS TO FRAME 9

1. sleighs (sounds like A)
2. receipt (follows C)
3. deceived (follows C) interviewer (usual)
4. patients' (usual) veins (sounds like A)
5. receiving (follows C)
6. Mischievous (usual)
7. reigned (sounds like A)
8. neighborhood (sounds like A)
9. perceive (follows C)
10. weighs (sounds like A)
11. friends (usual)
12. achieve (usual)

Frame 10   Spelling Rules

Rule 3b: Exceptions

Explanation

Only a few words do not meet the requirements of the preceding rule. Four of the most common exceptions and their definitions are listed below. They are also used in example sentences.

Example

1. Read the root word.
2. Study the definition(s).
3. Read the example sentence.

Root	*Meaning*
SEIZE	to take possession of; to take by force The police <u>seized</u> the stolen money. The soldiers <u>seized</u> the enemy's weapons.
FORFEIT	to give up, often dependent upon a penalty Convicted criminals <u>forfeit</u> their voting privileges.
COUNTERFEIT	not real; often an illegal substitute Thousands of <u>counterfeit</u> welfare checks were discovered during the raid.
HEIGHT	upward distance from a defined point: the ground, the floor, and so on The <u>height</u> of the file cabinet is 48 inches.

Exercise

1. Notice whether the space between the parentheses shows a suffix.
2. Select the correct word from the four listed above.
3. Write this word in the space between the parentheses.

Example

Suspecting that the customer's fifty-dollar bill was (   ), the cashier called the police.   <u>counterfeit</u>

1. The victorious troops (ed) the city.   _____
2. When the blizzard began, the team (ed) the game because its opponents were 40 points ahead in the fourth quarter.   _____
3. The (   ) coin became stuck in the vending machine.   _____
4. The (   ) of the World Trade Center in New York City is 1,210 feet.   _____

ANSWERS TO FRAME 10
1. seized   2. forfeited   3. counterfeit   4. height

Frame 11   Applying Your Knowledge (Proofreading Exercise)

Explanation

In Frame 11, you will apply all the rules (and exceptions) that you learned in this lesson. This frame requires you to proofread; that is, to locate and correct the errors.

Directions

1. Read the case upon which the proofreading exercise is based.
2. Proofread the exercise:
   a. Read each word to determine if it is misspelled.
   b. Correct the misspelled words by underscoring the incorrect word and writing the correct word below it.

CASE

Joe Rodriguez has just been promoted from machine operator to assistant foreman at the Federated Equipment Company. One of his duties is to write Critical Incident Reports explaining incidents of unusual employee behavior. These reports are placed in the employee's personal history file after being approved by the foreman. Assume that you are the foreman and proofread the body of Joe's report. Would you approve it? (You should find 25 errors.)

At approximately 9:00 A.M. on April 10, Bruce Jenkins was

driving his tractor dolly, loaded with eight crates of valueable

freight, from the Recieving Department through the storeage

areas to the Shiping Department. At the same time, Roosevelt

Walker was in Stageing Area A operating a crane to lift frieght

from the floor pads to spaces near the cieling. Bruce gave a

forcful shove to the "down" lever, and the crane droped about 10

feet, hitting the dolly load and clipping Roosevelt on the shoulder.

The noise of this occurence caused the men in the staging areas

to stop work. When I arrived, Roosevelt was hitting Bruce and

shoutting outragous and inexcusable language. The other men and

I stopped the fight. I saw that neither of the two men was truely injured,

so I discussed the incident with the two men. They admited that

their equipment was operateing properly and that they had been careless.

Roosevelt has not completed his probation period.

However, his improvement is noticable, and I believe that he

is benefitting from his in-service trainning. Bruce is also

profitting from his operator-training course. Both men are

excitable, but they can be creditted with being truthful.

Therefore, I did not require either man to forfiet his pay;

each will be held accountable for an equal share of the

damaged freight. I prefered handling the incident this

way, rather than refering it to managment.

Signed/Joe Rodriguez

ANSWERS TO FRAME 11

At approximately 9:00 A.M. on April 10, Bruce Jenkins was

driving his tractor dolly, loaded with eight crates of <u>valueable</u>
          valuable (Rule 1)

freight, from the <u>Recieving</u> Department through the <u>storeage</u>
    Receiving (Rule 3a)   storage (Rule 1)

areas to the <u>Shiping</u> Department. At the same time, Roosevelt
    Shipping (Rule 2a)

Walker was in <u>Stageing</u> Area A operating a crane to lift <u>frieght</u>
       Staging (Rule 1)   freight (Rule 3a)
from the floor pads to spaces near the <u>cieling.</u> Bruce gave a
                                     ceiling (Rule 3a)
<u>forcful</u> shove to the "down" lever, and the crane <u>droped</u> about 10
forceful (Rule 1)   dropped (Rule 2a)
feet, hitting the dolly load and clipping Roosevelt on the shoulder.

The noise of this <u>occurence</u> caused the men in the staging
                occurrence (Rule 2b)
areas to stop work. When I arrived, Roosevelt was hitting Bruce

and <u>shoutting</u> <u>outragous</u> and inexcusable language. The other men and
shouting (Rule 2a) outrageous (Rule 1a)
I stopped the fight. I saw that neither of the men was <u>truely</u> injured,
                                       truly (Rule 1b)
so I discussed the incident with the two men. They <u>admited</u>
                                  admitted (Rule 2b)
that their equipment was <u>operateing</u> properly and that they had
                           operating (Rule 1)
been careless.

   Roosevelt has not completed his probation period.

However, his <u>improvment</u> is <u>noticable</u>, and I believe that he
           improvement (Rule 1) noticeable (Rule 1a)
is <u>benefitting</u> from his in-service <u>trainning.</u> Bruce is also
  benefiting (Rule 2b)   training (Rule 2a)
<u>profitting</u> from his operator-training course. Both men are
 profiting (Rule 2b)
excitable, but they can be <u>creditted</u> with being truthful.
                    credited (Rule 2b)
Therefore, I did not require either man to <u>forfiet</u> his pay; each
                                   forfeit (Rule 3b)
will be held accountable for an equal share of the damaged

freight. I <u>prefered</u> handling the incident this way,
        preferred (Rule 2b)
rather than <u>refering</u> it to <u>managment.</u>
      referring (Rule 2b)   management (Rule 1)

If you missed a spelling error, check the applicable rule.

Lesson 3
Identification:
Parts of Speech

Pretest

Directions

Underscore the words that represent the part of speech shown at the right of the arabic number.

Example

VERB: He <u>received</u> a diploma from Dunbar High School in 1975 and <u>was graduated</u> from Oklahoma State University in 1980.

1. NOUN: The United States is called a republic because a president is elected to govern the population.
2. NOUN: Because the citizens elect people to represent them, this country is also called a democracy.
3. PRONOUN: A president is elected every four years; he may succeed himself in the presidency once.
4. PRONOUN: Congressmen and senators represent their constituents and try to satisfy them.
5. VERB: Many presidents have been educated as lawyers.
6. VERB: A president can veto a piece of legislation, but it may be passed over his veto.
7. ADJECTIVE: This large industrial nation has a high unemployment rate.
8. ADJECTIVE: Young people, eager and well trained, want to work in business organizations or government agencies that pay high salaries.
9. ADVERB: A highly paid person can usually speak and write well.
10. ADVERB: Young people who are looking for jobs should very carefully select as a role model someone who represents what they want to become.
11. PREPOSITION: In preparing for a career, one should read vocational material in the library and elsewhere.
12. PREPOSITION: Guidance specialists say that a person who begins work today may change jobs seven times during his or her lifetime.
13. CONJUNCTION: To find out more about the world in which you live, you should read books, newspapers, and professional journals.
14. CONJUNCTION: Many young people waste their spare time; therefore, they have little knowledge of history and current events.
15. INTERJECTION: Cheers! I will be graduated in three years.

Lesson 3
Identification: Parts of Speech

The parts of speech are the framework of any language. Our language has eight parts of speech, and you will use at least four of them in almost every sentence you write.

Why Learn the Parts of Speech?

To transmit ideas and facts so that others can understand them easily, you need to know how to identify and use the parts of speech. This lesson primarily shows you how to identify them. You will be shown how to use them in one or more lessons later in the book.

The eight parts of speech will be presented in this order: nouns, pronouns, verbs, adjectives, adverbs, prepositions, conjunctions, and interjections.

Frame 1   Nouns

Explanation

A *noun* names a person, place, thing, or quality. It may consist of one word (economy) or more (United States, Gross National Product). A noun may name one (person) or more (employees). Capitalization, plurals, and possessives of nouns are covered in Lessons 9, 10, and 11.

Example

1. Read the following paragraph.
2. Notice that each noun is underscored and labeled to show what it identifies.

The <u>economy</u> of the <u>United States</u> is classified according to business and
     (thing)   (place)
government <u>areas</u> that offer <u>goods</u> or <u>services</u> for <u>money</u>. The dollar
     (things)   (things)   (things)   (thing)
<u>value</u> of these <u>goods</u> and <u>services</u> is called <u>Gross National Product</u>
(thing)   (things)   (things)   (thing)
(GNP). <u>Economists</u> in the federal <u>government</u> compute the <u>GNP</u> on a
     (persons)   (thing)   (thing)
periodic <u>basis</u>. Their <u>honesty</u> in preparing these <u>data</u> is important because
    (thing)   (quality)   (things)
the <u>figures</u> illustrate the economic <u>health</u> of this <u>country</u>.
   (things)   (quality)   (place)

Exercise

1. Underscore each noun.
2. In the space below the line, label the noun to show what it identifies.

Example

<u>Mary Carter</u> lives in <u>Philadelphia</u> and works for a legal <u>firm</u>.
 (person)   (place)   (thing)

Every employed person in each state within the United States

is engaged in producing goods or offering services. The employees

who assemble the parts of a car are directly engaged in making

a product. The office personnel who work in the same plant do

not actually put their hands on a car, but they offer supporting

services to those employees who are directly engaged in production.

ANSWERS TO FRAME 1

Every employed <u>person</u> in each <u>state</u> within the <u>United States</u>
     (person)   (place)   (place)
is engaged in producing <u>goods</u> or offering <u>services</u>. The <u>employees</u>
               (things)   (things)   (persons)
who assemble the <u>parts</u> of a <u>car</u> are directly engaged in making
           (things)   (thing)
a <u>product</u>. The office <u>personnel</u> who work in the same <u>plant</u> do
  (thing)   (people)   (place)
not actually put their <u>hands</u> on a <u>car</u>, but they offer supporting
            (things)   (thing)
<u>services</u> to those <u>employees</u> who are directly engaged in <u>production</u>.
(things)   (persons)   (thing)

Frame 2   Pronouns

Explanation

A *pronoun* is a word that substitutes for a noun or another pronoun; in other words, it is used in place of a noun or another pronoun.

Example A

1. Read the following paragraph that is written without pronouns.
2. Notice the length, repetition, and grade school presentation.

A bank teller must be honest because a bank teller handles other people's money. Eleanour and Aaron are bank tellers; Eleanour and Aaron work at the Puget Sound Terminal Bank. Mr. Bradly, the manager, says Eleanour and Aaron are good employees because Mr. Bradly notices that Eleanour and Aaron perform the work accurately and treat the customers courteously.

Example B

1. Read this paragraph in which pronouns replace certain nouns.
2. Notice that the length and repetition are decreased and the presentation is more businesslike.

A bank teller must be honest because <u>he</u> or <u>she</u> handles other people's money. Eleanour and Aaron are bank tellers; <u>they</u> work at the Puget Sound Terminal Bank. Mr. Bradly, the manager, says <u>they</u> are good employees because <u>he</u> notices that <u>they</u> perform the work accurately and treat the customers courteously.

Exercise

In each numbered blank provided, write one pronoun that can be substituted for the noun(s) designated by that number in the paragraph.

Example

Potomac National Bank has $5 million in assets, and
<u>Potomac National Bank</u> has $2 million in liabilities.   (1) <u>it</u>
           (1)

Aaron and Eleanour are being considered for promotion to the position of   (1)_____

chief teller because <u>Aaron</u> and <u>Eleanour</u> are efficient and diligent. As only one   (2)_____
              (1)   (1)

person can be promoted, the manager must interview <u>Aaron</u> and <u>Eleanour</u> to   (3)_____
                               (2)   (2)

determine whether <u>Aaron</u> or <u>Eleanour</u> should get the job. <u>The</u> <u>manager</u> will
(3) (4) (5)

consider <u>Aaron's and Eleanour's</u> efficiency, diligence, cooperativeness,
(6)

and appearance.

(4)_____

(5)_____

(6)_____

ANSWERS TO FRAME 2

1.	they	3.	he	5.	He
2.	them	4.	she	6.	their

Frame 3 Antecedents of Pronouns

Explanation

A pronoun may have an *antecedent,* a word to which the pronoun refers. The antecedent usually comes before the pronoun in sentence order. It may even be in a preceding sentence.

Example

1. The pronouns are underscored and the antecedents are in capital letters.
2. Read each lettered sentence and the corresponding explanation under **Note.**

   (a) A BANK must close <u>its</u> doors if <u>it</u> does not make a profit.
   (b) The profit a BANK makes depends on the number of <u>its</u> CUSTOMERS and the amount of <u>their</u> deposits.
   (c) The CUSTOMERS expect prompt, courteous service because <u>they</u> enter a bank to transact business.
   (d) <u>They</u> also expect the employees to handle <u>their</u> transactions accurately.
   (e) Therefore, each EMPLOYEE is encouraged to take courses to improve <u>his</u> or <u>her</u> knowledge of banking procedures.

Note

   (a) The pronouns <u>its</u> and <u>it</u> refer to the noun BANK.
   (b) The pronoun <u>its</u> refers to the noun BANK, and the pronoun <u>their</u> refers to the noun CUSTOMERS.
   (c) The pronoun <u>they</u> refers to the noun CUSTOMERS.
   (d) The pronouns <u>they</u> and <u>their</u> refer to the noun CUSTOMERS (Sentence c).
   (e) The pronouns <u>his</u> and <u>her</u> refer to the noun EMPLOYEE.

Exercise

1. Write the antecedent for each numbered pronoun in the blank provided.
2. Write the letter of the sentence that contains the antecedent.

Example

(a) When a student graduates from high school, <u>he</u> or <u>she</u> should be
(1) (2)
prepared to enter a technical program or a collegiate institution.

(1) <u>student (a)</u>

(2) <u>student (a)</u>

(a) If a bank employee is encouraged to enter a training program, <u>he</u> or
(1)
<u>she</u> should take advantage of the opportunity.
(2)

(1)_____

(2)_____

(b) Some employees would rather spend <u>their</u> time enjoying <u>themselves</u>   (3)_____
     <u> </u>(3)   (4)
     than in trying to improve.   (4)_____

(c) <u>They</u> think that <u>their</u> superiors lack understanding.   (5)_____
     (5)   (6)
                                                                                    (6)_____

(d) However, the employee <u>whom</u> the bank promotes is likely to be the   (7)_____
                          (7)

     person <u>who</u> has completed a training program.   (8)_____
           (8)

ANSWERS TO FRAME 3

1. he: employee (a)   5. They: employees (b)
2. she: employee (a)   6. their: they (c)
3. their: employees (b)   7. whom: employee (d)
4. themselves: employees (b)   8. who: person (d)

Frame 4   Lists of Pronouns

Explanation

Because everything in the world has a name, the list of nouns is almost unending. As you have noticed, pronouns can be used over and over; therefore, our vocabulary includes fewer pronouns than nouns. Most of the pronouns in existence are listed below. In this frame you will be given practice in identifying pronouns; their usage is explained in Lessons 12, 13, & 14.

I	him	her	whom	somebody
you	her	its	which	all
he	it	mine	that	some
she	us	our	what	both
it	them	ours	another	few
we	my	their	anyone	many
they	your	theirs	anybody	others
me	his	who	someone	several
this	these	those	whose	myself
ourselves	yourself	yourselves	himself	herself
itself	oneself	themselves		

A pronoun may not always refer to an antecedent, either in the sentence that contains the pronoun or in a preceding sentence.

Example

Study the sentence and the explanation that accompanies it.

(a) Sam and Betty have been working at the bank since they graduated from high school. (The pronoun is <u>they</u>, and its antecedents are the two nouns <u>Sam</u> and <u>Betty</u>.)
(b) Your application should be sent to the Los Angeles office. (The pronoun <u>Your</u> does not have an antecedent.)

Exercise

1. Underscore each pronoun.
2. If a pronoun has an antecedent, first write the pronoun and then its antecedent in the blank provided.

Example

<u>He</u> injured <u>himself</u> with the paper knife.   <u>himself; he</u>

1. You yourself are responsible for preparing the budget.   _____
2. Tim Tuttle sent the contract to me.   _____
3. My subscription has expired.   _____
4. The clerks in the Shipping Department dislike their new work schedule.   _____
5. Amy sells farm equipment to the dealers in her territory.   _____
6. The manager and I went to the meeting.   _____
7. Her working is necessary because the family needs to increase its income.   _____
8. Who made the suggestion for improvement?   _____
9. Barney told me that he would send the form.   _____
10. These are the signed letters.   _____
11. Someone forgot to send the report.   _____
12. The person whom I called will contact you.   _____

ANSWERS TO FRAME 4

1. yourself: you	5. her: Amy	10. these: letters
2. me	7. Her; its: family	11. Someone
3. my	8. who	12. I; you; whom: person
4. their: clerks	9. me; he: Barney	

Frame 5   Verbs

Explanation

1. A *verb* is a word that expresses—
   a. action: walk, talk, compute, write
   b. being (or existence): is, am, was, were, be, been, are
   c. condition: become, seem, appear, look, taste, feel, smell (The last four are also called verbs of the senses.)
2. A verb may consist of—
   a. one word: wrote
   b. two words: has written
   c. three words or more: will have written
3. Each sentence must contain at least one verb. If it does not, it is unacceptable because it is not a complete thought. Agreement, voice, tense, and verbals are treated in Lessons 16, 17, 18, and 19.

Example

1. Read each sentence and notice the underscored verb.
2. The verb is labeled to show whether it expresses action, being, or condition.
   a. I <u>wrote</u> the report yesterday. (action)
   b. Elbert <u>is</u> the new manager. (being)
   c. Ellen <u>has worked</u> here for two years. (action)
   d. The corporate headquarters <u>will be moved</u> to Phoenix. (action)
   e. The computations <u>were</u> incorrect. (being)
   f. The sales representative <u>called</u> from the office in Reno and <u>sent</u> a telegram to Denver. (action)
   g. Frank Garth <u>will become</u> the new president when Mr. Ashton <u>retires.</u> (will become—condition; retires—action)

h. John, having organized the 96-page report during the past six weeks. (This sentence does not have a verb; therefore, it is not acceptable. The word having is a verb *form* that describes John and is not the verb of the sentence.)

i. The figures <u>appear</u> to be correct. (condition)

Exercise

1. Underscore each verb.
2. In the blank provided, write the word that identifies the verb: action, being, condition.

Example

The refinery fumes <u>smell</u> bad today.   <u>condition</u>

1. The letter was typed in the word processing center.   _____
2. I am in the process of packing my household goods.   _____
3. The truck crashed through the guard rail and fell into the river.   _____
4. The administrative assistant coordinates office activities and schedules work for the editors.   _____
5. She will have edited the chapters by Monday.   _____
6. Several people saw the accident.   _____
7. Without any previous knowledge of the subject and without having done any previous research to obtain a background.   _____
8. The weather has become very warm.   _____
9. The cafeteria food tastes worse each day.   _____

ANSWERS TO FRAME 5

1. The letter <u>was typed</u> in the word processing center.   <u>action</u>
2. I <u>am</u> in the process of packing my household goods.   <u>being</u>
3. The truck <u>crashed</u> through the guard rail and <u>fell</u> into the river.   <u>action</u>
4. The administrative assistant <u>coordinates</u> office activities and <u>schedules</u> work for the editors.   <u>action</u>
5. She <u>will have edited</u> the chapters by Monday.   <u>action</u>
6. Several people <u>saw</u> the accident.   <u>action</u>
7. Without any previous knowledge of the subject and without having done any previous research to obtain a background.   no verb; not <u>a sentence</u>
8. The weather <u>has become</u> very warm.   <u>condition</u>
9. The cafeteria food <u>tastes</u> worse each day.   <u>condition</u>

Frame 6   Adjectives

Explanation

An *adjective* is a word that describes a noun (*blue* dress) or restricts its meaning (*ten* men). It may also describe a pronoun. The use of an adjective makes the meaning of a noun or pronoun more precise and specific. A word that describes or limits the meaning of another word is called a *modifier;* therefore, an adjective is also a modifier. An adjective usually precedes a noun in sentence order; however, it may follow a noun or even the verb of a sentence.

The words *a, an,* and *the* are called *articles* and are treated as adjectives because they limit the nouns they modify. Adjectives are covered in detail in Lesson 20.

Example

1. Read each sentence.
2. Study the explanation that accompanies each sentence (or group).
    a. Notice that the noun (underscored) is changed by each adjective (capitalized) that is added.
        (1) THE <u>folder</u> is on the desk.
            (If eight folders are on the desk, to which one is the speaker referring?)
        (2) THE FILE <u>folder</u> is on the desk.
            (If all the folders are file folders, which one does the speaker mean?)
        (3) THE GREEN FILE <u>folder</u> is on the desk.
            (The folder is now identified—unless all the folders are green!)
    b. The adjectives may follow the noun or the pronoun.
        (1) THE <u>building,</u> OLD and DILAPIDATED, will be demolished soon.
        (2) THE <u>professor,</u> WELL KNOWN and CAPABLE, spoke at THE <u>meeting.</u>
        (3) THE <u>employees,</u> BROKE and DEJECTED after THE LONG <u>strike,</u> wanted to go to work.
    c. The adjective(s) may follow the verb.
        (1) THE <u>folder</u> is GREEN.
        (2) THE <u>building</u> has become OLD and DILAPIDATED.
        (3) THE <u>professor</u> is WELL KNOWN and CAPABLE.
        (4) <u>She</u> is PRETTY.
    Notice that each verb in Example C expresses either being or condition. An adjective (rather than an adverb) always follows these verbs.

Exercise

1. Underscore each adjective, each noun, and each pronoun.
2. Write A under each adjective, N under each noun, and P under each pronoun.

Example

Place <u>the</u> <u>incoming</u> <u>mail</u> in <u>the</u> <u>green</u> <u>basket.</u>
    A   A   N   A   A   N

1. The competent, efficient manager resigned last month.
2. The five-part form helps to capture most data at the source.
3. A picture, large, colorful, and scenic, hangs in the office.
4. She is capable, honest, and personable.
5. An applicant for this position needs some experience.
6. This agency sells commercial, farm, and ranch property.
7. The sound-absorbing panels are blue, green, and red.
8. Colorful, attractive packaging increases the cost of a product.

ANSWERS TO FRAME 6

1. <u>The</u> <u>competent,</u> <u>efficient</u> <u>manager</u> resigned <u>last</u> <u>month.</u>
  A   A   A   N   A   N
2. <u>The</u> <u>five-part</u> <u>form</u> helps to capture <u>most</u> <u>data</u> at <u>the</u> <u>source.</u>
  A   A   N   A   N   A   N
3. <u>A</u> <u>picture,</u> <u>large,</u> <u>colorful,</u> and <u>scenic,</u> hangs in <u>the</u> <u>office.</u>
 A N   A   A   A   A   N
4. <u>She</u> is <u>capable,</u> <u>honest,</u> and <u>personable.</u>
  P   A   A   A
5. <u>An</u> <u>applicant</u> for <u>this</u> <u>position</u> needs <u>some</u> <u>experience.</u>
 A   N   A   N   A   N

6. This agency sells commercial, farm, and ranch property.
   A   N   A   A   A   N

7. The sound-absorbing panels are blue, green, and red.
      A   A   N   A   A   A

8. Colorful, attractive packaging increases the cost of a product.
      A   A   N   A   N   A   N

Frame 7   *Adverbs*

Explanation

An *adverb* is a word that answers one of these questions: How? When? Where? Why? or How much? It modifies (describes or limits) a verb, an adjective, or another adverb. To determine if a word is an adverb, ask yourself one of these questions. Many adverbs end in *-ly;* others follow no particular pattern (*no, not, never, too, well*) and are identified by the words they modify. Adverbs are covered in detail in Lesson 21.

Example

1. Read the sentence.
2. Study the explanation.
   a. The editor proofreads pages rapidly.
      (1) What is the verb? Proofreads.
      (2) What is the answer to "Proofreads how?" Rapidly.
      (3) Rapidly adds something to proofreads by telling how the editor does it.
      (4) Rapidly modifies the verb and is an adverb.
   b. The vice president is a highly paid employee.
      (1) The word employee is a noun; what is the word that describes employee? Paid.
      (2) What is the answer to "How paid?" Highly.
      (3) Highly modifies the adjective and is an adverb.
   c. Some job-entry salaries are too low.
      (1) Which word in the sentence does low describe? Salaries.
      (2) Low is an adjective; what is the answer to the question, "How low?" Too.
      (3) Too modifies low, an adjective; therefore, it is an adverb.
   d. Grayson's new model of ranch truck is selling very well.
      (1) What is the verb? Is selling.
      (2) What is the answer to "Is selling how?" Well.
      (3) Well modifies the verb and is an adverb.
      (4) What is the answer to "How well?" Very.
      (5) Very modifies well, an adverb, and it is also an adverb.

Exercise

1. Underscore the adverbs in each sentence.
2. In the blank provided, write the word that each adverb modifies.

Example

Lois manages her department efficiently.

1. She transcribed her notes rapidly.
2. The sentence was too long to fit the crime.
3. The security device is extremely sensitive.
4. The new chemical additive is working well in the formula.
5. The accountant read the statement very carefully.

ANSWERS TO FRAME 7

1. She transcribed her notes <u>rapidly</u>.   <u>transcribed</u>
2. The sentence was <u>too</u> long to fit the crime.   <u>long</u>
3. The security device is <u>extremely</u> sensitive.   <u>sensitive</u>
4. The new chemical additive is working <u>well</u> in the formula.   <u>is working</u>
5. The accountant read the statement <u>very</u> <u>carefully</u>.   <u>carefully</u>
                                                                  <u>read</u>

Frame 8   Prepositions

Explanation

A *preposition* is a word that connects a noun or pronoun and its modifiers, adjectives and adverbs, to the rest of the sentence. The noun or pronoun that follows the preposition is called the *object of the preposition.* To be used correctly, a preposition must have an object. The preposition, its object, and the words that modify the object comprise a *prepositional phrase.*

To find the object of a preposition, ask the question *Who?* (for people) and *What?* (for things) after the preposition. The word that answers this question will be a noun or pronoun that is the object of the preposition.

Many prepositions show a location relative to another word: *in* the box, *by* the box, *inside* the box. Here are examples of some prepositions: <u>beside</u>, <u>from</u>, <u>upon</u>, <u>for</u>, <u>behind</u>, <u>into</u>, <u>at</u>, <u>on</u> and so on. Prepositions are discussed in detail in Lesson 23.

Example

1. Read the sentence.
2. Study the explanation.
    a. The bank is located on Oak Street.
        (1) If you believe that <u>on</u> is a preposition, what is the answer to the question "<u>On</u> what?" Oak Street.
        (2) <u>Oak Street</u> is the object of the preposition.
    b. Where is the bank located at?
        (1) If you believe that <u>at</u> is a preposition, what is the answer to the question "<u>At</u> where?" No answer!
        (2) The word <u>at</u> is used incorrectly; a preposition should have an object.

Exercise

1. Underscore the prepositions in each sentence.
2. Write the object of the preposition in the blank provided.

Example

I wrote the memo <u>for</u> him.   <u>him</u>

1. The switchboard operators transfer outside calls <u>to</u> the departments.
2. Supplies are obtained <u>by</u> requisition.
3. You must endorse (sign) your check <u>on</u> the back.
4. Electric cars may be manufactured <u>in</u> the future.
5. Where are you going to?

ANSWERS TO FRAME 8

1. The switchboard operators transfer outside calls <u>to</u> the departments.   <u>departments</u>
2. Supplies are obtained <u>by</u> requisition.   <u>requisition</u>
3. You must endorse (sign) your check <u>on</u> the back.   <u>back</u>
4. Electric cars may be manufactured <u>in</u> the future.   <u>future</u>
5. Where are you going <u>to</u>?   <u>no object;</u>
          <u>incorrect usage</u>

Frame 9   Conjunctions

A *conjunction* connects words, groups of words, (prepositional phrases, for example), or independent thoughts (sentences). The most common conjunctions are <u>and</u>, <u>but</u>, <u>or</u>, <u>for</u>, <u>nor</u>. They connect words, groups of words, or independent thoughts that are of equal rank.

Some conjunctions are used in pairs (either/or; neither/nor; both/and) to connect words, groups of words, or independent thoughts.

Other conjunctions (after, when, as, if) may begin a dependent thought within or at the beginning of a sentence.

Some conjunctions connect two independent thoughts. Examples of these conjunctions are <u>however</u>, <u>moreover</u>, <u>hence</u>, <u>yet</u>, <u>so</u>, <u>thus</u>, <u>consequently</u>, <u>therefore</u> and so on. A detailed discussion of conjunctions appears in Lesson 24.

Example

1. Read the sentence.
2. Study the explanation.
    a. Assets and liabilities are listed on the balance sheet.
        (1) <u>Assets</u> and <u>liabilities</u> are what parts of speech? Nouns.
        (2) They are of equal rank, and they are connected by <u>and</u>.
        (3) The word <u>and</u> is a conjunction.
    b. Either Gary or Isaac will represent the department.
        (1) <u>Gary</u> and <u>Isaac</u> are what parts of speech? Nouns.
        (2) They are of equal rank, and they are connected by <u>either</u> and <u>or</u>.
        (3) <u>Either</u> and <u>or</u> are conjunctions.
    c. I will write the report if you will prepare the graphic aids.
        (1) Which part of the sentence will not stand alone?
            (a) <u>I will write the report</u>, or
            (b) <u>if you will prepare the graphic aids</u>
        (2) Part (b) will not stand alone; it is dependent on part (a).
        (3) The word <u>if</u> introduces the dependent (subordinate) thought; it is a subordinate conjunction and connects the two thoughts.
    d. The snow was causing a traffic hazard; therefore, the employees were dismissed early.
        (1) Is the part of the sentence before <u>therefore</u> independent; that is, can it stand alone and make sense? Yes.
        (2) Is the part following <u>therefore</u> independent? Yes.
        (3) The word <u>therefore</u> is a conjunction that connects these two independent thoughts.

Exercise

Underscore the conjunction(s) in each sentence.

Example

The file is on the desk <u>or</u> in the cabinet.

1. The legal counsel was capable, ambitious, and loyal.
2. Neither the guard nor the employees could determine which person had the gun.
3. Four examiners were guilty of tampering with the books; consequently, they were fired.
4. The vote was taken after the chairman had left the meeting.
5. The flowchart was clearly presented, but the programmer was unable to follow it.

ANSWERS TO FRAME 9
1. The legal counsel was capable, ambitious, <u>and</u> loyal.
2. <u>Neither</u> the guard <u>nor</u> the employees could determine which person had the gun.
3. Four examiners were guilty of tampering with the books; <u>consequently</u>, they were fired.
4. The vote was taken <u>after</u> the chairman had left the meeting.
5. The flow chart was clearly presented, <u>but</u> the programmer was unable to follow it.

Frame 10   Interjections

Explanation

An *interjection* is a word that expresses feeling or emotion. The feeling or emotion may represent mild surprise or even shock. When the word shows strong emotion it is followed by an exclamation point; otherwise, it is followed by a comma.

An interjection is the least commonly used part of speech. It is used primarily in direct mail communications (letters that sell goods or services). It may also be used by a supervisor who writes critical incident reports about the behavior of employees; in these reports, the employee's exact words are used.

Example

1. Read the sentence.
2. Study the explanation.

    a. Oh, no! A cockroach just ran across the counter.
        (The two introductory words reflect the speaker's shock.)
    b. Well, the cafeteria manager should be told about this incident.
        (<u>Well</u> is a mild expression that is in itself meaningless; it is followed by a comma.)

Exercise

1. Underscore the interjections.
2. In the blank provided, write *mild* or *strong* to represent the degree of emotion shown by each word.

Example

<u>Congratulations</u>! You have just won a trip to Las Vegas, Nevada!   <u>strong</u>

1. <u>Hurry</u>! The last mail pickup is being logged now.   _____
2. Oh, I'll just put this letter in tomorrow morning's mail.   _____

ANSWERS TO FRAME 10

1. <u>Hurry</u>! The last mail pickup is being logged now.   <u> strong </u>
2. <u>Oh</u>, I'll just put this letter in tomorrow morning's mail.   <u> mild </u>

Frame 11   Review

Explanation

You have completed your practice in identifying each part of speech. Now you can practice identifying each word in a sentence.

Here is a brief reminder of what function each part of speech performs:

Part of Speech	*Function*
1. Noun	names a person, place, thing, or quality
2. Pronoun	is used as a noun substitute
3. Verb	shows action, being, or condition
4. Adjective	describes or restricts a noun or pronoun
5. Adverb	modifies a verb, adjective, or another adverb, and answers questions *how? when? where? why? how much?*
6. Preposition	connects its object (noun or pronoun) to the rest of the sentence; often shows location
7. Conjunction	connects words, groups of words, and sentences
8. Interjection	shows mild feeling or strong emotion

Exercise

1. Underscore each part of speech.
2. Under each part of speech, write the number keyed to that part in the Explanation.

Example

<u>Yes</u>! <u>He</u> <u>can perform</u> <u>the</u> <u>hard</u> <u>tasks</u> <u>very</u> <u>well</u> <u>without</u> <u>assistance</u> <u>or</u> <u>advice</u>.
 8   2   3   4   4   1   5   5   6   1   7   1

Of course, she was graduated from this college and is highly esteemed by the people in government.

ANSWER TO FRAME 11

<u>Of course</u>, <u>she</u> <u>was graduated</u> <u>from</u> <u>this</u> <u>college</u> <u>and</u> <u>is</u> <u>highly</u> <u>esteemed</u> <u>by</u> <u>the</u> <u>people</u> <u>in</u> <u>govern-</u>
   8   2   3   6   4   1   7   3   5   4   6   4   1   6   1

<u>ment</u>.

Frame 12   Word Position

Explanation

You have probably noticed that the same word may be shown as more than one part of speech. The position of any word in a sentence determines its part of speech.

Example

Read the sentences below and study the explanations which tell the part of speech and function of each underscored word.

1. I <u>work</u> on Third Avenue. (<u>work</u> is a verb here; it shows action)
2. The close <u>work</u> strains my eyes. (<u>work</u> is a noun here; it names something)
3. He made a <u>work</u> schedule. (<u>work</u> is an adjective here; it describes a noun)

Exercise

In the blank provided, write the part of speech for the underscored word.

Example

a.	A <u>college</u> education is a requirement for many executive positions.	<u>adjective</u>
b.	Joe attended a small <u>college</u> in Vermont.	<u>noun</u>

1.	a.	He did the job <u>for</u> me.	_____
	b.	I read the letter carefully, <u>for</u> I didn't want to make a poor impression.	_____
2.	a.	I bought a <u>green</u> dress.	_____
	b.	<u>Green</u> is my favorite color.	_____
3.	a.	The building is <u>too</u> close to the street.	_____
	b.	<u>Too</u> is usually an adverb.	_____

ANSWERS TO FRAME 12
1. a. preposition   2. a. adjective   3. a. adverb
   b. conjunction   b. noun   b. noun

Frame 13   Applying Your Knowledge

This proofreading exercise contains errors in content; that is, a statement may contain an error concerning the identification of a part of speech.

Directions

1. Read the case upon which the proofreading exercise is based.
2. Write True or False in the blank at the right to show that you believe or do not believe the statement. Not every sentence includes an error.
3. Correct the error and rewrite the sentence on the blank lines following the exercise.

Example

The English language is based on seven parts of speech.   <u>False</u>
<u>The English language is based on eight parts of speech.</u>

    CASE

    Chip is taking a speech course. His assignment requires that he prepare a two-minute speech containing specific information on a topic familiar to his classmates. Because he is also taking business English, he decided on the topic "Parts of Speech." After he hands the other students a copy of the speech, his instructor asks them to notice if he has made any incorrect statements. (He has made six errors!)

    a. A noun names a person, place, thing, or quality.   _____
    b. More pronouns than nouns exist in the English language.   _____
    c. Each pronoun must have an antecedent, a word to which it refers.   _____
    d. A verb may show action, being, or condition.   _____

    e.   Adjectives are words that describe or limit nouns.   _____

    f.   An adverb always ends in -ly.   _____

    g.   To be used correctly, a preposition should have an object.   _____

    h.   A conjunction connects words, groups of words (phrases), or independent thoughts.   _____

    i.   An interjection is most frequently used in letters of application.   _____

    j.   All eight parts of speech are found in most sentences.   _____

Now write the correct sentences on the lines provided.

_____

_____

_____

_____

_____

ANSWERS TO FRAME 13

a.   True

b.   False. More nouns than pronouns exist in the English language.

c.   False. A pronoun may have an antecedent, a word to which the pronoun refers.

d.   True

e.   False. Adjectives are words that describe or limit nouns and pronouns.

f.   False. Some adverbs end in -*ly*; others do not follow a pattern.

g.   True.

h.   True.

i.   False. An interjection is more frequently used in direct mail communications and reports that include a person's exact words.

j.   False. At least four of the eight parts of speech are found in most sentences.

Lesson 4
Sentence Construction: An Overview

Pretest

Directions

In the blank provided, write True if a statement is true and False if it is false.

1. This group of words has the characteristics of a sentence: The long, complex forms have been eliminated now.   _____

2. This group of words has the characteristics of a sentence: When the users recognize good and bad forms.   _____

3. In this sentence, (1) represents the independent clause: <u>Although a good attitude is a requisite for any job,</u> <u>it is especially important in an executive</u> setting.
   - (1) above "Although a good attitude is a requisite for any job,"
   - (2) above "it is especially important in an executive"   _____

4. The subject is identified by (2) and the verb by (1): Internship <u>programs</u> <u>have become</u> more popular in recent years and have accounted for a larger share of federal funds.
   - (2) above "programs"
   - (1) above "have become"   _____

5. The subject is identified by (2) and the verb by (1): The printouts for the <u>instructors</u> and the <u>students</u> <u>contain</u> discrepancies.
   - (2) above "instructors"
   - (2) above "students"
   - (1) above "contain"   _____

6. The subject of the dependent clause is labeled (2) and the verb of this clause is labeled (1): Students are often asked why <u>they</u> <u>want</u> to work for a certain company.
   - (2) above "they"
   - (1) above "want"   _____

7. The underscored words comprise a prepositional phrase: An application blank may be <u>obtained from the recruiter</u>.   _____

8. The underscored phrase is used as an adverb:
   Lana, an accounting major, went <u>to an interview</u>.   _____

9. The underscored phrase is used as an adjective:
   The man <u>in the blue suit</u> is an Apache Oil Company recruiter.   _____

10. The underscored phrase is used as an adverb:
    Please submit your application blank <u>to the Chicago office</u>.   _____

Lesson 4
Sentence Construction: An Overview

A sentence is the basic thought form in which words are used to convey facts and ideas. To construct a good sentence, the writer needs to be able to identify the parts of speech and understand the contribution of each part to a sentence.

You have had practice in identifying the parts of speech. In this lesson, you will learn how each part fits into various patterns to form different kinds of sentences. When you learn how sentences may vary in format, you can change the pattern to avoid monotony in your communications.

Frame 1   Recognizing a Sentence

Explanation

A sentence has these characteristics: (1) a group of grammatically related words, (2) a verb and a subject, and (3) a complete thought. A group of words that does not have these characteristics is a fragment, which is a partial sentence; or, it consists of meaningless words. Such constructions are not acceptable in business writing.

Example

Application 1

A sentence contains a group of grammatically related words.

To be grammatically related, words must form a logical, meaningful construction, such as a sentence, a clause, or a phrase. Which group of words is grammatically related? (a) ____? or (b) ____?

> (a) Supervisor the memo the employees a to wrote.
> (b) The supervisor wrote a memo to the employees.

ANSWER: (b) obviously! The point of asking you to make this selection was to illustrate the meaning of *grammatically related*, which is often misunderstood.

Application 2

A sentence contains a verb and a subject for that verb.
  a. Verb: a word that expresses action, being, or condition.
  b. Subject:
      1. is a noun or pronoun.
      2. usually precedes the verb in sentence order.
      3. can be identified by asking what? or who? before the verb.
  c. Simple Subject and Simple Verb: only the words that are used as the subject and the verb of the sentence.
  d. Complete subject and complete verb: the subject plus its modifiers and the verb plus its modifiers.

Note

The terms *simple predicate* and *complete predicate* are sometimes used instead of *simple verb* and *complete verb*.

  e. ALWAYS LOCATE THE VERB OF THE SENTENCE FIRST; THEN LOCATE ITS SUBJECT.

Which sentence contains a verb and a subject for that verb? (a) ____? or (b) ____?

> (a) The long, complex forms have been eliminated now.
> (b) The forms, long and complex, in every department of the company.

ANSWER: (a) Verb: *Have been eliminated*; Subject: *forms*. (b) does not contain a verb.

Application 3

A sentence represents a complete thought.
   Which of these groups of words consists of grammatically related words, contains a subject and verb, and represents a complete thought? (a) _____? or (b) _____?

   (a) If the initial sales are encouraging.
   (b) We shall develop a full-scale advertising campaign.

ANSWER: (b). It contains a group of grammatically related words, a verb (*shall develop*) and a subject for that verb (*we*, a pronoun). It also represents a complete thought. On the other hand, (a) is a group of grammatically related words and contains a verb (*are*) and a subject (*sales*), but it does not represent a complete thought. If you received a letter containing sentence (a) followed by a period, you would wonder if the writer had omitted something. If sentence (b) immediately followed (a), you would know the writer had punctuated (a) incorrectly. Whichever mistake the writer made will cause the reader to spend more time reading this communication than should be necessary.

Exercise

   1.   Identify the verb by writing V below it.
   2.   Identify the subject by writing S below it.
   3.   In the blank provided, write True if the group of words represents a sentence; write False if the group of words does not represent a sentence.

Example

If the shipment arrives as scheduled.   False
         S   V

   1.   Some forms can be completed easily.   _____
   2.   Other forms require a great deal of time and effort on the part of the users. _____
   3.   When the users recognize the poor forms.   _____
   4.   They may make suggestions for improving these forms.   _____
   5.   An analyst can construct good forms.   _____
   6.   If a file of forms is maintained by number.   _____

ANSWERS TO FRAME 1
   1.   Some forms can be completed easily.   True
            S   V
   2.   Other forms require a great deal of time and effort.   True
            S   V
   3.   When the users recognize the poor forms.   False
                  S   V
        (Although the sentence has a group of related words and contains a subject and verb, it does not represent a complete thought.)
   4.   They may make suggestions for improving these forms.   True
         S   V   V
        pronoun
   5.   An analyst can construct good forms.   True
            S   V   V
   6.   If a file of forms is maintained by number.   False
              S   V   V
        (Forms is not the subject; it is the object of the preposition *of* (it answers the question what? after the preposition). An object of the preposition cannot be the subject of a sentence.)

Frame 2   Independent and Dependent Clauses

A clause is a group of grammatically related words that contains a subject and verb.

Explanation

Two kinds of clauses exist:

1. *Independent:* This clause is a simple sentence. It is logical and meaningful when it stands alone.
2. *Dependent:* This clause depends upon the remainder of the sentence to give it a logical meaning because it cannot stand alone.

Example

Application 1

What is the number of the independent clause? (1) _____ ? or (2) _____ ?

> (Mr. Flynn wrote a letter of commendation to the personnel in
> (1)
> the Sales Department) (because they had won the coveted
> (2)
> national award.)

Prove your answer; fill in the blanks:

	(1)	(2)
Grammatically related words? (Yes? No?)	_____	_____
Verb and Subject? (List)	V: _____	V: _____
	S: _____	S: _____
Complete thought? (Yes? No?)	_____	_____

ANSWER: (1)   PROOF:

	(1)	(2)
Grammatically related words?	Yes	Yes
Verb and Subject?	V: wrote	V: had won
	S: Mr. Flynn	S: they
Complete thought?	Yes	No

Clause (2) depends upon the thought in clause (1) to complete its meaning. The word *because* is a subordinate conjunction; it introduces the dependent (subordinate) clause and connects it to the rest of the sentence.

Application 2

In the reversed sentence, which number indicates the independent clause? (1) _____ ? or (2) _____ ?

> (Because they had won the coveted national award,) (Mr.
> (1)   (2)
> Flynn wrote a letter of commendation to the personnel in the
> Sales Department.)

Prove your answer; fill in the blanks:

	(1)	(2)
Grammatically related words? (Yes? No?)	_____	_____
Verb and Subject? (List)	V: _____	V: _____
	S: _____	S: _____
Complete thought? (Yes? No?)	_____	_____

		(1)	(2)
ANSWER: (2)	PROOF:		
Grammatically related words?		Yes	Yes
Verb and Subject?		V: had won	V: wrote
		S: they	S: Mr. Flynn
Complete thought?		No	Yes

Changing the order of the clauses, but retaining the order of the words in each clause, does not change the characteristics of either clause. The word *because* remains a subordinate conjunction, even though it is at the beginning of the sentence. Notice that the introductory dependent clause is set off by a comma. This complies with the standard punctuation rule: Set off the introductory dependent clause with a comma.

Application 3

The dependent clause may be placed within a sentence. In this case, the independent clause begins the sentence, is interrupted by the dependent clause, and then completes the thought. In the following sentence, which numbered clause is dependent? (1) ____? or (2) ____?

> (Professor Jackson, (who wrote a book on management,) is now
>   (1)   (2)   (1)
> a consultant.)

Prove your answer; fill in the blanks:

	(1)	(2)
Grammatically related words? (Yes? No?)		
Verb and Subject? (List)	V:	V:
	S:	S:
Complete thought? (Yes? No?)		

	(1)	(2)
ANSWER: (2) PROOF:		
Grammatically related words?	Yes	Yes
Verb and Subject?	V: is	V: wrote
	S: Professor Jackson	S: who
Complete thought? (Yes?) (No?)	Yes	No

Occasionally, students say that a clause such as (2) is independent because it could form a question. However, the purpose of the sentence is to make a statement, not to ask a question. Never should the purpose of a sentence be distorted in identifying the clauses. Always be sure that the subject you select for a verb is in the same clause as the verb. A clause may be used as a part of speech; because this dependent clause modifies *Professor Jackson*, a noun, it is used as an adjective.

Application 4

In this sentence which numbered clause is dependent? (1) ____? or (2) ____?

> (The man (who wrote a book on management) is now a
>   (1)   (2)   (1)
> consultant.)

Prove your answer; fill in the blanks:

	(1)	(2)
Grammatically related words? (Yes? No?)	_____	_____
Verb and Subject? (List)	V: _____	V: _____
	S: _____	S: _____
Complete thought? (Yes? No?)	_____	_____

ANSWER: (2)   PROOF:

	(1)	(2)
Grammatically related words?	Yes	Yes
Verb and Subject?	V: is	V: wrote
	S: man	S: who
Complete thought? (Yes? No?)	Yes	No

Notice that in the previous sentence the dependent clause is set off by commas, and in this sentence it is not. The dependent clause is set off when the noun it modifies is specific (*Professor Jackson* names a person), but it is not set off if the noun it modifies is not specific (man). In this type of construction, you must be careful to select the subject and verb from the same clause.

Exercise

1. Place a set of parentheses around the independent clause and a set around the dependent clause.
2. Label the independent clause (1) and the dependent clause (2).
3. Prove your answer by completing the blanks below each sentence.

Example

Although the administrators prepare a great many communications, the majority are directed to faculty, staff, and other administrators within the institution.

(Although the administrators prepare a great many
(2)
communications,) (the majority are directed to faculty, staff,
(1)
and other administrators within the institution.)

PROOF:

	(1)	(2)
Grammatically related words? (Yes? No?)	Yes	Yes
Verb and Subject?	V: are directed	V: prepare
	S: majority	S: adminis- trators
Complete thought? (Yes? No?)	Yes	No

1. The board of regents is a university governing body that approves the budget for submission to the legislature.

PROOF: (1) (2)

Grammatically related words? _____ _____

Verb and subject? V:_____ V:_____

S:_____ S:_____

Complete thought? _____ _____

2. Although a good attitude is a requisite for any job, it is especially important in an executive setting.

    PROOF: (1) (2)

    Grammatically related words? _____ _____

    Verb and subject? V:_____ V:_____

    S:_____ S:_____

    Complete thought? _____ _____

3. Dr. Charbono, who has been president for ten years, is a former engineer and consultant.

    PROOF: (1) (2)

    Grammatically related words? _____ _____

    Verb and subject? V:_____ V:_____

    S:_____ S:_____

    Complete thought? _____ _____

4. The building that houses the chief administrators will be demolished.

    PROOF: (1) (2)

    Grammatically related words? _____ _____

    Verb and subject? V:_____ V:_____

    S:_____ S:_____

    Complete thought? _____ _____

ANSWERS TO FRAME 2

1. (The board of regents is a university governing body) (that approves the budget for sub-
    (1)   (2)
    mission to the legislature.)

PROOF:	(1)	(2)
Grammatically related words?	Yes	Yes
Verb and subject?	V: is	V: approves
	S: board of regents	S: that
Complete thought?	Yes	No

2. (Although a good attitude is a requisite for any job,) (it is especially important in an
   (2)   (1)
   executive setting.)

PROOF:	(1)	(2)
Grammatically related words?	Yes	Yes
Verb and subject?	V: is	V: is
	S: it	S: attitude
Complete thought?	Yes	No

3. (Dr. Charbono, (who has been president for ten years,) is a former engineer and consult-
    (1)   (2)   (1)
   ant.)

PROOF:	(1)	(2)
Grammatically related words?	Yes	Yes
Verb and subject?	V: is	V: has been
	S: Dr. Charbono	S: who
Complete thought?	Yes	No

4. (The building (that houses the chief administrators) will be demolished.)
    (1)   (2)   (1)

PROOF:	(1)	(2)
Grammatically related words?	Yes	Yes
Verb and subject?	V: will be demolished	V: houses
	S: building	S: that
Complete thought?	Yes	No

Frame 3   Compound Subjects in an Independent Clause

Both an independent clause and a dependent clause may have more than one subject
and more than one verb. Two of the same parts of speech are considered to be equal
in rank. A *coordinate conjunction* (and, but, or, for, nor) is a word that joins two words,
phrases, or clauses that are equal in rank.

Explanation

Two nouns or pronouns joined by a coordinate conjunction and used as the subjects
of a sentence are called a *compound subject*. Three or more words, phrases, or clauses of
equal rank form a series; the last two elements in the series are connected by a
coordinate conjunction.

Example

In each sentence:

1. Underscore the verb and label it (1).
2. Underscore the compound subject and label it (2).
3. Read the subjects and verb back to prove that you have made a logical choice.

Application 1

The following sentence contains a compound subject (<u>vice presidents</u> is a title, one word).

> The president and his vice presidents disagree on the subject of staff benefits.

ANSWER: The <u>president</u> and his <u>vice presidents</u> <u>disagree</u> on the subject of staff bene-
       (2)   (2)   (1)
fits.

READ BACK: president and vice presidents disagree.

Note

The pronoun *they* can be substituted for a compound subject, and *he, she,* or *it* for one subject. By substituting these words, you can prove your selection. For example, you would say *they* disagree (plural) but *he* (*she,* or *it*) disagrees (singular). A verb and its subject must always agree in number.

Application 2

The following sentence contains a compound subject and prepositional phrases. A prepositional phrase cannot contain the subject of a sentence.

> The printout for the instructors and the cards for the students contain discrepancies.

ANSWER: The <u>printout</u> for the instructors and the <u>cards</u> for the students <u>contain</u>
        (2)   (2)   (1)
discrepancies.

READ BACK: printout and cards contain. (They contain.)

Note

In this sentence the subjects are separated by several words; this construction is not unusual. You must be sure to ask what? or who? before the verb so that you do not select the wrong subject. The answer to <u>what contains?</u> is <u>printout</u> and <u>cards</u>. If you had asked who? you would have received an illogical answer: <u>instructors</u> and <u>students</u> <u>contain discrepancies</u>! Those nouns are the objects of prepositions.

Application 3

This sentence contains a series of subjects. Notice that the last two subjects are connected by a coordinate conjunction.

> The faculty, staff, and students gather in the auditorium for lectures.

ANSWER: The <u>faculty</u>, <u>staff</u>, and <u>students</u> <u>gather</u> in the auditorium for lectures.
         (2)   (2)   (2)   (1)
READ BACK: faculty, staff, students gather. (They gather.)

Exercise

1. Underscore the verb and subjects.
2. Label the verb (1) and the subjects (2).
3. Read back the sentence in subject/verb order to prove your choice.

Example

<u>David</u>, <u>Marsha</u>, and <u>Harold</u> <u>will receive</u> their awards on May 2.
  (2)   (2)   (2)   (1)

READ BACK: David, Marsha, and Harold will receive.

1. Scholarship organizations, professional clubs, and athletic organizations exist on most campuses.

    READ BACK:_____

2. Some college men and women can participate in few of these activities.

    READ BACK:_____

3. Membership fees, organization dues, and monetary assessments often create a burden on active students.

    READ BACK:_____

4. Membership in a professional club and participation in athletic activities comprise the extra-curricular interests of most students.

    READ BACK:_____

5. Many national politicians and professional people were active in student organizations during their college years.

    READ BACK:_____

ANSWERS TO FRAME 3

1. Scholarship <u>organizations</u>, professional <u>clubs</u>, and athletic <u>organizations</u> <u>exist</u> on most
                  (2)   (2)   (2)   (1)
    campuses.

    READ BACK: <u>organizations, clubs, and organizations exist</u>

2. Some college <u>men</u> and <u>women</u> <u>can participate</u> in few of these activities.
              (2)   (2)   (1)
    READ BACK: <u>men and women can participate</u>

3. Membership <u>fees</u>, organization <u>dues</u>, and monetary <u>assessments</u> often <u>create</u> a burden on
              (2)   (2)   (2)   (1)
    active students.

    READ BACK: <u>fees, dues, and assessments create</u>

4. <u>Membership</u> in a professional club and <u>participation</u> in athletic activities <u>comprise</u> the
      (2)   (2)   (1)
    extra-curricular interests of most students.

    READ BACK: <u>membership and participation comprise</u>

5. Many national <u>politicians</u> and professional <u>people</u> <u>were</u> active in student organizations
             (2)   (2) (1)
    during their college years.

    READ BACK: politicians and people were

Frame 4 *Compound Verbs in an Independent Clause*

Explanation

Like subjects, verbs may occur in a compound or series construction. The verbs may be separated only by the coordinate conjunction, or they may be separated by several words.

Example

Read through an entire sentence to assure yourself that you have found all the verbs. After you have selected the verb and its subject, read them back in subject/verb order to determine that they are logical and agree in number.

1. Underscore the verbs and subjects.
2. Label the verbs (1) and the subjects (2).

Application 1

The following sentence contains a compound verb.

> Jamie cleaned and oiled the microfilm processor.

ANSWER: <u>Jamie</u> <u>cleaned</u> and <u>oiled</u> the microfilm processor.
        (2)   (1)   (1)
READ BACK: Jamie cleaned and oiled

Application 2

In the following sentence, the compound verbs are separated by several words.

> Internship programs have become more popular in recent years and have accounted for a larger share of federal funds.

ANSWER: Internship <u>programs</u> <u>have become</u> more popular in recent years and <u>have</u>
                  (2)   (1)
<u>accounted</u> for a larger share of federal funds.
(1)
READ BACK: programs have become and have accounted

Application 3

The following sentence contains verbs in a series; the last two verbs are joined by a coordinate conjunction.

> The federal government recruits, trains, and hires graduates with internship experience.

ANSWER: The federal <u>government</u> <u>recruits</u>, <u>trains</u>, and <u>hires</u> graduates with intern-
             (2)   (1)   (1)   (1)
ship experience.

READ BACK: government recruits, trains, and hires

Exercise

1. Underscore each subject and verb.
2. Label each verb (1) and each subject (2).
3. Beside READ BACK write the words in subject/verb order to prove to yourself that you have selected the right subject.

Example

A college <u>student</u> <u>may earn</u> a salary, <u>acquire</u> work experience, and <u>gai</u> college
       (2)   (1)   (1)   (1)
credit in an internship program.

READ BACK: <u>student may earn, acquire, and gain</u>

1. Many firms have established internship programs and have actively recruited junior and senior students.

   READ BACK:_____

2. In some institutions, students spend one semester or quarter in an internship program and then write a report on their experience.

   READ BACK:_____

3. Marybeth Sipton sought and obtained a position in an internship program.

   READ BACK:_____

4. Many companies hire capable interns and provide them with additional training.

   READ BACK:_____

5. A college student needs, appreciates, and enjoys work experience.

   READ BACK:_____

ANSWERS TO FRAME 4

1. Many firms have established internship programs and have actively recruited junior
        (2)   (1)   (1)   (1)
   and senior students.

   READ BACK: firms have established and have recruited_____

2. In some institutions, students spend one semester or quarter in an internship program and
                          (2)   (1)
   then write a report on their experience.
        (1)
   READ BACK: students spend and write_____

3. Marybeth Sipton sought and obtained a position in an internship program.
        (2)   (1)   (1)
   READ BACK: Marybeth Sipton sought and obtained_____

4. Many companies hire capable interns and provide them with additional training.
        (2)   (1)   (1)
   READ BACK: companies hire and provide_____

5. A college student needs, appreciates, and enjoys work experience.
              (2)   (1)   (1)   (1)
   READ BACK: student needs, appreciates, and enjoys_____

Frame 5   Compound Subjects and Verbs in Independent and Dependent Clauses

Explanation

The subject for a verb must be in the same clause as the verb. The subject and verb must agree in number (singular and plural).

Example

Follow this procedure to identify the verbs and their subjects.

1. Place parentheses ( ) around the independent clause and label the clause IC.
2. Place parentheses ( ) around the dependent clause and label the clause DC.
3. Underline the subjects and verbs in each clause, labeling the verb(s) (1) and the subject(s) (2).

Application 1

The following sentence is an independent clause. It contains two verbs and two subjects. Both verbs take the same subjects.

> Freshmen and sophomores should attend career guidance classes and should also research careers of interest.

ANSWER: (Freshmen and sophomores should attend career guidance classes and
$\quad\quad$ (IC) $\quad$ (2) $\quad\quad\quad\quad\quad$ (2) $\quad\quad\quad$ (1)
should also research careers of interest.)
(1) $\quad\quad$ (1)

READ BACK: Freshmen and sophomores should attend and should research

The word *also* is an adverb, modifying the verb *should research*.

Application 2

The following sentence contains an independent and a dependent clause. Select the verb(s) and subject(s) for the independent clause and for the dependent clause.

> A career counselor who advises students on interviewing procedures is located in the Career Services Center.

ANSWER: (A career counselor (who advises students on interviewing procedures) is
$\quad\quad\quad$ IC $\quad\quad$ (2) $\quad\quad$ (2) $\quad$ (1) DC
located in the Career Services Center.)
(1)

READ BACK: IC: counselor is located
$\quad\quad\quad\quad\quad$ DC: who advises

Application 3

This sentence contains two independent clauses connected by a coordinate conjunction. It is called a *compound sentence*. Each independent clause has its own verb(s) and subject(s), of course. The conjunction "and" does not belong to either clause.

> Undergraduates want career counseling, and upperclassmen expect specific career advice.

ANSWER: (Undergraduates want career counseling,) and (upper classmen expect
$\quad\quad$ IC $\quad$ (2) $\quad\quad\quad$ (1) $\quad\quad\quad\quad\quad$ IC $\quad$ (2) $\quad\quad$ (1)

career advice.)

READ BACK: Undergraduates want; upperclassmen expect

Exercise

1. Place parentheses (   ) around the independent clause and label the clause IC.
2. Place parentheses (   ) around the dependent clause and label the clause DC.
3. Underline the subjects and verbs in each clause, labeling the verbs (1) and the subjects (2).

Example

(Young men and women (who hope to acquire entry-level management positions)
(IC) $\quad$ (2) $\quad\quad$ (2) $\quad\quad$ (2) (1) $\quad\quad\quad\quad\quad$ (DC)

should prepare well-organized résumés and show poise and courtesy during
(1) $\quad\quad\quad\quad\quad\quad\quad\quad\quad\quad$ (1)

interviews.)

READ BACK: Men and women should prepare and show; who hope

1. Business and government recruiters visit the campus and interview students who are interested in their organizations.

   READ BACK:_____

2. Recruiters tell the interviewee about the job, and they expect the student to ask pertinent, logical questions.

   READ BACK:_____

3. Students are often asked why they want to work for a certain company.

   READ BACK:_____

4. Before a student goes to the interview, he or she should read about the interviewing organization.

   READ BACK:_____

5. The recruiters and faculty expect students to dress in a businesslike way when they come to the interview session.

   READ BACK:_____

ANSWERS TO FRAME 5

1. (Business and government <u>recruiters</u> <u>visit</u> the campus and <u>interview</u> students)
   IC   (2)   (1)   (1)
   (<u>who</u> <u>are</u> <u>interested</u> in their organizations.)
    (2) (1) DC

   READ BACK: recruiters visit and interview; who are interested

2. (<u>Recruiters</u> <u>tell</u> the interviewee about the job,) and (<u>they</u> <u>expect</u> the student to ask
   IC (2)   (1)   (2) IC (1)
   pertinent, logical questions.)

   READ BACK: Recruiters tell; they expect

   The word *ask* is not a verb in this sentence; *to* and *ask* together form an infinitive. A verb

   that is immediately preceded by *to* is never the verb of the sentence.

3. (<u>Students</u> <u>are</u> often <u>asked</u> (why <u>they</u> <u>want</u> to work for a certain company.))
   IC (2)   (1)   (1)   DC (2)   (1)
   READ BACK: Students are asked; they want

   The word *often* answers the question when? and is an adverb. This entire sentence is in-

   dependent; that is, the dependent clause is essential to make the sentence complete. Here

   we have a dependent clause within an independent clause.

4. (Before a <u>student</u> <u>comes</u> to the interview), (<u>he</u> or <u>she</u> <u>should</u> <u>read</u> about the
   DC   (2)   (1)   (2) DC(2) (1)   (1)
   interviewing organization.)

   READ BACK: student comes; he/she should read

5. (The <u>recruiters</u> and <u>faculty</u> <u>expect</u> students to dress in a businesslike way) (<u>when</u>
   IC   (2)   (2)   (1)   DC
   <u>they</u> <u>come</u> to the interview session.)
   (2)   (1)
   READ BACK: recruiters and faculty expect; they come

Frame 6   *Recognizing a Phrase—Identification of Prepositional Phrases*

A *phrase* is a group of grammatically related words without a subject and a verb. A phrase may be located at the beginning, at the end, or in the middle of a sentence.

The first word of a phrase usually identifies the phrase. For example, a phrase beginning with a preposition and having an object and perhaps modifiers is called a prepositional phrase.

Some types of phrases can be used as a part of speech, just as a clause and a word can. The prepositional phrase can be used as an adjective or an adverb.

In this section, the prepositional phrase will be used as an example of (1) possible locations for a phrase, (2) how to determine if a phrase has an object (and modifiers), and (3) how to analyze a phrase to determine the part of speech it represents.

Explanation

As you probably recall, a *prepositional phrase* has an object. The object is found by asking what? or whom? after the preposition.

Example

Application 1

Underscore the prepositional phrase and label its object OP.

An application blank may be obtained from the recruiter.

ANSWER: An application blank may be obtained <u>from the recruiter</u>.

OP

The word <u>from</u> is a preposition; the answer to *from what?* is <u>recruiter</u>, the object of the preposition, and <u>the</u> is an adjective (article) that modifies the noun, <u>recruiter</u>.

Application 2

In this sentence, the preposition is used as an adverb and, therefore, does not take an object.

The price of corn is going up.

ANSWER: The price of corn is going <u>up</u>. The word is a preposition, but it is used as an adverb, telling *where* after the verb, <u>is going</u>.

Application 3

In this sentence, the preposition is used incorrectly. Why?

Where shall I send the check to?

ANSWER: Where shall I send the check <u>to</u>? The preposition <u>to</u> does not have an object. In fact, the preposition should not even be a part of the sentence. The addition of this word creates an ungrammatical sentence.

Exercise

1. Underscore the prepositional phrase and label the object OP.
2. If a preposition is not used as a preposition or if it is used incorrectly, explain on the line below. (A sentence may have more than one prepositional phrase.)

Example

Where will the interviews be held <u>at</u>?

The preposition <u>at</u> does not have an object, nor is it used as an adverb. It should be omitted from the sentence.

---

1. Interviews are held in the Administration Building.

---

2. You should take a résumé to the interview.

   _____

3. From the résumé, the interviewer will learn about your background.

   _____

4. The résumés of several applicants will be evaluated.

   _____

5. He asked if we could run off some copies.

   _____

6. Where is the office at?

   _____

ANSWERS TO FRAME 6
1. Interviews are held <u>in the Administration Building</u>.
                            OP
2. You should take a résumé <u>to the interview</u>.
                                 OP
3. <u>From the résumé</u>, the interviewer will learn <u>about your background</u>.
        OP   OP
4. The résumés <u>of several applicants</u> will be evaluated.
                        OP
5. He asked if we could run <u>off</u> some copies.
   In this sentence <u>off</u> is used as an adverb, modifying the verb <u>run</u>.
6. Where is the office <u>at</u>?
   The word <u>at</u> is used incorrectly. Its use makes the sentence ungrammatical. Correction:
   Where is the office?

Frame 7 Use of Prepositional Phrases

Explanation

A prepositional phrase can be used as an adjective or as an adverb. As an adjective, it modifies a noun or pronoun; as an adverb, it modifies a verb, an adjective, or another adverb.

The purpose of learning how a phrase is used (any phrase) helps you to determine if you have placed it in the proper position in a sentence. A phrase should always be close to the word it modifies.

Example

Each prepositional phrase is underscored.

1. Analyze the sentence to determine which word the phrase modifies.
2. Prove your answer by completing the blanks under the sentence.

Application 1

Lana, an accounting major, went <u>to an interview</u>.

This phrase modifies the word _____.

This word is a(an) _____. (Use *an* before words beginning with a vowel and *a* before words beginning with a consonant.)

A phrase that modifies a(an) _____ is used as a(an) _____.

ANSWER:
This phrase modifies the word <u>went</u>.
This word is a <u>verb</u>. (It answers the question *went where?*)
A phrase that modifies a <u>verb</u> is used as an <u>adverb</u>.

Application 2

The man <u>in the blue suit</u> is the Dixieland recruiter.

This phrase modifies the word _____.

This word is a(an) _____.

A phrase that modifies a(an) _____ is used as a(an) _____.

ANSWER:
This phrase modifies the word <u>man</u>.
This word is a <u>noun</u> (the subject of the sentence).
A phrase that modifies a <u>noun</u> is used as an <u>adjective</u>.

Application 3

Pleased <u>with the results</u>, Anne celebrated her first interview.

This phrase modifies the word _____.

This word is a(an) _____.

A phrase that modifies a(an) _____ is used as a(an) _____.

ANSWER:
This phrase modifies the word <u>Pleased</u>.
This word is an <u>adjective</u>. The word <u>Pleased</u> describes <u>Anne</u> ("Pleased Anne");
because <u>Anne</u> is a noun, the word that modifies it is an adjective.
A phrase that modifies an <u>adjective</u> is used as an <u>adverb</u>.

Application 4

She works efficiently <u>at all times</u>.

This phrase modifies the word _____.
This word is a(an) _____.
A phrase that modifies a(an) _____ is used as a(an) _____.

ANSWER:
This phrase modifies the word <u>efficiently</u>.
This word is an <u>adverb</u>. (It answers *works how?*)
A phrase that modifies an <u>adverb</u> is used as an <u>adverb</u>.

Note

In each example, the phrase modified a word that was adjacent to it. The word that a phrase modifies is usually adjacent to or near the phrase. Notice the situation when this order is violated: She said that she had two children <u>in the letter</u>. Does <u>in the letter</u> modify children? It does in this sentence, but that is why the sentence is amusing. What word should the phrase modify? The phrase should modify <u>said</u>: She

(e) A sentence may have two or more subjects and two or more verbs. (e)_____
(f) To find the subject, the writer asks the question *whom?* or *what?* before (f)_____
the verb. (g) To find the object of the preposition and the object of the (g)_____
verb, the writer asks the question *what?* or *whom?* after the preposition and
after the verb.

(h) A prepositional phrase consists of the preposition and its object (and (h)_____
may include modifiers of the object). (i) A prepositional phrase may be (i)_____
used as an adjective or as an adverb. (j) If it is used as an adjective, it (j)_____
modifies a pronoun; if it is used as an adverb, it modifies a verb, adjective, or
noun.

Now rewrite the incorrect sentences, giving the accurate information.

_____

_____

_____

_____

_____

ANSWERS TO FRAME 8

a. True
b. True
c. True
d. False. A dependent clause may be located at the beginning, in the middle, or at the end of an
    independent clause.
e. True
f. False. To find the subject, the writer asks the question *who?* or *what?* before the verb.
g. True
h. True
i. True
j. False. If it is used as an adjective, it modifies a noun or pronoun; if it is used as an adverb, it
    modifies a verb, an adjective, or an adverb.

Lesson 5
Dictionary Usage

Pretest

Directions

1. Read each sentence carefully.
2. If the sentence is true, write True in the blank provided.
3. If the sentence is false, write False in the blank.

1. One guide word is located in the upper left-hand corner and one in the lower right-hand corner of each page in most dictionaries. _____
2. Occasionally a vocabulary entry is followed by the same word spelled differently; this second spelling is an older version of the word and should never be used. _____
3. The *vi* which may follow a verb means *verb in transit* and refers to one that takes an object. _____
4. You should expect to find the past tense, past participle, and progressive tense for the word *work* in most dictionaries. _____
5. In some dictionaries, the first definition is the one which entered the English vocabulary first; and in other dictionaries, the first definition is the one most commonly used. _____
6. A synonym is a word that means the same or almost the same as the main vocabulary entry for which it is listed. _____
7. An acronym is usually in brackets and gives the anatomy, or history, of the main vocabulary entry for which it is listed. _____
8. Obsolete words are not listed in modern dictionaries. _____
9. The label *archaic* before a definition indicates that this definition is used primarily in architecture. _____
10. The word *ain't* is substandard English and therefore not listed in dictionaries. _____

Lesson 5
Dictionary Usage

What Can You Find in the Dictionary?

The dictionary is the most comprehensive reference book that you will ever use. Your success in many endeavors will depend upon your ability to speak and write clearly and correctly. You can use the dictionary as a tool to help you achieve this success.

Shown below are the kinds of facts you can obtain for each main vocabulary entry in a desk-type dictionary and the reasons these facts are important to you.

Facts	*Importance*
1. Correct spelling of words	Impresses readers (teachers and supervisors) favorably.
2. Word division	Shows you where to divide words at end of line.
3. Pronunciation	Clarifies your oral communication.
4. Parts of speech	Helps you use words correctly in a sentence.
5. Inflected word forms	Gives more assistance in spelling derivatives.
6. History of words	Helps you understand the English vocabulary.
7. Word usage	Shows you acceptable and unacceptable words.
8. Definitions	Permits you to choose the most appropriate word.
9. Synonyms	Decreases the monotony of your writing.
10. Antonyms	Makes your writing more precise.

In addition to the vocabulary listings, most desk dictionaries contain some or all of the following parts. (Place a check beside the parts that are contained in the desk dictionary you are using.)

1. An explanatory chart identifying the location of each item in the vocabulary listing
2. Explanatory notes illustrating the various facts under each vocabulary entry
3. A brief history of the English language
4. A list of abbreviations used in the dictionary
5. An explanation of the pronunciation symbols
6. A list of foreign words and phrases
7. A list of biographical names
8. A list of geographical names with a brief description of each location
9. A list of colleges and universities
10. A list and explanation of signs and symbols used in various fields
11. A handbook of style for business correspondence

How Should You Select a Dictionary?

The dictionary you select should meet your specific needs. Dictionaries are usually categorized as unabridged, abridged, or pocket-size.

Unabridged

This type of dictionary contains millions of entries and weighs over ten pounds. It is usually found on a pedestal or table in a library or in a central office location.

Abridged

Most desk dictionaries are abridged (condensed) to some extent. These dictionaries usually contain between one and two thousand pages. The vocabulary entries and reference information are sufficiently comprehensive for the purposes of most college students and business people; therefore, you should own an abridged desk-type dictionary.

Pocket-size

A dictionary of this size is published in paperback and fits easily into a purse, brief-case, or even a pocket. It is more convenient than a larger, heavier dictionary; therefore, it is generally used for in-class reference. To save space, this type of dictionary has fewer vocabulary entries than the abridged version; also, the explanatory material and vocabulary information are very concise.

We will use an abridged desk dictionary to construct this lesson. Various abridged desk dictionaries are on the market, and all perform the same function. If your desk dictionary is not the same as the one used in this lesson, you may detect minor differences in the presentation of some elements. These slight differences should not hinder you in completing the exercises. Instead, they should make you aware that (1) dictionary publishers may use different formats for the presentation of the various elements that identify words, and (2) dictionary editors, all experts, may define some words in a slightly different manner.

As you proceed through the frames, refer to the dictionary illustration page in this lesson and compare the presentation of each item with that in your desk dictionary. This information in this lesson is based primarily on *Webster's New Collegiate Dictionary*, 8th edition.

Frame 1   Locating a Specific Vocabulary Entry

Explanation

In a desk dictionary, locate the explanatory notes which serve as a guide to using the dictionary. Notes concerning dictionary usage precede the listed vocabulary. Read the explanations for *guide words* and *main vocabulary entries*. To locate a vocabulary entry easily, the user must be able to discern between which two guide words the entry would occur.

Two guide words are usually shown at the top of each dictionary page, above the main vocabulary entries. (Compare the dictionary page illustrated with a page in your dictionary.)

a. The word to the left is the first main vocabulary entry on the page: *accompanist*.
b. The word to the right is the last main vocabulary entry on the page: *accumulator*.

The main vocabulary entry consists of a word, letter, or combination of letters printed in boldface type against the left-hand margin of each column. The main vocabulary entries are in strict alphabetical order. Compare each of the following statements with the presentation in your dictionary.

1. A word or abbreviation beginning with a number is alphabetized as if the number were spelled out.
2. A single word precedes a compound word that begins with the single word: *follow* precedes *followup*.
3. A solid compound word precedes the same compound word in hyphenated form: *followup* precedes *follow-up*.
4. A hyphenated compound word precedes that compound word written as two words: *follow-up* precedes *follow up*.
5. A lowercase entry precedes the same entry in capitalized form: *french* precedes *French*.

Example

Many people cannot locate a main vocabulary entry rapidly because they do not use the guide words. This example exercise provides practice in locating an entry by using guide words. Because the guide words will be different if you are not using *Webster's New Collegiate Dictionary*, you are asked to select them from the examples that follow.

intended to give completeness or symmetry : COMPLEMENT **b** : an accompanying situation or occurence : CONCOMITANT

ac·com·pa·nist \ə-'kəmp-(ə-)nəst\ *n* : one (as a pianist) who plays an accompaniment

ac·com·pa·ny \ə-'kəmp-(ə-)nē\ *vb* **-nied; -ny·ing** [ME *accompanien*, fr. MF *acompaignier*, fr. *a-* (fr. L *ad-*) + *compaing* companion, fr. LL *companio*] *vt* **1** : to go with or attend as an associate or companion **2** : to perform an accompaniment to or for **3 a** : to cause to be in association : add or join to <*accompanied* his advice with a warning> **b** : to be in association with <the pictures that ~ the text> ~ *vi* : to perform an accompaniment
 syn ACCOMPANY, ATTEND, ESCORT *shared meaning element* : to go along with

ac·com·plice \ə-'käm-pləs, -'kəm-\ *n* [alter. (fr. incorrect division of *a complice*) of *complice*] : one associated with another esp. in wrongdoing

ac·com·plish \ə-'käm-plish, -'kəm-\ *vt* [ME *accomplisshen*, fr. MF *acompliss-*, stem of *acomplir*, fr. (assumed) VL *accomplēre*, fr. L *ad-* + *complēre* to fill up — more at COMPLETE] **1** : to bring to a successful conclusion : carry to completion <when they had ~*ed* their journey> <I hope to ~ much more today> **2** : to attain to (a measure of time or distance) : COVER <at that rate will ~ only half the distance> **3** *archaic* **a** : to equip thoroughly **b** : PERFECT ***syn*** see PERFORM — **ac·com·plish·able** \-ə-bəl\ *adj* — **ac·com·plish·er** *n*

ac·com·plished *adj* **1** : COMPLETED, EFFECTED <an ~ fact> **2 a** : complete in acquirements as the result of practice or training <an ~ dancer> **b** : having many social accomplishments

ac·com·plish·ment \ə-'käm-plish-mənt, -'kəm-\ *n* **1** : the act of accomplishing : COMPLETION **2** : something accomplished : ACHIEVEMENT **3 a** : a quality or ability equipping one for society **b** : a special skill or ability acquired by training or practice

1**ac·cord** \ə-'kȯ(ə)rd\ *vb* [ME *accorden*, fr. OF *acorder*, fr. (assumed) VL *accordare*, fr. L *ad-* + *cord-*, *cor* heart — more at HEART] *vt* **1** : to bring into agreement : RECONCILE **2 a** : to grant as suitable or proper **b** : to allow as a concession **c** : to confer something on as an award **d** : to assign as a portion ~ *vi* **1** *archaic* : to arrive at an agreement **2** *obs* : to give consent **3** : to exhibit perfect fitness in a relationship or association : adjust or fit harmoniously ***syn* 1** see AGREE ***ant*** conflict **2** see GRANT ***ant*** withhold

2**accord** *n* [ME, fr. OF *acort*, fr. *acorder*] **1 a** : AGREEMENT, CONFORMITY <acted in ~ with the company's policy> **b** : a formal act of agreement : TREATY **2** : balanced interrelationship : HARMONY **3** *obs* : ASSENT **4** : voluntary or spontaneous impulse to act <gave generously of their own ~>

ac·cor·dance \ə-'kȯrd-ᵊn(t)s\ *n* **1** : AGREEMENT, CONFORMITY <in ~ with a rule> **2** : the act of granting

ac·cor·dant \-ᵊnt\ *adj* **1** : CONSONANT, AGREEING **2** : HARMONIOUS, CORRESPONDENT — **ac·cor·dant·ly** *adv*

ac·cord·ing as *conj* **1** : in accord with the way in which **2 a** : depending on how **b** : depending on whether : IF

ac·cord·ing·ly \ə-'kȯrd-iŋ-lē\ *adv* **1** : in accordance : CORRESPONDINGLY **2** : CONSEQUENTLY, SO

according to *prep* **1** : in conformity with **2** : as stated or attested by **3** : depending on

1**ac·cor·di·on** \ə-'kȯrd-ē-ən\ *n* [G *akkordion*, fr. *akkord* chord, fr. F *accord*, fr. OF *acort*] : a portable keyboard wind instrument in which the wind is forced past free reeds by means of a hand-operated bellows — **ac·cor·di·on·ist** \-ē-ə-nəst\ *n*

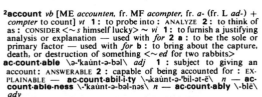

accordion

2**accordion** *adj* : folding or creased or hinged to fold like an accordion <an ~ pleat> <an ~ door>

ac·cost \ə-'kȯst, -'käst\ *vt* [MF *accoster*, deriv. of L *ad-* + *costa* rib, side — more at COAST] : to approach and speak to often in a challenging or aggressive way

ac·couche·ment \ˌa-ˌküsh-'mä^n, ə-'küsh-ˌ\ *n* [F] : LYING-IN; *esp* : PARTURITION

ac·cou·cheur \ˌa-ˌkü-'shər\ *n* [F] : one that assists at a birth <without President Truman as ~ there would have been no Israel —B. C. Crum>; *esp* : OBSTETRICIAN

1**ac·count** \ə-'kau̇nt\ *n* **1** *archaic* : RECKONING, COMPUTATION **2 a** : a record of debit and credit entries chronologically posted to a ledger page to cover transactions involving a particular item or a particular person or concern **b** : a statement of transactions during a fiscal period **3** : a collection of items to be balanced — usu. used in pl. **4** : a statement explaining one's conduct **5 a** : a periodically rendered calculation listing charged purchases and credits <a grocery ~ > **b** : the patronage involved in establishing or maintaining an account : BUSINESS<glad to get that customer's ~> **6 a** : VALUE, IMPORTANCE <a man of no ~> **b** : ESTEEM, JUDGMENT <he stands high in their ~> **7** : PROFIT, ADVANTAGE <turned his wit to good ~> **8 a** : a statement or exposition of reasons, causes, grounds, or motives <no satisfactory ~ of these phenomena> **b** : a reason for an action : BASIS <on all ~*s* you must do it> **c** : careful thought : CONSIDERATION <left nothing out of ~> **9** : a statement of facts or events : RELATION <a newspaper ~> **10** : HEARSAY, REPORT — usu. used in pl. <by all ~*s* a rich man> **11** : a sum of money or its equivalent deposited in the common cash of a bank and subject to withdrawal by the depositor — **on account of** : for the sake of : by reason of : because of — **on no account** : under no circumstances — **on one's own account 1** : on one's own behalf **2** : at one's own risk **3** : by oneself : on one's own

2**account** *vb* [ME *accounten*, fr. MF *acompter*, fr. *a-* (fr. L *ad-*) + *compter* to count] *vt* **1** : to probe into : ANALYZE **2** : to think of as : CONSIDER <~*s* himself lucky> ~ *vi* **1** : to furnish a justifying analysis or explanation — used with *for* **2 a** : to be the sole or primary factor — used with *for* **b** : to bring about the capture, death, or destruction of something <~*ed* for two rabbits>

ac·count·able \ə-'kau̇nt-ə-bəl\ *adj* **1** : subject to giving an account : ANSWERABLE **2** : capable of being accounted for : EXPLAINABLE — **ac·count·abil·i·ty** \-ˌkau̇nt-ə-'bil-ət-ē\ *n* — **ac·count·able·ness** \-'kau̇nt-ə-bəl-nəs\ *n* — **ac·count·ably** \-blē\ *adv*

ac·coun·tan·cy \ə-'kau̇nt-ᵊn-sē\ *n* : the profession or practice of accounting

ac·coun·tant \ə-'kau̇nt-ᵊnt\ *n* **1** : one that gives an account or is accountable **2** : one who is skilled in the practice of accounting or who is in charge of public or private accounts — **ac·coun·tant·ship** \-ᵊn(t)-ˌship\ *n*

account book *n* : a book in which accounts are kept : LEDGER

account executive *n* : a business executive (as in an advertising agency) responsible for the management of a client's account

ac·count·ing \ə-'kau̇nt-iŋ\ *n* **1** : the system of recording and summarizing business and financial transactions in books and analyzing, verifying, and reporting the results; *also* : the principles and procedures of accounting **2 a** : practical application of accounting **b** : an instance of applying the principles and procedures of accounting

accounting machine *n* : a business machine that is key-operated or uses stored data (as punch cards) and that tabulates, adds, subtracts, or totals

account payable *n, pl* **accounts payable** : the balance due to a creditor on a current account

account receivable *n, pl* **accounts receivable** : a balance due from a debtor on a current account

ac·cou·tre *or* **ac·cou·ter** \ə-'küt-ər\ *vt* **-cou·tred** *or* **-cou·tered; -cou·tring** *or* **-cou·ter·ing** \-'küt-ə-riŋ, -'kü-triŋ\ [F *accoutrer*, fr. MF *acoustrer*, fr. *a-* + *costure* seam, fr. (assumed) VL *consutura*, fr. L *consutus*, pp. of *consuere* to sew together, fr. *com-* + *suere* to sew — more at SEW] : to provide with equipment or furnishings : OUTFIT ***syn*** see FURNISH

ac·cou·tre·ment *or* **ac·cou·ter·ment** \ə-'kü-trə-mənt, -'küt-ər-mənt\ *n* **1** : the act of accoutering : the state of being accoutered **2 a** : an article of equipment or dress esp. when used as an accessory **b** : EQUIPMENT, TRAPPINGS; *specif* : a soldier's outfit usu. not including clothes and weapons — usu. used in pl. **3** : an identifying and often superficial characteristic

ac·cred·it \ə-'kred-ət\ *vt* [F *accréditer*, fr. *ad-* + *crédit* credit] **1** : to consider or recognize as outstanding **2** : to give official authorization to or approval of: **a** : to provide with credentials; *esp* : to send (an envoy) with letters of authorization **b** : to recognize or vouch for as conforming with a standard **c** : to recognize (an educational institution) as maintaining standards that qualify the graduates for admission to higher or more specialized institutions or for professional practice **3** : CREDIT ***syn*** see APPROVE — **ac·cred·i·table** \-ə-bəl\ *adj* — **ac·cred·i·ta·tion** \ə-ˌkred-ə-'tā-shən\ *n*

ac·crete \ə-'krēt\ *vb* **ac·cret·ed; ac·cret·ing** [back-formation fr. *accretion*] *vi* : to grow or become attached by accretion ~ *vt* : to cause to adhere or become attached : ACCUMULATE

ac·cre·tion \ə-'krē-shən\ *n* [L *accretion-*, *accretio*, fr. *accretus*, pp. of *accrescere* — more at ACCRUE] **1** : the process of growth or enlargement: as **a** : increase by external addition or accumulation (as by adhesion of external parts or particles) **b** : the increase of land by the gradual or imperceptible action of natural forces **2** : a product of accretion; *esp* : an extraneous addition <~*s* of grime> **3** : coherence of separate particles : CONCRETION — **ac·cre·tion·ary** \-shə-ˌner-ē\ *adj* — **ac·cre·tive** \ə-'krēt-iv\ *adj*

ac·cru·al \ə-'krü-əl\ *n* **1** : the action or process of accruing **2** : something that accrues or has accrued

ac·crue \ə-'krü\ *vb* **ac·crued; ac·cru·ing** [ME *acreuen*, prob. fr. MF *acreue* increase, fr. *acreistre* to increase, fr. L *accescere*, fr. *ad-* + *crescere* to grow — more at CRESCENT] *vi* **1** : to come into existence as a legally enforceable claim **2** : to come by way of increase or addition : arise as a growth or a result **3** : to be periodically accumulated whether as an increase or a decrease ~ *vt* : COLLECT, ACCUMULATE — **ac·cru·able** \-'krü-ə-bəl\ *adj* — **ac·crue·ment** \-'krü-mənt\ *n*

acct *abbr* account; accountant

ac·cul·tur·ate \ə-'kəl-chə-ˌrāt\ *vt* **-at·ed; -at·ing** [back-formation fr. *acculturation*] : to change through acculturation

ac·cul·tur·a·tion \ə-ˌkəl-chə-'rā-shən\ *n* **1** : a process of intercultural borrowing between diverse peoples resulting in new and blended patterns; *esp* : modifications in a primitive culture resulting from contact with an advanced society **2** : the process beginning at infancy by which a human being acquires the culture of his society — **ac·cul·tur·a·tion·al** \-shnəl, -shən-ᵊl\ *adj* — **ac·cul·tur·a·tive** \ə-'kəl-chə-ˌrāt-iv\ *adj*

ac·cu·mu·late \ə-'kyü-myə-ˌlāt\ *vb* **-lat·ed; -lat·ing** [L *accumulatus*, pp. of *accumulare*, fr. *ad-* + *cumulare* to heap up — more at CUMULATE] *vt* **1** : to heap or pile up : AMASS <~ a fortune> **2** : COLLECT, GATHER <a composer *accumulating* one award after another> ~ *vi* : to increase in quantity or number

ac·cu·mu·la·tion \ə-ˌkyü-myə-'lā-shən\ *n* **1** : the action or process of accumulating : the state of being or having accumulated **2** : increase or growth by addition esp. when continuous or repeated <~ of interest> **3** : something that has accumulated or has been accumulated

ac·cu·mu·la·tive \ə-'kyü-myə-ˌlāt-iv, -lət-\ *adj* **1** : CUMULATIVE <an age of rapid and ~ change> **2** : tending or given to accumulation — **ac·cu·mu·la·tive·ly** *adv* — **ac·cu·mu·la·tive·ness** *n*

ac·cu·mu·la·tor \ə-'kyü-myə-ˌlāt-ər\ *n* : one that accumulates: as **a** : SHOCK ABSORBER **b** *Brit* : STORAGE CELL **c** : a part (as in a computer) where numbers are totaled or stored

Webster's New Collegiate Dictionary, 8th edition, G & C Merriam Company, Springfield, Mass., 1977, p. 8.

Directions

1. Compare each letter in the vocabulary entry *accord* with each letter in *accuracy*, the left-hand guide word in the first numbered set that follows. Note that the "o" in *accord* precedes the "u" in *accuracy;* therefore, *accord* could not be on the page showing these guide words.
2. Then compare each letter in *accord* with those in *acceptability,* the first guide word in the second set. The "o" in *accord* follows the "e" in *acceptability.* Now compare each letter in *accord* with the second guide word, *accompaniment.* Because the "r" in *accord* follows the "m" in *accompaniment,* the word could not be on the page headed by this set of guide words either.
3. Compare each letter in *accord* with the first guide word in the third numbered set, *accompanist.* The "r" in *accord* follows the "m" in *accompanist,* so *accord* could be on the same page. To find out for certain, compare each letter in *accord* with the second guide word, *accumulator;* the "o" in *accord* precedes the "u" in *accumulator.*
4. Check the blank beside the third set of guide words, because the vocabulary entry occurs between these guide words.
5. Complete the remaining practice exercises using the same procedure.

a. accord
    1. accuracy   a cheval   _____
    2. acceptability   accompaniment   _____
    3. accompanist   accumulator   _____
b. NLRB (National Labor Relations Board)
    1. nit   noble   _____
    2. nightside   nit   _____
    3. naphthalenic   natatory   _____

ANSWER 1: Consider each letter in the abbreviation, not the standard words in parentheses. In strict alphabetical order, "l" follows "i" in *nit* and precedes "o" in *noble.*

c. 3-D (3-Dimensional)
    1. thirty-three   though   _____
    2. thought   three-master   _____
    3. three-mile limit   throttle   _____

ANSWER 2: Assume that 3 is spelled out; a single word precedes a compound word containing the single word.

d. A battery
    1. abash   abject   _____
    2. abjection   about   _____
    3. a   abasement   _____

ANSWER 1: In strict alphabetical order, the "t" in *battery* follows the "s" in *abash,* and the "a" in *battery* precedes the "j" in *abject.*

e. tourist
    1. tourist class   tow truck   _____
    2. tortoise beetle   totter   _____
    3. tottering   tourist card   _____

ANSWER 3: The "u" in *tourist* follows the "t" in *tottering,* and *tourist* precedes *tourist card.* One word precedes a compound having the first word as one of its parts.

Exercise

1. Look at the main vocabulary word.
2. Compare each consecutive letter with the corresponding letter in each set of guide words, eliminating the sets that do not "fit" the vocabulary word. Use the procedures illustrated in the preceding Example section.

3. Place a check in the blank beside the set of guide words that would be at the top of the page on which the vocabulary entry is located.

a. brine
   1. bridge   Brinell Number   _____
   2. brine shrimp   broad   _____
   3. breathtaking   bridge   _____
b. EOM (end of month)
   1. entertainment   enucleation   _____
   2. enumerability   epenthetic   _____
   3. epergne   epidermis   _____
c. T square
   1. TT   -tude   _____
   2. true   trust   _____
   3. trustability   tsutsugamushi disease   _____
d. 4-H
   1. fornices   fossicker   _____
   2. fossil   Fourier analysis   _____
   3. Fourierism   fractionally   _____
e. mother-in-law
   1. mosquito hawk   motley   _____
   2. morris chair   mosquito fish   _____
   3. motmot   mourner   _____

ANSWERS TO FRAME 1

a. ANSWER 1: "n" in *brine* follows the "d" in *bridge;* one word precedes another that has additional letter(s).
b. ANSWER 2: "o" in *EOM* follows "n" in *enumerability* and precedes "p" in *epenthetic.*
c. ANSWER 3: "s" in *square* follows "r" in *trustability,* and "q" precedes "u" in *tsutsugamushi.*
d. ANSWER 2: *Four* is spelled out; "u" in *four* follows "s" in *fossil,* and "H" precedes "i" in *Fourier.*
e. ANSWER 1: "t" in *mother* follows "s" in *mosquito,* and "h" precedes "l" in *motley.*

Frame 2 Syllabicating Words

Explanation

A word that must be divided at the end of a line of writing or print should be hyphenated between syllables.

1. *Syllable:* a single speech sound (Lesson 2)
   a. A syllable contains one or more letters.
   b. At least one of the letters must be a vowel.
2. *Hyphenate:* to place a hyphen, a short straight line (-), between syllables showing that the remainder of the word is on the following line.
3. Dictionary differences:
   In your dictionary: (a) read the explanatory notes pertinent to *syllabication*; (b) compare that presentation with the one below.
   a. Some dictionaries do not show syllabication of a single-letter syllable at the beginning or end of a word.
      (1) Locate the word *about.*
      (2) This word has two syllables: a·bout.
      (3) Some dictionaries will show the syllabication, and others will not.
      (4) The reason some dictionaries show *about* as a solid word is that one-letter syllables are never placed at the end or beginning of a line.
   b. Occasionally dictionaries will show the same word syllabicated differently. Under these circumstances, neither syllabication is incorrect; the editors simply have different ideas about how the word should be syllabicated.

Example (see dictionary illustration page)

1. Look at the main vocabulary entry: *accompanist.*
2. Notice that it is a four-syllable word, and centered dots separate the syllables.
3. Find *accompanist* in your dictionary.
4. Notice how the syllables are indicated.

Exercise

1. Find the following words in your dictionary.
2. Copy the syllabicated word in the blank (inserting the symbol between syllables).

a. accumulate_____

b. commercial_____

c. manacle_____

d. inimitable_____

e. organization_____

f. debit_____

g. post_____

h. towboat_____

ANSWERS TO FRAME 2

a. ac·cu·mu·late   d. in·im·i·ta·ble   g. post
b. com·mer·cial   e. or·ga·ni·za·tion   h. tow·boat
c. man·a·cle   f. deb·it

Frame 3 *Selecting from a Dual Entry*

Explanation

In your dictionary, read the explanatory notes concerning vocabulary entries to determine how your dictionary treats these dual entries, and compare that explanation with the one below.

1. Vertical dual entries:
   a. When two vocabulary entries spelled the same way immediately follow each other, the first may be the one that entered the English language earlier.
   b. However, in some dictionaries, such words may be entered according to the frequency of their usage.
2. Horizontal dual entries:
   a. When a main vocabulary entry is followed by *or* and the same word spelled differently:
      (1) Both spellings are standard English and may be used.
      (2) The first spelling is often more common than the second.
   b. When a main vocabulary entry is followed by *also* and the same word spelled differently:
      (1) Both spellings are standard English and may be used.
      (2) The first spelling is preferred and occurs more frequently than the second.

Example

1. On the dictionary illustration page, find the word *accoutrement*.
   a. It is joined by *or* to the second word *accouterment*.
   b. Both are standard English, and both are equal.
   c. Notice how these words are presented in your dictionary.
2. In your dictionary, find the word *encyclopedia*.
   a. Notice how *encyclopaedia* is shown; is it preceded by *also*?
   b. Both words are standard English, but the first is preferred.
3. In your dictionary, find the word *advisor*.
   a. If the word is not a main vocabulary entry in your dictionary, look under the verb *advise;* the words may be shown after the definitions.
   b. Some dictionaries show *advisor* as an alternative word, and others show it as a second preference.

Exercise

1. In your dictionary, locate each vocabulary entry listed below.
2. Notice if the word joined to it is equal or is a second preference.
3. If the words are equal, write the alternate word in the blank.
4. If they are not equal, write the preferred word in the blank.

1. theater_____
2. judgment_____
3. programmer_____
4. savor_____
5. intern_____

ANSWERS TO FRAME 3
1. theatre (Webster's); some dictionaries may show *theatre* as a second preference.
2. judgement (Webster's); some dictionaries may show *judgement* as a second preference.
3. programmer
4. savor
5. interne (Webster's); some dictionaries may show *interne* as an alternate word.

Frame 4   *Understanding Phonetic Spelling*

Explanation

In your dictionary, (1) read the explanatory notes pertinent to phonetic spelling (pronunciation); (2) compare that presentation with the one below.

The vocabulary entry is repeated in a form that illustrates the pronunciation. The *phonetic spelling, accent marks,* and *diacritics* are shown.

1. *Phonetic spelling.*   Located between two reverse diagonals immediately following the main vocabulary entry (dictionary illustration page). The syllables may or may not coincide with those in the main vocabulary entry. Examples of phonetic symbols and diacritics are usually shown at the bottom of each odd-numbered page or at the bottom of the left page and continuing on the bottom of the right page. When two phonetic spellings are joined by *also,* the first shows the more common pronunciation.
2. *Accent marks.*   Symbols that indicate the syllable to be accented when the word is pronounced.

3. *Diacritics.* Marks showing the shades of pronunciation for vowels and some consonants.
4. Symbols illustrating the phonetic spelling, accent marks, and diacritics may differ in various dictionaries.

Example

Compare these vocabulary entries on the dictionary illustration page and in your dictionary to determine if the presentation or symbols are different.

1. *accumulator:*
   a. The phonetic spelling is between two reversed diagonals.
   b. The high-set, short vertical mark is placed before the syllable(s) to be stressed in pronunciation.
   c. The low-set, short vertical mark is placed before the syllable(s) given minor stress in pronunciation.
2. *accouterment:*
   a. Two phonetic spellings are shown.
   b. As they are not connected by *also,* both are equal.

Exercise

1. Copy each word in the blank.
2. Divide it into syllables, using the symbols in your dictionary.
3. Place the symbol for the primary accent mark, as shown in your dictionary.

a. government_____

b. document_____

c. inexcusable_____

d. applicable_____

e. illustration_____

ANSWERS TO FRAME 4
a. gov′·ern·ment b. doc′·u·ment c. ap′·plic·a·ble d. in·ex·cus′·a·ble e. il·lus·tra′·tion

Frame 5   Recognizing Functional Labels

Explanation

In your dictionary, read the explanatory notes pertinent to *functional labels,* and compare that presentation with the one below.

Functional labels identify the parts of speech and other functions of words. These labels are usually found in light italic type after the pronunciation entry or the main vocabulary entry.

1. *Parts of speech*

Vocabulary entry	Functional label	Functional label meaning
man	n	noun
he	pro	pronoun
pretty	adj	adjective
rapidly	adv	adverb
aha	inter	interjection

Vocabulary entry	Functional label	Functional label meaning
in	prep	preposition
and	conj	conjunction
walk	vb	verb
set	vt	transitive verb (one that takes an object)
lie	vi	intransitive verb (one that does not take an object)

2. *Other functions*

Vocabulary entry	Functional label	Functional label meaning
CO	abbrev	abbreviation
tele-	comb. form	combining form
anti-	prefix	
-ness	suffix	
TT	symbol	

Example

Compare each numbered item on the dictionary illustration page and in your dictionary to notice if any part of this presentation is different.

1. *accretion*
    The label *n* (noun) follows the phonetic spelling.
2. *accost*
    The label *vt* (transitive verb) follows the phonetic spelling.
3. *accord*
    a. The label *vb* (verb) follows the phonetic spelling.
    b. *Accord* can be used as a transitive verb (*vt* before the first definition).
    c. It can be used as an intransitive verb (*vi* precedes three definitions showing this usage).
4. *accordion* (second entry)
    The label *adj* (adjective) follows the main vocabulary entry, as the phonetic spelling was given the first time the word was shown.
5. *acculturation*
    The functional labels for derivatives are placed after the definitions: *acculturational* and *acculturative* are adjectives.
6. *acct*
    The functional label *abbr* follows the main vocabulary entry.

Exercise

1. Locate each of the following vocabulary entries in your dictionary.
2. Write the functional label in the blank beside the word.

a. mktg_____

b. make up_____

c. intra_____

d. fivefold_____

e. too_____

f. withhold_____

g. analyst_____

h. at_____

i. but_____

j. hier-_____

ANSWERS TO FRAME 5

a.	abbr	e.	adv	h.	prep
b.	vt	f.	vb	i.	conj
c.	prefix	g.	n	j.	comb. form
d.	adj				

Frame 6   Locating Inflected Forms

Explanation

Inflected forms are merely changes in the root word or additions to it; either change creates a new word form. The inflected forms are usually shown in bold print after the functional usage.

In your dictionary: (1) read the explanatory notes pertinent to *inflected forms*; (2) compare that presentation with the one below.

Example

The following inflected forms are usually found in an abridged desk dictionary. Locate each underscored word in your dictionary. Notice how the inflected forms are shown.

1. *Nouns.*   Plurals are shown when:
   a. The spelling of the root word is changed to form the plural: <u>man</u>, <u>men</u>.
   b. A suffix is added to form the plural and the end of the root word is changed: <u>fly</u>, <u>flies</u>.
   c. The plural is formed in a way different from what the reader might expect: <u>tomato</u>, <u>tomatoes</u>.
   d. The noun is plural but considered singular in construction (meaning that it takes a singular verb): <u>genetics</u>.
   e. The noun is plural but considered singular or plural in construction, meaning that it can take either a singular or plural verb, depending upon how it is used in a sentence: <u>economics</u>.
   f. The noun is a Latin word: <u>addendum</u>, <u>addenda</u>.

2. *Verbs.*   The three principal parts and the progressive tense are usually shown for:
   a. Irregular verbs: <u>go</u> (present tense)
      <u>went</u> (past tense)
      <u>gone</u> (past participle)
      <u>going</u> (progressive tense—continuing action)
   b. Verbs that change their spelling in the formation of these tenses:
      <u>accompany</u> (present tense)
      <u>accompanied</u> (past tense)
      (The past participle is not usually shown if it is the same as the past tense.)
      <u>accompanying</u> (progressive tense)
      Some dictionaries also show the third person singular form (<u>goes</u>, <u>accompanies</u>).

3. *Adjectives and adverbs.* The comparative and superlative degrees of adjectives and adverbs are shown when they cause a change in the spelling of the root word or when they are irregular.

The positive degree refers to one person, thing, or quality, the comparative to two, and the superlative to three or more.

	Positive	*Comparative*	*Superlative*
Adjective	<u>pretty</u>	prettier	prettiest
Adverb	<u>early</u>	earlier	earliest
Irregular	<u>good</u>	better	best

Exercise

1. Locate the following vocabulary entries in your dictionary.
2. In the blank, write the part that is requested within the parentheses.

a. bad (comparative and superlative degrees)_____

b. company (plural)_____

c. accept (past tense)_____

d. draw (past tense and past participle)_____

e. data (singular)_____

f. accommodate (progressive tense)_____

g. hot (comparative and superlative degrees)_____

h. happy (comparative and superlative degrees)_____

i. attorney (plural)_____

j. analysis (plural)_____

ANSWERS TO FRAME 6

a.	worse, worst	e.	datum	h.	happier, happiest
b.	companies	f.	accommodating	i.	attorneys
c.	accepted	g.	hotter, hottest	j.	analyses
d.	drew, drawn				

Frame 7   Understanding the Etymology

Explanation

In your dictionary, read the explanatory notes concerning *etymology,* and notice particularly if your dictionary differs from the presentation below.

Etymology is the history of the vocabulary entry.

1. It is located in brackets immediately preceding the definition(s).
2. The word is traced as far back as possible to its origin.
3. The abbreviation *fr.* (from) precedes the language from which the word was borrowed.
4. The last entry is the word's origin or the last point to which the word can be traced.
5. For some words, the meaning in Old English and in other languages may be shown.
6. In some instances, the word is shown in its former spelling, along with the language forms that compose it.

Example

Compare the etymology of the following words as shown on the dictionary illustration page with that shown in your dictionary.

1. *accompany*
   a. ME—the word came into the English language from the Middle English period, where it was spelled *accompanien*.
   b. fr. MF—the word came into Middle English from Middle French, where it was spelled *accompaignier*.
   c. fr. *a-* (fr. L *ad-*)—the *a* came from the Latin *ad* (meaning *to*).
   d. + *compaing companion*—the French verb came from the French noun *compaing*, meaning *companion*.
   e. fr. LL—the word was borrowed into the Middle French language from the Late Latin language.
2. *accoucher*
   a. F—the word came from the French language.
   b. No previous indication of the word exists.
   c. It is spelled in the English language exactly as it is spelled in the French.

Exercise

1. In your dictionary, locate the word listed beside the arabic number.
2. Fill in the blanks in each sentence.

1. *tort:* came to the English language from the _____ language; it meant _____ in Latin.

2. *commerce:* came to the English language from the _____ language; it meant _____ in Latin.

3. *miscellaneous:* came to the English language from the _____ language, where it meant _____.

4. *stet* (abbr): came to the English language from the _____ language, where it meant _____.

5. *divan:* came to the English language from the _____ language; it meant _____.

ANSWERS TO FRAME 7
(Your dictionary may show derivatives and meanings that are either more or less complete than these.)
1. Middle English; twisted or distorted
2. Middle or Old French; merchandise
3. Latin; mixed
4. Latin; let it stand
5. Turkish or French; account book, register, office of accounts, council of state

Frame 8   Identifying Usage Labels

Explanation

In your dictionary, read the explanatory notes on *usage labels* and notice particularly if your dictionary differs from the presentation below.

Usage labels are italicized words identifying entries or definitions that are not common in English usage. This usage may be uncommon because of time period, regional area, or a difference in style.

Example

Compare the usage labels for the underscored vocabulary entries as directed.

1. Labels related to a time period (compare these terms on dictionary illustration page and in your dictionary).
   a. obsolete (*obs*): no evidence of use since 1755. Example: accord vb.—second definition
   b. archaic (*arch*): Once commonly used, but rarely used today. Example: accomplish—definitions 3a and b.
2. Labels related to regional area (compare presentation with that in your dictionary).
   a. Limited to specific region in the United States. Example: dogie—chiefly West
   b. Limited to an English-speaking country. Example: bilabong—Australia
   c. Used in several regions of the United States. Example: critter (*dial*)—dialect; labeled as *regional* in some dictionaries)
3. Stylistic (compare presentation with that in your dictionary).
   a. Slang: used only in very informal writing. Example: gyrene (meaning màrine)
   b. Nonstandard: disapproved of by many, but used by some people. Example: irregardless
   c. Substandard: not used by educated people. Example: ain't

Exercise

Place a check beside the letter that identifies the correct answer.

1. Which definition of coax (vb) is obsolete?
   a. to fondle or pet   _____
   b. to influence   _____
   c. to wheedle   _____
   d. to manipulate   _____
2. What is a football called by the British?
   a. rugby ball   _____
   b. soccer ball   _____
   c. football   _____
   d. goal ball   _____
3. Which usage label would you apply to rock in this sentence? Her rock almost blinded me.
   a. substandard   _____
   b. slang   _____
   c. chiefly British   _____
   d. dialect   _____
4. Which meaning of buxom (adj) is not obsolete?
   a. yielding   _____
   b. obedient   _____
   c. offering little resistance   _____
   d. plump   _____

ANSWERS TO FRAME 8
1. a   2. a or b (depending upon dictionary used)   3. b   4. d

Frame 9 **Selecting a Definition**

Explanation

In your dictionary, read the explanatory notes concerning *definitions*. Notice particularly the order and designation of the meanings.

1. A word may have more than one definition.
2. In some dictionaries, the definitions are shown in historical order, and in others, the most common usage is shown first.
3. In some dictionaries, the definitions are numbered, and in others, they are separated by punctuation or in a different way.
4. Rarely are derivatives of a word defined, unless the meaning is somewhat different from that of the main vocabulary entry.
5. In some dictionaries, the vocabulary entry is used in a partial or complete sentence.

Example

Compare the following presentation of the definitions on the dictionary illustration page with those shown in your dictionary. The definitions on the dictionary illustration page are in historical order.

1. accountancy
   a. The word is a noun.
   b. A colon precedes the single definition.
2. accord (n)
   a. It has four definitions.
   b. The definitions are numbered.
   c. Notice the swung (curved) dash between the angled brackets.
      (1) The dash represents the vocabulary entry word, showing how it is used according to that definition.
      (2) Definition 1a. is *agreement, conformity.*
      (3) The partial sentence would read: "acted in *accord* with the company's policy."
   d. The part of speech tells you how the word should be used in a sentence.
      (1) A noun should be used in a noun position.
      (2) Always check the functional usage that precedes a definition to assure yourself that you are using the word correctly in a sentence.
      (3) Example: Notice that *accord*, as a verb, has definitions for *vt* (when it requires an object) and *vi* (when it must not be given an object).

Exercise

1. Locate the following nouns in your dictionary.
2. Copy *one* of the standard usage definitions for each noun.
3. Employ the noun in a sentence, using the meaning you have chosen.

Example

demography

Definition: the statistical study of human populations, especially with reference to size and density, distribution and vital statistics.
Sentence: The marketing manager studied the demography of Pecos, Texas, and Carlsbad, New Mexico, to determine which would have the better market for Swedish modern furniture.

1. debenture

    Definition: _____
    Sentence: _____
2. administrator

    Definition: _____
    Sentence: _____
3. statistics

    Definition: _____
    Sentence: _____
4. hierarchy

    Definition: _____
    Sentence: _____
5. debtor

    Definition: _____
    Sentence: _____

ANSWERS TO FRAME 9

1. debenture
    Definition: a bond backed by the specific credit of a corporation, rather than a specific lien on particular assets.
    Sentence: Mrs. Aims holds a 5 percent debenture issued by a data systems organization.
2. administrator
    Definition: one who administers, especially school, business, or governmental affairs.
    Sentence: A superintendent is the chief administrator of a school system.
3. statistics
    Definition: A branch of mathematics dealing with the collection, analysis, interpretation, and presentation of masses of data.
    Sentence: Business students usually take at least one course in statistics.
4. hierarchy
    Definition: a body of persons in (or levels of) authority.
    Sentence: Reports travel upward through the hierarchy of the organization.
5. debtor
    Definition: one who owes a debt.
    Sentence: The Amalgamated Plumbing Supply Company sends collection letters to a debtor who has not paid a bill for three months.

Frame 10   Finding Synonyms and Antonyms

Explanation

In your dictionary, read the explanatory section on *synonyms* and *antonyms*. Compare that explanation with the one below.

1. A *synonym* (*syn*) is a word that has the same or similar meaning as the main vocabulary entry.
2. An *antonym* (*ant*) is a word that has the opposite meaning of the main vocabulary entry.
3. Synonyms and antonyms are usually in boldface type and located after the definition(s).

Example

Compare the presentation of the synonyms and antonyms on the dictionary illustration page with those shown in your dictionary. Some dictionaries may show more or fewer synonyms and antonyms than are listed in Webster's.

1. accompany
    a. The synonyms are attend and escort.
    b. Following the synonyms are these words: "shared meaning element: to go along with."
    c. The shared meaning element, to go along with, is common to all these synonyms.
2. accord (vb)
    a. After the *syn* abbreviation, the reader is told to "see AGREE," meaning that the list of synonyms is shown under that vocabulary entry.
    b. For a second synonym with a slightly different meaning, the reader is told to "see GRANT," meaning that the list of synonyms is shown under that vocabulary entry.
    c. The antonym for agree is conflict.
    d. The antonym for grant is withhold.

Exercise

1. Locate the following vocabulary entries in your dictionary.
2. In the columns to the right of each word, write a synonym and an antonym for each word.
3. If a word does not have a synonym or an antonym, write *none* in the appropriate column.

		Synonym	*Antonym*
1.	concise (adj)	_____	_____
2.	intricate (adj)	_____	_____
3.	standard (n)	_____	_____
4.	termination (n)	_____	_____
5.	mean (n)	_____	_____

ANSWERS TO FRAME 10
(Your dictionary may contain more or fewer synonyms and antonyms than shown.)
1. Syn.: terse, succinct, laconic, summary, pithy, compendious
    shared meaning element: very brief in statement or expression. Ant.: redundant
2. Syn.: complex. Ant.: (none)
3. Syn.: criterion, gauge, yardstick, touchstone
    shared meaning element: a means of determining what a thing should be. Ant.: (none)
4. Syn.: end. Ant.: inception, source
5. Syn.: average. Ant.: extreme

Frame 11   Applying Your Knowledge

Errors may consist of misspelled words, incorrect meanings, and incorrect usage—all of which can be corrected by reference to your dictionary.

Directions

1. Read the case.
2. Correct the errors in the letter by writing the correction below the incorrect item. (The letter contains 20 errors.)

CASE

Pamela Squires, a recent high school graduate, obtained a job as a correspondence secretary in the Planetary Insurance Company. She transcribes dictation in the word processing center. The letter below is one that she transcribed for you. Will you sign the letter?

January 18, 19____

Mr. Samuel Adams
1714 Grape Street
Berthoud, Colorado 80513

Dear Mr. Adams:

We welcome you as a new policy holder with the Planetary Life Insurance Company.

Your policy has been verifyied, and we are sending it to you with this letter. Like all insurance companys, we expect premeum payments to be made monthly, quarterly, or yearly. You payed your first monthly premium on December 31, and the second one should be post marked on or before the last day of this month.

If you can not make a payment by the end of a month, you you may take advantage of the 30-day gracing period. If your problem is severe, you may want to discussion it with your Planetary agent in Denver. Mr. Balinger, your agent, has been with Planetary for twenty five years and is well known for his compasion, understanding, and professionalness.

The Planetary Life Insurance Company offers endoughment, education, morgage, and key personnel insurance policys. Please mail the inclosed busness reply card to indicate your intrest in these other servises. It will be sent to Mr. Balinger, who will call you for an appointment.

Yours truely,
Henry Cisco, General Agent

ANSWERS TO FRAME 11

January 18, 19____

Mr. Samuel Adams
1714 Grape Street
Berthoud, Colorado 80513

Dear Mr. Adams:
   We welcome you as a new <u>policy holder</u> with the Planetary Life Insurance
policyholder
Company.

Your policy has been <u>verifyied</u>, and we are sending it to you with this letter. Like
verified

all insurance <u>companys</u>, we expect <u>premeum</u> payments to be made monthly, quarterly,
companies   premium

or yearly. You <u>payed</u> your first monthly premium on December 31, and the second
paid

one should be <u>post marked</u> on or before the last day of this month.
postmarked

If you <u>can not</u> make a payment by the end of a month, you may take advantage of
cannot

the 30-day <u>gracing</u> period. If your problem is severe, you may want to <u>discussion</u> it
grace   discuss

with your Planetary agent in Denver. Mr. Balinger, your agent, has been with

Planetary for <u>twenty five</u> years and is well known for his <u>compasion</u>, understanding,
twenty-five   compassion

and <u>professionalness</u>.
professionalism

The Planetary Life Insurance Company offers <u>endoughment</u>, education, <u>morgage</u>,
endowment   mortgage

and key personnel insurance <u>policys</u>. Please mail the <u>inclosed</u> <u>busness</u> reply card to
policies   enclosed business

indicate your <u>intrest</u> in these other <u>servises</u>. It will be sent to Mr. Balinger, who will
interest   services

call you for an appointment.

Yours <u>truely</u>,
truly

Henry Cisco, General Agent

Lesson 6
Vocabulary Building

Pretest

Directions

Write the word expressed by the sentence at the left. Use the proper prefix, suffix, or root to complete the part in parentheses.

Example

He read the chapter a second time (read).   reread

1. This organization meets twice yearly. (annually)   _____
2. A baby is not sensitive to morals, either good or bad. (moral)   _____
3. The students are studying the development of mankind. (logy)   _____
4. Page 2 comes before page 3. (cedes)   _____
5. The heads of the military services are located in a five-sided building in Washington. (gon)   _____
6. This account can be collected when it is due. (collect)   _____
7. Some people put off until tomorrow what should be done today. (crastinate)   _____
8. Some glass permits light to shine through, but one cannot see objects through it. (lucent)   _____
9. The recent reaction of the stock market to the high unemployment rate is not typical. (typical)   _____
10. An informational memo may be circulated between offices within a company. (office)   _____

Lesson 6
Vocabulary Building

Introduction: The Scope of Your Communications

Where will you become employed? Business firm or industrial organization? Some level of government? Self-employed? Regardless of your answer, at some time you will find yourself in a position to transmit facts or convey ideas to people within your organization or outside it. You may write letters and memos to subordinates and reports to superiors. You may write to suppliers, consumers, customers, applicants, other businesses, professional organizations, and certainly to the federal government.

What facts will you transmit? What ideas will you convey? You may write about products, personnel, funds, procedures, systems, equipment, raw materials—anything that is involved in your specific job.

Your ability to select the "right" word in transmitting information or conveying an idea will have these results:

1. *Clear communications.* The reader will understand the ideas or facts immediately.
2. *Favorable image.* It shows your interest in the job and your understanding of the topic under discussion.
3. *Cost-effectiveness.* Revising a communication requires time, and therefore increases the cost of creating it. Frequently, the time of reprocessing (retyping) is involved, which further increases the cost.

The purpose of this lesson is to help you learn methods by which you can increase your general and business vocabulary. The lesson consists of two parts:

1. *General vocabulary building.* You will learn the meanings of prefixes, suffixes, and root words, and how these elements can be interchanged to construct new words and their derivatives.

2. *Business vocabulary building.* Many words have several meanings; learning the meaning that is pertinent to business is important to a person who expects to communicate with other people in business. This lesson and each succeeding one will include a few words pertaining to an area of business.

Frame 1   How Prefixes Affect the Root Word

Explanation

The addition of a prefix to a word root changes the meaning of that root. The words formed by the addition of a prefix are called *derivatives* of the root word.

Example

Although a prefix may have more than one meaning, only one is used in this frame.

Word root	use, meaning to put into service.
Prefix	re-, meaning again
New word	reuse—to use again
Sentence	To save money, we can reuse the printout paper.

Prefix	mis-, meaning wrong
New word	misuse—wrong use
Sentence	The operator will be charged for his misuse of the equipment.

Prefix	<u>dis-</u>, meaning <u>absence of</u>
New word	<u>disuse</u>—the absence of use
Sentence	The <u>disuse</u> of the equipment will cause it to rust.

Prefix	<u>non-</u>, meaning not
New word	<u>nonuse</u>—not to use
Sentence	The <u>nonuse</u> of the equipment is a waste of money.

Exercise

1. Read each sentence carefully.
2. Using an appropriate prefix, rewrite the sentence without changing the meaning of the sentence.

Example

I read that book a second time this year.
I reread that book this year.

1. I frequently spell a word incorrectly.

    _____

2. This cleaner is not abrasive.

    _____

3. A person who steals from the supply room is not honest.

    _____

4. The reader does not interpret a sentence as the writer stated it.

    _____

5. The cafeteria serves beverages that have no alcoholic content.

    _____

6. The payroll clerk calculated Harry's pay incorrectly.

    _____

7. A clerk who tells confidential information is not loyal.

    _____

8. Due to rain, the baseball game must be scheduled for another time.

    _____

ANSWERS TO FRAME 1
1. I frequently <u>misspell</u> a word.
2. This cleaner is <u>nonabrasive</u>.
3. A person who steals from the supply room is <u>dishonest</u>.
4. The reader <u>misinterprets</u> a sentence.
5. The cafeteria serves <u>nonalcoholic</u> beverages.
6. The payroll clerk <u>miscalculated</u> Harry's pay.
7. A clerk who tells confidential information is <u>disloyal</u>.
8. Due to rain, the baseball game must be <u>rescheduled</u>.

Frame 2   How Suffixes Affect the Root Word

Explanation

The addition of a suffix to a word root makes the new word a different part of speech. Although the meaning of a suffix may be apparent from its use in a sentence, you should know the definitions of common suffixes. The new words formed by the addition of a suffix are called derivatives of the word root.

Example

The addition of a suffix may convert a word to one of these parts of speech: noun, verb, adjective, adverb. Below are some examples and definitions of some common suffixes.

a.   Noun
1.   kindness (kind + ness); -<u>ness</u>, state of (state of being kind)
2.   management (manage + ment); -<u>ment</u>, act of (act of managing)
b.   Verb
1.   working (work + ing); -<u>ing</u>, a continuing act (is working)
2.   worked (work + ed); -<u>ed</u> (past tense) (worked)
3.   terrorize (terror + ize); -<u>ize</u>, to cause (to cause terror)
c.   Adjective
1.   careful (care + ful); -<u>ful</u>, full of (full of care)
2.   helpless (help + less); -<u>less</u>, state of being without (without or not having help)
3.   taller (tall + er); -<u>er</u>, comparing two (taller than John)
d.   Adverb
1.   rapidly (rapid + ly); -<u>ly</u>, in the manner of (typing in a rapid manner)
2.   easiest (easi + est); -<u>est</u>, comparison of three or more (easiest test)

Exercise

Write the part of speech for the underscored word.

Example

Our company's sales are <u>greater</u> in Chicago than in Omaha.   <u>adjective</u>

1.   A hand calculator is a <u>useful</u> device for a student to own.   _____
2.   She is a <u>careless</u> typist.   _____
3.   Union and management reached an <u>agreement</u> on the benefits package.   _____
4.   Employment opportunities are becoming <u>increasingly</u> scarce in the metropolitan areas.   _____
5.   I shall be <u>reporting</u> this discrepancy to the Payroll Department before the end of the month.   _____
6.   The <u>politeness</u> of the employees was appreciated by the visitors.   _____
7.   Detroit is <u>larger</u> than Lincoln.   _____
8.   The applicant said that he was <u>grateful</u> for the interview.   _____
9.   My new assistant approaches her work <u>eagerly</u>.   _____
10.   The <u>management</u> of the Claims Department has improved during the last few months.   _____

ANSWERS TO FRAME 2

1.	adjective	5.	verb	8.	adjective
2.	adjective	6.	noun	9.	adverb
3.	noun	7.	adjective	10.	noun
4.	adverb				

Frame 3   Adding Second Prefixes and Suffixes

Explanation

More than one prefix and suffix may be affixed to a root word. Each additional prefix changes the meaning of the root, and each additional suffix changes its part of speech.

Example

Note the changes that can occur by adding a prefix or suffix:

Word root	<u>cycle</u> (noun or verb)
One prefix added	<u>recycle</u> (to cycle again): verb
One suffix added	<u>recyclable</u> (able to be recycled): adjective
Two prefixes added	<u>nonrecyclable</u> (not able to be recycled): adjective

Exercise

Complete the blank with a derivative of the word in parentheses.

Example

Alice agreed to _____ (pay) the loan in nine months.   <u>repay</u>

1. This loan is _____ (pay) on February 15.   _____

2. Most new cars require _____ (lead) gasoline.   _____

3. This subscription is _____ (new) as the publisher plans to discontinue operations.   _____

4. The dishonest sales manager _____ (appropriate) money from the advertising budget.   _____

5. A _____ (honor) discharge from the military service must be supported by facts.   _____

6. The _____ ([lack of] help) of a clerk should be reported to the management of the store in which that clerk works.   _____

7. Magic Toys are the strongest of their kind: they are _____ (break).   _____

8. The employees looked _____ (help) on while the file storage units crashed to the floor.   _____

9. The foreign officer had been assigned to a post, but after a civil war broke out in the area, he was _____ (assign) to another post.   _____

10. Merchandise from _____ (develop) countries is sold by many department stores.   _____

ANSWERS TO FRAME 3

1. payable or repayable	6. unhelpfulness
2. nonleaded or unleaded	7. nonbreakable or unbreakable
3. nonrenewable or unrenewable	8. helplessly
4. misappropriated	9. reassigned
5. dishonorable	10. underdeveloped or developing

Frame 4   Prefixes Listed in the Dictionary

Explanation

Prefixes are shown as vocabulary entries in most desk dictionaries. Many prefixes and suffixes have the same sections as word entries: pronunciation, label, etymology, and definition(s).

Example

1. Locate the prefix *ante-* in your dictionary.
2. Note that the prefix is listed below the word *ante.*
3. If your dictionary does not show a pronunciation section beside the prefix, you will probably find the pronunciation listed beside the word *ante.*
4. Many dictionaries will show a usage label (*prefix*) to identify the entry.
5. The etymology shows that this word was borrowed from Middle English and had come from Latin, where it was spelled *ante* and meant *before* or *in front of.* Notice that in Greek it was spelled *anti-* and meant *before* or *against.*
6. Most dictionaries will show more than one meaning for this prefix, although only a shade of difference may exist among them. This is true for most prefixes just as for other vocabulary entries.
7. These meanings will be listed in some dictionaries:
   a.   prior, or earlier: *antephase* (prior phase)
   b.   anterior, or forward: *anteroom* (room to the front)
   c.   prior to, or earlier than: *antedate* (a date prior to)
   d.   in front of, before: *antemeridian* (before midday, a.m.)
8. Locate *antelope.* Note that this word begins with the same letters as the prefix but that they do not form a prefix in *antelope.*

Exercise

Locate the prefix *semi-* in a desk dictionary and answer the following questions:
1.   What was the spelling and meaning of the prefix in Old High German?

_____

2.   What is the Greek word having the same meaning?_____
3.   What is the meaning of the prefix in each of these words?

   a.   semicircle:_____

   b.   semiannual:_____

   c.   semimoist:_____

   d.   semiconsciousness:_____
4.   In which of these words is *semi-* not a prefix?

   a.   semiclassical_____

   b.   seminarian_____

   c.   semipermanent_____

5.   What is the meaning of *hemisphere?*_____

ANSWERS TO FRAME 4
1.   sami-; half
2.   hemi-

3. a. semicircle: half a circle
    b. semiannual: twice a year
    c. semimoist: moist to some extent
    d. semiconsciousness: partial consciousness
4. b. seminarian
5. Meaning: half of a globe; half of the world (Western Hemisphere—the world divided by a meridian; Southern Hemisphere—the world divided at the equator.)

Frame 5   *Suffixes Listed in the Dictionary*

Explanation

Suffixes are vocabulary entries in most desk dictionaries. Usually they are shown with these sections: pronunciation, label, etymology, and definition(s).

Example

1. Locate *-ness* in your dictionary.
2. Because a suffix determines the part of speech of a word, a usage label will show what part of speech this is: *noun suffix,* in this case.
3. The etymology shows that *-ness* was borrowed from a Middle English word which came from Old English.
4. This suffix may mean *state, condition, quality,* or *degree.*
5. Sentence: The rud*eness* of the clerk alienated the customers.

Exercise

Locate *-able* in your dictionary and answer the following questions. (It may be followed by *-ible,* indicating that some words have that suffix but mean the same as *-able.*)

1. What is the usage label (if any) for *-able*?_____

2. From which language did it originate?_____

3. Give two concise definitions. _____, _____.

4. In which of these words is *able* not a suffix?

    a. cable_____

    b. workable_____

    c. receivable_____

ANSWERS TO FRAME 5
1. Adjective suffix
2. Latin
3. Definitions: capable of, fit for, worthy of, tending (*breakable*), given, or liable to (*collectible*)
4. a. cable

Frame 6   *Greek and Latin Word Roots with Prefixes and Suffixes*

Explanation

Prefixes and suffixes can be added to Greek and Latin word roots to form an English word and its derivatives.

Example

Word unit: *dict* (Latin): say, speak, tell

Examples of prefixes and suffixes that can be added to the word unit:

Prefixes	*Suffixes*
pre- (before)	-ate (shows action and makes the verb form)
un- (not)	-ion (the act of)
	-or (one who)
	-ing (ongoing action)
	-able (capable of, fit for, worthy of)

Notice how the underlined derivatives are used in these sentences:

1. A secretary transcribes the thoughts of the person who <u>dict</u>ates them.
2. A leader who tells his people how to react is called a <u>dict</u>ator.
3. When the weatherman gives a forecast, he pre<u>dict</u>s the weather for the next day.
4. Occasionally the weather trend cannot be identified; then it is said to be unpre<u>dict</u>able.
5. A student who writes shorthand as the instructor speaks the words is taking <u>dict</u>ation. The instructor is the <u>dict</u>ator. When the instructor is speaking, she is said to be <u>dict</u>ating to the class.

Exercise

Using the appropriate prefix(es) or suffix(es) with the Latin word unit *port* (*to carry*), form a derivative to complete the blanks in the following sentences.

Prefix	*Suffix*
re- (again, go back)	-able
trans- (across)	-or
im- (bring in)	-ed (past tense)
ex- (take out)	-er (one who)
de- (down, away)	-folio (leaf or sheet)

Example

The person working for a newspaper, radio station, or television network who visits a scene and then returns to the office to write the story is a <u>reporter.</u>

1. When a lightweight typewriter is placed in a case, it can be carried easily because it is _____.
2. Many computers, television sets, and transistor radios sold in this country have been _____ from Japan or West Germany.
3. A handy carrying case for loose papers is a _____.
4. Eleven shipping lines _____ cargo from Galveston to Liverpool.
5. Farmers hope that this country will _____ more wheat to Russia.
6. An undesirable alien may be _____ to his native land.

7. Few train stations or bus terminals have _____ to help travelers with their luggage.

8. An elephant would be difficult to _____ in an airplane.

9. _____ illegal drugs across international boundaries is a criminal offense.

ANSWERS TO FRAME 6

1.	portable	4.	transport	7.	porters
2.	imported	5.	export	8.	transport
3.	portfolio	6.	deported	9.	Transporting

Frame 7   *Greek Prefixes, Suffixes, and Roots*

Explanation

Many Greek prefixes, suffixes, and roots are used to form words in the English language. You should learn the more common forms, because they will help you to understand the derivation and meaning of many English words.

Example

Read each Greek prefix, suffix, and root. Study their meanings.

Prefixes and Suffixes	*Root**
a, an (without)	anthro, anthropo (man, mankind)
anti, ant (against)	chron (time)
dia (across, through)	dem, demo (people)
hyper (over, excessive)	log, logy (speech, study of,
hypo (under, less than)	collection of)
para, par (alongside)	micro (small)
syn, sym, syl, sys	the (god)
(together, with)	cracy (act of ruling)
nym (name)	
ist (follower)	

Exercise

Use the proper prefix, suffix, or root to complete the part in parentheses.

Example

The distance measured across a circle is its ___diameter___ (meter).

1. The course in which students study the development of mankind is

   (anthrop) _____.

2. Macroeconomics refers to the total economic system; the economics of an

   organization within the system is called _____. (economics)

3. Two equal lines drawn side by side are said to be _____. (llel)

---

*Jack S. Romine, *Vocabulary for Adults: A Self-Teaching Guide* (New York: John Wiley & Sons, 1975).

4. A(n) _____ (ist) does not believe in God.
5. When papers are filed in a time sequence according to the date, they are in

   _____ (ological) order.
6. A person who has an excessive amount of energy is hyperactive, but one

   who is always tired and has little energy is _____ (active).
7. America is ruled by the people through their elected representatives; there-

   fore, this country is called a _____ (cracy).
8. People who work against the ruling group, the establishment, frequently

   belong to _____ (establishment) organizations.
9. The name of a word that means the same or almost the same as another

   word is a(n) _____ (nym).

ANSWERS TO FRAME 7

1.	anthropology	4.	atheist	7.	democracy
2.	microeconomics	5.	chronological	8.	antiestablishment
3.	parallel	6.	hypoactive	9.	synonym

Frame 8   Latin Prefixes and Roots

Explanation

Many Latin prefixes and roots are used to form English words. Learning the meaning of these prefixes and roots will help you to understand the English words of which they are a part.

Example

1. Read the prefix and its meaning.
2. Read the root and its meaning.

Prefixes	*Roots**
dis, dif, di (down, away)	bene (good)
ex, ef, e (out)	cede, ceed, cess (go, move, yield)
inter (between)	cred (believe, trust)
intra (within)	grad, gress (step, go)
post (after)	jac, ject (throw, hurl)
pro (forward, in front of,	mal (bad)
in favor of)	scribe, script (write)
super (over)	fac, fact, fect, fict,
	feat, feas, fy (make, do)
	manu (hand)

Exercise

Complete each blank with a word formed from a Latin prefix, root, or combination of the two.

* *Ibid.*

Example

Joe always moves away from a topic he does not want to discuss; in other words, he _____digresses_____ (gresses).

1. The company can haul freight from Illinois to New York because it has a

   license to operate as a(an) _____ (state) carrier. A company whose license permits it to haul freight only within a state is a(an)

   _____ (state) carrier.
2. The man who created a disturbance in the cocktail lounge was unceremoni-

   ously _____ (jected) by the bouncer.
3. The United States will probably _____ (cede) between the two countries in an attempt to achieve a peaceful settlement of their differences.
4. The copy of a book written by an author and submitted to a prospective

   publisher is a _____ (script).
5. Craftsmen usually make an item by hand; however, we apply the same term to both machine-made and handmade items. The term is

   _____ (facture).
6. In mathematics and statistics, some numbers are written below the line

   (subscript position), but footnote numbers are in a(an) _____ (script) position.
7. You can purchase goods and pay for them later only if the merchant believes that you possess the attributes of a person who would make a good

   _____ (it) customer.
8. Employees believe that a company does something good for them when it

   increases their fringe _____ (fits).
9. If a machine is not functioning properly, we say that it is

   _____ (functioning).
10. The theater manager is my friend, and he said that I could

    _____ (ceed) to the head of the line.
11. A(an) _____ (dated) check cannot be cashed until the date placed upon it.

ANSWERS TO FRAME 8

1. interstate; intrastate	4. manuscript	7. credit	10. proceed
2. ejected	5. manufacture	8. benefits	11. postdated
3. intercede	6. superscript	9. malfunctioning	

Frame 9   Greek and Latin Numbers

Explanation

Among the most widely used prefixes derived from Greek and Latin are the first ten numbers. Learning these prefixes, particularly those from Latin, will help you to understand many words of which they are a part.

Example

Read the English number and the corresponding Latin and Greek prefixes shown on the same line.

English	Latin*	Greek*
one	uni-	mono-
two	du-	di-
three	tri-	tri-
four	quadr-	tetra-
five	quint-	penta-
six	sex-	hexa-
seven	sept-	hepta-
eight	oct-	oct-
nine	nov-	ennea-
ten	dec-	dec-

Exercise

Complete each blank with a number written in English.

Example

A unicycle has _____one_____ wheel(s).

1. If you are a triplet, you are one of _____ children.
2. The invading army decimated the population; that is, they killed one of

   every _____ people.

3. A duplex consists of _____ similar houses constructed under one
   roof.

4. A triangle has _____ sides.
5. A company that quadruples its earnings increases them by

   _____ times the previous amount.

6. A septennial celebration may last for _____ years.

7. The Pentagon in Washington has _____ sides.
8. A quadrangle on a campus is the section surrounded by

   _____ buildings, usually dormitories.

9. A sextet consists of _____ people.

10. An octogenarian is a person between _____ and

    _____ years old.

ANSWERS TO FRAME 9

1.	three	5.	four	8.	four
2.	ten	6.	seven	9.	six
3.	two	7.	five	10.	80 and 89
4.	three				

Frame 10   Business Vocabulary Building: Accounting

Explanation

Assets, liabilities, and net worth are recorded on a balance sheet, a financial statement that is prepared at the end of each month.

* *Ibid.,* p. 203.

Example

1. *Assets*
   a. Definition: An asset is something that is owned by an individual or an organization.
      (1) It is tangible (cash or inventory) as opposed to intangible (personality).
      (2) An asset has a value that can be identified in monetary terms.
   b. Kinds of assets
      (1) *Current assets:* cash, investments, accounts receivable, inventories.
      (2) *Long-term assets:* plant, equipment, and other long-term capital investments.
2. *Liabilities*
   a. Definition: A liability is an obligation owed by a person or organization.
   b. Kinds of liabilities:
      (1) *Current:* obligations that will be paid in a year or less: notes payable, taxes payable, for example.
      (2) *Long-term:* obligations resulting from borrowing money over long-term periods of a year or more.
3. *Net Worth* (also called *owner's equity*): net worth consists of two parts:
   a. Owner's investment
   b. Profit earned
4. *Balance Sheet*
   a. Definition: a financial statement constructed by taking the balance in each asset, liability, and net worth account at a certain point in time, usually the last day of the month.
   b. This equation is used to represent the balance sheet: Assets − liabilities = net worth.
   c. Example:

Super Office Supply Company
Balance Sheet, February 28, 1977

Assets		*Liabilities*	
Cash	$ 8,000	Notes payable	$20,000
Accounts receivable	12,000	*Net Worth:*	
Inventory	30,000	Owners' investment	10,000
		Earnings	20,000
	$50,000		$50,000

5. *Financial Statement:* A document showing the figures taken from various accounts and arranged in a format approved by the accounting profession. The most common financial statements are the balance sheet and the income statement.

Exercise

Tell whether each statement is true or false by writing T or F in the blank provided.

1. Assets are equal to liabilities plus net worth. _____
2. Honesty is a personal asset and should be recorded on the balance sheet under "Assets." _____
3. Assets include those which are current, such as cash, and those which depreciate, such as equipment. _____
4. A balance sheet shows changes in the financial condition over a period of time. _____
5. A check in payment is a financial statement. _____

Frame 11   Applying Your Knowledge

This proofreading exercise contains errors in spelling and word usage: general vocabulary and business vocabulary. Refer to your dictionary and the current lesson to assure that your answers are accurate.

Directions

1. Read the case upon which the proofreading exercise is based.
2. Underscore the incorrect word and write it correctly below the printed line.

CASE

Ralph is a capable accounting student who belongs to Beta Alpha Psi, the accounting honorary organization. He has been appointed to give a speech to students enrolled in a night class in beginning accounting. He also wants to provide them with a handout containing the important points of his speech. He asks Bob and Kathy, two friends, to read this handout and correct it. They find 15 errors!

THE ACCOUNTING PROFESSION

The accounting profession is disunderstood by many people. Anyone who plans to go into management or who is managing his own business should take a course in accounting. This course (BA 200) will not only help you to manage your own funds, but it will help you to discover when employees are disappropriating money. You will also learn about acceptable business practices; for example, you are not required to cash a check that has been antedated until the date shown on the check.

Each department in an organization is accountible for the money it spends. Usually, the department manager is asked to prepare a budget before preceeding with his prodetermined plans. Some managers are hyposensitive about their budgets and try to antecipate questions that may arise about the budgeted items. They fear the top management will deject some items; often intercompany rivalry exists because managers try to outdo each other in obtaining funds.

Some of you may want to become certified public accountants; this is a profession you can practice all your life. My father is a septegenarian, in his sixties, that is, and he practices from an office in our house. He advises his clients how to divest their principal, what the effect of different divestments may be, and how to cooperate with the Eternal Revenue Service.

Accounting is learned by the spiral method; in other words, what you learn about the balance sheet is true through all accounting courses; you simply learn more about each item that is placed on it. Therefore, the equation, assets always equal net worth minus liabilities, will remain true.

As my high school principal used to say, "I hope you'll consider me your pal and come to me with your questions."

Prepared by Ralph Easton

ANSWERS TO FRAME 11

THE ACCOUNTING PROFESSION

The accounting profession is <u>disunderstood</u> by many people. Anyone who plans to
        misunderstood
go into management or who is managing his own business should take a course in

accounting. This course (BA 200) will not only help you to manage your own funds,

but it will help you to discover when employees are <u>disappropriating</u> money. You will
                                misappropriating
also learn about acceptable business practices; for example, you are not required to

cash a check that has been <u>antedated</u> until the date shown on the check.
                    postdated
Each department in an organization is <u>accountible</u> for the money it spends. Usually,
                        accountable
the department manager is asked to prepare a budget before <u>preceeding</u> with his
                                proceeding
<u>prodetermined</u> plans. Some managers are <u>hyposensitive</u> about their budgets and try to
predetermined   hypersensitive
<u>antecipate</u> questions that may arise about the budgeted items. They fear the top
anticipate
management will <u>deject</u> some items; often <u>intercompany</u> rivalry exists because
            reject   intracompany
managers try to outdo each other in obtaining funds.

Some of you may want to become certified public accountants; this is a profession

you can practice all your life. My father is a septegenarian, in his <u>sixties</u>, that is, and
                                            seventies
he practices from an office in our house. He advises his clients how to <u>divest</u> their
                                        invest
principal, what the effect of different <u>divestments</u> may be, and how to cooperate with
                            investments
the <u>Eternal</u> Revenue Service.   investments
    Internal
Accounting is learned by the spiral method; in other words, what you learn about

the balance sheet is true through all accounting courses; you simply learn more about

each item that is placed on it. Therefore, the equation, assets always equal net worth

<u>minus</u> liabilities, will remain true.
plus

As my high school principal used to say, "I hope you'll consider me your pal and come to me with your questions."

Prepared by Ralph Easton

Lesson 7
Word Division

Pretest

Pretest Part I
Word Division Application

Directions

1. In the words listed below, a slash (/) represents a point where the word may be divided at the end of a line.
2. From each numbered list, choose the preferred word division and write the letter that corresponds to that word in the blank provided.

Example

a. thought
b. thou/ght
c. though/t   <u>   a   </u>

1. a. ship/ped
    b. shipped
    c. shipp/ed   _____

2. a. ad/vantage
    b. advan/tage
    c. advant/age   _____

3. a. cross-/ex/amine
    b. cross-/examine
    c. cross-exam/ine   _____

4. a. valu/able
    b. val/uable
    c. valua/ble   _____

5. a. referr/ing
    b. refer/ring
    c. re/ferring   _____

6. a. de/fensive
    b. defen/sive
    c. defens/ive   _____

7. a. manip/ulate
    b. manipu/late
    c. man/ipulate   _____

8. a. ap/plicant
    b. appli/cant
    c. applic/ant   _____

9. a. San Fran/cisco
    b. San Francisco
    c. San / Francisco   _____

10. a. Magdalene Hem/mingway
    b. Magda/lene Hemmingway
    c. Magdalene / Hemmingway   _____

111

11. a. Vice / President Gregory Kiddington
    b. Vice President / Gregory Kiddington
    c. Vice President Greg/ory Kiddington   ————
12. a. 2615 / Mulberry Street
    b. 2615 Mulberry / Street
    c. 2615 Mul/berry Street   ————
13. a. December / 25, 1975
    b. Dec/ember 25, 1975
    c. December 25,/ 1975   ————
14. a. couldn't
    b. could/n't
    c. coul/dn't   ————
15. a. TEX/ACO
    b. TEXACO
    c. TEXAC/O   ————
16. a. self-/control
    b. self-con/trol
    c. self-contr/ol   ————
17. a. intercontin/ental
    b. inter/continental
    c. intercontinent/al   ————
18. a. appropri/ately
    b. ap/propriately
    c. appropriate/ly   ————
19. a. commend/ing
    b. com/mending
    c. comm/ending
20. a. re/gressed
    b. regress/ed
    c. regressed   ————
21. a. reten/tion
    b. re/tention
    c. retent/ion   ————
22. a. pre/sent (noun)
    b. pres/ent (noun)
    c. present (noun)   ————
23. a. pract/ical
    b. prac/tical
    c. practi/cal   ————
24. a. be/ginning
    b. beginn/ing
    c. begin/ning
25. a. repaired
    b. re/paired
    c. repair/ed   ————

Pretest Part II
Word Division Rules

Directions

In the blank provided, write True if the statement is true or False if the statement is false.

1. Divided words may not appear at the ends of more than two consecutive lines. _____
2. A word may not be divided at the end of the last full line of a paragraph. _____
3. A word may be divided at the end of the last full line on a page if enough of the word is present so that it can be recognized. _____
4. A number should not be divided. However, if absolutely essential, a number separated by hyphens may be divided at a point where the hyphen occurs. _____
5. An abbreviation containing six or more letters may be divided. _____

Lesson 7
Word Division

Why Words Are Divided

The appearance of business communications is important because recipients notice the neatness and arrangement of letters, memorandums, or report pages even before reading them. These first impressions can affect their attitudes toward what is being communicated. A very uneven right margin, for example, is an obvious sign that the people who processed and signed the communication were either unaware of proper arrangement or did not care how it looked. This is one reason for dividing words at the ends of lines. However, words should be divided only when necessary, and learning the few simple, logical rules will help you to divide them correctly. The result will be a page on which the print is framed by approximately equal margins on the right and left side—a page that is attractive and easy to read.

Frame 1   Locations Where Words Cannot Be Divided

Explanation

Words are divided only between syllables. A hyphen is placed at the point of division to show that the word is completed on the following line.

  Words should NEVER be divided at certain locations on the page, because doing so would disrupt the reading process. Words are not divided at these locations:

1. Within an inside address.
2. At the end of the last full line in a paragraph.
3. At the end of the last full line on a page.
4. At the end of more than two consecutive lines in a paragraph.

Example

Read the following letter and the corresponding explanations below it.

Mr. Gordon Zeith, Tourist Manager
Tourist Information Bureau   (Inside Address)
Market and Chestnut Streets
Philadelphia, Pennsylvania 19100

Dear Mr. Zeith:

Thank you for providing tour guides, transportation, and literature for	1
the many hundreds of participants in the Executive Development	2
Business Seminar.	
The men and women who took part in the walking and bus tours were	3
pleased to see the historic buildings and hear the interesting, vivid	4
personal lectures given by your guides. Over 85 percent of the semi-	5
nar participants were from out of state, and many had never visi-	6
ted this city. The membership unanimously expressed its great	7
appreciation of the tours.	
Mr. Zeith, on behalf of the American Business Association, I commend	8
you for handling the logistics so well that 760 people could visit our	9
shrines of democracy and enjoy a catered dinner without a catastrophe	10

or even a minor problem. You certainly have made our   11
"Entertainment Night" one that they shall long remember.

Sincerely,

Betty Andrews, Chairman
Entertainment Committee

Inside Address

Notice that the lines happen to be about the same length. Even if the name of the organization is long, no word in it should be divided. Instead, the words of the title should be broken into logical groups and placed on two lines, as shown below:

> Mr. Gordon Zeith, Tourist Manager
> Tourist Information Bureau and
>   Historic Shrine Center
> Market and Chestnut Streets
> Philadelphia, Pennsylvania 19100

Line 2

The word <u>business</u> is not divided because it falls at the end of the last full line in the paragraph.

Line 5

The word <u>seminar</u> is divided; the word <u>visited</u> is started on line 6, but <u>appreciation</u> is not started on line 7 because division would occur at the end of more than two consecutive lines.

Line 11

The word <u>Entertainment</u> is not started on line 11 because that is the last full line of a paragraph.

Note

Assume that line 11 is the last line on the page. If <u>Entertainment</u> were divided, the reader would not know the complete word until the page was turned.

Exercise

Name the four locations in which words should not be divided because the reading process would be disrupted.

1. _____

2. _____

3. _____

4. _____

ANSWERS TO FRAME 1
1. Within the inside address
2. At the end of the last full line in a paragraph
3. At the end of the last full line on a page
4. At the end of more than two consecutive lines

Frame 2 *Words and Combinations that Cannot Be Divided*

Proper Nouns

Explanation

A proper noun names a specific person, place, or thing and, therefore, is capitalized. A proper noun may consist of one or more words, none of which may be divided at the end of a line. However, one or more complete words in the proper noun may be carried to the next line.

Some words—contractions and combinations, such as numbers, abbreviations, acronyms, and listings—are not divided.

Example

Read the explanations of the following types of proper nouns and notice how they are separated.

I. Proper Nouns
  A. Names of Persons
    1. The first name may be on one line and the last on the next line:
      The Vice President of Marketing is <u>Catherine</u>
      <u>Doyle</u>.
    2. The middle initial should be on the same line as the first name:
      The Vice President of Marketing is <u>Catherine A.</u>
      <u>Doyle</u>.
    3. A long title may be on one line and the name on the next, but a short title is preferably placed on the same line as the first name:
      The memo was delivered to <u>Lieutenant General</u>
      <u>Herman A. Cheryl</u>.
  B. Names of Places
    1. The city may be on one line and the state on the next:
      Mr. Graves has been transferred to <u>Atlanta,</u>
      <u>Georgia</u>.
    2. If necessary, a location consisting of more than one word may be broken into logical word groups and divided between two lines.
      The company has no offices west of the <u>Mississippi</u>
      <u>River</u>.
  C. Names of Things: Organizations
    1. In the body of a communication, the writer has little opportunity to carry "logical word groups" at the end of one line to the beginning of another; but regardless of the length of a word or a name, it is preferable not to divide within a word.
    2. Within the inside address, the processor should make an effort to keep the lines approximately equal for balance without dividing a word. See Example 1 in Frame 1 and notice the following:
      a. Line 2 of the letter in Frame 1 should not show a divided word for two reasons:
        i. it is the last full line of the paragraph
        ii. the word <u>Business</u> is part of the seminar name, a proper noun.
      b. Line 11 should not show a divided word because:
        i. it is the last full line of the paragraph
        ii. "<u>Entertainment Night</u>" is a proper noun, no word of which should be divided.
  D. Names of Things: Street Addresses
    The number of the street is not separated from the name of the street, but

the number and name may be separated from the word <u>street</u> or a synonym:

> The Post Office Building in Bellevue is at <u>605 Third</u>
> <u>Avenue</u>.

    E.   Names of Things: Dates

The day is not separated from the month; this combination may be divided after the day.

> The Citizens Mercantile Store burned on <u>April 11,</u>
> <u>1776</u>.

Other Words and Combinations

The following words and combinations cannot be divided:

Contractions

Two words joined into a solid compound and having an apostrophe in place of an omitted letter: *don't* (do not).

Abbreviations

The shortened form of a word or words in either lowercase or uppercase letters: *acct.* (account), *NLRB* (National Labor Relations Board).

Acronyms

The short form of a word or words that can be spoken: *CONOCO* (Continental Oil Company).

Numbers

No number combination (page, policy, license, and so on) should be divided. Some numbers are separated into groups by a hyphen, such as social security and credit card numbers. It is preferable not to divide these numbers between lines; if a division is essential, it should be made only where the hyphen already exists in the number sequence:

> The winner of the Lucky Superstakes is Number *508-*
> *27-8166*.

Listings

A numbered or lettered listing contained within a sentence may be divided before a number or letter:

> The letter lacks five important criteria of
> good writing: (1) conciseness, (2) completeness,
> (3) concreteness, (4) clarity, and (5) consideration.

Exercise

Draw a slanted line (/) between the parts of each of the following proper nouns to show where each should be divided at the end of a line.

Example

Alfonso E./ Erickson, Jr.

1. Congresswoman Dorthea M. Alberts
2. Oklahoma City, Oklahoma

3. Sierra Madre Mountains
4. (Inside address: name of an organization)
   Association of Records Managers and Administrators
5. 1805 Central Avenue
6. April 15, 1982
7. shouldn't
8. ILGWU
9. (Policy Number) 17437
10. (listing) Four items will be listed in the advertisement: (1) lingerie, . . .

ANSWERS TO FRAME 2

1. Congress/woman/ Dorthea M./ Alberts (either division is acceptable)
2. Oklahoma City,/ Oklahoma (preferably, the division would be at this point; however, if necessary, the words could be separated after Oklahoma.
3. Sierra Madre/ Mountains (preferable division); if necessary, the division could occur after Sierra.
4. Association of Records Managers/ and Administrators
5. 1805 Central/ Avenue
6. April 15,/ 1982
7. Cannot divide
8. Cannot divide
9. Cannot divide
10. Four items will be listed in the advertisement:/ (1) lingerie, . . .

Frame 3   Basic Word Division Rule

Explanation

Words are divided between syllables; often when pronouncing a word, you can determine the syllables. If you are in doubt about the point at which a word should be divided, consult a current dictionary. When a word can be divided at more than one point, place as much as possible of the word at the end of the line. This procedure will help the reader move to the next line easily.

Two basic rules govern word division:

1. Do not divide words of one syllable (*cloth*).
2. Divide a word so that a minimum of three letters falls at the end of a line and at the beginning of the next line (*pre/fix*).

Note

Some books give another rule: Do not divide a one-letter syllable at the beginning or at the end of a word. This rule is unnecessary now, because most current dictionaries do not show a division at this point, and following Rule (2), above, eliminates this decision.

Example

Study the following examples and explanations.

1. Do not divide one-syllable words. A one-syllable word is approximately a single speech sound; despite its length, it must not be divided.
   THOUGHT   BOUGHT   PASSED   WEIGHT
2. Do not divide a word of less than six letters even though it contains two or more syllables.
   REFER   DIET   ONLY

Exercise

1. If a word can be divided at the end of a line, write it in the blank and place a slash (/) at each acceptable division point.
2. If a word cannot be divided at the end of a line, write No in the blank at the right.

Example

condolence   <u>con/do/lence</u>

1. shipped	_____	7.	return	_____
2. primary	_____	8.	important	_____
3. perfect	_____	9.	kindness	_____
4. about	_____	10.	credit	_____
5. bough	_____	11.	balance	_____
6. estimate	_____	12.	regard	_____

ANSWERS TO FRAME 3

1. No	4. No	7. No	10. No
2. pri/mary	5. No	8. impor/tant	11. bal/ance
3. per/fect	6. esti/mate	9. kind/ness	12. No

Frame 4   *Preferred Word Division Points*

Explanation

Despite the fact that the dictionary may show more than one division point in a word, only one of these points may be preferable for end-of-line division. Four preferred word division points are applicable to compound words, prefixes and suffixes, internal vowels, and internal consonants.

Example

Study the rule and the example to which it applies.

I. Compound Words
   A. Divide a solid compound word between the words that comprise the compound:
      HOPELESS   CUPFUL   SALESMAN
      HOPE/LESS   CUP/FUL   SALES/MAN
   B. Divide a hyphenated compound word between the words that comprise the compound:
      SELF-/IMAGE   EYE-/CATCHING   PLAY-/BY-/PLAY
II. Prefixes and Suffixes
   A. Divide after a prefix (not within a prefix):
      PRE-/VENT   INTER-/NATIONAL   DIS-/APPEAR
   B. Divide before a suffix (not within a suffix):
      BREAK-/ABLE   COLLECT-/IBLE
   C. Divide after a prefix or before a suffix rather than within the root word. (The most meaningful division should be chosen.)
      COMMENDA-/TION   not   COMMEN-/DATION
   D. If a word has two suffixes, choose the division point that is the most meaningful:
      CONSIDERATE-/NESS   not   CONSIDER-/ATENESS

III. Vowels
    A. Divide after a one-letter syllable within a word:
        EXIGENT: EXI-/GENT   HOLIDAY: HOLI-/DAY
    B. Divide between two separately sounded vowels:
        APPROPRI-/ATE   MINI-/ATURE   VALU-/ABLE
IV. Double Consonants
If the final consonant is doubled when a suffix is added, separate the word between the double consonant IF the suffix is a separately pronounced syllable.
    PLAN-/NING   HIT-/TING   CONTROL-/LER
    Not: CONFER-/RED (The added *-ed* does not constitute another syllable.)
    C. Divide between a double consonant within a root word:
        COMIS-/SION   CON-/NOTE   BEL-/LIGERENT

Exercise

1. If a word can be divided at the end of a line, rewrite it, placing a slash (/) at the *preferred* point.
2. If a word cannot be divided at the end of a line, explain why. Keep the "Rule of Three" in mind.

Example

latecomer   late/comer

1. large-scale
2. pretest
3. amendment
4. passable
5. pressure
6. digressed
7. regular
8. transparent
9. appreciate
10. misspent
11. opposed
12. oppressing
13. conferring
14. succeed

ANSWERS TO FRAME 4
1. large-/scale (Divide at the point where the hyphen is located.)
2. pre/test (Divide after the prefix.)
3. amend/ment (Divide before the suffix.)
4. pass/able (Divide before and not within a syllable.)
5. pres/sure (Divide between an internal double consonant.)
6. digressed (The first syllable contains only two letters; the addition of *-ed* does not add another pronounceable syllable.)
7. regu/lar (Divide after a single vowel within a word.)

8. trans/parent (This division is better than *transpar/ent* because the syllable *trans-* is separated from the root word.)
9. appreci/ate (Divide between two pronounced vowels.)
10. mis/spent (Divide after a prefix.)
11. opposed (The first syllable contains only two letters; the *-ed* is not pronounced separately.)
12. oppress/ing (Divide after a double consonant at the end of a word.)
13. confer/ring (Divide between a double consonant created by the addition of a syllable if that consonant is pronounced.)
14. suc/ceed (Divide between an internal double consonant.)

Frame 5 Word Endings that Are Kept as Single Units

Explanation

Certain word endings, whether they form one or two syllables, should be kept as single units.

Example

-able	charge/able	-ible	illeg/ible	-tial	residen/tial
-cial	finan/cial	-ical	rad/ical	-tion	atten/tion
-cient	effi/cient	-sion	commis/sion	-tive	preven/tive
-cion	coer/cion	-sive	respon/sive		

Exercise

Place a slash (/) at *each* point where these words can be divided at the end of a line.

Example

residential_____ resi/den/tial_____

1. conducive_____

2. reliable_____

3. prevention_____

4. alternative_____

5. division_____

6. periodical_____

7. confidential_____

ANSWERS TO FRAME 5

1.	con/du/cive	3.	pre/ven/tion	5.	divi/sion	7.	con/fi/den/tial
2.	reli/able	4.	alter/na/tive	6.	peri/od/ical		

Frame 6 The Influence of a Change in Pronunciation

Explanation

Occasionally, a word that is used as a noun will be pronounced differently when it is used as a verb or as another part of speech. Incorrect word division under these circumstances would confuse the reader.

Example

As a noun, *record* is pronounced *rec/ord,* but as a verb, it is pronounced *re/cord.* Under these circumstances, the noun could be divided, but the verb could not.

Exercise

Write the word the way it should be divided when used as a noun and as a verb.

Example

	Noun	*Verb*
project	proj/ect	pro/ject

	Noun	*Verb*
1. present		
2. progress		
3. desert		

ANSWERS TO FRAME 6

1.	Noun:	pres/ent	Verb:	pre/sent
2.	Noun:	prog/ress	Verb:	pro/gress
3.	Noun:	des/ert (arid land), or desert (deserved reward— should not be divided)	Verb:	desert (to withdraw or leave —should not be divided)

Frame 7   Business Vocabulary

Explanation

To be successful, a business must have effective managers. Managers plan, organize, direct, and control the function to which they are assigned. Neither sex nor color nor ethnic background has any influence on one's ability to manage a function in the private sector (business and industry) or the public sector (federal, state, county, and city government agencies).

Example

Study the words and their definitions.

1. *Management:* Management is often defined as the art of "getting work done through people."
2. *Types of Managers*
   a. A *line manager* is one who manages a department that contributes directly to the product or service offered by the organization. The department this person manages is called a *line department.* Examples of line departments are production, finance, and marketing.
   b. A *staff manager* is one who acts in an advisory capacity and manages a department that provides services for the line departments. Examples of staff departments are personnel, administrative services, and research and development.
3. *Function:* A function is a group of similar jobs brought together in one unit under one manager. Examples of like duties are those pertaining to the employees (handled by the personnel department), and those involving the production of a product or the implementing of a service (handled by the production department).

Exercise

Select the word in parentheses that makes the statement correct, and write that word in the blank.

1. The data processing function in a manufacturing firm is a _____ (line, staff) function.

2. When all the duties involving records are brought together, they form the records management _____ (function, department).

3. The manager of the research and development department is a _____ (line, staff) manager.

4. Managers plan, organize, direct, and _____ (coordinate, control) the functions they are assigned.

5. A department that contributes directly to the product or service offered by the organization is a _____ (staff, line) department.

ANSWERS TO FRAME 7
1. staff   2. function   3. staff   4. control   5. line

Frame 8   *Applying Your Knowledge*

You are applying for a management position and have given your rough-draft application letter to another student to type in perfect format for your signature. You receive the letter perfectly typed, but with the right margin almost completely even because the typist has divided many, many words at the same margin position. Although the right margin is "even," the letter is extremely difficult to read.

Directions

1. If a word is divided incorrectly (or a proper noun separated incorrectly), write the correction directly next to it on the line.
2. Write the pertinent rule in a complete sentence next to the correction.
3. If the word is correct, write "C" in the blank to the right.
4. You will find 10 errors in this exercise.

Example

ap/plicant   appli/cant   Divide a word before the suffix.

semimonth/ly_____

Professor Albert/ Garland_____

person/nel_____

process/ing_____

gra/duate_____

refer/ring_____

product/ion_____

bus/iness_____

re/search_____

man/agement_____

market/ing_____

résu/mé_____

administra/tive_____

partici/pate_____

re/cords (noun)_____

indus/try_____

govern/ment_____

in/terview_____

comm/erce_____

advis/ory_____

proj/ect (noun)_____

depart/ment_____

ANSWERS TO FRAME 8

<u>semi/monthly</u>   Divide after a prefix; do not separate a two-letter syllable._____

Professor Albert/ Garland_____C_____

person/nel_____C_____

process/ing_____C_____

<u>gradu/ate</u>   Divide between two vowels that are sounded separately._____

refer/ring_____C_____

<u>produc/tion</u>   Divide before a suffix._____

<u>busi/ness</u>   Divide after a one-letter syllable; divide before a suffix._____

<u>research (cannot be divided)</u>   Do not separate a two-letter syllable._____

<u>manage/ment</u>   Divide before a suffix._____

market/ing_____C_____

<u>résumé (cannot be divided)</u>   Do not separate a two-letter syllable._____

administra/tive_____C_____

partici/pate_____C_____

<u>rec/ords</u>   The division of this word is dependent upon its pronunciation and part of speech.

indus/try_____C_____

govern/ment_____C_____

<u>inter/view</u>   Do not separate a two-letter syllable; divide after a prefix._____

com/merce   Divide between a double consonant within a word.

advis/ory   C

proj/ect (noun)   C

depart/ment   C

Lesson 8
Frequently Misused Words

Pretest

The pretest and posttest for this lesson are presented as an Applying Your Knowledge section. The presentation of the tests in this form permits you to determine if certain words are part of your writing vocabulary. The following frequently misused words are covered in this lesson:

1. principal, principle
2. effect, affect
3. capital, capitol
4. you're, your
5. ad, add
6. advise, advice
7. stationery, stationary
8. access, excess
9. envelope, envelop
10. assent, ascent
11. biannual, biennial
12. course, coarse
13. devise, device
14. emigrate, immigrate

Directions

1. Draw a line through each misused word.
2. Write the correct word in the space below the error.
3. After you have proofread the letter, write five sentences, each correctly using one of the words which you crossed out in the original letter.

Example

The bank's mechanical tellers allow customers 24-hour ~~excess~~ to check-cashing
                                                        access
_____

services. _____

Sentence: Mr. Bates will pay taxes in <u>excess</u> of $17,000 this year.

CASE

Joe, the publicity director of the student council, has prepared this letter for the council's approval. As a member, would you approve the letter? (5 errors)

January 27, 19____

Dear Businessperson:

As publicity director of the student council at Delaware

Junior College, I have been requested to solicit capital

for the initiation and publication of a new college journal,

Historic Delaware. The principal purpose of this journal, a biennial publication, to be distributed every fall and spring semester, is to make residents aware of the historical events that have occurred in this state. Our sponsor, Professor Bremer, especially wants us to show the affect that people who immigrated from other countries had on this state and how they influenced its course.

The stories will be written by students in English composition courses; these students have been given access to the archives at the capitol building in Wilmington. The campus Reproduction and Graphics Department has assented to devise the format of the magazine and provide advise in layout.

We do not plan to sell advertisements; instead, we hope that initial and succeeding contributions will provide the necessary funding. Each issue will be sold for an amount not in excess of a dollar, and this income wil' assist us to pay for postage and to purchase paper, stationery, envelops, and other supplies.

Would you like to read about historic Delaware? Your contribution to our capital is welcomed and will provide you and other citizens with an awareness of our state's past.

Sincerely,

Joseph Azzolita
Publicity Director

The first issue will be <u>free</u> to anyone who pledges $50.

Sentences

(1)_____

_____

(2)_____

_____

(3)_____

_____

(4)_____

_____

(5)_____

_____

Lesson 8
Frequently Misused Words

Five lessons in this textbook are devoted to words that are frequently misused. These words are confusing and troublesome for two reasons:

1. They are spelled and pronounced alike but have different meanings (*homonyms*).
2. They sound alike, or similar, but have different meanings and spellings (*homophones*).

In most instances, spelling rules do not apply to these words; therefore, the words must be studied in relation to their application in the English language. Practice in using these words is essential to anyone who expects to write business communications. Although each of the five lessons devoted to frequently misused words does provide practice, you might benefit from using the following procedure, designed to make a word part of your oral and written vocabulary:

1. Locate the word in the dictionary.
2. Copy it in syllables.
3. Place the accent mark(s).
4. Pronounce the word.
5. Identify its origin and meaning (from the etymology).
6. Notice the usage label: part of speech or other usage.
7. Read the definitions.
8. Select a definition that you want to apply.
9. Write a sentence using the word (and conveying the meaning of the definition you selected).
10. Use the word (or a derivative of it) orally within one day.

Once you have mastered these troublesome words, you will need to refer to the dictionary less frequently to determine their usage.

Frame 1

Explanation and Examples

Words that are spelled and pronounced alike but have different meanings are *homonyms* (example: *principal* and *principal*). Words that sound alike, or similar, but have different meanings and spellings are *homophones* (example: *affect, effect; advise, advice*). Read the explanations below and study each example.

Group 1   Homonym

PRINCIPAL   (adj) chief or most important.
              The PRINCIPAL crop is corn.
PRINCIPAL   (n) the money on which interest is earned or is due.
              I earned 6 percent interest on the PRINCIPAL.
PRINCIPAL   (n) a person who has controlling authority or is in a leading position—frequently applied to a school principal or an originator of correspondence.
              Mr. Stark is the PRINCIPAL of Laurel School.

Homophone

PRINCIPLE   (n) rule, law, doctrine, or code of conduct.
              The PRINCIPLE of effective management is this: When you give the person a job, also give him/her the power to perform it.

Mnemonic Devices

A mnemonic device is a memory aid. Such a device can be used to distinguish between some frequently misused words.

1. princi*pal*: school administrator or important person; this person can be your *pal*.
2. princip*al*: money; capit*al* also means money.
3. princi*ple*: law, rule; ru*le* also ends in *-le*.
4. princip*al* (*a*dj): the choice should be *al* (not *le*) when it is used in an *a*djective position.

Group 2   Homophones: AFFECT, EFFECT

AFFECT   (v): to influence
          Will the close election results AFFECT the senator's vote on this issue?
EFFECT   (n): result
          The EFFECT of increasing wages is that fewer people will be employed.
EFFECT   (v): to bring about
          The lawyers can EFFECT a settlement without going to court.

Group 3   Homophones: ADVISE, ADVICE

ADVISE   (v) to counsel or inform
          Mr. Reid pays a lawyer to ADVISE him correctly.
ADVICE   (n) opinion regarding action to be taken
          The cost of the lawyer's ADVICE depends upon many variables.

Exercise

Complete the meaning of each sentence by selecting one of the words within parentheses. Write this word in the blank provided.

Example

The (principle, principal) did not support the teachers when they brought their discipline problems to him.   _principal_

1. According to the surgeon general, smoking may (affect, effect) your health. _____
2. The President is attempting to (affect, effect) an agreement on his energy program. _____
3. Some people believe that certain diets (affect, effect) the body's nervous system. _____
4. The doctor (advices, advises) his patients to exercise. _____
5. The (principle, principal) reason for including this lesson is to help you increase your vocabulary. _____
6. Interest is computed on the full amount of the (principal, principle). _____
7. The (affect, effect) that new equipment will have on speeding the paperflow is unknown at this time. _____
8. The person who dictates to a secretary in person or through a recording device is often called a (principal, principle). _____
9. Someone who observes the ethics of his profession and maintains them even under duress is a person of (principals, principles). _____
10. The loan officer (adviced, advised) the applicant to improve his financial condition before reapplying for a loan. _____
11. The applicant took the loan officer's (advice, advise) seriously and immediately opened a savings account. _____

ANSWERS TO FRAME 1

1. affect	4. advises	7. effect	10. advised
2. effect	5. principal	8. principal	11. advice
3. affect	6. principal	9. principles	

Frame 2

Explanation and Example

In formal business communications, such as letters and reports, you should not abbreviate words or use contractions. Study the explanations and examples below.

1. AD (n) : this word is an abbreviation for *advertisement;* it should not be used in formal communications. A less formal communication may contain the word.

    > I placed an AD in the newspaper to solicit applications for this job. (memo)

    ADD (v) : to compile two or more figures.

    > ADD the expenses for labor and supplies to determine how much we should charge for this printing job.

2. YOUR: a personal pronoun showing possession.

    > I have YOUR letter.

    YOU'RE: a contraction of the words *you are;* an apostrophe is inserted at the point where a letter is omitted.

    > YOU'RE expected to attend the departmental meetings.

3. STATIONERY (n) : paper on which correspondence is prepared; for example, office stationery. (mnemonic device: compare l*etter* and station*ery*)

    > Our STATIONERY is white with blue print.

    STATIONARY (adj) : stays in one place; does not move (mnemonic device: compare station*ary* and *stay*).

    > The counter on the copy machine is STATIONARY and must be repaired.

Exercise

Complete the meaning of each sentence by selecting one of the words within parentheses. Write this word in the blank provided.

1. If a memo is written in an informal style, the writer may use the word (*ad, add*), but it is not acceptable for formal correspondence. _____
2. (Your, You're) job will be evaluated, and you may get a salary increase. _____
3. The restaurant on the top floor of the World Trade Center does not revolve; it is (stationery, stationary). _____
4. Graphic artists in a print shop may design (stationery, stationary) and envelopes. _____
5. Courtesy is appreciated; let us remember to say "(Your, You're) welcome" when someone thanks us for our cooperation. _____

ANSWERS TO FRAME 2
1. ad   2. Your   3. stationary   4. stationery   5. You're

Frame 3

Explanation and Example

These words are frequently misused: envelope, envelop; access, excess; capitol, capital.

1. ENVELOPE (n) : paper container in which letters and other communications are mailed (mnemonic device: <u>ope</u>n the envel<u>ope</u>).

   Place the letter in the ENVELOPE.

   ENVELOP (v) : to encompass

   The fumes from the punctured tank will ENVELOP the city.

2. ACCESS (n) : open to a person; admittance.

   The administrative secretary has ACCESS to the president's office.

   EXCESS (adj) : more than sufficient, required, or necessary; a surplus.

   The additional bag is EXCESS luggage.

   EXCESS (n) : (same meaning as the adjective, above).

   We drove in EXCESS of the speed limit.

3. CAPITOL (n) : a building that houses a legislative body (mnemonic device: capit*o*l, d*o*me).

   The CAPITOL has a gold dome.

   CAPITAL (n) : money; securities; an investment (mnemonic device: princip*a*l and capit*a*l refer to money).

   The company has CAPITAL to invest.

   CAPITAL (n) : city that is the official seat of government.

   The CAPITAL of Connecticut is Hartford.

   CAPITAL (adj) : first and foremost; chief; principal.

   The CAPITAL city of Iowa is Des Moines.

Exercise

Complete the meaning of each sentence by selecting one of the words within parentheses. Write this word in the blank provided.

1. The thief gained (access, excess) through an unlocked window.
2. The writer earned in (access, excess) of $20,000 a year.
3. The (capital, capitol) of the United States is Washington, D.C.
4. The (capital, capitol) building will be remodeled.
5. Assets that can be readily liquidated are considered (capital, capitol) assets.
6. Smog (envelops, envelopes) the city on humid days.
7. Only the authorized manager should have (access, excess) to the vital records of a company.
8. The (capital, capitol) is in need of repairs costing at least $100,000.
9. The (capital, capitol) of New Mexico is Santa Fe.
10. The consultant is taking an (accessive, excessive) amount of time to complete the systems survey.
11. All stationery, letterhead, and (envelops, envelopes) should be coordinated in design and color.
12. This company has insufficient (capital, capitol) to establish a new product line at this time.
13. To gain (access, excess) to the building, you must show your identification card.

ANSWERS TO FRAME 3

1.	access	5.	capital	8.	capitol	11.	envelopes
2.	excess	6.	envelops	9.	capital	12.	capital
3.	capital	7.	access	10.	excessive	13.	access
4.	capitol						

Frame 4

Explanation and Example

The ten words presented in this frame are ascent, assent; biannual, biennial; coarse, course; device, devise; and emigrate, immigrate.

1. ASSENT (v) : to concur; to agree.

>   He ASSENTED to my request after he considered it carefully.

   ASSENT (n) : agreement; the act of assenting.

>   He gave his ASSENT to the proposal.

   ASCENT (n) : the act of rising upward.

>   Her ASCENT in the organization was due to her persuasive abilities.

2. BIANNUAL (adj) : twice a year.

>   This is a BIANNUAL publication.

   BIENNIAL (adj) : once every two years (mnemonic device: cent*ennial* means once every hundred years; bi*ennial* means once every two years).

>   This flower is one of the few BIENNIAL plants in our collection.

3. COARSE (adj) : rough.

>   The fabric was a COARSE weave.

   COURSE (n) : part of a curriculum; part of a meal; a direction.

>   The main COURSE is pheasant with wild rice.

4. DEVICE (n) : a contrivance.

>   The counting DEVICE on the copier is malfunctioning.

   DEVISE (v) : to form by new applications of combinations; to invent; to plan.

>   Doctors have DEVISED a way in which they can alter the pacemaker's rhythm after it is installed in a person's body.

5. EMIGRATE (v) : to go from a country (usually followed by *from*).

>   Ms. Wells EMIGRATED from England to Australia.

   IMMIGRATE (v) : to come to a country (usually followed by *to*).

>   My grandfather IMMIGRATED to the United States from Germany in 1850.

   IMMIGRANT (n) : a person who immigrates.

>   The European IMMIGRANTS to the United States settled in the Northeast.

Exercise

Complete the meaning of each sentence by selecting one of the words within the parentheses. Write this word in the blank provided.

1. The refugees (emigrated, immigrated) from their war-torn country to the United States.
2. My supervisor finally (assented, ascented) to my request.
3. (Coarse, Course) fiber foods, such as bran, asparagus, and so on, are recommended in this diet.
4. This course is offered every two years; that is, it is offered on a (biannual, biennial) basis.
5. The managers (deviced, devised) a plan by which the company can obtain a long-term loan.
6. This magazine, which is (biannual, biennial), is published in June and December.
7. The Forsyth family (emigrated, immigrated) to the United States from New Zealand after World War II.
8. His (ascent, assent) in the financial world was almost as swift as his downfall.
9. The boat's captain steered a northeasterly (coarse, course), hoping to evade the rough seas.
10. He invented a (device, devise) that will measure the erosion created by water on rock formations.

ANSWERS TO FRAME 4

1. emigrated	5. devised	8. ascent
2. assented	6. biannual	9. course
3. Coarse	7. immigrated	10. device
4. biennial		

Lesson 9
Nouns:
Capitalization

Pretest

Pretest Part I
Noun Classifications

Directions

In each of the following sentences, underscore the type of noun indicated at the right of each number.

Example

Proper Noun: <u>John Crawford</u> has accepted a position with the <u>Magic Mannequin Agency</u> in <u>Minneapolis</u>.

1. *Common Noun:* The restaurant on the top floor of the World Trade Center is called Windows on the World.
2. *Proper Noun:* The meeting of the American Management Association is scheduled for Friday, May 26.
3. *Abstract Noun:* A lack of harmony exists between the two departments.
4. *Concrete Noun:* The book contains graphs, pictures, and forms.
5. *General Noun:* Can I help you in this matter?
6. *Specific Noun:* Shall I write a recommendation for you?
7. *Collective Noun:* The committee unanimously believes that more emphasis should be placed on the fundamentals in English courses.
8. *Verbal Noun:* Writing this report will require considerable time and effort.

Pretest Part II
Capitalization

Directions

Underscore each word that should be capitalized. If no words require capitalization, write C (correct) in the blank.

Example

The <u>agency</u> for <u>international</u> <u>development</u>, headquartered in <u>washington</u>, provides financial and educational assistance for many countries in <u>africa</u>, <u>south america</u>, and <u>asia</u>.

1. The company will not pay a dividend this year.   _____
2. I believe that father will pay my tuition this fall.   _____

3. I registered for Spanish, history, anthropology, and statistics 206. ⎯⎯⎯⎯
4. I purchased a china closet with the money from my income tax refund. ⎯⎯⎯⎯
5. The city of Philadelphia is located southeast of Harrisburg. ⎯⎯⎯⎯
6. The department of defense is directed by a civilian. ⎯⎯⎯⎯
7. The personnel director, Miss Bertha Carmadine, will interview you at 10:15. ⎯⎯⎯⎯
8. Mr. Smythe is a former lieutenant colonel. ⎯⎯⎯⎯
9. This book was written by professor James B. Lane. ⎯⎯⎯⎯
10. The defense attorney thought that judge Clark should expunge the record of the defendant. ⎯⎯⎯⎯
11. Send your report to the marketing department in the Comsat Company. ⎯⎯⎯⎯
12. Most student organizations meet in the long's peak room of the morgan student center. ⎯⎯⎯⎯
13. I plan to take flight no. 193 to Houston next week. ⎯⎯⎯⎯
14. In line 10 of paragraph 2 on page 23, you will find the answer to this question. ⎯⎯⎯⎯
15. The citrus crop in northern Florida has been damaged by the cold weather. ⎯⎯⎯⎯
16. The article, "the economy is looking up," was written by well-known economist, John Paul Swanson. ⎯⎯⎯⎯
17. The stone age is the first known stage of human development. ⎯⎯⎯⎯

Lesson 9
Nouns: Capitalization

The capitalization rules in this lesson are applicable to most business communications; however, an organization may vary some rules to meet specific needs, desires, or policies. Also, certain types of specialized communications, such as sales letters, legal documents, and technical reports, may contain additional capitalization for visual effect, emphasis, or clarification. You should be familiar with the basic rules, consistent in applying them, and aware of variations preferred by the organization in which you are employed.*

The first step in learning which words to capitalize is to be able to distinguish proper nouns from other noun classifications.

Frame 1   Classification of Nouns

Explanation

Nouns are classified as common, proper, concrete, abstract, general, specific, collective, or verbal. Understanding these classifications will help you to capitalize the correct words, and to write grammatical, specific, and interesting sentences.

Example

Study the following classifications and representative examples of nouns.

1. Common and Proper Nouns: A *common noun* names a person, place, or thing within a category; a *proper noun* names a specific person, place, or thing within a category. A proper noun is always capitalized; a common noun is not.

Type	Person	Place	Thing
Common	woman	city	car
Proper	Marsha Daws	Lincoln	Ford

2. Concrete and Abstract Nouns: A *concrete noun* is a common noun and names something that has substance and which appeals to one or more of the five senses—taste, smell, hearing, touch, sight. An *abstract noun* does not have substance and does not appeal to the five senses. It usually names a quality, trait, or characteristic.

Concrete	desk	shirt	paper
Abstract	honor	loyalty	courage

3. General and Specific Nouns: A *general noun* is a common noun that names a category in general, and a *specific noun* is a common noun that names a specific person, place, or thing in a category. If a specific noun is also a proper noun, it is capitalized. Specific nouns are preferable in business writing because they promote understanding between the reader and writer.

General	information	(in this) matter
Specific	brochures	checkbook

4. Collective Noun: A *collective noun* is a common noun that names a collection of something—persons, places, or things. This type of noun is plural in meaning,

* By permission. Lois Meyer and Ruth Moyer, *Machine Transcription in Modern Business* (New York: John Wiley & Sons, 1978), p. 28.

but it takes a singular verb if the members or parts are considered as one, and it takes a plural verb if the members or parts are considered separately.

Singular   The city *council agrees* on the street assessment. (The council is acting as a group or unit.)
Plural   The *faculty disagree* on this controversial subject. (The members are considered separately.)
Singular   The *group makes* its yearly contribution to the Community Fund in January. (The group acts as a unit.)
Plural   The *committee solicit* opinions from their respective departments. (Committee members act separately.)

5. Verbal Noun: A *verbal noun* is a verb form ending in *-ing* and used as a noun. This common noun is called a *gerund.*

Verb form   walk
Ending in -ing   walking
Used as a noun   *Walking* is good exercise. (subject)
                 The doctor recommended *walking* as good exercise. (object of the verb)
                 A good exercise for an overweight person is *walking*. (subjective complement)
                 He does not care to get his exercise by *walking*. (object of the preposition *by*)

Exercise

In each of the following sentences, underscore the noun(s) indicated at the right of each number.

Example

Proper: <u>Mr. Ballantine</u>, the marketing manager, attended a meeting in <u>St. Louis</u> on <u>Thursday</u>, <u>April</u> 25.

1. *Common:* The sales in that region have been decreasing this quarter.
2. *Collective:* The jury disagree regarding the guilt of the defendant.
3. *Verbal:* His favorite sport is swimming.
4. *Abstract:* The bank guard had the courage to stop the armed assailant.
5. *Concrete:* The bank guard had the courage to stop the armed assailant.
6. *General:* Joe asked the personnel director of the Amco Company to send him some information.
7. *Specific:* Joe asked the personnel director of the Amco Company to send him some brochures.
8. *Collective:* The committee, as a whole, believes that this policy should be changed.
9. *Proper:* Albert Eamonera suggested that the personnel department redesign the form.
10. *Verbal:* They were paid well for working during the strike.
11. *Abstract:* Honesty is an important virtue for any employee who handles cash.
12. *Concrete:* These statements have been evaluated by the analyst.

ANSWERS TO FRAME 1

1. <u>sales</u>, <u>region</u>, <u>quarter</u>
2. <u>jury</u>
3. <u>swimming</u>
4. <u>courage</u>
5. <u>guard</u>, <u>assailant</u>
6. <u>information</u>
7. <u>Joe</u>, <u>personnel director</u>, <u>Amco Company</u>, <u>brochures</u>
8. <u>committee</u>
9. <u>Albert Eamonera</u>
10. <u>working</u>
11. <u>Honesty</u>, <u>virtue</u>
12. <u>statements</u>, <u>analyst</u>

Frame 2 *Nouns with Other Parts of Speech*

Explanation

A noun that is the name of a specific person, place, or thing is a proper noun and is capitalized. The capitalization of other nouns is dependent upon the type of word (if any) that precedes them, the word from which they have been derived, or their usage in a sentence or word combination.

The word that precedes a noun may make it more specific, but does not necessarily make it a proper noun. Certain pronouns, adjectives, and the article *the* may make a common noun more specific, but they do not convert it into a proper noun—a noun that is the *name* of a specific person, place, or thing.

Example

Notice how a noun may become more specific but does not become a proper noun:

1. A common noun preceded by a possessive pronoun (our, ours, my, mine, your, yours, his, her, hers, their, theirs, its) becomes more specific, but it does not become a proper noun if it is not the *name* of a certain person, place, or thing. Some examples are:

   > A father should cooperate in disciplining his children.

   > (The word *father* is a common noun.)

   > My father is president of the Fastco Manufacturing Company.

   > (The words *my father* identify a specific person, but *father* is not a proper noun because it is not used as the *name* of this person.)

   > I believe Father said that he would loan me the money for tuition.

   > (Here, *Father* is not preceded by a pronoun; it is a proper noun and is capitalized to show that it *names* a specific member of the family.)

   > A *company* in this industry should make an average annual profit of 3 percent.

   > (The word *company* is a common noun, referring to any member of a category.)

   > Our *company* made a 3 percent profit last year.*

   > (The pronoun specifically identifies the subject, but the word *company* is not the name of a specific company, and it is not a proper noun.)

2. A common noun preceded by certain adjectives (this, that, these, those) is not capitalized. These words make the noun more specific, but they do not convert it to a proper noun.

   > This *company* made a 3 percent profit last year.*

3. A common noun preceded by the article *the* is not capitalized. The word *the* is the only article that identifies a specific person, place, or thing.

   > The *corporation* now has over 7,000,000 stockholders.*

---

* Sometimes the employing organization has a policy that requires capitalizing such words as *company, bank,* or *corporation* when they refer to the organization itself. Under these circumstances, the employee will need to comply.

4. An article, conjunction, or preposition within a proper noun or considered as part of it is not capitalized unless this word begins the proper noun.
   a. Proper noun including a capitalized article: *The Daily News* (*The* is part of the name.)
   b. Proper noun including an article not capitalized: *Top of the Park; Secretary of the Treasury*
   c. Proper noun including a preposition not capitalized: *Bureau of Land Management; Voice of America*
   d. Proper noun including a conjunction not capitalized: *Barton and Barton, Accountants*

Note

Often the ampersand (&) is used instead of the word *and*. The name of an organization should be capitalized in the same manner as is shown on the letterhead or in the telephone directory.

5. Substitution of a common noun for a proper noun: Except in legal documents or very formal communications, a common noun substituted for a proper noun is not capitalized.

> Alcorn International Freight Company has offices in 42 cities throughout the world. The *company* appreciates your patronage.
>
> The channel of the Missouri River was changed by the Corps of Engineers. The *river* now is navigable to barges and small boats.
>
> Use Form 72A to list your beneficiaries. This *form* is available from the Personnel Department.

Exercise

In the following sentences, underscore the words that should be capitalized. If a sentence has no words that require capitalization, write C (correct) in the blank provided.

Example

I believe <u>mother</u> will visit me soon.   _____

1. Our company will pay your moving expenses.   _____
2. You can transfer your account from this bank to your home bank very easily.   _____
3. The law firm of Harvey and Adams will handle the estate.   _____
4. The court is located in the city of Denver.   _____
5. According to the annual report, that corporation paid a dividend last year.   _____
6. To obtain data for their term papers, many students use publications from the bureau of labor statistics.   _____
7. The accounting firm of Henderson & Payne performs the corporate audit. This firm has been in business for ninety years.   _____

ANSWERS TO FRAME 2
1. C   2. C   3. C   4. C   5. C   6. <u>Bureau</u>, <u>Labor Statistics</u>   7. C

Frame 3   *Proper Nouns and Their Derivatives*

Explanation

A *proper adjective* is derived from a proper noun and is capitalized. In some cases, a proper noun or proper adjective may have become so common through usage that it is no longer capitalized.

Example

1. Capitalize the names of nations, races, and religions when they are used as proper nouns and proper adjectives. If in doubt, consult a current dictionary.

Proper noun	*Proper adjective*	*Neither a proper adjective nor a proper noun*
China	Chinese people	china, chinaware, china clay
France	French history	french fry*
Manila	Manila streets	manila folder

2. *Courses:* Capitalize a course only when it is specifically named. Do not capitalize an area or field of study.

> I am taking a *typewriting* course. BUT: I am taking *Typewriting II.*

> I took a course in *English composition.* I took *English Composition I.*

> Mr. Simon teaches the *English literature* courses. I am taking *English Literature 210.*

> I registered for *Russian, political science,* and *statistics.*

> I am taking *Russian, Political Science 105,* and *Statistics 206.*

3. *Brand Names:* Brand names and trademarks are capitalized. Through the years a brand name or trademark may become so common that all the items of its type are referred to by its name; that is, it becomes a generic term. When this happens, the brand name or trademark is not capitalized. If in doubt, consult a current dictionary.

> Our new syrup product, *Connoisseur's Delight,* is scheduled to be on the market by March 1.

> The word *Kleenex* is a trademark.

> A *mimeograph* is a duplicator that reproduces copies by the stencil method. (The etymology indicates that this word is from *Mimeograph,* which is a trademark.)

Exercise

Underscore the proper adjectives and proper nouns that should be capitalized in the following sentences. If no words in a sentence require capitalization, write C (correct) in the blank provided.

1. I took a course in english composition. _____
2. My advisor suggested that I add a spanish literature course and an art course to my schedule. _____
3. We purchased english pea soup at the market. _____
4. Are the words kleenex, mimeograph, and dictaphone generic terms? _____
5. Mai Takahashi sells chinese lanterns, chinaware, and other party and hostess items in her store, China Imports. _____
6. I plan to take a cost accounting course next year. _____
7. My major is finance. _____

ANSWERS TO FRAME 3

1. <u>English</u>   4. Kleenex, Dictaphone   7. C
2. <u>Spanish</u>   5. <u>Chinese</u>
3. <u>English</u>   6. C

* Some dictionaries show this word capitalized, and others do not.

Frame 4   Proper Nouns in Organization, Unit, and Job Titles*

Explanation

The names of organizations, subdivisions of organizations, and titles of individuals are capitalized.

Example

1. Capitalize the names of businesses, government agencies, organizations, associations, societies, clubs, and so on.

   > *Dixieland Convenience Stores, Incorporated,* owns many small stores.

   > The company's regulations must be coordinated with the *Environmental Protection Agency's* guidelines.

2. Capitalize the titles of departments, divisions, sections, committees, boards, and other subdivisions of the *employing organization* (your employer). Do not capitalize these titles if they refer to another organization's subdivisions or the subdivision is not that of a specific organization.

   > The *Training Department* will handle the details of this program. (your organization)

   > Will you please refer the questionnaire to the appropriate person in your *personnel department.* (in a letter to another company)

   > Recruitment and training are both functions of the *personnel department* of an organization. (does not refer to a subdivision of a specific organization)

3. Capitalize a job or position title when it precedes the name. Do not capitalize this title when it is used without a name or when it is in apposition to a name.

   > I will ask *Professor* Williams to speak at the faculty meeting.

   > Dr. Hans Williams, *professor of management,* will preside at the special faculty meeting. (in apposition)

   > The *chief auditor* will prepare the final audit report. (used without a name)

Exercise

Underscore each word that should be capitalized in the following sentences. If no words in a sentence require capitalization, write C (correct) in the blank provided.

1. A small firm in Arkansas, called citrus associates, is the only manufacturer of this particular formula. _____
2. The executive committee has decided that a training program should be instituted. [our organization] _____
3. The discrepancies in the reports of the robbery were first noticed by officer Clark. _____
4. Ms. Barrows will serve as chairperson of the group that will conduct the study. _____
5. The national association of realtors certifies sales associates as brokers. _____
6. The internal revenue service has ordered 5,000 of our calculators. _____
7. One of the functions of a research and development department is to conduct feasibility studies. _____
8. All questions regarding the advertising campaign should be referred to the manager of our marketing department. _____

* Ibid., p. 29.

9. The administrative management society in this city is particularly active. _____
10. The operations manager is responsible for scheduling the tellers in our bank. _____

ANSWERS TO FRAME 4
1. Citrus Associates
2. Executive Committee
3. Officer
4. C
5. National Association, Realtors
6. Internal Revenue Service
7. C
8. Marketing Department
9. Administrative Management Society
10. C

Frame 5   Compass Points*

Explanation

Capitalize compass points used as proper nouns and proper adjectives identifying specific geographical areas of cities, states, countries, or the world. Do not capitalize compass points that indicate direction; they are adverbs, not nouns.

Example

1. Some commonly recognized proper nouns and proper adjectives are:
   a. Cities: the South Side (Chicago), the East Side (New York)
   b. States: Southern California, West Texas
   c. United States regions: the East, the West, the North, the South, the West Coast, the Midwest, the Southwest, the Pacific Northwest, the Eastern Seaboard
   d. World regions: the Far East, the Middle East, Western Europe
2. Usage examples:
   a. Noun—specific geographical area:
      Our company is opening many new retail outlets in the *East.*
   b. Adjective—specific geographical area:
      Our *West Coast* sales are up by 10 percent.
   c. Adverb—a direction, not a specific geographical area:
      Freight charges to points *west* of Denver are generally higher.
   d. Adjective—not recognized as a specific geographical area:
      Weather conditions have delayed the sugar beet harvest in *eastern* Colorado.

Exercise

Underscore each word that should be capitalized. If no words in a sentence require capitalization, write C (correct) in the blank provided.

1. We presently have representatives in all areas of the country except the midwest.
2. Our newest plant will be located north of San Francisco. _____
3. Mr. Ryan will return to the Los Angeles office after three years in the middle east. _____
4. Jack Miller, who has been our east coast representative for ten years, will become the new sales manager for eastern Canada. _____
5. The northern section of the city is primarily industrial. _____

ANSWERS TO FRAME 5
1. Midwest 2. C (*north,* an adverb, is a direction) 3. Middle East
4. East Coast (*eastern,* an adjective, is not an identifiable area)
5. C (*northern section* is not an identifiable area)

* Ibid., pp. 31–32.

Frame 6   Proper Nouns and Adjectives Related to Time

Explanation

Capitalize the days of the week, holidays (legal and religious), months of the year, historical events, and descriptive expressions referring to eras. Do not capitalize the seasons or the names of decades or centuries.

Example

1. Capitalize the days of the week: Monday, Tuesday, Wednesday, Thursday, Friday, Saturday, Sunday.
2. Capitalize legal and religious holidays: legal—Veterans Day, the Fourth of July; religious—Good Friday, Passover.
3. Capitalize the months of the year: January, February, March, etc.
4. Capitalize the names of historical events, eras, and descriptive expressions:

the War of 1812	the Great Depression*	the Age of Diplomacy*
World War II	the Gay Nineties*	the Age of Reason*
Middle English	Old French	Old English

5. Do not capitalize the names of seasons or descriptive terms used as synonyms unless they are personified: fall, spring, winter, summer, autumn; but, Old Man Winter.

Exercise

Underscore each word that should be capitalized. If no words in a sentence require capitalization, write C (correct) in the blank provided.

1. On monday, august 2, Mr. Austin will return to his home in Germany. _____
2. A new catalog is printed each season—fall, winter, spring, and summer. _____
3. Great commercial ventures were undertaken during the middle ages. _____
4. I believe that easter will be early this year. _____
5. Many stores have sales prior to mother's day and after the fourth of july. _____

ANSWERS TO FRAME 6

1. <u>Monday, August</u>
2. C (seasons)
3. <u>Middle Ages</u>
4. <u>Easter</u>
5. <u>Mother's Day, Fourth of July</u>

Frame 7   Proper Nouns and Proper Adjectives as Identifiers†

Explanation

Capitalize the names of buildings and rooms, the word preceding an identifying number, and the word preceding an identifying letter.

Example

1. Capitalize the names of buildings and rooms:

    Today's meeting will be held in the *Fireside Room* of the *Greenville Community Center.*

    The work on our new *Perry Park Building* is scheduled for June.

---

* Some dictionaries do not include these expressions; others may not show them as proper nouns. However, to emphasize these expressions, the writer may capitalize them.

† Ibid., pp. 30–32.

2. Capitalize the word preceding an identifying number (with these exceptions—page, paragraph, line, and size).

> Please check each copy of *Form* 87 before it is routed to our office.

> Notice that *Item* 13 has been omitted from the list on *page* 12.

> The pros and cons of nuclear power are discussed in *Bulletin No.* 1.

3. Capitalize the word preceding an identifying letter.

> Our product contains a high concentration of *Vitamin C.*

> Be sure to attach a copy of *Schedules A* and *F* to *Form* 1040.

Exercise

Underscore each word that should be capitalized. If no words in a sentence require capitalization, write C (correct) in the blank provided.

1. Calculator model D is now obsolete; it has been replaced by model E.
2. We have ordered five more dresses, style 35 in size 10.
3. Please note paragraph 5 at the bottom of page 3.
4. The heaviest traffic on our direct flights from New York to Chicago is on flight nos. 173 and 204.
5. Our offices are located in suite 3013.
6. Following luncheon in the green room of the regency hotel, the group will move to the florentine room for the afternoon meeting.

ANSWERS TO FRAME 7

1. <u>Model D</u>, <u>Model E</u>	4. <u>Flight Nos.</u>
2. <u>Style 35</u>	5. <u>Suite 3013</u>
3. C	6. <u>Green Room</u>, <u>Regency Hotel</u>, <u>Florentine Room</u>

Frame 8   Source Titles*

Explanation

Capitalize each word in a *source title* (book, magazine, speech, and so on), with the exception of: (1) articles—a, an, the; (2) prepositions containing not more than three letters—for example, for, in, to, by, and (3) conjunctions—and, but, for, or, nor. The first and the last word of a title are always capitalized.

Example

1. A subscription to *U.S. News and World Report* will help an executive keep up to date on business news and current events.
2. This bulletin, *Vegetables and Your Health,* includes a chapter entitled "Potatoes and Your Health."
3. The topic of Ms. Carroll's speech is "Time Marches On."

Exercise

Underscore each word that should be capitalized.

1. The title of our new book is machine transcription in modern business.
2. Ms. Berger gave a lecture on "word processing concepts and careers."
3. Mr. M. L. Jones wrote the article, "when the consultant comes in."
4. Our new brochure, *the use of color in the modern office,* will be sent to you after it comes from the printer.

* Ibid., pp. 31-32.

5. Our latest industrial film is entitled "strange encounters between the corporation and the ad agency."

ANSWERS TO FRAME 8

1. <u>Machine Transcription</u> in <u>Modern Business</u>
2. "<u>Word Processing Concepts</u> and <u>Careers</u>"
3. "<u>When</u> the <u>Consultant Comes In</u>"
4. <u>The Use</u> of <u>Color</u> in the <u>Modern Office</u>
5. "<u>Strange Encounters Between</u> the <u>Corporation</u> and the <u>Ad Agency</u>"

Frame 9   Titles of Forms and Laws*

Explanation

Capitalize the nouns in the titles of forms, legal documents, and laws; also capitalize the adjectives that are derived from such titles.

Example

1. Form titles: Ask customers to complete the enclosed *Appliance Department Survey Form.*
2. Legal document titles: Please sign and return the enclosed *Confidentiality Agreement.*
3. Adjective derived from title of act: The *Equal Employment Opportunity* concept is not only a matter of business policy, but a moral and civic responsibility.
4. Name of act: Job applicants are protected by the *Fair Credit Reporting Act.*

Exercise

Underscore each word that should be capitalized.

1. The social security act of 1935 established the social security system for the United States.
2. Please complete the attached form, application for graduation, by April 1.
3. All industries are expected to follow the environmental protection agency's guidelines.
4. Each customer who purchases our furniture on credit must sign the conditional sales agreement.

ANSWERS TO FRAME 9

1. <u>Social Security Act</u>, <u>Social Security</u>
2. <u>Application</u> for <u>Graduation</u>
3. <u>Environmental Protection Agency's</u>
4. <u>Conditional Sales Agreement</u>

Frame 10   Miscellaneous Usages of Capitals

Explanation

The first word in most word groups is capitalized. The words in a subject line of a letter or memo are capitalized according to the rule that governs source titles.

Example

1. First word in a sentence:

   Secondary research should be concluded before primary research is begun.

2. First word in a direct quotation:

   The first clause in your insurance policy reads as follows: "*The*

---

* Ibid., p. 30.

insured car is to be driven only by the persons named in this policy. If the car is involved in an accident and the insured is in violation of this clause, the insurance benefits become void."

3. First word and proper nouns (or identifying words) in a salutation:

    Dear Mr. Carmen: *My* dear *Ms. Dose:*   *Dear Customer:*

4. First word in an outline division. (The remaining words in the main division and first subdivision are capitalized according to the rule that governs source titles.)

    I. Higher Wages in Des Moines
        A. More Professional People Employed
            1. In the medical profession and related professions
            2. In the technical professions
                a. Engineers
                b. Scientists

5. First word in a tabulated list:
    a. I have a 3.1 average in these courses:

        Accounting
        Management
        Human relations
        Data processing

    b. Three types of investments are recommended by the financial analyst:

        1. *Bonds*
        2. *Preferred* stocks
        3. *Real* estate investment trusts

Exercise

Underscore each word that should be capitalized.

dear reader:
your subscription to this periodical, *how to make money grow,* will expire with the next issue. my editor said, "tell the subscriber to plant the seed—$14." For this amount you will receive this year's quarterly publications that emphasize investments such as these:
1. off-shore oil blocks.
2. space vehicle manufacturing.
3. solar energy research firms.
Just check and mail the enclosed card to receive your first issue.

yours truly,

ANSWERS TO FRAME 10
<u>Dear Reader</u>:
<u>Your</u> subscription to this periodical, <u>How</u> to <u>Make Money Grow</u>, will expire with the next issue. <u>My</u> editor said, "<u>Tell</u> the subscriber to plant the seed—$14." For this amount you will receive this year's quarterly publications that emphasize investments such as these:
1. <u>Off-shore</u> oil blocks.
2. <u>Space</u> vehicle manufacturing.
3. <u>Solar</u> energy research firms.
Just check and mail the enclosed card to receive your first issue.

<u>Yours</u> truly,

Frame 11   Business Vocabulary

Explanation

Word processing terms are important for all employees to know if they are involved in creating communications or preparing them for processing. The most common words are these: word processing, originator or principal, processor, and text-editing typewriter.

Example

1. Word processing—the process of getting the idea on paper.
   Word processing equipment—a standard typewriter and a desk-type recording unit, or a sophisticated arrangement, such as an automatic typewriter and a telephone dictation system.
2. Originator or principal—the person who has the primary responsibility for creating or originating the communication. This responsibility also includes proofreading it for content and mechanics when it has been returned.
3. Processor—the person who transcribes the recorded dictation in proper format. This person should be a rapid typist; have an excellent understanding of grammar, spelling, punctuation, and other fundamentals; and should be a good proofreader.
4. Text-editing typewriter—any one of several brands of typewriters providing for the copy to be corrected by striking over an incorrect letter(s) or word(s). The typewriter can be programmed with communications that are routine and repetitive and occur in volume, such as form letters. This typewriter also has many logic functions, such as the ability to justify margins, insert words, and so on.
5. Word processing center—a room or area where two or more processors transcribe recorded dictation.

Exercise

Complete the blanks with a word explained in the Business Vocabulary.

1. A person who originates correspondence is called an originator or a

   _____.

2. The person who transcribes the recorded dictation is called a

   _____.

3. An automatic typewriter with the capacity for corrections by strikeover is a

   _____.

4. To assure error-free copy, the _____ and
   _____ should be able to proofread.

ANSWERS TO FRAME 11
1. principal
2. processor
3. text-editing typewriter
4. originator (or principal) and processor

Frame 12   Applying Your Knowledge

Directions

1. Read the case upon which the proofreading exercise is based.

2. Proofread the exercise:
    a. Underscore each word that should be capitalized.
    b. If a word is incorrectly capitalized, draw a line through the first letter.

Example

My Mother's office is located in <u>suite</u> 803 of the Howard Clark <u>building</u>.

> CASE
>
> This letter was prepared by Al Embry, a new administrative assistant in your department, Customer Relations. He dictated the letter to the Word Processing Center, received the rough draft copy, signed it, and placed it on your desk for approval. He understands that he is to proofread the copy, make corrections, and return it for preparation in proper format. The letter contains 25 errors.
>
> April 26, 1977
>
> Mrs. Paul Clarke
> Paradise Valley Road At
>   Mariposa County Line
> Littleton, Colorado 80200
>
> Dear Mrs. Clarke:
>
> Here is the booklet you requested, *The Greenhouse Of Tomorrow.*
>
> We are pleased to send you this booklet and to provide the following
>
> answers to your questions:
>
> 1. Must the greenhouse have a Southern exposure?
>   Yes, Mrs. Clarke, this model g is designed to be placed
>   against a solid construction, such as the side of your house.
>   Even though the temperatures in Eastern Colorado may not
>   exceed the limits mentioned in our advertisement, the most
>   desirable growing conditions exist when the greenhouse is
>   placed in this position.
> 2. Where can I learn more about greenhouses?
>   The department of agriculture has published bulletin no. 47,
>   *Raising a Greenhouse Garden,* which is free. This Bulletin
>   explains how vegetables and flowers can be started in a
>   greenhouse and later planted in the garden. Also, you can
>   visit your local nursery, Brandhoff and sons, to obtain
>   personal assistance. Mr. Brandhoff was formerly a Government
>   Horticulturalist, and he can tell you how to obtain additional
>   printed material free or at minimum cost. Brandhoff and Sons
>   also carries a complete line of our greenhouses, most of them
>   assembled for inspection by customers.

3. Can I use fertilizer in a greenhouse?

The use of fertilizer is dependent upon the content of the fertilizer and the manner in which you intend to apply it. Outdoor applications are best made when the plants are set out in the Spring. The Environmental protection agency's guidelines will be helpful to you in this respect. You can receive a copy from your Regional office.

4. How can I get my garden soil analyzed?

You can accomplish this task in three ways:

1. Purchase a kit from a local nursery. Instructions are inside the kit.

2. Send a sample to your County Agent, Mr. Gaylord Smith, in Yuma.

3. Send a sample to the College of agriculture at the University of Nebraska. Dr. Edward Jackman, Professor of Soil Management, will have it analyzed by the students for a small fee.

I appreciate your interest in our greenhouses and shall inform our Distributor, Mr. Brandhoff, of your desire to learn more about greenhouse gardening.

Yours Truly,

Samson Turnoff
Customer Relations

ANSWERS TO FRAME 12

Mrs. Paul Clarke
Paradise Valley Road A̶t
  Mariposa County Line
Littleton, Colorado 80200

Dear Mrs. Clarke:
Here is the booklet you requested, *The Greenhouse O̶f Tomorrow.* We are pleased to send you this booklet and to provide the following answers to your questions:
1. Must the greenhouse have a S̶outhern exposure?
   Yes, Mrs. Clarke, this model g is designed to be placed against a solid construction, such as the side of your house. Even though the temperatures in E̶astern Colorado may not exceed the limits mentioned in our advertisement, the most desirable growing conditions exist when the greenhouse is placed in this position.
2. Where can I learn more about greenhouses?
   The department of agriculture has published bulletin no. 47, *Raising a Greenhouse Garden,* which is free. This B̶ulletin explains how vegetables and flowers can be started in a greenhouse and later planted in the garden. Also, you can visit your local nursery, Brandhoff and sons, to obtain personal assistance. Mr. Brandhoff was formerly a G̶overnment H̶orticulturalist, and he can tell you how to obtain

additional printed material free or at minimum cost. Brandhoff and Sons also carries a complete line of our greenhouses, most of them assembled for inspection by customers.

3. Can I use fertilizer in a greenhouse?

   The use of fertilizer is dependent upon the content of the fertilizer and the manner in which you intend to apply it. Outdoor applications are best made when the plants are set out in the Spring. The Environmental <u>protection</u> <u>agency's</u> guidelines will be helpful to you in this respect. You can receive a copy from your Regional office.

4. How can I get my garden soil analyzed?

   You can accomplish this task in three ways:

   1. Purchase a kit from a local nursery. Instructions are inside the kit.
   2. Send a sample to your County Agent, Mr. Gaylord Smith, in Yuma.
   3. Send a sample to the College of <u>agriculture</u> at the University of Nebraska. Dr. Edward Jackman, Professor of Soil Management, will have it analyzed by the students for a small fee.

I appreciate your interest in our greenhouses and shall inform our Distributor, Mr. Brandhoff, of your desire to learn more about greenhouse gardening.

Yours Truly,

Samson Turnoff
Customer Relations

Lesson 10
Nouns: Plural Forms

Pretest

Directions

In the blank provided, write the plural form of the underscored word.

Example

This periodical lists 500 <u>corporation</u> according to their past year's sales.   <u>corporations</u>

1. Banks in some states are permitted to have <u>branch</u>.   _____
2. A government publication states that more than 100,000 additional <u>secretary</u> will be needed by the mid-1980s.   _____
3. The <u>Kelley</u> purchased property in West Virginia.   _____
4. Government agency staff members and their <u>wife</u> entertained the visiting dignitaries.   _____
5. A Manford truck containing over 60 <u>calf</u> was hijacked.   _____
6. The Dayton Music Company is having a sale on <u>cello</u>.   _____
7. The <u>cargo</u> of two ships were unloaded by men in the Carey Company.   _____
8. <u>Phonetics</u> is a good way to teach children to read.   _____
9. All <u>printout</u> made during the last week have been requested by the court.   _____
10. The company has a great number of outstanding <u>account receivable</u>.   _____
11. Three <u>follow-up</u> were sent after the original credit notice.   _____
12. Two law professors were formerly <u>attorney-at- law</u>.   _____
13. Schools are placing more emphasis on the <u>3 R</u>.   _____
14. The <u>AMA</u> throughout the country are discussing malpractice suits against doctors.   _____
15. Mr. Jones uses too many <u>and</u> when he lectures.   _____
16. In a formal report, do not abbreviate a word such as <u>dept</u>.   _____
17. Two <u>parenthesis</u> are used to surround words, phrases, clauses, or sentences that are explanatory.   _____
18. The <u>curriculum</u> in each college of the university are being studied.   _____
19. Mary and Jane are <u>alumna</u> of a women's college.   _____
20. You can analyze a financial statement only by using specific, predetermined <u>criterion</u>.   _____

Lesson 10
Nouns: Plural Forms

Nouns have three characteristics: case, number, and gender. In this lesson, we will discuss the number and gender of nouns; case will be discussed in Lesson 11.

Number refers to the singular and plural forms of a noun. These forms are easy to recognize in a sentence; the major problem you will encounter is deciding how to spell the plural form. The rules in this lesson are comprehensive and include many words you will use on your job.

Not all authors agree on the presentation of some plural forms, particularly abbreviations. When you are in doubt about the proper way to form a plural, consult a current dictionary. Most desk dictionaries show the plural form for all nouns with the exception of those that are formed by the addition of an *s*. The plural form is usually shown after the etymology and functional label.

Frame 1   Basic Rule for Forming Plurals of Common and Proper Nouns

Explanation

Most common and proper nouns form their plurals by the addition of *s*.

Example

1. *Common Nouns*

Singular	corporation	organization	bank	employee
Plural	corporations	organizations	banks	employees*

2. *Proper Nouns: Surnames (and other proper nouns).*   Never change the spelling of the singular proper noun to form its plural.

Singular	Meyer	Goodman	Anderson	O'Leary	Carolina
Plural†	Meyers	Goodmans	Andersons	O'Learys	Carolinas

3. *Proper Nouns: Given names*

Singular	Mary	Robert	Kay	Gerald
Plural	Marys	Roberts	Kays	Geralds

Exercise

Write the plural form of the underscored word in the blank provided.

1. The Poudre School District issued <u>bond</u> to obtain <u>fund</u> for a new building.   _____
2. The <u>Johnson</u> contribute regularly to the state and city <u>museum</u>.   _____
                                                                    _____
3. Both <u>Linda</u> excel in quantitative courses.   _____
4. The principal crop of the <u>Dakota</u> is wheat.   _____
5. The <u>Bradley</u> have three children.   _____

---

* At least one publisher of a business periodical has begun to spell *employe* with one *e*. The plural then is *employes*.

† The word *the* always precedes the plural form of a surname.

Frame 2 Common and Proper Nouns Ending in *s, x, ch, sh,* and *z*

Explanation

To form the plural of a common or proper noun ending in *s, x, ch, sh,* or *z,* add *-es.*

Example

1. *Common Nouns*

Singular	business	box	church	bush	buzz
Plural	businesses	boxes	churches	bushes	buzzes

2. *Proper Nouns: Surnames.* Never change the spelling of the singular form before adding *-es.*

Singular	Jones	Fox	Cratch	McCosh	Alvarez
Plural	Joneses	Foxes	Cratches	McCoshes	Alvarezes

3. *Proper Nouns: Given names*

Singular	Bess	Max	Birch	Josh
Plural	Besses	Maxes	Birches	Joshes

Exercise

Write the plural of the underscored word in the blank provided.

1. Business located near church have been requested not to open until noon on Sundays.
2. People who own ranch have been overburdened with tax.
3. The Rich and Messix have moved to Georgia.
4. Both Max, junior and senior, are architects.

Frame 3 Nouns Ending in *y*

Explanation

The way a common or proper noun ending in *y* forms its plural is dependent upon whether the *y* is preceded by a vowel or consonant.

Example

1. To form the plural of a noun ending in *y* preceded by a vowel (a, e, i, o, u), add only *s.*

Singular	attorney	valley
Plural	attorneys	valleys

2. To form the plural of a noun ending in *y* preceded by a consonant, change *y* to *i* and add *es*.

Singular	secretary	company	Canby	(Proper name)
Plural	secretaries	companies	Canbys	

Exercise

In the blank provided, write the plural form of the underscored word.

1. Many <u>industry</u> are installing pollution-control devices. _____
2. That law firm consists of eight <u>attorney</u>. _____
3. You are required to list your <u>beneficiary</u> on Form 76. _____
4. Some ex-military personnel are fighting in Africa and the Middle East as <u>mercenary</u>. _____
5. The Platte Poultry Farm sold over 8,000 <u>turkey</u> this year. _____
6. Since World War II, two <u>Germany</u> have existed. _____

ANSWERS TO FRAME 3
1. industries 3. beneficiaries 5. turkeys
2. attorneys 4. mercenaries 6. Germanys

Frame 4 Nouns Ending in f, fe, or ff

Explanation

Most nouns ending in *f, fe,* or *ff* form their plurals by the addition of an *s;* however, in some cases the plural is formed by changing *f* or *fe* to *ve* and adding *s.* Because this rule is not specific, you will need to consult a current dictionary to verify the accuracy of your spelling.

Example

1. Add *s* to form the plural.

Singular	staff	safe	chief
Plural	staffs	safes	chiefs

2. Change *f* or *fe* to *ve* and add *s* to form the plural.

Singular	calf	wife
Plural	calves	wives

Exercise

In the blank provided, write the plural form of the underscored word.

1. The <u>sheriff</u> will hold their meeting in Atlanta this year. _____
2. The <u>loaf</u> of bread were placed into the freezer. _____
3. The <u>knife</u> on the shredder cut the <u>leaf</u> into a fine mulch. _____
   _____
4. Both attorneys' <u>brief</u> mentioned the book <u>proof</u> as possible evidence. _____

5. The <u>calf</u> were driven to the <u>wharf</u> where they were loaded onto the cattle boats.   _____

    _____

ANSWERS TO FRAME 4

1. sheriffs
2. loaves
3. knives, leaves (secondary spelling is *leafs*)

4. briefs, proofs
5. calves, wharves (also *wharfs*—secondary)

Frame 5 Nouns Ending in o

Explanation

Like nouns ending in *y*, those ending in *o* also form their plurals according to whether the *o* is preceded by a vowel or consonant. Some exceptions to this rule exist; therefore, to verify the spelling of words not shown here, you should consult a current dictionary.

Example

1. To form the plural of a noun ending in o preceded by a consonant, add *s*. Words derived from the field of music are in this category. Some words ending in o preceded by a vowel also form the plural by the addition of an *s*.

Singular	alto	radio	piano	solo	commando
Plural	altos	radios	pianos	solos	commandos

2. Exceptions:
   a. A few words ending in *o* preceded by a consonant form their plural by the addition of *es*.

Singular	potato	tomato	embargo
Plural	potatoes	tomatoes	embargoes

   b. Some nouns ending in *o* may form their plurals by either the addition of an *s* or *es* to the singular.

Singular	cargo	zero
Plural	cargos or cargoes	zeros or zeroes*

Exercise

In the blank provided, write the plural of the underscored word.

1. The <u>embryo</u> of seed plants should be maintained at a temperature not less than 72 degrees.   _____
2. <u>Tomato</u> are raised from seed, and <u>potato</u> are raised from tubers.   _____ _____
3. <u>Cargo</u> may be loaded and unloaded from ships anchored at <u>embarcadero</u>.   _____ _____
4. Two <u>radio</u> were being played on adjacent <u>patio</u>.   _____ _____
5. The <u>piano</u> are on sale.   _____

ANSWERS TO FRAME 5

1. embryos
2. Tomatoes, potatoes
3. Cargoes (or *Cargos*), embarcaderos

4. radios, patios
5. pianos

  * Refer to Lesson 5, Dictionary Usage. A word connected to the main entry by *also* is a secondary spelling; a word connected by *or* is equally as acceptable as the main entry.

Frame 6   *Nouns that Do Not Conform to Rules*

Explanation

A few nouns do not form their plurals in compliance with any rules. This frame gives some examples of words that form their plurals in various ways.

Example

1. Nouns that form the plural through a change in internal spelling:

Singular	man	foot	tooth	mouse
Plural	men	feet	teeth	mice

2. Nouns that form the plurals by the addition of letters:

Singular	child	ox
Plural	children	oxen

3. Some nouns are singular whether or not they end in *s*:

    news   phonetics   phonics   economics*
    semantics*   statistics*

4. Some nouns are always plural:

    trousers   pants   cattle

5. Some nouns have the same singular and plural form:

    sheep   deer   aircraft

Exercise

Two verbs are shown in parentheses. In the blank provided, write the verb that agrees in number with the underscored word.

1. Many <u>women</u> (is, are) now gaining positions in middle and top management.   _____
2. A <u>child</u> who commits adult crimes (is, are) being treated as an adult by the courts.   _____
3. The <u>news</u> about the stock market (is, are) good.   _____
4. Men's <u>pants</u> (is, are) on sale at Teller's.   _____
5. Eight private <u>aircraft</u> (was, were) destroyed during electrical storms this year.   _____
6. Most <u>statistics</u> in the report (is, are) incorrect.   _____
7. <u>Economics</u> (is, are) a prerequisite to this course.   _____
8. The <u>cattle</u> (was, were) unloaded into eight feedlots.   _____
9. <u>Mathematics</u> (is, are) a requirement for engineers.   _____

ANSWERS TO FRAME 6

1.	are	4.	are	7.	is
2.	is	5.	were	8.	were
3.	is	6.	are	9.	is

* Dictionaries do not agree; some show that this word may be singular or plural in construction.

Frame 7   Compound Nouns

Explanation

A compound word is a combination of two or more words, written as a solid word, as two (or more) spaced words, or with a hyphen.

Example

1. Form the plural of a solid word on the last part of the combination:

Singular	letterhead	printout	businessman
Plural	letterheads	printouts	businessmen

2. Form the plural of words written separately on the most important word (usually a noun).

Singular	peace officer	account receivable
Plural	peace officers	accounts receivable

3. Form the plural of hyphenated words on the most important word (usually a noun).

Singular	yellow-dog contract	sister-in-law
Plural	yellow-dog contracts	sisters-in-law

4. Form the plural of hyphenated words on the last element if no word in the combination is a noun:

Singular	tie-in	follow-up	to-do
Plural	tie-ins	follow-ups	to-dos

5. A small number of words form their plural in two ways:

Singular	attorney general
Plural	attorneys general or attorney generals

Exercise

In the blank provided, write the plural form of the underscored word.

1. The new travel policy permits four <u>per diem</u> per month.   _____
2. The competing <u>textbook</u> explains <u>trademark</u> differently.   _____
                                                                                     _____
3. Both of our law professors have been <u>attorney-at-law</u>.   _____
4. The teller will subtract the amount of your <u>bank note</u> from your <u>bankbook</u>.   _____
                                                                                     _____
5. The ill man gave <u>power of attorney</u> to his lawyer and to his best friend. _____
6. A member on the board has <u>tie-in</u> with several other boards in the same industry.   _____
7. The carrier is responsible for writing the <u>bill of lading</u> for all shipments.   _____

ANSWERS TO FRAME 7

1. per diems
2. textbooks, trademarks
3. attorneys-at-law
4. bank notes, bankbooks
5. power of attorneys
6. tie-ins
7. bills of lading

Frame 8 **Forming the Plural of Abbreviations**

Explanation

Considerable variation exists in capitalizing and in forming the plurals of abbreviations. Consult a current dictionary and be consistent in the way you capitalize and form the plurals of abbreviations.

The plural of most abbreviations is formed by the addition of an *s*. If the plural form could be confused with another word or might not be easily read with the addition of an *s*, an apostrophe and *s* are used.

Example

1. Most abbreviations in lower case letters without internal periods form the plural by the addition of an s:

Singular	acct.	dept.	mo.	yr.
Plural	accts.	depts.	mos.	yrs.

2. Most abbreviations written in upper case letters, with or without internal periods, form the plural by the addition of a lower case *s*:

Singular	CPA	NLRB	PTA	AAA	Ph.D.
Plural	CPAs	NLRBs	PTAs	AAAs	Ph.D.s

Note

Some references will show capitalized abbreviations or those ending with a capital as forming their plurals with an apostrophe and *s*. The apostrophe and *s* should be used if an abbreviation might be confusing or could be misinterpreted with the addition of only an *s*.

Example: CPS   CPS's

3. Most abbreviations written in lower case with internal periods form the plural by the addition of an apostrophe and *s*. Only a few double the letter to form the plural.

Singular	c.o.d.	p. 7 [page 7]
	c.o.d.'s	pp. 7–9 [pages 7–9]

4. Capital letters and arabic numbers form the plural by the addition of an *s* (unless confusion would result).

Singular	C	1980
Plural	The seven Cs of effective writing	in the 1980s

5. Words representing parts of speech other than nouns form the plural by the addition of *s* or *es* (depending on their singular ending) when they are used as nouns:

Original part of speech	and	don't	pro and con
Plural noun usage	ands	don'ts	pros and cons

Note

If confusion would result from the application of this rule, an apostrophe and *s* should be used to form the plural:

Original part of speech   do
Plural noun usage   do's

6. Some abbreviations representing measurements have the same form in singular and plural:

Example: ft. (foot and feet)   in. (inch or inches)

Exercise

In the blank provided, write the plural form for the underscored word.

1. That course teaches the <u>ABC</u> of management. _____
2. More emphasis is being placed on the three <u>R</u>. _____
3. The child was intimidated by hearing so many <u>don't</u>. _____
4. We have three <u>Ed.D.</u> in the department. _____
5. Three <u>CPA</u> founded this firm in 1920. _____
6. [in a footnote] <u>p.</u> 25–26. _____
7. Invoices <u>No.</u> 12345–12390 are filed in the records center. _____
8. Three brands of <u>TV</u> are on sale. _____
9. The abbreviation for mortgages is <u>mtge.</u> _____

ANSWERS TO FRAME 8

1.	ABCs	4.	Ed.D.s	7.	Nos.
2.	Rs	5.	CPAs	8.	TVs
3.	don'ts	6.	pp. 25–26	9.	mtges.

Frame 9   Personal Titles

Explanation

Personal titles are those by which men and women are addressed in person or in written communications. The titles reflect the *gender* of the individual being addressed. The following genders exist: masculine (man), feminine (woman), neuter (desk), and common (employees). *Common gender* describes nouns that include both men and women, or those whose identities and gender are unknown by the writer.

Care must be taken to address a reader in the way he or she would expect or desire to be addressed. Therefore, you must recognize which forms of address are highly formal and not likely to be used in business communications; in addition, you must recognize the modern usage in addressing women.

Example

1. Masculine titles:

Common: Mr. Smith and Mr. Carry
Formal: Messrs. Smith and Carry

2. Feminine titles (married women):

Common: Mrs. (or Ms.) Adams and Mrs. (or Ms.) Charman
Formal: Mmes. Adams and Charman

3. Feminine titles (single women):

> Common: Miss (or Ms.) Cabrey and Miss (or Ms.) Dorman
> Formal: the Misses Cabrey and Dorman

4. Sometimes the sex of the reader is unknown, or more than one person (men and women) will read the same letter.
    a. Sex of the reader is unknown.
        (1) Eliminate the courtesy title in the inside address:
             Use: M. Vestman   Not: Mr. M. Vestman
        (2) Eliminate the salutation and complimentary closing. This type of letter (called *simplified*) is becoming more and more acceptable.
    b. Both men and women may read the letter; for example, a letter to the members of an organization.
        (1) Eliminate the courtesy title in the inside address.
        (2) Make the salutation *Dear Member,* for example.
    c. The addressee may be a single or married woman, or the marital status is unimportant.
        (1) Use *Ms.* before the name in the inside address: *Ms. Kay Walls*
        (2) Make the salutation *Dear Ms. Walls.*

Exercise

In the blank provided, write the title requested beside each number.

1. Common form (plural): Messrs. Flora and Watrous   _____
2. Common form (plural): Mmes. Hanks and Bass   _____
3. Common form (plural): Misses Bay and Lind   _____
4. Sex is unknown or irrelevant: E. V. Barr   _____
5. What are your alternatives if the letter may be read by both men and women?

_____

_____

ANSWERS TO FRAME 9

1. Mr. Flora and Mr. Watrous
2. Mrs. Hanks and Mrs. Bass, or Ms. Hanks and Ms. Bass
3. Miss Bay and Miss Lind, or Ms. Bay and Ms. Lind
4. E. V. Barr (See a.)
5. The courtesy title (Mr., Mrs., Ms.) can be eliminated from the inside address and the letter can be prepared without a salutation and complimentary closing. If the addressees can be classified, such as members, readers, subscribers, and so on, the salutation could be *Dear Member,* for example.

Frame 10   Foreign Nouns

Explanation

As a person who wants to succeed in business, the professions, government, or some other line of work, you will want to recognize and be able to use a few foreign words and their plural forms. You will notice that many of these words are used in the newspaper, on television, and in your textbooks.

Example

Some foreign words have both a foreign and an English plural. The plural of foreign words is formed at the end of the word. Some words do not have a plural form in the English language.

1. Words ending in *a*: add *e* to form the foreign plural; add *s* to form the English plural.

Singular	*Foreign Plural*	*English Plural*
alumna (feminine)	almunae	
agenda		agendas
formula	formulae	formulas (more common)

2. Words ending in *um:* change *um* to *a* to form the foreign plural; add *s* to form the English plural.

Singular	*Foreign Plural*	*English Plural*
addendum	addenda	
curriculum	curricula* (more common)	curriculums
datum	data* (more common)	datums
medium	media†	mediums
memorandum	memoranda	memorandums

3. Words ending in *x*: change *x* to *c* and add *es* to form the foreign plural; and add *es* to form the English plural.

Singular	*Foreign Plural*	*English Plural*
appendix	appendices	appendixes*
index	indices	indexes*

4. Words ending in *is:* to form the foreign plural, change *i* to *e*. These foreign plurals have been absorbed into the English language and are used as the English plural forms also.

Singular	*Foreign Plural*
analysis	analyses
axis	axes
basis	bases
parenthesis	parentheses
synopsis	synopses

5. Words ending in *us:* change *us* to *i* to form the foreign plural.

Singular	*Foreign Plural*
alumnus	alumni (masculine; also used to refer to groups containing both men and women graduates)

6. Words ending in *on;* change *on* to *a* to form the foreign plural.

Singular	*Foreign Plural*	*English Plural*
criterion	criteria (more common)	criterions

* Some dictionaries show both as acceptable; others show this form as preferred.
† This plural is preferred in referring to a communication mode that carries advertising.

7. Words ending in *eau*: add x to form the foreign plural; add *s* to form the English plural.

Singular	*Foreign Plural*	*English Plural*
bureau	bureaux	bureaus (more common)

Exercise

In the blank provided, write the plural of the underscored foreign word.

1. Does your school print a magazine for its <u>alumnus</u>?   _____
2. Conciseness is one of the <u>criterion</u> of effective writing.   _____
3. You will be responsible for writing <u>memorandum</u>.   _____
4. A chart has two <u>axis</u>, vertical and horizontal.   _____
5. The <u>synopsis</u> of both reports should be no longer than one page.   _____
6. The <u>agenda</u> for the next two meetings have been completed.   _____
7. Do you know the <u>formula</u> for square root and chi square?   _____
8. Only two government <u>bureau</u> returned my questionnaire.   _____
9. Television is the better of the two <u>medium</u>.   _____
10. Two <u>parenthesis</u> are required to enclose an explanatory statement.   _____

ANSWERS TO FRAME 10

1. alumni
2. criteria
3. memorandums or memoranda
4. axes
5. synopses
6. agendas
7. formulas or formulae
8. bureaus
9. media
10. parentheses

Frame 11 Business Vocabulary: Investments

Explanation

People who have surplus disposable income (that amount left over after bills, living expenses, and budgeted items are subtracted) often invest it in securities—bonds or common or preferred stock. Newspapers and business periodicals give daily changes in the stock market; these changes are also announced on television newscasts.

Example

The vocabulary listed below is common to the investment business:

1. Stock—A corporation's securities which are divided into shares and sold to the public and to institutional investors, such as insurance companies. Those who buy stock become owners of the firm in proportion to their investment. Two classes of stock exist: common and preferred.
2. Preferred stockholders—Those who receive fixed dividends rather than speculate on the potential gains that may increase dividends beyond the fixed amount. These stockholders also have preference over common stockholders if the firm is liquidated (goes out of business).
3. Common stockholders—Those who elect to receive dividends that may fluctuate with the earnings of the firm. These dividends are paid after the fixed dividends are paid to the preferred stockholders; these stockholders are the last to be paid off if the corporation is liquidated.

Stocks are traded (sold) on the New York and American Stock Exchanges. The fluctuations in the market caused by the buying and selling of stocks and bonds (corporate and municipal) result from economic conditions, domestic and foreign actions, and speculation. These fluctuations give rise to two common terms:

1. Bear—An investor who sells stock when a decline in the market is expected.
2. Bull—An investor who buys stock when a price rise is expected.

Exercise

Complete the blank with the appropriate word from the business vocabulary.

1. The stockholder who receives fixed returns in the form of dividends and who receives payment first if the firm goes out of business is a _____ stockholder.

2. If a firm is forced to go out of business, it is said to have been _____.

3. The names of two exchanges where stock is traded are the _____

4. An investor is called a _____ if he sells his stock when a decline is expected.

5. A corporation's securities sold to the public consist of _____ and _____.

ANSWERS TO FRAME 11

1. preferred
2. liquidated
3. American and New York Stock Exchanges
4. bear
5. stocks, bonds

Frame 12   *Applying Your Knowledge*

Directions

1. Read the case below.
2. In the exercise, underscore each word that represents an incorrect singular or plural form.
3. Write the correct form of the word in the space below it.

CASE

Three young couples decided to pool their income and begin a stock brokerage firm, selling stocks and bonds to people in their locality. To solicit customers, they are sending this letter to a mailing list containing the names of people in the middle-income bracket who might logically use their services. The young couples are Jean and Paul Bench, Cal and Kay Cash, and Larry and Ann Murray. Paul, as the secretary of the new firm, drafts this letter for the others' approval. The name of the firm is Murcaben, a combination of the owners' names. The letter will be processed by a secretarial service and sent to 1,000 people. (15 errors)

May 1, 19____

Mr. & Mrs. John Stapleton
2413 Canfield Drive
Topeka, Kansas 64132

Dear Mr. & Mrs. Stapleton:

You have undoubtedly read in the newspaper and heard over
television that Murcaben is the first and only brokerage house
in this city. We want to perform a service for the people, like
you, who have disposable income. We can help you make that
income grow.

The man and women who receive this letter are encouraged to
consider investing in securitys such as stocks and bonds. Murcaben
can obtain instant market prices from the Kansas City office,
which has a direct line to the New York Stock Exchange. In this
way, Murcaben can tell you at any time how the stock of
corporations, companys, and firms in all industrys is trading.
The Murries are the stock analysts, and they have established
several criterions upon which they base their various analysis.
In addition, Murcaben uses the services of two financial data
bank to obtain up-to-date reports on companies.

Murcaben is authorized to trade in common stocks, preferred
stocks, and municipal bonds; in the future, we expect to be able
to give some assistance to those of you interested in the
commoditys market. Our role in the community is to help you
establish a bases upon which to make investment decisions.

The red, white, and blue banners, presented by the Chamber
of Commerce, will be flying across the front of 1917 Flint Hills
Street on June 1, our first day of business. Please come in and
talk with us about investing, trading, or "learning the ropes"
of the business. We expect to open the second of our three
proposed branchs in the fall.

In conclusion, may I introduce the members of our company:
The Benchs handle the records and administrative details; the

Cashes, bond investments, and the Murrays, stock investments.

All of us have degrees in finance and experience in financial

counseling; in addition, our wifes are CPA.

Paul Bench
Secretary
P.S. On opening day we will be giving away giant sunflowers.

Bring your family, even all your sister-in-laws and brothers-in-law!

ANSWERS TO FRAME 12

May 1, 19____

Mr. & Mrs. John Stapleton
2413 Canfield Drive
Topeka, Kansas 64132

Dear Mr. & Mrs. Stapleton:

You have undoubtedly read in the newspaper and heard over television that

Murcaben is the first and only brokerage house in this city. We want to perform a

service for the people, like you, who have disposable income. We can help you make

that income grow.

The <u>man</u> and women who receive this letter are encouraged to consider
men
investing in <u>securitys</u> such as stocks and bonds. Murcaben can obtain instant
securities
market prices from the Kansas City office, which has a direct line to the New York

Stock Exchange. In this way, Murcaben can tell you at any time how the stock of

corporations, <u>companys</u>, and firms in all <u>industrys</u> is trading. The <u>Murries</u> are the
companies   industries   Murrays
stock analysts, and they have established several <u>criterions</u> upon which they base their
criteria
various <u>analysis</u>. In addition, Murcaben uses the services of two financial data
analyses
<u>bank</u> to obtain up-to-date reports on companies.
banks
Murcaben is authorized to trade in common stocks, preferred stocks, and municipal

bonds; in the future, we expect to be able to give some assistance to those of you

interested in the <u>commoditys</u> market. Our role in the community is to help you
commodities
establish a <u>bases</u> upon which to make investment decisions.
basis
The red, white, and blue banners, presented by the Chamber of Commerce, will

be flying across the front of 1917 Flint Hills Street on June 1, our first day of business.

Please come in and talk with us about investing, trading, or "learning the ropes"

of the business. We expect to open the second of our three proposed <u>branchs</u> in the fall.
branches
In conclusion, may I introduce the members of our company: The <u>Benchs</u> handle
Benches
the records and administrative details; the Cashes, bond investments, and the

Murrays, stock investments. All of us have degrees in finance and experience in

financial counseling; in addition, our <u>wifes</u> are <u>CPAS</u>.
                                          wives   CPAs

Paul Bench
Secretary

P.S. On opening day we will be giving away giant sunflowers. Bring your family,

even all your <u>sister-in-laws</u> and brothers-in-law!
                           sisters-in-law

Lesson 11
Nouns: Possessives

Pretest

Pretest Part I

Directions

Identify the case of each underscored word by writing one of the following abbreviations in the blank provided:

N—Nominative   O—Objective   P—Possessive

Example

The corporation's income statement shows a net profit of $2,000,000, a   (1)___P___ (2)___N___
(1)   (2)   (3)
20 percent increase over last year.   (3)___O___

1. The company's insurance plan includes major medical expenses.   (1)_____ (2)_____
(1)   (2)   (3)
2. The advertising coordinator sent the Art Department a schedule.   (3)_____ (4)_____
(4)   (5)
3. Mr. Bailey is the advertising coordinator.   (5)_____ (6)_____
(6)

Pretest Part II

Directions

If a form is incorrect, rewrite it correctly in the blank. If the sentence is correct, write C in the blank.

Example

Ms. Herrick has been employed in this firm for three months'.   __months__

7. The person who applies for this job should have at least two years experience in writing copy.   _____
8. Most secretarys job descriptions are being evaluated this month.   _____
9. Ms. Doss vacancy will be filled before the end of the month.   _____
10. The state's welfare burden is the highest in the nation.   _____
11. During the bus strike, Helen had a miles walk to the office.   _____
12. All savings and loan associations' new interest rates will be effective next month.   _____
13. The nurses new contract will provide for more input to the hospital administration.   _____
14. Klein's and Newport's new designs will be shown at the city mart this spring. (separate ownership)   _____
15. Are you taking an economics class?   _____

16. Pete going to Hawaii will leave us without an auditor for two weeks.   _____
17. Most credit card holder's delinquencies are thoroughly investigated.   _____
18. A navy yeoman's job consists primarily of administrative work.   _____
19. Three CPA's papers will be read at the next meeting.   _____
20. The File-Right Co.s' new modular equipment is being shown in May.   _____

Lesson 11
Nouns: Possessives

Each word in a sentence represents one of the eight parts of speech. Nouns (and pronouns) have an additional identifying property called *case*. The case of a noun (or pronoun) shows the relationship of this word to other words in a sentence. The use of a word and its location in a sentence guide you in determining its case.

Three cases exist: nominative, objective, and possessive. In this lesson, you will be shown how to identify these cases. However, the most emphasis will be placed on the possessive case (which most frequently shows ownership—*John's* car). A word in the possessive case ends in *s* and requires an apostrophe. The placement of the apostrophe depends upon the number (singular or plural) of the possessive word. Because a word containing a misplaced apostrophe can confuse the reader, this lesson provides practice in recognizing the possessive case and inserting the apostrophe.

Frame 1   Identifying Nominative, Objective, and Possessive Case

Explanation

To identify the case of a noun, you must first determine its use and its location in relation to other words in a sentence.

Example

1. *Nominative Case* (also called *Subjective Case*): The nominative case applies to a word used as a subject, a subjective complement, or an appositive to the subject.
   a. Subject

      The *bank* will be closed on May 30.

   b. Subjective complement. The subjective complement follows a linking verb and renames the subject. (Review: Linking verbs include these forms of *to be:* is, am, was, were, be, been, are; verbs of the senses; and verbs of condition: appears, seems, and so on.)

      A bank is a financial *institution*.

   c. Appositive to the subject. (Review: *Appositive* comes from a Latin root meaning "put in a position near to." An appositive to the subject is located near the subject and explains it further.)

      Mr. Sealy, the *manager*, would not authorize the payment.

2. *Objective Case:* The objective case applies to a word used as a direct object, an indirect object, an object of the preposition, or an appositive to the object.
   a. Direct object. (Review: The direct object is found by asking *What?* or *Whom?* after a verb of action.)

      Mr. Wheland discharged the inefficient *representative*.

   b. *Indirect Object:* An indirect object receives action indirectly from the verb. It can usually be made the object of the preposition *to*. In this position it answers the question *What?* or *Whom?* after the preposition.

      The president gave *Mrs. Benedict* an award.

      The sentence could be revised to read as follows:

      The president gave an award to *Mrs. Benedict.* The direct object is *award.*

   c. Object of the preposition:

      Some of the *employees* are absent.

d. Appositive to an object: A noun in apposition to the object is located near the object.

The Midwestern region has one salesperson, *Mrs. Michaels*.

3. *Possessive Case:* A possessive noun has these characteristics:
   a. It is used as an adjective and describes or limits the noun it modifies.

   The *clerk's* desk is near the door.

   b. Usually, it immediately precedes the noun.

   clerk's desk

   c. It always ends in *s*.

   clerk's desk   men's work

   d. Most frequently, it shows possession (*Ann's* suit), but it may show other relationships as well:
   (1) Measurement: a *year's* experience, an *hour's* work
   (2) Type: *women's* suits
   (3) Authorship: *Meyer's* book
   (4) Identification: *representative's* sales
   (5) Source: *manager's* memo

4. A noun in possessive case can be used in a phrase as the object of a preposition (usually the prepositions *by, of*):

Possessive Case	*Object of Preposition*
John's car	the car owned *by John*
men's work	the work *of the men*
a year's experience	the experience *of a year*
men's suits	suits *of the men*
Meyer's book	the book written *by Miss Meyer*
representative's sales	the sales *of the representative*
manager's memo	the memo written *by the manager*

Exercise

Using the following symbols, identify both the use and case of each underscored word. Write the symbols in the blank provided.

Use
S   Subject
DO   Direct Object
IO   Indirect Object
OP   Object of Preposition
SC   Subjective Complement
AS   Appositive of Subject
AO   Appositive of Object
Adj Adjective

Case
N   Nominative
O   Objective
P   Possessive

Example

The bank's <u>assets</u> are three times greater than its liabilities.   Use S   Case N

1. A <u>job description</u> lists the <u>qualifications</u> required by the <u>person</u> who performs the job.
   (1) _____ _____
   (2) _____ _____
   (3) _____ _____

Use   Case

2. An <u>employee's</u> <u>work</u> is evaluated on the basis of the <u>job description</u>. (4)___ ___
    (4)   (5)   (6)   (5)___ ___
                                                                            (6)___ ___
3. Our <u>director</u> gave <u>Al</u> a <u>recommendation</u>.   (7)___ ___
    (7)   (8)   (9)   (8)___ ___
                                                                         (9)___ ___
4. Al had three <u>years'</u> experience prior to becoming an analyst.   (10)___ ___
    (10)
5. Al, the <u>analyst</u>, evaluates the <u>company's</u> systems and procedures. (11)___ ___
    (11)   (12)   (12)___ ___
6. The report was given to Ms. Plat, the <u>assistant</u>.   (13)___ ___
    (13)
7. Mr. Evans is the <u>manager</u>.   (14)___ ___
    (14)

ANSWERS TO FRAME 1

(1) S; N	(4) Adj.; P	(7) S; N	(10) Adj.; P	(13) AO; O
(2) DO; O	(5) S; N	(8) IO; O	(11) AS; N	(14) SC; N
(3) OP; O	(6) OP; O	(9) DO; O	(12) Adj.; P	

Frame 2   Singular Possessive

Explanation

The *singular possessive* of a noun is made from the singular form of a noun, and the *plural possessive* is made from the plural form of a noun. A noun that does not end in *s* forms its possessive by the addition of an apostrophe and an *s*.

Example

1. The singular possessive is made by adding an apostrophe and *s* to the singular form of the noun:

Singular	*Singular Possessive*
bank	bank's assets
man	man's job
child	child's toys
company	company's sales
attorney	attorney's office
Ms. Smith	Ms. Smith's home
Mr. Bently	Mr. Bently's car

2. Words ending in *s* or *z:*
    a. Add an apostrophe and *s* to the noun if an additional syllable is formed in the pronunciation of the possessive:

boss	boss's desk
Adams	Adams's job
waitress	waitress's uniform

    b. Add only an apostrophe to the noun if an additional syllable makes the noun difficult to pronounce:

Mr. Acrocopolus	Mr. Acrocopolus' store
Mr. Hopkins	Mr. Hopkins' report

Application 1

To determine if a word is possessive, you must analyze the word(s) preceding it. Read the following sentence and answer the questions about it.

This firms profit has increased.

a. Which word ends in *s*, is used as an adjective, and is in

   the possessive case?————————firms————————

b. Which word tells you that this possessive noun must be

   singular?————————This————————

c. Can the word *firms* be made the object of a preposition?

   ————————Yes, profit of this firm————————

d. When it is the object, does it end in *s*?————No————

   Decision: Add an apostrophe before the *s* to form the singular

   possessive: ————————firm's————————

Application 2

Read the following sentence and answer the questions about it.

A womans job is likely to be more interesting today than previously.

a. Which word ends in *s*, is used as an adjective, and is in

   the possessive case?————————————————

b. Which word tells you that this possessive must be

   singular?————————————————

c. Can the possessive noun be made the object of the

   preposition?————————————————

d. When it is the object, does it end in *s*?————————————

ANSWERS:
a. womans
b. A
c. Yes; the job held by a woman
d. No; it ends in n.
DECISION: Add an apostrophe and s to woman to form the singular possessive.

Exercise

If a sentence contains an error in the use of the singular possessive form, rewrite the word correctly in the blank to the right. If the sentence does not contain an error, write C (Correct) in the blank.

Example

Our company's representative to the Rotary Club is Don Eloquent.   C

1. An employees' goals should be in agreement with the goals of the company. ————
2. The presidents memo was copied and placed on all bulletin boards. ————
3. Mr. Jacksons' briefcase was found by a policeman. ————
4. The experts identified Mr. Tompkins's writing. ————

5. One weeks' pay is deducted from the salary of any employee who violates company regulations for the third time.
6. A year's rent must be paid in advance by all tenants.
7. An hours work is required to complete the monthly reports.
8. Ms. Ross car was damaged when it was struck by two others.
9. The federal government's debt has increased to over one trillion dollars!
10. This administrations policies have been criticized by some people.

ANSWERS TO FRAME 2

1. employee's	5. week's	8. Ms. Ross's
2. president's	6. C	9. C
3. Jackson's	7. hour's	10. administration's
4. Tompkins'		

Frame 3   Plural Possessive

Explanation

The plural possessive is formed from the plural of a noun. The plural forms of most nouns end in *s;* to these nouns, add an apostrophe to form the possessive. The plural forms of a very few nouns do not end in *s;* to these nouns add an apostrophe and *s.*

Example

1. The plural possessive is formed by adding an apostrophe to the plural form of a noun ending in *s:*

Plural	*Plural Possessive*
banks	banks' charters
companies	companies' labor contracts
attorneys	attorneys' cases
Joneses	the Joneses' reunion

2. If the plural does not end in *s,* add an apostrophe and *s.*

men	men's gym suits
children	children's toys

Application 1

Read the following sentence and answer the questions about it.

The two (secretarys, secretaries) schedules will be heavy during the meeting days.

a. Which word ends in *s* and is used as an adjective?_____

b. Which word tells you that this possessive noun must be plural?_____

c. Can (secretarys, secretaries) be made the object of a preposition?_____

d. When it is the object, does it end in *s?*

ANSWERS:
a. Both end in s.
b. two
c. Yes; the schedules of the two secretaries, NOT the schedules of the two secretary!
d. yes

DECISION: Add an apostrophe after the *s* in *secretaries.*

Application 2

Read the following sentence and answer the questions about it.

The (businessmans, businessmens) association is sponsoring two student scholarships.

a. Which word ends in *s* and is used as an adjective? _____

b. Which word tells you that this possessive noun must be plural?_____

c. Can the word that you think is a possessive noun be made the object of a preposition?_____

d. When it is the object of a preposition, how does it end?_____

e. Where will you place the apostrophe?_____

ANSWERS:
a. Both end in s and are used as adjectives.
b. The sentence sense tells us that no club or association could belong to one person: businessmen is the correct form.
c. Yes; association of the businessmen.
d. It ends in n.
e. Because the word does not end in s, the apostrophe and s are added to form the plural possessive, businessmen's.

Exercise

If a sentence contains an error in the use of singular or plural possessive form, write the word correctly in the blank provided. If the sentence does not contain an error, write *C* in the blank.

Example

Twenty minutes' time is required to complete the test.   ___C___

1. The applicant had three years experience with computer equipment.   _____
2. The wife's personalities were evaluated before the men were promoted.   _____
3. The children's scholarships were awarded at our company's banquet.   _____
4. All interviewee's scores are ranked and recorded.   _____
5. Student's grades are posted after all tests have been corrected.   _____
6. Many investor's attitudes have changed since the recession.   _____
7. The clerk posts each recruiters' schedule daily.   _____
8. The steel industries' goal is to upgrade its mills.   _____
9. The cities' debt is excessive, and the city may become bankrupt.   _____
10. The department's budget has been decreased.   _____

ANSWERS TO FRAME 3
1. years'   5. Students'   8. industry's
2. wives'   6. investors'   9. city's
3. C   7. recruiter's   10. C
4. interviewees'

Frame 4   Common and Proper Nouns

The possessive forms of some common and proper nouns require special attention, as do the possessive forms of compound words.

Explanation

Common and/or proper nouns that require special attention are:

a. Those showing single or joint ownership
b. Understood nouns
c. Collective nouns
d. Nouns without apostrophes
e. Inanimate nouns
f. Nouns in apposition
g. Verbal nouns

Example

In the corresponding list that follows are some examples of the above types of nouns.

a. *Single or joint ownership.* To show separate ownership, make each noun possessive. To show joint ownership, make the last noun possessive.

> Separate ownership: The Marketing *Club's* and the Data Processing *Club's* rooms have been renovated.
> Joint Ownership: *Joe and Sam's* car has been stolen.

b. *Understood nouns.* Use the appropriate singular or plural possessive form before an understood noun.

> Singular: The equipment in this room is the *company's* (equipment).
> Plural: The fund is the employees' (fund).

c. *Collective nouns.* These nouns name a collection or group of people or items, but they form the possessive in the same manner as other nouns: if the plural form does not end in *s,* add an apostrophe and *s;* if it does end in *s,* add only an apostrophe to form the possessive.

> Singular: The *jury's* verdict will come in soon.
> Plural: The two *juries'* notices have been sent.

d. *Nouns without apostrophes.* Some nouns do not use apostrophes even though they seem to be possessive.
   (1) Names of organizations, periodicals, and so on. The name of an organization should be written in exactly the same way that it is shown on the letterhead or in the telephone directory. The name of an item should be written in the way the organization owning the item determines that it shall be presented.

> Denver Classroom Teachers Association
> *The Reader's Digest*

   (2) Some nouns ending in *s* are merely descriptive, not possessive. They do not use the apostrophe. Applying the rules of proof to these words makes an amusing phrase.

> Examples: news report   sports jacket   savings account.
> Proof (prepositional phrases): report of the new(s);
> jacket of the sport(s); account of the saving(s)

e. *Inanimate nouns:* To show possession, an inanimate noun is often better expressed as a descriptive adjective or in a phrase as an object of the preposition rather than in the usual form of an apostrophe plus *s.*

> Compare: The table's leg is broken.
>   The table leg is broken.
>   The leg of the table is broken.

f. *Nouns in apposition:* Rather than make a possessive form of a noun in apposition, the writer can usually state the sentence more clearly by placing the noun in a phrase or revising the sentence completely.

> Apposition: Mr. Healy, a stockholder's, dividend check was lost.
> Phrase: The dividend check belonging to Mr. Healy, a stockholder, was lost.

g. *Verbal nouns:* A verbal noun is always preceded by a possessive form. A verbal noun has these characteristics: It is a verb form (*walk*), ends in *-ing* (*walking*), and is used in a noun position. (You will study these nouns in Lesson 19.)

> Sam doesn't appreciate his supervisor's *correcting* him. (object of verb)
> The clerk's *working* overtime is appreciated by everyone. (subject)

Exercise

If a possessive form is incorrect in any of the following sentences, rewrite it correctly in the blank provided. If the sentence is correct, write C in the blank provided.

Example

My managers' leaving at this time will cause chaos.   manager's

1. The mens and womens meetings are scheduled at different times. (separate ownership) _____
2. This office is Harrys _____
3. The three panels' reports will be collected at the end of the meeting. _____
4. Joe flowcharting the new system so quickly was appreciated. _____
5. Hall & Company is selling sports' coats for children now. _____
6. Some of the book's pages have been torn. _____
7. The presidents retiring surprised everyone. _____
8. Ms. Dennison, the personnel director's, daughter also works here. _____
9. The sales' department employs nine field representatives. _____
10. The Boulton and Post's condominium is for sale. (joint ownership) _____

ANSWERS TO FRAME 4
1. men's, women's
2. Harry's
3. C
4. Joe's
5. sports (descriptive, not possessive)
6. C; preferably change to: Some of the pages in the book have been torn.
7. president's
8. C; preferably change to: The daughter of Ms. Dennison, the personnel director, also works here.
9. sales department (descriptive, not possessive)
10. C (one condominium with joint ownership)

Frame 5   Compound Nouns

Explanation

Solid and hyphenated compound nouns form their possessives the same way as do solid nouns. If the compound word does not end in *s,* add an apostrophe and *s;* if it does end in *s,* add only the apostrophe.

Example

Singular   *Plural*

policyholder, policyholder's   policyholders, policyholders'
brother-in-law, brother-in-law's   brothers-in-law, brothers-in-law's

Exercise

If a possessive form is correct, write C in the blank provided. If the possessive form is incorrect, write the correct form in the blank.

1. The value of a stockholder's ownership in a corporation is dependent upon the number of shares he owns in proportion to the number sold. _____
2. The commander-in-chief's role is undertaken by the President. _____
3. The countermen and counterwomens' duties require them to meet the public. (joint responsibility) _____
4. A farmhands' pay is not great. _____
5. The outpatients' forms should be signed by their doctors. _____

ANSWERS TO FRAME 5
1. C   2. C   3. counterwomen's   4. farmhand's   5. C

Frame 6   Abbreviations

Explanation

To form the singular possessive of an abbreviation, add an apostrophe and *s* to the singular noun; to form the plural possessive, add an apostrophe to the plural noun.

Example

Singular	CPA	M.D.	John Peyton, Jr.	The Leydon Co.
Possessive	CPA's	M.D.'s	John Peyton, Jr.'s	The Leydon Co.'s
Plural	CPAs	M.D.s	AMAs	
Plural Possessive	CPAs'	M.D.s'	AMAs'	

Exercise

If the possessive form in each of the following sentences is correct, write C in the blank provided. If the possessive form is incorrect, write the correct form in the blank provided.

1. Michigan State University's (MSU's) law school is well known. _____
2. Twenty L.L.B.'s diplomas were lost. _____
3. The Teledyne Co.s' products are sold from coast to coast. _____
4. Lee Products, Inc.'s new filing system is efficient. _____

ANSWERS TO FRAME 6
1. C   2. L.L.B.s'   3. Co.'s   4. C

Frame 7   Business Vocabulary: *Direct Mail Advertising*

Explanation

Advertising through the mass media (publications, radio and television commercials) and by direct mail presents new products to potential customers. It also encourages use or consumption of familiar products by keeping the brand names before the public. Direct mail advertising is that which is specifically planned and constructed to be sent to people on a mailing list. The following terms are common to direct mail advertising.

Example

Mailing list—a list of names that is purchased from a service company or gathered by the sending company. A mailing list usually includes a specific population: housewives, farmers, executives, professors, college students, and so on.

Direct mail letter—its purpose is to sell a specific product (bracelets) or service (carpet cleaning).

Sales campaign—a series of two or more letters, budgeted for and planned in advance, sent to the same list at predetermined intervals to encourage purchases of an item or service (example: magazine subscriptions).

Envelope fillers—the brochures, flyers, and other illustrated pieces that are added to the envelope to make the reader concretely aware of the product or service.

Central selling point—the most important characteristic of the product or service that is emphasized in the letter.

Exercise

Complete the blanks with the appropriate terms:

1. A letter designed to sell a specific product or service through the mail is a

   _____

2. The main feature of a product or service, its _____, is often placed in the first paragraph.

3. The brochures, folders, miniature replicas of the product, and so on that are enclosed with a statement or direct mail letter are _____.

4. Two or more mailing pieces, budgeted and planned in advance, and sent at predetermined intervals, constitute a _____.

5. Advertisements in publications and radio and television commercials are ways to reach the public through _____.

ANSWERS TO FRAME 7

1. direct mail letter	3. fillers	5. mass media
2. central selling point	4. sales campaign	

Frame 8 *Applying Your Knowledge*

Directions

Underscore the incorrect word(s) and write the correct form in the space below it.

CASE

Josephine was graduated from college last summer and is now working for College Jewelry Co., a nationwide firm that sells class rings, fraternity and sorority jewelry, and college identification jewelry by direct mail and through district representatives. A recent survey showed that chains are "in" and that students would like "personal identification" jewelry. As an assistant to the Advertising Manager, Jo has been asked to develop the appropriate direct mail letter. On a trial basis, it will be sent to ten representative schools; their responses will determine the success of the letter. (15 errors)

Dear Student:

Are YOU wearing a SILVER IDENTIFICATION KEY around your neck? On your wrist? Around your ankle? On your belt? In one ear or in both ears'? NO? Well, here is how you can get a key and open the door to new friendships!

College Jewelry Co.s' surprise this year is a personal identification key. This conversation piece is sterling silver, as are the key's chain and its clasp. These keys and chains are made by Abbott and Clark; our firms' twenty years' experience with Abbott and Clarks' manufacturing system assures us that CJC will be selling you quality merchandise at minimum cost. We know that is what you want because a college man's or womans' operating capital is usually at a low ebb.

The keys' range from 1 inch to 6 inches in length, and you may select a chain 2, 7, 10, 14, or 22 inches in length. Ms. Foss, our advertising manager's, idea was that you could purchase one or more keys or chains and "mix and match" the jewelry.

We have probably engraved your relatives', friends', and also your own college jewelry during our forty year's existence. Therefore, you know that we stand behind the accuracy and quality of the engraved jewelry.

To help you add some "small change" to your budget, we will send one set (chain and key) of your selection if you will include four additional orders with your order. A friend's, relative's, or even a faculty persons' order will count toward the free set.

This original offer is being made to ten schools located in the Northeast, Midwest, and Pacific Northwest. Should you like to be your schools' representative, taking order's for the regional salesperson's, just mark the box at the botton of the enclosed form.

Send in your order before 10 day's time has elapsed, and you will receive a 10 percent discount on the cost of your silver identification keys' and chains.

ANSWERS TO FRAME 8
Dear Student:

Are YOU wearing a SILVER IDENTIFICATION KEY around your

neck? On your wrist? Around your ankle? On your belt? In one ear or in both

ears'? NO? Well, here is how you can get a key and open the door to new
ears
friendships!

College Jewelry <u>Co.s</u>' surprise this year is a personal identification key.
Co.'s
This conversation piece is sterling silver, as are the <u>key's chain</u> and its clasp.
chain of the key
These keys and chains are made by Abbott and Clark; our <u>firms</u>' twenty years'
firm's
experience with Abbott and <u>Clarks</u>' manufacturing system assures us that
Clark's
CJC will be selling you quality merchandise at minimum cost. We know that

is what you want because a college man's or <u>womans</u>' operating capital is
woman's
usually at a low ebb.

The <u>keys</u>' range from 1 inch to 6 inches in length, and you may select a
keys
chain 2, 7, 10, 14, or 22 inches in length. <u>Ms. Foss, our advertising manager's,</u>
The idea of Ms. Foss, our advertising manager,
<u>idea</u> was that you could purchase one or more keys or chains and "mix and

match" the jewelry.

We have probably engraved your relatives', friends', and also your own

college jewelry during our forty <u>year's</u> existence. Therefore, you know that we
years'
stand behind the accuracy and quality of the engraved jewelry.

To help you add some "small change" to your budget, we will send one set

(chain and key) of your selection if you will include four additional orders

with your order. A friend's, relative's, or even a faculty <u>persons</u>' order will
person's
count toward the free set.

This original offer is being made to ten schools located in the Northeast,

Midwest, and Pacific Northwest. Should you like to be your <u>schools</u>'
school's
representative, taking <u>order's</u> for the regional <u>salesperson's</u>, just mark the box
orders   salespersons
at the bottom of the enclosed form.

Send in your order before 10 <u>day's</u> time has elapsed, and you will receive
days'
a 10 percent discount on the cost of your silver identification <u>keys</u>' and chains.
keys

Lesson 12
Using Personal Pronouns

Pretest

Directions

1. In the blank beside *Usage,* write the usage of the pronoun required to complete the sentence (for example, subject, direct object, object of the preposition, possessive before gerund, and so on).
2. In the blank beside *Case,* supply the case of the pronoun needed in the sentence. Use these symbols: N—Nominative; O—Objective; P—Possessive.
3. In the blank beside *Choice,* write the pronoun which meets the requirements you set down beside *Usage* and *Case.*

Example

I believe that (you, your) being transferred to the home office will provide you with more opportunities.

    Usage: <u>possessive before gerund</u> Case: <u>P</u>   Choice: <u>your</u>

1. Another accountant and (I, me) have been selected to perform the Smith and Judson audit.

    Usage: _____ Case: _____ Choice: _____

2. Harold, Mabel, and (he, him) will work on the advertising campaign for the new account.

    Usage: _____ Case: _____ Choice: _____

3. The dean gave each of us, Bud and (I, myself, me), a certificate of appreciation for our work on the city committee.

    Usage: _____ Case: _____ Choice: _____

4. The personnel director suggested that I talk with (he, him, himself) personally.

    Usage: _____ Case: _____ Choice: _____

5. I have checked (their, them) tax returns carefully and noted the errors.

    Usage: _____ Case: _____ Choice: _____

6. This department is permitted to select (its, it's) own part-time help from the pool.

    Usage: _____ Case: _____ Choice: _____

7. Harry said that the calculator is (his, his').

    Usage: _____ Case: _____ Choice: _____

8. Between you and (I, myself, me), I believe that we will not be asked to work on Monday.

    Usage: _____ Case: _____ Choice: _____

9. The supervisor said that (you, your) being off duty for six weeks had created a backlog in the Payroll Department.

    Usage: _____ Case: _____ Choice: _____

10. The courier and (I, myself, me) handed the envelope marked "confidential" to John.

    Usage: _____ Case: _____ Choice: _____

11. The vice president appointed Bill and (I, myself, me) to the committee.

    Usage: _____ Case: _____ Choice: _____

12. The president said in the press release that (it's, its) impossible to relocate the urban branch at this time.

    Usage: _____ Case: _____ Choice: _____

13. The unpaid account is (her's, hers).

    Usage: _____ Case: _____ Choice: _____

14. Two people, Margo and (I, myself, me), won the "Employee of the Week" award.

    Usage: _____ Case: _____ Choice: _____

15. The recruiter spoke to three groups, chemistry students, business students, and (they, them).

    Usage: _____ Case: _____ Choice: _____

16. The farmers are complaining because (their, them) crop prices are depressed.

    Usage: _____ Case: _____ Choice: _____

17. (It's, Its) your responsibility to compare the invoices and verify their accuracy.

    Usage: _____ Case: _____ Choice: _____

18. They sent the bill to (we, us, ourselves).

    Usage: _____ Case: _____ Choice: _____

19. Had it been (I, myself, me) who found that error, I would have reported it.

    Usage: _____ Case: _____ Choice: _____

20. He gave a copy to the branch manager, administrative assistant, and (she, her).

    Usage: _____ Case: _____ Choice: _____

Lesson 12
Using Personal Pronouns

A pronoun is a word that is used in place of a noun (*pro-* means *of* or *for*). Because a pronoun substitutes for a noun, it may be used in any noun position—subject, object, and so on. Therefore, if you have learned the noun characteristics and usages well, you will easily be able to place the correct pronoun in the correct position.

Frame 1 Characteristics: Nominative Case

Personal pronouns refer to persons or things. They have these characteristics: case, person, number, and gender.

Pronouns in the nominative (subjective) case are used in the same positions as are nouns in the nominative case: subject of a sentence, subjective complement, and in apposition with the subject. Also, like the noun it replaces, a pronoun in the nominative case may be singular or plural in number, and masculine, feminine, neuter, or common in gender. In addition, this pronoun is designated by person: first person is the person speaking or writing (I, we); second person is the person to whom you are speaking or writing (you); and third person is the person or thing about which you are speaking or writing (he, she, it, they).

Characteristics of the Nominative Case

	Nominative Case	
Number	Singular	Plural
First person	I*	we
Second person	you	you
Third person:		
Masculine	he*	they
Feminine	she*	they
Neuter	it*	they
Common**		they

* You will notice that the form of the personal pronoun changes from singular to plural for first and third persons and that the second person (you) is the same in singular and plural.

** Common gender is used when a group consists of both sexes or when the writer is unaware of which sex constitutes the group.

Example

A pronoun is used in place of a noun and must have the same characteristics (case, person, number, and gender) as the noun it replaces.

Study the examples and answer the practice questions in the following applications.

Application 1

Pronoun used as a subject:

John completed the application blank.

_____ completed the application blank.

1. What is the verb of the first sentence?_____

2. What is the subject of that verb?_____

3. This subject belongs to which person? _____

   Number? _____ Gender? _____

4. Which pronoun (from the chart) has these characteristics and can replace the subject of the first sentence? _____

ANSWERS:
1. completed
2. John
3. third; singular; masculine
4. He (<u>He</u> completed the application blank.)

Application 2

Pronoun used as subjective complement: (Review: A subjective complement follows a linking verb and renames the subject.)

> The professor is Ms. Andrews.
>
> The professor is _____.

1. What is the verb of the first sentence? _____

2. What kind of verb is it? _____ Which case must follow this kind of verb? _____

3. What is a noun in this position called? _____

4. The subjective complement belongs to which person? _____

   Number? _____ Gender? _____

5. Which pronoun (from the chart) has these characteristics and can replace the subjective complement in the first sentence?

ANSWERS:
1. is
2. linking; nominative
3. subjective complement
4. third; singular; feminine
5. she (The professor is <u>she</u>.)

Application 3

Pronoun used in apposition to the subject: (Review: A pronoun in apposition stands near the subject and explains it.)

> Two editors, Jim and Bob, were formerly regional salespersons.
>
> Two editors, Jim and _____, were formerly regional salespersons.

1. What is the verb of the first sentence? _____

2. What is the subject of this verb? _____

3. The words in apposition explain *editors* and are in which case?

   _____

4. The words in apposition belong to which person? _____

   Number? _____ Gender? _____

5. Which pronoun has these characteristics and can replace the word in apposition

   (*Bob*) in the first sentence? _____

ANSWERS:
  1. were
  2. editors
  3. nominative
  4. third, singular, masculine
  5. he (Two editors, Jim and he, were formerly regional salespersons.)

Exercise

  1. Complete each sentence with a pronoun in the nominative case and having the characteristics requested.
  2. In the blank provided, designate the usage of the pronoun, using the following symbols: S—Subject; SC—Subjective Complement; AS—Apposition to the Subject.

Example   *Usage*

Third person, plural:
<u>They</u>, the administrative assistants, and the department heads will meet on Wednesday.   ___S___

  1. First person, plural:

     The Doses and _____ will move to Detroit this summer.   _____

  2. Second person, singular:

     Mr. Bordan and _____ will remain here as part of the skeleton
     staff.   _____

  3. Third person, plural:

     The instructor and _____ are invited to attend the ceremonies.   _____

  4. Third person, singular, feminine:

     It was _____ who found the error.   _____

  5. First person, singular:

     The manager and _____ went to the meeting.   _____

  6. Third person, singular, masculine:

     The messengers, Joe and _____, have been promoted.   _____

  7. Third person, singular, feminine:

     The supervisor requested that Angelo and _____ arrange the
     meeting.   _____

  8. Third person, singular, neuter:

     _____ is not my place to make the decision.   _____

  9. Third person, singular, feminine:

     Had I been _____, I would have asked for a refund.   _____

 10. Second person, plural:

     _____ can enter the next training section.   _____

ANSWERS TO FRAME 1

1. We; S	5. I; S	8. It; S
2. you; S	6. he; AS	9. she; SC
3. they; S	7. she; S	10. You; S
4. she; SC		

Frame 2 Characteristics: Objective Case

Explanation

Pronouns in the objective case are used in the same position as are nouns in the objective case: direct object of the verb, indirect object of the verb, object of the preposition, and in apposition to the object. Like the noun it replaces, a pronoun in the objective case may be singular or plural in number, and masculine, feminine, neuter, or common in gender. In addition, a pronoun is designated by person: first person is the person speaking or writing (me, us); second person is the person to whom you are speaking or writing (you); and third person is the person or thing about which you are speaking or writing (him, her, it, them).

Characteristics of the Objective Case

	Objective Case	
Number	Singular	Plural
First person	me*	us
Second person	you	you
Third person:		
Masculine	him*	them
Feminine	her*	them
Neuter	it*	them
Common		them

* You will notice that the form of the personal pronoun changes from singular to plural for the first and third persons and that the second person (you) is the same in singular and plural.

Example

Read the following examples of the different ways in which pronouns in the objective case are used in a sentence, and answer the questions that follow each example.

Application 1

Pronoun used as the direct object of a verb: (Review: The direct object receives action from the verb. To find the direct object of a verb, ask *whom?* if people are involved, and *what?* if things are involved.)

The clerk in our Customer Service Department called Maxine.

The clerk in our Customer Service Department called

_____.

1. What is the verb of the first sentence? _____

2. What is the direct object of the verb? _____ _____

3. This direct object belongs to which person? _____

Number? _____ Gender? _____

4. Which pronoun (from the chart) has the same characteristics as the direct object in the first sentence? _____

ANSWERS:
1. called
2. Maxine
3. third; singular; feminine
4. her (The clerk in our Customer Service Department called <u>her</u>.)

Application 2

Pronoun used as indirect object of the verb: (Review: An indirect object receives indirect action from the verb. It can usually be preceded by an understood *to*. Ask *to whom?* or *to what?* after the verb to find the indirect object.)

The company sent John and Bill application blanks.

The company sent _____ application blanks.

1. What is the verb of the first sentence? _____

2. What is the direct object of the verb? _____

3. What is the indirect object? _____

4. This indirect object belongs to which person? _____

   Number? _____ Gender? _____

5. Which pronoun (from the chart) has the same characteristics as the indirect object in the first sentence? _____

ANSWERS:
1. sent
2. blanks
3. John and Bill (compound indirect object)
4. third; plural; masculine
5. them (The company sent <u>them</u> application blanks.)

Application 3

Pronoun used as object of the preposition:

I made a mistake on the statement.

I made a mistake on _____.

1. What is the preposition in the first sentence? _____

2. What is the object of the preposition? (Review: found by asking *what?* or *whom?* after the preposition.) _____

3. The object of the preposition belongs to which person? _____

   Number? _____ Gender? _____

4. Which pronoun (on the chart) has the same characteristics as the object of the preposition in the first sentence? _____

ANSWERS:
1. on
2. statement
3. third; singular; neuter
4. it (I made a mistake on <u>it</u>.)

Application 4

Pronoun in apposition to an object:

> Jose wrote to two customers, Ms. Barracks and Mr. Sims.
>
> Jose wrote to two customers, Ms. Barracks and
>
> _____ .

1. What is the preposition in the first sentence? _____
2. What is the object of this preposition? _____
3. Which words are in apposition with the object? _____
4. The word in apposition belongs to which person? _____

   Number? _____ Gender? _____
5. Which pronoun on the chart has the same characteristics as the word in apposition in the first sentence? _____

ANSWERS:
1. to
2. customers
3. Ms. Barracks and Mr. Sims
4. third; singular; masculine
5. him (Jose wrote to two customers, Ms. Barracks and <u>him</u>.)

Exercise

1. Complete each sentence with a pronoun that is in the objective case and has the characteristics requested.
2. In the blank at the right, designate the usage of the pronoun, using the following symbols: DO—Direct Object; IO—Indirect Object; OP—Object of the Preposition; AO—Apposition to an object.

Example

Usage

First person, singular:
The bank did not send <u>me</u> a statement this month.

<u>IO</u>

1. Third person, singular, neuter:

   I deposited _____ in my savings account.

   _____

2. First person, plural:

   The bank opened a joint account for _____ .

   _____

3. Second person, singular:

   The school will send _____ an enrollment application.

   _____

4. First person, singular:

   The bank cashes checks for _____. _____

5. Third person, singular, feminine:

   The store sent charge account applications to two family members, my mother and _____. _____

6. Third person, singular, masculine:

   The accident report must be completed by the policeman and

   _____. _____

7. Third person, singular, feminine:

   The supervisor struck _____ during the argument. _____

8. Second person, plural:

   The corporation will give _____ a bonus at Christmastime. _____

9. First person, singular:

   The Internal Revenue Service sent _____ a tax refund. _____

10. Third person, plural, common:

    The state pays the utilities for _____. _____

ANSWERS TO FRAME 2

1. it; DO	5. her; AO	8. you; IO
2. us; OP	6. him; OP	9. me; IO
3. you; IO	7. her; DO	10. them; OP
4. me; OP		

Frame 3   Characteristics: Possessive Case

Explanation

A word in the possessive case is used as an adjective—*John's* car; *his* car. The possessive case formed from a noun requires an apostrophe. However, the possessive case of a pronoun NEVER takes an apostrophe. A possessive pronoun shows case, person, number, and gender, just as the possessive case of a noun does.

Characteristics of the Possessive Case

	Possessive Case	
Number	Singular	Plural
First person	my, mine	our, ours
Second person	your, yours	your, yours
Third person:		
Masculine	his	their, theirs
Feminine	her, hers	their, theirs
Neuter	its	their, theirs
Common		their, theirs

Example

Compare the usage of the possessive form of the noun and the possessive pronoun in the examples.

1. First person, singular (assume the speaker is Ruth):

   Ruth's book was stolen.   *My* book was stolen.
   The book is *Ruth's.*   The book is *mine.*

2. Third person, singular, feminine:

   Betty's book was stolen.   *Her* book was stolen.
   The book is *Betty's.*   The book is *hers.*

3. Third person, singular, masculine:

   *John's** hurrying is unnecessary.   *His* hurrying is unnecessary.

Exercise

Complete the blank with the correct form of the possessive pronoun.

Example

Third person, singular, neuter:
The Women's Faculty Association has not received <u>its</u> account number.

1. First person, singular:

   I forgot _____ assignment.

2. Second person, singular:

   Do you have _____ assignment?

3. Third person, singular, neuter:

   _____ bell does not ring at the margin.

4. Third person, singular, feminine:

   The purse is _____.

5. First person, plural:

   The car is _____.

6. Third person, singular, masculine:

   _____ arm was broken in the accident.

7. Third person, plural:

   The reports are _____.

8. First person, singular:

   _____ tax refund is late.

9. Second person, plural:

   The tests are _____.

10. Third person, plural:

    _____ combat uniforms are olive drab in color.

ANSWERS TO FRAME 3

1. my	4. hers	7. theirs	10. Their
2. your	5. ours	8. My	
3. Its	6. His	9. yours	

* The possessive case is used preceding a gerund (a verb form ending in *-ing* and used as a noun).

Frame 4 Characteristics: Nominative, Objective, and Possessive Cases

Explanation

The following chart shows the characteristics of the nominative, objective, and possessive cases of personal pronouns.

Personal Pronoun Characteristics

Case:	Nominative		Objective		Possessive	
Number:	Singular	Plural	Singular	Plural	Singular	Plural
First person	I	we	me	us	my, mine	our, ours
Second person	you	you	you	you	your, yours	your, yours
Third person:						
Masculine	he	they	him	them	his	their, theirs
Feminine	she	they	her	them	her, hers	their, theirs
Neuter	it	they	it	them	its	their, theirs
Common		they		them		their, theirs

Example

Read the following examples of pronouns used in the three different cases, and answer the questions that follow each example.

Application 1

(He, Him) and the manager went to the meeting.

  a. The verb of the above sentence is _____.

  b. Does the verb have a subject? _____ What is it?

_____

  c. The choice needs to be a pronoun in the _____ case.

  d. The choice is _____.

ANSWERS:

  a. went
  b. Yes; *manager* and the pronoun to be chosen.
  c. nominative (subject of sentence)
  d. He (<u>He</u> and the manager went to the meeting.)

Application 2

It was (her, she).

  a. What is the verb? _____

  b. What is the subject? _____ The subject is a pronoun in the

_____ case.

  c. The pronoun to be selected follows a verb that (does, does not) take an object.

Therefore, the pronoun selected should be in the _____ case.

  d. Another reason the pronoun should be in this case is that it renames the subject

and is a _____.

  e. The correct pronoun is _____.

ANSWERS:
a. was
b. it; nominative
c. does not; nominative
d. subjective complement
e. she (It was <u>she</u>.)

Application 3

(She, Her) working is necessary.

a. What is the verb of the sentence? _____

b. What is its subject? _____

c. What kind of word is working? _____

d. Which case should precede working? _____

e. The correct pronoun is _____.

ANSWERS:
a. is
b. working
c. gerund (Review: A gerund is a verb form ending in *-ing* and used as a noun.)
d. possessive
e. Her (<u>Her</u> working is necessary.)

Application 4

The manager discharged (I, me).

a. What is the verb? _____

b. Does it have a subject? _____

c. What is the case of the pronoun needed in the blank? _____

   Why? _____

d. Which pronoun is in this case and should be selected? _____

ANSWERS:
a. discharged
b. yes; manager
c. objective; The pronoun is the direct object of the verb.
d. me (The manager discharged <u>me</u>.)

Exercise

1. In the blank beside *Use*, write the usage of the pronoun required to complete the sentence (for example: subject, direct object, object of the preposition, possessive before gerund, and so on).
2. In the blank beside *Case*, supply the case of the pronoun needed in the sentence. Use these symbols: N—Nominative; O—Objective; P—Possessive.
3. In the blank beside *Choice*, write the pronoun which meets the requirements you set down beside *Usage* and *Case*.

Example

Barney sent the forms to John and (I, me).
　　Use: <u>object of the preposition</u>　Case: ___O___　Choice: _____me_____

1.　To (I, me), the memo is meaningless.

　　Use: _____ Case: _____ Choice: _____

2.　(He, His, Him) submitting the report late is disgusting.

　　Use: _____ Case: _____ Choice: _____

3.　It is (he, him) who checks the invoices.

　　Use: _____ Case: _____ Choice: _____

4.　He has worked here longer than (me, I).

　　Use: _____ Case: _____ Choice: _____

5.　It was (they, them) who pilfered from the stockroom.

　　Use: _____ Case: _____ Choice: _____

6.　Denise reviewed the evaluation; then (she, her) signed it.

　　Use: _____ Case: _____ Choice: _____

7.　The form must be completed by the victim and (she, her).

　　Use: _____ Case: _____ Choice: _____

8.　The speaker called on two people, John and (I, me).

　　Use: _____ Case: _____ Choice: _____

9.　Eliot, the new agent, and (I, me) conducted the course.

　　Use: _____ Case: _____ Choice: _____

10.　(They, Them, Their) striking now is unlawful.

　　Use: _____ Case: _____ Choice: _____

11.　Between you and (I, me), I believe that the company is losing money.

　　Use: _____ Case: _____ Choice: _____

12.　One of the new employees, Cal or (he, him), is the president's cousin.

　　Use: _____ Case: _____ Choice: _____

13.　The auditors are preparing to review (their, there) client loads this quarter.

　　Use: _____ Case: _____ Choice: _____

14.　(They, Them) and the Retailers' Association reached an agreement yesterday.

　　Use: _____ Case: _____ Choice: _____

15.　The advertising agency sent Tom and (he, him) checks for their work.

　　Use: _____ Case: _____ Choice: _____

16.　It was (he, him) who designed the new equipment.

　　Use: _____ Case: _____ Choice: _____

17.　If we were (they, them), we could purchase stock now, too.

　　Use: _____ Case: _____ Choice: _____

18. (We, Us) employees never get a chance to participate in the important decisions.

    Use: _____ Case: _____ Choice: _____

19. Jim has worked here longer than (he, him).

    Use: _____ Case: _____ Choice: _____

20. (You, Your) conserving energy is important in this time of scarcity.

    Use: _____ Case: _____ Choice: _____

ANSWERS TO FRAME 4

1. Object of the preposition; O; me
2. Possessive preceding a gerund; P; His
3. Subjective complement; N; he
4. Subject of understood verb *have worked;* N; I
5. Subjective complement; N; they
6. Subject; N; she
7. Object of the preposition; O; her
8. Apposition to object of the preposition; O; me
9. Subject; N; I
10. Possessive preceding a gerund; P; Their
11. Object of preposition; O; me
12. Apposition to object of the preposition; O; him
13. Shows ownership; P; their
14. Subject; N; They
15. Indirect object of the verb; O; him
16. Subjective complement; N; he
17. Subjective complement; N; they
18. Subject; N; We
19. Subject of understood verb *has worked;* N; he
20. Possessive preceding a gerund; P; Your

Frame 5   Contractions and Personal Pronouns

Explanation

A contraction is a solid word that has been made from two words; an apostrophe is used in place of an omitted letter(s); *it* and *is* become *it's,* and mean *it is.* A pronoun in the possessive case <u>does not</u>—REPEAT—<u>does not</u> use an apostrophe to show possession. Many people confuse the two usages, particularly the contraction *it's* and the possessive form *its.*

Example

To determine whether a word is a contraction or a possessive pronoun, follow these instructions: When in doubt, mentally replace the construction *its* with *it is.* If the construction makes sense, you have a contraction and need the apostrophe. If the construction does not make sense, you have a personal pronoun and must not use an apostrophe.

Application

1. (It's, Its) branches are located throughout the world.
   (Read: *It is* branches. Does this construction make sense? No. The word is a possessive pronoun and cannot take an apostrophe.)
2. He said that (it's, its) this department's problem to solve.
   (Read: *It is* this department's problem. Does this construction make sense? Yes. Use the apostrophe.)

Exercise

Select the correct word in the parentheses and write it in the blank provided.

1. The knob must be released from (it's, its) normal position, or the variable line spacer will not work.
2. (It's, Its) too late to apply for the job that appeared in the classified section a week ago.
3. The guard dog injured (it's, its) foot.
4. The book was damaged; (it's, its) cover had been torn.
5. The bank branch manager told me that (it's, its) not possible to obtain a loan simply on one's signature.

ANSWERS TO FRAME 5

1. its 2. It's 3. its 4. its 5. it's

Frame 6   Compound Personal Pronouns

Explanation

Compound personal pronouns are formed by the addition of *-self* (singular) or *-selves* (plural) to eight personal pronouns.

Person	Singular	Plural
First	myself*	ourselves
Second	yourself	yourselves
Third		
Masculine	himself	themselves
Feminine	herself	themselves
Neuter	itself	themselves
Common		themselves

* Use *myself* only if *I* has been used previously in the sentence.

These pronouns perform two functions:

1. They intensify or emphasize the noun or pronoun with which they are in apposition:

> I *myself* will give the instructions.
> We *ourselves* did the work.

2. They reflect the action back to the subject.

> I injured *myself.*

When the compound pronouns are used in ways other than to intensify a noun or pronoun or to reflect action to a previously named noun or pronoun, they provide an awkward construction. Choose the regular personal pronoun for these cases:

> Kim and (I, myself) will use the tickets. (Use *I.*)
> The article reported the incident about Annie and (me, myself). (Use *me.*)

Exercise

Select the correct pronoun and write it in the blank provided.

1. He gave the report to Joe and (me, myself).

2. Jose (himself, he) authorized the expenditure. _____
3. They surprised (them, themselves) by writing perfect examination papers. _____
4. They sent the bill to (us, ourselves). _____
5. I did not save anything for (me, myself). _____

ANSWERS TO FRAME 6
1. me (objective)
2. himself (intensive or emphatic)
3. themselves (reflexive: reflects action to subject)
4. us (object of preposition)
5. myself (reflects action from subject *I*)

Frame 7   Business Vocabulary

Explanation

The personnel department in an organization is responsible for the following activities: recruiting, training, safety, benefits, wage and salary administration, and employee relations.

Example

The activities of the personnel department are described briefly here.

Recruiting—The selection of qualified employees to fill the jobs in the organization. Applicants may be solicited by newspaper or journal advertisements, announcements on bulletin boards, or institutional visits.

Training—The development of an employee to the benefit of the employee and the organization. Training is provided for line, staff, and executive employees.

Safety—The safeguarding and the protection of employees from hazards inherent in their jobs or in the physical environment of the organization.

Benefits—The security provided for employees on the job and upon retirement— pension, insurance, health care, and so on.

Employee relations—The firm's compliance with legislation governing such areas as union contracts, the Equal Opportunity Employment Act, the Occupational Health and Safety Act, and so on.

Wage and salary administration—The responsibility to maintain the wages and salaries of the organization's employees on a level that is equal to the level of each job performed and comparable with those paid in the locality for similar work.

Exercise

In the blank provided, write the appropriate word from the business vocabulary.

1. Name the personnel department activity that involves providing insurance, pension programs, and so on for the welfare of the employees: _____.

2. Training provided by the personnel department, regardless of the level, is to _____ the employee to the benefit of the employee and the organization.

3. Compliance with legislation which is for the protection of the employee and for the employee's present and future benefit falls under which personnel department program? _____

4.   Maintaining wages and salaries that are commensurate with the level of the job performed and comparable with those paid in the locality falls under which program? _____

ANSWERS TO FRAME 7

1.   benefits
2.   develop
3.   employee relations
4.   wage and salary administration

Frame 8   Applying Your Knowledge

Directions

1.   Proofread the letter and underscore each error in use of pronouns.
2.   Write the correction in the space below.

    CASE

    You are the director of recruiting in a large manufacturing company located in the Southwest. You need to respond to a letter from an applicant who has been turned down by the company. The original letter to him did not clearly state why his application was rejected. He wants to know and has the right to know. The reason for the rejection was that the applicant, Ronald Eagleton, did not show on his résumé that he could speak or write the Spanish language. This qualification is essential because he applied for an administrative position in which he would be responsible for writing the operating and equipment procedures in English and Spanish. You gave Ronald's letter to your assistant, who composed this response and submitted it to you for approval. (15 errors).

    May 8, 19____

    Mr. Ronald Eagleton
    2221 Plymouth Street
    Stamford, Connecticut 06902

    Dear Mr. Eagleton:

    Yes, Mr. Eagleton, you are well qualified for an administrative position with the El Paso Structural Steel Company. However, our advertisement in *The Wall Street Journal* requested that an applicant have the ability to speak and write Spanish. Your résumé does not show that you meet this requirement.

    The director of recruiting and me have reevaluated your résumé, and its our conclusion that you not being bilingual was the primary reason for us not inviting you to El Paso for an interview. In addition, you wrote on your application as follows: "Us business students aren't required to take a language."

    EPSSCO needs college graduates who can speak and write Spanish.

because over 50 percent of the employees have obtained there naturalization papers within the last two years. Naturally, English vocabulary is not familiar to many of them. A person in the position for which you applied must be able to write procedures (directions) they can read easily and rapidly.

Approximately seven of our bilingual administrators are natives of Mexico and have learned their English in Texas schools. Regardless of an applicant's native language, him or her attends a six-week training session to become acquainted with the company. During this time, the trainee is given practice in writing letters and memoranda in the Spanish and English languages.

Because you want to work for EPSSCO, the director and myself suggest that you come here and take a job on the assembly line to support you while you're taking a Spanish course. Should you want to do that, write to Ms. Margaret Sonda, supervisor of labor recruiting, or I. When you arrive here, call one of us, she or myself. Either of we will be glad to talk with yourself.

Very truly yours,

Leroy Brown
Recruiting Director

ANSWERS TO FRAME 8

Mr. Ronald Eagleton
2221 Plymouth Street
Stamford, Connecticut 06902

Dear Mr. Eagleton:

Yes, Mr. Eagleton, you are well qualified for an administrative position with the El Paso Structural Steel Company. However, our advertisement in *The Wall Street Journal* requested that an applicant have the ability to speak and write Spanish. Your résumé does not show that you meet this requirement.

The director of recruiting and me [I] have reevaluated your résumé, and its [it's] our conclusion that you [your] not being bilingual was the primary reason for us [our] not inviting you to El Paso for an interview. In addition, you wrote on your application as follows: "Us [We] business students aren't required to take a language."

EPSSCO needs college graduates who can speak and write Spanish, because over 50 percent of the employees have obtained there [their] naturalization papers within the last two years. Naturally, English vocabulary is not familiar to many of them. A person in the position for which you applied must be able to write procedures (directions) they can read easily and rapidly.

Approximately seven of our bilingual administrators are natives of Mexico and have learned their English in Texas schools. Regardless of an applicant's native language, <u>him</u> or <u>her</u> attends a six-week training session to become
<small>he   she</small>
acquainted with the company. During this time, the trainee is given practice in writing letters and memoranda in the Spanish and English languages.

Because you want to work for EPSSCO, the director and <u>myself</u> suggest
<small>I</small>
that you come here and take a job on the assembly line to support <u>you</u> while
<small>yourself</small>
you're taking a Spanish course. Should you want to do that, write to Ms. Margaret Sonda, supervisor of labor recruiting, or <u>I</u>. When you arrive here,
<small>me</small>
call one of us, <u>she</u> or <u>myself</u>. Either of <u>we</u> will be glad to talk with <u>yourself</u>.
<small>her   me   us   you</small>

Very truly yours,

Leroy Brown
Recruiting Director

Lesson 13
Antecedents of Pronouns

Pretest

Pretest Part I
Person of Pronouns

Directions

Underscore each personal pronoun and write below it whether it is first (1), second (2), or third (3) person.

Example

<u>He</u> wrote the letter quickly.
(3)

1. The inflation rate is at its highest in history.

2. When Doreen reported for work, she was told to see the personnel officer.

3. The customer representative talks with customers to solve their problems and retain them as customers.

4. They asked me to prepare a résumé, but they did not specify how I should prepare it.

Pretest Part II
Specific Pronoun Reference

Directions

Rephrase the following sentence to make the pronoun reference specific.

Example

John and Bert had an argument, and he left the meeting.
Revised: John and Bert had an argument, and Bert left the meeting.

5. Al and Tom disagreed with the recommendation, but he did not have an alternative suggestion.

   Revised: _____

_____

Pretest Part III
Identifying Third Person Pronouns and Their Antecedents

Directions

Underscore the personal pronouns and their antecedents in the following sentences. Then write each pronoun under its antecedent.

Example

When <u>John</u> looked for the <u>file</u>, <u>he</u> realized <u>it</u> was missing.
      he   it

6. Mr. Jones bid on an original painting, but his bid was exceeded by another person's.

7. Some states are sponsoring off-track betting to supplement their income from taxes.

8. Mrs. Fenlon, the new assignment manager at WPOT-TV, received her degree from the University of Nebraska.

9. A patient who receives Medicaid assistance is expected to pay his or her expenses that are not covered by this benefit.

10. When this building was constructed, it was the showplace of the city.

Pretest Part IV
Agreement of Pronouns and Antecedents in Number, Person, and Gender

Directions

Select the pronoun with the same person and number as the antecedent and write it in the blank provided.

Example

Either Don or Emil will sign (his, their) name.   <u>his</u>

11. Many a person has lost (his, his or her, their) money by speculating in the market.   _____

12. The Smithsons plan to invest (his, his or her, their) income in real estate.   _____

13. Neither the broker nor his associates could sell the new stock issue (he, he or she, they) had contracted.   _____

14. The committee voted unanimously to retain (its, their) chairman.   _____

15. Each shipping clerk, as well as the receiving clerks, was cautioned about (his, his or her, their) violation of safety precautions.   _____

16. The faculty disagreed on (its, their) choice of a council president.   _____

17. The Apex Company declared bankruptcy in (its, their) tenth year of operation.   _____

18. Everybody must attend the meeting or assign (his, his or her, their) proxy to someone else.   _____

19. The corporation sold (its, their) patent for the new design.   _____

20. Neither Ben Adams, a councilman, nor Harold Parsons, the mayor, received (his, their) company's approval to file for a second term.   _____

Pretest Part V
Appropriate Pronouns

Directions

In each of the following sentences, fill in the blank with the appropriate pronoun. If a selection would make the sentence reflect a sex bias, rewrite the sentence.

Example

Each student must bring his book to the examination.
Revised: Each student must bring his or her book to the examination.

21. A person who does not understand the fundamentals of photography will not be able to take _____ pictures with technical competence.

22. An unlicensed real estate associate must submit _____ credentials to the district board before _____ can sell in this agency.

23. Every insurance agent is expected to sell _____ annual quota of policies before _____ can be named to the Executive Sales Club.

24. The savings and loan association guarantees _____ depositors' savings up to $40,000.

25. In the first picture Eloise directed, _____ demonstrated _____ leadership and managerial ability.

Lesson 13
Antecedents of Pronouns

As you learned in the preceding lesson, the case of a pronoun is determined by its use in the sentence; for example, as a subject, an object, or a possessive form.

When a pronoun is used as a noun substitute, it must agree in person, number, and gender with its *antecedent* (a noun or pronoun to which it refers). If this rule is violated, a sentence will be confusing, difficult to interpret, or even meaningless. In most instances, the selection of the appropriate pronoun is simply a matter of logically applying the grammatical principles you have learned so far. However, in a few cases, the sentence structure must be studied carefully so that the proper choice is made.

A variety of pronoun classifications and their antecedents will be presented in this lesson. However, the emphasis will be on third person pronouns and their antecedents, because this group usually causes the most problems.

Frame 1   Agreement of Pronouns and Antecedents in Person

Explanation

An antecedent is the noun or pronoun to which a pronoun refers. A pronoun must have the same person, number, and gender as its antecedent.

A first person pronoun (I, me, we, us, our, ours) replaces the name of the speaker or writer. A second person pronoun (you, your, yours) replaces the name of the person to whom you are speaking or writing. A third person pronoun (he, she, it, they, theirs, their, them) replaces the name of a person, place, or thing about which you are speaking or writing. A pronoun must agree in person, number, and gender with a noun (or pronoun) which has already been named and to which it refers.

Example

1. A *first person pronoun* is used in place of the speaker's or writer's name.

    > *I* carried *my* briefcase with *me*.
    > (*I* is the antecedent of *my* and *me*.)

2. A *second person pronoun* is used in place of the reader's or listener's name.

    > *You* should carry *your* briefcase with *you* on the airplane.
    > (*You* is the antecedent of *your* and *you*.)

3. A *third person pronoun* is used in place of a noun (or pronoun) naming a person, place, or thing about which you are speaking.

    > *He* took *his* briefcase with *him*.
    > (*He* is the antecedent of *his* and *him*.)

4. *Indefinite reference:* A reference is indefinite when the reader cannot determine the antecedent to which the pronoun refers. To clarify this, the sentence may need to be revised, using a noun in place of a pronoun.
    a. Harry told John that *he* was expected to moderate a panel at the meeting. (Who was expected to moderate?)
        When Harry wrote to John, he explained that *John's* responsibility was to moderate a panel at the meeting.
    b. Sue and Lana talked with the professor, but *she* did not understand his explanation. (Who didn't understand the explanation?)
        Sue and Lana talked with Professor Jackson, but *Sue* did not understand his explanation.

5. *Unspecific reference:* The reference is unspecific when the reader does not know who or what the pronoun represents.
    a. *They* say that the rate of inflation will increase this year. (Who says?)
       The President's *advisors* say that the rate of inflation will increase this year.
    b. *It* is not known how many were drowned in the flood. (Not known by whom?)
       The *police department* does not know how many people were drowned in the flood.

Part I
Identifying the Person of Personal Pronouns

Exercise

Underscore each personal pronoun in the following sentences, and write below each pronoun whether it is first (1), second (2), or third (3) person.

Example

I gave him a book.
(1)   (3)

1. He placed the file in the tray.
2. I spoke to him about his making errors in comparing the charts.
3. She was promoted twice in one year.
4. Place your check in the enclosed envelope and send it today.
5. You are required to make a down payment of $2,000.

Part II
Identifying the Antecedent of Third Person Pronouns

Directions

Underscore each pronoun and its antecedent in the following sentences. Then write the pronoun under its antecedent.

Example

When John looked for the file, he realized that it was missing.
     he   it

1. The supervisor spoke to Carl about his making errors in comparing the charts.
2. The employees lost some of their benefits during the negotiations.
3. When Denise submitted her report, she noticed that she had not signed it.
4. The insurance company representative spoke to the personnel, giving them the facts about the new contract.
5. The sales agents forfeited their right to participate in the contest.
6. The German shepherd purchased for the night watchman has not yet had its obedience training.

7. The city agreed to negotiate with its unions according to the priority established by the labor-management representatives.

8. The newly promoted manager had moved her family from California to New York before she had thoroughly investigated her job responsibilities.

9. Carlos received many job offers, but he wanted to attend graduate school.

10. The book was better in its first printing than it is in its second.

Part III
Indefinite Reference

Directions

Rewrite each sentence to make the noun reference specific.

Example

Bert and John had an argument, and he left the meeting.
Revised: Bert and John had an argument, and Bert left the meeting.

1. The Keystone Building was sold to the McCracy Company, and it will be demolished soon.

    Revised: _____

    _____

2. The production manager told the foreman that he needed to replace the damaged tools.

    Revised: _____

    _____

Part IV
Unspecific Reference

Directions

Revise the following sentences, making the pronouns specific.

Example

They tell us that the machine will work properly after they repair it.
Revised: The Madden Company repairmen tell us that the machine will work properly after they repair it.

1. They sold more machinery in the Southwestern Division this year than they sold last year.

    Revised: _____

    _____

2. They voted to increase the Social Security tax.

    Revised: _____

ANSWERS TO FRAME 1

Part I.   Identifying the Person of Personal Pronouns

1. He   2. I, him, his   3. She   4. your, it   5. You
   (3)   (1) (3) (3)   (3)   (2)   (3)   (2)

Part II.   Identifying the Antecedent of Third Person Pronouns

1. his; antecedent: Carl
2. their; antecedent: employees
3. her, she, she; antecedent: Denise
   it; antecedent: report
4. them; antecedent: personnel
5. their; antecedent: sales agents

6. its; antecedent: German shepherd
7. its; antecedent: city
8. her, she, her; antecedent: manager
9. he; antecedent: Carlos
10. its, it, its; antecedent: book

Part III.   Indefinite Reference

1. The Keystone Building, which was sold to the McCracy Company, will be demolished soon.
2. When the production manager spoke with Peter Smith, the foreman, he told Peter to replace the damaged tools.

Part IV.   Unspecific References

1. The salesmen in the Southwestern Division sold more machinery this year than they sold last year.
2. The members of Congress voted to increase the Social Security tax.

Frame 2   Agreement of Pronouns and Antecedents in Number

Explanation

A pronoun must agree with its antecedent in number. In the preceding frame, you identified pronouns according to first, second, and third person, and identified antecedents for third person pronouns. In this frame, you will need to *select* a singular or plural pronoun in the third person to correspond with its antecedent.

Example

1. A singular antecedent requires a singular pronoun.

    > *Paula* reads the papers carefully before *she* makes the daily report.

2. A plural antecedent requires a plural pronoun.

    > *Students* must pass the quantitative test with a score of 500, or *they* cannot enroll in this course.

3. Antecedents modified by *each, every, many a,* and *many an* are singular and require a singular pronoun. Compound antecedents modified by these words also require a singular pronoun.

    > Each *member* is expected to pay *his* or *her* dues before June 1.

    > Each *man, woman,* and *child* contributes *his* or *her* annual share to the national debt.

4. Antecedents connected by *and*:
   a. require a plural pronoun when two persons, places, or things are involved.

    > The *copywriter* and the *artist* have finished *their* work on the advertisement.

b. require a singular pronoun when one person, place, or thing is the antecedent.

> The *supervisor and committee chairman,* Mr. Waller, gave *his* report. (One person performs in two capacities.)

5. Antecedents connected by *or* or *nor:*
a. require a singular pronoun.

> *John or Hank* will sign *his* name to the requisition.

> Either the *box or* the *envelope* can be closed by *its* self-sealing tape.

> Neither *Priscilla nor Cathy* could translate *her* notes.

b. require a plural pronoun if the nearest antecedent is plural.

> Neither the lawyer nor his *associates* believe that *their* client was innocent.

> Either the mayor or his *administrators* should clarify *their* stand on the urban renewal program.

6. Antecedents are not located within parenthetical expressions. Such expressions are not essential to the meaning of the sentence and are set off by commas. Examples of phrases that begin parenthetical expressions are these: as well as, in addition to, and rather than.

> *Mr. Delozier,* as well as his fellow brokers, sold *his* stock before the price fell.

> The *students,* in addition to the instructor, requested that *their* personal data not be disseminated.

7. An antecedent that is a collective noun requires:
a. a singular pronoun when the group is considered as one.

> The *jury* submitted *its* verdict.

b. a plural pronoun when the group is divided (or does not act as one).

> The executive *board* were divided in *their* opinion.

> The city *council* disagree in *their* assessment of the tax issue.

c. a singular or plural pronoun, depending upon usage.
(1) a singular pronoun:

> The *company* will sell *its* new stock issue to the public on June 15.

> The *department* is in need of personnel, but *it* can function with a minimum staff for a brief time.

(2) a plural pronoun (for logic and sentence sense):

> Send the letter to *Orlando Company* and tell *them* [not *it*] that we can deliver the oil before July 1.

8. Indefinite singular pronouns used as antecedents require singular pronoun references:

> *Everybody* must sign *his* or *her* name to verify that *he* or *she* has attended the meeting.

Exercise

Underscore the antecedent in each of the following sentences. Then select the pronoun that agrees with this antecedent and write the pronoun in the blank provided.

Example

The potted *plants* in this office are losing (its, their) leaves.   ___their___

1. All employees must show (his, their) identification when entering the building.   _____
2. Neither the desk nor the chair has been moved from (their, its) position by the janitors.   _____
3. Every driver must show (his or her, their) license before passing the barricade.   _____
4. Each congressman and senator has moved (his or her, their) office to the new building.   _____
5. Neither of the editors cooperated with (his or her, their) authors well.   _____
6. The branch manager, as well as the tellers, is expected to have (his or her, their) fingerprints taken.   _____
7. The committee has lost (its, their) power.   _____
8. Neither the letterhead paper nor the envelopes are in (their, its) usual location.   _____
9. The principal, in addition to the faculty, is required to attend the meeting or send (his or her, their) proxy.   _____
10. Everyone must present (his or her, their) identification at the door.   _____
11. Anyone can install (their, his or her) equipment for less than $25,000.   _____
12. The corporation announced (their, its) plans to establish a branch in Sao Paulo.   _____
13. The company changed (its, their) investment policy.   _____
14. When the company didn't send my check, I wrote to (it, them).   _____
15. Neither of the publishing companies can afford to have (his, its, their) newspaper stopped by a strike.   _____

ANSWERS TO FRAME 2

1. <u>employees</u>; their
2. <u>desk</u> (nor) <u>chair</u>; its
3. <u>driver</u>; his or her
4. <u>congressman</u> and <u>senator</u>; his or her
5. <u>Neither</u>; his or her
6. <u>manager</u>; his or her
7. <u>committee</u>; its
8. <u>paper</u> (nor) <u>envelopes</u>; their
9. <u>principal</u>; his or her
10. <u>Everyone</u>; his or her
11. <u>Anyone</u>; his or her
12. <u>corporation</u>; its
13. <u>company</u>; its
14. <u>company</u>; them
15. <u>Neither</u>; its

Frame 3 Agreement of Pronouns and Antecedents in Gender

Explanation

A pronoun must agree with its antecedent in gender, as well as in person and number. Quite obviously, an antecedent in the masculine gender requires a pronoun in the masculine gender, an antecedent in the feminine gender requires a pronoun in the feminine gender, and an antecedent in the neuter gender requires a pronoun in the neuter gender.

Common gender refers to a noun or pronoun antecedent of unknown sex, or to a noun or pronoun antecedent that could include either or both sexes. Such nouns as *student, employee,* and *person* and pronouns as *one, everyone,* and *each* are examples of these antecedents. Formerly, the pronouns most frequently used to show agreement with a common gender antecedent were *he* and *his.* These pronouns were considered generic, meaning that they applied to persons as a group (without regard to the sex or sexes that constituted this group). Modern usage discourages this concept. In this frame, you will be shown how to make unbiased references to antecedents.

Example

1. An antecedent in the masculine gender requires a pronoun in the masculine gender.

    Joe gave up *his* job to return to school.

2. An antecedent in the feminine gender requires a pronoun in the feminine gender.

     Mary requested *her* transcripts from the college.

3. An antecedent in neuter gender requires a pronoun in the neuter gender.

     The advantage of this *radio* over others of comparable price is *its* chrome case.

4. Common gender
   a. Ways to avoid the sexual bias of *his*:*

        Everyone must sign *his* identification card.

      (1) his or her: Everyone must sign *his or her* identification card.†
      (2) his/her: Everyone must sign *his/her* identification card. (awkward)
      (3) plural: Employees must sign *their* identification cards.
      (4) Unacceptable: Everyone must sign *their* identification card.
   b. Ways to avoid sexual bias of *he*:*

        A *teacher* must understand the students *he* is trying to help.

      (1) he or she: A teacher must understand the students *he or she* is trying to help.†
      (2) plural: *Teachers* must understand the students *they* are trying to help.
      (3) awkward and not encouraged: A teacher must understand the students *he/she* is trying to help.

Exercise

1. Write a third person pronoun of the proper number, gender, person, and case in each of the blanks in the following sentences.
2. If sexual bias could be obvious, remedy it by completing the blank or rewriting the sentence using a plural form.

Example

Many employees prefer to take their vacations during the summer months.

1. Katherine is the new sales representative for the Mountain-Plains states; _____ territory includes 11 states.

2. Sam's oil paintings of the Maine seacoast won for _____ the scholarship _____ needed to continue _____ education.

3. Each student must bring _____ own blue book to the examination.

4. To become a certified public accountant, _____ must pass a six-part examination.

5. The Aldone Company won _____ suit against the city.

* *Wiley Guidelines on Sexism in Language* (New York: John Wiley & Sons, 1977).
† If this construction is used frequently in a communication, it becomes cumbersome.

6. Everyone will save _____ tax refund if _____ believes that a recession is near.

7. A financial analyst must show that _____ is capable not only of performing the common analyses but also of using them in computer simulation models.

8. A person who does not take modern social thought into account when _____ writes memos and letters creates a poor image for _____ .

9. Each new pilot is expected to complete _____ physical examination before _____ is scheduled to fly the trans-Atlantic route.

10. The fortunate man or woman who is named to the position of vice president of sales will need to express _____ opinions forcefully.

ANSWERS TO FRAME 3

1. her
2. him, he, his
3. his or her
4. one (or) he or she
5. its
6. People will save their tax refunds if they believe that a recession is near. (Using *his or her* and *he and she* in the same sentence would make a cumbersome construction.)
7. he or she
8. People who do not take modern social thought into account when they write memos and letters create a poor image for themselves.
9. New pilots are expected to complete their physical examination before they are scheduled to fly the trans-Atlantic route.
10. his or her

Frame 4   Business Vocabulary—Internal Communications

Explanation

The most common internal communication in any organization is the office memorandum, informally called a *memo* (*memos, memoranda,* plural). Everyone who is authorized to originate a communication, from the company president or top government administrator to the lowest-ranking supervisor, writes memos. The majority of these memos are brief, factual, and routine. Some, however, are more lengthy and distinguished by names that indicate that they are reports.

Often a memo is read and its contents noted; then it is discarded. Some memos, however, are considered *formal* in nature because of their contents or their importance to the writer. Others become the basis for action or a decision and are regarded as *official records*.

Example

A memo has a minimum of four identifying words in the heading. The following four words (or their synonyms) are likely to be found in the heading of all memoranda. In either a preprinted or typed format, these words are shown in capital letters.

1. DATE.   The current date is typed in the space provided across from the word

DATE. Except for very informal memoranda, the date is presented in this form: month, day, year (May 26, 1978).

2. TO.   Across from the TO element is the name of the individual to whom the memo is to be sent. The title, department, and location are shown if the organization is large, the memo is formal, or the memo will be maintained as an official record.

> TO: Wallace Ally, Training Director
> Personnel Department, Building 4-C

3. FROM.   Across from the FROM element is the name of the sender. If any of the circumstances mentioned in 2 above is present, this element should be complete, as shown:

> FROM: Mary Rose, Claims Evaluator
> Fire, Theft, and Casualty Division
> Room 123

4. SUBJECT.   The subject line is a brief heading that reflects the contents of the memo. It is used in subject filing to identify the topic of the correspondence. The subject line may be shown in capital letters; or the first letter of each word, except conjunctions, articles, and short prepositions, should be capitalized. If the memo concerns a case or file having a number or name designation, that reference may be shown in the subject line or elsewhere above the body of the memo.

Exercise

1. What are the four elements that are shown in the heading of a memo?

   _____   _____   _____   _____

2. Under what circumstances should more information than the sender's name be shown?

   (1) _____

   (2) _____

   (3) _____

3. How should this subject line be capitalized?
   progress toward the completion of equipment overhaul

   _____

   _____

ANSWERS TO FRAME 4
1. TO:, FROM:, DATE:, SUBJECT:
2. More information than the sender's name should be shown under these circumstances: (1) the memo is formal; (2) the organization is large; (3) the memo is an official record.
3. PROGRESS TOWARD THE COMPLETION OF EQUIPMENT OVERHAUL (or) Progress Toward the Completion of Equipment Overhaul

---

Frame 5   Applying Your Knowledge

Directions

1. Read the memo in the following case and underscore the errors.
2. Write the corrections in the space below.

3. If an error cannot be corrected by changing a word, revise the sentence on the lines provided at the end of the memo.

CASE

You, the training director of Sunrise Insurance Company, have just drafted this memo to the new trainees in the Sunrise management training program. The 20 trainees (11 men and 9 women) will meet together for orientation on Monday, the first day of the nine-month program. This memo, which will be handed to them, contains information that they will need to know and instructions that they must follow. (15 errors)

DATE: May 16, 19____
TO: Trainees
FROM: Andrew Winner, Training Director
SUBJECT: Policies Governing Trainees—Memo No. 1

These policies will acquaint you with the operations of the Sunrise Insurance Company, and it will help you to realize the importance of your job here.

1.   Security: During this week, each trainee is expected to obtain their permanent identification card from the Personnel Department (Room 605). A guard is on duty around the clock. Every person who enters the building is expected to show their identification card to this guard and to sign the register.

 If your card is lost or stolen, call the Security Department (Ext. 492) for instructions. Because this identification card is also a passcard and will open certain doors, losing them creates a security risk.

2.   Absenteeism: Trainees are expected to be in his or her assigned departments and ready to begin work at 9:30 and to remain until 5:30.

 If you are unable to come to the office, for whatever reason, you are expected to call Ms. Corn, my administrative assistant, no later than 9:00. He will, in turn, inform the department manager to whom you have been assigned. The Sunrise Insurance Company looks unfavorably upon unnecessary absenteeism, and their policy is to include such absences in a trainee's file.

3.   Smoking: Smoking is permitted only in the blue section of the cafeteria. This policy was established at the request of the majority of the employees, and they would appreciate your honoring them, I'm sure.

4. <u>Theft</u>: The correspondence, as well as reports and other written, printed, reproduced, or filmed records, is company property, and they cannot be removed from the premises, except by authorized personnel. Each manager-coach will provide his/her trainees with notebooks, file folders, and whatever study material he/she believes is essential. A trainee may ask for and, at the discretion of the manager, receive additional material. A trainee who removes any record or other company property will be dismissed from the training program if proof of the theft is established. Additional penalties may be assigned by the court, depending upon the value of the item or their importance to the company.

5. <u>Loyalty</u>: Loyalty is expected from all trainees. Information relative to the company, that is obtained from or deduced from figures, correspondence, conversations, and meetings, is not for public dissemination.

   Proof of a trainee's passing on such information shall be sufficient for its discharge from the training program. A manager-trainee committee will be selected and will render their decision by evaluating the nature of the information and the resulting damage to the company's image, sales, and so on.

Now revise the incorrect sentences on the lines below.

_____

_____

_____

_____

_____

_____

_____

_____

_____

_____

_____

_____

_____

_____

ANSWERS TO FRAME 5

DATE: May 16, 19____
TO: Trainees
FROM: Andrew Winner, Training Director
SUBJECT: Policies Governing Trainees—Memo No. 1

These policies will acquaint you with the operations of the Sunrise Insurance

Company, and <u>it</u> will help you to realize the importance of your job here.
_{they}
1.   <u>Security</u>: During this week, each trainee is expected to obtain <u>their</u>
                                                                    _{his or her}
     permanent identification card from the Personnel Department (Room

     605). A guard is on duty around the clock. Every person who enters the

     building is expected to show <u>their</u> identification card to this guard and to sign
                                  _{his or her}
     the register.

     If your card is lost or stolen, call the Security Department

     (Ext. 492) for instructions. Because this identification card is also a passcard

     and will open certain doors, losing <u>them</u> creates a security risk.
                                          _{it}
2.   <u>Absenteeism</u>: Trainees are expected to be in <u>his or her</u> assigned
                                                         _{their}
     departments and ready to begin work at 9:30 and to remain until 5:30.

     If you are unable to come to the office, for whatever reason, you are

     expected to call Ms. Corn, my administrative assistant, no later than 9:00.

     <u>He</u> will, in turn, inform the department manager to whom you have been
     _{She}
     assigned. The Sunrise Insurance Company looks unfavorably upon

     unnecessary absenteeism, and <u>their</u> policy is to include such absences in a
                                   _{its}
     trainee's file.

3.   <u>Smoking</u>: Smoking is permitted only in the blue section of the cafeteria. This policy

     was established at the request of the majority of the employees, and they would

     appreciate your honoring <u>them</u>, I'm sure.
                              _{it}
4.   <u>Theft</u>: The correspondence, as well as reports and other written, printed,

     reproduced, or filmed records, is company property, and <u>they</u> cannot be
                                                             _{it}
     removed from the premises, except by authorized personnel.

     <u>Each manager-coach</u> will provide <u>his/her</u> trainees with notebooks, file
     _{Manager-coaches}   _{their}
     folders, and whatever study material <u>he/she</u> <u>believes</u> is essential. A
                                          _{they   believe}
     trainee may ask for and, at the discretion of the manager, receive

     additional material. A trainee who removes any record or other

     company property will be dismissed from the training program if proof of

     the theft is established. Additional penalties may be assigned by the

     court, depending upon the value of the item or <u>their</u> importance to the
                                                     _{its}
     company.

5. <u>Loyalty</u>: Loyalty is expected from all trainees. Information relative to the company, that is obtained from or deduced from figures, correspondence, conversations, and meetings, is not for public dissemination.

Proof of a trainee's passing on such information shall be sufficient for

<u>its</u> discharge from the training program.
his or her

A manager-trainee committee will be selected and will render <u>their</u>
                                                              its

decision by evaluating the nature of the information and the resulting damage to

the company's image, sales, and so on.

Lesson 14
Using Other Pronouns

Pretest

Directions

Write the correct word from the parentheses in the blank to the right of each sentence.

1. (Who's, Whose) the new personnel director? _____
2. He is the person (who, which, whom) will become an asset to the company. _____
3. She is the type of manager (who, that) will organize this department properly. _____
4. Of the three applicants, (who, whom) do you think we should hire? _____
5. The author (who's, whose) book I read has now published a sequel. _____
6. Employee benefits accrue to the employees upon their retirement or to the beneficiaries (who, whom) they name. _____
7. (Whoever, Whomever) receives a jury summons has the right and responsibility to serve on the jury. _____
8. The retailers' association elected a new president (who, whom) hopes to change the collection policy. _____
9. The manufacturing company was sold to the two executives (who, whom) the chairman of the board favored. _____
10. The award will be given to (whoever, whomever) the students select. _____
11. The new energy administrator (who, whom) the President appointed is in favor of developing solar energy sources. _____
12. (These, This) classes of cruise fares do not permit the passenger to use the first-class salon or dining room. _____
13. (These, This) kind of television commercial costs over $30,000. _____
14. The theory of socialism advocates collective or government ownership of the means of production and distribution; each citizen is to be rewarded with goods and pay according to the work he does. (This, This theory) does not motivate a desire to accumulate personal wealth. _____
15. (Anyone, Any one) of the books will be interesting reading. _____
16. (Somebodys' Somebody's) tools are frequently not replaced at the end of the duty day. _____
17. Each of the supervisors (is, are) responsible for evaluating his or her subordinates this month. _____
18. Many a person (has, have) become ill due to the inhalation of fumes from gases. _____
19. Most of the sugar crop (have, has) been destroyed by insects. _____
20. The contract should be returned to (whoever, whomever) signed it. _____

Lesson 14
Using Other Pronouns

The English language has fewer pronouns than nouns, and these pronouns are divided into classifications (such as the personal pronouns) that serve specific purposes in our writing.

People who make their living directing others, making important decisions, and speaking publicly use proper grammar. They cannot afford to convey their ideas improperly or ungrammatically. The incorrect use of pronouns and verbs is probably the most likely "give-away" of a person's weakness in using the English language; therefore, diligent application in the pronoun lessons is essential to anyone wanting to present a favorable image.

Frame 1 Pronoun Classifications: Relative and Interrogative Pronouns

Pronouns can be classified into distinctive groups for use under specific circumstances. The name of each pronoun classification indicates how the group of words in that classification is used. Because the majority of problems are caused by just a couple of pronouns *(who, whom)*, you will be given more practice on them than on the others which are quite easy to use.

General Comments

Explanation

Refer to the table entitled "Relative and Interrogative Pronouns" and notice that:

1. All the pronouns except *that* may be used as interrogative pronouns, meaning that they may introduce questions.
2. All the pronouns may be used as relative pronouns. A relative pronoun is "related" to another word in the sentence.
3. The pronouns *that, what,* and *which* are the same in the nominative and objective cases; therefore, they very rarely create trouble for the writer.

Relative and Interrogative Pronouns

Pronoun Classification	Nominative	Objective	Possessive
Relative and Interrogative	who	whom	whose
Relative and Interrogative	which	which	
	what	what	
Relative	that	that	

Example

1. Who/Whom
   a. *Who* will sort the mail?
      (1) Who is in the nominative case; it is the subject of the sentece.
      (2) A personal pronoun in the nominative case *(I, you, she, he, it, we, they)* can logically be substituted for *who*:

      I will sort the mail.
      (NOT: *Me* will sort the mail.)

   b. *Whom* do you suggest we select for the award?
      (1) Rephrase a question to place the main subject at the beginning:

      You do suggest we select whom for the award?

      (2) <u>Whom</u> is in the objective case; it is the direct object of the verb <u>select</u>.

      (3) A personal pronoun in the objective case *(me, you, it, her, him, us, them)* can logically be substituted for *whom.* (Mnemonic device: who*m* and hi*m* both end in *m;* use <u>whom</u> if <u>him</u> could logically be substituted for the word.)

> You do suggest we select <u>him</u> for the award.
> (NOT: select <u>he</u> for the award).

  c. She is the person *who* called.

      (1) <u>Who</u> is in the nominative case; it is the subject of the dependent clause <u>who called</u>.

      (2) A personal pronoun in the nominative case can be substituted for <u>who</u>.

> <u>She</u> called.
> (NOT: <u>Her</u> called.)

      (3) In this sentence, <u>who</u> is a relative pronoun and relates to its antecedent (<u>person</u>) in the preceding clause.

  d. She is the woman *whom* I recommended for promotion.

      (1) <u>Whom</u> is in the objective case: it is the direct object of the verb <u>recommended</u>:

> I recommended <u>whom</u> for promotion.

      (2) A personal pronoun in the objective case can be substituted for <u>whom</u>.

> I recommended <u>her</u> for promotion.
> (NOT: I recommended <u>she</u> for promotion.)

      (3) In this sentence, <u>whom</u> is a relative pronoun and relates to its antecedent (<u>woman</u>) in the preceding clause.

2. Which/That

  a. Dora's synopsis, *which* I read yesterday, is well written.

      (1) The word <u>which</u> is used to refer to places, things, and animals.

      (2) The clause starting with <u>which</u> is NOT ESSENTIAL to the sentence and is set off by commas.

  b. The dog *that* I found in the park is a collie.

  c. He is the *type* of employee *that* is an asset to the company.

      (1) The word <u>that</u> is used to refer to places, things, and animals; it is also used to refer to a person(s) mentioned by type, kind, or class.

      (2) A *that* clause is usually a noun clause and is ESSENTIAL to the sentence. Such a clause is not set off by commas.

3. Whose (possessive)/Who's (contraction)

  a. *Whose* book was left on the desk? (possessive)

  b. *Who's* responsible for the safety program? (contraction: *who is*)

Exercises

A. Who/Whom

In the blank provided, write one personal pronoun that can be substituted for <u>who</u> or <u>whom</u> in the following sentences.

Example

She is the processor <u>who</u> proofreads accurately.   <u> she </u>

1. Mr. Wallich is the person <u>who</u> gave me the report.   <u>   </u>
2. Steve is the administrator <u>whom</u> I dislike.   <u>   </u>

3. The employees <u>who</u> signed for the deduction are listed here. _____
4. The students <u>who</u> pass the CPA examination will become certified public accountants. _____
5. Several people, <u>whom</u> I listed below, have not contributed to the community fund drive. _____

B. That/Which

If the underlined word is used incorrectly, write the correct word(s) in the blank provided. If it is used correctly, write C in the blank.

Example

Soren, <u>that</u> I saw in the cafeteria, just returned from a buying trip. ___whom___

1. She is the kind of accountant <u>that</u> may someday become a partner in the firm. _____
2. The dog <u>whom</u> I saw near the building is Carla's. _____
3. The December 19 letter, <u>which</u> was directed to the wrong addressee, has been returned. _____
4. The memo <u>that</u> has been revised is ready for your approval. _____
5. She is the clerk <u>that</u> insulted the customer. _____

C. Whose/Who's

If the underlined word is used incorrectly, write the correct word in the blank provided. If it is written correctly, write C in the blank.

Example

<u>Whose</u> scheduled to work tomorrow? ___Who's___

1. <u>Who's</u> the new committee chairperson? _____
2. I need to know <u>who's</u> responsible for the new schedule. _____
3. These are the employees <u>whose</u> efforts contributed to our winning the efficiency award. _____
4. <u>Whose</u> the new secretary? _____
5. The people <u>who's</u> homes are near the shopping center are concerned about the proposed construction. _____

ANSWERS TO FRAME 1

A. Who/Whom	B. That/Which	C. Who's/Whose
1. he	1. C	1. C
2. him	2. that	2. C
3. they	3. C	3. C
4. they	4. C	4. Who's
5. them	5. who	5. whose

Frame 2 Pronoun Classifications: Relative and Interrogative Pronouns

Who/Whom

Explanation

If you can use the nominative and objective cases of the personal pronouns correctly, you will be able to use *who* and *whom* correctly. The method of proving the accuracy of the selection is the same.

Example

Application 1

(Who, Whom) is the new manager?

a. What is the verb of the sentence? _____

b. Does that verb have a subject? _____

c. The word to be selected will become the subject. It is in the _____ case.

d. Which of the pronouns is in the nominative case and can be used as a subject?

_____

e. Which personal pronoun(s) can logically be substituted to prove your selection?

_____

ANSWERS:
a. is   d. Who
b. No   e. He [or She] is the new manager.
c. nominative

Application 2

The decision was made by Mr. Davenport, (who, whom) is responsible for the results.

Always divide a sentence into clauses.
Independent clause: The decision was made by Mr. Davenport.
Dependent clause: (who, whom) is responsible for the results.

a. What is the verb of the dependent clause? _____

b. Does that verb have a subject? _____

c. Which pronoun is in the nominative case and must be selected for the subject?

_____

d. Which personal pronoun can logically be substituted to prove your selection?

_____

ANSWERS:
a. is   c. who
b. No   d. (he) is responsible for the results.

Application 3

(Who, Whom) do you think we should send on this trip? Rephrased: You do think we should send (who, whom) on this trip?

a. What is the verb of the sentence? _____

b. Does this verb have a subject? _____

c. Does the sentence have another verb? _____

d. Does this verb have a subject? _____

e. Does it need an object? _____

f.   Which pronoun is in the objective case and must be se-
     lected?_____

g.   Which personal pronoun(s) can logically be substituted for your selec-
     tion?_____

ANSWERS:
a.   do think   e.   Yes
b.   Yes; you   f.   whom
c.   Yes; should send   g.   him or her [We should send him (her) on this trip.]
d.   Yes; we

Exercise

In the appropriate blanks below each of the following sentences, write the correct
word from the parentheses, and its case and use. Write N (nominative) or O (objective) to identify its case.

Example

The employees (who, whom) wish to take their vacations in July must sign the
attached Vacation Request Form.

Choice: _____who_____ Case: _____N_____ Use: _____subject_____

1. (Who, Whom) is the chairman of the security committee?

    Choice:_____ Case:_____ Use:_____
2. The report was signed by Mr. Frantic, (who, whom) is the new watchman.

    Choice:_____ Case:_____ Use:_____
3. The committee chairpersons (whom, who) report to the vice president of per-
    sonnel must hold meetings before August 1.

    Choice:_____ Case:_____ Use:_____
4. (Who, Whom) do you believe is responsible for the peak load we are experienc-
    ing?

    Choice:_____ Case:_____ Use:_____
5. The company hired Mr. Goodsen, (who, whom) formerly worked for the Yan-
    kee Dog Biscuit Company.

    Choice:_____ Case:_____ Use:_____
6. The secretary asked, "(Who, Whom) is calling?"

    Choice:_____ Case:_____ Use:_____
7. To (who, whom) is the toll call to be charged?

    Choice:_____ Case:_____ Use:_____
8. The employees (who, whom) work at the Gary plant have formed carpools.

    Choice:_____ Case:_____ Use:_____
9. (Who, Whom) do you think we should elect to the board?

    Choice:_____ Case:_____ Use:_____
10. For (who, whom) is the new building named?

    Choice:_____ Case:_____ Use:_____

ANSWERS TO FRAME 2

1. who; N; Subject   6. who; N; Subject
2. who; N; Subject   7. whom; O; Object of preposition
3. who; N; Subject   8. who; N; Subject
4. who; N; Subject   9. whom; O; Direct object
5. who; N; Subject   10. whom; O; Object of preposition

Frame 3   Pronoun Classifications: Relative and Interrogative Pronouns

Compound Relative Pronouns

Explanation

The compound relative pronouns are *whoever* and *whomever,* and they are in the nominative and objective cases, respectively. To verify your choice, you can substitute a personal pronoun in the nominative case for *whoever* and one in the objective case for *whomever.*

Example

Application 1

I will appoint (whomever, whoever) will do the job.

a.   The main verb of the sentence is _____.

b.   Does this verb have a subject?_____

c.   The remaining part of the sentence is a dependent clause; it is the

_____ of the verb *will appoint.*

d.   The verb of this clause is _____.

e.   Does this verb have a subject?_____

f.   Which word should be selected for the subject?_____

g.   Which personal pronoun(s) can be substituted to prove the answer?

_____

ANSWERS:

a.	will appoint	e.	No
b.	Yes; I	f.	whoever
c.	object	g.	he, she, they
d.	will do		

Application 2

I will give the letter to (whoever, whomever) asks for it.

a.   The main verb of the sentence is _____.

b.   Does this verb have a subject?_____

c.   You know that *to* is a preposition and must take an object; the object is not just

a word, it is a _____.

d.   The verb of this clause is _____.

e.   The verb needs a subject; therefore, _____ must be selected.

f.   Which personal pronoun(s) can be substituted to prove the answer?

_____

ANSWERS:

a.	will give	d.	asks
b.	Yes; I	e.	whoever
c.	clause	f.	he, she

Exercise

In the blanks provided below each of the following sentences, write the correct word from the parentheses, and its case and use.

Example

I will vote for (whoever, whomever) you recommend.

Choice: _____whomever_____ Case: _____O_____ Use: _____object_____

1. (Whoever, Whomever) you name will be allowed to take the day off.

    Choice:_____ Case:_____ Use:_____
2. (Whoever, Whomever) made the call should pay for it.

    Choice:_____ Case:_____ Use:_____
3. We will select (whoever, whomever) you name for the training program.

    Choice:_____ Case:_____ Use:_____
4. The money will be paid to (whoever, whomever) is named as beneficiary.

    Choice:_____ Case:_____ Use:_____
5. (Whoever, Whomever) ordered the book should pay the postage.

    Choice:_____ Case:_____ Use:_____

ANSWERS TO FRAME 3

1. Whoever; N; Subject   3. whomever; O; Object   5. Whoever; N; Subject
2. Whoever; N; Subject   4. whoever; N; Subject

Frame 4   *Pronoun Classifications: Demonstrative Pronouns*

Explanation

The words *this, that, these,* and *those* are pronouns when they are used in place of nouns. They are adjectives when they point out or identify a noun, thereby making it more specific.

   Using any one of these four words as a pronoun is acceptable only as long as the word or thought to which it refers is readily grasped. Many times, however, the writer uses one of these pronouns to refer to a remote word or idea, and the reader becomes confused.

   This and *these* refer to something close at hand or recent; *that* and *those* refer to something remote from the writer or earlier in time.

Example

1. Pronoun Usage:
    a. Studio apartments rent for $450. This is extremely high. Better usage: Studio apartments rent for $450; this price is extremely high. (The word this is an adjective and specifically identifies a named noun.)
    b. The concept of capitalism is based on a free-market system and is dependent on the supply of goods and the demand for them. This is often difficult to understand. (Exactly *what* is difficult to understand?) Better usage: This concept is often difficult to understand.
2. Adjective Usage: Singular and Plural
    An adjective should have the same number as the noun it identifies.
    a. Singular: this, that

        This kind of furniture will not endure rough treatment.

        That type of machine has a history of malfunctions.

b. Plural: <u>these</u>, <u>those</u>

> <u>These</u> classes of plane fares do not include meals.
>
> <u>Those</u> sorts of office arrangements are not conducive to employee communications.

Exercise

Write the correct word from the parentheses in the blank to the right of each sentence.

1. (This, These) kinds of records should be safeguarded.   _____
2. (That, Those) type of box is not maintained in inventory.   _____
3. (Paragraph 1 of a report) The doctrine of laissez-faire opposes governmental interference in the economic affairs of the country, except where noninterference causes the destruction of property or the disturbance of the peace. (Two more sentences follow.)
   (Paragraph 2) (This, This doctrine) literally means that the members of society may do as they please.   _____
4. I received a good citizenship award. (This, This award) is considered an honor.   _____
5. (This, These) forms have been changed and are easier to use.   _____

ANSWERS TO FRAME 4
1. These   2. That   3. This doctrine   4. This award   5. These

---

Frame 5   *Pronoun Classifications: Indefinite Pronouns*

Explanation

An *indefinite pronoun* names an indefinite person, place, or thing. The form of indefinite pronouns is the same in the nominative and objective cases. The indefinite pronouns in the possessive case follow the noun rule for the formation of the possessive: if a word does not end in s, add an apostrophe and s.

Indefinite pronouns are always in the third person.

Example

1. Singular Indefinite Pronouns
   a. Many singular indefinite pronouns are compound words; the last part of the compound may be -*one*, -*body*, -*thing*. Because the pronoun is singular, its verb must also be singular:

anyone*	someone*	everyone*
anything	something	everything
anybody	somebody	everybody

      > This ticket will admit <u>anyone</u>.
      >
      > <u>Everybody</u> is present.
      >
      > <u>Someone's</u> car was stolen.
      >
      > <u>Something</u> must be done about this procedure.

* These words are written separately when they are followed by *of*. (*Any one* of the answers may be correct. *Every one* of the students is qualified for graduation.)

b. Other singular pronouns: *each, one, either, neither, every.*

> <u>Each</u> is permitted one day of sick leave.

> <u>Neither</u> has earned his pay today.

c. Singular pronouns as adjectives: The pronouns listed in 1b can also be used as adjectives modifying a singular noun.

> <u>Each</u> person is responsible for a portion of this work.

> <u>Every</u> paper must be thoroughly analyzed.

2. Plural Indefinite Pronouns
   a. Very few of the indefinite pronouns are plural: *both, few, several, others, many.**

> <u>Both</u> of us are in the same department.

> <u>Few</u> saw the orientation movie.

> <u>Many</u> were selected for professional jobs in this city.

3. Indefinite Pronouns that May Be Singular or Plural
   a. A few pronouns may be either singular or plural: *some, most, none, all.*
   Two points help to choose the verb that should accompany the noun:
   (1) If an *of* phrase follows the pronoun, the number of the object of the preposition determines the number of the verb;
   (2) Bulk items (milk, cereal) or those which cannot be easily counted (corn) are singular in number.

Singular	<u>All</u> of the information <u>was</u> taken into consideration.
Plural	<u>All</u> of the reports <u>have been</u> graded.
Singular	<u>Most</u> of the corn <u>has</u> not been harvested due to snow.
Plural	<u>Most</u> of the departments <u>have</u> submitted their budgets.
Singular	<u>None</u> of the milk <u>is</u> contaminated.
Plural	<u>None</u> of the cars <u>were</u> damaged.†

Exercise

Each of the following sentences contains an error. Explain in a complete sentence how the error can be corrected.

Example

Anyone of the answers could be right.

<u>The compound indefinite pronoun "anyone" should be written as two</u>

<u>words when it is followed by a prepositional phrase beginning with "of."</u>

1. Each of your payments are to be made to the realty company.

___

___

* <u>Many</u> followed by <u>a</u> is singular: <u>Many</u> <u>a</u> person has faced a severe physical problem and lengthy hospitalization.

† If you wish to emphasize the word none, a singular verb can be used. Some texts give this permission only for cases where the object is a person. (<u>None</u> of the students <u>is</u> eligible for the award from the professional society.)

2. Most of the material have been sent to the Production Department.

   _____

   _____

3. Someones' check was left on the desk.

   _____

   _____

4. Everybody in the company are ready to protest the action.

   _____

   _____

5. All of the reports has been graded.

   _____

   _____

ANSWERS TO FRAME 5

1. The subject <u>Each</u> is singular; therefore, the verb should be <u>has been sent</u>.
2. The object of the preposition <u>of</u> is <u>material</u>; this word represents a bulk item which cannot be counted. Because it is considered singular, the verb should be <u>has been sent</u>.
3. An indefinite pronoun forms the possessive by the addition of an apostrophe and <u>s</u>: <u>Someone's</u>.
4. The subject <u>Everybody</u> is singular; the verb should be <u>is</u>.
5. The object of the preposition <u>of</u> is <u>reports</u> (plural); it requires a plural verb, <u>have been graded</u>.

Frame 6   Business Vocabulary: Training Program

Explanation

In their senior year of college, many young men and women attempt to obtain jobs in companies that have training programs for new employees. The competition for these trainee positions is quite high, and the lucky student who receives an offer believes that the months of training will make the transition from college to work easier.

Terms

Orientation—All new employees, whether or not they are in a training program, are told about the background of the company, its products or services, goals, philosophy, and so on. Those in a training program are given additional orientation focused on their duties and activities during the training period.

Training period—A training program may last from a few weeks to several months. Some companies have six- or nine-month training programs for new employees. During this time, the trainee receives a comprehensive orientation to various jobs in one or more departments. After the training period, the successful trainees are placed in jobs appropriate to their ability and interest.

Training activities—Trainees may be *rotated* (moved) from one position in a department to another or from one department to another. During a tour in a department, a trainee may be *coached* by the manager or person appointed to coordinate the trainee's activities. The trainee is expected to perform under supervision many of the duties that are performed by the coach.

Discussion groups—The trainees sit in on staff and department meetings to learn how the managers solve the variety of business problems and how they coordinate activities among departments. In addition, discussion groups are scheduled so that these trainees can discuss problems they encountered in the departments to which they are assigned.

Evaluation—The moderator of the trainees' discussion groups, each manager who has worked with a trainee, and other persons with important input evaluate each trainee's contribution and the value each gained from the training program. Those trainees who have performed satisfactorily are retained, and the remainder must seek jobs elsewhere.

Exercise

Answer each of the following questions in one or more complete sentences.

1. Why is competition for entry into company training programs so great?

   _____

   _____

2. Is a person who completes a training program guaranteed a job with the company?

   _____

   _____

3. What might be three reasons that a trainee is not retained?

   _____

   _____

   _____

4. What is the advantage to the trainee of listening to managers solve problems in a staff meeting?

   _____

   _____

ANSWERS TO FRAME 6

1. Students believe that the counsel and guidance they receive in a training program will make a job easier than if they accept one immediately after graduation without such training.
2. No; a trainee is not guaranteed a job.
3. The trainee may not have been punctual, may not have performed assigned jobs to the satisfaction of a manager, or may not have gotten along with other trainees, superiors, and co-workers.
4. By listening to different managers solve problems, the trainee gains a comprehensive view of the nature of problems that can occur in the organization and hears how professional managers solve them.

Frame 7   *Applying Your Knowledge*

Directions

In the exercise below, underscore each error, and write the correction in the space below it.

CASE

Simone is an assistant training director of IOM, International Office Machines, Inc. She has gathered and organized all the information regarding a training program and has just completed a first draft of her memo to department heads. The memo is directed to the department heads as a group, because 42 departments of various sizes exist at the headquarters manufacturing site. (10 errors)

DATE: May 10, 19____
TO: Department Heads
FROM: Simone Algier, Assistant Training Director
SUBJECT: Training Program on Internal Written Communications

1. Purpose

    The purpose of establishing this program is to meet a need that almost every department head recognizes. Over 90 percent of the 40 department heads who completed our recent questionnaire acknowledge an immediate need for improving the ability of first-line supervisors to present clear, readable reports and memos.

2. Topics

    All of the topics in the program are the one's selected by department heads as being important to supervisors: a review of English fundamentals; memos; progress, justification and analytical reports; and feasibility studies.

3. Instructors

    The faculty members whom have been chosen are Dr. Harry Gibbons and Dr. Maureen Ringo from Montrose Community College. Each of them have taught several writing courses in business and industry. Professors from three institutions were shown the questionnaire results, and Professors Gibbons and Ringo were the only ones who discerned our needs and prepared an outline that was acceptable to us. Both professors will share the instruction. This is in agreement with Mr. Neidt, who will supervise them. The professors will give this types of ratings during and at the conclusion of the course: outstanding, satisfactory, unsatisfactory. Each employee whose participating is expected to check his or her grade with the instructors at the end of the course.

4. Schedule

    Our plans are to schedule the course in Classroom H, located on the first floor of the Wingate Building. The class will meet from 4 P.M. to

6 P.M. on Tuesdays and Thursdays for 16 weeks. One hour of the class will be held on duty-time and one hour on the participant's time. Sessions will begin on June 15, October 17, and February 18. Roll will be taken at the beginning of each class meeting, and everyone of the participants is expected to be prompt.

5. Action Required

    First-line supervisors are required to attend one of the three sessions unless excused by their department head or by an acting department head who has this authority. You may select no more than five employees from those whom volunteer to take a class. Schedule first-line supervisors by giving consideration to their convenience and your department's work requirements. The line employees who volunteer are motivated, and we shall try to give consideration to everyone of them. Please submit the attached Employee Training Schedule, Form 82, by May 20. To save your time and ours, be especially careful to present every body's name and corresponding data correctly.

ANSWERS TO FRAME 6

DATE: May 10, 19____
TO: Department Heads
FROM: Simone Algier, Assistant Training Director
SUBJECT: Training program on Internal Written Communications

1. Purpose

    The purpose of establishing this program is to meet a need that almost every department head recognizes. Over 90 percent of the 40 department heads who completed our recent questionnaire acknowledge an immediate need for improving the ability of first-line supervisors to present clear, readable reports and memos.

2. Topics

    All of the topics in the program are the <u>one's</u> selected by department heads as
    ones
    being important to supervisors: a review of English fundamentals; memos; progress, justification and analytical reports; and feasibility studies.

3. Instructors

    The faculty members <u>whom</u> have been chosen are Dr. Harry Gibbons and
    who
    Dr. Maureen Ringo from Montrose Community College. Each of them
    <u>have</u> taught several writing courses in business and industry. Professors
    has
    from three institutions were shown the questionnaire results, and Professors
    Gibbons and Ringo were the only ones who discerned our needs and prepared an

outline that was acceptable to us. Both professors will share the

instruction. <u>This</u> is in agreement with Mr. Neidt, who will supervise them.

This procedure
The professors will give <u>this</u> types of ratings during and at the conclusion

these
of the course: outstanding, satisfactory, unsatisfactory. Each employee

<u>whose</u> participating is expected to check his or her grade with the

who's
instructors at the end of the course.

4. Schedule

Our plans are to schedule the course in Classroom H, located on the first floor of

the Wingate Building. The class will meet from 4 P.M. to 6 P.M. on Tuesdays and

Thursdays for 16 weeks. One hour of the class will be held on duty-time and one

hour on the participant's time. Sessions will begin on June 15, October 17, and

February 18. Roll will be taken at the beginning of each class meeting, and

<u>everyone</u> of the participants is expected to be prompt.

every one

5. Action Required

First-line supervisors are required to attend one of the three sessions

unless excused by their department head or by an acting department

head who has this authority. You may select no more than five

employees from those <u>whom</u> volunteer to take a class. Schedule first-line

who
supervisors by giving consideration to their convenience and your

department's work requirements. The line employees who volunteer

are motivated, and we shall try to give consideration to <u>everyone</u> of

every one
them. Please submit the attached Employee Training Schedule,

Form 82, by May 20. To save your time and ours, be especially careful

to present <u>every body's</u> name and corresponding data correctly.

everybody's

Lesson 15
Frequently Misused Words

Pretest

The pretest that follows and the posttest for this lesson are presented in the form of an Applying Your Knowledge section. The presentation of the tests in this form permits you to determine if certain words are part of your writing vocabulary. The following frequently misused words are covered in this lesson:

1. All ready, Already	9. Personal, Personnel
2. All together, Altogether	10. Their, There, They're
3. Almost, Most	11. To, Two, Too
4. All right, Alright	12. Addition, Edition
5. All ways, Always	13. Role, Roll
6. All, All of	14. Sometime, Some time, Sometimes
7. Former, Latter	15. Accede, Exceed
8. Formerly, Formally, Formal	

Directions

1. Draw a line through each misused word in the Performance Evaluation that follows and write the correct word in the space below the error.
2. Then write five sentences, each correctly using one of the words which you crossed out in the original.

Example

The Happy Hands Janitorial Service has hired an employee relations consultant to help them with their ~~personal~~ problems.
          personnel

Sentence

Using the direct long-distance telephone line for <u>personal</u> calls is against company regulations.

> CASE
>
> Dave Carlson, the marketing manager, has written this evaluation of Mary Cupolat, a department secretary. At the end of her six-month probationary period, this narrative evaluation, plus a performance checklist, will be discussed with Mary and placed in her file. Dave asks you to check the narrative evaluation for accuracy; you find five errors.

> *PERFORMANCE EVALUATION*
>
> I recommend that Mary Cupolat, Secretary B, be given permanent employment with the John F. Folger Publishing Enterprises.

Mary's typing speed (80 wpm) exceeds that of my former secretary, and her ability to proofread is almost perfect. She has all ready learned how to prepare the payroll for computer processing and has begun typing the new edition of the advertising personnel assignment sheet.

Because Mary formally worked for another publishing company, at first she was some time too eager to tell us how she did a similar job there. However, she is rapidly learning and accepting our procedures. The department personnel are all together in there desire to welcome Mary as a permanent employee. Her attitude, efficiency, and personality, in addition to her secretarial ability, indicate that she will have an important roll in this department.

Sentences

1. _____

_____

2. _____

_____

3. _____

_____

4. _____

_____

5. _____

_____

Lesson 15
Frequently Misused Words

In this lesson, fifteen groups of words are presented in five frames.

Explanation

Words beginning with *all* or *al-* confuse even people who write messages daily. When these combinations are studied at the same time, however, the distinction between them becomes more apparent. The following words will be considered: *all ready, already; all right, alright; all together, altogether; all ways, always.* The word *all* followed by an *of* phrase is common, but it is not concise; this construction, too, will be considered.

Example

1. ALL READY/ALREADY
   a. ALL READY (adv)—a phrase meaning all are ready; completely prepared.

      The letters are ALL READY for your signature.

      The seniors are ALL READY to celebrate their completion of school.

   b. ALREADY (adv)—previously; usually related to time.

      The move has ALREADY been completed.

      We cannot cash our checks because the cash has ALREADY been locked in the safe.

2. ALL TOGETHER/ALTOGETHER
   a. ALL TOGETHER (phrase)—all are together.

      The family is ALL TOGETHER for the first time in years.

      The people at this reunion became friends when they were ALL TOGETHER in Da Nang during the war.

   b. ALTOGETHER (adv)—wholly or thoroughly.

      You are ALTOGETHER right.

      Hal states that his high salary is ALTOGETHER sufficient compensation for the stress he undergoes while fighting oil fires.

3. ALMOST/MOST
   a. ALMOST (adv)—very nearly.

      We are ALMOST through extracting the data.

   b. MOST (adv)—majority. This word should NOT be used in place of *almost.*

      I have looked through MOST of the periodicals.

      MOST of the students passed the examination.

      NOT: We are MOST through extracting the data.

4. ALL RIGHT/ALRIGHT
   a. ALL RIGHT (adv)—well enough. ALL RIGHT is not used in formal writing, such as reports and letters.

      The book is ALL RIGHT for children (acceptable, all correct).

   b. ALRIGHT and ALL-RIGHT are NOT acceptable.

5. ALL WAYS/ALWAYS
   a. ALL WAYS (phrase)—all methods.

      We tried in ALL WAYS to contact him.

      ALL WAYS to reach Chicago—air, rail, and automobile—are blocked by the snow.

   b. ALWAYS (adv)—at all times.

      The employees in this department are ALWAYS friendly.

      ALWAYS remember to lock the door when you work late at the office.

6. ALL/ALL OF
   The construction of ALL followed by a prepositional phrase beginning with OF is not concise; the preposition usually can be omitted from the construction.

      ALL OF the apartments have been rented.

      Revised: ALL the apartments have been rented.

Exercise

Select the correct word from the parentheses in each of the following sentences and write it in the blank provided.

Example

(All, All of) the contractors have been paid.   ___All___

1. Your answers are (alright, all right).   _____
2. (Most, Almost) all the sanitation workers helped remove the snow after the blizzard.   _____
3. Place the leases (all together, altogether) in the vault.   _____
4. (All, All of) the street vendors purchase licenses from the city.   _____
5. The market has (all ready, already) dropped seven points this week.   _____
6. I am (most, almost) through reading the books on the bibliography list.   _____
7. The day's reports have (all ready, already) been microfilmed.   _____
8. The answers are (all together, altogether) correct.   _____
9. She was dependable in (all ways, always).   _____
10. (All, All of) the dangerous products have been removed from the shelves.   _____

ANSWERS TO FRAME 1

1. all right	5. already	8. altogether
2. Almost	6. almost	9. all ways
3. all together	7. already	10. All
4. All		

Frame 2

The words to be studied in this frame are *latter, former; formerly, formally, formal;* and *personal, personnel.*

Example

1. FORMER/LATTER
   a. FORMER (adj)—coming before in time; preceding in place or arrangement.

      The FORMER directive has been rescinded.

b. LATTER (adj)—the second of two groups or the last of several.

> Of the Data Processing Club and the Marketing Club, the LATTER has the greater number of guest speakers and field trips.

2. FORMERLY/FORMALLY/FORMAL
    a. FORMERLY (adv)—at an earlier time; previously.

> Justine FORMERLY worked for the Ballard Company.

    b. FORMALLY (adv)—ceremoniously.

> You are requested to dress FORMALLY for the banquet.

    c. FORMAL (adj)—conventional (applied to language); often third person and does not include nonstandard words, slang, or jargon.

> The report should be written in a FORMAL style.

3. PERSONAL/PERSONNEL
    a. PERSONAL (adj)—private.

> Your PERSONAL life is not pertinent to your job unless it affects your performance.

    b. PERSONNEL (n)—a body of persons employed in a specific factory, office, company, and so on.

> The PERSONNEL have been informed about the change in benefits.

Exercise

Select the correct word from the parentheses in each of the following sentences and write it in the blank provided.

1. Reports prepared by outside consultants are usually written in (former, formal) style.
2. Jane Brown is the (former, latter) Mrs. Alexander Cronin.
3. (Personnel, Personal) business should not be transacted during working hours.
4. You are expected to be (formerly, formally) attired for the banquet.
5. (Personal, Personnel) having less than one year of service with the company do not get a vacation with pay.
6. The sales manager was Mary Ann Noll; she resigned the (former, latter) part of April.
7. (Personal, Personnel) are allowed three days' sick leave each month.
8. (Personal, Personnel) correspondence should not be written on duty time.
9. The (former, latter) of your two statements showed a balance of $545, and the latter, $242.
10. (Former, Formal) language is usually in the third person.

ANSWERS TO FRAME 2

1. formal	5. Personnel	8. Personal
2. former	6. latter	9. former
3. Personal	7. Personnel	10. Formal
4. formally		

Frame 3

Explanation

These words are often confused because they sound alike: *their, they're,* and *there.*

Example

1. THEIR (possessive pronoun)

   They lost THEIR licenses.

2. THEY'RE (contraction)—they are.

   THEY'RE three weeks behind in the mailings.

3. THERE (expletive)—takes the position of the real subject of a sentence.

   THERE are several errors in this letter. [The real subject is <u>errors</u>. <u>This letter contains several errors.</u>]

4. THERE (adv)—indicating where.

   He placed the mail THERE.

Exercise

Select the correct word from the parentheses in each of the following sentences and write it in the blank provided.

1. (Their, They're, There) unable to meet the requirements established for promotion.
2. The employees on strike may lose (their, they're, there) benefits.
3. (Their, They're, There) is a section of files that is unavailable for evaluation.
4. (Their, They're, There) passing the legislation at this time is essential.
5. The analyst said that the minicomputer could be placed (their, they're, there).
6. (Their, They're, There) unsure about the amount of the dividend.
7. (Their, They're, There) are three people eligible for promotion.
8. (Their, They're, There) obligated by the contract if they sign it.
9. I found the lost check (their, they're, there).
10. Three employees lost (their, they're, there) bonuses because of violating the agreement.

ANSWERS TO FRAME 3

1.	They're	5.	there	8.	They're
2.	their	6.	They're	9.	there
3.	There	7.	There	10.	their
4.	Their				

Frame 4

Explanation

The seven words presented in this frame are *to, two, too; addition, edition;* and *role, roll.*

1. TO/TWO/TOO
   a. TO (prep)—toward.

      He took the file TO the record center.

   b. TWO (adj.)—the sum of one and one.

      TWO analysts were discharged.

   c. TOO (adv)—more than; also.

      He worked on the problem TOO long.

      I am going TOO.

2. ADDITION/EDITION
   a. ADDITION (n)—the summing of one or more columns of figures.

      He made an error in ADDITION.

   b. EDITION (n)—a copy or version of a publication.

      The fifth EDITION of this book will be published next year.

3. ROLE/ROLL
   a. ROLE (n)—a part in a play, society, or group.

      She played the ROLE of Bess in "Good Queen Bess."

      Ms. Stanton attended a seminar dealing with the ROLE of a supervisor in a modern molybdenum mine.

   b. ROLL (n)—list of names or related items.

      The class ROLL does not show your name.

   c. ROLL (n)—a small piece of baked yeast dough.

      The company provides free cinnamon ROLLS to employees who must begin work at 6:30 A.M.

   d. ROLL (v)—to revolve.

      The pencil ROLLED under the desk.

Exercise

Select the correct word from the parentheses in each of the following sentences and write it in the blank provided.

1. The teacher took the (role, roll) to determine who was absent. _____
2. The play stars Richard Burton in the (role, roll) of Hamlet. _____
3. Inflation has caused the price of movies to become (to, two, too) high for many people. _____
4. The Sunday (addition, edition) of the newspaper has many classified advertisements. _____
5. You can perform (addition, edition) on all calculators in approximately the same way. _____
6. He is acting in the (role, roll) of moderator during this session of the meeting. _____
7. The sentence is (to, two, too) long, and the reader loses the thought. _____
8. The (addition, edition) to the building will cost approximately $100,000. _____
9. The president of the Chamber of Commerce read the (role, roll) of organizations that had contributed to the campaign. _____
10. I used the twentieth (addition, edition) of that book. _____

ANSWERS TO FRAME 4

1.	roll	5.	addition	8.	addition
2.	role	6.	role	9.	roll
3.	too	7.	too	10.	edition
4.	edition				

Frame 5

Explanation

The frequently misused words in this frame are *sometime, some time, sometimes;* and *accede, exceed.*

1. SOMETIME/SOME TIME/SOMETIMES
    a. SOMETIME (adv)—a point in time; not specified or definitely known time.

        He will arrive by plane SOMETIME tomorrow.

    b. SOME TIME (n)—a period of time; if *little* can logically be inserted between the words, use SOME TIME.

        He visited each branch for SOME TIME to obtain the data regarding the experiment.

    c. SOMETIMES (adv)—on occasion; now and then.

        SOMETIMES the computer printout is extremely light and difficult to read.

2. ACCEDE/EXCEED
    a. ACCEDE (v)—to express approval or give consent in response to urging.

        The foreman ACCEDED to the request of the line personnel.

    b. EXCEED (v)—to surpass; to be greater than or superior to; to extend outside.

        The patrolman said that I EXCEEDED the speed limit by 27 miles per hour.

Exercise

Select the correct word from the parentheses in each of the following sentences, and write it in the blank provided.

1. He will leave for the Paris office (some time, sometime, sometimes) soon. _____
2. The file had been removed from the office for (some time, sometime, sometimes). _____
3. The disagreement was settled after the employees (acceded, exceeded) to the safety requirements upon which the manager had insisted. _____
4. (Some time, Sometime, Sometimes) the president conducts the meetings instead of the chairman of the board. _____
5. When the river (acceded, exceeded) the flood stage, the small industries along the waterfront were severely damaged. _____
6. When Hiram (acceded, exceeded) the speed limit, he received a ticket. _____
7. I shall be graduated (some time, sometime, sometimes) next year. _____
8. The new editor spent (some time, sometime, sometimes) in California before he transferred to this office. _____
9. If you will (accede, exceed) to the new credit terms, we will increase your line of credit as you requested. _____
10. (Some time, Sometime, Sometimes) the publication is directed to my home instead of my office. _____

ANSWERS TO FRAME 5

1. sometime	5. exceeded	8. some time
2. some time	6. exceeded	9. accede
3. acceded	7. sometime	10. Sometimes
4. Sometimes		

Lesson 16
Verbs: Agreement with Subject

Pretest

Directions

Underscore the subject(s) of each of the following sentences. Then select the correct word from the parentheses and write it in the blank provided.

Example

Either the <u>instructor</u> or the <u>student</u> (is, are) responsible for the charge on the late book.   <u>is</u>

1. The refrigerator, as well as the other household appliances, (is, are) on sale. _____
2. Neither of the books (is, are) in the stacks. _____
3. Some of the utility costs (has, have) been paid by the renters. _____
4. The architecture of the houses in this subdivision (is, are) interesting. _____
5. The price of the calculator, along with the recharger, (is, are) over $100. _____
6. The committee (has, have) signed their names to the petition. _____
7. Most of the unleaded gasoline (is, are) transported by truck. _____
8. The editor of this magazine (seem, seems) to be biased on the topic of rent control. _____
9. The class (was, were) dismissed at nine. _____
10. He (doesn't, don't) contribute to the community fund. _____
11. The company (has, have) established a branch office in Tampa. _____
12. Both the furnace and the gas heater in each condominium (was, were) replaced. _____
13. Either the dealer or a salesperson (quote, quotes) a price that is based on the condition of the used car and its depreciated value. _____
14. The pant suit and skirt combination (sell, sells) for $150. _____
15. In the storeroom there (is, are) supplies, office equipment, and steel shelving. _____
16. Neither the nursery nor the seed company (has, have) sold hanging plants in the spring. _____
17. George, as well as his family, (plan, plans) to vacation in Mexico this year. _____
18. Each agency of the federal government (comply, complies) with the Privacy Act. _____
19. One of the departments located in the Lory Building (boast, boasts) of having no absenteeism for two months. _____
20. The committee chairman and the parliamentarian (consider, considers) Jack a rude person. _____
21. Only one of the employees (has, have) volunteered to stay overtime during the peak period. _____
22. Neither Professor Tate nor his students (see, sees) the evaluation results until they are printed in the paper. _____
23. The foreman (don't, doesn't) report all discipline problems to the plant superintendent. _____
24. If this (was, were) Sunday, we could not receive a reduced fare. _____
25. The president and founder of the company (hope, hopes) to retire and spend his time traveling. _____

Lesson 16
Verbs: Agreement with Subject

Verbs are the "workhorses" of our language. They have these characteristics:

1. *Tense:* the time when an action occurs or a condition exists.
2. *Mood:* the manner in which the action or condition is presented.
3. *Voice:* the sentence structure that shows the subject performing or receiving the action.
4. *Form:* the ability to be converted into three verbals: gerund, participle, and infinitive.
5. *Principal Parts:* the three forms—present, past, and past participle—which can be taken by a root verb.

A word without these five characteristics is not a verb.

Each sentence must have a verb and a subject for that verb. The main verb is often called the *simple predicate,* and the main subject is called the *simple subject.* The subject with its modifiers is the *complete subject,* and the verb with its modifiers is the *complete predicate.*

> The two men began their landscaping business after graduation.

Simple subject: men
Simple verb: began
Complete subject: The two men
Complete predicate (comprised of all remaining words after the complete subject has been identified): began their landscaping business after graduation

The subject and verb must agree in number. The frames in this lesson will help you make decisions regarding the agreement of the subject and its verb.

Frame 1   Subject and Verb Agreement

Agreement of One Subject and Its Verb(s)

Explanation

A noun or pronoun used as a subject agrees with its verb in number. You will remember that the majority of nouns ending in s are plural, but that identification is not true of verbs. A singular noun or pronoun in the third person requires a verb that ends in s if the action occurs in the present.

he, she	works	John	writes
it	is	a student	enrolls

The auxiliary (helping) verb used with a *singular* noun or pronoun in the third person ends in *s:*

he, she	has worked	it	was true
John	has written	he, she	is working
it	has been done	John	is writing
he, she	was late	it	is going
John	was late		

Notice the application of this rule in the sentences illustrating the agreement between subjects and their verbs.

Example

1. Agreement between one subject and its verb: Ask *who?* or *what?* before the verb to locate its subject.

   Singular   The <u>letter</u> <u>is</u> ready for your signature.
   Plural   The <u>letters</u> <u>are</u> ready for your signature.

2. Agreement between one subject and an auxiliary verb: An auxiliary verb helps the main verb, and together they constitute a <u>verb phrase</u>.

   Singular   The <u>administrative assistant (has) completed</u> the work schedule.
   Plural   The <u>administrative assistants (have) completed</u> the work schedule.

3. Agreement between one subject and a compound verb: A compound verb consists of two verbs or verb phrases connected with a conjunction.

   Singular   <u>Greta</u> <u>has checked</u> the figures and <u>has found</u> them to be correct.
   Plural   <u>They</u> <u>have checked</u> the figures and <u>have found</u> them to be correct.

4. Agreement between a subject and its verb that are separated by phrases and modifiers:

   Singular   A <u>list</u> of the full-time employees now on the payroll <u>is</u> available from the Accounting Department.
   Plural   The <u>salaries</u> of the personnel in Job Classification V <u>are being adjusted</u> so that they will be comparable with those in the locality.

5. Agreement between a subject and verb that are separated by a parenthetical expression: A parenthetical expression consists of a word or group of words that are explanatory but not essential to the sentence. It is set off by commas. The existence of this expression does not affect the choice of a verb.

   Singular   This <u>department</u>, in addition to the Marketing Department, <u>is being evaluated</u> this fall.
   Plural   The <u>students</u>, as well as the faculty, <u>have been asked</u> to complete evaluation questionnaires.

6. Agreement between a collective noun as a subject and its verb: A collective noun considered or acting (or being acted upon) as a unit requires a singular subject, but when a collective noun represents people acting separately, it requires a plural verb.

   Singular   The temporary <u>committee</u> <u>was appointed</u> by the chairperson of the standing committee.
   Plural   The <u>committee</u> <u>were</u> in disagreement about the correct parliamentary procedure.

7. Agreement between a quantity as a subject and its verb: A quantity requires a singular verb if it expresses a single unit.

   Singular   <u>Five thousand dollars is</u> too much to pay for that car.
   Plural   <u>Forty typewriters were stolen</u> last week.

   Singular   <u>Six feet</u> of wire <u>is</u> the minimum allowed for a telephone connection.
   Plural   The <u>six feet</u> of this insect <u>have</u> suction devices that permit it to cling to a surface.

8. A fraction may be singular or plural, depending upon the word it modifies.

Singular   <u>Three-fourths</u> of a (pie graph) <u>represents</u> 75 percent of the pie.

Plural   <u>Three-fourths</u> of the (people) in this room <u>represent</u> 75 percent of the class.

9. Agreement between a title as a subject and its verb:

Singular   <u>Forty Thousand Words</u> <u>is</u> the title of a book on word division.

Plural   <u>Forty thousand words</u> <u>comprise</u> a lengthy article.

Singular   <u>Loper, Ballard, and Associates</u> <u>is</u> now located on Elm and Fifth Streets.

Plural   <u>Mr. Loper and Mr. Ballard</u>, as well as their associates, <u>are</u> members of this organization.

10. Agreement between a subject and its verb in a contraction: A contraction is one word that has been constructed from two words; an apostrophe is inserted at the point where a letter(s) has been omitted. The most common error is incorrect usage of *don't* (do not) and *doesn't* (does not). Third person singular nouns or pronouns agree with *doesn't,* and other nouns and pronouns agree with *don't.* Notice that the s rule applies.

Singular   <u>He</u> <u>doesn't</u> understand the rule. (He doe<u>s</u> not.)

Plural   <u>They</u> <u>don't</u> understand the rule. (They do not.)

11. Agreement between a singular subject ending in s and its verb: Some nouns ending in s are singular: mathematics, news, phonetics, genetics, politics.

The <u>news</u> from the Middle East <u>is</u> good.

Exercise

Underscore the subject in each of the following sentences. Then select the correct verb and write it in the blank provided.

Example

My <u>supervisor</u>, along with the personnel in the Data Processing Division, (doesn't, don't) believe that our firm should merge with Maxipro, Inc.   <u>doesn't</u>

1. The cafeteria (make, makes) 36 percent profit on the food it sells.   _____
2. The doors to the corridor (was, were) still locked at 8:30 this morning.   _____
3. I (has, have) purchased the car and (has, have) applied for insurance.   _____
4. Ms. Johnson's house, which is located on the corner of Fifth and Lake Streets, (is, are) for sale.   _____
5. The salesperson with the greatest number of verified sales during the month of June (is, are) Herbert Siegel, who transferred from the Atlanta office.   _____
6. The jury (has, have) presented its verdict to the bailiff.   _____
7. Ten miles (is, are) the distance between my home and my office.   _____
8. Half the inventory (has, have) been sold to the Redding Company.   _____
9. *Two for the See-Saw* (is, are) a play that appeared on Broadway some years ago.   _____
10. There (is, are) a list of student names and grades taped to the door.   _____
11. Mr. Symington (doesn't, don't) know if he can obtain business-interruption insurance on that type of inventory.   _____
12. The class (has, have) completed their reports.   _____
13. He (doesn't, don't) ever follow directions in preparing an assignment.   _____
14. The students in that class (was, were) given the wrong room number.   _____

15. The sales of the eight clerks and three salespersons on commission (amount, amounts) to more than $80,000 for May. _____
16. The pilots, as well as the stewardesses and the maintenance personnel, (has, have) announced their intention to stop work on Friday. _____
17. The airmail envelope, in addition to the two cartons sent by air freight, (has, have) arrived safely. _____
18. The criteria (is, are) used as major division headings in an analytical report. _____
19. The faculty (is, are) voting for a new chairman today. _____
20. Mathematics (is, are) difficult for people who are not quantitatively inclined. _____

ANSWERS TO FRAME 1

1. <u>cafeteria</u>, makes
2. <u>doors</u>, were
3. <u>I</u>, have, have
4. <u>house</u>, is
5. <u>salesperson</u>, is
6. <u>jury</u>, has
7. <u>miles</u>, is
8. <u>inventory</u>, has
9. *Two for the See-Saw*, is
10. <u>list</u>, is
11. <u>Mr. Symington</u>, doesn't
12. <u>class</u>, have
13. <u>He</u>, doesn't
14. <u>students</u>, were
15. <u>sales</u>, amount
16. <u>pilots</u>, have
17. <u>envelope</u>, has
18. <u>criteria</u>, are
19. <u>faculty</u>, are
20. <u>Mathematics</u>, is

Frame 2   Subject and Verb Agreement

Agreement of an Indefinite Pronoun and Its Verb

Explanation

An *indefinite pronoun* names an indefinite person, place, or thing. This pronoun may be a singular compound word, a singular word, a plural word, or a singular or plural word, depending upon its use in a sentence.

Example

1. A singular compound indefinite pronoun requires a singular verb.

   <u>Everyone</u> <u>works</u> at his or her own desk during the examination.

   <u>Nobody</u> <u>is</u> allowed to leave the room after the test begins.

2. Certain other singular pronouns require singular verbs: *each, one, neither, either, every*.

   <u>Each</u> <u>is</u> expected to do his or her own work.

   <u>One</u> <u>has</u> been graded.

   When one of these pronouns is used as an adjective, the noun it modifies is singular and requires a singular verb.

   (Each) <u>employee</u> and <u>department head</u> <u>has read</u> the announcement.

   (Every) <u>retailer</u> <u>wonders</u> what happened to this year's profit.

3. A plural indefinite pronoun requires a plural verb: *several, few, both, others, many*.

   <u>Several</u> from your school <u>have passed</u> this test.

   <u>Few</u> <u>understand</u> the importance of this certification.

4. Some indefinite pronouns are either singular or plural: *most, some, none, all, any.* The number of the verb is determined by the number of the object of the preposition which the subject modifies.

    Singular   <u>Some</u> of the corn <u>is</u> not yet <u>harvested</u>.
    Plural   <u>Some</u> of the people <u>are scheduled</u> to attend the second meeting.

    Singular   <u>None</u> of the milk <u>is</u> contaminated.
    Plural   <u>None</u> of the students <u>were</u> present at the seminar.

Exercise

Underscore the subject in the following sentences. Then select the correct word and write it in the blank provided.

1. Everybody (is, are) expected to comply with the company policy.   _____
2. Of the two candidates, neither (is, are) present to defend his or her paper.   _____
3. Many (was, were) absent during the nice weather.   _____
4. Many a house (has, have) been appraised for double its cost.   _____
5. All the information (has, have) been abstracted for the report.   _____
6. Most of the employees (was, were) not in favor of the holiday schedule.   _____
7. None of the oil (has, have) been piped into this area.   _____
8. Any of the report formats (is, are) acceptable.   _____
9. Something in the compound (kill, kills) the insects but (do, does) not damage the roses.   _____
                                                                                                            _____
10. Some of the inhabitants in that city (do, does) not approve of the casino's being located there.   _____

ANSWERS TO FRAME 2

1. <u>Everybody</u>, is   5. <u>information</u>, has   8. <u>Any</u>, are
2. <u>neither</u>, is   6. <u>Most</u>, were   9. <u>Something</u>, kills, does
3. <u>Many</u>, were   7. <u>None</u>, has   10. <u>Some</u>, do
4. <u>house</u>, has been

Frame 3   Subject and Verb Agreement

Agreement Between a Compound Subject and Its Verb

Explanation

A compound subject consists of two subjects connected with a conjunction, such as *and, or,* or *nor.*

Example

1. Compound subjects connected with *and* require a plural verb.

    <u>Mary</u> and <u>Paul</u> <u>are borrowing</u> money to buy their car.

2. Compound singular subjects connected with *or* or *nor* require a singular verb.

    Either the <u>instructor</u> or the <u>student</u> <u>is</u> responsible for the charge on the late book.

    The loan <u>officer</u> or his <u>assistant</u> <u>is</u> responsible for the error.

3. A compound subject containing a singular and a plural word requires a verb that agrees with the closer of the two subjects.

Singular   Neither his <u>associates</u> nor the <u>lawyer</u> <u>has prepared</u> the brief.
Plural   Neither the <u>lawyer</u> nor his <u>associates</u> <u>have prepared</u> the brief.

4. Compound subjects connected with *and* that have become a common term require a singular verb.

Singular   <u>Bread and butter</u> <u>is</u> hard to earn these days.
Plural   <u>Bread</u> and <u>butter</u> <u>were</u> two of the items on sale.

Singular   <u>Bacon and eggs</u> <u>is</u> on the menu.
Plural   <u>Bacon</u> and <u>eggs</u> cost more at the Wonder Grocery than at the Food Basket.

Exercise

Underscore the compound subject in each of the following sentences. Then select the correct verb and write it in the blank provided.

1. Neither the car dealer nor the salespeople (was, were) aware that the customer's car had been stolen.   _____
2. Barbara and her sister (is, are) the beneficiaries of the annuity.   _____
3. Either the employees or the landscape architect (has, have) selected the wrong type of trees for the lawn.   _____
4. Bacon and eggs (has, have) increased in price by 12 and 8 cents, respectively.   _____
5. The driver of the moving van or his partner (is, are) responsible for checking the condition of the household goods.   _____

ANSWERS TO FRAME 3
1. <u>dealer, salespeople</u>, were
2. <u>Barbara, sister</u>, are
3. <u>employees, architect</u>, has
4. <u>bacon, eggs</u>, have
5. <u>driver, partner</u>, is

Frame 4   Subject and Verb Agreement

Agreement Between the Subject and a Verb in the Subjunctive Mood

Explanation

Mood indicates the manner in which a verb of action or being is used. Three moods exist: *indicative, imperative,* and *subjunctive.* A verb in the indicative mood is used in a sentence that makes a statement or asks a question; a verb in the imperative mood is used in a sentence that makes a command or a request. The subjunctive mood is used to express a condition that is contrary to fact or to state a wish. The verb *were* is used under these circumstances, even though the subject is singular. It may be helpful to note that *were* always follows *as if, as though,* and *wish* (and sometimes *if*).

Example

1. Subjunctive mood is used to express a condition contrary to fact.

   If <u>I</u> <u>were</u> John, I certainly would not sign the contract.

   If the <u>police officer</u> <u>were</u> here, he would give the reckless driver a ticket.

2. Subjunctive mood is used to express a wish.

    I wish I <u>were</u> able to take a vacation this year.

    I wish that <u>statement</u> <u>were</u> true.

3. Subjunctive mood is not used when stating a fact.

    If the <u>letter</u> <u>was</u> not <u>received</u> yesterday, we may not hear from them until after the holiday. (The writer does not know if the letter was received yesterday; the statement is not contrary to fact.)

4. A pronoun in the nominative case follows *were.*

    If I <u>were</u> <u>he</u>, I would sell some of the rental property.

Exercise

In each of the following sentences, select the proper word from the parentheses and write it in the blank provided.

1. If today (was, were) a holiday, the prime time television commercial would be replaced with a safety message.
2. If Mr. Barnes (was, were) out of town yesterday, he will probably return your call today.
3. If you were (he, him), you could afford to fly to Hawaii for a weekend.
4. I wish that the check (was, were) made out to us.
5. If the book (was, were) required last semester, you may be able to buy a used copy.

ANSWERS TO FRAME 4
1. were   2. was   3. he   4. were   5. was

Frame 5   Business Vocabulary: Collection Agency

Explanation

A *collection agency* is a service business that collects money from a debtor and then pays the creditor—the person or company to which the debt is owed.

An agency may retain from 30 to 60 percent of the money it collects for its time, effort, and administrative expenses.

Terms

Debtor—one who owes a sum of money.
Administrative expenses—the cost of paper, stamps, advertising, printing, and so on, that can be allocated to each account presented for collection.
Operating expenses—taxes, utilities, salaries, and other expenses that are necessary for the agency to operate.
Collection letter—a communication sent by the agency to the debtor requesting payment of a specific account by a certain time.
Collection series—a group of routine form letters, each more forceful than the preceding, sent to a debtor in an effort to encourage payment.
Bill collector (collection advisor or specialist)—an agency employee who writes letters or talks with the debtor, attempting to persuade the debtor to make a partial payment or pay the account in full.

Delinquent debt—a sum of money that has been owed for a period of time longer than the financial contract between the debtor and creditor permits.

Creditor—the person or organization to which the money is owed.

Garnishment (n)—the stoppage of a specific sum from wages to satisfy a creditor.

Garnishee (n)—one who is served with a garnishment or an order.

Garnishee (v)—to attach wages.

Exercise

In each of the following sentences, write the correct business vocabulary term in the blank provided.

1. A _____ is the person who owes money.

2. A _____ is the person to whom the money is owed.

3. An agreement whereby a creditor and a debtor's employer agree to withhold an amount from an employee's wages is called _____.

4. An overdue debt is described as being _____.

5. A group of form letters sent at intervals to the debtor is called a _____.

ANSWERS TO FRAME 5

1. debtor 2. creditor 3. garnishment 4. delinquent 5. collection series

Frame 6   Applying Your Knowledge

Directions

Proofread the following letter and underscore each error in usage. Then write the correct usage in the space below.

CASE

As a new employee of the Recoup Collection Agency, you have been assigned some accounts, each in various stages of delinquency. You have reviewed the accounts and assigned a priority to each of them. Having just completed this first draft of a letter to Don Jakes, you are now prepared to revise it so that it is clear and accurate. (10 errors)

August 30, 19____

Mr. Don Jakes
2114 Alameda Boulevard
Big Spring, Texas, 79720

Dear Mr. Jakes:

Western Department Stores, Inc., have just submitted your account to this agency for collection. As a collection advisor, I am responsibile for reviewing your credit record with Western to assure that it is accurate and to collect the balance of your overdue account.

You established your account with Western on April 30 of this year, and the records submitted to us by Western shows that in May and June you paid the minimum amount required under the financial agreement: $20. In July you charged additional merchandise, amounting to $210.40, bringing your balance to $350.50. Your payment record indicates that Western sent you a statement in July and another in August, as well as three collection letters during the two months.

I, as well as the credit manager at Western, has tried to call you at home and also at Union Industries, which you listed as your place of employment. The personnel director at Union Industries inform me that you were discharged on July 5. The telephone company service representative said that your telephone were disconnected on June 30 because you had not paid for service in May and June.

Mr. Jakes, neither Western Department Stores, Inc., nor this agency want to place a hardship on you; however, this delinquent debt must be paid. I have been authorized to offer you two payment plans, and I request that you select one of these plans as the basis on which to pay your overdue account:

(1) Mail a certified check for $350.50 to this agency no later than September 30.

(2) Mail a certified check for $175 and the enclosed 30-day promissory note for $175.50 to this agency no later than September 30.

If neither of these plans are satisfactory, please call me within five days of receiving this letter, and I shall discuss the problem with you. Should you fail to respond to this letter or to select one of the plans, you will receive a letter giving you notice that I shall discuss with your new employer the feasibility of garnisheeing your wages.

For your convenience, two business reply envelopes and a duplicate promissory note is enclosed. Should you choose Plan 2, the copy of the note will be your record of this transaction.

By the way, Mr. Jakes, for a nominal charge you may obtain a certified check at any bank. One of the tellers or a bank service representative accept your cash and prepare a check payable to this agency.

Sincerely,

ANSWERS TO FRAME 6

The corrected letter appears on the next page.

Body of Letter:

Dear Mr. Jakes:

Western Department Stores, Inc., <u>have</u> just submitted your account to this
_{has}
agency for collection. As a collection advisor, I am responsibile for reviewing your credit record with Western to assure that it is accurate and to collect the balance of your overdue account.

You established your account with Western on April 30 of this year, and the records submitted to us by Western <u>shows</u> that in May and June you paid the minimum
_{show}
amount required under the financial agreement: $20. In July you charged additional merchandise, amounting to $210.40, bringing your balance to $350.50. Your payment record indicates that Western sent you a statement in July and another in August, as well as three collection letters during the two months.

I, as well as the credit manager at Western, <u>has</u> tried to call you at home and
_{have}
also at Union Industries, which you listed as your place of employment. The personnel director at Union Industries <u>inform</u> me that you were discharged on July 5. The
_{informs}
telephone company service representative said that your telephone <u>were</u> disconnected
_{was}
on June 30 because you had not paid for service in May and June.

Mr. Jakes, neither Western Department Stores, Inc., nor this agency <u>want</u> to place
_{wants}
a hardship on you; however, this delinquent debt must be paid. I have been authorized to offer you two payment plans, and I request that you select one of these plans as the basis on which to pay your overdue account:

(1)   Mail a certified check for $350.50 to this agency no later than September 30.

(2)   Mail a certified check for $175 and the enclosed 30-day promissory note for
       $175.50 to this agency no later than September 30.

If neither of these plans <u>are</u> satisfactory, please call me within five days of
_{is}
receiving this letter, and I shall discuss the problem with you. Should you fail to respond to this letter or to select one of the plans, you will receive a letter giving you notice that I shall discuss with your new employer the feasibility of garnisheeing your wages.

For your convenience, two business reply envelopes and a duplicate promissory
note <u>is</u> enclosed. Should you choose Plan 2, the copy of the note will be your
_{are}
record of this transaction.

By the way, Mr. Jakes, for a nominal charge you may obtain a certified check at any bank. One of the tellers or a bank service representative <u>accept</u> your cash
_{accepts}
and <u>prepare</u> a check payable to this agency.
_{prepares}

Sincerely,

Lesson 17
Verbs: Voice and Principal Parts

Pretest

Pretest Part I
The Voice of a Verb

Directions

Rewrite the following sentences, changing the voice of each from active to passive, or from passive to active. Add words where necessary to make the sentence meaningful and businesslike.

Example

I asked Howard to deliver the letter.
Passive: Howard was asked by me to deliver the letter.

1. The Dudley Company shipped your order on June 1.

   _____

2. This merchandise has been inspected by the Quality Control Department.

   _____

   _____

Pretest Part II
Transitive and Intransitive Verbs

Directions

1. Place a check in the proper column to show whether the verb is used in a transitive or intransitive form.
2. Underscore the direct object if one exists.

Example	Transitive	Intransitive
Dr. Dowson dismissed the <u>class</u> early today.	X	_____
1. Green Discount Appliance Stores, Inc., consists of four branch grocery stores in a metropolitan area.	_____	_____
2. The Green brothers established the first store in 1960.	_____	_____

259

3. Each store is in a suburb of the metropolitan area.   _____ _____
4. Green Discount Appliance Stores, Inc., is a retailing organization.   _____ _____
5. The appliances sold in the stores are purchased from various manufacturers.   _____ _____
6. Some of these manufacturers sell merchandise direct from the plant.   _____ _____
7. Some damaged merchandise can be sold at a discount.   _____ _____
8. All appliances should be carefully inspected by the quality control department of the manufacturing firm.   _____ _____
9. Bill Green is the president of Green Discount Appliance Stores, Inc.   _____ _____
10. Nathaniel Green, their father, gave Bill and his brother some financial assistance. _____ _____
11. The brothers located their first store on Roslyn Street.   _____ _____
12. Each store has four departments: large appliances, small appliances, appliance parts, and appliance repair.   _____ _____
13. All but one store in the corporation seems to be prospering.   _____ _____
14. The brothers have talked about opening a fifth store in a town 60 miles away.   _____ _____
15. The general offices of this corporation are located in the Fairway Plaza Building.   _____ _____
16. The personnel director hires many part-time employees.   _____ _____
17. Three stores have been robbed during the past year.   _____ _____
18. The corporation is installing security devices at each of the stores.   _____ _____

Pretest Part III
Principal Parts

Directions

Choose the correct form of the verb in parentheses and write it in the blank provided.

1. Linda now (teach) at one of the junior high schools in Detroit.   _____
2. The auditor had (report) the discrepancy to the company president before the Internal Revenue Service recognized it.   _____
3. Herbert has (do) his part of the work without complaining.   _____
4. The new microfilm readers (cost) 20 percent more than we anticipated.   _____
5. The Potter Company currently (plan) to construct a plant in Milwaukee.   _____
6. The motorcycle has been (ride) only 219 miles.   _____
7. When we bought the property, we (pay) $500 to the lawyer for a clear title.   _____
8. Ms. Elmwood was (strike) with paralysis after the accident.   _____
9. The Pure Lite Company has (hang) the new fixtures in the lobby.   _____
10. Mark had (be) on the road for a week before he reported the loss of his credit card. _____

Lesson 17
Verbs: Voice and Principal Parts

To present the relationship of a verb to its subject or its object, as well as the principal parts a verb may take, we need to use several grammatical terms. You will not find the terms difficult to understand because you have been introduced to linking (verbs of being), transitive, and intransitive verbs previously; and all terms are explained and illustrated.

Most verbs form their principal parts by the addition of a -d or -ed. Others form their principal parts in an irregular manner. For this latter group, even people with many years' experience in writing occasionally need to refer to the dictionary to verify that they have selected the proper form. You, too, are likely to find that the dictionary is a valuable reference in determining the correct form of these verbs.

Frame 1   A Verb in Relation to a Subject or an Object

Review

A sentence consists of a group of grammatically related words containing a subject and a verb and expressing a complete thought. A verb may or may not have an object.

A Verb in Relation to Its Subject: Voice

Explanation

The term *voice* is used to show the relationship between a verb and its subject. A verb is used in *active voice* when the subject performs the action, and it is in *passive voice* when the subject receives the action.

Example

1. *Active Voice:* used more frequently in business writing than passive voice. Sentences in active voice are more concise and direct than those in passive voice.

   Mrs. Flory purchased her groceries at the discount grocery
        S   V   O
   store.

   The subject, Mrs. Flory, is performing the action.

2. *Passive Voice:* used when the writer wishes to vary the style of writing, or desires to state a negative thought without angering or embarrassing the reader.

   The groceries were purchased at the discount grocery store by
      S   V
   Mrs. Flory.

   Active   You computed the discounts incorrectly.
                S   V   O
   Passive   The discounts were computed incorrectly.
                   S   V

3. Converting Active Voice to Passive Voice:
   a. A verb in the active voice always has an object.
   b. A verb in the passive voice never has an object.
   c. A verb in the passive voice is always preceded by one of these words: *is, am, was, were, be, been, are.*
   d. The direct object in active voice becomes the subject in passive voice.

   Active   Jay wrote the memo about absenteeism.
               S   V   O
   Passive   The memo about absenteeism was written by Jay.
                 S   V

Active   The <u>company</u> <u>has sold</u> its preferred <u>stock</u>.
                S   V   O

Passive   The preferred <u>stock</u> <u>has been sold</u> by the company.
                         S   V

Active   <u>Mimi</u> <u>had written</u> the weekly <u>report</u> by noon.
             S   V   O

Passive   By noon the weekly <u>report</u> <u>had been written</u> by Mimi.
                                 S   V

Active   <u>You</u> <u>transcribed</u> the wrong <u>letter</u>.
            S   V   O

Passive   The wrong <u>letter</u> <u>was transcribed</u>.
                  S   V

Exercise

Rewrite the following sentences, changing the voice from active to passive, or from passive to active. Where necessary, add the appropriate words to make the sentence meaningful and businesslike.

Example

The 8:30 bus is taken by Mary every morning.
Active: Mary takes the 8:30 bus every morning.

1. The report was sent to the home office by the branch manager.

    _____

2. Mary was complimented by her supervisor for her outstanding performance.

    _____

    _____

3. This property was sold by the Houseman Agency.

    _____

4. The transportation company was directed by the government commission to change its routes.

    _____

    _____

5. You sent two books instead of one to each respondent.

    _____

ANSWERS TO FRAME 1

1. Active: The branch manager sent the report to the home office.
2. Active: The supervisor complimented Mary for her outstanding performance.
3. Active: The Houseman Agency sold this property.
4. Active: The government commission directed the transportation company to change its routes.
5. Passive: Two books instead of one were sent to each respondent.

Frame 2   A Verb in Relation to a Subject or Object

Verbs can be classified as transitive and intransitive, depending primarily upon whether they can be used with objects.

Transitive Verbs

Explanation

A *transitive verb* is a verb of action that can be used in either active or passive voice. It requires a noun or pronoun to complete its meaning.

Example

1. A transitive verb is a verb of action: <u>type</u>
2. It can be used in active or passive voice.
   Active: The verb needs a noun or pronoun (an object) to complete its meaning:
   <u>Phyllis</u> <u>typed</u> the <u>manuscript</u>.
     S   V   O
   Passive: The direct object in active voice becomes the subject; remember that the verb in passive voice will always be in a phrase and will include a verb of being *(is, am, was, were, be, been, are)*: The <u>manuscript</u> <u>was typed</u>
                                    S   V
   by Phyllis.
3. In the dictionary, transitive verbs are identified by *vt* (verb transitive). *Webster's New Collegiate Dictionary* shows this label* after the pronunciation section:

> **ver·i·fy** \'ver-ə-ˌfī\ *vt* **-fied; -fy·ing** [ME *verifien,* fr. MF *verifier,* fr. ML *verificare,* fr. L *verus* true — more at VERY] **1 :** to confirm or substantiate in law by oath **2 :** to establish the truth, accuracy, or reality of *syn* see CONFIRM — **ver·i·fi·er** \-ˌfī(-ə)r\ *n*

Verify is a transitive verb.

Active   The <u>auditor</u> <u>can verify</u> the <u>accuracy</u> of your statement.
                  S   V   O
Passive   The <u>accuracy</u> of your statement <u>can be verified</u> by the auditor.
                   S   V

Intransitive Verbs: Action Verbs

Explanation

An *intransitive verb* does not require a noun or pronoun to complete its meaning; it may or may not be followed by such modifiers as prepositional phrases, adjectives, or adverbs. This verb can be used only in the active voice and cannot be used with an object.

Example

1. An intransitive verb can be used only in the active voice.

   <u>I</u> <u>walked</u> from the office to the shopping center.
   S   V

   <u>You</u> <u>may talk</u> with me after class.
    S   V

2. *Webster's New Collegiate Dictionary* shows that *die** is an intransitive verb *(vi)*:

   He <u>died</u> of malnutrition despite his great wealth.

> **¹die** \'dī\ *vi* **died; dy·ing** \'dī-iŋ\ [ME *dien,* fr. or akin to ON *deyja* to die; akin to OHG *touwen* to die, OIr *duine* human being] **1 :** to pass from physical life : EXPIRE **2 :** to pass out of existence : CEASE <their anger *died* at these words> **3 a :** to suffer or face the pains of death **b :** SINK, LANGUISH <*dying* from fatigue> **c :** to long keenly or desperately <*dying* to go> **4 :** to cease to be subject <let them ~ to sin> **5 a :** to pass into an inferior state or situation <they have developed competence which we . . . must utilize lest it wither and ~ —Ruth G. Strickland> **b :** STOP <the motor *died*>

*By permission. From *Webster's New Collegiate Dictionary* ©1977 by G. & C. Merriam Co., Publishers of the Merriam-Webster Dictionaries.

Intransitive Verbs: Linking Verbs

Explanation

A *linking verb* is a verb of being (*is, am, was, were, be, been, are*); a verb of the senses (*feels, tastes, looks, smells*); or a word expressing a condition (*seem, become, appear*). A linking verb is never used with an object; instead, it is followed by the nominative form of a noun or pronoun (subjective complement) or by an adjective (predicate adjective).

Example

1. Linking verb followed by a subjective complement:

   > Harry <u>is</u> the new office manager. (The linking verb is followed by <u>office manager</u>, a subjective complement.)

   > The person who wrote the check <u>is</u> she. (The linking verb is followed by <u>she</u>, a pronoun in the nominative case.)

2. Linking verb followed by an adjective:

   > The new building <u>is</u> the tallest in the city. (The linking verb is followed by <u>tallest</u>, an adjective describing <u>building</u>.)

   > The chocolate cake <u>tastes</u> good. (The linking verb is followed by <u>good</u>, an adjective describing <u>cake</u>.)

   > The mountains <u>appear</u> purple at dusk. (The linking verb is followed by <u>purple</u>, an adjective describing <u>mountains</u>).

Transitive and Intransitive Verbs

Explanation

Many verbs are used in both the transitive and intransitive form, but usually one or the other is more common.

Example

Webster's New Collegiate Dictionary shows the more common usage first.* Notice that the *vt* meanings follow the inflected forms (in bold print), and the *vi* meanings are shown next.

> **or·ga·nize** \'òr-gə-ˌnīz\ *vb* **-nized; -niz·ing** *vt* **1** : to cause to develop an organic structure **2** : to arrange or form into a coherent unity or functioning whole : INTEGRATE <trying to ~ her thoughts> **3 a** : to set up an administrative structure for **b** : to persuade to associate in an organization; *esp* : UNIONIZE **4** : to arrange by systematic planning and united effort <*organized* a field trip> ~ *vi* **1** : to undergo physical or organic organization **2** : to arrange elements into a whole of interdependent parts **3** : to form an organization; *specif* : to form or persuade workers to join a union *syn* see ORDER *ant* disorganize — **or·gan·iz·able** \-ˌnī-zə-bəl\ *adj*

Transitive

Active   The police department organized a community patrol system.
Passive   A community patrol system was organized by the police department.

---

*By permission. From *Webster's New Collegiate Dictionary* ©1977 by G. & C. Merriam Co., Publishers of the Merriam-Webster Dictionaries.

Intransitive

The management's attitude changed after the employees organized.

Exercise

1. Place a mark in the proper column to show whether the verb is used in a transitive or intransitive form.
2. Underscore the direct object if one exists.

Example	*Transitive*	*Intransitive*
Ralph completed his <u>tour</u> in the service.	X	

	Transitive	*Intransitive*
1. Please list your assets in the space provided.		
2. The police department is expecting more applicants.		
3. During his last television appearance, the president looked tired.		
4. She receives $1,500 for each performance.		
5. The applicant most likely to be selected is she.		
6. The late checks have been a constant source of irritation to me.		
7. Bert sold his quota before the end of the month.		
8. The students are now selecting their report topics.		
9. The financial analysis will be completed by the end of the month.		
10. The cost of living in Washington exceeds that in New York.		

ANSWERS TO FRAME 2

	Object	*Transitive*	*Intransitive*
1.	<u>assets</u>	X	
2.	<u>applicants</u>	X	
3.			X
4.	<u>$1,500</u>	X	
5.			X
6.			X
7.	<u>quota</u>	X	
8.	<u>topics</u>	X	
9.	(passive)	X	
10.	<u>that</u>	X	

Frame 3   *Principal Parts of a Verb*

All verbs have three principal parts:

1. *Present tense,* representing an action occurring in the present (I *talk*);
2. *Past tense,* representing an action started and finished in the past (I *talked*); and
3. A *past participle,* representing an action that has been completed; this form is always used with a helping verb (I *have talked*).

Some verbs form their three principal parts in a regular manner (by the addition of
-d or *-ed*) and are called *regular* verbs. Others, called *irregular* verbs, form their three
principal parts in a variety of ways.

The editors of dictionaries differ in their presentation of the inflected forms (principal parts) of verbs. In *Webster's New Collegiate Dictionary,* the inflections are shown if
a change in spelling occurs or if the principal parts are formed in an uncommon
manner.

Regular Verbs

Explanation

A *regular verb* forms the past tense and past participle by the addition of a *-d* or
-ed. Most verbs are regular and pose no problem to the user. The third principal part
requires an auxiliary (helping) verb (has, have, and so on).

1. Examples of the principal parts of some regular verbs:

Present	*Past*	*Past Participle*
account	accounted	accounted
benefit	benefited	benefited
credit	credited	credited
capture	captured	captured
donate	donated	donated

2. Dictionary Presentation of Regular Verbs: The third principal part is not
    shown if it is spelled the same as the second principal part. Note these examples
    previously shown:
    a. *Verify*: An inflection is shown because the spelling changes from the first to
        the second principal part. The third principal part is not shown because it
        is the same as the second. The spelling of the progressive tense (*-fying*) is
        usually shown. This tense represents a continuing action.
    b. *Die* and *organize*: Both show the second principal part and the progressive
        tense. The third principal part is not shown because it is the same as the
        second.
    c. *Credit*: The principal parts and progressive tense are not shown because the
        second and third principal parts are formed by the addition of *-ed,* and
        spelling does not change.*

> ²**credit** *vt* [partly fr. ¹*credit;* partly fr. L *creditus,* pp.] **1 :** to supply
> goods on credit to **2 :** to trust in the truth of : BELIEVE **3** *archaic*
> : to bring credit or honor upon **4 :** to enter upon the credit side
> of an account **5 a :** to consider usu. favorably as the source,
> agent, or performer of an action or the possessor of a trait <∼ *s* him
> with an excellent sense of humor> **b :** to attribute to some person
> <they ∼ the invention to him> *syn* see ASCRIBE

3. Usage: *Credit*
    a. Present tense, first principal part: I <u>credit</u> you with discovering the error.
    b. Past tense, second principal part: You <u>credited</u> my account when I re-
        turned the merchandise.
    c. Past participle, third principal part: The Telcon Company <u>has credited</u>
        your account for the merchandise you returned.

Exercise

Write the correct form of the verb in parentheses in the blank provided. Consult your
dictionary, if necessary.

1. We have (donate) money and food to the Christmas fund.   _____
2. This product line has (account) for 60 percent of the sales.   _____

*By permission. From *Webster's New Collegiate Dictionary* ©1977 by G. & C. Merriam Co., Publishers of the Merriam-Webster Dictionaries.

3. Before coming here, he (work) in Cincinnati.
4. Jim (pass) five parts of the CPA examination.
5. Ms. Hans (analyze) the report thoroughly.

ANSWERS TO FRAME 3
1. donated 2. accounted 3. worked 4. passed 5. analyzed

Frame 4   Principal Parts of a Verb

Irregular Verbs

Explanation

A few verbs form their principal parts by changes in vowels or endings; some become different words, and others remain the same.

An *irregular verb* forms its past tense and past participle by some method other than the addition of *-d* or *-ed*. You can learn the principal parts of the words you use frequently by checking them in the dictionary and making those words a part of your vocabulary.

Example

1. Some examples of irregular verbs:

Present	*Past*	*Past Participle*
be (is, am, are)	was (were)	been
become	became	become
begin	began	begun
break	broke	broken
buy	bought	bought
choose	chose	chosen
cost	cost	cost
deal	dealt	dealt
do	did	done
draw	drew	drawn
eat	ate	eaten
get	got	gotten
give	gave	given
go	went	gone
lend	lent	lent
lose	lost	lost
see	saw	seen
send	sent	sent
teach	taught	taught
write	wrote	written

2. Dictionary Presentation of Irregular Verbs: The three principal parts and the progressive tense are shown. Most desk dictionaries also show the form used with a third person singular noun or pronoun.*

¹do \(')dü, də(-w)\ *vb* did \(')did, dəd\; done \'dən\; do·ing \'dü-iŋ\; does \(')dəz\ [ME *don,* fr. OE *dōn;* akin to OHG *tuon* to do, L *-dere* to put, *facere* to make, do, Gk *tithenai* to place, set] *vt* 1: to bring to pass : carry out 2: PUT — used chiefly in *do to death* 3 a : PERFORM, EXECUTE <~ some work> <*did* his

*By permission. From *Webster's New Collegiate Dictionary* ©1977 by G. & C. Merriam Co., Publishers of the Merriam-Webster Dictionaries.

3. Usage: *do* (*vt*—most common usage)
   Present: I <u>do</u> the report regularly.
   Past: I <u>did</u> the report last month.
   Past Participle: I <u>have done</u> the report many times.

Exercise

In the following sentences, choose the correct form of the verb in parentheses and write it in the blank provided.

1. Claus has (write) the audit report. _____
2. Last semester (begin) on September 2. _____
3. Melissa has (teach) in a government school for six years. _____
4. I have (take) the oral examination to defend my thesis. _____
5. Yesterday the committee (choose) its new chairperson. _____
6. The union has (strike) this textile mill three times in the past two years. _____
7. Sam (withdraw) all the money from his savings account. _____
8. Ms. Osborne (quit) after the supervisor reprimanded her. _____
9. The company (pay) the consultant $30,000 for his past services. _____
10. The mayor (freeze) the rents in Yorktown. _____

ANSWERS TO FRAME 4

1. written
2. began
3. taught
4. taken
5. chose
6. struck
7. withdrew
8. quit
9. paid
10. froze

Frame 5 Business Vocabulary: Channel of Distribution

Explanation

Products find their way from the manufacturer to the retailer through the *channel of distribution* the manufacturer has selected. A retailer may purchase from the manufacturer direct or from a wholesaler. Other channels exist as well, all with the goal of moving a product to its destination for sale to the consumer.

Terms

Manufacturer—the person or company that makes a product (from soap to automobiles) with the use of manual or machine labor.
Retailer—the person who is the last link in the channel of distribution; this person sells to the consumers.
Consumer—a member of the buying public who purchases manufactured goods for personal use.
Wholesaler—a person or organization that purchases from the manufacturer and sells to the retailer. However, some manufacturers wholesale their own products, and some wholesalers handle a variety of products.
Distribution center—the warehouse or storage facility for merchandise that has been shipped from the manufacturer to the retailer—usually a chain of stores. From this point, it is distributed to the chain's branch stores.

Exercise

Complete each sentence with the proper term from the preceding vocabulary list.

1. Manufactured goods are moved from the manufacturer to the retailer through

   the _____ selected by the manufacturer.

2. The person or organization that sells goods to the public is the

_____.

3. A member of the buying public is a _____.

4. A manufacturer may or may not operate its own outlet for quantity purchase or lots. In either case, the business person from whom quantity lot purchases (and sometimes lesser ones) are made is called a _____.

5. Some very large chain stores or discount stores maintain locations where they store a variety of products that are sent to the branch stores as needed. These locations are called _____.

ANSWERS TO FRAME 5

1. channel of distribution
2. retailer
3. consumer
4. wholesaler
5. distribution centers

Frame 6   *Applying Your Knowledge*

Directions

Underscore the errors in the following letter. Then write the correction in the space below each sentence.

CASE

Bill and Joe Green own Green Discount Appliances, Inc., consisting of four appliance stores in a metropolitan area. They buy their appliances direct from the manufacturer, place some in their showrooms, and store the remainder in a large warehouse. As their warehouse manager, you have discovered that a shipment of 150 refrigerators from the Frio Company includes 80 that are damaged. After careful inspection of the refrigerators, you compose this letter for the approval of Bill Green, the president. (10 errors)

Body of Letter:

Our order No. 157920 for 150 Frio refrigerators in assorted models and colors (as shown on the attached invoice) was received on May 26. Each refrigerator has been uncrated, and 80 of the 150 were found to be damaged.

The receiving crew begun uncrating this order immediately after its arrival. None of the crates were damaged, either in transit or by the receiving crew. However, the majority of the refrigerators have obvious exterior or interior defects, which our crew seen when they done the uncrating.

Here is a list of the defects:

1. The doors on 26 Model B refrigerators have been springed and do not close.

2. Fourteen Model 10A refrigerators do not have motors! The housing and hose are in place, but the assemblers did not sit the motor into the housing.

3. Ten Model 4B refrigerators have frozen food compartments without doors; on these same refrigerators, the freezer control unit was builded into the spot where the temperature control should have been installed.

4. On 20 Model B8 refrigerators the shelves have been hanged 4 inches apart.

5. Ten white refrigerators (Model G6) come with avocado green doors.

You have never shipped us an order that had more than 5 percent defective items. Is it possible that the refrigerators in this shipment could have been chose from rejects that were destined for salvage? Ninety of these refrigerators were to have been delivered to our four stores for a sale beginning on June 4, and the remainder were to be delivered as needed during the week of the sale.

I have recommended to the credit manager that our June 1 order be stopt until we are assured of replacements for these 80 refrigerators. In addition, the freight charges should be prorated to cover only the 70 salable refrigerators.

Please respond by letter, explaining the circumstances surrounding the defects in this order and telling us how you propose to handle the merchandise and freight costs.

ANSWERS TO FRAME 6

Our order No. 157920 for 150 Frio refrigerators in assorted models and colors (as shown on the attached invoice) was received on May 26. Each refrigerator has been uncrated, and 80 of the 150 were found to be damaged.

The receiving crew begun uncrating this order immediately after its arrival.
began

None of the crates were damaged, either in transit or by the receiving crew.

However, the majority of the refrigerators have obvious exterior or interior defects,

which our crew seen when they done the uncrating.
saw   did

Here is a list of the defects:

1. The doors on 26 Model B refrigerators have been springed and do not close.
sprung

2. Fourteen Model 10A refrigerators do not have motors! The housing and hose are in place, but the assemblers did not sit the motor into the housing.
set

3. Ten Model 4B refrigerators have frozen food compartments without doors; on these same refrigerators, the freezer control unit was <u>builded</u> into the spot
built
where the temperature control should have been installed.

4. On 20 Model B8 refrigerators the shelves have been <u>hanged</u> 4 inches apart.
hung

5. Ten white refrigerators (Model G6) <u>come</u> with avocado green doors.
came

You have never shipped us an order that had more than 5 percent defective items. Is it possible that the refrigerators in this shipment could have been <u>chose</u> from
chosen
rejects that were destined for salvage? Ninety of these refrigerators were to have been delivered to our four stores for a sale beginning on June 4, and the remainder were to be delivered as needed during the week of the sale.

I have recommended to the credit manager that our June 1 order be <u>stopt</u> until
stopped
we are assured of replacements for these 80 refrigerators. In addition, the freight charges should be prorated to cover only the 70 salable refrigerators.

Please respond by letter, explaining the circumstances surrounding the defects in this order and telling us how you propose to handle the merchandise and freight costs.

Lesson 18
Verbs: Tenses

Pretest

Pretest Part I
Primary Tense

Directions

From the verb in parentheses in each of the following sentences, select the proper form of the primary tense required by the designation at the left. Use only active voice.

Example

Simple: Joe (work) for the Atlas Company last year.   worked

1. Simple: The clerk (insult) the customer yesterday.   _____
2. Progressive: I (evaluate) his grades when he came in.   _____
3. Emphatic: He (work) on the night shift.   _____
4. Simple: The safety director (issue) an announcement about the accident tomorrow.   _____
5. Simple: The Kramer Company (purchase) a microfilm processor two years ago. _____
6. Progressive: The customers (enter) the store as soon as the doorman unlocks the door.   _____
7. Simple: The doctor (discharge) the patient this morning.   _____
8. Simple: The United States Air Force (test) the experimental helicopter next month.   _____
9. Progressive: The copy center (reproduce) our syllabus again next year. _____
10. Simple: The administrative assistants usually (check) all the word processing center's output.   _____

Pretest Part II
Perfect Tense

Directions

Fill in the blank at the right of each sentence with the perfect form of the verb in parentheses that is required by the designation at the left. Use only active voice.

Example

Simple: Joe (work) for the Atlas Company at least ten years.   has worked

1. Simple: Before the loan came due, he (pay) it and had borrowed additional money.   _____
2. Simple: The publishing company (establish) its production department in California before the summer.   _____

3. Simple: Aggie Benson (win) the Most Valuable Employee Award again this year. _____
4. Simple: I (send) my suggestion before you had. _____
5. Simple: The sales representative (visit) your campus before the end of this semester. _____
6. Simple: The labor mediator (fly) here before next month to try for a settlement. _____
7. Progressive: The agency head (misappropriate) funds for two years before he was caught. _____
8. Progressive: Ms. Perkins (represent) this department at the weekly staff meetings. _____
9. Simple: Before the trial next month, he (analyze) the handwriting. _____
10. Simple: The previous foreman (assign) Bert to the Quality Control Department before the new foreman took over. _____

Lesson 18
Verbs: Tenses

A *verb* shows an action or existence and when it occurs. The time expressed by a verb or verb phrase is called *tense*. Two main verb tenses exist: the primary tense and the perfect tense. Although you have used these tenses all your life, you may not have thought of the specific application of each tense. In this lesson, you will be shown how to recognize each tense and will be given illustrations of its usage.

Frame 1   Primary Tenses

The *primary tense* consists of the present, past, and future tenses.

Present Tense

Explanation

Refer to Chart 1 and notice the location and characteristics of each of the following numbered items.

In the active voice, the *present tense* consists of (1) the simple present, (2) the present progressive, and (3) the present emphatic tenses. In the passive voice, the present tense consists of (4) the simple present and (5) the present progressive tenses.

Example

A. Simple present tense—active and passive [numbers (1) and (4) in Chart 1]: used for two purposes:
1. To make a statement about a fact, a truth, or routine activity that occurs in the present or to express an action that will occur in the future.

> Mr. Simpson <u>departs</u> on the early shuttle tomorrow. (active)

> A physical count of the inventory <u>is made</u> each month. (passive)

> The bank <u>takes</u> possession of the property on which the debtor owes money. (active)

> You <u>are driven</u> to the plane by the hotel courtesy car. (passive)

2. To express an action that was true and continues to be true. This usage is important in all writing, and particularly in business report writing when explaining completed research.

> The tabulation <u>shows</u> that 60 percent of the respondents <u>prefer</u> X brand of soap. (This statement was true two weeks ago when the tabulation was originally made, and it is true today when you are writing your report.)

> The data <u>show</u> that the financial condition of X company <u>is</u> better than that of Y company.

B. Present progressive tense—active and passive voices [numbers (2) and (5) in Chart 1]: used to express an action continuing in the present.

> I <u>am writing</u> the report now. (active)

> He <u>is preparing</u> the analysis. (active)

> You <u>are being given</u> another chance to compete for the job. (passive)

> The grain <u>is being weighed</u> by the elevator workers. (passive)

CHART 1 Present Tense

Principal parts of the verb *take*: Present tense—*take*; Past tense—*took*; Past participle—*taken*

Primary Tense

Active Voice

Person	Singular	Plural
	Simple (1)	

Characteristics:
a. Verb: first principal part: *take*

1	I take	We take
2	You take	You take
3	He/She/It takes	They take

Progressive (2)

Characteristics:
a. Verb: ends in -*ing* (*taking*)
b. Helping verb: first principal part of *be* (i.e., *is, am, are*)

1	I am taking	We are taking
2	You are taking	You are taking
3	He/She/It is taking	They are taking

Emphatic (3)

Characteristics:
a. Verb: first principal part (*take*)
b. Helping verb: first principal part of *do*

1	I do take	We do take
2	You do take	You do take
3	He/She/It does take	They do take

Passive Voice

Person	Singular	Plural
	Simple (4)	

Characteristics:
a. Verb: third principal part: *taken*
b. Helping verb: first principal part of *be* (i.e., *is, am, are*)

1	I am taken	We are taken
2	You are taken	You are taken
3	He/She/It is taken	They are taken

Progressive (5)

Characteristics:
a. Verb: third principal part: *taken*
b. Verb: preceded by *being*
c. Helping verb: first principal part of *be* (i.e., *is, am are*)

1	I am being taken	We are being taken
2	You are being taken	You are being taken
3	He/She/It is being taken	They are being taken

Emphatic

NOT USED IN PASSIVE VOICE

C. Present emphatic tense—active voice [number (3) in Chart 1]: used to emphasize a statement about a fact, truth, or routine activity.

I <u>do take</u> my pills daily.

Mary <u>does believe</u> that her opinion is correct.

Pearl and I <u>do expect</u> to be paid promptly.

Exercise

1. Underscore the verb or verb phrase in each sentence.
2. Use the symbols below to identify the tense of the verb:

    S Simple present   P Present progressive   E Present emphatic

3. Place an A (active) or P (passive) in the Voice column to show the correct voice of the verb.

Example	*Tense*	*Voice*
He <u>works</u> in the suburbs.	S	A

1.	I am working on the project now.		
2.	The immigrant does believe in democracy.		
3.	The course is listed in the class schedule.		
4.	Ms. George is being taken to the hospital.		
5.	The supervisor never asks employees for suggestions.		
6.	The employees in the Production Department are given a percentage increase in pay each year.		
7.	You are being called to the personnel office to discuss this incident.		
8.	The store does accept coupons.		
9.	Mildred is preparing a workshop on this topic.		
10.	Hank supervises nine employees in the Shipping Department.		

ANSWERS TO FRAME 1

1. <u>am working</u>; P; A
2. <u>does believe</u>; E; A
3. <u>is listed</u>; S; P
4. <u>is being taken</u>; P; P
5. <u>asks</u>; S; A
6. <u>are given</u>; S; P
7. <u>are being called</u>; P; P
8. <u>does accept</u>; E; A
9. <u>is preparing</u>; P; A
10. <u>supervises</u>; S; A

Frame 2 Primary Tenses

Past Tense

Explanation

Refer to Chart 2 and notice the location of each of the following numbered items.

In the active voice, the *past tense* consists of (1) simple past, (2) the past progressive, and (3) the past emphatic tenses. In the passive voice, the past tense consists of the (4) simple past and (5) past progressive tenses.

CHART 2 Past Tense

Principal parts of the verb *take*: Present tense—*take*; Past tense—*took*; Past participle—*taken*

Primary Tense

Active Voice

Person	Singular	Plural
	Simple (1)	

Characteristics:
a. Verb: second principal part (*took*)

1	I took	We took
2	You took	You took
3	He, She, It took	They took

	Progressive (2)	

Characteristics:
a. Verb: ends in *-ing* (*taking*)
b. Helping verb: second principal part of *be* (*was, were*)

1	I was taking	We were taking
2	You were taking	You were taking
3	He/She/It was taking	They were taking

	Emphatic (3)	

Characteristics:
a. Verb: first principal part (*take*)
b. Helping verb: second principal part of *do*

1	I did take	We did take
2	You did take	You did take
3	He/She/It did take	They did take

Passive Voice

Person	Singular	Plural
	Simple (4)	

Characteristics:
a. Verb: third principal part (*taken*)
b. Helping verb: second principal part of *be* (*was, were*)

1	I was taken	We were taken
2	You were taken	You were taken
3	He, She, It was taken	They were taken

	Progressive (5)	

Characteristics:
a. Verb: third principal part (*taken*)
b. Verb: preceded by *being*
c. Helping verb: second principal part of be (*was, were*)

1	I was being taken	We were being taken
2	You were being taken	You were being taken
3	He/She/It was being taken	They were being taken

	Emphatic	

NOT USED IN PASSIVE VOICE

Example

A.   Simple past tense—active and passive voices [numbers (1) and (4) in Chart 2]: used to make a statement about a fact, truth or routine activity that occurred in the past.

> He <u>went</u> to college in Nebraska. (active)
>
> The teller <u>exchanged</u> his domestic currency for foreign currency. (active)
>
> You <u>were taken</u> to the airport by the sales representative. (passive)
>
> Four letters <u>were written</u> in class during the semester. (passive)

B.   Past progressive tense—active and passive voices [numbers (2) and (5) in Chart 2]: used to express a continuing action that occurred in the past.

> She <u>was attending</u> summer session last year. (active)
>
> This section <u>was estimating</u> costs at an unrealistically low level. (active)
>
> The data <u>were being fed</u> into the computer during the night. (passive)
>
> We <u>were being affected</u> by the high pollution count in the area. (passive)

C.   Past emphatic tense—active voice only [number (3) in Chart 2]: used to emphasize a past action.

> I <u>did take</u> the graduate qualifying examination before.
>
> The department <u>did requisition</u> the additional furniture.
>
> We <u>did place</u> your name on the list for apartment referrals.

Exercise

1.   Underscore the verb or verb phrase in each sentence.
2.   Use these symbols below to identify the tense of the verb:

   SP   Simple past   PP   Past progressive   PE   Past emphatic

3.   Place an A (active) or P (passive) in the Voice column to show the correct voice of the verb.

Example	*Tense*	*Voice*
I <u>took</u> the test yesterday.	SP	A
1. After the meeting, Karen went to her office.		
2. Jim was being harassed by the collection agency.		
3. The patrol officer did issue a ticket to the negligent driver.		
4. We were expecting a raise this year.		
5. This department was given a commendation.		

	Tense	Voice
6. Homer was being reprimanded for his carelessness.	_____	_____
7. The salesperson made a high commission.	_____	_____
8. The employees donated one day's pay to the community fund.	_____	_____
9. The television commentator was being sued for libel.	_____	_____
10. He did make a derogatory statement about the judge.	_____	_____

ANSWERS TO FRAME 2

1. went; SP; A
2. was being harassed; PP; P
3. did issue; PE; A
4. were expecting; PP; A
5. was given; SP; P
6. was being reprimanded; PP; P
7. made; SP; A
8. donated; SP; A
9. was being sued; PP; P
10. did make; PE; A

Frame 3   Primary Tenses

Future Tense

Explanation

Refer to Chart 3 and notice the location and characteristics of each of the following numbered items.

In the active voice, the *future tense* consists of (1) the simple future and (2) the future progressive tenses. In the passive voice, the future tense consists only of (3) the simple future tense.

In formal writing, *shall* is used with the first person singular and plural; and in informal writing, *will* is used with first person singular and plural. Truthfully, many people do use *will* with all three persons to express future tense. In this book *shall* is used; however, your instructor can make the decision whether to require *shall* or *will* with first person singular and plural. See Lesson 22 for information regarding the use of *shall* and *will* to express determination, a requirement, or an obligation.

Example

A. Simple future tense—active and passive voices [numbers (1) and (3) in Chart 3]: used to express an action or condition that will occur.

> I shall take the deposit to the bank. (active)
>
> Julia will be brought to the office in the car pool. (passive)
>
> We shall order pictures of each faculty member. (active)
>
> The designs will be constructed by Josephine's Art Design Company. (passive)

B. Future progressive tense—active voice only [number 2 in Chart 3]: used to show that an action or condition will begin and continue in the future.

> I shall be taking the train to Los Angeles.
>
> She will be soliciting orders for the fall style lines.
>
> The technicians will be taking X-rays of his leg tomorrow.

CHART 3 Future Tense

Principal parts of the verb *take*: Present tense—*take*; Past tense—*took*; Past participle—*taken*

Primary Tense

Active Voice

Person	Simple (1)	
	Singular	Plural
1	I shall take	We shall take
2	You will take	You will take
3	He/She/It will take	They will take

Characteristics:
a. Verb: first principal part (*take*)
b. Helping verbs: (1) *shall*; (2) and (3) *will*

Person	Progressive (2)	
	Singular	Plural
1	I shall be taking	We shall be taking
2	You will be taking	You will be taking
3	He/She/It will be taking	They will be taking

Characteristics:
a. Verb: ends in -*ing* (*taking*)
b. Verb: preceded by first principal part of *be*
c. Helping verbs: (1) *shall*; (2) and (3) *will*

Passive Voice

Person	Simple (3)	
	Singular	Plural
1	I shall be taken	We shall be taken
2	You will be taken	You will be taken
3	He/She/It will be taken	They will be taken

Characteristics:
a. Verb: third principal part (*taken*)
b. Verb: preceded by first principal part of *be*
c. Helping verbs: (1) *shall*; (2) and (3) *will*

Progressive

NOT USED IN PASSIVE VOICE

Exercise

1. Underscore the verb or verb phrase in each sentence.
2. Use the symbols below to identify the tense of the verb:

   SF   Simple future   FP   Future progressive

3. Place an A (active) or P (passive) in the Voice column to show the correct voice of the verb.

Example	*Tense*	*Voice*
You <u>will be scheduling</u> each phase of the production activity.	FP	A

	Tense	*Voice*
1. I shall be spending over a hundred dollars each month for household assistance.		
2. The government will be taking the census in two years.		
3. The property will be appraised by the assessor.		
4. Helen will take her oral examination about her thesis tomorrow.		
5. This plane will be flown on the trans-Atlantic route.		
6. You will need additional help during the tax season.		
7. The auditors will be going to the Parton Company in May.		
8. We will close our books at the end of the fiscal year.		
9. The lots in this subdivision will be sold in one-acre parcels.		
10. We shall be arriving in Des Moines at 8:45 Tuesday night.		

ANSWERS TO FRAME 3

1. <u>shall be spending</u>; FP; A
2. <u>will be taking</u>; FP; A
3. <u>will be appraised</u>; SF; P
4. <u>will take</u>; SF; A
5. <u>will be flown</u>; SF; P
6. <u>will need</u>; SF; A
7. <u>will be going</u>; FP; A
8. <u>will close</u>; SF; A
9. <u>will be sold</u>; SF; P
10. <u>shall be arriving</u>; FP; A

Frame 4   Primary Tenses

Selecting the Proper Primary Tense

Explanation

This frame is included so that you can apply what you have learned about the primary tense.

Exercise

From the verb shown within parentheses in each of the following sentences, select the proper form of the primary tense required by the designation at the left. Use only the active voice.

Example

Progressive: Mary (take) accounting this semester.   is taking

1. Progressive: Allan (plan) his schedule now.   _____
2. Simple: The clerk (overcharge) the customer yesterday.   _____
3. Simple: Most of the employees (live) in the Piedmont area now.   _____
4. Simple: I (appraise) your property within the next week.   _____
5. Progressive: The troupe (appear) here next fall.   _____
6. Emphatic: I (call) the bank about the error.   _____
7. Simple: When you (select) the format for the letterhead, we (print) it for you. _____
                                                                      _____
8. Simple: The clerk (sell) me the wrong paper.   _____
9. Progressive: I (prepare) the copy when he called.   _____
10. Simple: The technicians (repair) the computer tomorrow.   _____

ANSWERS TO FRAME 4

1. is planning   5. will be appearing   8. sold
2. overcharged   6. did call   9. was preparing
3. live   7. select, will print   10. will repair
4. shall [will] appraise

Frame 5   Perfect Tenses

Present Perfect Tense

Explanation

Refer to Chart 4 and notice the location and characteristics of each of the following numbered items.

In the active voice, the *present perfect tense* consists of (1) the simple perfect and (2) the perfect progressive tense. The passive voice includes only (3) the simple perfect tense.

Example

A. Simple present perfect tense—active and passive voices [numbers (1) and (3) in Chart 4]: used to express an action that has been completed by the present time.

> I have finished analyzing the credit reports. (active)
>
> I have taken over his responsibilities. (active)
>
> Precautions have been used to prevent pilfering. (passive)
>
> The trailer has been moved to the construction site. (passive)

B. Present perfect progressive tense—active voice only [number (2) in Chart 4]: used to express an action or condition that was begun in the past and is continuing in the present time; and to express an action that is occurring at the same time as another action.

> I have been taking my vacation in July.
>
> The trainees have been selecting their assignments.
>
> You have been acting as department head for six months.

CHART 4 Present Perfect Tense

Principal parts of the verb *take*: Present tense—*take*; Past tense—*took*; Past participle—*taken*

Perfect Tense

Active Voice

Person	Singular	Plural
	Simple (1)	

Characteristics:
a. Verb: third principal part (*taken*)
b. Verb: preceded by first principal part of *have*

Person	Singular	Plural
1	I have taken	We have taken
2	You have taken	You have taken
3	He/She/It has taken	They have taken

Progressive (2)

Characteristics:
a. Verb: ends in *-ing* (*taking*)
b. Verb: preceded by third principal part of *be* (*been*)
c. Helping verb: first principal part of *have*

Person	Singular	Plural
1	I have been taking	We have been taking
2	You have been taking	You have been taking
3	He/She/It has been taking	They have been taking

Passive Voice

Person	Singular	Plural
	Simple (3)	

Characteristics:
a. Verb: third principal part (*taken*)
b. Verb: preceded by third principal part of *be* (*been*)
c. Helping verb: preceded by first principal part of *have*

Person	Singular	Plural
1	I have been taken	We have been taken
2	You have been taken	You have been taken
3	He/She/It has been taken	They have been taken

Progressive

NOT USED IN PASSIVE VOICE

Barney <u>has been reviewing</u> the accounts.

While I <u>have been typing</u> the letters, he <u>has been reading</u> the mail.

Exercise

1. Underscore the verb or verb phrase in each sentence.
2. Use the symbols below to identify the tense of the verb:

    SPP   Simple present perfect   PPP   Present perfect progressive

3. Place an A (active) or P (passive) in the Voice column to show the correct voice of the verb.

Example	*Tense*	*Voice*
I have been taking my vacation in July.	PPP	A

		Tense	*Voice*
1.	Elvis has worked in New York for three years.	_____	_____
2.	The city has been using its surplus money to fund a recreation program.	_____	_____
3.	Judge Pickett has heard five probation cases today.	_____	_____
4.	Mitchell has been identifying handwriting for twenty-five years.	_____	_____
5.	This company has developed a new type of cat litter.	_____	_____
6.	The Barry School of Cosmetology has been operating for ten years.	_____	_____
7.	The dietitian has planned the meals for the next month.	_____	_____
8.	The firm of Simon & Blade has been auditing our books during the past week.	_____	_____
9.	The book has been scheduled for January publication.	_____	_____
10.	Jerry has been informed of his promotion.	_____	_____

ANSWERS TO FRAME 5

1. <u>has worked</u>; SPP; A
2. <u>has been using</u>; PPP; A
3. <u>has heard</u>; SPP; A
4. <u>has been identifying</u>; PPP; A
5. <u>has developed</u>; SPP; A
6. <u>has been operating</u>; PPP; A
7. <u>has planned</u>; SPP; A
8. <u>has been auditing</u>; PPP; A
9. <u>has been scheduled</u>; SPP; P
10. <u>has been informed</u>; SPP; P

Frame 6   Perfect Tenses

Past Perfect Tense

Explanation

Refer to Chart 5 and notice the location of each of the following numbered items.

In the active voice, the *past perfect tense* consists of (1) the simple past perfect and (2) the progressive past perfect tenses. The passive voice includes only (3) the simple past perfect tense.

CHART 5 Past Perfect Tense

Principal parts of the verb *take*: Present tense—*take*; Past tense—*took*; Past participle—*taken*

Perfect Tense

Active Voice

Simple (1)

Person	Singular	Plural
1	I had taken	We had taken
2	You had taken	You had taken
3	He/She/It had taken	They had taken

Characteristics:
a. Verb: third principal part (*taken*)
b. Helping verb: second principal part of have (*had*)

Progressive (2)

Person	Singular	Plural
1	I had been taking	We had been taking
2	You had been taking	You had been taking
3	He/She/It had been taking	They had been taking

Characteristics:
a. Verb: ends in *-ing* (*taking*)
b. Verb: preceded by third principal part of be (*been*)
c. Helping verb: second principal part of have (*had*)

Passive Voice

Simple (3)

Person	Singular	Plural
1	I had been taken	We had been taken
2	You had been taken	You had been taken
3	He/She/It had been taken	They had been taken

Characteristics:
a. Verb: third principal part (*taken*)
b. Verb: preceded by third principal part of be (*been*)
c. Helping verb: second principal part of have (*had*)

Progressive

NOT USED IN PASSIVE VOICE

Example

A. Simple past perfect tense—active and passive voices [numbers (1) and (3) in Chart 5]: used to express an action completed prior to a particular time in the past.

>   By noon he <u>had completed</u> the report. (active)
>
>   By noon the report <u>had been completed</u>. (passive)
>
>   He <u>had sold</u> his stock before the bottom fell out of the market. (active)
>
>   The stock <u>had been sold</u> before the bottom fell out of the market. (passive)

B. Past perfect progressive tense—active voice only [number (2) in Chart 5]: used to express an action that had been continuing while another action occurred.

>   He <u>had been driving</u> for six hours before the accident happened.
>
>   Because Dell & Company <u>had been hauling</u> freight from coast to coast, the commission revoked its license.

Exercise

1. Look at the underscored verb or verb phrase in each sentence.
2. Use the symbols below to indicate the tense of the verbs:

    SPAP   Simple past perfect   PAPP   Past perfect progressive

3. Place an A (active) or P (passive) in the Voice column to show the correct voice of the verb.

Example	*Tense*	*Voice*
I <u>had taken</u> temperature readings before the doctor arrived.	SPAP	A

	Tense	*Voice*
1. Mary Ann <u>had worked</u> in a military installation for three years before she was married.		
2. Ronald <u>had been flying</u> jets prior to his recall.		
3. He <u>had been selling</u> insurance during the time he was under investigation.		
4. The store and its inventory <u>had been purchased</u> under a loan from the Small Business Administration.		
5. The furniture <u>had been arranged</u> by Office Design Consultants, Inc., before the records were moved to the premises.		
6. Maria <u>had been nominated</u> for the office before Bill.		
7. The commission hearings <u>had been closed</u> to reporters for a week before they objected.		
8. By the time the spring fabric arrived, the winter fabric <u>had been returned</u> to the wholesaler.		

	Tense	*Voice*
9. Keith <u>had been entertaining</u> his girl friend on his expense account money until the sales manager commented on his high expenses.	_____	_____
10. The college <u>had sought</u> accreditation prior to last year.	_____	_____

ANSWERS TO FRAME 6

1. SPAP; A	4. SPAP; P	7. SPAP; P	10. SPAP; A
2. PAPP; A	5. SPAP; P	8. SPAP; P	
3. PAPP; A	6. SPAP; P	9. PAPP; A	

Frame 7   Perfect Tenses

Future Perfect Tense

Explanation

Refer to Chart 6 and notice the location and characteristics of each of the following numbered items.

In the active voice, the *future perfect tense* consists of (1) the simple future perfect and (2) the progressive future perfect tenses. The passive voice includes only (3) the simple future perfect tense.

Example

A. Simple future perfect tense—active and passive voices [numbers (1) and (3) in Chart 6]: used to express an action that will be completed prior to a time in the future.

> By September I <u>shall have worked</u> here for 20 years. (active)
>
> The report <u>will have been completed</u> by the end of the month. (passive)
>
> Before spring comes, the roses <u>will have been planted.</u> (passive)
>
> By May 17 I <u>shall have used</u> this typewriter for two months. (active)
>
> The bill <u>will have been passed</u> before spring. (passive)
>
> By the time we submit the manuscript, we <u>shall have written</u> over 40,000 words. (active)
>
> By four o'clock, they <u>will have been gone</u> an hour. (passive)

B. Future perfect progressive tense—active voice only [number (2) in Chart 6]: used to express an action or condition that is continuing or progressing at a point in the future.

> By August, the engineers <u>will have been surveying</u> this property for six months.
>
> By the time this case comes to trial, <u>we shall have been working</u> on it for over a year.
>
> By the time I get to Phoenix, I <u>shall have been driving</u> for six hours.

CHART 6 Future Perfect Tense

Principal parts of the verb *take*: Present tense—*take*; Past tense—*took*; Past participle—*taken*

Perfect Tense

Active Voice

Simple (1)

Characteristics:
a. Verb: third principal part (*taken*)
b. Verb: preceded by first principal part of *have*
c. Helping verb: (1) *shall*; (2) and (3) *will*

Person	Singular	Plural
1	I shall have taken	We shall have taken
2	You will have taken	You will have taken
3	He/She/It will have taken	They will have taken

Progressive (2)

Characteristics:
a. Verb: ends in *-ing* (taking)
b. Verb: preceded by *have* + third principal part of *be* (*been*)
c. Helping verb: (1) *shall*; (2) and (3) *will*

Person	Singular	Plural
1	I shall have been taking	We shall have been taking
2	You will have been taking	You will have been taking
3	He/She/It will have been taking	They will have been taking

Passive Voice

Simple (3)

Characteristics:
a. Verb: third principal part (*taken*)
b. Verb: preceded by *have* + third principal part of *be* (*been*)
c. Helping verb: (1) *shall*; (2) and (3) *will*

Person	Singular	Plural
1	I shall have been taken	We shall have been taken
2	You will have been taken	You will have been taken
3	He/She/It will have been taken	They will have been taken

Progressive

NOT USED IN PASSIVE VOICE

289

Exercise

1. Look at the underscored verb or verb phrase in each sentence.
2. Use the symbols below to indicate the tense of the verb:

    SFP Simple future perfect   PFP Progressive future perfect

3. Place an A (active) or P (passive) in the Voice column to show the correct voice of the verb.

Example	*Tense*	*Voice*
By dinner, I <u>shall have written</u> ten pages.	SFP	A

	Tense	Voice
1. On June 10, Clemencia <u>will have been married</u> for six months.	_____	_____
2. By fall, she <u>will have supported</u> her parents for ten years.	_____	_____
3. By nightfall, the crowds <u>will have left</u> the scene of the wreckage.	_____	_____
4. When you receive that amount, the balance <u>will have been paid</u>.	_____	_____
5. By 1980, the postal department <u>will have been selling</u> this stamp for thirty-one years.	_____	_____
6. Thousands of people <u>will have visited</u> the exhibit before it closes.	_____	_____
7. By noon, the choir <u>will have been practicing</u> for three hours.	_____	_____
8. The bank <u>will have received</u> your check by Friday.	_____	_____
9. The court clerk <u>will have been working</u> on the docket before the session begins.	_____	_____
10. Your contribution <u>will have been received</u> before the testimonial dinner.	_____	_____

ANSWERS TO FRAME 7

1. SFP; P	5. PFP; A	8. SFP; A
2. SFP; A	6. SFP; A	9. PFP; A
3. SFP; A	7. PFP; A	10. SFP; P
4. SFP; P		

Frame 8   Perfect Tenses

Selecting the Proper Perfect Tense

Explanation

This frame is included so that you can apply what you have learned about the perfect tense.

Exercise

From the verb shown within parentheses in each of the following sentences, select the proper form of the perfect tense required by the designation at the left. Write it in the blank provided. Use only active voice.

Example

Simple: We (walk) six blocks before it rained.   had walked

1. Progressive: Carrie and I (employ) high school students in the ice cream shop. _____
2. Simple: Before the letter was processed, he (dictate) a second one. _____
3. Simple: The personnel director (discharge) four minority employees before the law was passed. _____
4. Simple: I (analyze) the new system before the end of the month. _____
5. Simple: The patient (undergo) a series of tests. _____
6. Progressive: By April, the minister and his assistant (sponsor) this festival for three years. _____
7. Simple: They (credit) your account for your purchases until the error was discovered. _____
8. Progressive: The decorator's assistants (paint) the office for three days. _____
9. Progressive: Emilia (teach) for six years in May. _____
10. Simple: By the time we received your letter, we (sell) the equipment locally. _____

ANSWERS TO FRAME 8

1.	have been employing	6.	will have been sponsoring
2.	had dictated	7.	had credited
3.	had discharged	8.	have been painting
4.	shall (will) have analyzed	9.	will have been teaching
5.	has undergone	10.	had sold

Frame 9   *Business Vocabulary: Credit Department (Adjustments Section)*

Explanation

In addition to maintaining the records of credit customers, the credit department of a large retail organization also has the responsibility to approve or disapprove credit applications, communicate with paying and delinquent customers, and grant or refuse requests for adjustments on credit sales.

In some organizations, each of the duties is handled by a separate group of employees in a designated unit, such as a section or department.

Terms

Adjustment Department (Section)—the unit comprised of employees who respond to customer complaints about merchandise. They may write informative letters to the complainant, ask that person to bring the merchandise to the store for inspection, or send an inspector to the customer's premises.

Claim—a customer's statement (written or oral) that an item or piece of merchandise is defective, malfunctions, and so on.

Credit memo—a form given to the customer whose claim has been accepted. The credit memo contains a statement informing the customer that his/her account will be adjusted (decreased) for the amount of his claim.

Guarantee—an assurance of the quality or length of use to be expected from a product offered for sale (often with the promise of reimbursement).

Warranty—a written guarantee of the integrity of a product and of the maker's responsibility for the repair or replacement of defective parts.

Exercise

Fill in each blank in the following sentences with the correct word from the preceding business vocabulary list.

1. If a piece of fabric carries a tag stating that this fabric will not shrink more than 2 percent, the tag is the manufacturer's _____.

2. If a new car malfunctions within a specified period due to a defective part, the owner may have the part installed without making a payment for the part or the labor because the car is under a _____.

3. The owner who is dissatisfied with an item makes an oral or written _____ to the retailer and asks for an adjustment.

4. If you order a pair of shoes and find that they don't fit properly, you may receive an adjustment from the company. This form is called a _____.

ANSWERS TO FRAME 9
1. guarantee   2. warranty   3. claim   4. credit memo

Frame 10   Applying Your Knowledge

Directions

Underscore each incorrectly used verb or verb phrase in the following letter. Then write the correct verb or verb phrase in the space below the sentence.

CASE

You have received a letter from Ben Ferrera, a college student, who claims that batter sticks to the surface of his newly purchased electric doughnut maker. He asks you to send him a replacement (without charge, of course). This letter is a rough draft of your response to Ben. (10 errors)

Mr. Ben Ferrera
150 East 39th Street, #302
New York, New York 10017

Dear Mr. Ferrera:

The craze for homemade doughnuts is sweeping the country, and you were one of over 700,000 persons who own a HANSCO DOUBLE BARREL DONUT MAKER.

An instruction/recipe booklet had been enclosed in the box with the DOUBLE BARREL DONUT MAKER. On page 6 of this booklet were instructions on the use of this appliance. The first two directions pertain to the preparation of the donut maker for the first batch of donuts: "(1) Wash the nonstick surfaces with hot sudsy water, rinse thoroughly, and dry. (2) Condition these surfaces before the first use with salad oil or unsalted shortening." If these two directions had been followed prior to the first use, the batter would not have stucken to the surface of the donut maker.

Because this donut maker had been used for only two weeks, you can almost eliminate the tendency of the batter to stick if you will follow these instructions: (1) Wipe the surfaces with a cloth saturated with salad oil or unsalted shortening. (2) Plug the cord into a 120-volt wall outlet. (3) Heat the appliance while it is closed for 5 or 6 minutes. (4) Repeat steps (1), (2), and (3) hourly for five hours.

The DOUBLE BARREL DONUT MAKER makes delicious bagels, muffins, and biscuits, as well as tasty doughnuts. Look at the recipes in the instruction booklet enclosed with this letter. The recipes had been developed by a home economist and tested in the home economics departments of six large universities. The men and women in the classes, as well as their lucky friends, vote these recipes a blue ribbon.

If the batter continues to stick to the surface of your donut maker, send the appliance to the HANSCO plant in Birmingham, Alabama, along with a letter requesting that the surfaces be reconditioned. For a nominal amount ($3 plus shipping costs), the surfaces of your DOUBLE BARREL DONUT MAKER shall be refinished.

The enclosed brochure has shown other HANSCO appliances; these appliances are sold at a 10 percent discount next month.

Sincerely,

Barbara Woods
Adjuster

ANSWERS TO FRAME 8
Body of letter:

Dear Mr. Ferrera:

The craze for homemade doughnuts is sweeping the country, and you <u>were</u> one of (are) over 700,000 persons who own a HANSCO DOUBLE BARREL DONUT MAKER.

An instruction/recipe booklet <u>had been enclosed</u> in the box with the DOUBLE (was enclosed) BARREL DONUT MAKER. On page 6 of this booklet <u>were</u> instructions on the use of (are) this appliance. The first two directions pertain to the preparation of the donut maker for the first batch of donuts: "(1) Wash the nonstick surfaces with hot sudsy water, rinse thoroughly, and dry. (2) Condition these surfaces before the first use with salad oil or unsalted shortening." If these two directions had been followed prior to the first use, the

batter would not have <u>stucken</u> to the surface of the donut maker.

stuck

    Because this donut maker <u>had</u> been used for only two weeks, you can almost

                                                             has

eliminate the tendency of the batter to stick if you will follow these instructions: (1)

Wipe the surfaces with a cloth saturated with salad oil or unsalted shortening. (2) Plug

the cord into a 120-volt wall outlet. (3) Heat the appliance while it is closed for 5 or 6

minutes. (4) Repeat steps (1), (2), and (3) hourly for five hours.

    The DOUBLE BARREL DONUT MAKER makes delicious bagels, muffins, and

biscuits, as well as tasty doughnuts. Look at the recipes in the instruction booklet

enclosed with this letter. The recipes <u>had</u> been developed by a home economist and

                                                   have

tested in the home economics departments of six large universities. The men and

women in the classes, as well as their lucky friends, <u>vote</u> these recipes a blue ribbon.

                                                                  voted

    If the batter continues to stick to the surface of your donut maker, send the

appliance to the HANSCO plant in Birmingham, Alabama, along with a letter

requesting that the surfaces be reconditioned. For a nominal amount ($3 plus shipping

costs), the surfaces of your DOUBLE BARREL DONUT MAKER <u>shall</u> be refinished.

                                                                                                   will

    The enclosed brochure <u>has shown</u> other HANSCO appliances; these appliances

                                                          shows

<u>are sold</u> at a 10 percent discount next month.

will be selling

Lesson 19
Verbals

Pretest

Pretest Part I
Gerunds

Directions

1. In each of the following sentences, underscore the gerund or gerund phrase, if one exists.
2. In the blank provided, write one of these symbols to show how the gerund is used:

S   Subject   A   Apposition
OV   Object of the Verb   SC   Subjective Complement
OP   Object of the Preposition

3. If a sentence does not contain a gerund, write No in the blank.

Example

<u>Supervising this group</u> requires leadership ability.   _____S_____

1. Working in the excavated area is dangerous.   _____
2. The teller was dismissed for embezzling money.   _____
3. Ann's job, teaching day school for children of working mothers, is being abol-
   ished.   _____
4. One of Jay's favorite sports is swimming.   _____
5. He liked watching the quotations appear on the screen.   _____
6. Helmut's new job is hauling household goods from coast to coast.   _____
7. He is managing a branch office operation now.   _____
8. Ms. Padilla is responsible for hiring clerical and professional personnel. _____
9. Safeguarding the company's records is the job of the corporate records manager. _____
10. The city council anticipates rezoning this residential area.   _____

Pretest Part II
Participles

Directions

1. In each of the following sentences, underscore the participle or participial phrase, if one exists.
2. In the blank provided, write the word that the participle or participial phrase modifies.
3. One sentence does not contain a participle; write No in the blank for that sentence.

Example

The new plaza will have a <u>sunken</u> garden.   garden

1. Attending school in Paris for a year, Monte became accustomed to French food.   _____
2. The registrar, having explained the tuition requirements to out-of-state students, asked them to complete the enrollment forms.   _____
3. The accountant, hunting for specific financial records, became disgusted with the company's system.   _____
4. Having filmed the records, the technician placed the originals in a secure place.   _____
5. The filmed records will be duplicated.   _____
6. The driver, having been warned about the faulty brake system, is responsible for the damage.   _____
7. The judge, being unaware of the defendant's sudden movement, was shocked by the screams of those present.   _____
8. Paco, having been evicted from his apartment, sought legal advice.   _____
9. This department will be having its annual party during Thanksgiving vacation.   _____
10. Having lost the election, the state senator returned home and practiced law.   _____

Pretest Part III
Infinitives

Directions

1. In each of the following sentences, underscore the infinitive or infinitive phrase, if one exists.
2. In the blank provided, write the part of speech that identifies the usage of the infinitive.
3. One of the sentences contains a prepositional phrase instead of an infinitive; identify it by writing No in the blank.

Example

<u>To advertise your merchandise widely</u>, you should purchase radio time.   Adjective
Mrs. Sangria reported to the personnel office upon her arrival.   No

1. To be named to the post is an honor.   _____
2. To be accepted for admission, you must be in the upper third of your graduating class.   _____
3. A word processor is expected to be a good proofreader.   _____
4. The building to be located on this property will be constructed by Avon Associates.   _____
5. His goal is to become a career diplomat.   _____
6. To be hired by this company, the applicant for a professional job must undergo rigid training.   _____
7. To have been named to the committee was an honor.   _____
8. He wanted to be sent to the California office.   _____
9. Ms. James wrote this memo to the staff.   _____
10. To be represented on the community board, each subdivision must elect one qualified member before July 1.   _____

Pretest Part IV
Misplaced Modifiers

Directions

Two of the following sentences are correct; identify them by writing C after the sentence. If a sentence contains a misplaced modifier, revise the sentence.

Example

The sprinklers should be placed at the edge of the lawn to work effectively.
Revised: <u>To work effectively, the sprinklers should be placed at the edge of the</u>
<u>lawn.</u>

1. The secretary, noticing the error in the report, called the committee chairperson.

   _____

   _____

2. To have rearranged the office properly, the furniture should have been placed in groupings to facilitate communication among the functions.

   _____

   _____

   _____

3. The price of this commodity, having been affected by foreign imports, is now lower than the domestic equivalent.

   _____

   _____

4. To enter the training program, the classification of the employee must be Class IV or higher.

   _____

   _____

5. Alexander quit his job, having been embarrassed by losing an important advertising account.

   _____

   _____

Lesson 19
Verbals

A *verbal* is a verb form: gerund, participle, or infinitive. The verbal may be used by itself or in a phrase. All verbals have the characteristics of the verb which they include; for example, if the verb can occur with an object, the verbal can also occur with an object.

The framework of our language is such that one can hardly discuss a part of speech without referring to another one or a usage without referring to another usage. For this reason, you have been exposed to gerunds and participles in previous lessons. However, in this lesson you will concentrate on identifying and using these two verbals and infinitives.

Frame 1   Verbals: Gerunds

A verbal may be used as a part of speech: a gerund is used as a noun; a participle is used as an adjective; and an infinitive is used as a noun, adjective, or adverb. Logically, when a verbal is used as a certain part of speech, it is in the position of the part of speech it represents and modifies the same word(s) as that part of speech modifies.

A *gerund* is a verb form ending in *-ing* that is used as a noun.

Usage: Gerund

Explanation

Like a noun, a gerund can be:

1. The subject of a sentence
2. Object of the verb
3. The object of a preposition
4. An appositive
5. A subjective complement

A word that modifies the gerund must be in the possessive case.

Example

1. Subject: <u>Sewing</u> is my hobby.
2. Direct object: He enjoys <u>working</u>.
3. Object of the preposition: I won the award by <u>studying</u>.
4. Apposition with noun: Her job, <u>typing</u>, strains her back.
5. Subjective complement: Seeing is <u>believing</u>.
6. Gerund preceded by possessive form: <u>Mary's writing</u> has improved.

Exercise

1. Underscore the gerund in each of the following sentences.
2. In the blank provided, write one of the symbols below to show how the gerund is used.

S	Subject	A	Apposition
OV	Object of the verb	SC	Subjective complement
OP	Object of the preposition		

Example

<u>Swimming</u> is good exercise.   <u>S</u>

1. Programming requires the ability to think logically.
2. His job is supervising.
3. He was arrested for speeding.
4. He enjoys swimming.
5. His major problem in English, spelling, has not improved.

ANSWERS TO FRAME 1

1. <u>Programming</u>; S   3. <u>speeding</u>; OP   5. <u>spelling</u>; A
2. <u>supervising</u>; SC   4. <u>swimming</u>; OV

Frame 2   Verbals: Gerunds

Usage: Gerund Phrase

Explanation

A *gerund phrase* consists of a gerund plus any objects and modifiers. This phrase is used in the same positions in which the gerund is used.

Example

1. <u>Maintaining discipline in the classroom</u> is essential.
   a. The phrase is used as the subject of the sentence.
   b. <u>Maintaining</u> is a gerund.
   c. The answer to *Maintaining what?* is <u>discipline</u>, the object of the gerund.
   d. The prepositional phrase <u>in the classroom</u> answers *Where?* and modifies the gerund phrase.
   e. The gerund phrase consists of the gerund <u>maintaining</u> plus its object <u>discipline</u> and the modifier, the prepositional phrase <u>in the classroom</u>.
2. <u>Reading business periodicals and books</u> will help you to improve your business vocabulary.
   a. The phrase is the subject of the sentence.
   b. <u>Reading</u> is a gerund.
   c. The answer to *Reading what?* is <u>periodicals and books</u>.
   d. <u>Business</u> is an adjective that describes both nouns and is a modifier.
   e. The gerund phrase consists of the gerund plus its object and modifiers.
3. <u>By ordering now</u>, you can save $6 on a subscription to *Business Times*.
   a. <u>By ordering now</u> is a prepositional phrase that contains a verbal: <u>ordering</u>.
   b. <u>Ordering</u> is a gerund (object of the preposition <u>by</u>), and <u>now</u> is an adverb modifying <u>ordering</u>.

Exercise

1. Underscore the complete gerund or verbal phrase in each of the following sentences.
2. In the blank provided, write one of the symbols below to show how the gerund is used.

    S   Subject   A   Apposition
    OV   Object of the verb   SC   Subjective complement
    OP   Object of the preposition

3. If a sentence does not contain a gerund, write No in the blank.

Example

<u>Supervising</u> requires leadership ability.   _____S_____

1.   Selecting good employees is the personnel manager's job.   _____
2.   He was disciplined for disobeying the order.   _____
3.   This job, washing cars, does not pay well.   _____
4.   Yancy, an Army pilot, has been flying jets for many years.   _____
5.   This policy discourages placing calls during duty time.   _____
6.   You can supplement your income by obtaining a second job.   _____
7.   I was surprised by his winning the spelling contest.   _____
8.   One of Joy's best skills is typing statistical reports.   _____
9.   He liked working in his garden.   _____
10. On reaching his next birthday, James will inherit $50,000.   _____

ANSWERS TO FRAME 2
1.   <u>Selecting good employees</u>; S
2.   <u>disobeying the order</u>; OP
3.   <u>washing cars</u>; A
4.   No (<u>has been flying</u> is a verb)
5.   <u>placing calls</u> (during duty time), OV (prepositional phrase modifies <u>placing</u>)
6.   <u>obtaining a second job</u>; OP
7.   <u>winning the spelling contest</u>; OP (Note that the gerund is preceded by a possessive pronoun.)
8.   <u>typing statistical reports</u>; SC
9.   <u>working</u> (in his garden)—<u>working</u> is OV; the prepositional phrase modifies <u>working</u>.
10. <u>reaching his next birthday</u>; OP.

Frame 3   Verbals: Participles

A *participle* is a verb form used as an objective. The participle may be used by itself or in a participial phrase. In either case, it is located in an adjective position and modifies a noun or pronoun. A participle must always be located in proximity to the noun or pronoun it modifies. Failure to observe this principle results in a misplaced (or dangling) participle.

Properties of Participles

Explanation

A participle retains these properties of a verb: tense, voice, and the ability to take an object.

Example

A.   Active Voice:
1.   The present participle always ends in *-ing* (purchasing).
2.   The perfect participle uses the third principal part of the verb preceded by *having* (having purchased).
B.   Passive Voice:
1.   The present participle uses the third principal part of the verb preceded by *being* (being purchased).
2.   The past participle uses the third principal part of the verb (purchased).
3.   The perfect participle uses the third principal part of the verb preceded by *having been* (having been purchased).

Voice	Present	Past	Perfect
Active	purchasing		having purchased
Passive	being purchased	purchased	having been purchased

C. Usage:

1. Use the present participle to express an action that is occurring at the same time as the action expressed by the main verb.

   Purchasing the car in January, John saved considerable money.

2. Use the past participle to express an action that has been completed.

   The car *purchased by John* is blue.

3. Use the perfect participle to express an action that occurred prior to the action expressed by the verb in the main clause.

   Having purchased a car in June, John took a trip in July.

4. The passive voice of the present, past, and perfect participle is used to express an action reflected upon the subject.

   Having been purchased by John, the car was removed from the showroom. (perfect tense and passive voice)

   The *purchased* car was removed from the showroom.

Exercise

Each participial phrase is underscored in the sentences below. Any object or modifier is also underscored.

1. In the Voice column, write A (active) or P (passive) to identify the voice of the underscored participle.
2. In the Modified Word column, write the word which the participle or participial phrase modifies.

	Voice	*Modified Word*
Example		
<u>Purchasing the car in January,</u> John saved considerable money.	A	John
1. <u>Having gone to Hong Kong by ship,</u> Charlie decided to fly home.	_____	_____
2. Ann, <u>having been scheduled to work overtime,</u> was unhappy.	_____	_____
3. The clerk, <u>having found the receipt,</u> called Mr. Thompson.	_____	_____
4. This figure, <u>having been entered in the wrong column,</u> caused the trial balance to be incorrect.	_____	_____
5. <u>Anticipating an increase in population of the city,</u> Mr. Andrews, the developer, tried to have the Mantz Subdivision rezoned for commercial purposes.	_____	_____
6. <u>Having been handed a subpoena,</u> Ms. Alvarez had no choice but to appear in court.	_____	_____
7. <u>Having worked for the state government,</u> the retiring administrator expected to collect his pension.	_____	_____

	Voice	*Modified Word*
8. <u>Establishing her own business</u>, Joan discovered how much paperwork is required by the various governmental agencies at all levels.	_____	_____
9. The program <u>being written now</u> is for your new computer-output-microfilm system.	_____	_____
10. <u>Reconditioned by the factory</u>, the used computer functioned as well as a new one.	_____	_____

ANSWERS TO FRAME 3

1. A; Charlie	4. P; figure	7. A; administrator	10. P; computer
2. P; Ann	5. A; Mr. Andrews	8. A; Joan	
3. A; clerk	6. P; Ms. Alvarez	9. P; program	

Frame 4   Verbals: Participles

Location of Participles

Explanation

A participle or participial phrase may precede or follow the noun it modifies.

Example

1. Her <u>written</u> report was better than her oral report.
   The past participle <u>written</u> is the third principal part of the verb.
2. The report <u>written by Jane</u> was better than the one <u>written by Bruce</u>.
   The underscored phrases begin with a past participle, and each modifies the noun that precedes it.
3. <u>Preparing the telegram</u>, Marge saw the error.
   The sentence begins with a present participle that modifies <u>Marge</u>.
4. The company honored the employees <u>having five or more years of service</u>.
   The sentence ends with a participial phrase that modifies <u>employees</u>.

Exercise

1. Underscore the participle or participial phrase in each of the following sentences.
2. In the blank provided, write the word that the participle or participial phrase modifies.
3. One sentence does not contain a participle; write No in the blank for that sentence.

Example

<u>Having been stolen from the police</u>, the car was easily recognized.   car

1. Recognized by the school for outstanding academic performance, Gregory was pleased and proud.   _____
2. The renovated building has been purchased by the realty company.   _____
3. Enrique, drawing plans for the new highway system, discovered a better location for the thoroughfare.   _____
4. The employees have been pilfering supplies.   _____
5. Some of the small pilfered appliances have been sold to fences.   _____

6. The dean read the names of students having received a 4.0 average during their college careers. _____

7. Being located in the warehouse district, the restaurant caters to truck drivers, warehouse workers, and local office workers. _____

8. The property situated on the crest of Lookout Mountain is not currently for sale. _____

9. The Osbornes, having been on a cruise, could not provide any information about the robbery. _____

10. The chemical contaminated the city water supply, making many residents ill. _____

ANSWERS TO FRAME 4

1. <u>Recognized by the school for outstanding academic performance</u>; Gregory
2. <u>renovated</u>; building
3. <u>drawing plans for the new highway system</u>; Enrique
4. No
5. <u>pilfered</u>; appliances
6. <u>having received a 4.0 average during their college careers</u>; students
7. <u>Being located in the warehouse district</u>; restaurant
8. <u>situated on the crest of Lookout Mountain</u>; property
9. <u>having been on a cruise</u>; Osbornes
10. <u>making many residents ill</u>; water supply

Frame 5   Verbals: Infinitives

An *infinitive* consists of a verb form preceded by *to* (usually written but sometimes understood). Like other verbals, an infinitive may be part of a phrase, and as such, it may have an object and modifiers. An infinitive or infinitive phrase is used as a noun, adjective, or adverb.

Properties of an Infinitive

Explanation

An infinitive retains these properties of a verb: tense, voice, and the ability to take an object.

Example

A. Active Voice
   1. The present tense uses the first principal part of the verb (to repair).
   2. The perfect tense uses the third principal part of the verb preceded by *have* (to have repaired).
B. Passive Voice
   1. The present tense uses the third principal part of the verb preceded by *be* (to be repaired).
   2. The perfect tense uses the third principal part of the verb preceded by *have been* (to have been repaired).

Voice	Present	Perfect
Active	to repair	to have repaired
Passive	to be repaired	to have been repaired

C. Usage
   1. Use the present tense to express an action that occurs at the same time as the action of the main verb.

To repair the typewriter properly, you need to remove the carriage.

2. Use the perfect tense to express an action that occurs before the action expressed by the main verb.

To have repaired the car before yesterday was his job.

3. The passive voice of the infinitive is used to express an action reflected upon the subject.

The refrigerator to be repaired is on the patio. (present tense and passive voice)

The refrigerator to have been repaired has now been sold. (perfect tense and passive voice)

Exercise

In the blank provided, write A (active) or P (passive) to identify the voice of the infinitive in the underscored phrases.

Example	*Voice*
The paper to be typed is Bella's.	P

		Voice
1.	To be accepted into this organization, you must have the vote of 95 percent of the members.	_____
2.	To succeed in business is her goal.	_____
3.	Carl wants to attend college.	_____
4.	To have managed the firm for five years is remarkable.	_____
5.	The man to have been appointed by the mayor died suddenly.	_____

ANSWERS TO FRAME 5
1. P   2. A   3. A   4. A   5. P

Frame 6   Verbals: Infinitives

Recognizing Infinitive Usages

Explanation

The infinitive may be used as a noun, adjective, or adverb.

Example

1. Noun:

To drive in a professional race may be dangerous. (subject)

His goal is to succeed. (subjective complement—renames goal)

The Prongonza family wants to work in this city. (direct object)

2. Adjective:

The paper to be read at the meeting is Frank's. (modifies noun paper)

3. Adverb:

Grace was too nervous to speak. (modifies adjective nervous)

Exercise

1. Underscore the infinitive or infinitive phrase in each of the following sentences.
2. Then indicate how it is used by writing *adjective, adverb,* or *noun* in the blank provided.
3. One of the sentences contains a prepositional phrase; identify it by writing No in the blank.

Example   *Usage*

To advertise your merchandise widely, you should purchase radio time.   adjective

1. Mary is too excited to work.   _____
2. To have been passed over for promotion was humiliating.   _____
3. Ms. Atkins is the woman to be seen about the job.   _____
4. Betty Broome is the person to hire for the position.   _____
5. He hoped to pay his bill this month.   _____
6. To be selected for the honor, you must have applied before July. _____
7. His aim is to play on the varsity team.   _____
8. He walked from the office to the bank.   _____
9. The deposit is to be made today.   _____
10. You are required to pay one month's deposit in advance.   _____

ANSWERS TO FRAME 6
1. to work; adverb (modifies adjective excited)
2. To have been passed over for promotion; noun (subject)
3. to be seen about this job; adjective (modifies noun woman)
4. to hire for the position; adjective (modifies noun person)
5. to pay his bill this month; noun (object of verb hoped)
6. To be selected for the honor; adjective (modifies pronoun you)
7. to play on the varsity team; noun (subjective complement renames aim)
8. No; to the bank is a prepositional phrase
9. to be made today; adjective (predicate adjective, modifies the subject deposit)
10. to pay one month's deposit in advance; adverb (modifies the verb are required)

Frame 7   Verbals: Infinitives

Flexibility of the Infinitive

Explanation

Grammarians believe that no word should "split" the infinitive; that is, be placed immediately after *to.* "Splitting the infinitive" usually results in an awkward construction.

Example

1. Split infinitive:

    The doctor asked me to rapidly read the chart. (awkward)
    The doctor asked me to read the chart rapidly. (revised)

2. Subject of the infinitive: used in the objective case.

    The sales clerk asked me to sign my name. (me is the direct object of asked, and it is the subject of the infinitive)

Exercise

Revise the following sentences to eliminate the split infinitives.

Example

Marilyn hopes to someday become a CPA.
Revised: <u>Marilyn hopes to become a CPA someday</u>.

   a.   The manager asks Jerry to usually work late.

     _____

   b.   The secretary told the applicant to very thoroughly read the directions.

     _____

     _____

   c.   To easily have recorded the charge sale, you could have used the customer's credit account number.

     _____

     _____

Exercise

Underscore the subject of the infinitive.

Example

This university requires all <u>students</u> to pass an English proficiency test before they can be graduated.

   d.   I told him to requisition more supplies.

ANSWERS TO FRAME 7
   a.   The manager usually asks Jerry to work late.
   b.   The secretary told the applicant to read the directions very thoroughly.
   c.   To have recorded the charge sale easily, you could have used the customer's credit account number.
   d.   <u>him</u>

Frame 8   *Misplaced Modifiers*

Explanation

A word, phrase, or clause used as a modifier should be as close to the word that it modifies as possible. A violation of this rule causes the construction to be awkward, confusing, and sometimes amusing (at the writer's expense). Verbals, particularly participles, can easily be misplaced in a sentence. Careful writers are alert for these *misplaced modifiers* and revise the sentence to correct the construction.

Example

   1.   Misplaced (or dangling) participle:

      Original   <u>Running to the meeting</u>, the memo was read by Jane. (The participial phrase should modify <u>Jane</u>; instead, it modifies <u>memo</u>.)
      Revision   <u>Running to the meeting</u>, Jane read the memo.

Original <u>Making the trial balance</u>, the error was noticed. (The participial phrase has no logical modifier in the sentence; a noun or pronoun modifier needs to be included in the revision.)
Revision <u>In making the trial balance</u>, <u>he</u> noticed the error.

2. Misplaced infinitive:

Original A person must be capable of performing his job <u>to be successful</u>. (The infinitive phrase should modify <u>person</u>, not <u>job</u>.)
Revision <u>To be successful</u>, a <u>person</u> must be capable of performing his job.

Original <u>To have been elected</u>, one more vote was needed by Bernie.
Revision <u>To have been elected</u>, Bernie needed one more vote.

Exercise

1. Revise any of the following sentences that contain misplaced modifiers.
2. Two of the sentences are correct; identify them by writing C in the blank provided.

Example

Hearing the burglar alarm, the police were immediately called by the night watchman.
Revised: <u>Hearing the burglar alarm, the night watchman immediately called the police.</u>

1. Not being able to pay the taxes, the house was sold.

2. Dr. Witkind was honored at a banquet, having been named the Business Professor of the Year.

3. To arrive in Albuquerque before lunch, you will need to take an early flight.

4. Having once been wrecked, Joe knew that the used car was not a good buy.

5. Ms. Benzito, having worked for the city, was aware of the poor image that most city offices have.

ANSWERS TO FRAME 8

(Some sentences can be revised in more than one way.)
1. Not being able to pay the taxes, (noun or pronoun—<u>Mr. Benedict</u>, for example) sold the house.
   (Noun or pronoun—<u>Mr. Benedict</u>), not being able to pay the taxes, sold the house.
2. Dr. Witkind, having been named Business Professor of the Year, was honored at a banquet.
3. C
4. Joe knew that the used car, having once been wrecked, was not a good buy.
5. C

Frame 9   Business Vocabulary: Education

Explanation

A hierarchy of levels and positions exists in an educational institution, just as in business organizations and government agencies. Like the organizations and agencies, these educational institutions have line and staff personnel.

Terms

Line personnel—those persons who direct others, make decisions, or otherwise affect the academic behavior of the final product, the student.

President (or Chancellor)—top-ranking administrator of a collegiate institution.

Vice presidents—administrators responsible for certain activities that are part of or contribute to the institution's mission; for example, instruction, research, finance, extension, and so on.

Deans—administrators of colleges within the institution. A dean has a broad background in a discipline and expertise in one or more areas of instruction offered by the specific college; for example, business, arts and sciences, home economics, forestry, agriculture, and so on.

Department chairpersons—administrators of departments within a college. A department chairperson is responsible for the quality of instruction and performance of related activities within a department; for example, marketing, finance, management, information systems.

Faculty—personnel who teach classes in one or more areas of expertise, and also perform other professional and scholarly activities as deemed important by the department, the college, and the institution as a whole. Faculty members are divided into four ranks designated by these titles: instructor, assistant professor, associate professor, and professor. Progression from one rank to the next depends upon one's educational background, advanced degrees, teaching ability, and contribution to the department, college, and institution.

Staff personnel—persons in those offices that support the line personnel in carrying out their functions. Many staff offices exist. Three examples follow:

Personnel Office—maintains records pertinent to faculty and staff employment, benefits, compensation, safety, and so on.

Office of Academic Advising—offers assistance and guidance to students who need help in deciding on their goals and the curriculum that will help them to achieve these goals.

Office of Admissions and Records—evaluates records to determine which students shall be admitted; also maintains and transmits student records.

An educational institution usually needs many committees to gather information and offer suggestions for the improvement of operations and instruction. For instance, there are committees on faculty benefits, student life, faculty improvement, and academic instruction.

Exercise

Complete each of the following sentences with the correct word from the preceding business vocabulary list.

1. Name the top administrator of a post-high school institution:

   _____.

2. The title of a top-ranking faculty member is _____.

3. A dean serves in a (line, staff) function. _____

4. The Office of Admissions and Records performs a (line, staff) function.

_____

5. The lowest administrative line unit is an educational institution is the

_____.

ANSWERS TO FRAME 9

1. president (or chancellor)   3. line   5. department
2. professor   4. staff

Frame 10 *Applying Your Knowledge*

Directions

1. Underscore the incorrectly constructed sentences in the following case.
2. Rewrite the five incorrect sentences on the lines provided at the end of the letter.

CASE

Mabel DiConza, the assistant to the president of Excelsior University, has been asked to prepare a personal letter that can be adapted and sent to six students who are to be graduated with high distinction in June.

Dear Ms. Banderra:

Congratulations! On June 1 you will be graduated with high distinction.

To have been accorded this honor upon graduation, your family, relatives, and friends should be exceedingly proud of you. Your superior academic record reflects diligence, perseverance, and ambition. Having these qualities, your future is sure to be one of accomplishment and success.

Cecelia, I have met you many times during your four years at Excelsior University; therefore, I am especially proud to honor you. A student must have sustained a superior grade average, as you know, to be graduated with honors. This honor should be exceptionally meaningful to you for two reasons: you have demonstrated outstanding scholastic ability, and you have also exhibited strong leadership traits.

The phrase with high distinction will be engraved upon your diploma, which I will hand to you after conferring the degrees upon you and the five other students being given this honor. Dr. Alan Brady, Dean of the College of Engineering, will lead the graduates with high distinction to their appropriate seats on the stage, being the marshal of the procession.

After completing the graduation ceremony, a reception for honor graduates will be held at the President's residence. Three admission cards are enclosed for your use.

My most sincere best wishes for a happy and successful future.

Cordially,

Morgan T. Standish
President

Revised Sentences

1. _____
   _____

2. _____
   _____

3. _____
   _____

4. _____
   _____

5. _____
   _____

ANSWERS TO FRAME 10

1. <u>To have been accorded this honor upon graduation, your family, relatives, and friends should be exceedingly proud of you.</u>

   REVISED: Because you are being accorded this honor upon graduation, your family, relatives, and friends should be exceedingly proud of you.

2. <u>Having these qualities, your future is sure to be one of accomplishment and success.</u>

   REVISED: Having these qualities, you can anticipate a future of accomplishment and success.

3. <u>A student must have sustained a superior grade average, as you know, to be graduated with honors.</u>

   REVISED: To be graduated with honors, a student must have sustained a superior grade average, as you know.

4. <u>Dr. Alan Brady, Dean of the College of Engineering, will lead the graduates with high distinction to their appropriate seats on the stage, being the marshal of the procession.</u>

   REVISED: Dr. Alan Brady, Dean of the College of Engineering, being the marshal of the procession, will lead the graduates with high distinction to their seats on the stage.

5. <u>After completing the graduation ceremony, a reception for honor graduates will be held at the President's residence.</u>

   REVISED: After completing the graduation ceremony, honor graduates will be given a reception at the President's residence.

Lesson 20
Adjectives

Pretest

Pretest Part I
Descriptive Adjectives

Example

Assume that you have been working for one week and that you are describing your supervisor (whom you like) to a friend. List five logical, businesslike adjectives to describe your supervisor's traits.

1. capable   3. honest   5. diligent
2. efficient 4. likable

Assume that you need to write a recommendation for a student who performed as follows: never submitted papers on time, often submitted the wrong assignment, talked when you were lecturing, and cheated on two assignments. Write three logical, businesslike adjectives to describe this student's traits.

(1)_____ (2) _____ (3) _____

Pretest Part II
Limiting Adjectives

Directions

Some of the underscored limiting adjectives in the following sentences are used correctly; some are not. If one is not, write the correct word in the blank provided; if one is correct, write C in the blank. If the adjective should be omitted, write Omit in the blank.

Example

Writing this kind of <u>a</u> report is a valuable experience for you.	omit
<u>This</u> correspondence should be filed today.	C
<u>An</u> hyphen should be used in that compound adjective.	A

1. <u>These</u> type of information is not concrete. _____
2. Al is <u>an</u> husky man. _____
3. This man thought that he saw <u>an</u> UFO (unidentified flying object). _____
4. I bought <u>an</u> umbrella from a street vendor. _____
5. <u>An</u> outcome of the research is that we found an error in our accounting system. _____
6. <u>A</u> hourglass may be filled with sand or colored water. _____
7. <u>A</u> hyperactive person usually has an active thyroid condition. _____
8. A microfiche is <u>a</u> unitized microfilm. _____
9. A native of New England is known as <u>an</u> Yankee. _____
10. You probably learned to make <u>a</u> histogram in your first statistics class. _____

Pretest Part III
Compound Adjectives

Directions

In each pair of sentences, one combination forms a compound adjective and is written correctly. In the blank provided, write the letter that identifies the correct sentence.

Example

a. A better than average student should be selected.
b. The student selected should be better than average. ____b____

1. a. A ten-year-old child could understand that concept.
   b. A child who is ten-years-of-age could understand that concept. _____
2. a. The error is no-fault of mine.
   b. Most states require drivers to carry no-fault insurance. _____
3. a. Harvey was given a three-day pass.
   b. Harvey was given a pass for three-days. _____
4. a. The side-by-side benches are uncomfortable.
   b. The benches were sitting side-by-side. _____
5. a. The secretary took the dictation word-for-word.
   b. Word-for-word dictation is not easy to take. _____
6. a. The hard-bound book sells for more than the other version.
   b. The hardbound book sells for more than the other book. _____
7. a. Sample ready-made suits are shown in the fabric department.
   b. Sample suits that have already been made are shown in the fabric department. _____
8. a. Just read the easy-to-follow directions on the package.
   b. The package directions are easy-to-follow. _____
9. a. A report that is easy-to-read saves the manager's time.
   b. An easy-to-read report saves the manager's time. _____
10. a. The Brett Company is a well-known manufacturer of cosmetic supplies.
    b. The Brett Company is well-known as a manufacturer of cosmetic supplies. _____

Pretest Part IV
Comparison of Regular Adjectives

Directions

In one sentence of each of the following pairs, a degree of comparison is used correctly. In the blank provided, write the letter designating the correct sentence.

Example

a. Joe is the more capable of the two applicants.
b. Joe is the most capable of the two applicants. ____a____

1. a. This reference book is longer than that one.
   b. This reference book is the longest of the two. _____
2. a. Our stock has sold higher than the Brown Company.
   b. Our stock has sold higher than the Brown Company's. _____

3. a. She is younger than the other employees in the group.
    b. She is more younger than the other employees in the group. _____
4. a. The Reynor Company's image is better than the Baker Company's.
    b. The Reynor Company's image is better than the Baker Company. _____
5. a. This year's report is more comprehensive than last year's.
    b. This year's report is the most comprehensive of the two. _____
6. a. This microfilm processor is more expensive than the REIMAGE processor.
    b. This microfilm processor is the most expensive of the two processors. _____
7. a. This chair is the newest of the three.
    b. This chair is the newer of the three. _____
8. a. This task is the most difficult one I have ever undertaken.
    b. This task is the difficultest one I have ever undertaken. _____
9. a. Of the 50 cities, New York City is the largest.
    b. Of the 50 cities, New York City is the larger. _____
10. a. Ms. Sanfelipo is more progressive than any other manager in this group.
    b. Ms. Sanfelipo is most progressive than any other manager in this group. _____

Pretest Part V
Adjective Clauses

Directions

1. Underscore the adjective clause in each of the following sentences.
2. In the blank provided, write the noun or pronoun that this clause modifies.

Example

The person <u>who removed the barricade</u> has been found. <u>person</u>

1. This assignment, which I just graded, cannot be accepted. _____
2. The employee whose car was stolen works in this department. _____
3. The county clerk said that anyone who had the payment could purchase a special license plate. _____
4. I spoke to the clerk whom you recommended for a promotion. _____
5. Claude Aiken is the professor whom I met at the meeting. _____

Lesson 20
Adjectives

If we compare a piece of furniture with our language, we might say that the nouns, pronouns, and verbs, along with the complete thought, are required in its construction. The adjectives, however, motivate our interest in this piece of furniture: Early American, Mediterranean, or French Provincial represent the style; classic, modern, or period represent the design; large, cumbersome, or graceful represent the appearance.

The use of adjectives can make a sentence more concise. For example, "He saw the supervisor, who was angry, rip the report to shreds," can be shortened to "He saw the angry supervisor rip the report to shreds."

Adjectives can also make our writing more specific: "We need to requisition more paper" does not answer the question, *What kind?* To make it more specific, we could change it to "We need to requisition more (bond) (letterhead) (printout) paper."

Frame 1: Adjectives: Relationships to Nouns

Adjectives are easily identified because they are always considered in relation to a noun (or pronoun).

An adjective is versatile in nature. It may describe, limit, or specifically name a noun (to review proper adjectives—see Lesson 9 on capitalization). The placement of an adjective within a sentence adds variety and interest to our writing.

Functions of Adjectives

An *adjective* always functions in relation to a noun (or pronoun). An adjective describes a noun (bond paper), limits it (this machine), or specifically names it (English class).

Descriptive Adjectives

Explanation

A *descriptive adjective* describes a noun; it makes the noun easier to recognize. A descriptive adjective answers the question, *What kind?*

Example

The desk is being replaced. (What kind?)
The old desk is being replaced.
The old green desk is being replaced.

Exercise

Assume that you have been working for one week and that you are describing your supervisor (whom you like) to a friend. List five logical, businesslike adjectives to describe the supervisor's traits.

1. capable   3. honest   5. diligent
2. efficient   4. likable

1. Assume that you are a customer representative and have just talked with a customer who is extremely dissatisfied with your company's service. Write three

317

adjectives that you might use in a report to your supervisor to describe this customer's attitude.

(1) ——————— (2) ——————— (3) ———————

2. Assume that the customer in the previous example is grateful for your explanation of the company's service. This person listens eagerly and asks appropriate questions. Write three adjectives that you might use in a report to your supervisor to describe this customer's attitude.

(1) ——————— (2) ——————— (3) ———————

3. Assume that the office in which you work is noisy beyond reason; that the system, if one exists, is poor; that no one appears to know what his or her job is. Because you dislike the way this company operates, you decide to obtain another job. Write three adjectives describing this office that you can use in explaining to the personnel director during your exit interview why you are leaving.

(1) ——————— (2) ——————— (3) ———————

4. Assume that a management trainee has been assigned to you. No amount of written or oral explanation has persuaded this young man to do his work accurately, promptly, or efficiently. Write three adjectives that you can use in a recommendation report to describe him.

(1) ——————— (2) ——————— (3) ———————

5. A subordinate has just handed you an excellent report which was based on a difficult project and required considerable research. Write five adjectives that you could use in complimenting the subordinate on the quality of this report.

(1) ——————— (2) ——————— (3) ———————

ANSWERS TO FRAME 1

Several adjectives would be appropriate for these answers. Following are some of the more likely choices.

1. (1) belligerent (2) antagonistic (3) angry (4) acrimonious (5) illogical
2. (1) understanding (2) logical (3) reasonable (4) interested (5) appreciative
3. (1) noisy (2) chaotic (3) unbusinesslike (4) disorganized (5) disruptive
4. (1) inaccurate (2) inefficient (3) lackadaisical (4) inattentive (5) disorganized
5. (1) comprehensive (2) readable (3) concise (4) scholarly (5) accurate

Frame 2   Adjectives: Relationship to Nouns

Limiting Adjectives

Explanation

The three most common classes of *limiting adjectives* are demonstrative adjectives—those that point out or identify the noun—*this, that, these,* and *those;* articles—*a, an,* and *the;* and possessive pronouns used as adjectives.

This, That, These, and Those

Example

1. *This* and *that* are singular adjectives and are used with singular nouns. For example: this desk, that type of program.
2. *These* is the plural of *this,* and *those* is the plural of *that.* For example: these desks, those types of programs.

A, An, and The

Example

1. *The:* a definite article that identifies a person, place, or thing within a category.
2. *A, An:* indefinite articles that simply name a category of persons, places, or things.

> This contribution will help to purchase <u>a</u> guide dog.
> <u>An</u> electrician can repair the damaged circuit.

a. Use <u>a</u> before words beginning with a consonant sound:

> <u>a</u> balance sheet   <u>a</u> roster   <u>a</u> cost accountant   <u>a</u> figure

b. Use <u>a</u> before words beginning with one of these sounds:

> sounded h: <u>a</u> house, <u>a</u> history lesson, <u>a</u> hog
>
> long u: <u>a</u> union contract, <u>a</u> unit of measure
>
> *o* sounded as *w:* <u>a</u> one-hour test

c. Use <u>an</u> before words beginning with a vowel sound (except long u, which requires <u>a</u>):

> <u>an</u> egg, <u>an</u> aptitude test, <u>an</u> income statement, <u>an</u> underpass

d. Use <u>an</u> before words beginning with a silent h: <u>an</u> hour, <u>an</u> honorable person

e. Use the articles <u>a</u> and <u>an</u> only when they are necessary.

> Incorrect   What kind of <u>a</u> test do you give?
> Correct   What kind of test do you give?

Possessive Pronouns

Example

A *possessive pronoun* may be used as an adjective. In this usage, it limits the noun it modifies:

> <u>My</u> book is lost. <u>Her</u> assignment is late. <u>His</u> car was stolen. <u>Their</u> annual reports are not up to date.

Exercise

In the following sentences, the limiting adjectives are underscored. If the underscored adjective is used correctly in a sentence, write C in the blank provided, if not, write the correct form in the blank. Write Omit in the blank if the adjective should be omitted.

Example

Writing this kind of <u>a</u> report is a valuable experience for you.	Omit
<u>This</u> correspondence should be filed today.	C
<u>An</u> hyphen should be used in that compound adjective.	A

1. The bank wants to purchase <u>an</u> new computer.   _____
2. <u>These</u> fares will not be applicable after May 30.   _____
3. Intracompany mail should be placed in <u>a</u> routing envelope.   _____

4. <u>A</u> envelope of this kind is used by all departments. _____
5. Snyder is taking bets on <u>an</u> hockey game. _____
6. The vegetable growers lost <u>a</u> onion crop again this year. _____
7. <u>Those</u> kind of furniture is not durable. _____
8. The committee members made <u>an</u> united stand against the council's suggestion. _____
9. <u>An</u> elementary algebra book was found in this classroom. _____
10. The consultant will be paid <u>a</u> honorarium for his effort. _____

ANSWERS TO FRAME 2

1. a	4. An	7. That	10. an
2. C	5. a	8. a	
3. C	6. an	9. C	

Frame 3   Adjectives: Relationship to Nouns

Placement of Adjectives

Explanation

Adjectives may precede or follow the noun. Most frequently, an adjective precedes a noun; however, for variety it may follow a noun or a verb of being.

Example

1. Adjectives preceding a noun:

    The <u>enthusiastic</u> and <u>diligent</u> employee is an asset.

    The <u>enthusiastic, diligent</u> employee is an asset.

    <u>Enthusiastic</u> and <u>diligent</u>, the employee is an asset.

2. Adjectives following a noun:

    The employee, <u>enthusiastic</u> and <u>diligent</u>, is an asset.

    The employee is <u>enthusiastic</u> and <u>diligent</u>; therefore, he is an asset. (Predicate adjective—follows verb of being and describes the subject.)

Exercise

1. Underscore each adjective in the following sentences (exclude articles).
2. Assign one number to all the adjectives that modify a particular noun, and write that number below each.
3. In the blank provided, write the noun modified by this (these) adjective(s).
4. Do this for each noun that has modifying adjectives.

Example

The play, <u>unique</u> and <u>exciting</u>, received an <u>excellent</u> rating.   <u>(1) play </u>
        (1)   (1)   (2)   <u>(2) rating</u>

1. The lengthy, incomprehensible, and inaccurate report was given a grade of F. _____
    _____
2. The new professor, young, arrogant, and intelligent, won a fellowship. _____
    _____
3. The United Nations building is imposing, large, and modernistic. _____
    _____

4. Glass-enclosed and solar-heated, this house is the example of future architecture. _____
5. The system is unfeasible, erratic, and inaccurate. _____

ANSWERS TO FRAME 3

1. <u>lengthy, incomprehensible, inaccurate</u> (1)   (1) report
2. <u>new, young, arrogant, intelligent</u> (1)   (1) professor
3. <u>United Nations, imposing, large, modernistic</u> (1)   (1) building
4. <u>Glass-enclosed, solar-heated, this</u> (1) <u>future</u> (2)   (1) house
                                                      (2) architecture
5. <u>unfeasible, erratic, inaccurate</u> (1)   (1) system

Frame 4   Compound Adjectives

Explanation

A *compound adjective* is composed of two or more words that modify the same noun. When these words precede the noun, they are joined by a hyphen; when the words follow a noun, they are written separately.

Example

1. Hyphenated compound adjectives:

   Preceding   The editor is also a <u>well-known writer</u>.
   Following   The <u>editor</u> is also <u>well known</u> as a writer.

   Preceding   An <u>up-to-date report</u> is expected monthly.
   Following   Each month I expect a <u>report that is up to date</u>.

   Preceding   We have <u>one-</u>, <u>two-</u>, and <u>three-bedroom houses</u> for sale.
   Following   <u>Houses</u> with <u>one</u>, <u>two</u>, or <u>three bedrooms</u> are for sale.

   Preceding   He pitched a <u>no-hit</u> game.
   Following   <u>No-hit</u>, like many other words, cannot be used easily following the noun.

2. Compound adjectives that are not hyphenated:
   Some compound adjectives are not hyphenated. To assure that you spell compound adjectives correctly, consult a dictionary.

   sportswear   *thickset*   *windproof*   *foursquare*   *madcap*

Exercise

In one sentence in each of the following pairs, a compound adjective is used correctly. In the blank provided, write the letter that identifies the correct sentence.

Example

a. A better-than-average student should be selected for this nomination.   _____a_____
b. The student selected for this nomination should be better-than-average.

1. a. A $40,000-a-year salary for middle management personnel is typical in this industry.
   b. He made a salary of $40,000-a-year when he was a systems manager. _____
2. a. Most states require drivers to carry no-fault insurance.
   b. This mistake is no-fault of mine. _____

3. a. Present-day morals are not acceptable to some senior citizens.
   b. The history of the present-day will reflect these morals. _____
4. a. The one-way streets in this city confuse me.
   b. The oneway streets in this city confuse me. _____
5. a. A ten-day leave was granted to Mr. Selmer.
   b. A leave of ten-days was granted to Mr. Selmer. _____
6. a. His missing the bus is an every day occurrence.
   b. His missing the bus is an everyday occurrence. _____
7. a. The open-door policy permits goods to enter this country with little or no import tax.
   b. My department chairman has an open-door, thereby welcoming faculty and students. _____
8. a. The anniversary banquet is a white-tie affair.
   b. This affair requires that gentlemen wear a white-tie. _____
9. a. These shingles are fire-proof.
   b. These fireproof shingles are only slightly more expensive than others. _____
10. a. The budget ready-to-wear garments are in the basement.
    b. The garments have been cleaned and are ready-to-wear. _____

ANSWERS TO FRAME 4

1. a	4. a	7. a	10. a
2. a	5. a	8. a	
3. a	6. b	9. b	

Frame 5   Comparison of Adjectives

Descriptive adjectives are used to compare the qualities of persons, places, and things. Three degrees of comparison are used: positive, comparative, and superlative.

Most adjectives form these degrees in a regular manner: by the addition of a suffix or use of *more* or *most* preceding the adjective. A few adjectives form these degrees by the use of completely different words. The latter group requires careful attention.

Regular Adjectives

Explanation

The three degrees of adjectives are used in the following ways:

Positive: Used to make a statement about one person, place, or thing.
Comparative: Used to compare two persons, places, or things.
Superlative: Used to compare three or more persons, places, and things.

Example

1. Positive: Used to make a statement about one person, place, or thing:

   Ronald is a <u>tall</u> man.

   Mount McKinley is a <u>high</u> mountain.

   This is an <u>expensive</u> car.

2. Comparative: Used to compare two persons, places, or things:
   a. Most one-syllable and some two-syllable adjectives form the comparative degree by the addition of -*er*.

   Ronald is <u>taller</u> than Joe.

   Mount McKinley is <u>higher</u> than Mount Rushmore.

b. Most adjectives of two or more syllables must be used in combination with the word *more* to show a greater increase in the descriptive quality and *less* to show a greater decrease in the descriptive quality.

My car is <u>more expensive</u> than yours.

Your car is <u>less expensive</u> than mine.

c. In comparing persons, places, or things, be certain that a complete comparison has been made.

Incorrect   Our sales figures are higher than the Bertrand Company. (<u>Figures</u> cannot be higher than a company!)

Correct   Our sales figures are higher <u>than those</u> of the Bertrand Company. (<u>Those</u> refers to <u>sales figures</u>.)

Correct   Our sales figures are higher than the Bertrand <u>Company's</u>. (The words <u>sales figures</u> are understood.)

d. In comparing one person with a group or class of which he/she is a part, use the comparative degree. Also, the words *other* or *else* should appear in the sentence.

Joe is <u>more</u> intelligent than the <u>other</u> students.
(The term <u>other students</u> comprises a group, and Joe is one of the students.)

Ed sold <u>more</u> merchandise than did the other sales representatives. (Ed is one of the sales representatives.)

e. When *other* or *else* is not included, use the superlative degree.

Joe is the <u>most</u> intelligent student in the class.

Of all the sales representatives, Ed sold the <u>most</u> merchandise.

f. Most desk dictionaries show the comparative forms of regular adjectives only if a change in spelling occurs in the comparative and superlative degrees, or if the spelling is uncommon.*

> ¹**easy** \ˈē-zē\ *adj* **eas·i·er; -est** [ME *esy,* fr. OF *aaisié,* pp. of *aaisier* to ease, fr. *a-* ad- (fr. L *ad-*) + *aise* ease] **1** : causing or involving little difficulty or discomfort <an ~ problem> **2 a** : not severe : LENIENT **b** : not steep or abrupt <~ slopes> **c** : not difficult to endure or undergo <an ~ penalty> **d** : readily prevailed on <~ prey> **e** (1) : plentiful in supply at low or declining interest rates <~ money> (2) : less in demand and usu. lower in price <bonds were *easier*> **3 a** : marked by peace and comfort <the ~ course of his life> **b** : not hurried or strenuous <~ pace> **4 a**

3. Superlative: Used to compare three or more persons, places, and things.
   a. Most one-syllable and some two-syllable adjectives form the superlative degree by the addition of *-est.*

   Ronald is the <u>tallest</u> student in the class.

   Mount McKinley is the <u>highest</u> mountain in the United States.

   b. Most adjectives of two or more syllables must be used along with *most* to show the greatest positive distinction and with *least* to show the greatest negative distinction in a quality.

   John made the *most* effective sales presentation.

   This product line is the *least* lucrative of the four.

*By permission. From *Webster's New Collegiate Dictionary* ©1977 by G. & C. Merriam Co., Publishers of the Merriam-Webster Dictionaries.

4. Example Comparisons:

Positive	*Comparative*	*Superlative*
bright	brighter	brightest
easy	easier	easiest
beautiful	more beautiful	most beautiful
	less beautiful	least beautiful
comprehensive	more comprehensive	most comprehensive
	less comprehensive	least comprehensive

Exercise

In one sentence of each of the following pairs, a degree of comparison is used correctly. In the blank provided, write the letter designating the correct sentence.

Example

a. Joe is the most capable of the two applicants.
b. Joe is the more capable of the two applicants.   b

1. a. Our unit cost is greater than the Borman Company.
   b. Our unit cost is greater than that of the Borman Company.   _____
2. a. The income statement for May shows a greater profit than does April's.
   b. The income statement for May shows a greater profit than April.   _____
3. a. The Datacron computer is more expensive than the Datatype computer.
   b. The Datacron computer is the most expensive of the two computers.   _____
4. a. Helen is a faster typist than the other girls in the word processing center.
   b. Helen types more fast than Kay.   _____
5. a. This is the most difficult assignment of the four.
   b. This assignment is the more difficult of the four.   _____
6. a. Tuesday was the most cold day of the year.
   b. Tuesday was the coldest day of the year.   _____
7. a. Your salary is higher than that of any other consultant on the staff.
   b. Your salary is highest than any of the other four consultants'.   _____
8. a. Belmont is the longest of the two streets leading to the highway exit.
   b. Belmont is the longer of the two streets leading to the highway exit.   _____
9. a. Pearl is more enthusiastic about her job than is Marilyn.
   b. Pearl is enthusiasticer about her job than is Marilyn.   _____
10. a. Mike is neater than the other accountants in the firm.
    b. Mike is more neat than the other accountants in the firm.   _____

ANSWERS TO FRAME 5

1. b	4. a	7. a	10. a
2. a	5. a	8. b	
3. a	6. b	9. a	

Frame 6   Comparison of Adjectives

Irregular Comparative Forms

Explanation

Only a few adjectives do not form the comparative and superlative degrees by the addition of -er and -est or by being used with *more* and *most*. These adjectives have irregular comparative forms. Because they are very frequently misused, they are presented in Lesson 22, which is devoted to frequently misused words.

Adjective Clauses

Explanation

A clause is a group of grammatically related words containing a subject and verb. A clause that modifies (describes, limits) a noun or pronoun is used as an adjective clause. Notice that an adjective clause usually follows the noun or pronoun it modifies. This clause often begins with one of these pronouns: *who, whom, which, whose.*

Example

1. An employee <u>who signs the insurance release form before June 30</u> will not be required to pay the indemnification charge. (modifies <u>employee</u>, a noun)
2. This paper, <u>which I read at the professional meeting</u>, has been published. (modifies <u>paper</u>, a noun)
3. I gave the check to Andrea, <u>whom I met in the hall</u>. (modifies <u>Andrea</u>, a noun)
4. Anyone <u>who pays his tax before the deadline</u> will not be required to pay a penalty. (modifies <u>anyone</u>, a pronoun)

Exercise

Underscore the adjective clause in each of the following sentences. In the blank provided, write the noun or pronoun that this clause modifies.

Example

The person <u>who removed the barricade</u> has been found.   <u>person</u>

1. A bonus will be granted to anyone who has sold the prescribed minimum quota. _____
2. Alicia gave her secretary, whom she likes, a raise this month. _____
3. The woman whose place I took has been promoted. _____
4. The new corporate headquarters will be moved to Lincoln, which is in eastern Nebraska. _____
5. Emmett, who is selling real estate, formerly worked for the Homewood Savings and Loan Association. _____

ANSWERS TO FRAME 6
1. <u>who has sold the prescribed minimum quota</u>   anyone
2. <u>whom she likes</u>   secretary
3. <u>whose place I took</u>   woman
4. <u>which is in eastern Nebraska</u>   Lincoln
5. <u>who is selling real estate</u>   Emmett

Frame 7   *Business Vocabulary: Marketing—Product Analysis*

Explanation

Before any advertising can be created for a product or service, that product or service must be analyzed in relation to those which will be its closest competitors.

Terms

Product analysis—an evaluation of each feature of a product (or service) in relation to equivalent features in competitors' products (or services) to determine the central and subordinate selling points.

Central selling point—the feature or characteristic that one product has in a greater quantity or to a greater degree than another product. This major advantage is emphasized in mass advertising and in direct mail advertising.

Subordinate selling points—the features or characteristics of a product (or service) that may be the same as (or similar to) those of competitors' products. These subordinate selling points are mentioned in the advertising to support the central selling point and describe the product.

Exercise

In the blank provided, write the letter that designates the most appropriate answer.

1. The central selling point of a car described as a "compact" is most likely to be which of the following features? _____
   a. High gas mileage
   b. Long-lasting paint
   c. Maneuverability
   d. Leather upholstery
2. To the average consumer, which of the following characteristics would be least likely to be a central selling point for an item of clothing? _____
   a. Color
   b. Price
   c. Fit
   d. Brand
3. Mass advertising is persuasive written or oral communication directed toward and available to almost all people in a designated locality: a city, trading area, or country. Which of the following is least likely to be considered mass advertising media? _____
   a. 30-second radio commercial
   b. 15-second television commercial
   c. An advertisement in a local newspaper distributed to a large trading area
   d. An advertisement in a publication directed to farmers
4. Which of the following facts can a product analysis not disclose? _____
   a. Central selling point
   b. Number of prospective buyers
   c. Subordinate selling points
   d. Location of prospective buyers

ANSWERS TO FRAME 7
1. a   2. d   3. d   4. b and d

Frame 8   *Applying Your Knowledge*

Directions

Proofread the following letter and underscore each error in adjective usage. Write the correction in the space below the sentence.

CASE

You have been given the product analysis that shows how a broiler manufactured by the Argo Company, for which you work, compares with two other broilers. This is your first draft of a letter to be used in direct mail advertising. (10 errors)

Body of Letter:

Dear Reader:

Dinner for one or dinner for a crowd—the ARGOWARE BROILER/ROTISSERIE can handle it for you with EASE and CONVENIENCE!

With this *one* electrical appliance, your meat can broil or roast while you do other work or visit with your guests. You can broil steak and chops on the lowest level of the two level rack, reverse it, and broil chicken, franks, or bacon. When the rotisserie motor and elements are attached, you can place a roast or chicken on the spit and anticipate a main course prepared to your satisfaction but without effort on your part.

Tested in the ARGO kitchens, the ARGOWARE BROILER/ ROTISSERIE is the most compact, lighter, and easier to use than other rotisserie/broilers now on the market. The stainless-steel body will retain the heat and divert the juices from the broiler into an aluminum drip tray, situated on the base frame.

Broiled food has been found to retain its flavor without retaining the fats that are a part of fried or oven roasted meat. The broiling chart in the guidebook gives the approximate time for broiling poultry, at least ten cuts of meat, and a variety of fish. This most unique ARGOWARE BROILER/ROTISSERIE is available in two sizes: 9″ × 15″ and 9″ × 11″. The largest of the two will accommodate a 13-pound turkey or a 6-pound roast.

This easy to clean appliance is completely immersible; in fact, every piece except the motor and heating element can be placed in the dishwasher. Any particles that stick to the stainless steel body can be removed with steel wool.

For only $49.95 (for 9″ × 15″ and $39.95 for 9″ × 11″), you can have the joy of broiled food without the spatter and smoke that result from skillet or oven cooking. Without opening an oven door or removing a skillet lid, you can see your food being broiled or roasted. The flavor of spit roasted meats is greater than other meats because as the spit turns, the meat is basted in its own juice.

Visit your favorite hardware or department store and ask to see the ARGOWARE BROILER/ROTISSERIE. Take advantage of the

ARGOWARE sale from June 15–July 15 and make your life one of EASE and CONVENIENCE with an ARGOWARE BROILER/ROTISSERIE.

ANSWERS TO FRAME 8

Dear Reader:

Dinner for one or dinner for a crowd—the ARGOWARE BROILER/ ROTISSERIE can handle it for you with EASE and CONVENIENCE!

With this *one* electrical appliance, your meat can broil or roast while you do other work or visit with your guests. You can broil steak and chops on the <u>lowest</u> level of the
lower
<u>two level</u> rack, reverse it, and broil chicken, franks, or bacon. When the rotisserie
two-level
motor and elements are attached, you can place a roast or chicken on the spit and anticipate a main course prepared to your satisfaction but without effort on your part.

Tested in the ARGO kitchens, the ARGOWARE BROILER/ROTISSERIE is <u>the most</u> compact, lighter, and easier to use than other rotisserie/broilers now on
more
the market. The <u>stainless-steel</u> body will retain the heat and divert the juices
stainless steel
from the broiler into an aluminum drip tray, situated on the base frame.

Broiled food has been found to retain its flavor without retaining the fats that are a part of fried or <u>oven roasted</u> meat. The broiling chart in the guidebook gives the
oven-roasted
approximate time for broiling poultry, at least ten cuts of meat, and a variety of fish.

This <u>most unique</u> ARGOWARE BROILER/ROTISSERIE is available in two sizes:
unique
9″ × 15″ and 9″ × 11″. The <u>largest</u> of the two will accommodate a 13-pound turkey
larger
or a 6-pound roast.

This <u>easy to clean</u> appliance is completely immersible; in fact, every piece except the
easy-to-clean
motor and heating element can be placed in the dishwasher. Any particles that stick to the stainless steel body can be removed with steel wool.

For only $49.95 (for 9″ × 15″ and $39.95 for 9″ × 11″), you can have the joy of broiled food without the spatter and smoke that result from skillet or oven cooking. Without opening an oven door or removing a skillet lid, you can see your food being broiled or roasted. The flavor of <u>spit roasted</u> meats is greater <u>than</u> other meats because
spit-roasted   than that of
as the spit turns, the meat is basted in its own juice.

Visit your favorite hardware or department store and ask to see the ARGOWARE BROILER/ROTISSERIE. Take advantage of the ARGOWARE sale from June 15–July 15 and make your life one of EASE and CONVENIENCE with an ARGOWARE BROILER/ROTISSERIE.

Lesson 21
Adverbs

Pretest

Pretest Part I
Adverbs as Modifiers

Directions

1. In the first column, write an adverb from the sentence at the left.
2. In the second column, write the word that the adverb modifies.
3. In the third column, write the part of speech that identifies the modified word.
4. If a sentence contains more than one adverb, repeat the procedure for each of them, using the blanks provided.

Example

	Adverb	Modified Word	Part of Speech
The postage machine has	efficiently	operates	verb
been repaired, and it	very	efficiently	adverb
operates very efficiently.			
1. These plants will bloom very early in the spring.			
2. Working ten hours a day is quite exhausting.			
3. This letter is entirely too long.			
4. Bob closed the deal with Abermarle Enterprises today.			
5. She worked competently and swiftly to complete the article by the deadline.			

Pretest Part II
Adverbs with Linking Verbs

Directions

Select the correct word and write it in the blank provided.

Example

The perfume smells (fragrant, fragrantly).   fragrant

1. She feels (bad, badly) today.   _____
2. He smelled the air (cautious, cautiously), trying to detect gas fumes.   _____
3. Benito does (good, well) in quantitative subjects.   _____
4. Ms. Reid is recuperating, and we expect her to be (good, well) enough to return
   to work soon.   _____
5. Harmon seems (disinterested, disinterestedly) in this project.   _____

Pretest Part III
Degrees of Comparison

Directions

Select the correct word and write it in the blank provided.

Example

My office is (less, least) efficiently arranged than yours.   less

1. Helen types (more fast, faster) than the other typists in the department.   _____
2. He works (more quickly, quicker) than I do.   _____
3. This company is (the less, the least) autocratically managed organization in the
   entire textile industry.   _____
4. The machine can be operated (more easier, more easily) than the brand X
   machine.   _____
5. Patricia, a case worker, visits some families (more frequently, frequenter) than
   others.   _____

Pretest Part IV
Double Negatives

Directions

1. If the sentence contains a double negative, underscore the negative words.
2. If the double negative is used correctly, write C in the blank provided; if not,
   write one of the negative words (or the combination) and the positive word that
   should replace it.

Example

Though not unenthusiastic, Marilyn did not contribute as much to the discussion as
her group had anticipated she would.   C

1. I cannot hardly read the print on this lease.   _____
2. The manager said that we did not need no more help during the night shift.   _____

3. The woman did not have neither the education nor the experience to become a licensed practical nurse. _____
4. I don't know nobody in this city yet. _____
5. This is not a nonalcoholic drink. _____

Pretest Part V
Adverbial Phrases and Clauses

Directions

1. In the first column, write P (phrase) or C (clause) to identify the underscored words.
2. In the second column, write the word that the underscored words modify.
3. In the third column, write the part of speech that identifies the modified word.

Example

	Phrase or Clause	Modified Word	Part of Speech
The accountant analyzed the report <u>to find the error</u>.	P	analyzed	verb
1. The rental agency increased the rent <u>to pay the higher taxes</u>.	_____	_____	_____
2. Jan was late <u>because she missed the bus</u>.	_____	_____	_____
3. <u>When the real estate appreciates</u>, we will sell the Collins property.	_____	_____	_____
4. Read the agenda <u>before you go to the meeting</u>.	_____	_____	_____
5. Please sign for the package <u>when it is delivered</u>.	_____	_____	_____

Lesson 21
Adverbs

An *adverb* is an explanatory word, usually answering one of these questions: *How?* *When?* *Where?* *Why?* or *How much?*

Adverbs create images that make our writing interesting, vivid, and clear. Notice the different image presented by each sentence within the following pairs. (The adverbs are underscored.)

a. He walked to the bank.
b. He walked <u>rapidly</u> to the bank.

a. She awaited the response to her application.
b. She <u>anxiously</u> awaited the response to her application.

a. He wants you to reply to the letter.
b. He wants you to reply to the letter <u>immediately</u>.

Although adverbs are used to explain, intensify, or clarify, in business writing they should be used sparingly. The immoderate use of adverbs causes a sentence to become unwieldy and difficult to read. Also, the overuse of adverbs in a business communication may distract from the main idea and convey an exaggerated opinion.

Exaggerated: <u>Devastatingly</u> beautiful but <u>obviously</u> <u>extremely</u> expensive, the office furniture is the focal point in the executive suite.
Less exaggerated: The office furniture, beautiful but obviously expensive, is the focal point in the executive suite.

Frame 1 Adverbs: Identification

Adverbs are easily recognized, but problems can occur in using them correctly. In these frames, adverbs will be identified, illustrated as modifiers, shown in comparisons, and used in phrases and clauses.

Explanation

An *adverb* is an explanatory word that answers one of these questions: *How?* *When?* *Where?* *Why?* or *How much?* *(To what extent?)*. Many adverbs that answer the question *how?* end in *-ly*. Others are recognized by their position in the sentence and the word which each modifies. The word to which the question pertains is the word that the adverb modifies.

Example

The word that the adverb modifies in each of the following example sentences is underscored within the parentheses.

1. Some adverbs answer the question *How?* Examples: rapidly, carefully, well, peacefully, energetically.

   She typed the manuscript <u>rapidly</u>. (<u>typed</u> how?)
   The teller counted the cash <u>quickly</u>. (<u>counted</u> how?)

2. Some adverbs answer the question *When?* Examples: now, soon, then, immediately, yesterday, often.

   I am going to the reproduction center <u>now</u>. (<u>am going</u> when?)
   Answer this letter <u>immediately</u>. (<u>Answer</u> when?)

333

3. Some adverbs answer the question *Where?* Examples: there, here, anywhere, somewhere.

> The meeting will be held <u>there</u> again. (<u>will be held</u> where?)
> Place the desk <u>here</u>. (<u>Place</u> where?)

4. Some adverbs answer the question *How much?* (*To what degree?*). Examples: extremely, too.

> The report is <u>extremely</u> long.
> The distance is <u>too</u> far to walk.

5. Other commonly used adverbs: no, not, never, very, quite.

> Harry <u>never</u> arrives on time. (<u>arrives</u> when?)
> The work is <u>quite</u> difficult. (how <u>difficult</u>?)

Exercise

Underscore the adverb in each of the following sentences. In the blank provided, write the word the adverb modifies.

Example

The clerk counted the change <u>rapidly</u>.   <u>counted</u>

1. The administrator completed the report quickly.   _____
2. She is eagerly awaiting a response to her application letter.   _____
3. The store has finally reordered the items which were not in the inventory. _____
4. Your tax return will be due soon.   _____
5. Shelly is very interested in joining a professional organization.   _____

ANSWERS TO FRAME 1

1. <u>quickly</u>; completed	3. <u>finally</u>; reordered	5. <u>very</u>; interested
2. <u>eagerly</u>; awaiting	4. <u>soon</u>; due	

Frame 2   *Adverb Use: Modifying a Verb, Adjective, or Adverb*

Explanation

The adverb is used to modify a verb, adjective, or another adverb. To locate the adverb, ask one of the identifying questions.

Example

1. Adverbs that modify verbs answer the questions *How? When?* or *Where?*

> She edited the manuscript <u>carefully</u>. (<u>edited</u> how?)
> Jerry sent the telegram <u>immediately</u>. (<u>sent</u> when?)
> The student placed the book <u>there</u>. (<u>placed</u> where?)

2. Adverbs modify descriptive adjectives, those which name a quality. In this case, the adverb tells to what degree the quality exists and answers the question *How much?*

> Be <u>especially</u> careful in operating this machine.
> This is the <u>most</u> expensive car on the lot.
> It is <u>extremely</u> late to return this questionnaire.

3. Occasionally, an adverb may modify another adverb. In this case, the adverb answers the question *To what extent?*

> She was <u>very</u> thoroughly prepared for the job. (<u>very</u> modifies <u>thoroughly</u>, an adverb)

> He drove <u>too</u> rapidly and missed the exit. (<u>too</u> modifies <u>rapidly</u>, an adverb)

Exercise

1. In the first column, write an adverb from the sentence at the left.
2. In the second column, write the word that the adverb modifies.
3. In the third column, write the part of speech that identifies the modified word.
4. If a sentence contains more than one adverb, repeat the procedure for each of them, using the blanks provided.

Example

	Adverb	Modified Word	Part of Speech
The postage machine has been repaired, and it operates very efficiently.	efficiently	operates	verb
	very	efficiently	adverb

1. The cab driver drove slowly through the traffic.

2. Becky very capably presented the slide demonstration to the sales representatives.

3. This is the most efficiently managed office that I have inspected today.

4. The customer spoke angrily to the counter clerk.

5. The check has not been located anywhere.

6. Ms. Green is un-
   believably happy
   about being named
   to this position.

   _____ _____ _____

   _____ _____ _____

   _____ _____ _____

   _____ _____ _____

7. This report is en-
   tirely too long.

   _____ _____ _____

   _____ _____ _____

8. This form would be
   more useful if
   the information
   were arranged
   differently.

   _____ _____ _____

   _____ _____ _____

   _____ _____ _____

   _____ _____ _____

   _____ _____ _____

9. The revision of the
   forms series could be
   done more rapidly if
   we had additional
   help.

   _____ _____ _____

   _____ _____ _____

   _____ _____ _____

   _____ _____ _____

   _____ _____ _____

10. Tabulating the
    questionnaire man-
    ually is quite time-
    consuming.

    _____ _____ _____

    _____ _____ _____

    _____ _____ _____

    _____ _____ _____

ANSWERS TO FRAME 2

	Adverb	*Modified Word*	*Part of Speech*
1.	slowly	drove	verb
2.	capably	presented	verb
	very	capably	adverb
3.	efficiently	managed	adjective
	most	efficiently	adverb
	today	have inspected	verb
4.	angrily	spoke	verb
5.	not	has been located	verb
	anywhere	has been located	verb
6.	unbelievably	happy	adjective
7.	too	long	adjective
	entirely	too	adverb
8.	more	useful	adjective
	differently	were arranged	verb
9.	rapidly	could be done	verb
	more	rapidly	adverb
10.	manually	tabulating	gerund (verb form)
	quite	time-consuming	adjective

Frame 3   Adverb Use: Adverbs with Linking Verbs

Explanation

Adverbs do not modify *linking verbs,* such as verbs derived from *be: is, am, was, were, been, are;* verbs of the senses: *feel, look, sound, smell, taste;* or such words as *seem, appear, become.* Linking verbs link a noun or pronoun to its modifier, usually an adjective.

Example

1. From *be:* is, am, was, were, been, are

    The attendance is <u>small</u>. (adjective modifying <u>attendance</u>)
    She was <u>late</u>. (adjective modifying <u>She</u>)
    The response is <u>good</u>. (adjective modifying <u>response</u>)

Note

The word *good* is always an adjective; *well* is an adjective when it refers to a state of health, but at other times it is an adverb.

    She is <u>well</u> after the operation. (adjective modifying <u>She</u>)
    He did <u>well</u> on the examination. (adverb modifying <u>did</u> and answering the question How?)

2. Verbs of the senses: feel, look, sound, smell, taste.

    The surface feels <u>rough</u>. (adjective, modifying <u>surface</u>; the surface can't do the feeling)
    The milk tastes <u>sour</u>. (adjective modifying <u>milk</u>; the milk can't do the tasting)

Note

If the verb conveys the idea that the subject is performing the action, an adverb is used with the verb of the senses.

    He felt the surface <u>gingerly</u>, trying to avoid splinters. (adverb telling how <u>he</u> performed the action)

    The dog smelled his dinner <u>eagerly</u>. (adverb telling how the <u>dog</u> performed the action)

3. Other verbs, such as appear, seem, become.

    This furniture becomes <u>dark</u> (not darkly) with age. (adjective, modifying <u>furniture</u>)

    These people seem <u>strange</u> (not <u>strangely</u>). (adjective modifying <u>people</u>)

Exercise

Select the correct word in each of the following sentences and write it in the blank provided.

Example

This perfume smells (fragrant, fragrantly).   <u>fragrant</u>

1. She looks (different, differently) with her new hairdo.   _____
2. Ms. Alonza manages her division (good, well).   _____

3. Mr. Sims has been ill, but we expect him to be (good, well) by spring. _____
4. Despite the accident, Mr. Sorenson appeared (calm, calmly). _____
5. He felt the envelope (careful, carefully) to determine if it contained coins. _____
6. The child ate the food (greedy, greedily). _____
7. The crackers stored in the emergency shelter became (moist, moistly) because of the dampness. _____
8. The coffee tastes (strong, strongly) this morning. _____
9. He tasted the coffee (cautious, cautiously), fearing that it had been spiked. _____
10. She feels (bad, badly) about the mistake. _____

ANSWERS TO FRAME 3

1. different	5. carefully	8. strong
2. well	6. greedily	9. cautiously
3. well	7. moist	10. bad
4. calm		

Frame 4   Degrees of Comparison

Common Comparisons

Explanation

Like adjectives, adverbs have three degrees of comparison: positive, comparative, and superlative. Many adverbs, in fact, are formed from adjectives.

Example

1. Positive degree: Used to make a statement about a person, place, or thing. In many cases, the positive degree of the adverb is formed by adding -*ly* to the adjective.

    Mary is a rapid typist. (adjective)

    Mary types rapidly. (adverb)

    He is a careful driver. (adjective)

    He drives carefully. (adverb)

    The customer was angry. (adjective)

    He spoke angrily to the clerk. (adverb)

Although all dictionaries label each vocabulary entry with its part of speech, the comparative and superlative degrees are not likely to be shown beside the positive form unless they are irregular or the spelling of the root word is changed. Therefore, the degrees of *early* are shown, but those of *soon (sooner, soonest)* are not.*

¹ear·ly \'ər-lē\ *adv* ear·li·er; -est [ME *erly,* fr. OE *ǣrlice,* fr. *ǣr* early, soon — more at ERE] **1 :** near the beginning of a period of time or of a process or series **2 a :** before the usual time **b** *archaic* : SOON **c :** sooner than related forms <these apples bear ∼>

*By permission. From *Webster's New Collegiate Dictionary* ©1977 by G. & C. Merriam Co., Publishers of the Merriam-Webster Dictionaries.

2. Comparative degree: Used to compare two persons, places, or things. To form the comparative degree of a one-syllable adverb, add *-er* to the positive form.

Positive	*Comparative*
soon	sooner
fast	faster
late	later

To form the comparative degree of a two-syllable adverb, either add *-er* to the positive form, or insert *more* (or *less*) before the positive form.

Positive	*Comparative*
often	oftener (or) more often (or) less often
early	earlier
warmly	more (or less) warmly
greatly	more (or less) greatly

3. Superlative degree: Used to compare three or more persons, places, or things. To form the superlative degree of a one-syllable adverb, add *-est* to the positive form.

Positive	*Superlative*
soon	soonest
late	latest
fast	fastest

To form the superlative degree of a two-syllable adverb, either add *-est* to the root word or insert *most* (or *least*) before the positive form.

Positive	*Superlative*
often	oftenest (or) most/least often
early	earliest
warmly	most/least warmly
greatly	most/least greatly

To form the superlative degree of an adverb containing three or more syllables, insert *most* (or *least*) before the positive form.

Positive	*Superlative*
conveniently	most/least conveniently
frequently	most/least frequently
efficiently	most/least efficiently

4. Never use these comparisons together:
   a. Two superlative forms.

Incorrect	He drives the <u>most fastest</u> of anyone on the team.
Correct	He drives the <u>fastest</u> of anyone on the team.

   b. The words *more* or *most* before a one-syllable adverb.

Incorrect	He drives <u>more fast</u> than I.
Correct	He drives <u>faster</u> than I.

Exercise

Fill in the blank provided for each sentence with the correct word from within the parentheses.

Example

My office is (less, least) efficiently arranged than yours.   ___less___

1. She maintains the (more, most) orderly office in this three-office department. _____
2. Ms. James works the (fastest, most fastest) of the three sorters. _____
3. He inspects this office (less, least) often than the other government inspectors do. _____
4. Ms. Alden was the (most expensively, expensivest) attired woman at the meeting. _____
5. The hand calculator with a slanted frame can be operated (more easy, more easily) than the one with a flat frame. _____

ANSWERS TO FRAME 4
1. most   2. fastest   3. less   4. most expensively   5. more easily

---

Frame 5 *Degrees of Comparison*

Problem Comparisons: Adjectives and Adverbs

Explanation

Problems in comparing adverbs arise for these reasons: some adverbs, like some adjectives, cannot be compared; some words are both adjectives and adverbs; and some adverbs have two forms.

Example

1. Some adverbs, such as completely, universally, and never, cannot be compared.

    This answer is <u>completely</u> wrong. (No answer can be <u>more completely wrong</u>.)

2. Adjective/Adverb Confusion:
    a. Some adjectives (as well as adverbs) end in -*ly;* such words are labeled as adjectives in the dictionary. For instance: friendly, motherly, costly.

        Customers appreciate a <u>friendly</u> employee. (adjective)

    b. Some words ending in -*ly* are both adjectives and adverbs; the part of speech depends upon their usage in the sentence. Many desk dictionaries define, and may even illustrate, each usage. For instance: only, weekly, daily, monthly, yearly.

        A <u>weekly</u> report is presented to the controller. (adjective; what kind of report?)

        You are expected to prepare this report <u>weekly</u>. (adverb; prepare when?)

3. Some adverbs have two forms; each form is listed in the dictionary as an adverb: slow, slowly; direct, directly; short, shortly.

    Drive <u>slowly</u> through the school zone. (adverb)

    Drive <u>slow</u> through the school zone. (adverb)

It is possible for the two forms to have different meanings:

> Please ship the merchandise <u>direct</u> from the factory. (modifies <u>ship</u>, a verb, and means that the merchandise is not to be shipped to a wholesaler who will ship it onward)

> He is <u>directly</u> involved with the management of the casino. (modifies <u>involved</u>, a verb, and means that he personally is involved with the management)

Exercise

Select the correct sentence in each pair. In the blank provided, write the letter that identifies this sentence.

Example

  a. She always answers the questions perfectly.
  b. She always answers the questions more perfectly than anyone else.   a

1. a. The idea that the world is round is universally accepted.
   b. The idea that the world is round is more universally accepted than the idea that it is flat.   _____
2. a. Sam most never attends regional meetings.
   b. Sam never attends regional meetings.   _____

Directions

In each sentence that follows, an adjective or adverb is underscored. In the first column, write the word that the underscored word modifies. In the second column, write the part of speech of the underscored word.

Example

	Word	*Part of Speech*
The <u>yearly</u> sale will be held in December.	sale	adjective

3. The dentist sends his bills <u>monthly</u>. _____ _____
4. <u>Only</u> the dock superintendent can tell you if this merchandise was received in good condition. _____ _____
5. The employees on this floor are very <u>friendly</u>. _____ _____
6. The petty cash must be counted <u>daily</u>. _____ _____
7. The <u>slow</u> return of the questionnaire is due to the lack of a deadline on the letter of transmittal. _____ _____
8. He eased the lever <u>slowly</u> to the "Off" position. _____ _____
9. The planned expansion will be <u>costly</u>. _____ _____
10. The plane arrived <u>late</u>, and some of the passengers could not make their connections. _____ _____

11. The newspapers are being delivered ear-
    ly in the day now. _____ _____

12. The mail was late due to the storm which
    dropped five feet of snow on the metro-
    politan area. _____ _____

13. I haven't read the financial column
    lately. _____ _____

14. Your grade will be docked 10 percent for
    each late paper. _____ _____

15. Simon is closely related to the company
    president. _____ _____

ANSWERS TO FRAME 5

1.	a		8.	eased	adverb
2.	b		9.	expansion	adjective
3.	sends	adverb	10.	arrived	adverb
4.	dock superintendent	adjective	11.	are being delivered	adverb
5.	employees	adjective	12.	mail	adjective
6.	must be counted	adverb	13.	haven't read	adverb
7.	return	adjective	14.	paper	adjective
			15.	is related	adverb

Frame 6   Double Negatives

Explanation

Two negative words in one clause create a *double negative* expression and result in a positive meaning. In some instances, such an expression is used to emphasize a point, but in other cases this usage is incorrect and nonstandard. Some negative expressions are created by the use of negative words (no, not, never, none, nothing, and so on) and others by negative prefixes dis-, un-, and non-. Certain words can never be used with a negative word or prefix.

Example

1. Using the negative expression to emphasize a point:

    He is not disinterested in his job. (emphasizing that he is inter-
    ested in his job)

    Somewhat opinionated, Ms. Baca is not unprepared to discuss this
    subject on any occasion. (meaning that she is prepared at all
    times)

2. Using the double negative correctly:
    a. Some adverbs, such as scarcely, hardly, and barely, have a negative mean-
       ing and should not be used with another negative word. To correct the
       sentence, the first negative word should be changed to positive.

    Incorrect   I haven't hardly any social security credits.
    Correct   I have hardly any social security credits.

    Incorrect   I can't barely see the print in this contract.
    Correct   I can barely see the print in this contract.

b. Using two negative expressions in the same clause is incorrect. To correct the sentence, change one of the words (expressions) to the positive. (N—Negative; P—Positive)

Incorrect   He <u>didn't</u> see <u>no one</u> in the hall.
              N   N

Correct   He <u>didn't</u> see <u>anyone</u> in the hall.
             N   P

Incorrect   When the requisition was prepared, she
        said that she did <u>not</u> want <u>nothing</u>.
                    N   N

Correct   When the requisition was prepared, she
        said that she did <u>not</u> want <u>anything</u>.
                    N   P

Incorrect   The clerk <u>cannot</u> do <u>neither</u> the posting
                 N   N
        <u>nor</u> the comparing correctly. (neither/nor
        N
        is considered one negative expression)

Correct   The clerk <u>cannot</u> do <u>either</u> the posting
                 N   P
        <u>or</u> the comparing correctly. (either/or
        P
        is considered one positive expression)

Incorrect   <u>Neither</u> the president <u>nor</u> his top execu-
        N   N
        tives <u>cannot</u> appreciate the importance
             N
        of a good communications network.

Correct   <u>Neither</u> the president <u>nor</u> his top execu-
        N   N
        tives <u>can</u> appreciate the importance of
           P
        a good communications network.

Incorrect   The messengers <u>never</u> take <u>none</u> of the
                 N   N
        outgoing mail before ten o'clock.

Correct   The messengers <u>never</u> take <u>any</u> of the
                 N   P
        outgoing mail before 10 o'clock.

Exercise

1. If one of the following sentences contains a double negative that is used to emphasize a point:
   a. Underscore the negative words.
   b. Write C in the blank provided.
2. If the sentence contains a double negative that is used incorrectly:
   a. Underscore the negative words.
   b. In the blank provided, write one of the negative words (or the combination) and the positive word that should replace it.

Example

1. Though <u>not unenthusiastic</u>, Marilyn did not contribute as much to the discussion as her group had anticipated she would.   <u>   C   </u>
2. The night supervisor had <u>not</u> told <u>no one</u> on the shift about the new policy.   no one—<u>anyone</u>

1. The director did not like nothing that either manager did.   <u>   </u>

2. This new law does not affect neither wholesalers nor retailers. _____
3. I cannot hardly appreciate what you have done for me, Professor Rand. _____
4. The discount store did not have nothing in its flyer about a tire sale. _____
5. Not unaccustomed to luxury, the family now finds that one salary is insufficient. _____
6. At the committee meeting, the chairperson told the group never to call her at home before 7:00 A.M. nor after 9:00 P.M. _____
7. I did not work neither in the Baton Rouge plant nor in the Houston plant. _____
8. I have not yet placed no one on suspension for an infraction of this rule. _____
9. The customer had neither written nor called the company about this claim before he visited the Credit Department yesterday. _____
10. The buyer said she did not need no more merchandise. _____

ANSWERS TO FRAME 6

1. not, nothing   nothing—anything
2. not, neither/nor   neither/nor—either/or
3. cannot hardly   cannot—can
4. not, nothing   nothing—anything
5. not unaccustomed   C
6. never, nor   nor—or
7. not, neither/nor   neither/nor—either/or
8. not, no one   no one—anyone
9. (neither/nor is considered   C
   one negative expression,
   not a double negative)
10. not, no   no—any

Frame 7   Adverbial Phrases

Explanation

A *phrase* is a group of grammatically related words without a subject and verb. When infinitive and prepositional phrases are used in the same positions as adverbs, they modify an adjective, a verb, or an adverb. In these cases, they function as adverbs.

Example

1. Infinitive Phrase: used in an adverb position when it modifies a verb or an adjective. Often these phrases answer the question *Why?*

   > The salesclerk was eager to make the sale. (modifies eager, an adjective)

   > The accountant analyzed the report to find the error. (modifies analyzed, a verb)

2. Prepositional Phrase: functions as an adverb when it modifies a verb, adjective, or adverb.

   > The report will be completed in a month. (modifies the verb, will be completed)

   > Careful about her appearance, Ms. Martinez sets a good example. (modifies Careful, an adjective)

   > He works well at all times. (modifies well, an adverb)

Exercise

1. In the following sentences, the underscored phrases function as adverbs. In the first column, identify the type of phrase with an I (infinitive) or P (preposition).

	Modified Word	Part of Speech

6. Barron was happy <u>because he had received a commendation from the department manager</u>. _____ _____

7. The mail arrived early, <u>although the streets were almost impassable</u>. _____ _____

8. The new employees are slow <u>because the changed operation requires more steps than the previous one</u>. _____ _____

9. <u>When this merchandise is sold</u>, we shall order a different brand. _____ _____

10. <u>Before the property was placed on the market</u>, Scarborough Realty had received three offers to purchase it. _____ _____

ANSWERS TO FRAME 8

	Modified Word	Part of Speech			Modified Word	Part of Speech
1.	must be paid	verb		6.	happy	adjective
2.	late	adjective		7.	early	adverb
3.	smiled	verb		8.	slow	adjective
4.	must be signed	verb		9.	shall order	verb
5.	efficiently	adverb		10.	had received	verb

Frame 9   Selecting Adjectives and Adverbs

Explanation

In deciding whether to use an adjective or an adverb in a sentence, we need to know what word the selection will modify. An adjective modifies only a noun or a pronoun; an adverb modifies a verb, adjective, or another adverb.

Example

Which word should be selected in this sentence?

> Peter performed more (capably, capable) than the other trainees.

Making the decision: (a) the word to be chosen modifies the verb <u>performed</u>; (b) only an adverb can modify a verb; (c) <u>capable</u> is an adjective, and <u>capably</u> is an adverb; (d) therefore, the selection should be <u>capably</u>.

Exercise

In each of the following sentences, select the correct word in the parentheses and write it in the blank provided.

1. The supervisor operated this department very (efficient, efficiently). _____
2. Mike, a statistician, used formulas (expert, expertly) without reference to a textbook. _____
3. The insurance adjuster (inaccurate, inaccurately) appraised the damage to my roof. _____
4. The fumes from the chemical smell (bad, badly). _____
5. He feels (bad, badly) about the rumor. _____
6. To write letters (effective, effectively), you need a good basis in grammar. _____
7. The company had (real, very) good sales this month. _____

8. The building will be condemned unless the plumbing is repaired (expeditious, expeditiously). _____
9. He is not (adequate, adequately) qualified for the job. _____
10. The (rapid, rapidly) declining population of this metropolitan area is caused by high taxes and a high crime rate. _____

ANSWERS TO FRAME 9

1. efficiently
2. expertly
3. inaccurately
4. bad
5. bad
6. effectively
7. very
8. expeditiously
9. adequately
10. rapidly

Frame 10   Business Vocabulary: Market Analysis

Explanation

Before goods or services are offered for sale, the company offering them needs to know who and where the potential customers are. To obtain this information, an employee in the marketing department performs a *market analysis.*

Terms

Market analysis—an evaluation of the characteristics of the population to determine who the potential buyers of this product may be. Characteristics evaluated are age, income, profession or job (if pertinent to this product), and location (according to geographic areas and population centers—rural, suburban, or urban).

Demographic study—a study of the population with reference to size, density, distribution, and vital statistics. The study is part of the market analysis.

Bureau of the Census—a bureau within the federal government that takes and publishes the census statistics on various kinds of products and services; for example, number of retailers in an area, population of various cities, ages of population by area, and income of population according to age and area.

Universe—the total population. The universe is whatever the investigator determines that it shall be: the country, a state, a city, a market area. The demographic study of this universe provides the answers to this question: Who are and where are the potential customers?

Exercise

1. A complete market analysis requires that a _____ study of the population be made.

2. From this study, statistics are derived to identify the potential customers; these statistics pertain to what population characteristics? (name three)

   _____   _____   _____

3. In a market analysis, the total population of a country, city, and so on, is called the _____.

4. If you wanted an answer to each of these questions, to what publication(s) would you go? _____

   a. What is the average income of doctors in Atlanta?

   b. How many senior citizens live in Phoenix?

c.   What is the population of Butte, Montana?

d.   How many savings and loan associations are located in New York City?

e.   What is the population distribution according to age in West Texas?

5.   Whether your company is manufacturing hair dryers, cornpickers, cars, or novelty jewelry, what information can be determined by a market analysis, in addition to the characteristics of the potential customer? _____

ANSWERS TO FRAME 10
1.   demographic
2.   income, age, profession, according to the location of the customer
3.   universe
4.   Bureau of the Census
5.   where the customers are located and, therefore, where the product might be placed (dealership, specialty store, department store, and so on) for sale to the customer.

Frame 11   Applying Your Knowledge

Directions

Underscore each error in adverb or adjective usage in the following letter and write the correction in the space below it.

CASE

After a thorough study of the market, ASMD Electronics has decided to sell its new product, an electronic calculator called THE WHIZ, direct to high school students. Read this first draft of a letter written by the company's marketing specialist and correct the errors. (10 errors)

Dear Student:

Are you a WHIZ at math? Whether you answer this question Yes or No, THE WHIZ, ASMD's newly-designed electric calculator, is for you. Why?

If you are good at math, you can become even better, because THE WHIZ will help you to arrive at the answer more quick than would a manual method.

If you are not a WHIZ (and can use all the help you can get), THE WHIZ will help you to become one; just read the easy-to-follow directions.

With THE WHIZ you won't need to use neither a great amount of time nor a tremendous effort to arrive at the correct solution to a problem. The symbols on the keys correspond to those shown in the programmed directions that accompany THE WHIZ. By following these directions careful, you can practice solving square-root problems, find the standard deviation, compute variances, and perform many other operations.

THE WHIZ is 5 inches long, 4 inches wide, and ¾-inch thick—just the right size to fit in a pocket or a purse easy. If math bores or frustrates you, THE WHIZ will add zip to your day. The calculator comes in six colors: Chinese red, sky blue, delicate pink, avocado green, sunshine yellow, and midnight black. The key faces are in a contrasting color, and the symbols are the same color as the calculator frame. THE WHIZ is encased in a highly-textured suede folder that opens like a book.

You can find the keys easy and position your fingers on them quick because of the deep concave centers. Also, the frame is constructed at a 30-degree angle, permitting you a real good view of the red numbers as they appear on the dark screen at the top of THE WHIZ.

All these features would make THE WHIZ a good buy at $9.95, but you will receive even more—your name and address engraved on a plate of genuine copper and glued to the top of the frame.

Just fill out the enclosed card and send it with your check in the business reply envelope. In ten days, you can be computing your problems more competent than before.

Sincerely,

Betsy Purdue, Director
High School Marketing Division

ANSWERS TO FRAME 11

Dear Student:

Are you a WHIZ at math? Whether you answer this question Yes or No, THE WHIZ, ASMD's <u>newly-designed</u> electric calculator, is for you. Why?
           newly designed
If you are good at math, you can become even better, because THE WHIZ will help you to arrive at the answer <u>more quick</u> than would a manual method.
               more quickly
If you are not a WHIZ (and can use all the help you can get), THE WHIZ will help you to become one; just read the easy-to-follow directions.

With THE WHIZ you won't need to use <u>neither</u> a great amount of time <u>nor</u>
                            either   or
tremendous effort to arrive at the correct solution to a problem. The symbols on the keys correspond to those shown in the programmed directions that accompany THE WHIZ. By following these directions <u>careful</u>, you can practice solving square-root
                                  carefully
problems, find the standard deviation, compute variances, and perform many other operations.

THE WHIZ is 5 inches long, 4 inches wide, and ¾-inch thick, just the right size to

fit in a pocket or a purse <u>easy</u>. If math bores or frustrates you, THE WHIZ will add
easily
zip to your day. The calculator comes in six colors: Chinese red, sky blue, delicate

pink, avocado green, sunshine yellow, and midnight black. The key faces are in a

contrasting color, and the symbols are the same color as the calculator frame. THE

WHIZ is encased in a <u>highly-textured</u> suede folder that opens like a book.
highly textured
    You can find the keys <u>easy</u> and position your fingers on them <u>quick</u> because of the
easily   quickly
deep concave centers. Also, the frame is constructed at a 30-degree angle, permitting

you a <u>real</u> good view of the red numbers as they appear on the dark screen at the top
very
of THE WHIZ.

All these features would make THE WHIZ a good buy at $9.95, but you will receive

even more—your name and address engraved on a plate of genuine copper and glued

to the top of the frame.

Just fill out the enclosed card and send it with your check in the business reply

envelope. In ten days, you can be computing your problems <u>more competent</u> than
more competently
before.

Sincerely,

Betsy Purdue, Director
High School Marketing Division

Lesson 22
Frequently Misused Words

Pretest

The pretest and posttest for this lesson are presented in the form of an Applying Your Knowledge section. The presentation of the tests in this form permits you to determine if certain words are part of your writing vocabulary. The following frequently misused words are covered in this lesson:

1. of, have
2. ought with a helping verb
3. can, may
4. could, might
5. shall, will
6. should, would
7. lie, lay
8. sit, set
9. rise, raise
10. bad (ill), worse, worst
11. good (well), better, best
12. far, farther, further, farthest, furthest
13. unique, round, perfect
14. little, less, least
15. many (much), more, most
16. only
17. real, very, really

Directions

Draw a line through each misused word in the letter that follows and write the correct word in the space below it. Then write five sentences, each correctly using one of the words which you crossed out in the original letter.

Example

John and Martin are marketing a ~~most~~ unique product: pet punk rocks,
omit <u>most</u>

complete with safety pins and little leather jackets.

Sentence: Our lawnmower is <u>unique</u> because it runs on gasohol instead of gasoline.

CASE

As a cost accountant in a manufacturing firm, you have supervised a student from the cooperative program at the local high school for the past semester. You are required to write a brief account of this student's contribution to the firm and evaluate the knowledge he has gained. Here is the first draft of your letter to the student's instructor. (5 errors)

Ms. Harriet Charlton, Co-op Advisor
Mountain View High School
1821 Vestman Road
Bethesda, Maryland 21218

Dear Ms. Charlton:

Co-op Student—Joe Burns

Joe's efforts in the Cost Accounting Department are to be commended. He performed his assigned tasks real well.

As a messenger, he learned the route more quickly than did the other new messengers; in addition, he had a more perfect record for accurate deliveries. His pleasant attitude and cheerful manner made everyone's day very pleasant.

After completing his mail delivery, Joe worked in the department copy center. His attention to detail, ability to grasp the procedures quickly, and initiative in handling problems were commendable. Before Joe's arrival, the copy center had been noted for its chaotic operation. Joe lay all the reams of paper in labeled locations on the shelves and set the machines in different positions to improve the workflow. More employees are pleased with the center now because they can expect to pick up their reproduction orders on time.

In the afternoons, Joe has helped my assistants check inventory cards and prepare the computer input. He worked faster than the others and made less errors—only one per 500 cards compared!

Even though Joe's efforts were outstanding, he could improve his performance in two ways:

1. He should be more modest about his accomplishments.
2. He might of made a better impression by not flirting with the women employees.

I have appreciated and benefited from Joe's contribution to this department and will be pleased to participate in the program again next year.

Lesson 22
Frequently Misused Words

In this lesson, seventeen groups of words are presented in frames.

Frame 1

Explanation

These verb constructions should not be used:

(1) *of* in place of *have* in a verb phrase
(2) the verb *ought* with a helping verb

Example

1. OF/HAVE
   In a verb phrase, *could, should, might, will,* and *would* are followed by HAVE rather than OF.

   Correct: She SHOULD HAVE called me yesterday.
   I COULD HAVE finished the work if I had stayed at the office.

2. OUGHT
   This verb does not have principal parts. It should never be preceded by a helping verb.

   Correct: He OUGHT to plan his time better.
   Incorrect: He HAD OUGHT to plan his time better.

Exercise

Correct each of the following sentences by writing the incorrect word and the correction in the blank provided. If a sentence is already correct, write C in the blank.

Example

Janet may of been overreacting to the sportscaster's comments when she threw the brick at the television screen.   <u>of—have</u>

1. The supervisor should of known about Jay's absence.   _____
2. He had ought to write a memo on this topic.   _____
3. I might have won the award if I had submitted my entry.   _____
4. Kelly ought to speak to Ms. Sana about his problem.   _____
5. The newspaper account of the accident could of been incorrect. _____

ANSWERS TO FRAME 1
1. of—have   2. omit *had*   3. C   4. C   5. of—have

Frame 2

Explanation

The frequently misused words in this frame are verbs: can, may; could, might; should, would; shall, will.

1. CAN (COULD)/MAY (MIGHT)
   CAN and COULD imply capability; MAY and MIGHT imply permission or possibility.

   > I CAN complete the work by 4:30. (capability)

   > He COULD pass the course if he tried. (capability)

   > MAY I take compensatory leave from June 1–5? (permission)

   > I MAY go to the meeting in Washington. (possibility)

   > I MIGHT be able to pay the bill this month. (possibility)

2. SHALL/WILL
   Many years ago spoken and written English was much more formal than it is today; an example of this formality is the distinction between the uses of SHALL and WILL to express future action. Today, especially in conversational English, WILL is used far more extensively than SHALL. However, some organizations prefer that certain written communications reflect the formality of the occasion. Therefore, both the formal and the informal usage are explained.
   a. To express future action:
      (1) Formal: SHALL is used with first person; WILL is used with second and third persons.

      > I (We) SHALL appreciate your completing the questionnaire.

      > You WILL benefit from learning the results of the survey.

      > He (She, It, They) WILL come to the office tomorrow.

      (2) Informal: WILL is used for first, second, and third person.

   b. To express determination or a requirement:
      (1) Formal: WILL is used with first person, and SHALL is used with second and third person.

      > I (We) WILL not pay the bill until I (we) am (are) satisfied with the appliance.

      > You SHALL not leave the department without signing the control sheet.

      > He (She, They) SHALL be discharged for unsatisfactory performance.

      (2) Informal: WILL is used with first, second, and third person.
      (3) To show willingness, the word WILL is used in all three persons: I WILL be glad to help you.

3. SHOULD/WOULD
   SHOULD is used in place of SHALL, and WOULD is used in place of WILL:
   a. To show future action
   b. To show determination
   c. To imply willingness

Exercise

The word in parentheses at the beginning of each sentence tells what is to be expressed. Select the word from the parentheses that best expresses this and write it in the blank provided.

Example

(requirement) You (shall, will) attend the final examination at its regularly scheduled time. ___shall___

1. (permission) (May, Can) I have an appointment to discuss how my background in records management can be applied to the job of records administrator in your company? _____
2. (future) The payroll clerk (shall, will) complete the weekly payroll before the holiday. _____
3. (requirement) The insured (will, shall) notify this company by mail within ten days of the date from which the listed address has been changed. _____
4. (informal) I (should, would) like to hear from you before July 15 if you are interested in this job. _____
5. (permission) (Can, May) I use you as a reference? _____
6. (future) He (shall, will) return your call tomorrow. _____
7. (capability) (May, Can) I walk without a limp after my leg brace is removed? _____
8. (willingness) I (shall, will) be happy to write a recommendation for you. _____
9. (informal) I (should, would) appreciate your returning this questionnaire by July 1. _____
10. (determination) I (shall, will) report this incident to the department head. _____

ANSWERS TO FRAME 2

1. May	4. would	7. Can	10. will
2. will	5. May	8. will	
3. shall	6. will	9. would	

Frame 3

Explanation

Three pairs of commonly used verbs, along with their principal parts, are presented in this frame: *sit, set; lie, lay; rise, raise.*

Example

1. LIE/LAY
   LIE (v)—to recline
   LAY (v)—to place an object on a surface
   a. Principal Parts

Present	*Past*	*Past Participle*
lie	lay	lain
lay	laid	laid

   b. Usage:
      (1) LIE—intransitive verb; cannot take an object.

         Because of its spiral binding, the handbook <u>lies</u> open at any page. (present)

         The file <u>is lying</u> on the counter. (progressive)

         The file could have been stolen; it <u>lay</u> on the counter all day. (past)

         He <u>has lain</u> in a coma for three months. (past participle)

(2)   LAY—transitive verb; can take an object.

> Please <u>lay</u> the book on the desk. (present)
>
> He <u>is laying</u> bricks for the patio. (progressive)
>
> I <u>laid</u> the book on the desk last night. (past)
>
> He <u>has laid</u> the book on the desk. (past participle)

2.   SIT/SET
   SIT (v)—to be in a sitting position.
   SET (v)—to place an object on a surface.
   a.   Principal Parts:

Present	*Past*	*Past Participle*
sit	sat	sat
set	set	set

   b.   Usage:
      (1)   SIT—intransive verb; cannot take an object.

> I usually <u>sit</u> on the swivel chair. (present)
>
> She <u>is sitting</u> in the car. (progressive)
>
> The machine <u>sat</u> on the table yesterday. (past)
>
> I <u>have sat</u> in the second row at the theater many times. (past participle)

      (2)   SET—transitive verb; can take an object.

> <u>Set</u> the typewriter on the desk. (present)
>
> Harold <u>is setting</u> type for the newspaper now. (progressive)
>
> I <u>set</u> my purse on the desk an hour ago. (past)
>
> Mr. Gregory <u>has set</u> a tentative date for our meeting. (past participle)

3.   RISE/RAISE
   RISE (v)—to travel upward without help.
   RAISE (v)—to move an object upward.
   a.   Principal Parts:

Present	*Past*	*Past Participle*
rise	rose	risen
raise	raised	raised

   b.   Usage:
      (1)   RISE—intransive verb; cannot take an object.

> I <u>rise</u> at 6 a.m. every day. (present)
>
> The speaker <u>is rising</u> from his chair. (progressive)
>
> The smoke <u>rose</u> to the top of the building. (past)
>
> For the past three years, prices <u>have risen</u> steadily. (past participle)

(2)   RAISE—transitive verb; can take an object.

I <u>raise</u> a garden each year. (present)

The military guard <u>is raising</u> the flag. (progressive)

The tow truck <u>raised</u> the car from the river. (past)

Vegetable gardeners <u>have raised</u> cauliflower in this area for many years. (past participle)

Exercise

Select the correct word in parentheses in each sentence that follows and write it in the blank provided.

1.   The price of the farm (rose, raised) 8 percent during the last decade.   _____
2.   The repairman (set, sat) the machine in the storeroom.   _____
3.   The contract is (laying, lying) on the desk.   _____
4.   Prices always (raise, rise) more rapidly in the summer.   _____
5.   People could (sit, set) down at the bus stop if the city government would (sit, set) benches there.   _____
6.   The manager (lay, laid) the letter in the secretary's basket.   _____
7.   (Laying, Lying) in the sun causes some people to freckle and others to tan.   _____
8.   The bed of the truck can be (risen, raised) to dump the grain.   _____
9.   Pieces of the plane (had laid, had lain) on the mountain all winter.   _____
10.   The Gross National Product (rose, raised) 2 percent during the last quarter.   _____
11.   Some of the furniture has been (sitting, setting) in the showroom for the past month.   _____
12.   The refuse has been (laying, lying) in the street all day.   _____
13.   The chairperson (rose, raised) the issue of appointing an ad hoc committee.   _____
14.   The unopened letter (lay, laid) on his desk until he returned.   _____
15.   The store manager said that the workers could (lie, lay) the carpet this week.   _____
16.   Construction costs have (raised, risen) sharply during the past year.   _____
17.   The customers can (sit, set) in the covered arcade and relax from their shopping.   _____
18.   Some plants should be (set, sat) in the light to receive nourishment from the sun.   _____
19.   Hemlines have been (raised, risen) at the whim of designers.   _____
20.   During last year's epidemic, some patients (lay, laid) in the hospital corridors.   _____

ANSWERS TO FRAME 3

1.	rose	6.	laid	11.	sitting	16.	risen
2.	set	7.	Lying	12.	lying	17.	sit
3.	lying	8.	raised	13.	raised	18.	set
4.	rise	9.	had lain	14.	lay	19.	raised
5.	sit, set	10.	rose	15.	lay	20.	lay

Frame 4

Explanation

The comparative and superlative degrees of these adjectives are frequently misused: *bad, good; far, little; many, much.* Also certain adjectives, because they do not have comparative and superlative degrees, are misused.

The dictionary shows* the comparative and superlative degrees of irregular adjectives:

> **¹bad** \'bad\ *adj* **worse** \'wərs\; **worst** \'wərst\ [ME] **1 a** : failing to reach an acceptable standard : POOR **b** : UNFAVOR-ABLE <make a ~ impression> **c** : not fresh or sound : SPOILED. DILAPIDATED <~ fish> <the house was in ~ condition> **2 a** : morally objectionable **b** : MISCHIEVOUS. DISOBEDIENT **3** : inadequate or unsuited to a purpose <a ~ plan> <~ lighting> **4** : DISAGREEABLE. UNPLEASANT <~ news> **5 a** : INJURIOUS. HARMFUL **b** : SEVERE <a ~ cold> **6** : INCORRECT. FAULTY <~ grammar> **7 a** : suffering pain or distress <felt generally ~> **b** : UNHEALTHY. DISEASED <~ teeth> **8** : SORROWFUL. SORRY **9** : INVALID. VOID <a ~ check> — **bad** *adv* — **bad·ly** *adv* — **bad·ness** *n*

Example

1. BAD (ILL)—positive   WORSE—comparative   WORST—superlative

    He is in ILL health. He has a BAD cold.

    He has a WORSE cold than I. (not worser!)

    This is the WORST cold I've had all winter.

2. GOOD (WELL)—positive   BETTER—comparative   BEST—superlative
    a. The word GOOD is an adjective, and the word WELL is an adverb, except when it refers to a person's health. The adjective GOOD is usually used after a verb of the senses (feels, tastes, and so on).

        Your answer was GOOD. (adjective describing answer)

        Your answer was BETTER than Joe's. (adjective describing answer)

        Your answer was the BEST in the class. (adjective describing answer)

    b. He writes WELL. (WELL modifies the action verb writes and is an adverb.)

        Since he had the operation, he looks WELL. (WELL refers to his state of health and is used as an adjective.)

        The candy made from this recipe tastes GOOD. (GOOD modifies candy, follows a verb of the senses, and is an adjective.)

3. FAR—positive   FARTHER, FURTHER—comparative
    FARTHEST, FURTHEST—superlative
    a. FAR, FARTHER, and FARTHEST are used to refer to distance. FURTHER and FURTHEST are used when "additional" or "to a greater degree" is meant.

        Dallas is FARTHER from Denver than from Oklahoma City.

        This paper needs FURTHER attention.

        Of all the cities, San Diego is the FARTHEST distance from Bangor, Maine.

*By permission. From *Webster's New Collegiate Dictionary* ©1977 by G. & C. Merriam Co., Publishers of the Merriam-Webster Dictionaries.

4. LITTLE—positive   LESS—comparative   LEAST—superlative

> I have LITTLE money to spend for entertainment.
>
> She has LESS money than I.
>
> In the entire club, the Johnsons have the LEAST money to spend for entertainment.

a. LESS and FEWER are sometimes confused. LESS always refers to uncountable (or mass) nouns, and FEWER refers to countable nouns.

> We have LESS wheat this year than we had last year.
>
> FEWER people attended the meeting this month than last month.

5. MANY (MUCH)—positive   MORE—comparative   MOST—superlative

> I have MANY books.
>
> She has MORE books than I.
>
> Of all the personal libraries, Bud's has the MOST books.
>
> Jamie has MUCH talent.
>
> Alice has MORE talent than does Jamie.
>
> The winner has the MOST talent.

6. Some adjectives cannot be compared because the positive degree cannot be exceeded. Examples: UNIQUE, ROUND, PERFECT.

> This is a UNIQUE piece of furniture. (Another piece of furniture cannot be more or less unique.)
>
> The table is ROUND.
>
> You have a PERFECT paper. (No one can have a paper that is more perfect!)

Exercise

In each of the following sentences, select the correct word from the parentheses and write it in the blank provided.

1. He is (good, well) after his long illness.
2. The corridor in this building has (good, better) lighting than the corridor in the Jax Building.
3. Ms. Brentano explains the lesson (well, good).
4. The water does not taste (well, good).
5. No (farther, further) payments will be necessary.
6. (Less, Fewer) corn was planted this year.
7. Polly has (less, fewer) pupils in her class this year.
8. The colors in this picture are (unique, more unique).
9. I have many hobbies, but she has (more, the most).
10. Has he had any (farther, further) symptoms of cancer?
11. This is the (better, best) of the two opportunities.
12. (Less, Fewer) sugar is being used in many foods now.
13. The bank is (farther, further) from my residence than is the savings and loan association.
14. You will need to make (farther, further) changes in your report before it can be accepted.

15. Harlan feels (good, well) today, but he is still recovering from a virus. _____
16. (Fewer, Less) students were graduated this year than last. _____
17. This damage is the (worsest, worst) we have ever suffered from hail. _____
18. His spelling is (good, well). _____
19. You will find Mr. Semple in the (farthest, furthest) office on the right side of the corridor. _____
20. This advertisement is (more unique, uniquer, unique) and more persuasive than the other one. _____

ANSWERS TO FRAME 4

1.	well	6.	Less	11.	better	16.	Fewer
2.	better	7.	fewer	12.	Less	17.	worst
3.	well	8.	unique	13.	farther	18.	good
4.	good	9.	more	14.	further	19.	farthest
5.	further	10.	further	15.	well	20.	unique

Frame 5

Explanation

Some adverbs are frequently misused because:
a. They are placed in the wrong position in the sentence to modify the correct word and convey the meaning intended.
b. They are used to modify adjectives or other adverbs rather than verbs.
c. They are hyphenated.

Example

1. ONLY (adj, adv)—solely.
   Many writers misuse this word by placing it incorrectly within a sentence. Because ONLY can act as an adjective or as an adverb, careless writers often place it in an adverb position when they intend it to modify a noun or pronoun, or they place it in an adjective position when they intend it to modify a verb.

   > ONLY Kay read the report. (meaning: No one else read this report; ONLY is used as an adjective, modifying <u>Kay</u>.)

   > Kay ONLY read the report. (meaning: Kay did not write, type, or extract information from the report—she read it. In this sentence, ONLY is an adverb, modifying <u>read</u>.)

   > Kay read ONLY the report. (meaning: Kay read nothing other than this report. Here ONLY is an adjective modifying <u>report</u>.)

   > Kay read the report ONLY. (meaning: Kay read no reports other than this report. Here ONLY is an adjective modifying <u>report</u>.)

2. REAL/VERY
   The adjective REAL is frequently misused because it is placed in a sentence to modify an adjective or adverb. Because REAL is an adjective, it can modify only a noun or pronoun.

Incorrect	Porter is a REAL good student. (modifies <u>good</u>, an adjective)
Correct	Porter is a VERY good student. (modifies <u>good</u>, an adjective)
Correct	Porter is a GOOD student. (modifies <u>student</u>, a noun)
Correct	Porter is a REALLY good student. (an adverb, modifies <u>good</u>, an adjective)

3. An adverb ending in -*ly* is not hyphenated before the word it modifies.

> He is a HIGHLY paid executive.

> This is an EXTREMELY long report.

Exercise

In the blank provided, write the letter designating the sentence that correctly expresses the meaning of the numbered sentence.

Example

No one but John read the report.

    a. Only John read the report.
    b. John only read the report.   <u> a </u>

1. Mary typed but did not proofread or correct the letter.
    a. Mary only typed the letter.
    b. Mary typed only the letter.   <u>   </u>
2. Mary did not type other correspondence.
    a. Mary typed only the letter.
    b. Mary only typed the letter.   <u>   </u>
3. No one but Mary typed the letter.
    a. Only Mary typed the letter.
    b. Mary typed the letter only.   <u>   </u>

Directions

Select the correct word from the parentheses and write it in the blank to the right of each of the following sentences.

Example

She works (real, very) hard to make a living.   <u> very </u>

4. We received a (really, real) fine response to this direct mail letter.   <u>   </u>
5. The product is (widely advertised, widely-advertised) in the mass media.   <u>   </u>
6. This book is (real, very) interesting.   <u>   </u>
7. Jack, you did a (real, very) fine job on this report.   <u>   </u>
8. Dr. Hodges is a (highly-respected, highly respected) physician.   <u>   </u>
9. I bought this (intricately woven, intricately-woven) tapestry in Pakistan last summer.   <u>   </u>
10. Jennifer looked (real, really) tired this morning.   <u>   </u>

ANSWERS TO FRAME 5

1.	a	5.	widely advertised	8.	highly respected
2.	a	6.	very	9.	intricately woven
3.	a	7.	very	10.	really
4.	really				

Lesson 23
Prepositions

Pretest

Pretest Part I
Identifying Prepositions and Objects

Directions

1. Underscore the preposition and its object in each of the following sentences.
2. If the object is correct, write C in the blank provided. If it is not, write the incorrect object and the correction in the blank.

Example

The·company sent the same memo to him and I.   <u> I—me </u>

1. Arrange the files in the drawer.   <u>   </u>
2. On behalf of the club, I commend you.   <u>   </u>
3. The director spoke to Ben and I.   <u>   </u>
4. The accountant wrote to her family and her.   <u>   </u>
5. The high scores were made by Jim and she.   <u>   </u>

Pretest Part II
Preposition Usage

Directions

If the underscored word is used correctly in each sentence that follows, write C in the blank provided; if not, write Omit.

Example

Where is Mr. Crowley's file <u>at</u>?   <u> Omit </u>

1. All <u>of</u> the reports have been completed.   <u>   </u>
2. Captain Black was passed <u>over</u> for promotion.   <u>   </u>
3. The last student to leave the room is required to turn <u>off</u> the master switch.   <u>   </u>
4. Where should I send the letter <u>to</u>?   <u>   </u>
5. The accountant doesn't know why Ms. Anner sent the money <u>for</u>.   <u>   </u>

Pretest Part III
Reviewing Prepositional Phrases

Directions

1. In the first column, write the word which is modified by the underscored prepositional phrase.
2. In the second column, write the part of speech of the modified word.

Example

	Modified Word	*Part of Speech*
The tax returns <u>in the basket</u> are to be checked.	returns	noun

1. The questionnaire contains an error <u>on line 15</u>. _____ _____
2. Ms. Morgan performed adequately <u>during the trial period</u>. _____ _____
3. Anyone <u>in the Payroll Department</u> will be able to help you. _____ _____
4. The lease buyer works <u>in Tulsa</u> now. _____ _____
5. J. B. is slow <u>in paying</u> his bills. _____ _____

Pretest Part IV
Selecting the Correct Preposition

Directions

In each of the following sentences, select the correct word from the parentheses and write it in the blank provided.

1. I have not corresponded (to, with) this customer since July. _____
2. The training director talked (to, with) each member of the team individually. _____
3. The city council differed (with, from) the city manager about the need for a new municipal building. _____
4. The book was accompanied (by, with) a letter and a statement. _____
5. The patient's dosage does not correspond (with, to) the doctor's prescription. _____

Pretest Part V
Confusing Prepositions

Directions

In each of the following sentences, select the correct word from the parentheses and write it in the blank provided.

1. I assure you that (between, among) the three products, you will like this one the best. _____
2. I completed the tax form (like, as) the representative said I should. _____
3. Write your response (in, into) the blank provided. _____
4. (Beside, Besides) the financial statements, we would appreciate having the names of your current creditors. _____
5. Ms. Oragana reacted to the comment (like, as) I anticipated. _____

Lesson 23
Prepositions

As you have learned, a preposition is a connective word; it connects its object—and any modifiers of the object—to the remainder of the sentence, thus forming a prepositional phrase. The emphasis in this lesson is on learning how to distinguish correct from incorrect prepositional usages. In preparing communications directed to internal or external readers, a writer often needs to make a decision about which preposition to use to express an idea. The choice of a wrong preposition reveals a writer's weak background in English fundamentals.

Frame 1 Identifying Prepositions and Objects

The writer who can identify and use prepositions and prepositional phrases correctly can present ideas clearly—a goal of all writers. Even though the subject, verb, and modifiers carry the weight of a sentence, the prepositional phrase connects essential ideas to the sentence. If an incorrect preposition or phrase is used, the thought is distorted.

Explanation

The preposition itself may consist of one word or a combination of words. The object of a preposition is usually a noun or pronoun; however, it may be a gerund or even a clause.

Example

1. One-word preposition: Many prepositions are listed in Lesson 3. These are examples: *in, about, for, among, between, by, into, upon, with, from.* Some instructors tell students to place the word they believe is a preposition in a phrase with the word *box(es)* as its object. If the phrase that results is logical, the word can be identified as a preposition.

    Arrange the files <u>in</u> the <u>box</u>.   Send the list <u>with</u> the <u>box</u>.

    Take the papers <u>from</u> the <u>box</u>.   He asked <u>for</u> a <u>box</u>.

2. Combination preposition: For example: *in spite of, in addition to, with reference to, on behalf of, according to.* The usage of a combination preposition is the same as that of a one-word preposition. Note that the last preposition in the combination requires an object.

    We went to the meeting <u>in spite of</u> the <u>weather</u>.

    The lecturer spoke <u>on behalf of</u> a new conservation <u>policy</u>.

    Memos, <u>in addition to letters</u>, should be routed to interested personnel through the intracompany mail system.

3. Noun(s) as the object:

    Technical publications should not be removed <u>from</u> the <u>room</u>.

    The reports were given <u>to Mary</u>.

    The annual report is sent <u>to stockholders</u> and other interested <u>persons</u>. (compound object)

4. Pronoun(s) as the object: Remember that a pronoun in the objective case is used as the object of the preposition.

    The petition was signed <u>by him</u> and two other employees.

5. A gerund as the object:

> Mrs. Ames was paid $150 <u>for</u> <u>consulting</u>.

6. A noun clause as the object:

> We will give the award <u>to</u> <u>whoever has the most points</u>.

> We will give the award <u>to</u> <u>whomever the committee chooses</u>.

Exercise

1. Underscore the preposition and its object in each sentence that follows.
2. If the object is correct, write C in the blank provided; if not, write the incorrect object and the correction in the blank.

Example

He was reprimanded <u>for</u> <u>being</u> late.	C
The company sent the memo <u>to</u> <u>him</u> and <u>I</u>.	I—me
The stock prospectus will be sent <u>to</u> potential <u>buyers</u>.	C

1. Enclose the brochure with the letter. _____
2. The personnel director placed the advertisement in the newspapers and journals. _____
3. Ms. Strong is responsible for hiring clerical personnel. _____
4. Between Bill and I, we have sorted 30,000 cards today. _____
5. He wrote with reference to our claim. _____
6. Place the desk by the window. _____
7. Lower the machine into the crate carefully. _____
8. According to this letter, the customer did not follow the operating instructions. _____
9. Send this form to whoever requests it. _____
10. I plan to request a leave in spite of the new policy. _____

ANSWERS TO FRAME 1

1.	<u>with</u>, <u>letter</u>	C	6.	<u>by</u>, <u>window</u>	C
2.	<u>in</u>, <u>newspapers</u>, <u>journals</u>	C	7.	<u>into</u>, <u>crate</u>	C
3.	<u>for</u>, <u>hiring</u>	C	8.	<u>According to</u>, <u>letter</u>	C
4.	<u>Between</u>, <u>Bill</u>, <u>I</u>	I—me	9.	<u>to</u>, <u>whoever requests it</u>	C
5.	<u>with reference to</u>, <u>claim</u>	C	10.	<u>in spite of</u>, <u>policy</u>	C

Frame 2   Using Prepositions Correctly

Explanation

Some usages of prepositions require special attention:

1. Distinguishing between a word used both as a preposition and as an adverb.
2. Using unnecessary prepositions.
3. Ending a sentence with a preposition.

Example

1. Preposition or adverb: Some words may be used both as a preposition and as an adverb. The part of speech of these words is dependent upon their function in a sentence.

> Your interest is computed <u>by</u> the day. (preposition)

He jumped <u>up</u> when the alarm sounded. (adverb modifying <u>jumped</u>)

The fireman climbed <u>up</u> the ladder. (preposition)

The customer came <u>up</u> when I called his name. (adverb modifying <u>came</u>)

2. Unnecessary prepositions: A preposition should be used only if it is necessary to the meaning of a sentence.

Incorrect   Take your feet <u>off</u> of the desk.
Correct   Take your feet <u>off</u> the desk.

Incorrect   All <u>of</u> the employees received a bonus.
Correct   All the employees received a bonus.

Incorrect   Where is Mr. Crowley's file <u>at</u>?
Correct   Where is Mr. Crowley's file?

3. Ending a sentence with a preposition: Grammarians recommend that a sentence not end with a preposition, and educated writers usually observe this rule. Most sentences can be revised to relocate the preposition within the sentence.

Poor   <u>Whom</u> did you send the memo <u>to</u>?
Revised   <u>To whom</u> did you send the memo?

Occasionally, however, the only logical way to express an idea is to locate the preposition at the end of a sentence.

Logical   He doesn't know <u>what</u> the medicine is <u>for</u>.
Illogical   He doesn't know <u>for</u> <u>what</u> the medicine is.
Revised   He doesn't know why the medicine was prescribed.

Amusingly, Winston Churchill, a grammarian as well as a soldier and statesman, was criticized because he wrote an article in which he ended a sentence with a preposition. To show that the rule is not always applicable, he is reported to have made this comment in response: "A preposition at the end of the sentence is something up with which I shall not put!"

Exercise

Part I

If the underscored word in each of the following sentences is used as a preposition, write P in the blank provided; if it is used as an adverb, write A in the blank.

Example

Your check is <u>in</u> the office.   P

1. The price of corn went <u>up</u> today.
2. A tornado is expected to pass <u>over</u> between 7 P.M. and 10 P.M.
3. When do you believe the inspection team will pass <u>through</u>?
4. To conserve energy, please turn <u>off</u> the lights when you leave your office.
5. The calculator is damaged because Joe knocked it <u>off</u> the desk.

Part II

If the underscored word in each sentence that follows is used correctly, write C in the blank to the right; if not, write Omit.

Example

The messenger doesn't know where the memo is <u>at</u>.   <u>Omit</u>

1. All <u>of</u> the questionnaires have been tabulated.   _____
2. Tear the form off <u>of</u> the bottom of the letter.   _____
3. Where is the property located <u>at</u>?   _____
4. How many respondents should I send the questionnaire <u>to</u>?   _____
5. The new salesclerk is hard to get along <u>with</u>.   _____

ANSWERS TO FRAME 2
Part I
1. A 2. A 3. A 4. A 5. P
Part II
1. Omit 2. Omit 3. Omit
4. C (However, the sentence would be improved if it were revised: "To how many respondents should I send the questionnaire?")
5. C

Frame 3   Reviewing Prepositional Phrases

Explanation

A preposition, its object, and the object's modifiers constitute a prepositional phrase. Such phrases may be used to modify a noun, pronoun, adjective, verb, or adverb.

Example

1. Prepositional phrase modifying a noun or pronoun: used in an adjective position.

    The chairperson gave a report <u>on the committee's activities</u>. (modifies <u>report</u>)

    The teller <u>at Window 3</u> is faster than the one <u>at Window 4</u>. (first phrase modifies <u>teller</u>, a noun; second phrase modifies <u>one</u>, a pronoun)

2. Prepositional phrase modifying a verb, adjective, or adverb: used in an adverb position.

    You will receive a statement <u>in June</u>. (modifies verb, <u>will receive</u>)

    Excited <u>about her promotion</u>, Jean wrote to her friends. (modifies an adjective, <u>Excited</u>)

    Margaret Mary works efficiently <u>at all times</u>. (modifies an adverb, <u>efficiently</u>)

Exercise

1. In the first column, write the word which is modified by the underscored prepositional phrase.
2. In the second column, write the part of speech of the modified word.

Example

	Modified Word	Part of Speech
The tax returns <u>in the basket</u> are to be checked.	returns	noun

1. The account executive is bitter <u>about the company's attitude</u>.

2. I know someone <u>in our Accounting Department</u> who can help you.

3. The trainee worked <u>under adverse conditions</u>.

4. The insurance policy is <u>in Mr. Greene's name</u>.

5. The information <u>in these brochures</u> will be helpful.

6. His office is located <u>on the seventh floor</u>.

7. She waited <u>for a call</u>.

8. In this book, you will find directions <u>for using the appliance</u>.

9. Don was delinquent <u>in paying his note</u>.

10. J & B Construction Company had the low bid <u>for constructing the new building</u>.

ANSWERS TO FRAME 3

Modified Word	Part of Speech		Modified Word	Part of Speech
1. bitter	adjective	6.	is located	verb
2. someone	pronoun	7.	waited	verb
3. worked	verb	8.	directions	noun
4. policy	noun	9.	delinquent	adjective
5. information	noun	10.	bid	noun

Frame 4 *Using Prepositions to Convey Correct Meaning*

Prepositions with Verbs and Adjectives

Explanation

A preposition often follows a verb or adjective. Frequently, either of two prepositions can follow this word, and each can represent a logical, correct meaning. The problem that occurs is this: Is the meaning that is represented the one that the writer wants to convey?

Example

Notice that the meaning in the following examples is dependent upon the preposition that follows the verb.

1.   a.   Accompany with: used for things.

   > The report is <u>accompanied with</u> the supporting documents.

     b.   Accompany by: used for people.

   > The president was <u>accompanied by</u> his wife and daughters.

2.   a.   Correspond to: to match.

   > The numbers of this claim do not <u>correspond to</u> those on the printout.

     b.   Correspond with: to write.

   > I <u>corresponded with</u> the customer three times before we agreed on a settlement.

3.   a.   Differ from: unlike.

   > An analytical report <u>differs from</u> a justification report; the former is assigned, and the latter is initiated.

     b.   Differ with: disagree.

   > The controller <u>differed with</u> the executive committee on the amount of capital that could be used for expansion.

4.   a.   Talk to: a group.

   > The tax research consultant <u>talked to</u> a large crowd comprised of faculty, accounting students, and managers of local businesses.

     b.   Talk with: individual.

   > The marketing specialist <u>talked with</u> Ms. Abbott to determine her reaction to the new package.

Exercise

In each of the following sentences, select the correct word from the parentheses and write it in the blank provided.

Example

The inspector was accompanied (by, with) an assistant when he visited the production line.   <u>by</u>

1. A handbook differs (from, with) a textbook; the former is used as a reference, and the latter is used as an instructional aid.   _____
2. The lecturer talked (to, with) a group of 500 enthusiastic conservationists.   _____
3. The personnel director talked (to, with) many applicants before she found one suitable for this position.   _____
4. The student differed (from, with) the instructor about his final grade.   _____
5. The numbers in the key do not correspond (to, with) those in the lessons.   _____

ANSWERS TO FRAME 4
1. from   2. to   3. with   4. with   5. to

Frame 5   *Using Prepositions to Convey Correct Meaning*

Confusing Prepositions

Explanation

Some prepositions, often considered in pairs, are frequently misused because the writer does not understand the difference between the meanings of the two words.

Example

1. AMONG/BETWEEN
   a. AMONG is used when the writer speaks about three or more persons, places, or things.
   b. BETWEEN is used when the writer speaks about two persons, places, or things.

   > BETWEEN John and me, there is no disagreement.

   > The bonus was distributed AMONG the employees in the department.

2. LIKE/AS
   a. LIKE is a preposition and is followed by a noun or pronoun.
   b. AS is a conjunction and is followed by a phrase or clause.

   > Mr. Thompson, the manager, acts LIKE a director.

   > Even though it has been repaired, this machine does not perform AS it should.

3. BESIDE/BESIDES
   a. BESIDE—next to.
   b. BESIDES—in addition to.

   > At the ceremony, Ms. Andrews sat BESIDE the speaker.

   > BESIDES the income statement, we also expect to see your balance sheet.

4. IN/INTO
   a. IN—inside of.
   b. INTO—moving or being moved from outside to inside.

   > The manager is IN his office.

   > The manager just walked INTO his office.

Exercise

In each of the following sentences, select the correct word from the parentheses and write it in the blank provided.

Example

(Between, Among) the two of us, we have $5.   Between

1. You would think that at least one person (between, among) the six employees could speak Spanish.   _____
2. While he was in the training program, Mr. Jordan performed (like, as) I would have expected.   _____
3. (Beside, Besides) the forms, we shall need file folders and computer-prepared labels.   _____
4. Lower the machine carefully (in, into) the box.   _____
5. The differences (between, among) him and me have been settled.   _____
6. Mr. Ballerica's desk is (beside, besides) the window.   _____
7. When the applicant arrived, he walked briskly (in, into) Mr. Syme's office. _____
8. Josephine is a student, but she has an attitude (like, as) a professional.   _____
9. (Like, As) the police officer said, "Crime does not pay."   _____
10. Programs were distributed (between, among) the audience.   _____

ANSWERS TO FRAME 5

1. among	4. into	7. into	10. among
2. as	5. between	8. like	
3. Besides	6. beside	9. As	

Frame 6 Business Vocabulary: Questionnaire Preparation

Explanation

A business, professional organization, or student researcher may want to survey a target population for the following reasons:

1. Up-to-date information on the topic under consideration is not available in textbooks or other published sources.
2. Information with respect to this topic and under these restrictions has not been gathered previously.

Terms

Survey (n)—an instrument used to gather facts.

Mail survey—an instrument, usually a questionnaire, sent through the mail to a predetermined or randomly selected list of recipients.

Telephone survey—calls placed to a predetermined or randomly selected list of recipients. The same telephone survey questionnaire is used as a basis in eliciting information from all recipients.

Questionnaire—a page or pages containing questions which can be answered by checking a blank, circling a figure, or writing a word(s).

Letter of transmittal—a letter that accompanies a questionnaire. This letter should interest the recipient, explain the problem being investigated, and persuade the reader to comply with the writer's request.

Exercise

Fill in the blanks in the following sentences with the appropriate word(s) from the preceding vocabulary list.

1. Name two common types of surveys:

   _____   _____

2. A questionnaire is always accompanied with a _____ .

3. What is the purpose of the letter of transmittal? _____

   _____

   _____

ANSWERS TO FRAME 6

1. telephone survey; mail survey
2. letter of transmittal
3. a. to interest the recipient
   b. to explain the problem being investigated
   c. to persuade the reader to comply with the writer's request

Frame 7   Applying Your Knowledge

Directions

Underscore each error in the following letter. Write the correction in the space below the error.

CASE

Barbara Cada will be graduated with a major in accounting. She is trying to make a decision between entering an accounting firm and working as an accountant in industry. Because she is enrolled in a business communications class and has an assignment requiring her to write a report, she is basing the report topic on the major question confronting her. She has prepared a questionnaire to be sent to ten selected accounting firms and to ten industries. Here is the first draft of her letter of transmittal. (10 errors)

Note

A letter without a salutation or complimentary closing, but with a subject line, is called a *Simplified Letter.*

620 South Shields
Fort Collins, CO 80521
April 16, 19____

Ms. Joan B. Harris, Partner
Harris & Harris
2222 Jackson Street
El Paso, Texas 77777

SUBJECT: To Enter an Accounting Firm or Become an Industrial
Accountant

As an accounting major planning to graduate this spring, I need to make a career decision: whether to enter an accounting firm or become an industrial accountant.

Because I am also enrolled into a business communications class and have been assigned a report, I am investigating the two accounting areas. Specifically, the purpose of my report is to compare a job-entry position in an accounting firm with a similar position in industry to determine which is more feasible for a person with my background. The decision will be derived upon the duties, salary, working conditions, and opportunities for advancement. To determine how one position differs with the other, I have read books and periodicals, beside talking to three accountants in each area.

Between the people I have interviewed, I have discovered some conflicting ideas. I have been told that if I put forth the effort and perform like a good accountant should, I may or may not have the opportunity to become an auditor. I enrolled in accounting because my long-term goal is to become an auditor.

This letter is accompanied by a questionnaire and a self- addressed envelope. The number in the upper left-hand corner of the questionnaire corresponds with the name of your organization; however, I would appreciate your signing the questionnaire as well. If you are interested in receiving a synopsis of my report, please complete all of the blanks below the dotted line. If I receive your response before July 1, I shall have your synopsis to you before July 15.

Barbara Cada

ANSWERS TO FRAME 7

Body of letter:

As an accounting major planning to graduate this spring, I need to make a career decision: whether to enter an accounting firm or become an industrial accountant.

Because I am also enrolled into a business communications class and have been
<u>in</u>
assigned a report, I am investigating the two accounting areas. Specifically, the purpose of my report is to compare a job-entry position in an accounting firm with a similar position in industry to determine which is more feasible for a person with my background. The decision will be derived upon the duties, salary, working conditions,
<u>from</u>
and opportunities for advancement. To determine how one position differs <u>with</u> the
<u>from</u>
other, I have read books and periodicals, <u>beside</u> talking <u>to</u> three accountants in each
<u>besides</u>   <u>with</u>
area.

<u>Between</u> the people I have interviewed, I have discovered some conflicting ideas. I
<u>Among</u>
have been told that if I put forth the effort and perform <u>like</u> a good accountant should,
<u>as</u>
I may or may not have the opportunity to become an auditor. I enrolled in accounting because my long-term goal is to become an auditor.

This letter is accompanied <u>by</u> a questionnaire and a self-addressed envelope. The
<u>with</u>
number in the upper left-hand corner of the questionnaire corresponds <u>with</u> the name
<u>to</u>
of your organization; however, I would appreciate your signing the questionnaire as well. If you are interested in receiving a synopsis of my report, please complete all <u>of</u>
<u>(omit)</u>
the blanks below the dotted line. If I receive your response before July 1, I shall have your synopsis to you before July 15.

Lesson 24
Conjunctions

Pretest

Pretest Part I
Identifying Conjunctions

Directions

1. In the following sentences, underscore each word that is used as a conjunction.
2. In the blank provided, identify each conjunction with one of the following abbreviations:

   CO   Coordinate conjunction   SC   Subordinate conjunction
   CA   Conjunctive adverb   CR   Correlative conjunction

3. If a sentence does not contain a word used as a conjunction, write No in the blank.

Example

Either the bank president or a member of the Board of Directors will give the address.   CR

1. When you return the equipment, please sign the customer release form.   _____
2. The price of bread has increased, but the price of wheat has decreased.   _____
3. The company will be closed not only on the day before the holiday but also on the day after the holiday.   _____
4. I did not pass the driver's examination; consequently, I shall need to retake it.   _____
5. Both Monte and Mohammed plan to work for the airlines.   _____
6. Many ranchers, however, have been unable to recoup the losses they incurred during the drought.   _____
7. The systems analyst has worked either in New York or in Boston.   _____
8. Homer studied hard; however, he did not pass the test.   _____
9. Your check will be cashed if you can show the proper identification.   _____
10. The claims adjuster appraised the damaged car carefully, for he believed the client had caused some of the fender dents previously.   _____

Pretest Part II
Usage

Directions

One sentence in each of the following pairs contains a conjunction that is used incorrectly. In the blank provided, write the letter designating the correct sentence.

Example

a. Your grade was 65; however, 70 is considered passing.
b. Your grade was 65; consequently, 70 is considered passing.   <u>a</u>

1. a. The equipment was damaged by the bomb; moreover, the company cannot conduct business until the police have completed their investigation.
   b. The equipment was damaged by the bomb; therefore, the company cannot conduct business until the police have completed their investigation.   _____

2. a. Ms. Adamson directed the previous advertising campaign; however, it pulled only a 40 percent response.
   b. Ms. Adamson directed the previous advertising campaign; moreover, it pulled only a 40 percent response.   _____

3. a. Mr. Prosko has worked in Venezuela for two years; furthermore, he cannot speak Spanish.
   b. Mr. Prosko has worked in Venezuela for two years; nevertheless, he cannot speak Spanish.   _____

4. a. She is an excellent proofreader; however, she would not have been hired.
   b. She is an excellent proofreader; otherwise, she would not have been hired.   _____

5. a. The editor either wrote to the author or to the sales representative.
   b. The editor wrote either to the author or to the sales representative.   _____

6. a. He both saw the World Trade Center and the Statue of Liberty when he visited New York.
   b. He saw both the World Trade Center and the Statue of Liberty when he visited New York.   _____

7. a. Bill came neither to work nor called the office.
   b. Bill neither came to work nor called the office.   _____

8. a. His writing is not only illegible but also ungrammatical.
   b. His writing is not only illegible but also is ungrammatical.   _____

9. a. The stolen money was found in both his home and in his car.
   b. The stolen money was found in both his home and his car.   _____

10. a. His itinerary includes not only Colorado but he will also go to California.
    b. His itinerary includes not only Colorado but also California.   _____

Pretest Part III
Sentence Identification

Directions

Identify the type of sentence construction by writing one of the following abbreviations in the blank provided:

S	Simple	CX	Complex
CO	Compound	CC	Compound Complex

Example

We will send you our sales forecast by next Tuesday; our subsidiaries will send theirs before the end of the month.   <u>CO</u>

1. I always prepare an outline before I write a report, and if I have prepared a good outline, the report is well organized.   _____
2. The chief administrative assistant maintains the records and schedules the work of the other assistants.   _____
3. Before the end of the year, you will need to pay your estimated tax.   _____

4. The prefabricated houses are manufactured by the Justin Company, and the utilities are installed by I&R Contractors. _____

5. The legal counsel is responsible for advising us about our records retention requirements; consequently, he is on the Records Retention Committee. _____

6. Punctuation clarifies the meaning of a sentence; however, excessive punctuation confuses the reader. _____

7. When you mail merchandise to customers, be certain that you insure the package for an amount commensurate with the value of the contents. _____

8. You will not be permitted to take compensatory leave if you do not check with your supervisor first. _____

9. When the report is submitted, please check it, and if you find an error, notify me immediately. _____

10. The bonds will be sold in August, but construction of the grade school begins in July. _____

Lesson 24
Conjunctions

Conjunctions are connecting words that permit the writer to add thoughts to a sentence, change the direction of a thought, and to present concise, but clear statements.

Without conjunctions, our writing would be choppy, repetitive, and juvenile.

No conjunction   Mary went to the meeting. Kemper went to the meeting.
Conjunction   Mary <u>and</u> Kemper went to the meeting.
No conjunction   Mary went to the meeting. Kemper did not go to the meeting.
Conjunction   Mary went to the meeting, <u>but</u> Kemper did not go.

In this lesson, conjunctions will be identified and discussed according to their usage in four types of sentence constructions.

Frame 1   Identification: Coordinate Conjunctions

These four types of conjunctions are presented in this lesson: coordinate, conjunctive adverbs, correlative, and subordinate.

Explanation

A *coordinate conjunction* connects words, phrases, or clauses of equal rank (of equal importance). The five coordinate conjunctions are *and, but, for, or,* and *nor.*

Example

1. Coordinate conjunction connecting words:

    > The assets <u>and</u> liabilities are shown on the balance sheet. (connects two nouns)

    > Shy <u>but</u> determined, the secretary persevered until the job was completed. (connects two adjectives)

2. Coordinate conjunction connecting phrases:

    > The copy is on the desk <u>or</u> in the file. (connects two prepositional phrases)

    > Supervising the production department <u>and</u> chairing the committee permit Ms. Aldridge little time to handle details. (connects two gerund phrases)

3. Coordinate conjunction connecting clauses:

    > She plans to attend night school, <u>but</u> she cannot afford to do so now. (connects two independent clauses)

    > The customer wrote that he had followed the operating instructions <u>and</u> that he had contacted our service department. (connects two dependent clauses)

Exercise

Underscore the coordinate conjunction in each sentence that follows. In the blank provided, write the type of construction that is connected by this conjunction.

Example

My supervisor said that I should complete the project <u>and</u> that I should determine the number of reports needed.

dependent
<u>clauses</u>

1. Having worked in the Classified Section but having been discharged, William did not want to work for another newspaper. _____
2. Joyce was promoted, but Harry was not. _____
3. Mitzi attended the training session, and she prepared herself for promotion. _____
4. Janice or Doreen will be transferred this month. _____
5. I understand that he has been employed by the Jeffrey Company and by the Cole Company. _____

ANSWERS TO FRAME 1

1.	<u>but</u>	participial phrases	4.	<u>or</u>	nouns
2.	<u>but</u>	independent clauses	5.	<u>and</u>	prepositional phrases
3.	<u>and</u>	independent clauses			

Frame 2   Identification: Conjunctive Adverbs

Explanation

An adverb that connects two independent clauses is used as a conjunction and is called a *conjunctive adverb*. The meaning of a conjunctive adverb is significant to the thought of the entire sentence; therefore, this word must be chosen with care so that it represents the idea the writer wants to convey.

   Commonly used conjunctive adverbs are these: *moreover, consequently, furthermore, however, nonetheless, therefore, hence, still, yet, so, thus, otherwise.*

Example

1. The conjunctive adverb connects two independent clauses (IC):

   <u>Your score was 72</u>; however, <u>75 is considered passing</u>.
   (IC)   (IC)

2. The conjunctive adverb and the second clause modify the first clause:

   <u>Ms. Simpson was not promoted</u>; therefore, <u>she resigned</u>.
   (Note that <u>she resigned</u> pertains to the first clause.)

3. The meaning of a conjunctive adverb is significant to the thought the writer wants to convey.
   a. MOREOVER and FURTHERMORE—indicate that the idea in the second clause is in addition to that in the first clause.

      The association will not accredit the college; <u>moreover</u>, the consensus is that the president should be removed. (<u>Moreover</u> means <u>in addition</u>.)

   b. THEREFORE and CONSEQUENTLY—introduce the reason or result presented in the second clause.

      The broker said that Zerplex was not a growth stock; <u>therefore</u>, I did not purchase any shares. (<u>Therefore</u> means <u>for that reason</u>.)

   c. HOWEVER and NEVERTHELESS—place restrictions on the first clause.

      You passed the final examination; <u>however</u>, your final grade is below that required to pass the course.

(<u>However</u> may have any one of these meanings: but, yet, nevertheless, still.) The reader recognizes <u>however</u> as a clue to the thought in the second clause; if a positive thought was expressed in the first clause, a negative thought will follow <u>however</u>, and vice versa.

    d. OTHERWISE—explains a contrary situation.

> Ms. Plinko has had six years' experience with an accounting firm; <u>otherwise</u>, she would not have been hired for this position.

Exercise

1. For each of the following sentences, write the conjunctive adverb that gives the sentence a logical meaning.
2. Choose from one of the following conjunctive adverbs: therefore, however, moreover, otherwise.

Example

The property has been appraised; _____, we have not been informed of the current value.   <u>however</u>

1. Ms. Simpson was not promoted; _____, she resigned.   _____

2. Harvey is about to retire; _____, he would be asked to resign.   _____

3. These agricultural students established this business; _____, they are planning to expand it in the near future.   _____

4. Loneta was named the beneficiary; _____, she will not obtain any money until she reaches the age of 21.   _____

5. The council did not pass the rezoning ordinance; _____, they voted to table this resolution indefinitely.   _____

6. The consultant has an outstanding reputation; _____, we certainly would not pay her $500 a day.   _____

7. The doctor said that Mr. Shak's leg would not need to be amputated; _____, it is possible that his leg may remain paralyzed.   _____

ANSWERS TO FRAME 2

1.	therefore	4.	however	6.	otherwise
2.	otherwise	5.	moreover	7.	however
3.	moreover				

Frame 3   *Identification: Correlative Conjunctions*

Explanation

Correlative conjunctions are used in pairs to join words, phrases, or clauses that are parallel in construction. The latter word of the pair is a coordinate conjunction—*and, but, for, or, nor.*

    The most common correlative conjunctions are: *either/or, neither/nor, both/and, not only/but also.*

The words following each element of the pair must be parallel in construction. To be parallel, the construction must consist of two of the same type words, phrases, or clauses.

Example

1. EITHER/OR

    Incorrect   The registrar (either) <u>wrote to the student's</u> parents (or) <u>to the student</u>. (not parallel: <u>either</u> is followed by a verb, and <u>or</u> is followed by a prepositional phrase)

    Correct   The registrar wrote (either) <u>to the student's parents</u> (or) <u>to the student</u>. (Note that both <u>either</u> and <u>or</u> are followed by prepositional phrases.)

2. NEITHER/NOR

    Incorrect   He (neither) <u>worked for the federal government</u> (nor) <u>for the state government</u>. (not parallel; <u>neither</u> is followed by a verb, and <u>or</u> is followed by a prepositional phrase)

    Correct   He worked (neither) <u>for the federal government</u> (nor) <u>for the state government</u>. (correlative conjunction connects two prepositional phrases)

3. BOTH/AND

    Incorrect   An error was found in (both) <u>the manual computations</u> (and) <u>in the computer program</u>. (not parallel)

    Correct   An error was found (both) <u>in the manual computations</u> (and) <u>in the computer program</u>. (prepositional phrase follows each element)

4. NOT ONLY/BUT ALSO

    Incorrect   The action is (not only) <u>unethical</u> (but also) <u>does not conform to the law</u>. (the first element is followed by an adjective; the second is followed by a verb)

    Correct   The action is (not only) <u>unethical</u> (but also) <u>illegal</u>. (both elements are followed by adjectives)

Exercise

In the following sentences, the first conjunction of the correlative pair has been omitted.

1. Judging from the location of the second conjunction, determine where the first conjunction should be inserted.
2. In the blank provided, write the first conjunction plus the word preceding it.

Example

This student's paper is to be regraded or to be recorded.   <u>is either</u>

1. Your statement is accurate nor logical.   _____
2. Regina won the university scholarship and the president's special scholarship.   _____

3. While he is touring the country, the foreign businessman will visit corporations but also federal agencies. _____
4. I believe that the chairman of the board nor the president really wants an open stockholders' meeting. _____
5. Send this price list to our wholesalers and to our retailers. _____
6. I received the letter and the brochure on the same day. _____
7. The car has air conditioning but also has power-glide windows. _____
8. The professor said that we could accept the grade we have at this point or could take the final examination to try to improve the grade. _____
9. The Random Company will provide the training program but also the accommodations for trainees. _____
10. The writer of the recommendation letter stated, "She was graduated in June, or she will be graduated this summer." _____

ANSWERS TO FRAME 3

1.	is neither	5.	list both	8.	we either
2.	won both	6.	received both	9.	provide not only
3.	visit not only	7.	car not only	10.	stated, "Either
4.	that neither				

Frame 4   Identification: Subordinate Conjunctions

Explanation

A *subordinate conjunction* introduces a dependent (subordinate) clause. Some of the more common subordinate conjunctions are listed:

if	when	as	while	that
since	than	where	though	
although	unless	because	before	

Example

1. Subordinate clause at the end of a sentence:

   Many taxpayers will be displeased <u>if the court reverses its decision</u>.

2. Subordinate clause within a sentence:

   The report <u>that I read today</u> concerns the economic implications of overproduction.

3. Subordinate clause at the beginning of a sentence:

   <u>Before the demolition squad arrived</u>, the bomb had exploded.

Exercise

Underscore the dependent clause in each sentence that follows. Then write the subordinate conjunction in the blank provided.

Example

<u>Because monthly overtime expenses were incurred</u>, the company changed to the cycle billing system.   <u>Because</u>

1. When the last half of the real estate tax is due, you must pay it in full or receive a penalty. _____

2. Late papers, as you were told previously, cannot be accepted for full credit. _____
3. Since he joined the company two years ago, he has given many lectures to professional associations. _____
4. The retailers in this city are more progressive than are the retailers in that city. _____
5. Proceed immediately to the Mulberry Street exit when the fire alarm rings. _____
6. The statue will be erected where the two streets converge. _____
7. While the dictation is entering the central station, the transcriber is transcribing from a desk unit. _____
8. His decision, although it is logical, cannot be implemented at this time. _____
9. Unless we hear from you before July 1, we shall ship your order collect. _____
10. The police officer, though she was thorough, did not detect the driver's well-concealed contraband. _____

ANSWERS TO FRAME 4

1.	When the last half of the real estate tax is due	When
2.	as you were told previously	as
3.	Since he joined the company two years ago	Since
4.	than are the retailers in that city	than
5.	when the fire alarm rings	when
6.	where the two streets converge	where
7.	While the dictation is entering the central station	While
8.	although it is logical	although
9.	Unless we hear from you before July 1	Unless
10.	though she was thorough	though

Frame 5   Conjunctions in Simple Sentences

As you have learned, a conjunction itself adds to or changes the meaning of a sentence; its location and manner of punctuation in the sentence structure also contribute to its meaning.

The next frames illustrate how conjunctions are used in four types of sentences: simple, compound, complex, and compound/complex.

Explanation

A *simple sentence* is an independent clause; therefore, it has a subject and verb and expresses a complete thought. A group of words that does not have these characteristics is called a fragment. A simple sentence may have one subject and one verb, one subject and a compound verb, a compound subject and one verb, or a compound subject and a compound verb.

Example

The subject(s) and verb(s) are underscored in the sentences that follow.

1. One subject and one verb:

    The unit cost has risen by two cents.

2. One subject and a compound verb:

    The mail clerk sorted and delivered the mail. (verbs joined by coordinate conjunction and)

3. Compound subject and one verb:

    Either the manager or one of the supervisors will represent this department. (subjects joined by a correlative conjunction, either/or)

4. Compound subject and compound verb:

> Neither <u>employees</u> nor <u>visitors</u> <u>may park</u> in Lot 4 or <u>enter</u> from Olive Street. (compound subject joined by coordinate conjunction, <u>nor</u>; compound verb joined by coordinate conjunction, <u>or</u>)

Exercise

Write the subject(s), the verb(s), and the conjunction, if any, in the appropriate blanks. If the words do not comprise a sentence, write No in the appropriate blank to show which part (subject or verb) is missing.

Example

	Subject	*Verb*	*Conjunction*
Ted and Greg, despite their lengthy friendship and years of having worked in this company.	Ted/Greg	No	and
The landscaping company has completed the plaza garden.	company	has completed	

1. Neither the books nor the periodicals have been moved into the new library.
2. All employees are expected to attend one of the scheduled meetings and are also expected to sign the secretary's attendance roster.
3. Not having bid on the construction contract, Palmer Company may be going out of business.
4. The judge asked for order and then assigned the sentence.
5. Either Ms. Reid or Ms. Dunn worked Sunday to complete the project.
6. Managers of small businesses and members of the business faculty will meet to discuss the impact of the new regulation.
7. Students and faculty are encouraged to submit items to the college newspaper.

	Subject	Verb	Conjunction
8. Jane, having been graduated from the teaching hospital with a degree in nursing.	_____	_____	_____
9. The accounting staff worked overtime but did not complete the audit.	_____	_____	_____
10. Mr. Dale or Mr. Smith is responsible for this error.	_____	_____	_____

ANSWERS TO FRAME 5

Subject	Verb	Conjunction
1. books, periodicals	have been moved	Neither . . . nor
2. employees	are expected, are expected	and
3. Palmer Company	may be going	
4. judge	asked, assigned	and
5. Ms. Reid, Ms. Dunn	worked	Either . . . or
6. Managers, members	will meet	and
7. Students, faculty	are encouraged	and
8. Jane	No	
9. staff	worked, did complete	but
10. Mr. Dale, Mr. Smith	is	or

Frame 6   *Conjunctions in Compound Sentences*

Explanation

A *compound sentence* contains two or more independent clauses. To reflect unity, the clauses must be closely related. The clauses may be connected by a coordinate conjunction or a conjunctive adverb, or may include no connective word.

Example

To verify that each underscored clause in the following sentences is independent (IC), read each without considering the connective word.

1. Compound sentence connected with a coordinate conjunction:

    The unit cost has risen by 2 cents, but the company will
    (IC)
    not raise the selling price.
    (IC)

2. Compound sentence connected with a conjunctive adverb:

    The unit cost has risen by 2 cents; however, the company
    (IC)
    will not raise the selling price.
    (IC)

The word *however* is not a conjunctive adverb in the following sentence because it does not connect two independent clauses. To verify this, read the words to the left of *however* and notice that they cannot stand alone; neither can the words to the right of *however*.

    The unit price, however, has risen 2 cents.
    (In this sentence however is a parenthetical expression and not a conjunctive adverb.)

Exercise

Underscore the clauses in the sentences that follow; label them IC (independent clause) and DC (dependent clause).

Example

<u>I hope that we can recruit several new employees</u>; <u>if we cannot</u>, <u>some of our people</u>
  (IC)   (DC)   (DC)
<u>will have to work overtime</u>.
      (IC)

1. This company maintains a fleet of cars for its sales agents; and what is more, these cars are traded every two years.

2. You are expected to attend the staff meeting; however, if you cannot, please let me know.

3. This building does not have adequate facilities to house the new equipment; but if more outlets are installed, we shall be able to accommodate it.

4. The superintendent of a city school system is well paid, and as he has a great .responsibility, he deserves the money.

5. Ms. Tweed, who was promoted to financial vice president, declined to comment on the promotion; furthermore, she asked not to be interviewed.

ANSWERS TO FRAME 8

1. <u>This company maintains a fleet of cars for its sales agents</u>; and <u>what is more,</u> <u>these cars are</u>
             (IC)   (DC)
<u>traded every two years</u>.
    (IC)

2. <u>You are expected to attend the staff meeting</u>; however, <u>if you cannot,</u> <u>please let me know</u>.
         (IC)   (DC)   (IC)

3. <u>This building does not have adequate facilities to house the new equipment</u>; but <u>if more</u>
                    (IC)
<u>outlets are installed,</u> <u>we shall be able to accommodate it</u>.
     (DC)   (IC)

4. <u>The superintendent of a city school system is well paid,</u> and <u>as he has a great responsibility,</u>
          (IC)   (DC)
<u>he deserves the money</u>.
    (IC)

5. <u>Ms. Tweed,</u> <u>who was promoted to financial vice president,</u> <u>declined to comment on the</u>
 (IC—   (DC)   —IC)
<u>promotion</u>; furthermore, <u>she asked not to be interviewed</u>.
                        (IC)

Frame 9   Sentence Identification

Explanation

Variety is the spice of life, as the saying goes; it also makes a communication more interesting and readable. Therefore, in a letter, memorandum, or report, a good writer attempts to use at least two of the sentence types illustrated in the preceding frames.

Example

Following are some combinations which can comprise the four different types of sentences:

1. Simple sentence: One independent clause.

2. Compound sentence:
    a. Independent clause, coordinate conjunction, independent clause.
    b. Independent clause, conjunctive adverb, independent clause.
    c. Independent clause, independent clause.
3. Complex sentence:
    a. Dependent clause, independent clause.
    b. Independent clause, dependent clause.
4. Compound complex sentence: Independent clause, dependent clause, coordinate conjunction, independent clause.

Exercise

In the blank provided, identify the type of sentence construction by using one of these abbreviations:

S   Simple   CX   Complex
CO Compound   CC   Compound Complex

Example

We will send you our sales forecast by next Tuesday; our subsidiaries will send theirs before the end of the month.   <u> CO </u>

1. Your approval is required before the group health insurance becomes effective for your family.   <u>   </u>
2. The young graduate tried to be alert and efficient, for he was hoping to be promoted.   <u>   </u>
3. Abby Randolph is a good typist and takes dictation rapidly.   <u>   </u>
4. I heartily recommend Betty Quincy for the position of administrative assistant; moreover, I am certain you will be pleased with her performance.   <u>   </u>
5. To obtain full vesting rights, you generally need to work for the same firm at least five years.   <u>   </u>
6. I called him and also sent an adjuster.   <u>   </u>
7. I shall not be able to attend the January meeting; therefore, I shall give you my proxy.   <u>   </u>
8. Although it has extended into the grace period, this policy will cover your hospital expenses.   <u>   </u>
9. No unlicensed brokers will be permitted to assist new clients unless the vice president gives his approval.   <u>   </u>
10. The property will be sold to the highest bidder, and that person is required to pay the back taxes.   <u>   </u>

ANSWERS TO FRAME 9

1.	CX	4.	CC	7.	CO	10.	CO
2.	CO	5.	S	8.	CX		
3.	S	6.	S	9.	CX		

Frame 10   *Business Vocabulary: Real Estate*

Explanation

The vocabulary in this frame is used by real estate salespeople, brokers, managers, and others within and outside the real estate profession.

Terms

Appreciate—the value of property may appreciate, or increase; on the other hand, the value may *depreciate,* or decrease. These changes in value may be due to rezoning, the surrounding area, or property improvements (or lack thereof).

Appraise—the condition and surroundings of property are evaluated, usually by someone licensed to do so, to determine its market value; a corresponding selling price is established.

Lease—a contract by which one person conveys real estate, equipment, or facilities for a specified time and at a specified rate. A *lessor* owns the property and conveys it to a *lessee,* the person who rents it.

Condominium—a unit in a multi-unit structure. A condominium is similar to an apartment in physical layout; however, a condominium is owned by an individual(s), and an apartment is rented.

Exercise

Complete each sentence that follows with the appropriate word from the preceding vocabulary list.

1. When the value of property has increased, it is said to have

   _____.

2. A lessor owns the property, and the person who rents it is called a

   _____.

3. The difference between a condominium and an apartment is that a condominium is _____, and an apartment is _____.

4. To evaluate property is to _____ it.

ANSWERS TO FRAME 10
1. appreciated 2. lessee 3. owned, rented 4. appraise

Frame 11   Applying Your Knowledge

Directions

In the letter that follows, underscore each error in conjunction usage. Then write the correction in the space below.

CASE

This letter was written by a real estate sales associate (agent) to a prospective buyer who is moving into the city. (10 errors)

Mr. Gregory Abbott
2735 Harvard Avenue
Tacoma, Washington 98466

Dear Mr. Abbott:

   Yes, Mr. Abbott, Keystone Realty can meet your needs not only for a house or apartment but also a condominium.

   The condominiums in the Lexington Green area range from $50,000 for a two-bedroom split-level home to $90,000 for a four-bedroom split-level home. Our contracts specify that 30 percent of the price be paid upon purchase and that the balance be paid by a 20-year mortgage.

In beautiful surroundings and decorated with taste. The apartments in Bellaire Courts are leased by the year. The lessee either may pay the total sum upon signing the lease or pay the rent by the month. The monthly rent on these apartments ranges from $500 for a studio to $1500 for a four-bedroom apartment. The apartments can be rented either furnished or without furniture; otherwise, furnished apartments are more costly than unfurnished ones.

According to your letter, you would prefer to either live in a condominium or an apartment for one year before purchasing a private dwelling. The value of property is appreciating by 5 percent per year in this city; moreover, I urge you to make a decision soon. Apartment rents in both the metropolitan area and in the suburban area have been frozen by the city; however, we anticipate that the new administration will attempt to remove this restriction.

I am enclosing brochures, pamphlets, city maps. Will you please study the pictures or read the property descriptions. Before you leave Tacoma, please call me to make an appointment. I shall try to spend a week helping you to get settled in the city.

Sincerely,

Rudolph Behrends
Sales Associate

ANSWERS TO FRAME 11

Body of letter:

Yes, Mr. Abbott, Keystone Realty can meet your needs not only for a house or
for not only
apartment but also a condominium.

The condominiums in the Lexington Green area range from $50,000 for a two-bedroom split-level home to $90,000 for a four-bedroom split-level home. Our contracts specify that 30 percent of the price be paid upon purchase and that the balance be paid by a 20-year mortgage.

In beautiful surroundings and decorated with taste. The apartments in Bellaire
taste, the
Courts are leased by the year. The lessee either may pay the total sum upon signing
may either pay
the lease or pay the rent by the month. The monthly rent on these apartments ranges from $500 for a studio to $1500 for a four-bedroom apartment. The apartments can be rented either furnished or without furniture; otherwise, furnished apartments are
unfurnished   however
more costly than unfurnished ones.

According to your letter, you would prefer <u>to either live in</u> a condominium or an
to live in either
apartment for one year before purchasing a private dwelling. The value of property is

appreciating by 5 percent per year in this city; <u>moreover,</u> I urge you to make a
therefore,
decision soon. Apartment rents <u>in both</u> the metropolitan area and in the suburban area
both in
have been frozen by the city; however, we anticipate that the new administration will

attempt to remove this restriction.

I am enclosing brochures, <u>pamphlets, city</u> maps. Will you please study the pictures
pamphlets, and city
<u>or</u> read the property descriptions. Before you leave Tacoma, please call me to make
and
an appointment. I shall try to spend a week helping you to get settled in the city.

Lesson 25
Effective Writing: Unity, Coherence, and Emphasis

Pretest

Pretest Part I
Achieving Sentence Unity

Directions

Rewrite the following sentences to achieve unity of expression. You may add to or change each sentence to make it meaningful and businesslike.

Example

Original   While the workers on the production line met their quota, maintained high productivity, and attained a low defect rate, according to Mr. Zest, the production manager.

Revision   The workers on the production line met their quota, maintained high productivity, and attained a low defect rate, according to Mr. Zest, the production manager.

1. Return contract—envelope—September 20.

   _____

2. Having completed the report in the morning.

   _____

3. The realtor sold a million dollars' worth of real estate this year; he handled the Bascom ranch transaction.

   _____

   _____

4. The retailer, having announced a sale of used stereos.

   _____

Pretest Part II
Revising for Coherence

Directions

1. In the blank provided, write the reason for the lack of coherence in each sentence. Use these symbols:

P	Parallelism	V	Voice
T	Tense	MM	Misplaced modifier

2. Then revise each sentence, using the blank lines below it.

Example

You will either get a promotion or Ms. Allison will get it.
Revised: Either you or Ms. Allison will get the promotion.   P

1. I believe that she formerly either worked as a teacher or as an editor.   _____

   _____

   _____

2. I will write the report, and Carrie is going to proofread it.   _____

   _____

   _____

3. Before using the calculator, the battery should be tested.   _____

   _____

   _____

4. He wrote the policy, and it was checked by a lawyer.   _____

   _____

   _____

Pretest Part III
Emphasis

Directions

In the blank provided, write the letter (a or b) designating the sentence which best answers each question.

Example

Which sentence should the company president select to call attention to pilfering?
a. Pilfering cannot be condoned by this company.
b. This company cannot condone the pilfering of office supplies, merchandise, and furniture.   a

1. Which sentence should a professor use in a letter of recommendation to emphasize a student's strength?
   a. Perseverance is Mr. Bell's greatest strength.
   b. Of all the strengths exhibited by Mr. Bell, perseverance is his greatest strength.   _____

2. Which sentence should a loan manager use to inform a customer that her loan has been approved?
   a. I am happy to take this opportunity, Ms. Puls, to inform you that the loan for which you applied in June has been approved.
   b. The bank officers approved your loan, Ms. Puls, and you may continue your negotiation for the property.   _____

3. Which sentence should a credit department correspondent use in replying to a customer who asked for a refund?
   a. Our Repair Department found that the springs in your sofa were not properly tied; therefore, a refund is in order.
   b. Your money will be refunded because our Repair Department discovered that the springs in your sofa were not properly tied.   _____

4. Which sentence should a correspondent in the claims department use to tell a customer that the refrigerator he purchased is no longer under warranty?
   a. If this refrigerator had been under a warranty when the motor stopped, the company would have been happy to have furnished the part and repaired the appliance without charge.
   b. Your refrigerator was not under warranty when the motor stopped; therefore, we can neither furnish the part nor repair the refrigerator without charge.   _____

Pretest Part IV
Conciseness: Eliminating Words

Directions

1. Draw a line through the unnecessary word(s) in each sentence that follows.
2. If the unnecessary expression can be stated more concisely, write the new expression in the blank provided.

Example

During the ~~course of the~~ year, he accumulated 13 traffic violations.   _____

1. The meeting began promptly at the hour of eight.   _____
2. I wish to take this opportunity to say that you have done an admirable job as a training director.   _____
3. During the year of 1978, Ms. Bogart was employed as a theatrical agent.   _____
4. This class will be dismissed on August 3 due to the fact that on this date Colorado became a state.   _____
5. Please be assured that your check will be in the mail before June 30.   _____

Pretest Part V
Changing Constructions

Directions

1. In each of the following sentences, underscore the construction (clause, phrase, words) that can be made more concise.
2. Revise the sentence to make it more concise.

Example

The supervisor <u>helped and assisted me in making</u> the schedule.
<u>Revision: The supervisor helped me make the schedule.</u>

1. The county clerk's records which are outdated have been sent to the state archives.

   _____

   _____

2. The house belonging to the Barret family is in the condemned area.

   _____

   _____

3. Students enrolled in classes in accounting are encouraged to attend the speech by Ms. Agra, a CPA.

   _____

   _____

4. The bulbs are easy to plant and do not need to be taken up before winter.

   _____

   _____

Lesson 25
Effective Writing: Unity, Coherence, and Emphasis

Only by recognizing the constructions that destroy unity and coherence can the writer revise a communication to convey the intended meaning. The soaring costs of written communications require that anyone who creates them be aware of the criteria of effective writing.

Frame 1   Achieving Sentence Unity

Unity is defined as a close relationship between all parts of the whole.

Explanation

The unity of a sentence is destroyed under these circumstances: the sentence is not complete; the ideas are not related; the sentence is telegraphic.

Example

1. Express an idea in a complete sentence.

    Incorrect   While the workers on the production line met their quota, maintained high productivity, and attained a low defect rate, according to Mr. Zest, their production manager. (does not express a complete thought)

    Correct   The workers on the production line met their quota, maintained high productivity, and attained a low defect rate, according to Mr. Zest, the production manager.

2. The ideas in the first and second clauses of a sentence should be closely related.

    Incorrect   The water board met on Tuesday; energy sources were also discussed.

    Correct   The water board met on Tuesday; in addition to watering restrictions, the members also discussed local energy sources.

    Incorrect   Ted bought a new car, and he has six children.

    Correct   Ted bought a station wagon because he needed a vehicle that would accommodate his family.

3. Use the words necessary to express an idea clearly. Telegraphic sentences (those omitting articles, modifiers, the subject, or the verb) destroy unity.

    Incorrect   Application accepted; registration August 20.

    Correct   Your application has been accepted; please register for classes during the week of August 20.

Exercise

Using the lines provided, rewrite each sentence to achieve unity of expression. Construct logical, businesslike sentences.

1. Upon removing the letter from the typewriter.

    _____

    _____

2. All federal, state, and local government offices will be closed on the Fourth of July, but Sooper Grocery is on College Avenue.

---

3. Return contract—envelope—September 20.

ANSWERS TO FRAME 1
(Other answers could be correct; read the criteria required for the correct revision of each sentence.)

1. Upon removing the letter from the typewriter, the secretary discovered the error.

    The original group of words constitutes a fragment rather than a complete sentence. The fragmentary part needs to be followed by an independent clause; in other words, a subject, verb, and complete thought must be added to the fragment. The subject must be a noun that is logical; it must identify a person who can perform the action of "removing."

2. All federal, state, and local government offices will be closed on the Fourth of July; however, the Sooper Grocery on College Avenue will be open.

    Although you probably revised your sentence differently, your first and second clauses should be closely related and meaningful.

3. Will you please return your contract in the enclosed envelope before September 20.

    As an experiment to save time, employees in a large insurance company were permitted to write internal and some external communications in a telegraphic manner. Insureds complained, saying that the letters were curt and often meaningless. Within the organization, these telegraphic messages resulted in many employees' acting or reacting in a manner not intended by the writer. The experiment was discontinued in favor of the conventional sentence structure.

    Sentence 3 is an example of such a telegraphic communication. To have corrected it, you should have inserted the necessary words to express a meaningful idea.

Frame 2   Coherence

Coherence requires that all parts of a sentence "fit" or "stick" together and express a logical, meaningful idea.

Revising for Coherence

Explanation

To achieve coherence, the writer must be able to detect and eliminate these errors: lack of parallelism, misplaced modifiers, changes in tense, and changes in voice.

Example

a. *Parallelism:* The parts of a sentence that express a parallel thought should be constructed in the same manner; that is, they should begin with the same part of speech.

Incorrect	To pursue his hobby, to travel to Europe, and writing a book will keep Mr. Dalton busy. (two infinitive phrases and a gerund phrase)
Correct	To pursue his hobby, to travel to Europe, and to write a book will keep Mr. Dalton busy. (infinitive phrases)

Correct   Pursuing his hobby, traveling to Europe, and writing a book will keep Mr. Dalton busy. (gerund phrases)

Incorrect   The person who was hired can type material rapidly, proofread copy well, and also can take dictation accurately. (<u>can</u> should not be repeated in the third verb phrase)

Correct   The person who was hired can type material rapidly, proofread copy well, and take dictation accurately. (three verb phrases without repetition)

b. *Misplaced modifiers:* A modifier is placed as closely as possible to the word it modifies.

Incorrect   <u>To be inviting to potential buyers</u>, Ms. Gordon should renovate and repaint the house. (modifies <u>Ms. Gordon</u>)

Correct   <u>To be inviting to potential buyers</u>, the house should be renovated and repainted by Ms. Gordon. (modifies <u>house</u>)

Correct   Ms. Gordon, to make the house inviting to potential buyers, should renovate and repaint it.

Incorrect   <u>Having money to invest</u>, it is logical that Chi, a financial analyst, would purchase stocks. (modifies <u>it</u>)

Correct   <u>Having money to invest</u>, Chi, a financial analyst, would logically purchase stocks. (modifies <u>Chi</u>)

Incorrect   The manager saw the dog <u>sitting at his desk</u>. (modifies <u>dog</u>—the dog is sitting at the manager's desk?)

Correct   Sitting at his desk, the manager saw the dog.

Incorrect   <u>Only</u> Jane won the top scholastic award. (Only one <u>top</u> scholastic award exists; therefore, only one person can logically win it.)

Correct   Jane won <u>only</u> the top scholastic award. (meaning that other awards were given, but Jane won this award)

c. *Changes in tense:* To express actions occurring at the same time, use the same tense.

Incorrect   I <u>will take</u> the course in the spring, and he <u>is going</u> to take it in the fall. (future tense in the first clause and present progressive in the second)

Correct   I <u>will take</u> the course in the spring, and he <u>will take</u> it in the fall. (future tense in both clauses)

Incorrect   Miss Goff <u>has hired</u> ten employees for this job, and Mr. Merrick <u>tested</u> them. (present perfect tense in the first clause and simple past in the second)

Correct   Miss Goff <u>has hired</u> ten employees for this job, and Mr. Merrick <u>has tested</u> them. (present perfect tense in both clauses)

d. *Change in voice:* In some cases, changing the voice of the verb from the first to the second clause can cause an awkward construction.

Poor   He wrote the justification report, and it was typed by Mary.
Better   He wrote the justification report, and Mary typed it.

Poor   Angela sold five insurance policies, and they were sent to the home office today.
Better   Angela sold five insurance policies and sent them to the home office today.

Exercise

1. In the blank provided, write the reason for the lack of coherence in each sentence. Use these symbols:

   P   Parallelism   V   Voice
   T   Tense   MM   Misplaced modifier

2. Then revise each sentence, using the blank lines below it.

Example

Analyzing the paperwork, the idea suddenly came to me.   MM
The idea suddenly came to me as I was analyzing the paperwork.

1. Chip installed the wiring, and it was checked by the inspector today.   _____

   _____

   _____

2. I believe that his former experience was obtained in either a print shop or a
   newspaper plant.   _____

   _____

   _____

3. Having an engine malfunction prior to takeoff, the pilot returned the plane to
   the hangar.   _____

   _____

   _____

4. I will check the schedule, and Bill is going to compare the figures.   _____

   _____

   _____

5. We are looking for an employee who is industrious, who is capable, and one
   who is efficient.   _____

   _____

   _____

6. Ms. Stover has designed the advertising campaign, and Mr. Benson prepared
   the copy.   _____

   _____

   _____

7. Jim both wrote the stage play and the television script.   _____

   _____

   _____

ANSWERS TO FRAME 2

1. Chip installed the wiring, and the inspector checked it today.   V
2. I believe that his former experience was obtained either in a print shop or in a newspaper
   plant.   P
3. Having an engine malfunction prior to takeoff, the plane was returned to the hangar by the
   pilot.   MM

4. I will check the schedule, and Bill will compare the figures.

_____ T _____

5. We are looking for an employee who is industrious, capable, and efficient. (or) We are looking for an employee who is industrious, who is capable, and who is efficient.

_____ P _____

6. Ms. Stover has designed the advertising campaign, and Mr. Benson has prepared the copy. (or omit *has*)

_____ T _____

7. Jim wrote both the stage play and the television script.

_____ P _____

Frame 3 Emphasis

Explanation

The reader assumes that certain ideas are important because the writer has handled them in a manner commensurate with their importance. As a result, the reader attaches significance to these ideas. If the writer does not emphasize the important ideas, the reader is left to filter them from the many words and sentences in a communication.

An idea may be emphasized by its position in a sentence and by its location in a certain sentence construction. Two or more significant ideas may be tabulated or numbered within a sentence.

Mechanical methods (underscoring, quotation marks, dashes, capitalization, ellipses, and exclamation points) are also used to emphasize a word(s).

Example

1. The first and last word in a sentence are in important positions; however, the first word is often considered more emphatic.

    Integrity is his primary virtue.

    His primary virtue is integrity.

2. An independent clause represents a more important idea than does a dependent clause or a phrase.

    Ray will attend the university after he leaves the service.

3. Active voice carries more impact than does passive voice. Also, a sentence in active voice is shorter than one in passive voice.

    This analysis justifies our purchasing the equipment. (active)

    Our purchasing the equipment is justified by this analysis. (passive)

Note

The passive voice is especially useful, however, in de-emphasizing a negative point. This technique is important in retaining customer goodwill.

    Active: Because you did not operate the machine according to the directions, we cannot repair it without charge.

    Passive: If the machine had been operated according to the directions on page 7 of the manual and had malfunctioned, we would have been glad to repair it without charge.

4. A very short sentence serves to emphasize an idea or fact.

    We sold 4,000,000 copiers last year!

5. Listing several points within a sentence or in tabulated form serves to emphasize each point and makes the total sentence more readable.

   a. The following items from the furniture department will be on sale during August: (1) bedroom suites, (2) dining sets, (3) upholstered occasional chairs, (4) patio furniture, and (5) loveseats.
   b. The following items from the furniture department will be on sale during August:
      1. Bedroom suites
      2. Dining sets
      3. Upholstered occasional chairs
      4. Patio furniture
      5. Loveseats

   The items may be tabulated and centered, placed at the margin and preceded by numbers, or placed at the margin and preceded by letters.

   c. Your responsibilities are to:
      a. Coordinate the work of your assistants.
      b. Schedule reviews and books in process.
      c. Pay reviewers.
      d. Reimburse authors.
      e. Compute royalties.

   Notice that the construction of the list is parallel; the first word in each section completes the infinitive (*to coordinate,* and so on).

Exercise

In the blank provided, write the letter designating the sentence which answers the question.

Example

Which sentence should the company president select to call attention to a serious crime against the company?

a. Pilfering cannot be condoned by this company.
b. This company cannot condone the pilfering of office supplies, merchandise, and furniture.   a

1. Which sentence should the Claims Department correspondent use in replying to a customer who asked for a refund?
   a. Your money will be refunded because we found the appliance to be defective.
   b. Because we found the appliance to be defective, your money will be refunded.   _____
2. Which statement should a production manager use to inform the workers about a positive point?
   a. Despite an exhausting schedule and many hours of overtime, we made our quota this month.
   b. We made our quota this month.   _____
3. Which statement should a credit manager use in informing a credit applicant that her application for credit has been approved?
   a. We are pleased that you have chosen the Paramount Department Store in which to open your account, Ms. Bowen.
   b. We have opened an account for you, Ms. Bowen, and you may begin charging to it immediately.   _____

4. Which sentence should a professor use in a letter of recommendation to emphasize a student's positive quality?
   a. Creativity is the greatest of Mr. Baker's many strengths.
   b. Of Mr. Baker's many strengths, creativity is the greatest.
5. Which sentence should a company accountant use in telling a business customer that the discount does not apply to this order? The company does not want to anger this customer!
   a. The 10 percent discount does not apply to your order because we received your payment after the discount period.
   b. If your payment had been received prior to the end of the discount period, we would have been glad to allow the 10 percent discount.

ANSWERS TO FRAME 3

1. <u>a</u> The customer asked about a refund; that is the customer's primary interest. Naturally, a company would prefer to de-emphasize the fact that a product is defective.
2. <u>b</u> The workers know that their schedule was exhausting and that they were required to work overtime.
3. <u>b</u> Sentence a. is a rather oblique way to tell Ms. Bowen that an account has been opened for her. In fact, Ms. Bowen may not even be certain the sentence implies that an account has been opened for her.
4. <u>a</u> An outstanding quality is placed in a position of importance, not buried within a sentence.
5. <u>b</u> Sentence a. is blunt; to retain the goodwill of the customer, the accountant uses an introductory dependent clause in passive voice to soften the bluntness and follows it with a positive statement.

Frame 4   Conciseness: Eliminating Words

Explanation

The reader of a business communication expects it to be clear and concise. To achieve conciseness, the writer eliminates trite, lengthy, and meaningless words and phrases.

Example

1. Some clauses and phrases can be reduced to one or two words. The left-hand column contains a long expression, and the right-hand column contains a concise expression of the same thought.

Lengthy	*Concise*
at all times	always
at the hour of eight	at eight
at a later date	later
at an early date	soon
at a price of $10	at $10
long period of time	long time
enclosed herewith	enclosed
during the course of	during
in the state of Alaska	in Alaska
during the year of 1981	during 1981
in regard to	about
due to the fact that	because
in the event that	if
will you kindly, be so kind	please

The preceding list contains only some examples of reducing lengthy phrases to words or short phrases.

2. During the revision process, any words that do not contribute to the meaning or intent of the message are eliminated.

   a. <u>Please be assured that</u> your order will be shipped on July 15. Revised: Your order will be shipped on July 15.

   b. <u>As a matter of fact</u>, I called the Payroll Department yesterday. Revised: I called the Payroll Department yesterday.

   c. <u>The fact of the matter is that</u> the committee has taken no action on your proposal. Revised: The committee has taken no action on your proposal.

   d. <u>I should like to assure you that</u> the confidentiality of your response will be maintained. Revised: The confidentiality of your response will be maintained.

   e. <u>I wish to take this opportunity to say that</u> we welcome you as a credit customer. Revised: We welcome you as a credit customer.

Exercise

Each of the following sentences contains a lengthy expression. Draw a line through the unnecessary words in each sentence. If the unnecessary expression can be shortened, write the short expression in the blank provided.

Example

During ~~the course of~~ the year, he accumulated 14 traffic violations. _____

1. We will sell this car for a price of $4,500. _____
2. Please be assured that this coat is made of genuine mink. _____
3. Please return this questionnaire at an early date. _____
4. The customer wrote in regard to his delinquent account. _____
5. As a matter of fact, I wrote to Mr. Compo yesterday. _____
6. In the event that you cannot attend the meeting, will you please name a proxy. _____
7. Due to the fact that your account is in arrears, you are requested to pay the finance charges immediately. _____
8. The secretary tried in every way possible to open the large box. _____
9. Will you be so kind as to reply before August 1. _____
10. Enclosed herewith is a sample of April perfume. _____

ANSWERS TO FRAME 4

Eliminate	*Concise*
1. a price of	
2. Please be assured that	
3. at an early date	soon or by X date
4. in regard to	about or concerning
5. As a matter of fact	
6. In the event that	If
7. Due to the fact that	Because
8. in every way possible	
9. Will you be so kind as to	Please
10. herewith	

Frame 5   Conciseness: Changing Constructions

Explanation

Occasionally, a construction can be changed to make a sentence shorter and yet retain the same meaning.

Example

1. The words in a clause can be converted into a compound adjective.

   The child, <u>who is ten years old</u>, has been missing for a week.

   The <u>ten-year-old</u> child has been missing for a week.

2. The words in a clause can be converted into modifiers.

   The mail cart, <u>which was heavily laden</u>, lost a wheel.

   The <u>heavily laden</u> mail cart lost a wheel.

3. The number of consecutive prepositional phrases can be reduced.

   The residents <u>of a city in California</u> voted to decrease property taxes.

   The residents <u>of a California city</u> voted to decrease property taxes.

4. A possessive pronoun or noun can be substituted for a prepositional phrase.

   The car <u>which was damaged</u> belonged <u>to Ben</u>.

   <u>Ben's</u> car <u>was damaged</u>.

5. A synonym can be eliminated.

   We are reviewing and <u>rechecking</u> your order.

   We are reviewing your order.

A sentence can be changed in more than one way to achieve conciseness. Again, during the revision phase, the writer seeks to "tighten" the construction without losing the meaning or intent of the message.

Exercise

Each sentence in the following exercise can be made more concise by changing the construction.

1. In each of the following sentences, underscore the construction (clause, phrase, words) that can be made more concise.
2. Revise the sentence to make it more concise.

Example

The supervisor <u>helped and assisted me in making</u> the schedule.
<u>The supervisor helped me make the schedule.</u>

1. The equipment, which was old, was sold to the Browning Company.

   _____

   _____

2. The directions are easy to read and can be followed by a child who is five years old.

   _____

   _____

3. Employees in the traffic department of the plant in Texas are requesting a hearing.

_____

_____

4. The stock of this company is rapidly increasing in value.

_____

5. The corporate executives are highly esteemed, and the decision they make is sure to be accepted.

_____

_____

6. We want to be of assistance and service to you.

_____

ANSWERS TO FRAME 5
1. The old equipment was sold to the Browning Company.
2. The easy-to-read directions can be followed by a five-year-old child.
3. Traffic Department employees in the Texas plant are requesting a hearing.
4. This company's stock is rapidly increasing in value.
5. The decision made by the highly esteemed corporate executives is sure to be accepted.
6. We want to be of service to you.

Frame 6   Business Vocabulary: Production Department

Explanation

The terms in this frame are common to the *production department* of a manufacturing firm.

Terms

Production department—the part of the organization in which a product is made, assembled, inspected, and packaged, or prepared for sale. Some large corporations have numerous production departments scattered throughout the country, and others locate each phase of production at a different site.

Work-in-process—the bulk product (paint, for example) or the individual product that is currently undergoing one of the phases in the production department.

Finished goods—the completed product that is ready for sale to a wholesaler, retailer, or consumer.

Inventory— a stock of goods or materials on hand. An inventory of finished goods includes a list of the number and nature of the product to be sold. A parts inventory consists of the number and kind of parts for use.

Raw material—the resource from which the product is made: fabric, iron, steel, wood, and so on. An inventory of raw materials is also maintained.

Exercise

Complete each sentence with the appropriate term from the preceding vocabulary list.

1. If petroleum is used in making plastic, it is called a _____.
2. A stock of goods or material on hand is an _____.
3. Those goods ready for sale are called _____.

4. Material which is undergoing one of the phases of production is _____

_____

5. Which of the following is not work-in-process? _____
   a. a car on the assembly line.
   b. beer in a bottle which is being labeled.
   c. a mattress being packaged.
   d. a gross of games awaiting shipment.

ANSWERS TO FRAME 7

1. raw material   3. finished goods   5. d
2. inventory   4. work-in-process

Frame 8   Applying Your Knowledge

Directions

1. Read the following memorandum and underscore each error in unity, coherence, or conciseness.
2. Write the corrections in the space below.
3. If a sentence needs revision, revise it on the blank lines which follow the exercise.

CASE

The production manager has written this progress report to inform the plant superintendent about progress toward the completion of a large order. (10 errors)

July 5, 19____

TO: Hiram Anderson, Plant Superintendent
FROM: Edmund Asher, Production Manager
SUBJECT: Progress on Completion of Government Order No. 74829

This report presents the progress toward the completion of the federal government's order for 20,000 desk-type calculators.

Present Status:

1. The order was received on April 30, and the inventory was checked immediately to determine if all components were available in sufficient number to begin production. As a matter of fact, during the course of the year, had I not been purchasing in quantity to take advantage of lower steel prices, we would not have had the raw materials to begin production.

2. At this point in time, at least 10,000 calculators are in the finished goods inventory; the remainder are in various and different stages of production.

<u>Problems Encountered</u>:

Approximately 1,000 hours of overtime work will be required to wire the components and transistors. Due to the fact that many employees are on vacation and the remainder prefer not to spend their summer evenings at the plant, I am having a difficult time finding people for the night shift. Being required to train unskilled employees, the calculators may not be wired and in readiness for the next stage at the proper time. Which of the following alternatives do you recommend?

a. To keep the production moving smoothly and swiftly, I either shall need to pay a higher night differential rate or to extend the day shift.

b. Another alternative is to hire students enrolled in the electronics classes at the Briarwood Technical School. Mr. Wood, who is the president of the school, said that eighty students who are well trained and capable are available.

<u>Anticipated Progress</u>:

If sufficient work-hours are expended, this order will be completely finished by September 1.

Revise the sentences on these lines.

_____

_____

_____

_____

_____

ANSWERS TO FRAME 8

July 5, 19____

TO: Hiram Anderson, Plant Superintendent
FROM: Edmund Asher, Production Manager
SUBJECT: Progress on Completion of Government Order No. 74829

This report presents the progress toward the completion of the federal government's order for 20,000 desk-type calculators.

<u>Present Status</u>:

1. The order was received on April 30, and the inventory was checked immediately to determine if all components were available in sufficient number to begin production. <u>As a matter of fact</u>, during <u>the course of</u> the year, had I not been
   (delete)   (delete) During
   purchasing in quantity to take advantage of lower steel prices, we would not have had the raw materials to begin production.

2. <u>At this point in time,</u> at least 10,000 calculators are in the finished goods inventory;
(delete)
the remainder are in various <u>and different</u> stages of production.
(delete)

<u>Problems Encountered</u>:

Approximately 1,000 hours of overtime work will be required to wire the components

and transistors. <u>Due to the fact that</u> many employees are on vacation and the
Because
remainder prefer not to spend their summer evenings at the plant, I am having a

difficult time finding people for the night shift. Being required to train unskilled

employees, <u>the calculators may not be</u> wired and in readiness for the next stage at the
I may not have the calculators
proper time. Which of the following alternatives do you recommend?

a. To keep the production moving smoothly and swiftly, I <u>either shall need</u> to pay a
shall need either
higher night differential rate or to extend the day shift.

b. Another alternative is to hire students enrolled in the electronics classes at the

Briarwood Technical School. <u>Mr. Wood, who is the president of the school</u>, said
President Wood
that <u>80 students who are well trained and capable</u> are available.
80 well-trained, capable students

<u>Anticipated Progress</u>:

If sufficient work-hours are expended, this order will be <u>completely finished</u> by
completed
September 1.

Lesson 26
Number Usage

Pretest

Directions

Correct any incorrectly written numbers in the following sentences by writing the correction in the blank provided. If no numbers need to be corrected, write C in the blank.

Example

The insurance company has 250 agencies.   C

1. The Records Management Department now consists of 3 supervisors, 6 analysts, and 17 information specialists. _____
2. We have 250 items in the finished goods inventory, and ten are in some stage of production. _____
3. Approximately 150 people participated in the 10 seminars. _____
4. According to the personnel director, the retirement age in this company will remain at 65. _____
5. Forty-five percent of the respondents did not answer this question; fifteen percent misinterpreted Question 14, and ten percent did not check Question 17. _____
6. Ms. Adams took out this policy when James was two years 11 months and 14 days old. _____
7. Most people want a nine to five job; that is why we have difficulty recruiting for the four o'clock shift. _____
8. The Reproduction Center can assemble 1,000 five-page pamphlets in 15 minutes. _____
9. My car insurance is due on the 20th of this month. _____
10. The 2nd National Bank is now located at One Maiden Lane. _____
11. Anchor Savings and Loan now pays 8.5 percent interest on a $7,000 certificate. _____
12. Only .3 of an inch of rainfall was recorded during this month. _____
13. We have received four-fifths of the pledges. _____
14. Ms. Bundy moved from 412 Tenth Street to 1820 3rd Avenue. _____
15. The restaurant is now located at 130 East 39th Street. _____
16. Add two tablespoons of liquid for each gallon of Riot Weed Killer. _____
17. Please enclose 75 cents to cover the handling and mailing costs. _____
18. The city has a $4 million dollar surplus. _____
19. During the month of the sale, ladies' coats will be reduced from $200 to $135.00. _____
20. The unit cost of Product A is 7 cents; Product C, $1.75, and Product D, $1.90. _____
21. The consultant has had 18 years' experience in a management position. _____
22. To secure this debt, we request that you sign a 90-day promissory note. _____
23. You can purchase this car for only $89.95 and pay the same amount monthly for 36 months. _____
24. We have 250 boxes of letterhead paper, 190 boxes of envelopes, and 9 preprinted memo pads in the supply room. _____
25. According to the statistical report, the average male will live to be 72. _____

Lesson 26
Number Usage

This lesson emphasizes the commonly accepted number-writing practices in business communications. Legal documents, technical reports, and statistical presentations do not comply with all the listed rules.

In legal documents, numbers are often written in figures as well as in words to assure accuracy and to clarify the content.

Most technical reports contain a vast amount of quantitative data. These numbers are usually written in figures to facilitate rapid reading and also to coincide with equipment, experiment, or project data. To save space and also to coincide with the technical data, these reports often include symbols (%, #, $, and so on) that represent words.

In statistical presentations—tables, other graphic aids, and tabulated formats within a communication—figures are used to save space. Symbols are considered acceptable in all statistical presentations.

The business writer uses a number-writing style that complies with the organization policy and which may be illustrated in its correspondence manual. The rules in this lesson may be adapted to conform to company policies and different types of communication. Regardless of the number-writing style selected, the business writer is consistent in applying it to all numbers in a communication. The rules and exercises in this lesson are adapted from *Machine Transcription in Modern Business*.*

Frame 1   Basic Rule for Number Usage

Explanation

One basic rule governs the expression of numbers in business communications: Numbers through ten are written as words, and numbers above ten are written in figures. The exceptions to this basic rule form the rules for the specific usages.

Example

1. Basic rule:
   a. Express numbers through ten in words.

      This department now has <u>nine</u> employees.

   b. Express numbers over ten in figures.

      The insurance company has <u>250</u> agencies.

2. Exceptions:
   a. Express related numbers in figures. Related numbers may consist of either construction:
      (1) Series of three or more numbers.
      (2) Two or more numbers joined by one of these connecting words: *and, or, to.*

      The requisition includes <u>8</u> condensers, <u>24</u> transistors, and <u>10</u> porcelain insulators. (Related, series—one number above ten)

      We now have <u>45</u> salespersons and <u>4</u> supervisors. (Related, connecting word—<u>and</u>; one number above ten)

*By permission. Lois Meyer and Ruth Moyer, *Machine Transcription in Modern Business* (New York: John Wiley & Sons, 1978).

b. Write unrelated numbers according to the basic rule. Unrelated numbers do not have either of these constructions:
   (1) Series of three or more numbers.
   (2) Two or more numbers joined by *and, or,* or *to.*

> Our first <u>ten</u> sessions attracted more than <u>250</u> people.
> (Unrelated, not in a series; no connecting word)

c. Express in words a number when it begins a sentence. If the number cannot be expressed in one or two words, revise the sentence.

> <u>Sixty-five</u> people attended the meeting.

Incorrect	<u>Three hundred sixty-five</u> people attended the meeting.
Revised	The meeting was attended by <u>365</u> people.

Exercise

Some of the following sentences have incorrectly written numbers. Write the corrections in the blanks provided. If a sentence is correct, write C; if it needs to be revised, write R.

Example

Seven mowers were sold today.   <u>C</u>

1. I am sure that this speaker would attract at least fifty people to the conference. _____
2. This year we added six new salespersons to our staff. _____
3. We listed eight sets of china, 16 vases, and 19 serving dishes on the order form. _____
4. The inventory consists of 95 private dwellings and 5 commercial buildings. _____
5. The Wilson Company has more than six thousand independent insurance agents. _____
6. 53 of the administrative office managers had been in their present positions for 10 years or more. _____
7. Mobile Home Communities owns 26 parks with over 7,300 spaces in 9 states. _____
8. The type of equipment we select will determine whether we need ten or 25 employees. _____
9. Four hundred thirty-three firms had fires resulting in serious losses. _____

ANSWERS TO FRAME 1

1. 50   5. 6,000
2. C   6. Fifty-three; ten
3. 8   7. nine
4. C   8. 10
9. R (Example: Last year, 433 firms had fires resulting in serious losses.)

Frame 2   Ages

Explanation

Ages are expressed as words except when they have a contractual or statistical significance, or when they are exact.

Example

1. Express ages of persons, places, and things in words.

> The Whiteside Company declared bankruptcy shortly after its president died of a heart attack at the age of <u>forty-five</u>.

2. Exceptions:
   a. Express ages in figures when they have a contractual or statistical significance (in personnel matters, for example).

   > The minimum age for employment as a sales clerk at Miller's Department Store is 18. (contractual significance)

   b. Express exact ages (years, months, days) in figures.

   > One of our policyholders received retirement benefits each month until his death at the age of 99 years 11 months and 28 days.

Exercise

Some of the following sentences have incorrectly written numbers. Write the corrections in the blanks provided; write C if a sentence is correct.

Example

John Wilson, who is 30, is the youngest executive in the organization.   thirty

1. The Martins moved to Denver recently because their doctor recommended a dry climate for their 15-year-old son.   _____
2. An employee with 30 years' experience may retire with full benefits at the age of 62.   _____
3. Mr. Kelly embarked upon a new career at the age of 54, when most men start looking toward retirement.   _____
4. Frank Jones took out an insurance policy on the life of his daughter when she was only one year two months and 15 days old.   _____
5. Of the 90 questionnaires returned, 25 respondents did not include their names; 9, their titles; and 30, the names of their companies.   _____

ANSWERS TO FRAME 2
1. fifteen-year-old   2. C   3. fifty-four   4. 1 year 2 months   5. C

Frame 3   Clock Time

Explanation

Clock time is expressed in figures when A.M. or P.M. or the word *o'clock* follows the time; otherwise, it is expressed in words. A colon is used to separate hours from minutes when both hour and minutes are stated.

Example

1. Clock time in figures:

   > Our plane leaves Madison at 11:30 A.M. and arrives in Chicago at 12:10 P.M.

   > Advertising copy for our big Sunday issue is accepted until 4 o'clock on Friday.

2. Exception: clock time in words.

   > Half our employees will work from eight to four, while the other half will work from nine to five.

Exercise

In the blanks provided, write the corrections for all incorrectly expressed numbers; if a sentence is correct, write C in the blank.

Example

We should like all conference participants to be our guests for lunch at twelve-thirty.   _____C_____

1. Hector's will remain open from 6:00 A.M. to 10:00 P.M. on Monday, Tuesday, and Wednesday for the special sale.   _____
2. I have made a tentative appointment with Mr. Frank for 3 o'clock.   _____
3. Employment interviews are scheduled on Wednesdays and Fridays from 2 until 5.   _____
4. The new branch bank will be open from 7:30 A.M. to 6 P.M., Monday through Friday.   _____
5. Our next meeting will be held at 8:30 A.M.   _____

ANSWERS TO FRAME 3
1. 6, 10   2. C   3. two, five   4. C   5. C

Frame 4   Combination Numbers

Explanation

When two numbers appear consecutively in a sentence and one is used as an adjective, express one of the numbers in words and the other in figures. Generally, the first number is expressed in words and the second in figures.

Example

1. Express the first number of a consecutive combination as a word and the second in figures.

   The downtown parking problem has been eased by the recent erection of two 5-story garages.

2. Exception: If the second number is much shorter than the first, express the second number in words and the first in figures.

   We will need enough large envelopes to mail 250 five-page bulletins.

Exercise

In the blanks provided, write the corrections for all incorrectly expressed numbers; if a sentence is correct, write C in the blank.

Example

An employee with five years' service or more may take two 15-day vacations in one year.   _____C_____

1. The management training seminar will consist of three two-hour sessions.   _____
2. About 125 20-foot poles will be needed at the construction site on Lake Street.   _____
3. We have just received a shipment of 10 5-piece bedroom suites.   _____
4. Our employees are allowed two fifteen-minute coffee breaks daily.   _____
5. The book consists of three chapters, each over 100 pages long.   _____

ANSWERS TO FRAME 4
1. 3   2. twenty   3. ten   4. 15   5. C

Frame 5   Dates

Explanation

Express dates in figures, using one of these endings (*st, nd, rd, th*) when the day precedes the month or when it is used alone.

Example

1. Express dates in figures:

   > We notified you October <u>20</u> that your payment was overdue.

2. Use *st, nd, rd,* or *th* after the date when the day precedes the month and when it is used without the month:

   > Please let us have your decision before the <u>15th</u> of November. Mr. Smith will be out of town until the <u>20th</u>.

Exercise

In the blanks provided, write the corrections for all incorrectly expressed numbers; if a sentence is correct, write C in the blank.

Example

We are enclosing a copy of our quarterly report for the period ending May 31st.   <u>31</u>

1. The new rates for long distance calls will go into effect on January 3rd.   _____
2. Construction of our new facilities should be completed by the thirtieth of next month.   _____
3. Our order of May 12th was not received until the 20th.   _____
4. Your promotion will be effective as of September first.   _____
5. Our next meeting will be on the 17th.   _____

ANSWERS TO FRAME 5
1. 3   2. 30th   3. 12   4. 1.   5. C

Frame 6   *Decimals and Percentages*

Explanation

Decimals are expressed in figures. If a whole number does not precede the decimal point, write *0* before the decimal point, unless the decimal itself begins with *0*.

Example

1. Express a decimal in figures:

   > The report shows that our sales increased 2.6 percent during the month of October.

2. Alternative: If a whole number does not precede the decimal point, write *0* before the decimal point, unless the number with a decimal begins with *0*.

   > The cost of living index rose <u>.09</u> last month, compared with 1.2 the previous month.
   > Precipitation for the entire month of November measured <u>0.5</u> (not <u>.5</u>) inches.

3. Express percentages in figures:

> By purchasing now, you can take advantage of the <u>10 percent</u> discount.

Exercise

In the blanks provided, write the corrections for all incorrectly expressed numbers; if a sentence is correct, write C in the blank.

Example

The price of hamburger rose eight percent last month.   <u>8</u>

1. Our sales dropped from 1.3 percent last month to .9 this month.   _____
2. We cannot accept Order No. 254 because the specifications of the machine part show an .08 variation from the tolerance level.   _____
3. The country's two largest banks raised their prime interest rate from 6.25 to 6.5 percent.   _____
4. The rain gauge shows that this area had 0.02 inches of rain last night.   _____
5. Sale prices are 20 to 30 percent off the retail price.   _____

ANSWERS TO FRAME 6
1. 0.9   2. C   3. C   4. .02   5. C

Frame 7   Fractions

Explanation

Fractions are expressed in words with a hyphen between the two parts, unless (1) the fraction is combined with a whole number, or (2) a fraction cannot be written in one or two words.

Example

1. Express a fraction in words with a hyphen between the two parts.

> We have reached only <u>three-fourths</u> of our sales quota at this time.

2. Exceptions:
    a. Write a mixed number (fraction combined with a whole number) as a figure.

> Last year the average employee missed 2 ½ working days due to illness.

Note

In a typed format, the mixed number and whole number are separated by a space.

    b. Write a fraction as a figure if it cannot be expressed in one or two words.

> The specifications for this precision measuring instrument must be accurate to 197/200 of an inch.

Note

Such fractions are not followed by *th, nd,* or *rd,* even though the syllable is pronounced in speaking.

Exercise

In the blanks provided, write the corrections for all incorrectly expressed numbers; if a sentence is correct, write C in the blank.

Example

The company pays 1/2 of the cost of the employee's health insurance, and one-half is deducted from the employee's paycheck.   <u>one-half</u>

1. The votes cast in the city election represented about 1/3 of the eligible voters.   _____
2. Our best camera has shutter speeds to 1/1000th of a second.   _____
3. Four-fifths of the exterior of this briefcase is leather; the trim is nylon.   _____
4. We will need two and one-half boxes of letterhead stationery for the special sales promotion we are preparing.   _____
5. The Tiger delivered seventeen percent more fuel economy than the car that came in second on the economy run.   _____

ANSWERS TO FRAME 7
1. one-third   2. 1/1000   3. C   4. 2 1/2   5. 17

Frame 8   *Identification Numbers*

Explanation

Serial and location numbers are identifiers and are usually expressed in figures. They are not written with commas.

A *serial number* identifies a specific item in a sequential series; for example, policy, page, invoice, purchase order, and check.

Location numbers identify houses, buildings, and streets.

Example

1. Write a serial number in figures without commas.

> Invoice Nos. <u>4571</u> and <u>8672</u> were both paid last month with Check No. <u>301</u>.

> The first two paragraphs in Section <u>6</u> of the <u>Employee Manual</u> cover sick-leave policies.

2. Write house and building numbers in figures, with the exception of the number *one*. The most common usage of these numbers is in the inside address of letters.

> Miss Mary Green
> <u>3548</u> Canyon Road
> Toledo, OH 45387

> Mr. Harold H. Turner
> Wilson and Company
> <u>10</u> Commerce Building
> Portland, OR 97209

> Mr. J. C. Stern
> <u>One</u> Park Lane
> Tacoma, WA 98411

3. Write street names that are numbers through ten in words; write street names that are numbers above ten in figures with *st, nd, rd,* or *th.* (If a discrepancy occurs between this rule and the way the address is shown on a company's letterhead, use the letterhead presentation.)

Mr. Howard L. Bond
314 Eighth Street
Lake Charles, LA 70601

Mr. Michael Young
Personnel Manager
The Larsen Appliance Company
3859 18th Street
Denver, CO 80200

Mr. A. C. Miller, Manager
Miller's Men's Shop
1600 East 18 Street
Pierre, SD 57501

Note

Street names that are numbers above ten may be expressed without *st, nd, rd,* or *th* when another word separates the house number and the street number.

Exercise

In the blanks provided, write the corrections for the incorrectly expressed numbers; if a sentence is correct, write C in the blank.

Example

The premium on Policy No. 532879 is $70.50.   C

1. Our new Model Nine computer is now on the market.   _____
2. Your order No. 488 for 100 reams of letterhead should reach you by July 10.   _____
3. Ms. Sara Barnes
   Sixteen Cedar Lane
   Belleville, IL 62220   _____
4. Mr. Oscar Day, Manager
   Bass and Company
   Five Parker Lane
   Waterloo, IA 50701   _____
5. Mr. George C. Mills
   1 Gulf Drive
   Beaumont, TX 77704   _____
6. Ms. Alice White
   Regional Sales Manager
   King's Office Equipment
   2000 Fiftieth Avenue
   St. Paul, MN 55101   _____
7. Mr. Daniel Davis
   3859 North 18th Street
   Oklahoma City, OK 73100   _____
8. Mr. Carl Yates
   Marketing Manager
   Emerson Equipment Company
   540 35th Street
   Wichita, KS 67202   _____

ANSWERS TO FRAME 8

1. 9	3. 16	5. One	7. 18
2. C	4. 5	6. 50th	8. C

Frame 9   Measurements

Explanation

Measurements are expressed in figures:

Measurement	Unit of Measurement—Examples
Dimensions	feet, inches, yards
Temperatures	degrees of Centigrade and Fahrenheit
Weights	pounds, grams, ounces
Sizes	size
Distance	miles, kilometers, knots
Fluid Measures	pint, quart, liter
Electrical Measures	volt, watt

Example

Express measurement in figures:

The storage area measures <u>9 feet</u> by <u>3 feet</u>.

Exposure of aerosol cans to temperatures above <u>120 degrees Fahrenheit</u> may cause them to burst.

We do not have the <u>12-volt</u> ignition coils that were ordered last week.

New York is over <u>1,500 miles</u> from Denver. (Use comma to designate thousands.)

Exercise

In the blanks provided, write the corrections for all incorrectly expressed numbers; if a sentence is correct, write C in the blank.

Example

The temperature of seven degrees was a record low for this date.   7

1. The entire order of two-inch brass screws is being returned because the screws did not meet our specifications.
2. We used only 2 hundred gallons of gas in driving five thousand miles.
3. Our new copier weighs thirty-seven pounds and requires only two feet of counter space.
4. One-hundred watt bulbs in all corridors are being replaced with 70-watt bulbs in an attempt to save electricity.
5. During the dense fog, the petroleum-laden vessel traveled at 10 knots.

ANSWERS TO FRAME 9
1. 2-inch   2. 200; 5,000   3. 37; 2   4. C   5. C

Frame 10   Money

Explanation

Amounts of money are expressed in figures.

426 · Business English Basics

1. Express amounts of $1 or more in figures preceded by a dollar sign. Express even dollar amounts without a decimal point and ciphers (zeros).

    The hard-cover edition of this book sells for $12.50.

    The prize for the first-place sales team will be $1,000.

2. Express amounts under $1 in figures followed by the word *cents*. When amounts over and under $1 appear in a series, write each amount with a dollar sign and a decimal point for the sake of consistency.

    Be sure to enclose 50 cents to cover the handling costs.

    The sales tax on the three products amounted to $.85, $1.24, and $.75.

3. Even amounts of $1 million or more may be expressed by writing the dollar sign and number plus the word *million, billion,* or *trillion.* This rule may also be applied to numbers of a million or more (other than money) which would normally be expressed in figures.

    Since the founding of this company, our policyholders have been reimbursed for more than $2 billion in financial losses.

    The new budget figure of $20 million appears to be completely unrealistic.

    Last year our airline transported more than 18 million passengers.

Exercise

In the blanks provided, write the corrections for all incorrectly expressed numbers; if a sentence is correct, write C in the blank.

Example

The cost of the damage caused by the flood was over 16 million dollars.	$16 million
1. We have safe-deposit boxes of all sizes, ranging in price from five dollars to $50 a year.	_____
2. Advertising pens with your company name imprinted in black are only $.45 each in lots of 25.	_____
3. You gave an estimate of $500, but the invoice shows charges of $563.90.	_____
4. The small picture frames about which you inquired are available at the following prices: Style A, $2.29; Style B, 98 cents; and Style C, $1.79.	_____
5. The annual statement of the Farmer's National Bank shows assets of almost $5 billion.	_____
6. Please return this premium notice, together with your check for $35.00, in the enclosed envelope.	_____
7. Copies of this brochure are available at 75¢ each.	_____

ANSWERS TO FRAME 10

1.	$5	3.	C	5.	C	7.	75 cents
2.	45 cents	4.	$.98	6.	$35		

Frame 11   Ordinals

Explanation

An *ordinal number* indicates a position in a sequence; for example, *first, fifteenth, twenty-*

second, and so on. Ordinal numbers that consist of one or two words are expressed in words; others are expressed in figures.

Example

1. Express an ordinal number in words if it can be written in one or two words.

> The accounting offices have been moved to the <u>third</u> floor.
>
> We are planning a special issue of our magazine to observe our <u>fiftieth</u> year of publication.
>
> On the occasion of our <u>twenty-fifth</u> anniversary, we pledge to continue our policy of prompt, efficient service to our customers.

Note

Compound numbers above 20 are hyphenated.

2. Express an ordinal number in figures if it cannot be written in one or two words. The endings *st, nd, rd,* or *th* follow the figures.

> During our special sales promotional week, a surprise gift will be given to the <u>150th</u> customer.

3. Express ordinal dates in figures.

> Please let us have your decision before the <u>15th</u> of November.

Exercise

In the blanks provided, write the corrections for all incorrectly expressed numbers; if a sentence is correct, write C in the blank.

Example

The 1st National Bank offers full service to its depositors.   <u>First</u>

1. Currently in its 95th year, Park College continues to strive for greater academic and professional excellence.   _____
2. The Executive Committee will meet on the fourth Monday of each month.   _____
3. We have scheduled a special meeting on June 10 to make plans for our 30th year in business.   _____
4. The largest voter turnout occurred in the 221st precinct.   _____
5. Your payment is due on the eighteenth.   _____

ANSWERS TO FRAME 11
1. ninety-fifth   2. C   3. thirtieth   4. C   5. 18th

Frame 12   Periods of Time

Explanation

Periods of time are expressed in words when they consist of one or two words. When they refer to credit terms, discount periods, or interest rates, they are expressed in figures.

Example

1. Periods of time are expressed in words.

> Sales have increased from $1 million to $30 million during the past <u>fifteen</u> years.

2. Exceptions: Periods of time are expressed in figures if they —
   a. require more than two words:

   > Our claim service is as near as your telephone 365 days of the year. (three hundred sixty-five has 3 words)

   b. refer to credit terms, discount period, or interest rates:

   > You may deduct 10 percent upon payment of the invoice in 10 days.

Exercise

In the blanks provided, write the corrections for all incorrectly expressed numbers; if a sentence is correct, write C in the blank.

Example

Earnings for the first 6 months were 20 percent above earnings of the same period two years ago.   <u>six</u>

1. The National Clothing Company has been in business for over forty-seven years.   _____
2. Even though our planes were grounded for six weeks by a strike, we transported more than 18 million passengers last year.   _____
3. Could you spare 20 minutes of your busy day for a demonstration of the Blitz calculator?   _____
4. Roger Hunter comes to us from KHTV, Houston, where he has worked in television production for 16 years; he has served as production manager for the past six years.   _____
5. A Hamilton stereo can be yours for only $50 down and $25 a month for twenty-four months.   _____

ANSWERS TO FRAME 12
1. C 2. C 3. twenty 4. sixteen 5. 24

Frame 13   *Business Vocabulary: Transportation*

Explanation

Goods are transported by air and sea, on land, and even under the ground (pipelines).

Terms

Cargo—goods (freight) that are transported by plane, ship, or other vehicle (plural: cargos or cargoes).

Hold—the portion below the deck of a ship or the compartment of a plane where cargo is stored during shipment.

Piggyback—the procedure of placing a truck trailer on a railroad flatcar or in the hold of a ship. The trailer is brought to the location attached to a truck cab, and when the ship or railroad car reaches its destination, the trailer is removed and again attached to a truck cab.

Deadhead—making a return trip, usually by truck, without a load of goods.

Port of entry—a station or location where foreign goods are cleared through customs or where interstate carriers stop for inspection of freight, vehicle, or licenses.

Traffic manager—an employee who schedules freight on various carriers from point of origin to point of destination.

Exercise

Complete each blank in the following sentences with the appropriate term from the preceding vocabulary list.

1. Freight that is transported by plane, ship, or other vehicle is called

   _____.

2. In a ship, this freight is placed in the _____, which is below

   deck.

3. When a trailer is placed below deck in a ship or on a flatcar, it is riding

   _____.

4. Driving on the return trip without a load, called _____, creates

   an expense without gaining any income.

5. At this station, the _____, foreign goods may be cleared through

   customs, and interstate carriers stop for inspection of freight, vehicle, and li-

   censes.

6. ·A person who schedules freight on various carriers from point of origin to point

   of destination is a _____.

ANSWERS TO FRAME 13
1. cargo 2. hold 3. piggyback 4. deadheading 5. port of entry 6. traffic manager

---

Frame 14   Applying Your Knowledge

Directions

In the letter that follows, underscore each error in number usage. Write the correction in the space below the error.

CASE

The traffic manager of Plywood Prefabs, Inc., prepared this letter regarding a shipment. Read the letter carefully to determine which numbers have not been written in accordance with good business practices. (10 errors)

July 8, 19____

Mr. Philip Obeski, Manager
Klondike Construction Company
1 Main Street
Fairbanks, Alaska 99999

Dear Mr. Obeski:

   Your order No. 40,952 for 300 unassembled prefabricated houses,

concrete slabs, and supplies for the utilities will arrive at your construction

site on July 16. It is being shipped to Seattle on July 10 via Pacific

Northwest Freight Lines.

The shipment will arrive at Pier 14 on July 11 at approximately two o'clock. Stevedores will remove the cargo and place it in the hold of the Funston, which will transport it through the Inland Passage to Portage, Alaska. The expected time of arrival in Portage is between 10 A.M. and 11 A.M. on the 15th. The trailers will be loaded onto flatcars of the Alaskan Railroad for transportation to Fairbanks, where they are expected to arrive on July 16 at 6 in the afternoon. Ptarmigan Fast Freight will have a crew at the station to unload the trailers, attach them to the cabs, and drive them the one hundred miles to your construction site.

As we discussed, the credit terms of this order are as follows: ten percent will be deducted from the total cost if we receive payment within 30 days, and 5 percent if we receive payment within 60 days.

All utility supplies, wire, pipes, and slabs have been prepared to your specifications. Approximately 95 percent of the wire is of top quality, and the remaining five percent is second-run wire, but it is guaranteed to meet your needs. Over three fourths of the concrete slabs are reinforced to endure the perma-frost, as well as minus 40 degrees Fahrenheit temperature. The remainder are crated with reinforced wire for your installation.

Your order is the 134th we have shipped to an Arctic site, and only .2% have been more than three days late in arriving. This year, our forty-fifth in the business, we expect to handle over 14 million dollars in shipments to Alaska. Generous credit terms, expeditious shipment, and outstanding products qualify us to achieve this business and increase your profit.

Sincerely,

Tom Brad
Traffic Manager

ANSWERS TO FRAME 14

July 8, 19____

Mr. Philip Obeski, Manager
Klondike Construction Company
1 Main Street
One
Fairbanks, Alaska 99999

Dear Mr. Obeski:

Your order No. 40,952 for 300 unassembled prefabricated houses, concrete slabs, and
40952

supplies for the utilities will arrive at your construction site on July 16. It is being shipped to Seattle on July 10 via Pacific Northwest Freight Lines.

The shipment will arrive at Pier 14 on July 11 at approximately <u>two</u> o'clock.
2
Stevedores will remove the cargo and place it in the hold of the Funston, which will transport it through the Inland Passage to Portage, Alaska. The expected time of arrival in Portage is between 10 A.M. and 11 A.M. on the 15th. The trailers will be loaded onto flatcars of the Alaskan Railroad for transportation to Fairbanks, where they are expected to arrive on July 16 at <u>6</u> in the afternoon. Ptarmigan Fast Freight
six
will have a crew at the station to unload the trailers, attach them to the cabs, and drive them the <u>one hundred</u> miles to your construction site.
100

As we discussed, the credit terms for this order are as follows: <u>ten</u> percent will be
10
deducted from the total cost if we receive payment within 30 days, and 5 percent if we receive payment within 60 days.

All utility supplies, wire, pipes, and slabs have been prepared to your specifications. Approximately 95 percent of the wire is of top quality, and the remaining <u>five</u> percent
5
is second-run wire, but it is guaranteed to meet your needs. Over <u>three fourths</u> of the
three-fourths
concrete slabs are reinforced to endure the perma-frost as well as minus 40 degrees Fahrenheit temperature. The remainder are crated with reinforced wire for your installation.

Your order is the 134th we have shipped to an Arctic site, and only <u>.2%</u> have been
0.2 percent
more than three days late in arriving. This year, our forty-fifth in the business, we expect to handle over <u>14 million dollars</u> in shipments to Alaska. Generous credit
$14 million
terms, expeditious shipment, and outstanding products qualify us to achieve this business and increase your profit.

Sincerely,

Tom Brad
Traffic Manager

Lesson 27
Punctuation: Period, Question Mark, Exclamation Point, Hyphen, Apostrophe

Pretest

Directions

1. Some of the following sentences are correctly punctuated. Write C in the blank provided if both the end-of-sentence and internal punctuation are correct.
2. When the end-of-sentence punctuation is incorrect, write the correct punctuation mark in the blank provided.
3. When the internal punctuation is incorrect, rewrite the word and insert or omit the punctuation, as appropriate.

Example

The I.R.S. has announced a change in the tax structure.   <u>IRS</u>

1. Will you please complete and return the application blank?   <u>   </u>
2. The customer asked if the Stone Company would refund her money because the appliance was defective?   <u>   </u>
3. How would your family survive if you died without life insurance?   <u>   </u>
4. I wonder if you would tell me the name of your representative in the Pittsburgh area?   <u>   </u>
5. Ms. Mills came to us with high recommendations from her former employer.   <u>   </u>
6. Although he recently retired from active management of the company, Carl Scott, Sr, will continue as a member of the board of directors.   <u>   </u>
7. Ms. Helen Wiley (MA, University of Michigan) has been awarded a fellowship to pursue her doctoral study.   <u>   </u>
8. Over-the-counter pain relievers have recently been judged ineffective by the A.M.A.   <u>   </u>
9. Prof. Mitchell and Colonel McKay will serve as co-chairpersons of the fund-raising drive.   <u>   </u>
10. John Wilson & Sons, Inc, has just opened three branch offices.   <u>   </u>
11. I absolutely refuse to move to another office; this is the <u>third</u> time I have been asked to move this month. (said with anger)   <u>   </u>
12. Thirty four items in the last shipment were found to be defective.   <u>   </u>
13. Three fourths of the questionnaires were returned by July 15.   <u>   </u>
14. Our ex-secretary is now an administrative assistant.   <u>   </u>

15. A cooperative, not a self-ish, attitude is expected in this department. ———————
16. The office furniture will be recovered in pale blue. ———————
17. Ones success is equivalent to one's effort. ———————
18. If you don't dot your is, I can't tell them from your e's. ———————
19. Four local companies employees are on strike. ———————
20. Three PTA's presidents have signed the petition. ———————

Lesson 27
Punctuation: Period, Question Mark, Exclamation Point, Hyphen, Apostrophe

Punctuation is a tool used to help clarify the meaning of written communications. It can also change the emphasis and give more than one meaning to the same sequence of words. A writer or processor of business communications should be able to present thoughts clearly so that the reader can understand them easily and quickly. Therefore, an ability to apply punctuation rules is essential.

Notice the difference in meaning of these two sentences:

> He asked who called. (a statement referring to a previous question)

> He asked, "Who called?" (a statement repeating a previous question)

Frame 1   Period: End-of-Sentence Punctuation

The period, question mark, and exclamation point not only are end-of-sentence punctuation marks but also serve other purposes within the sentence. The most common usages of the hyphen and apostrophe have been discussed in previous lessons; however, other usages of these marks are illustrated in this lesson.

A period is used to separate statements containing ideas that are expressed in complete thoughts, to clarify certain abbreviations, and to emphasize enumerations.

Explanation

A *period* follows a declarative sentence and an imperative sentence. It also follows a question that is phrased as a courteous request.

Example

1. A *declarative sentence* is a statement that expresses a fact. It is followed by a period.

   > The accountant prepared the financial report.

2. An *imperative sentence* is a statement that gives a command; to soften the bluntness of the statement, the word *please* is frequently used. It ends with a period.

   > Please return the contract by September 1.

3. A *courteous request* is a statement that is phrased as a courteous question. It ends with a period. Suggestions, commands, or requests may be phrased as courteous questions. If the reader is expected to respond by action, rather than with an oral or written reply, a courteous request has been made.

   > Will you please complete and return the enclosed application blank.

Note

Here, the reader is not expected to reply, saying that the blank will be returned; instead, he or she is expected to perform the *action* of completing and returning it.

4. A *meaningful fragment* is followed by a period. Such fragments are often responses to questions. In business writing, these fragments are used when the exact or implied words of the speaker are recorded; such usages could occur in reports that record the comments of an employee and in direct mail letters.
   a. Report:

   > Supervisor: Did you strike Ms. Jenner with the stapler?
   > Clerk: No.

b.   Direct-mail letter:

Do you need another hour each day? Of course.

5.   An *indirect question* is followed by a period. This statement indicates that a question has been asked.

The manager asked when you will return from the sales meeting.

Exercise

1.   In the first column, write the end-of-sentence punctuation. Write No if punctuation is not necessary.
2.   In the second column, write the symbol identifying the construction of the sentence:

D	Declarative	MF	Meaningful fragment
I	Imperative	F	Fragment
CR	Courteous request	IQ	Indirect question

Example

	Punctuation	Sentence Construction
Please distribute this memo to all employees in this department	_____	_____ I _____
1. Please route this directive to the listed departments	_____	_____
2. Your federal tax return should be sent to the regional office in Albuquerque	_____	_____
3. Will you please notify the insured that his policy has lapsed	_____	_____
4. To save the Monroe Company more than $500 in transportation expenses during the first quarter of the year	_____	_____
5. Of course not	_____	_____
6. The customer asked when her refund would be mailed	_____	_____

ANSWERS TO FRAME 1

1.	.	I	4.	NO	F
2.	.	D	5.	.	MF
3.	.	CR	6.	.	IQ

Frame 2   Period: Abbreviations

Explanation

Abbreviations are shortened forms of words, groups of words, or names.

Some abbreviations are commonly understood and used by everyone. Others, such as short forms of organization names and business terms, may not be understood by people outside a particular organization. Therefore, the writer must consider whether a message will be clear to the reader when abbreviations are used.

Some dictionaries show certain abbreviations with periods, and other dictionaries show the same abbreviations written in solid form. The writer must follow organization policy or a style guide and be consistent in writing abbreviations.

Example

1. Courtesy titles and family designation abbreviations are followed by a period: Mr., Mrs., Ms., Messrs., Jr., Sr.

    Ms. Ray has been appointed to the board.

    The new committee chairman, Robert Anderson, Jr., will contact the committee members within the next week.

2. With the exception of the title *Doctor* (*Dr.*), do not abbreviate professional, military, or civilian titles when used with a surname.

    The seminar will be conducted by Professor Long.

Note

Usage varies when a professional, military, or civilian title is used with the full name of an individual. (Follow organizational policy.)

3. Academic degrees and professional designations: An educational institution awards an academic degree to its graduates; a professional organization awards a professional designation to a person who has successfully qualified through tests and experience.
    a. Some dictionaries show the letters in abbreviations of some academic degrees separated by periods, and other dictionaries show these degrees written in solid form. In this book, the letters in academic degrees are separated by periods.

        Professor Harold Smith, Ph.D., will leave the faculty at the end of the school year. (The words Professor and Ph.D. may be used because they do not have the same meaning; however, Dr. John Zach, M.D., is not used because both titles have the same meaning.)

    b. Professional designations are not separated by periods.

        Dwayne expects to become a CPA.

4. Abbreviate the names of well known organizations and agencies (business, government, military, professional, educational, and others). Periods and spaces are not generally used with these abbreviations.

GM	General Motors
IBM	International Business Machines
AT&T	American Telephone and Telegraph
NASA	National Aeronautics and Space Administration
IRS	Internal Revenue Service
FCC	Federal Communications Commission
CBS	Columbia Broadcasting System
AMA	American Medical Association
USAF	United States Air Force
UCLA	University of California at Los Angeles
USDA	United States Department of Agriculture

    The regional USDA office is located in Kansas City.

5. Business names: The words Company (Co.), Corporation (Corp.), Incorporated (Inc.), and Limited (Ltd.) are often abbreviated in business writing. Follow the form shown in the official name of the organization. A period at the end of an abbreviation is part of that abbreviation; therefore, any other mark of punctuation may follow the period (with the exception of another period at the end of a sentence).

> Have we received a reply from Richmond Co.?

> I have an appointment with Charles Edmund of Edmund & Co.

> General Products, Inc., is expanding its operations in the western states.

6. Business terms: Commonly abbreviated business terms are expressed in capital letters without periods. Some examples are:

LIFO	Last in, first out
FIFO	First in, first out
PERT	Program Evaluation and Review Technique
COBOL	Common Oriented Business Language
FORTRAN	Formula Translation System
MICR	Magnetic Ink Character Recognition
OCR	Optical Character Recognition
GNP	Gross National Product
PR	Public Relations

> This company uses the FIFO method of inventory evaluation.

> The value of the GNP has risen by 4 percent this year.

7. Other abbreviations:
    a. Zip codes: Two capital letters without spaces or periods.

    > NY—New York   CO—Colorado

    b. Initials in names: Each initial in a person's name is followed by a period and a space.

    > The letter was signed by B. J. Doran.

Exercise

In the blanks provided, write the corrections for the incorrectly punctuated abbreviations in the following sentences. If a sentence is correct, write C in the blank.

Example

Please report to Mr Smith in the Personnel Department as soon as you arrive.   ___Mr.___

1. The designation PLS (Professional Legal Secretary) is achieved upon satisfactory completion of a comprehensive examination.   _____
2. John B Simpson, Sr., has turned the firm over to his son, John B. Simpson, Jr.
3. Miss Mary White was formerly a receptionist in the office of Dr. Robert Wells, DDS (Doctor of Dental Surgery).   _____
4. The firm of Smythe & Smythe, Ltd, has offices in London, Antwerp, and New York.   _____
5. The value of the G.N.P. is expected to increase during the next year.   _____
6. Many business organizations use the C.O.B.O.L. language.   _____
7. The applicant has changed his address to 1706 Vine Street, Denver, CO, according to recent letters.   _____

8. Professor Switzer formerly taught at LSU (Louisiana State University). _____
9. The I.R.S. has changed its rules regarding capital gains. _____
10. David King will take the C.A.M. (Certified Administrative Manager) examination. _____

ANSWERS TO FRAME 2

1.	C	4.	Ltd.	7.	C	10.	CAM
2.	B.	5.	GNP	8.	C		
3.	D.D.S.	6.	COBOL	9.	IRS		

Frame 3   Period: Enumerations

Explanation

Periods are used after numerals and letters that designate items in an outline or tabulated list unless the letters or numbers are enclosed within parentheses. Use a period at the end of a line only if it completes the sentence.

Example

1. Periods are not used at the end of a line in a tabulation if that line does not complete the sentence.

> The company promoted three employees:
> 1. Tom Jones
> 2. Mary Brown
> 3. Joe Yates

2. Periods are used at the end of a line in a tabulation if that line completes the sentence.

> Use a period after a (an):
> a. Declarative sentence.
> b. Imperative sentence.
> c. Courteous request.

Exercise

One of the following two tabulated formats requires periods at the end of each line. In the blank provided, write the number (1 or 2) designating the format which requires periods.

1. Follow these directions in submitting your test:
   a. Write your name in the upper left-hand corner
   b. Write your section number below your name
   c. Fold the paper vertically
   d. Hand it to the test monitor
2. Five cities are shown on his itinerary:
   a. Philadelphia
   b. St. Louis
   c. Grand Rapids
   d. Helena
   e. Portland

_____

ANSWER TO FRAME 3

1.

Frame 4 Question Mark

Explanation

The question mark is used after a direct question, a rhetorical question, an expression about which the writer is doubtful, and a question within a sentence.

Example

1. Use a question mark after a direct question. A direct question is one that requires an oral or written answer.

    When will the meeting be held?

2. Use a question mark after a rhetorical question. This question does not require an oral or written response, but the reader is required to "think" about the answer. This type of question is often used in persuasive letters to get attention.

    What will be your take-home pay in the year 2000?

3. A question mark is used at the end of a question that follows a statement.

    My records indicate that you agreed to become a member of the Speakers' Bureau; is that correct, Mr. Smith?

4. For emphasis, use a question mark after brief questions within a sentence.

    Ask what? or whom? after the verb; the noun or pronoun that answers this question is the direct object.

5. Use a question mark within parentheses to show that the preceding fact is questionable.

    Sam is the oldest of the three (?) children.

6. CAUTIONS:
    a. Use a *period* after a statement that shows interest. Such statements often begin with the words "I wonder. . . ." or "I would like to know . . . ."

        I would like to know the dimensions of the modular desk.

        These constructions reflect poor usage because they are not concise; a direct question is more to the point.

        What are the dimensions of the modular desk?

    b. Place the question mark after the period that follows an abbreviation.

        May I change my appointment to 3 P.M.?

Exercise

This exercise requires the use of both periods and question marks. In the blank provided, write the word preceding the punctuation mark(s), as well as the mark(s).

Example

What would happen to your family if you were killed in an accident today   <u>today?</u>

1. You are one of the three candidates for the position, Miss Sana; do you want me to schedule an interview with Mr. Franklin of the home office   _____
2. How will the Federal Reserve Board react to another increase in the rate of inflation   _____

3. Will you please reply to Mr. Evans' letter   _____
4. Where will the ABCA meeting be held   _____
5. What is your company policy on the use of Ms   _____
6. I wonder if you can tell me the cost of the Model 44 camera   _____
7. To find the object of the preposition, ask the question what or whom after the preposition   _____
8. Five employees were ill with the flu last week (The writer is unsure of the illness that caused the employees' absences.)   _____
9. Did he arbitrate the decision for the teachers and the NEA   _____

ANSWERS TO FRAME 4

1.	office?	4.	held?	7.	what? whom? preposition.
2.	inflation?	5.	Ms.?	8.	flu (?) week.
3.	letter.	6.	camera.	9.	NEA?

Frame 5 *Exclamation Point*

Explanation

An *exclamation point* may follow a word, phrase, or clause that reflects strong emotion. This mark is infrequently used in business communications. The most common usages, as mentioned previously, are in reports written about employees (such as critical incident reports) and in direct mail letters. Lesson 33 illustrates the use of exclamation points with quotation marks. Exclamation points should be used sparingly; otherwise, their impact is decreased.

Example

1. Use an exclamation point after a word, phrase, or clause that shows strong emotion (anger, shock, exhilaration, and so on).
   Direct mail letter:

   > Free! A bargain!

   > With all these outstanding features, the WHIZ is only $49.95!

   Reports:

   > No!   I resign!

   > I did not make that statement!

2. Use only one ending punctuation mark; choose the strongest of three possibilities. The strongest marks (in order) are the:
   a. Exclamation point
   b. Question mark
   c. Period

   > Did you say that this recorder is only $9.95!

Exercise

One sentence in each pair could be expressed with strong emotion and punctuated with an exclamation point. In the blank provided, write the letter designating this sentence.

1. a. The Personnel office is on the first floor
   b. I insist upon seeing my personnel file   _____

2. a. How many workers were injured in the accident
    b. How can you possibly expect this company to make restitution for damages when our equipment was removed prior to the accident

ANSWERS TO FRAME 5
1. b.   2. b. (The writer is obviously shocked, angered, and vehement.)

Frame 6 *Hyphen*

Explanation

The *hyphen* has been discussed in the lessons concerning word division (7), compound words (20), and fractions and compound numbers (26). These usages are reviewed in this lesson.

1. Use a hyphen to show the division of a word at the end of a line.
2. Use a hyphen to separate the elements of a compound word preceding a noun. The hyphen is usually not used when the words forming the compound follow the noun.

> Mr. Jones is a <u>well-known</u> lecturer.

> As a lecturer, Mr. Jones is <u>well known</u>.

3. To determine whether certain nouns or verbs are compounds and should contain hyphens, consult a current dictionary. For example, passbook (one word); bank book (two words); to-do (hyphenated).
4. Use a hyphen to separate numbers from 21 to 99 that are written as words.

> He took out this life insurance policy at the age of twenty-seven.

Do not hyphenate even numbers of hundreds, thousands and millions that are written as words.

> <u>One hundred</u> items were defective.

> <u>Two million</u> tires were subject to recall.

5. Use a hyphen between the numerator and denominator of a fraction written as words.

> <u>Three-fourths</u> of the respondents did not answer this question.

6. Use a hyphen between the prefixes *self-* and *ex-* and the following word. (Selfish, selfless, and their derivatives are the only *self* words that are not hyphenated.)

> His <u>self</u>-esteem was badly shaken after the meeting.

> The <u>ex</u>-president frequently offers advice to the executives.

> His <u>selflessness</u> is evidenced by his numerous volunteer activities.

7. Use a hyphen to join a prefix to a proper adjective or noun: neo-Nazism, anti-American.
8. Use a hyphen to prevent misunderstanding, particularly in certain words beginning with the prefix *re-* (meaning *again*). Hyphenating such words is especially important when the meanings of the hyphenated and unhyphenated word are different. Examples: <u>recover</u> (to get back) and <u>re-cover</u> (to cover again).

> The chair in the faculty lounge will be <u>re-covered</u>.

> The stolen property was <u>recovered</u>. (not re-covered)

9. CAUTION: Do not use a hyphen between an adverb ending in -*ly* and the following word.

> He is a highly paid executive.

Exercise

If the underscored words in each of the following sentences are expressed correctly, write C in the blank provided; if not, write the correction in the blank.

Example

Helen is celebrating her <u>twenty first</u> birthday today.   <u>twenty-first</u>

1. This product has been <u>widely advertised</u> in the mass media.   _____
2. I <u>recollect</u> that the memo was given to me a couple weeks ago.   _____
3. <u>One-thousand</u> items are shown on the inventory.   _____
4. The <u>exsupervisor</u> of this department is now the advertising manager. _____
5. This trainee exercises great <u>selfcontrol</u> under stress.   _____
6. The personnel department is offering a clinic to <u>reform</u> smokers.   _____
7. The fiscal year ends in <u>mid-July</u>.   _____
8. Before taking the examination, you should <u>reread</u> the chapters.   _____
9. <u>One eighth</u> of the voters selected Mr. Brawn.   _____
10. The employes in this department do not <u>co-operate</u> with the department manager.   _____

ANSWERS TO FRAME 6
1.	C	5.	self-control	8.	C
2.	C	6.	C	9.	One-eighth
3.	One thousand	7.	C	10.	cooperate
4.	ex-supervisor				

Frame 7 *Apostrophe*

Explanation

The apostrophe has been discussed in previous lessons: to form possessives (11), to form contractions (12). It will be reviewed in this lesson.

Example

1. Use the apostrophe to form the possessive case of a noun.

> The sales <u>manager's</u> report is optimistic.

2. Use the apostrophe to form the possessive case of indefinite pronouns.

> <u>Someone's</u> key was left on the desk.

3. Use the apostrophe in lieu of an omission in a contraction.

> The auditor <u>isn't</u> responsible for this error.

4. To form the singular possessive of an abbreviation, add an apostrophe and s to the singular noun. To form the plural possessive, add an apostrophe to the plural noun.

Singular	CPA	M.D.
Possessive	CPA's	M.D.'s
Plural	CPAs	M.D.s
Possessive	CPAs'	M.D.s'

5. To form the plural of abbreviations, numbers, and letters, do not use the apostrophe unless confusion would result from its omission.

CPAs   PTAs   Ph.D.s   in the 1980s

The Seven Cs of Effective Writing

The three Rs

BUT: CPS's (certified professional secretaries)

Dot the i's and cross the t's. (not is and ts)

6. If confusion would result, use the apostrophe when words other than nouns are used as nouns.

The sentence contains too many the's and ands.

Exercise

If the underscored words in each of the following sentences are expressed correctly, write C in the blank provided; if not, write the correction in the blank.

Example

Ms. <u>Adano's</u> job will be in jeopardy if she does not change her attitude.   _____C_____

1. You used too many <u>and's</u> during your speech.   _____
2. <u>Aren't</u> the customers being unreasonable?   _____
3. Ms. <u>Andersons</u> résumé is the best of the three.   _____
4. <u>Everyones</u> insurance forms must be submitted before August 1.   _____
5. This police department has two <u>APBs</u> out on this person.   _____
6. Three state <u>AMAs</u> have condemned the high cost of malpractice insurance.   _____
7. You will be expected to take a portion of the two <u>CPAs</u> cases during the peak period.   _____
8. The grade school enrollment is expected to increase by the <u>mid-1990s</u>.   _____
9. You spelled Mississippi with too many <u>is</u>.   _____
10. The <u>as</u> in your writing look like <u>os</u>.   _____

ANSWERS TO FRAME 7
1. ands   5. C   8. C
2. C   6. C   9. i's
3. Anderson's 7. CPAs'   10. a's, o's
4. Everyone's

Frame 8   Business Vocabulary: Information Systems

Explanation

The terms defined in this frame are used in an information systems department as well as throughout an organization.

Terms

System—a whole entity consisting of a network of subsystems (digestive system, nervous system, planetary system, information system), all of which contribute to the function of the whole system.

Information system—the collection and distribution of information within an organization for the purpose of record or decision making. This term is broader in concept than data processing, which, strictly speaking, refers only to the processing of the information.

Procedure—comprised of steps to be performed by one or more persons to complete an operation that is part of a system (registration procedure; procedure for preparing computer input; procedure for preparing hard copy to be filmed).

Method—the manner in which an operation is performed; the method may be general (performed by typing, writing, filming) or specific (informing in detail how something shall be typed, written, filmed, and so on).

CRT (cathode ray tube)—a piece of equipment similar to a television set; through electronic means, hard copy, film, or computerized data at a remote location can be called for by a user and will appear on the desk-set screen.

Feasibility study—an evaluation of two or more systems to determine the feasibility (or practicality) of converting to or adopting a different system.

Exercise

Complete each of the following sentences with the correct term from the preceding vocabulary list.

1. To determine whether the company should maintain its records on paper or install a micrographics system, an analyst would perform a

    _____.

2. A _____ is a set of steps performed by one or more persons which contributes to the operation of a _____.

3. The manner in which the steps are performed is called the

    _____.

4. A _____ screen shows data from a remote point.

ANSWERS TO FRAME 8
1. feasibility study 2. procedure, system 3. method 4. CRT

Frame 9   Applying Your Knowledge

Directions

1. Proofread the following memorandum and underscore each punctuation error.
2. Write the correction in the space below.
3. If a punctuation mark should be omitted, write Omit and the punctuation mark in the space below.

    CASE

    This memo was prepared by a systems analyst for the head of an information systems department. (10 errors)

July 10, 19____

TO: Herbert Poma, Manager, Information Systems Department
FROM: Pamela Downing, Systems Analyst
SUBJECT: Problems Encountered in Converting Payroll System

The following problems have been encountered in converting to the new system:

1.   Department heads have reclassified employees and not notified us

2.   Notification of employee increases has not been timely.

3.   Two CRT's in the personnel office are out of order.

1.   To help us solve the first problem, will you please notify all departments that the date of all classification changes must be reported to this department?

2.   This problem is created for us by two departments: Production and Marketing. Twenty four employees from the two departments were standing in line for two hours while we attempted to locate errors in the programming of their data. Naturally, the data were not on the printout or in the data bank because we <u>had never been informed</u> of the salary changes; can you imagine that? I strongly recommend that you write a memo to these department managers, emphasizing the need either to send a copy of the Personnel Action Form or to send the specific data to be changed.

3.   For three days the Personnel Department has been tying up our phones asking for information to use in responding to employees who want to know why their checks don't correspond to their PAF's. Today the assistant personnel manager, Ms Carerra, told me that two CRTs' are malfunctioning. I called Dalton Data Repair, Inc, to report the malfunction.

These problems are obviously not due to the system but to managers not yet becoming adjusted to the changes.

ANSWERS TO FRAME 9

July 10, 19____

TO: Herbert Poma, Manager, Information Systems Department
FROM: Pamela Downing, Systems Analyst
SUBJECT: Problems Encountered in Converting Payroll System

The following problems have been encountered in converting to the new system:

1.   Department heads have reclassified employees and not notified <u>us</u>.
           us.

2.   Notification of employee increases has not been timely.

3.   Two <u>CRT's</u> in the personnel office are out of order.
           CRTs

1. To help us solve the first problem, will you please notify all departments that the

   date of all classification changes must be reported to this <u>department?</u>
   department.

2. This problem is created for us by two departments: Production and Marketing.

   <u>Twenty four</u> employees from the two departments were standing in line for two
   Twenty-four
   hours while we attempted to locate errors in the programming of their data.

   Naturally, the data were not on the printout or in the data bank because we <u>had</u>

   <u>never been informed</u> of the salary changes; can you imagine <u>that?</u>
   that!
   I strongly recommend that you write a memo to these department managers,

   emphasizing the need either to send a copy of the Personnel Action Form or to

   send the specific data to be changed.

3. For three days the Personnel Department has been tying up our phones asking for

   information to use in responding to employees who want to know why their checks

   don't correspond to their <u>PAF's.</u> Today the assistant personnel manager, <u>Ms</u>
   PAFs   Ms.
   Carerra, told me that two <u>CRTs'</u> are malfunctioning. I called Dalton Data Repair,
   omit '
   <u>Inc,</u> to report the malfunction.
   Inc.,
   These problems are obviously not due to the system but to <u>managers</u> not yet becoming
   managers'
   adjusted to the changes.

Lesson 28
Frequently Misused Words

Pretest

The pretest which follows and posttest for this lesson are presented in the form of an Applying Your Knowledge section. The presentation of the tests in this form permits you to determine if certain words are part of your writing vocabulary. The following frequently misused words are discussed in this lesson:

1. provided, providing
2. where, that
3. try to, try and
4. sight, cite, site
5. morale, moral, morals
6. imply, infer
7. alter, altar
8. accept, except
9. credible, creditable
10. anxious, eager
11. adopt, adapt, adept
12. teach, learn

Directions

1. Draw a line through each misused word in the following letter and write the correct word in the space below the error.
2. After you have proofread the letter, write five sentences, each correctly using one of the words which you crossed out in the original letter.

  CASE

  You are a construction supervisor in a large construction company. Some of the laborers work half a day on jobs you supervise and then attend a technical school for half a day. This letter is your recommendation of Alice Alder for continuation in this program. (5 errors)

  Mr. Benjamin Zebbs, Director
  Industrial Construction Management Division
  Blender Technical School
  Cheyenne, Wyoming 82001

  Dear Mr. Zebbs:

  Alice Alder has been working under my supervision on the Green Lake cite for eight weeks. Except for a minor detail, her work has been excellent. She follows a crew chief's orders precisely and learns procedures rapidly. Moreover, she has not been requested to alter any carpentry work or try and correct a deviation because of improper planning. In fact, Alice is especially adept at reading blueprints; she often detects potential problems and informs her crew chief of their existence.

Alice is an anxious, enthusiastic carpenter trainee. Completing the framing on the houses at this site before the scheduled date is creditable to Alice because she worked overtime on several occasions. In addition, her appreciation of the experience and her enthusiasm for the work contribute to the morals of any crew to which she has been assigned.

Occasionally, Alice implies to her crew chief or me that someone is "goofing off." These instances have caused some hard feelings between Alice and the regular workers. I discussed this situation with her, and she now understands that she was wrong.

I sincerely recommend that Alice be allowed to continue her on-the-job training with us; the crew chiefs and I will continue to learn her the methods and techniques of good craftsmanship.

Sentences

1. _____
   _____

2. _____
   _____

3. _____
   _____

4. _____
   _____

5. _____
   _____

Explanation

This frame illustrates the proper usage of certain commonly used subordinate and coordinate conjunctions.

Example

1. PROVIDED/PROVIDING
   a. PROVIDING (v)—usually means supplying or equipping.

      We have been PROVIDING office supplies without requisitions.

      By PROVIDING clothing, food, and toys to the city's poor, the Cosmopolitan Club is performing a vital service.

   It is not considered good usage to use this word as a subordinate conjunction.

   b. PROVIDED (vt)—past tense of provide.

      We PROVIDED the refreshments for the meeting.

      The PROVIDED funds have been allocated. (participal)

   c. PROVIDED (subordinate conjunction)—on the condition, if. PROVIDED should be used as a conjunction only when it expresses a requirement. It is often followed by *that*.

      You may go PROVIDED that you complete the report before-hand.

   When a possibility is expressed, IF is preferable to PROVIDED.

      You may attend the meeting IF approval is granted.

2. THAT/WHERE
   a. THAT, as a subordinate conjunction, is sometimes repeated unnecessarily.

      The doctor believed THAT under the circumstances THAT Mr. Payne should be permitted to work half days. (omit the second THAT)

   b. WHERE is an adverb and refers to location. It should not be used in the place of a subordinate conjunction.

      Incorrect   I read WHERE the new community center will be completed before August.
      Correct   I read THAT the new community center will be completed before August.

3. TRY AND/TRY TO
   TRY followed by the coordinate conjunction AND plus an action verb is con-tradictory. One TRIES TO perform an action.

      The sales manager will TRY TO initiate the campaign next month.

Exercise

Select the correct word(s) in each sentence that follows and write it (them) in the blank provided.

1. The university president said that the system (that, omit that) he advocated was used by 90 percent of the large universities. _____
2. Ms. Bacon will try (to, and) work until she is 65. _____
3. We can install a microfilm system (providing, if, provided) the controller will supply the necessary funds. _____
4. By (provided, providing) free trees to the residents, the bank has improved its image. _____
5. Please try (and, to) schedule my appointment for 10:30. _____

ANSWERS TO FRAME 1
1. omit *that* 2. to 3. if 4. providing 5. to

Frame 2

Explanation

The frequently misused words illustrated in this frame are: *sight, cite, site; morale, moral, morals;* and *imply, infer.*

Example

1. SIGHT/CITE/SITE
   a. SIGHT (n)—the process, power, or function of seeing.

      This memo is for your SIGHT only.

   b. SIGHT (vt)—to see.

      The guard SIGHTED the two men as they entered the bank.

   c. CITE (v)—to quote; to commend; to give a citation.

      The lawyer CITED the first amendment as an example.
      The police officer was CITED for bravery.

   d. SITE (n) location.

      The SITE of the accident is marked by a red flag.

2. MORAL/MORALS/MORALE
   a. MORAL (n)—significance of a practical lesson; the lesson to be drawn from a story.

      The MORAL of this play is that crime does not pay.

   b. MORAL (adj)—pertaining to principles of right and wrong; ethical.

      Young children should be taught how to make MORAL judgments.

   c. MORALS (n)—modes of conduct.

      This person does not have high MORALS.

   d. MORALE (n)—a mental or emotional condition reflected by enthusiasm, confidence, or loyalty toward a task; often used in respect to the common purpose of a group; esprit de corps.

      The MORALE will improve now that John is the supervisor.

3. IMPLY/INFER
    a. IMPLY (vt)—to express indirectly.

        His silence IMPLIED consent.

    b. INFER (v)—to draw a conclusion from facts or premises.

        I INFER from your letter that you prefer not to be named to this committee.

Exercise

Select the correct word from the parentheses in each of the following sentences and write it in the blank provided.

1. A politician's (morales, morals) are important to his conduct in office. _____
2. To support his statements about the economy, the speaker (sighted, sited, cited) excerpts from three government reports. _____
3. The department manager (implied, inferred) that we are to pay for our transportation to the Chicago meeting. _____
4. The (moral, morale) of the employees is low, and I believe that a strike is imminent. _____
5. The (moral, morale) is this: Don't put the payroll funds and the operating funds in the same bank. _____
6. I (imply, infer) from this report that our sales in the Southeastern Division are slipping. _____
7. His patience exhausted, the judge (sighted, cited, sited) the defendant for contempt. _____
8. Many people believe that they have (sighted, cited, sited) UFOs (unidentified flying objects). _____
9. The lawyer's action was neither ethical nor (moral, morale). _____
10. The foreman (implied, inferred) that I should resign before the hearing takes place. _____

ANSWERS TO FRAME 2

1. morals	4. morale	7. cited	10. implied
2. cited	5. moral	8. sighted	
3. implied	6. infer	9. moral	

Frame 3

Explanation

The words illustrated in this frame are: *alter, altar; accept, except; credible, creditable; anxious, eager.*

Example

1. ALTER/ALTAR
    a. ALTER (vt)—to change.

        We may need to ALTER the requirements for this job.

    b. ALTAR (n)—a table which serves as the center of religious ceremonies.

        Flowers were placed upon the ALTAR.

2. ACCEPT/EXCEPT
   a. ACCEPT (v)—to take, undertake, receive with consent.

      Ms. Baca ACCEPTED the job offer.

   b. EXCEPT (vt)—to omit; leave out.

      We should EXCEPT this item from the expense sheet.

   c. EXCEPT (prep)—with exception of; excluding.

      This office is open daily EXCEPT Sundays.

   d. EXCEPT (conj)—on any other condition than that.

      I would contribute to the fund EXCEPT that I shall be leaving the city soon.

3. CREDIBLE/CREDITABLE
   a. CREDIBLE (adj)—believable; reasonable.

      This is a CREDIBLE account of the circumstances surrounding the missent order.

   b. CREDITABLE (adj)—worthy of merit, esteem, praise; capable of being assigned.

      Gaining the new account was CREDITABLE to the station manager's persistence.

4. ANXIOUS/EAGER
   a. ANXIOUS (adj)—worried.

      Mary is ANXIOUS about her grade.

   b. EAGER (adj)—enthusiastic or impatient.

      The trainees are EAGER to begin their assignments.

Exercise

Select the correct word from the parentheses in each of the following sentences and write it in the blank provided.

1. The collection was placed upon the (alter, altar).
2. The employees are (eagerly, anxiously) awaiting the awards banquet.
3. Everyone (accept, except) Greer received a satisfactory rating.
4. The witness' story is (credible, creditable).
5. An (altared, altered) legal document is open to question by the court.
6. The high sales in Division 3 are (credible, creditable) to the representatives' efforts.
7. Mr. Gleeson has (excepted, accepted) a position with a soft-drink company in Indiana.
8. The secretary is (anxious, eager) about her mother, who was taken to the hospital today.
9. I would vote (accept, except) that I don't really care who wins the election.
10. All punctuation marks (except, accept) the exclamation point are used in most business communications.

ANSWERS TO FRAME 3

1. altar	4. credible	7. accepted	10. except
2. eagerly	5. altered	8. anxious	
3. except	6. creditable	9. except	

Frame 4

Explanation

Two sets of misused words are presented: *adopt, adept, adapt; teach* and *learn.*

Example

1. ADOPT/ADEPT/ADAPT
    a. ADOPT (vt)—to take as one's own; to put into effect; to take and use freely.

        The Ho Chin family ADOPTED a child.

        The government will ADOPT new measures to preserve our natural resources.

        The instructor ADOPTED a new textbook last fall.

    b. ADEPT (adj)—thoroughly proficient.

        Rocco is ADEPT in quantitative courses.

        Joe is more ADEPT in handling subordinates than is Mary.

    c. ADAPT (v)—to make something fit the circumstances; to adjust.

        We ADAPTED the form used by the Parker Company to our needs.

        He became ADAPTED to the severe climate of the Arctic.

2. TEACH/LEARN
    a. TEACH (vt)—to instruct.

        The instructor TAUGHT the participants in the seminar to forecast under fluctuating economic conditions.

    b. LEARN (vt)—to gain knowledge or understanding through instruction, study, or experience.

        The students LEARNED the lesson well.

        The children in the outdoor survival course LEARNED how to exist under trying circumstances. (the clause following LEARNED is the direct object)

Note

A teacher TEACHES and a student LEARNS.

Incorrect   The teacher LEARNED me to write effective letters.
Correct   The teacher TAUGHT me to write effective letters.

Exercise

Select the correct word from the parentheses in each of the following sentences and write it in the blank provided.

1. He is (adapt, adept, adopt) at repairing mechanical devices.   _____
2. Ms. Abrams (teached, taught, learned) the children of migrant workers to speak English.   _____

3. Yesterday the students (learned, learnt, learn) how to set up laboratory equipment.   _____

4. The ad hoc committee (will adopt, will adapt, will adept) the rules of the standing committee to make them more pertinent to small group activity.   _____

5. I (adopted, adapted, adepted) Plan B in the company insurance program.   _____

6. Mr. Azza will (adopt, adapt, adept) his wife's son by a former marriage.   _____

7. You can (adopt, adapt, adept) the spring schedule and use it in the fall.   _____

8. Holcomb is more (adopt, adapt, adept) at writing programs than is anyone else in the section.   _____

9. Harley (teach, teached, taught) in the city recreation program.   _____

10. By the end of the summer, the children had (learnt, learned) many games.   _____

ANSWERS TO FRAME 4

1. adept	4. will adapt	7. adapt	10. learned
2. taught	5. adopted	8. adept	
3. learned	6. adopt	9. taught	

Lesson 29
Comma Usage

Pretest

Pretest Part I
Identifying Sentence Construction

Directions

1. In the first blank that follows each sentence, write the letter that correctly identifies the underscored construction:

   A. Direct address
   B. Consecutive coordinate adjective
   C. Series

   D. Introductory element containing a verbal (word or phrase)
   E. Introductory clause
   F. None of these

2. In the second blank, write the word that precédes the comma and the comma; write No if a comma is not required.

Example

	Construction	Correction
The <u>old green</u> sofa has been re-covered.	F	No

1. <u>Disgusted</u> the employees talked about the problem of disparate wages within the department. _____ _____

2. <u>First</u> on the agenda is the topic of tuition increases. _____ _____

3. <u>Students</u> you are expected to submit your papers on the date shown on your assignment sheet. _____ _____

4. An <u>affable interested</u> salesperson makes more sales than one who is noncommunicative and disinterested. _____ _____

5. <u>However</u> excited about your upcoming vacation you may be, please complete your assigned duties before leaving. _____ _____

6. <u>On March 27</u> Ms. Andros will have worked here for one year. _____ _____

7. <u>By the way</u> please bring your employee manuals to the meeting. _____ _____

	Construction	*Correction*

8. Neither your <u>assignments nor your tests nor your class participation</u> shows that you have performed the required research.   _____ _____

9. The modular furniture has <u>easily adjustable</u> seats and backs.   _____ _____

10. <u>To be approved for a loan</u> Ms. Browner, you must have a checking account in this bank.   _____ _____

11. Zeb is taking <u>accounting, finance, information systems, etc.</u> during the evening.   _____ _____

12. <u>If the customer calls</u> please give him the information I've obtained.   _____ _____

13. <u>Walking from her apartment</u> Ellen arrived at work before employees who rode the bus an equal number of blocks.   _____ _____

14. <u>If acceptable</u> I would appreciate your approving the leave request before August 1.   _____ _____

15. <u>Attending workshops</u> will enhance your opportunity for promotion.   _____ _____

Pretest Part II
Applying Punctuation Rules

Directions

1. If a sentence in the following group is punctuated correctly, write C in the blank provided.
2. If a comma is used incorrectly, underscore it and write the applicable rule on the blank line below the sentence.

Example

The old<u>,</u> green sofa has been re-covered.   _____
<u>Do not use a comma between consecutive adjectives that are not</u>

<u>coordinate.</u>

1. The impatient, discourteous customer shouted at the teller, Ms. Yardley.   _____

   _____

   _____

2. Sorting, indexing, and filing, correspondence is the job of Clerk A.   _____

   _____

   _____

3. Being dissatisfied the customer said that she would never order from this company again.

    _____

    _____

4. In the middle of the lobby, will be a giant gazebo containing cut flowers and seating capacity for ten.

    _____

    _____

5. The 200 exhibits of records management equipment will provide additional value to the registrants.

    _____

    _____

6. For working overtime, the remodeling crew was paid $7.75 per hour.

    _____

    _____

7. If the complimentary copies are insufficient, you may obtain an additional 100 copies for only 10 cents a copy.

    _____

    _____

8. Whichever paper is the best, will be sent to the state competition.

    _____

    _____

9. I believe, ladies and gentlemen, that you will receive great satisfaction from contributing to this worthwhile cause.

    _____

    _____

10. Before the first session, of the semester, each student must have purchased the following items: three-ring binder, graph paper, calculator, etc.

    _____

    _____

Lesson 29
Comma Usage

The comma is the most frequently used—and most frequently misused—punctuation mark. The omission of a necessary comma can cause the reader to reread a sentence to obtain the idea that the writer wanted to convey. Placing a comma in the wrong position can create a confusing sentence and sometimes an amusing one.

Notice these examples of incorrect comma usage:

> All your children you see will be protected under this policy. (Without punctuation the sentence gives the impression that only the children in view will be protected.)

> All your children, you see, will be protected under this policy. (In this sentence, the commas surround a parenthetical thought that interrupts the sentence and is not necessary to its meaning.)

This lesson illustrates comma usage in direct address, with consecutive coordinate adjectives, in a series of words, and after introductory elements. Some examples and exercises in this lesson were abstracted from *Machine Transcription in Modern Business.*

Frame 1   Direct Address

A comma is used to set off words, phrases, and clauses. To "set off" means that a comma precedes and follows an expression. However, if the expression is at the beginning of a sentence, a comma follows it to set it off. If the expression is at the end of a sentence, a comma precedes it to set it off.

Explanation

A comma is used to set off a noun in direct address. The noun may be (1) a person's surname preceded by a courtesy title, (2) a person's first name, (3) a substitute for a person's name (courtesy, position, or job title), or (4) a substitute for the names of persons receiving the communication, as shown in the inside address (legal firm or club).

Example

Use a comma to set off a noun in direct address.

> Yes, <u>Mr. Curtano</u>, your order will be shipped before July 17.

> We are happy, <u>Ann</u>, that you decided to join our staff.

> Yes, <u>sir</u>, this complete package is only $10.95.

> <u>Gentlemen</u>, our lawyer advises us not to comply with your firm's request.

Exercise

In the blank provided, write the word preceding the comma and the comma. If a sentence does not require a comma, write No in the blank.

Example

We appreciate your remittance Mrs. Granby.   <u>remittance,</u>

---

* By permission. Lois Meyer and Ruth Moyer, *Machine Transcription in Modern Business* (New York: John Wiley & Sons, 1978).

1. You know Mr. Mason that we pay the shipping charges when you order in quantity. _____
2. Ms. Abbott we are pleased to extend credit to you. _____
3. This is your chance ladies to make some additional money for your club. _____
4. Under the circumstances Bob we should develop a policy to cover absences due to mental health problems. _____
5. Mr. Keegan has been promoted to another position. _____

ANSWERS TO FRAME 1
1. know, Mason, 3. chance, ladies, 5. No
2. Abbott, 4. circumstances, Bob,

Frame 2 Consecutive Coordinate Adjectives

Explanation

A comma is used to separate two consecutive coordinate adjectives.

Example

Use a comma to separate two consecutive adjectives (a) if they can be reversed and the sentence is logical, and (b) if the word *and* can be inserted between them and the sentence is logical. Notice that a comma is not used between the last adjective and the noun it modifies.

Test He is a diligent enthusiastic employee.
    (a) Reversed: He is an enthusiastic diligent employee.
    (b) *And* inserted: He is a diligent and enthusiastic employee.
    The adjectives are coordinate; separate them with a comma. He is a diligent, enthusiastic employee.
Test The old brick building will become a museum.
    (a) Reversed: The brick old building will become a museum. (Not logical— the second test becomes unnecessary.)

Exercise

Write the word preceding the comma and the comma in the blank provided. If a comma is not required, write No in the blank.

Example

The top executives have large oak desks with overhanging surfaces.   __No__

1. Repetitive routine tasks have been eliminated by computers. _____
2. The red plastic file folder should be inserted where a file has been removed. _____
3. Fascinating challenging jobs are available to the person who transfers to our foreign branch. _____
4. The new analyst can prepare clear concise feasibility studies. _____
5. To employ competent efficient personnel, we must establish effective recruiting procedures. _____

ANSWERS TO FRAME 2
1. Repetitive, 2. No 3. Fascinating, 4. clear, 5. competent,

Frame 3 *Series*

Explanation

A comma is used to separate the elements within a series. A *series* consists of three or more words, phrases, or clauses of equal rank; for example, three nouns, prepositional phrases, or dependent clauses.

If the elements are connected with a conjunction, this word takes the place of the comma.

Example

1. Use a comma to separate elements in a series.
    a. Words in a series (the last element is not separated from the verb by a comma):

    > The president, vice president, and the corporate secretary were present at the last meeting. (nouns in a series)

    b. Phrases in a series:

    > To type reports, to file correspondence, and to answer the phone are the receptionist's duties. (infinitive phrases in a series)

    > Having transcribed the letters, having filed the correspondence, and having cleaned her desk, Mary was ready to go home. (participial phrases in a series)

    > Cora reported to me that she had looked on the desk, in the folder, and under the cabinet for the missing file. (prepositional phrases in a series)

    c. Clauses in a series:

    > Employees who have worked for the company for one year, who have a satisfactory performance rating, and who are recommended by their supervisors may apply for training under this program. (clauses in a series)

2. Do not use a comma to separate the elements of a series if these elements are joined by a coordinate conjunction *(and, but, or, for, nor)*.

    > Cora reported to me that she had not looked on the desk or in the folder or under the cabinet for the missing file.

3. Use a comma before and after *etc.* when it ends a series.

    > Books, periodicals, cassettes, videotapes, etc., are available in the library.

    > In addition to books on this topic, the library provides periodicals, cassettes, videotapes, etc. (Only one period is used at the end of a sentence; a comma does not follow an abbreviation at the end of a sentence.)

Exercise

Write the word preceding the comma and the comma in the blank provided. If a comma is not required, write No in the blank.

Example

Oil coal and gas can be extracted only under the guidelines established by the federal government.   Oil, coal,

1. To qualify for the job, the applicant must be able to type 50 words per minute to pass a clerical competence test with a score of 65 and to proofread accurately.   _____

2. A correspondence manual shows examples of company correspondence illustrates the format of communications and provides instructions regarding the maintenance of records.   _____

3. A company which pays employees according to the local standards which treats them fairly and which provides acceptable benefits can achieve a favorable image in the community.   _____

4. Computing ratios, preparing financial statements and writing analytical reports are duties of the financial analyst.   _____

5. A secretary should maintain a tickler file and a calendar of events.   _____

6. Having read the current newspapers having scanned the stock reports and having dictated replies to his correspondence, the president was ready to meet with his executives.   _____

7. The trays and the bottles and the old advertisements displayed in the company's corporate archives interested many visitors.   _____

8. Ms. Kelly was promoted because she had experience in the Word Processing Center in the Accounts Payable Department and in the Microfilm Section.   _____

9. Dean Namath said that the College would furnish the paper stamps and envelopes for students who send questionnaires based on research of general interest.   _____

10. The Peapod Company, Inc., of Des Moines, Iowa, sells garden seeds, such as peas turnips carrots etc. throughout the United States.   _____

ANSWERS TO FRAME 3

1. minute, 65,
2. correspondence, communications,
3. standards, fairly,
4. statements,
5. No

6. newspapers, reports,
7. No
8. Center, Department,
9. paper, stamps,
10. peas, turnips, carrots, etc.,

Frame 4   Introductory Words

Introductory elements—words, phrases, and clauses—are set off under certain circumstances, not all of which are applicable to each element. Therefore, words, phrases, and clauses are discussed in separate frames.

Explanation

An introductory word is set off when it is not necessary to the thought of the sentence (parenthetical). Many introductory parenthetical words are transitional in nature and are set off.

Example

1. Set off an introductory word.

> Furthermore, no brokers shall be permitted to assist new clients without the approval of the vice president.

> First, check the electric cord to see that it is plugged securely into the socket.

2. Do not set off an introductory word that is necessary to the sentence.

> <u>However</u> important these test results may be, they must be substantiated by additional screening procedures.

> <u>Next</u> in order of importance is the recruiting method used for the selection of clerks.

3. Set off an introductory participle.

> <u>Excited</u>, Mary punched the cards incorrectly.

Exercise

Write the word preceding the comma and the comma in the blank provided. If a comma is not required, write No in the blank.

Example

However the passing score on the employment test was 75.   <u>However,</u>

1. Next move the variable line spacer to the forward position.   _____
2. Obviously crying at her desk, the secretary was told by the office manager that she could leave work early.   _____
3. Obviously the depreciation expense was recorded incorrectly last month.   _____
4. First in the manual should be the current organizational chart.   _____
5. Moreover we are prepared to install a new air-conditioning system without charge for materials or labor.   _____
6. Enthusiastic the sales personnel listened to the manager's briefing.   _____

ANSWERS TO FRAME 4
1. Next, 2. No 3. Obviously, 4. No 5. Moreover, 6. Enthusiastic,

---

Frame 5   Introductory Phrases

Explanation

A phrase is a group of grammatically related words without a subject and verb. Gerund, infinitive, participial, and prepositional phrases frequently occur at the beginning of a sentence. An introductory phrase is set off by a comma unless it is required to complete or clarify the meaning of a sentence or it contains the subject of a sentence.

Example

1. Set off a long introductory prepositional phrase with a comma. Often two or three prepositional phrases occur in succession; without a punctuation mark after the last phrase, the meaning could be unclear.

> <u>In the plan for the new building</u>, all the offices are located on the top floor.

> BUT: <u>In the middle of the room</u> stands the computer. (No comma follows <u>room</u> because the remainder of the sentence, <u>stands the computer</u>, would not be clear.)

2. Set off a short prepositional phrase if it is not necessary to the sentence.

> <u>By the way</u>, your payment has not been received.

> BUT: <u>On March 1</u> the promotion will become effective. (The phrase is important to the meaning of the sentence.)

3. Set off an introductory infinitive phrase unless it contains the subject of the sentence.

> <u>To understand the organization of the company</u>, the consultant must be provided with an organization chart.

> BUT: <u>To explain the organization of the university</u> is a difficult task. (The infinitive phrase is the subject and cannot be separated from the verb by a comma.)

4. Set off an introductory participial phrase.

> <u>Having become aware of the increase in prices</u>, the dealer canceled his order.

5. Do not set off an introductory gerund phrase because it contains the subject of the sentence.

> <u>Having modern mail-processing equipment</u> contributes to the efficiency of the office.

6. Set off a phrase that contains a verbal.

> By <u>ordering</u> now, you can save $9.95.

> Before <u>registering</u>, read the directions carefully.

Exercise

1. Underscore the introductory phrase in each sentence that follows.
2. Write the word preceding the comma and the comma in the first blank provided. If a comma is not required, write No in the blank.
3. In the second blank, write one of these letters to identify the introductory construction that is (or is not) being set off:
   A. Prepositional phrase(s)
   B. Infinitive phrase
   C. Participial phrase
   D. Phrase containing a verbal (word)
   E. Gerund phrase

Example

	Correction	*Construction*
<u>To arrive in Houston before 10:30 A.M.</u> you will need to take Flight No. 173.	A.M.,	B
1. Computing the ratios is his job.		
2. Of all the employees in the company Elbert has twice won a prize for a suggestion.		
3. By working for the airlines you are entitled to one free trip during your first year of service.		

		Correction	*Construction*

4. Having evaluated the system thoroughly Ms. Simpson recommended that the payroll be included in the microfilm system. _____ _____

5. To be eligible for promotion you must have served in this position for three years. _____ _____

6. For your convenience we are sending along a pad of order blanks. _____ _____

7. On May 21 we shall start publication of a regular Saturday edition of this newspaper. _____ _____

8. To enter graduate school is his goal. _____ _____

9. Working in our Records Department Mr. Boone soon learned the organization and procedures used in the company. _____ _____

10. In preparing your report please include the variances between the estimated and actual budget figures. _____ _____

ANSWERS TO FRAME 5

		Correction	*Construction*
1.	Computing the ratios	No	E
2.	Of all the employees in the company	company,	A
3.	By working for the airlines	airlines,	D
4.	Having evaluated the system thoroughly	thoroughly,	C
5.	To be eligible for promotion	promotion,	B
6.	For your convenience	convenience,	A
7.	On May 21	No	A
8.	To enter graduate school	No	B
9.	Working in our Records Department	Department,	C
10.	In preparing your report	report,	D

Frame 6   Introductory Clauses

Explanation

An independent clause is a group of grammatically related words that contain a subject and verb and express a complete thought. A dependent clause is a group of grammatically related words that contain a subject and verb but do not express a complete thought. An introductory dependent clause used as an adverb (adverbial clause) is followed by a comma.

Example

1. Set off an introductory dependent clause used as an adverb.

> When you come to Albany next week, the sales figures will be ready for analysis. (modifies ready, an adjective)

468 · Business English Basics

2. Do not set off an introductory clause that is used as the subject.

> <u>Whomever you name as your guest</u> will be invited to attend the showing of the new models. (clause used as the subject)

3. Set off an elliptical clause (one in which the subject and verb are implied).

> <u>If so</u>, please let us know immediately. (The actual clause might be as follows: <u>If that is so</u>.)

Exercise

Write the word preceding the comma and the comma in the blank provided. If a comma is not required, write No in the blank.

Example

After you finish the capital budget analysis please let met know which project the company should undertake.

<u>analysis,</u>

1. Since we discussed the morale in the department I have decided to visit with each employee. _____
2. If not where can I purchase an adaptor for this calculator? _____
3. Whichever person is selected must pay his or her accommodations during the meeting. _____
4. Because the report was late the data cannot be included in this month's analysis. _____
5. When you enter the building please sign the guard's record sheet immediately. _____

ANSWERS TO FRAME 6
1. department, 2. not, 3. No 4. late, 5. building,

Frame 7 Comma Usage Rules

Explanation

To punctuate accurately, the writer should understand the reason for each punctuation mark. To do this, the writer must know the punctuation rules, be able to identify various sentence constructions, and apply the rules to these constructions.

Example

1. Set off a noun in direct address.

> Yes, <u>Mr. Barry</u>, we will be glad to talk with you.

2. Separate consecutive coordinate adjectives with a comma.

> The <u>diligent, capable</u> employee was promoted.

3. Separate the elements in a series with commas.

> <u>Going to classes, working in the store, and participating in activities</u> required Marianne to organize her time well.

4. Set off an introductory element consisting of a word or phrase used as a verbal unless that element is the subject of the sentence (verbal: gerund, infinitive, participle).

> By <u>working</u> hard, you will achieve your goal.

5. Set off a long introductory prepositional phrase or two or more consecutive prepositional phrases.

> <u>In the event of a violent electrical storm</u>, unplug the television monitors in your office.

6. Set off a dependent clause used as an adverb.

> <u>When the report is due</u>, please submit it to Mr. Henry.

Exercise

1. In the first blank to the right of each sentence, write the letter that identifies the underscored construction:

A. Direct address
B. Consecutive coordinate adjectives
C. Series

D. Introductory element containing a verbal word or phrase
E. Introductory clause
F. None of these

2. In the second blank, write the word that precedes the comma and the comma. If a comma is not required, write No in the blank.

Example	*Construction*	*Correction*
The <u>old green</u> sofa has been re-covered.	F	No

1. Under the circumstances <u>class</u> we can offer the examination at only one time. | ___ | ___
2. Ms. Patton is a <u>morose unhappy</u> individual. | ___ | ___
3. Neither <u>her ratings nor her attitude nor her work</u> is satisfactory. | ___ | ___
4. The <u>old wooden</u> table will be replaced by a piece of modular furniture. | ___ | ___
5. The core requirements, <u>accounting, business law, etc.</u> are listed in the catalog. | ___ | ___
6. <u>To qualify for this job</u> an applicant must have three years' experience. | ___ | ___
7. <u>Soliciting assistants to canvass the territory</u> Ms. Anderson called upon a campus organization. | ___ | ___
8. <u>In spite of the lengthy delay in processing her check</u> Ms. Durant maintained a co-operative attitude. | ___ | ___
9. <u>Working for an accounting firm</u> will provide the experience needed to qualify you for the examination. | ___ | ___
10. <u>When the manager of the Research and Development Department comes to the library</u> give him all the assistance he needs. | ___ | ___
11. Sooper Seeds are guaranteed to germinate within 30 days if you will <u>plant them according to directions, water the plot daily and hoe it when necessary.</u> | ___ | ___

	Construction	*Correction*
12. <u>On your transcript</u> you will find a notarized statement showing that you have completed the courses required for certification.	_____	_____
13. <u>Moreover</u> you can be sure that this company will repair your car during the warranty period without charge for parts or labor.	_____	_____
14. <u>Elated</u> Max showed his award to the other employees.	_____	_____
15. <u>However</u> important you believe this score to be, the interview is even more important.	_____	_____

ANSWERS TO FRAME 7

1. A circumstances,	5. C etc.,	9. D No	13. F Moreover,
2. B morose,	6. D job,	10. E library,	14. D Elated,
3. C No	7. D territory,	11. C daily,	15. F No
4. F No	8. D check,	12. F No	

Frame 8   Business Vocabulary: Commercial Banking

Explanation

A *commercial bank* provides many services for its customers. The terms identifying these services are the same whether the customer is an individual, a business organization, or an institution (government, foundation, etc.).

Terms

Bank statement—a form prepared by the bank in which a depositor has a checking account. The statement shows the deposits, withdrawals, service charges, and other items.

Reconciliation—the comparison of a customer's checkbook (or ledger) with the bank statement to verify the items and to confirm the current balance.

Line of credit—the maximum credit allowed to a borrower. In many modern banks, this line of credit is shown on the bank statement, along with the total amount deducted from it.

Principal—the amount of money on which interest is earned or paid.

Interest—the cost of borrowing money or the income from loaning money.

Finance charge—the interest charged on the money borrowed by the customer under his approved line of credit.

Exercise

Complete each of the following sentences with the appropriate word from the preceding vocabulary list.

1. A form that shows the customer's deposits and withdrawals, as well as other additions or deductions, is a _____.

2. The customer compares the figures on the form with those in the checkbook to verify the items and confirm the balance on hand. This comparison is called a

_____.

3. The cost of borrowing money or the income from loaning money is called

   _____.

4. The _____ is the amount of money on which interest is paid.

5. The interest charged on a line of credit is a _____.

ANSWERS TO FRAME 8

1. bank statement   3. interest   5. finance charge
2. reconciliation   4. principal

Frame 9 Applying Your Knowledge

Directions

1. If a comma is used incorrectly, underscore it.
2. If a comma is omitted, insert it in the proper place.
3. Write the applicable rule on the blank line below the sentence.

Example

Among the many services a bank provides, are checking
A comma should not separate the subject *(services)* from the

accounts, savings accounts, credit lines, and so forth.
verb *(are)*.

CASE

The marketing director of the Fifth National Bank prepared this letter to be sent to a new customer, encouraging her to apply for a line of credit with the bank. (10 errors)

Mrs. Roger Loper
2812 Morningside Drive
Houston, TX 99999

Dear Mrs. Loper:

We are pleased, Mrs. Loper that you have selected the Fifth National

_____

Bank as "your bank." This letter explains one of our very popular services,

_____

the Balance-Plus Account.

_____

Having a Balance-Plus Account, is like having a second checking

_____

account. When you need to pay a bill, and do not have sufficient funds in

_____

your checking account, you can "borrow" from the Balance-Plus Account

_____

simply by writing a check on your regular checking account. The bank

will transfer the necessary amount from your Balance-Plus Account to your

checking account, pay the check and show this payment on your statement

as a deduction from your line of credit.

By using this service you will not need to obtain small loans or pay high

interest for unsecured loans. The periodic rate used in computing the

finance charge is 1.5 percent per month on the average daily outstanding

balance of the Balance-Plus Account since the prior account statement

date. The finance charge is computed at an annual percentage rate of 18.0

percent.

To apply for a Balance-Plus Account simply follow these concise

easy-to-understand directions:

1. Complete the attached form.

2. Sign it.

3. Place it in the enclosed envelope.

4. Return the envelope within 10 days.

Having been approved for a Balance-Plus Account you will receive a

letter telling you the maximum amount which can be transferred to your

account. The administrative details are handled by the bank; you need no card or other identification to "prove" that you are a Balance-Plus

---

customer. However, important this may be to you, the recipient will never

---

know whether it is being paid from your checking account or from your

---

Balance-Plus Account.

Within one week after applying for the Balance-Plus Account you will

---

be able to supplement your regular checking account.

Sincerely,

Dan Bartram
Marketing Director

ANSWERS TO FRAME 8

Mrs. Roger Loper
2812 Morningside Drive
Houston, TX 99999

Dear Mrs. Loper:

We are pleased, Mrs. Loper, that you have selected the First National Bank as

Set off a noun in direct address.

"your bank." This letter explains one of our very popular services, the Balance-Plus
Account.

Having a Balance-Plus Account__ is like having a second checking account. When

Do not separate the subject (a gerund phrase) from the verb (is).

---

you need to pay a bill__ and do not have sufficient funds in your checking account,

Set off <u>the complete</u> introductory dependent clause.

---

you can "borrow" from the Balance-Plus Account simply by writing a check on your
regular checking account. The bank will transfer the necessary amount from your
Balance-Plus Account to your checking account, pay the check, and show this

Use a comma before the coordinate conjunction that joins
the last two elements in a series.

---

payment on your statement as a deduction from your line of credit.

By using this service, you will not need to obtain small loans or pay high interest

---
Set off an introductory phrase containing a verbal (<u>using</u>— a gerund).
---

for unsecured loans. The periodic rate used in computing the finance charge is 1.5

percent per month on the average daily outstanding balance of the Balance-Plus

Account since the prior account statement date. The finance charge is computed at

an annual percentage rate of 18.0 percent.

To apply for a Balance-Plus Account, simply follow these concise,

---
Set off an introductory infinitive phrase that does not contain the subject.
Use a comma between consecutive adjectives that are coordinate.
---

easy-to-understand directions:

1. Complete the attached form.

2. Sign it.

3. Place it in the enclosed envelope.

4. Return the envelope within 10 days.

Having been approved for a Balance-Plus Account, you will receive a letter telling

---
Set off an introductory participial phrase.
---

you the maximum amount which can be transferred to your account. The

administrative details are handled by the bank; you need no card or other

identification to "prove" that you are a Balance-Plus customer. However__important

---
Do not set off an introductory word that is essential
to the meaning of the sentence.
---

this may be to you, the recipient of your check will never know whether it is being paid

from your checking account or from your Balance-Plus Account.

Within one week after applying for the Balance-Plus Account, you will be able to

---
Set off an introductory phrase containing a verbal (<u>applying</u>).
---

supplement your personal checking account.

Sincerely,

Dan Bartram
Marketing Director

Lesson 30
Comma Usage Continued

Pretest

Directions

1. In the first blank to the right of each of the following sentences:
   a. Write C if the underscored element is punctuated correctly.
   b. Write the word preceding each comma and the comma if punctuation is needed.
2. In the second blank, write one of the following symbols to identify the under-scored element:

C	Compound sentence	NR	Nonrestrictive phrase or clause
P	Parenthetical expression	O	Other than listed

Example	*Correction*	*Construction*
Boucher's development on the east side of town and the one on the west side contain show homes that are open until 9 P.M.	C	O
1. Mr. Holter, who is an account executive, resigned in August.	_____	_____
2. All students having a B average or above are excused from the final examination.	_____	_____
3. The departmental meeting will be held at 9 A.M. on Friday August 29.	_____	_____
4. The landscape designers planted the bushes on the east side of the building and then they planted the trees on the north side.	_____	_____
5. An employee who signs the indemnification form will have his or her salary indemnified for a minimal deduction.	_____	_____
6. This procedure which has always been awkward to implement should be changed.	_____	_____
7. I called the customer at 5:30 P.M. not 5:30 A.M.	_____	_____
8. The police officer said that Denning had been swerving into the right lane and that he had been driving over the speed limit.	_____	_____
9. We have a high turnover rate for this month don't we?	_____	_____
10. The more inventory we purchase the greater our asset value becomes.	_____	_____
11. Ms. Altman resigned and moved to Philadelphia, Pennsylvania last month.	_____	_____
12. I believe on the other hand that we need to increase our sales and use the slack capacity we have in this plant.	_____	_____

475

	Correction	*Construction*

13. My mother <u>who is 82</u> sold her stock in the Relathon Company. _____ _____
14. The Production Department will be able to operate at full capacity <u>if we can move 14 employees into it through lateral transfer.</u> _____ _____
15. Ms. Bonney <u>by the way</u> is no longer with this firm. _____ _____
16. Our union steward <u>who was recently elected</u> has been encouraging the employees to take advantage of the training programs offered through the Personnel Department. _____ _____
17. The assignment for tomorrow includes this reference: <u>Chapter III, Section 32.4, page 81.</u> _____ _____
18. <u>Federal, state, and local government offices will be closed on the Fourth of July but the banks will be open.</u> _____ _____
19. Inflation <u>so they say</u> will become even more of a burden during the 1980s. _____ _____
20. The president of this corporation <u>who retired last year</u> has become a member of the board of directors of a petroleum company. _____ _____
21. Ms. Symonds <u>of the San Francisco branch</u> has been visiting our facilities. _____ _____
22. All employees <u>whom the manager has designated as fire guards</u> will meet in Room 214 at 9 A.M. _____ _____
23. The office equipment <u>all of which is old</u> will be sold through a classified advertisement. _____ _____
24. Our CPA firm <u>Harrison and Brown</u> will not take the responsibility for this mistake. _____ _____
25. The supervisor had <u>no doubt</u> about the manner in which the accident happened. _____ _____
26. Ms. Southern <u>having been instructed to wear goggles during the hazardous descent into the mine</u> complied with the request cheerfully. _____ _____
27. Elected representatives <u>who neglect their constituents' wishes and demands</u> place themselves in a precarious political position. _____ _____
28. <u>The payroll data are on the computer but the inventory data are not.</u> _____ _____
29. Seventy-four percent of the residents voted for Stephens; <u>21 percent for Johnson; and 5 percent for Anchou.</u> _____ _____
30. The color <u>red</u> is painted above all equipment which cannot be operated by apprentices. _____ _____

Lesson 30
Comma Usage Continued

Three rules for comma usage are presented and illustrated in this lesson:

1. Use a comma before a coordinate conjunction that connects two independent clauses.
2. Set off a parenthetical element with commas.
3. Set off a nonrestrictive element in apposition with commas.

In addition, a few miscellaneous usages are illustrated; logic and common sense dictate the use of a comma in certain constructions rather than does a specific rule.

In this lesson, as in all lessons devoted to punctuation, the writer needs to understand sentence construction, have a knowledge of punctuation rules, and be able to apply these rules to specific constructions.

The use of commas in quoted material is presented in Lesson 33.

Frame 1 Compound Sentence

Explanation

A compound sentence consists of two or more independent clauses connected with a coordinate conjunction: *and, but, or, for, nor.*

Example

1. Use a comma before a coordinate conjunction that connects two independent clauses. To determine that two independent clauses exist, read the clause to the left of the coordinate conjunction; if it is independent, read the clause to the right of the conjunction. If both clauses are independent, place a comma before the coordinate conjunction.

   > We are pleased with all aspects of the construction in our new building, <u>and</u> we shall call you when we are ready to begin planning our Altus factory.

2. Do not use a comma before a coordinate conjunction that does not connect two independent clauses. To determine if the coordinate conjunction connects two independent clauses, apply the tests that follow.
   a. Compound Dependent Clauses:

   > I believe that many employees have been reporting to work late <u>and</u> that the supervisors should call a meeting to discuss this problem.

   TEST: Does an independent clause precede the conjunction? Yes. Does an independent clause follow the conjunction? No. Result: Do not use a comma before the conjunction.
   b. Compound Verb:

   > The accountant completed his cost reports <u>and</u> compared them with the predetermined standard costs.

   TEST: Does an independent clause precede the conjunction? Yes. Does an independent clause follow the conjunction? No. Result: Do not use a comma before the coordinate conjunction.

c. Compound Subject:

> The plant located in Baton Rouge <u>and</u> the plant located in Tacoma are using flexible scheduling procedures on a trial basis.

TEST: Does an independent clause precede the conjunction? No. The second question is unnecessary. The sentence is not compound, and a comma is not used before the conjunction.

3. Use a comma before the coordinate conjunction that connects the independent clauses in a compound-complex sentence. As you may recall, this type of sentence has two or more independent clauses and one or more dependent clauses.

> If Ms. Simmons responds before the end of the month, please approve her account, <u>but</u> if she does not respond by that time, write to her and encourage her further consideration of our offer.

Note

A semicolon rather than a comma may be used before the coordinate conjunction (1) if a compound-complex sentence would be confusing or (2) if the writer desires to emphasize the clauses.

> We requisitioned Forms 76, 92, and 103; but Forms 86, 93, and 102 were received in today's delivery.

Exercise

1. If the sentence is punctuated correctly, write C in the blank provided.
2. Underscore punctuation marks which are used incorrectly.
3. If punctuation marks are omitted, insert them in the proper places.
4. On the blank line below the sentence, write a complete sentence explaining your corrections.

Example

Boucher's development on the east side of town, and the one on the west side contain show homes that are open until 8 P.M.
<u>No comma is required; the sentence contains a compound subject.</u> _____

1. The supervisor checked the letter but he did not find the mistake. _____

2. The sales reports were submitted by the sales associates, and evaluated by Mr. McNally, the vice president. _____

3. The training director and the department heads have arranged seminars for the employees in each department. _____

4. The calendars will be used for advertising all product lines but the retailer's name will be printed on the bottom of each page. _____

5. The new price list has been sent to wholesalers and all dealers in District 8, but they have been instructed that these prices are not effective until August 1. _____

ANSWERS TO FRAME 1

1. The supervisor checked the letter, but he did not find the mistake.
   Use a comma before a coordinate conjunction that connects two independent clauses.
2. The sales reports were submitted by the sales associates, and evaluated by Mr. McNally, the vice president.
   Do not use a comma to separate a compound verb.
3. C
4. The calendars will be used for advertising all product lines, but the retailer's name will be printed on the bottom of each page.
   Use a comma before a coordinate conjunction that connects two independent clauses.
5. The new price list has been sent to wholesalers, and all dealers in District 8, but they have been instructed that these prices are not effective until August 1.
   The misplaced comma was inserted before a coordinate conjunction that connected two objects of the preposition.
   Use a comma before a coordinate conjunction that connects two independent clauses.

Frame 2 Parenthetical Expression

Explanation

A *parenthetical expression* consists of a word, phrase, or clause that is unnecessary to complete the structure or clarify the meaning of a sentence. Such an expression is an interrupting thought when it appears in the middle of a sentence or an afterthought when it appears at the end of a sentence. A parenthetical introductory expression may be a transitional word, phrase, or clause. To emphasize that a parenthetical expression is not necessary, the writer sets it off with commas.

Example

1. Set off a parenthetical expression with commas. To determine if a word, phrase, or clause is parenthetical:
   a. Read the sentence with the expression.
   b. Read the sentence without the expression.
   c. Set off the expression if it is unnecessary to the structure or meaning of the sentence.

   > I do think, <u>however</u>, that production should be increased before next year.

   > <u>However</u>, I do think that production should be increased before next year.

   > I do think that production should be increased before next year, <u>however</u>.

   BUT: I think that production should be increased before next year; <u>however</u>, the decision must be based on the effective plant capacity at our disposal. In this sentence, <u>however</u> connects two independent clauses and is preceded by a semicolon. Notice that it is followed by a comma, but a comma does not follow a one-syllable conjunctive adverb (*here, yet, still, or, so*) unless the writer wants to stress it.

   > He was, <u>in my opinion</u>, a very hard worker.

   > He was a very hard worker, <u>in my opinion</u>.

   > The new product line, <u>so they say</u>, is expected to bring considerable profit.

The new product line is expected to bring considerable profit, <u>so they say</u>.

I am going too. (When <u>too</u> is used as <u>also</u> at the end of a sentence, the comma is usually omitted. If <u>too</u> is an interrupter, it is set off.)

She, <u>too</u>, will attend the meeting.

2. Place a comma after a parenthetical expression that introduces a second independent clause.

The price of a loaf of bread has increased 5.2 percent, but <u>on the other hand</u>, the price of wheat cereal has increased only 3.2 percent.

Note

A comma does not follow the coordinate conjunction; only the comma after the parenthetical expression is necessary.

Exercise

If punctuation is needed in any of the following sentences, write the word preceding the comma and the comma in the blank provided. If no correction is required, write C in the blank.

Example

You too can obtain reimbursement for business expenses.   <u>you, too,</u>

1. The IRS representative can, I'm sure, answer your questions.   _____
2. Joe Kala I admit had a good reason for being late.   _____
3. I have no doubt about the new supervisor's ability to make decisions.   _____
4. On the contrary you have not complied with the recent directive concerning maintenance of records.   _____
5. Clark has been preparing his résumé no doubt.   _____
6. On the other hand were three cuts that occurred when the saw whipped from his grasp.   _____
7. Supervisors have been asked to attend the meeting too.   _____
8. As predicted we had a 10 percent increase in sales this month.   _____
9. I agree that the recent regulation does not permit us to increase salaries more than 5.5 percent.   _____
10. The income statement it appears has been prepared without consideration to acceptable accounting practices.   _____
11. We are unable to meet the contract deadline; however we are certain that we can complete the construction by August 15.   _____
12. I shall appreciate your responding to this letter before December 1, and by the way will you please indicate the payment plan you intend to accept.   _____
13. The plant manager in Knoxville will be expecting a call from you; hence you must obtain the answer to his question as soon as possible.   _____
14. Also please include one additional manual with each machine.   _____
15. In the first place, you did not endorse the check as it was made out, and in the second place you did not include a deposit slip in the envelope.   _____

ANSWERS TO FRAME 2

1.	C	6.	C	11.	however,
2.	Kala, admit,	7.	C	12.	way,
3.	C	8.	predicted,	13.	C
4.	contrary,	9.	C	14.	Also,
5.	résumé,	10.	statement, appears,	15.	place,

Frame 3   Words in Apposition

A word, phrase, or clause is in *apposition* when it renames, explains, or identifies the word (usually a noun) by which it stands.

Explanation

If the word, phrase, or clause in apposition is not necessary to the construction or meaning of the sentence, it is considered nonrestrictive, meaning that it does not restrict the meaning of the sentence. Nonrestrictive elements are set off by commas.

If the word in apposition is necessary to the construction or meaning of the sentence, it is considered restrictive, meaning that it restricts the meaning of the sentence. Restrictive words are not set off by commas.

To make the punctuation decision, read the sentence with and without the element in apposition. If the element is not necessary to the construction or meaning (the reader would understand the sentence easily), set off the element.

A word in apposition is nonrestrictive and is set off:

1. When it is specifically identified:
   a. By title or proper noun
   b. By one of these words: *this, that, these, those*
   c. By a personal pronoun, such as: *my, your, his,* and so on
2. When it renames or explains a noun.

Example

1. Set off a nonrestrictive word(s) in apposition:
   a. A noun in apposition identified by a title.

      > The sales manager, <u>Mr. Usellit</u>, said that sales increased this quarter.

   b. Words in apposition identified by a proper noun.

      > Mr. Usellit, <u>head of the sales department</u>, said that sales increased this quarter. (A proper noun is an identifier; therefore, the words in apposition are set off.)

   c. Word in apposition identified by a demonstrative adjective: *this, that, these, those.*

      > This calculator, <u>a Model 4MC</u>, was made in Japan.

   d. Word in apposition identified by a personal pronoun.

      > My only son, <u>Paul</u>, is in the service.

   e. Word(s) explaining a noun.

      > Our leading product, <u>Clean-it-up Sooper Soap</u>, is now being sold in 48 states.

   f. Word(s) renaming or defining a noun.

      > The criterion, or unit of measurement, should be selected before the research is begun.

2. Do not set off a word(s) in apposition if it is necessary to the construction or meaning of the sentence (restrictive).

   > The word *check* has many meanings. (Surrounded by commas, the word *check* would appear to be unimportant or unnecessary.)

My Aunt Sophia works for this company. (Rarely is this type of one-word apposition set off; the two words are usually considered as proper nouns.)

Barbara herself wrote the article. (Intensive pronouns are not set off.)

The book <u>How to Raise Vegetables</u> sells for 95 cents. (The title is not set off because the book is not identified by any distinctive word(s).)

Exercise

1. If punctuation is required in any of the following sentences, write the word preceding each comma and the comma in the blank provided; if punctuation is not required, write C in the blank.
2. Using the line provided below sentences 6, 7, 8, 11, and 15, write a complete sentence explaining your reason for the answer written in the blank at the right.

Example

Paul Wayne the vice president in charge of sales will retire on May 30.   <u>Wayne, sales,</u>
<u>Set off words in apposition identified by a proper noun.</u>

1. Mr. Tavoli a well-known writer will give a lecture tomorrow night.   _____
2. The town's main street College Avenue will become a part of the new mall area.   _____
3. Cole himself assumed charge of the department during the emergency.   _____
4. My alma mater the University of Nebraska is located in Lincoln.   _____
5. He spelled the word *accommodate* incorrectly.   _____
6. My car a Ford was stolen from the parking lot.   _____

7. Ms. Smithson the new buyer has many ideas for improving the department.   _____

8. The dean of the College of Business Dr. Kilmer Bench once taught at Harvard.   _____

9. The cable address JONWIL is printed on the company stationery.   _____
10. *Strictly Speaking* a book by Edwin Newman has received acclaim from book reviewers.   _____
11. The cafeteria is now serving crepes suzette or French pancakes.   _____

12. Our guard dog a German shepherd caught the intruder and maimed him.   _____
13. The primary export of the UAR petroleum is creating a deficit balance of trade for the Western World.   _____
14. That aircraft the SST has received both negative and positive reviews by technicians.   _____
15. The year 1945 marked the end of World War II and the beginning of economic assistance to war-torn nations.   _____

ANSWERS TO FRAME 3

1. Tavoli, writer,   4. mater, Nebraska,
2. street, Avenue,   5. C
3. C
6. car, Ford, (The word <u>car</u> is identified by a personal pronoun.)

7. Smithson, buyer, (A proper noun identifies the person.)
8. Business, Bench, (The title identifies the individual.)
9. C
10. *Speaking*, Newman,
11. suzette, (The noun is defined or explained by the element in apposition.)
12. dog, shepherd,
13. UAR, petroleum,
14. aircraft, SST,
15. C (The year is necessary to the meaning of the sentence; it is not identified in any way.)

Frame 4   Phrases in Apposition

Explanation

Phrases in apposition may be restrictive or nonrestrictive. As with words in apposition, phrases are set off if they are totally unnecessary (nonrestrictive) to the construction and meaning of a sentence; otherwise, they are not set off.

Introductory phrases were discussed in the preceding lesson. Phrases in apposition may occur in the middle or at the end of a sentence. The decision to set off a phrase in apposition is based on the same test as that used to make the determination regarding a word(s) in apposition: Read the sentence with and without the phrase. If the phrase is not necessary to the construction or meaning, set it off.

A phrase is in apposition when it renames, explains, or identifies the noun by which it stands. The clues may be:

1. A proper noun
2. A demonstrative adjective: *this, that, these, those*
3. A personal pronoun
4. A title or other specific term

Example

Set off a phrase in apposition.

Eleanour Gregory, <u>having been graduated from a university in France</u>, worked as an interpreter at the United Nations. (participial phrase: identified by a proper noun)

A young woman <u>having been graduated from a university in France</u> can become an interpreter at the United Nations. (not set off because the noun is not specifically identified; the sentence would read, "A young woman can become an interpreter at the United Nations.")

Mr. Balzac, <u>of the Miami office</u>, is visiting our Legal Department. (prepositional phrase identified by a proper noun)

A staff member <u>of the Miami office</u> is visiting our Legal Department. (not set off because the noun is not specifically identified)

This typewriter, <u>having been damaged in the fire</u>, has minimum salvage value. (participial phrase; the noun is identified by a demonstrative adjective)

A typewriter <u>having been damaged by fire</u> usually has minimum salvage value. (The noun is not specific.)

My car, <u>parked in level D of the parking garage</u>, was stolen yesterday. (participial phrase; noun is identified by a personal pronoun)

A car <u>parked in level D of the parking garage</u> was stolen yester-day. (the noun is not specifically identified)

Jan Evans, <u>to show her enthusiasm for the project</u>, prepared a preliminary research report. (infinitive phrase identified by a proper noun)

One of the project staff prepared a preliminary research report <u>to show her enthusiasm for the project</u>. (noun is not specifically iden-tified)

This tape recorder, <u>made in Taiwan</u>, has a locater device. (parti-cipial phrase; noun is identified by a demonstrative adjective)

I purchased a tape recorder <u>made in Taiwan</u>. (noun is not specif-ically identified)

Exercise

The sentences in this exercise are not punctuated.

1. In each sentence that follows, underscore the phrase in apposition.
2. Read the sentence with and without this phrase.
3. In the first blank provided, write R (restrictive) or NR (nonrestrictive) to iden-tify the phrase.
4. If the phrase is nonrestrictive, use the second blank to write the word preceding each comma and the comma.

Example

	R/NR	Correction
I purchased a tape recorder <u>made in Taiwan</u>.	R	
My supervisor <u>having become ill yesterday</u> will not be able to represent the department at the staff meeting.	NR	supervisor, yesterday,

1. Lulu Benton having become president of the fashionable clothing house estab-lished new policies regarding spring showings.
2. This copier purchased from you a year ago does not print clean, clear copies.
3. A graduate of Columbia was hired for the job.
4. An error in the letter was brought to my attention.
5. The employees having the longest record of service with the company will be given special awards at the forthcoming ban-quet.
6. My property having been appraised by Ms. Bolton is now on the market.
7. Mr. Grant to be eligible for promotion to a top management position must divest himself of $30,000 in company stock.
8. A person to be eligible for promotion to a top management position must sell his or her stock or place it in trust.

	R/NR	Correction

9. His goal to become a CPA was shattered when he lost his eyesight in the automobile accident.

10. Some cars manufactured in Germany are assembled in the United States.

ANSWERS TO FRAME 4

	R/NR	Correction
1. having become president of the fashionable clothing house	NR	Benton, house,
2. purchased from you a year ago	NR	copier, ago,
3. of Columbia	R	
4. in the letter	R	
5. having the longest record of service with the company	R	
6. having been appraised by Ms. Bolton	NR	property, Bolton,
7. to be eligible for promotion to a top management position	NR	Grant, position,
8. to be eligible for promotion to a top management position	R	
9. to become a CPA	NR	goal, CPA,
10. manufactured in Germany	R	

Frame 5 Clauses in Apposition

Explanation

Clauses in apposition may be restrictive or nonrestrictive. Like words and phrases in apposition, clauses are set off if they are totally unnecessary (nonrestrictive) to the construction and meaning of a sentence; otherwise, they are not set off.

Introductory clauses (adverbial) were discussed in the preceding lesson. Clauses in apposition may occur in the middle or at the end of a sentence. The decision to set off a clause in apposition is based on the same test as that used to make the determination regarding words and phrases: Read the sentence with and without the clause. If the clause is not necessary to the construction or meaning of the sentence, set it off with commas.

A clause is in apposition when it renames, explains, or identifies the noun by which it stands. The clues may be:

1. A proper noun
2. A demonstrative adjective
3. A personal pronoun
4. A title or other specific term
5. The initial word in a clause

Example

1. Set off nonrestrictive clauses.
   a. Noun clause:
      Rarely is a noun clause beginning with *that* set off because it is usually essential to complete the meaning of a sentence.

      The concept <u>that management is getting work done through people</u> is well established in the business world.

b. Clause identified by a proper noun:

> Mr. Vissenberg, <u>who operates a travel agency in this city</u>, is the new president of the association.

> A man <u>who operates a travel agency in this city</u> is the new president of the association. (noun is not specifically identified)

c. Noun identified by a personal pronoun:

> My father, <u>who is president of the Barker Corporation</u>, hopes that I will begin my career in that organization.

> The man <u>who is the president of the Barker Corporation</u> hopes that I will begin my career in that organization. (noun is not specifically identified)

d. A title or other specific term:

> The president of the Sunshine Corporation, <u>who appeared before the court on Tuesday</u>, refused to testify. (position title specifically identifies the noun; a company has one president)

> An officer of the Sunshine Corporation <u>who appeared in court on Tuesday</u> refused to testify. (noun is not specifically identified)

e. Demonstrative adjective:

> This city, <u>which we are considering as our convention headquarters</u>, has 23,000 hotel rooms.

> Any city <u>which we consider as convention headquarters</u> should have at least 20,000 hotel rooms. (noun is not specifically identified)

2. Certain words identify clauses that are always nonrestrictive; for example: *all of which, although, for, no matter (why,* or *how), none of which, some of whom,* and *whereas.*

> We have three candidates for the position, <u>all of whom are well qualified</u>.

3. Set off an adverbial clause at the end of a sentence if it is definitely not necessary to the construction or meaning of the sentence.

> The headquarters will be moved to Phoenix, <u>as you know</u>.

> You will not receive your certification <u>until you pass Part VI of this examination</u>. (clause is necessary to the meaning of the sentence)

Exercise

The sentences in this exercise are not punctuated.

1. Underscore the clause in apposition in each sentence that follows.
2. Read the sentence with and without this clause.
3. In the first blank, write R (restrictive) or NR (nonrestrictive) to identify the clause.
4. If the clause is nonrestrictive, use the second blank to write the word preceding each comma and the comma.

Example

	R/NR	Correction
This city <u>which we are considering as convention headquarters</u> has 23,000 hotel rooms.	NR	city, headquarters,

1. The professor who conducted the seminar is on the faculty of the University of Colorado.
2. The city which we choose as a site for the assembly plant must be a rail center.
3. Mr. Stapleton who transferred from the Boston office is a legal aide in this office.
4. This automatic typewriter which the company just purchased was identified as stolen property.
5. The reason that he gave is not credible.
6. His father who is the company president made him the manager of the plant in Paris, France.
7. This policy although it has extended into the grace period will cover your hospital expenses.
8. The quality control clerk inspected 150 invoices all of which were accurate.
9. The results of our new advertising campaign were negative as you predicted they would be.
10. All D shift employees will receive overtime pay if they work more than 40 hours this week.

ANSWERS TO FRAME 5

		R/NR	Correction
1.	<u>who conducted the seminar</u>	R	
2.	<u>which we choose as a site for the assembly plant</u>	R	
3.	<u>who transferred from the Boston office</u>	NR	Stapleton, office,
4.	<u>which the company just purchased</u>	NR	typewriter, purchased,
5.	<u>that he gave</u>	R	
6.	<u>who is the company president</u>	NR	father, president,
7.	<u>although it has extended into the grace period</u>	NR	policy, period,
8.	<u>all of which were accurate</u>	NR	invoices,
9.	<u>as you predicted they would be</u>	NR	negative,
10.	<u>if they work more than 40 hours this week</u>	R	

Frame 6   Other Comma Usages

Explanation

A few comma usages do not fall under one of the previous rules. However, like the preceding usages, they demonstrate the need to clarify the meaning of a sentence by the use of punctuation.

Example

1. Use commas to set off items in dates, locations, and sources.

    I was graduated on August 20, <u>1967</u>.

    The meeting was held on Monday, <u>April 21</u>, 1776.

    Jasper lives at <u>2100 Oak Street</u>, <u>Pocatello</u>, <u>Idaho</u>.

    The district office in Columbia, <u>South Carolina</u>, was destroyed in the hurricane.

    This quote is from <u>Chapter II, Section 281.4, page 42</u> of the handbook.

Note

Commas are not used when the date is reversed: <u>10 January 1888</u>.

2. Use commas to set off abbreviations that follow names of people, places, or things.

    John Henry, <u>Jr.</u>, is the president's grandson.

    Maple Leaf, <u>Ltd.</u>, is a Canadian company.

    John Spurlin, <u>D.D.S.</u>, established an office in Kansas City.

    Cynthia Holmes, <u>CPA</u>, is a partner in that prestigious firm.

3. Use commas to set off identical or repeated words.

    This department is overworked, <u>overworked</u>, <u>overworked</u>.

    Many taxpayers who pay, <u>pay</u> because they are frightened to do otherwise.

4. Use commas to set off contrasting expressions.

    The more I get paid, <u>the less I save</u>.

    He agreed to rewrite the contract, <u>not to ignore it</u>.

    He always jogs during weekends, <u>never during the week</u>.

5. Use commas to show the omission of words within a sentence.

    District 3 exceeded last year's sales by 21 percent;
    District <u>4,</u> by 24 percent; and District <u>1,</u> by 26 percent.

6. Use commas to facilitate reading—to prevent the reader's having to reread a sentence.

    The judge cautioned, "Above all tell the truth."
    "Above, all tell the truth."
    "Above <u>all</u>, tell the truth."

7. Use commas to separate a question that follows a statement.

You are working during the convention, <u>aren't you</u>?

Exercise

In the blank provided, write the word preceding each comma and the comma.

Example

He was born on October 27 1945.   <u>27, </u>

1. The branch manager is leaving for El Paso Texas tomorrow. _____
2. The regional sales meeting will be held on Monday January 20. _____
3. Ramond Marcus CRM will interview records management students on Thursday and Friday. _____
4. Allen Bundt Jr. has been elected to a state office. _____
5. This example can be found in Chapter III Section 32.2 page 53. _____
6. The lawyer agreed to work with us not against us. _____
7. Many students who cheat cheat because they have not prepared the lesson. _____
8. Eighty-three percent of the respondents indicated that their offices had centralized records management programs; 15 percent decentralized programs; and 2 percent a combination of both. _____
9. On the whole office procedures have changed drastically over the last ten years. _____
10. You will write to the treasurer won't you? _____

ANSWERS TO FRAME 6

1. Paso, Texas,
2. Monday,
3. Marcus, CRM,
4. Bundt, Jr.,
5. III, 32.2,
6. us,
7. cheat,
8. percent, percent,
9. whole,
10. treasurer,

Frame 7   *Business Vocabulary: Sales Personnel*

Explanation

The existence of an organization that offers goods or services depends on the profit from its sales. In some instances, the sales are not made through the normal channel of distribution, but rather by individuals who represent the company in the field. Such persons explain the product or service and encourage the target population to purchase it.

Terms

Outside sales representative—(1) a person who is stationed in a designated location to serve a specific population, or (2) one who spends a day or week or longer away from the office visiting customers and potential customers to demonstrate or explain the company's product or service.

Manufacturer's representative—an outside sales representative who represents the company's product to professional persons or retailers or companies that might logically be interested in purchasing it. Examples are representatives of pharmaceutical firms who visit doctors, hospitals, and medical supply outlets and representatives of computer manufacturers who visit large organizations to explain the equipment and systems they represent.

Publisher's sales representative—an outside sales representative who represents a publishing company in a specific territory. This representative visits educational institutions and explains the content and features of forthcoming publications and takes orders.

Payment of outside sales representatives—some of these representatives are paid a straight salary that is negotiated when they are hired. Others work on a salary plus commission basis, meaning that they receive a commission or percentage of each sale, in addition to a salary.

Expense account—money budgeted for expenditure by the outside sales representative to promote the company or its product. The representative draws upon the expense account. The company credit card plus the expense account is expected to cover most of the representative's expenses.

Reimbursement—a repayment to an individual who has spent his or her money to benefit another. Upon presenting a receipt of payment, outside salespersons are reimbursed for taxi fare, intracity transportation, and so on.

Itinerary—a schedule showing the traveler's proposed route during a journey. A complete itinerary may include cities, accommodations, times of arrival and departure, and people to be called upon.

Exercise

Complete each of the following sentences with the appropriate word from the preceding vocabulary list.

1. Selling that is not done on premises or through the regular channels of distribution may be performed by an _____.

2. A _____ representative demonstrates and explains the manufacturer's product to a potential customer.

3. A _____ sales representative is responsible for selling to the territory which he or she represents. The selling involves visiting educational institutions, explaining the content and features of a book and taking orders.

4. The amount that is budgeted for the representative's travel, accommodations, and other expenses, and upon which the representative may draw, is called an

    _____.

5. The representative is _____ for out-of-pocket money spent to benefit the company.

6. The schedule showing a traveler's proposed route is an _____.

ANSWERS TO FRAME 7

1. outside sales representative	3. publisher's	5. reimbursed
2. manufacturer's	4. expense account	6. itinerary

Frame 8   Applying Your Knowledge

Directions

1. Insert any commas which have been omitted in the following memorandum.
2. If a comma is inserted incorrectly:
    a. Underscore the comma and, if necessary, insert it in the correct position.
    b. On the blank line below the sentence, write a complete sentence explaining your reason for underscoring placed commas.

Example

I stopped the car, and attempted to turn off the ignition.
A comma should not separate the parts of a compound verb.

CASE

This report was written by a publisher's representative to justify her spending approximately $700 over the maximum expense account allocation for the period. (10 errors—two commas needed to set off an internal element count as *one* error.)

DATE: July 15, 19____
TO: Robert Hey, Sales Manager
FROM: Marcia Denton, Sales Representative, District 6
SUBJECT: Justification of Overexpenditure on Expense
Account

This is a justification for the overexpenditure on my expense account for

the period from June 15 to July 15.

1. As you suggested, I am spending the summer visiting institutions to

solicit orders for the fall term. From Tuesday, June 26 through

Thursday, June 28, I visited the public and proprietary schools in

Phoenix, Arizona. I was approximately 50 miles west of Albuquerque,

New Mexico on Friday when the air conditioner began exuding hot

not cold, air. I pulled into the safety lane, and moved the transmission

lever to the "Park" position. Steam suddenly spewed from under the

dashboard; I jumped from the car and waited for the steam to stop. A

passing motorist, who noticed my predicament, stopped to help. Using

his CB radio, he called the XYZ Garage which sent a mechanic. He discovered that the compressor had malfunctioned and said that a new

---

one was needed. Unfortunately he also discovered that the

---

transmission needed overhauling.

---

2. The new compressor and the labor to install it amounted to $250. The

---

cost for overhauling the transmission was $200. Mesquite, the town in

---

which my car was stranded, has no motels, but the mechanic gave me

---

a ride to Albuquerque. Because the Sunset Motel in Albuquerque

---

had lost my reservation and had no vacancies, I stayed at the Yucca

---

which charged $50 a night.

---

3. The overexpenditure I admit is considerable, but it was unavoidable.

Therefore I would appreciate your approving this request for

---

supplementary funds.

ANSWERS TO FRAME 8
Body of Memorandum

This is a justification for the overexpenditure on my expense account for the period from June 15 to July 15.

1. As you suggested, I am spending the summer visiting institutions to solicit orders for the fall term. From Tuesday, June 26, through Thursday, June 28, I visited the public and proprietary schools in Phoenix, Arizona. I was approximately 50 miles west of Albuquerque, New Mexico, on Friday when the air conditioner began exuding hot, not cold, air. I pulled into the safety lane, and moved the

   A comma should not separate compound verbs.

   transmission lever to the "Park" position. Steam suddenly spewed from under the dashboard; I jumped from the car and waited for the steam to stop. A passing

motorist, who noticed my predicament, stopped to help. Using his CB radio, he
A clause in apposition should not be set off if the noun it explains
is not specifically identified.
called the XYZ Garage, which sent a mechanic. He discovered that the compressor

had malfunctioned and said that a new one was needed. Unfortunately, he also

discovered that the transmission needed overhauling.

2. The new compressor and the labor to install it amounted to $250. The cost for

overhauling the transmission was $200. Mesquite, the town in which my car was

stranded, has no motels, but the mechanic gave me a ride to Albuquerque. Because

the Sunset Motel in Albuquerque had lost my reservation and had no vacancies, I

stayed at the Yucca, which charged $50 a night.

3. The overexpenditure, I admit, is considerable, but it was unavoidable. Therefore,

I would appreciate your approving this request for supplementary funds.

Lesson 31
Semicolon and Colon

Pretest

Pretest Part I
Semicolon—Compound Sentences

Directions

1. If a sentence in the following group requires punctuation, write the word preceding each punctuation mark and the punctuation mark in the first blank to the right. If punctuation is not required, write No.
2. In the second blank, write the letter given below that corresponds to the reason for your answer in the first blank.
   - A   Used   ,   preceding coordinate conjunction
   - B   Used   ;   preceding conjunctive adverb
   - C   Used   ;   because no connective word exists
   - D   Used   ;   because sentence would be confusing with only a comma
   - E   Used   ,   after conjunctive adverb containing two or more syllables
   - F   Used   .   because the two clauses are not closely related
   - G   None of these answers

Example

	Correction	Reason
The report is due on September 1 consequently you will need to complete the research prior to August 13.	1; consequently,	B, E

1. The sales campaign was successful moreover the response far exceeded our estimates.
2. The monthly cost of utilities has increased by 10 percent this increase affects our variable costs of operation.
3. Julia Helms, the managing editor, is responsible for thirteen books and she has three top sellers.
4. The pollution index for some cities has increased hence the government is encouraging those cities to control polluting devices.
5. The memo was written by the systems analyst the payroll system will be the next one to be computerized.

	Correction	Reason

6. You will note however that I have recommended you be retained on a consultant's fee.

7. The trainee appears interested yet he has a poor rating in each department to which he has been assigned.

8. Having received her degree, Mary Helen was offered a job by the Balsam Company but she did not accept it.

9. To be repaired are Locust, Juniper, and Heather Streets and Jackson, Bent, and Pine Streets are to be widened.

10. Sales meetings will be held in San Diego, El Paso, Chicago, and Albany and will be scheduled at a Marlborough Hotel in each city.

Pretest Part II
Semicolon and Colon Usages

Directions

1. In the blank to the right of each of the following sentences, write the word preceding each required punctuation mark and the punctuation mark—semicolon, colon, or comma.
2. If a blank line is shown below a sentence, use it to explain why you punctuated the sentence as you did.

Example

The Dodgers scored a 2 to 1 victory over the Giants.   2:1
Use a colon to represent *to* in a ratio.

1. Members of the Selection Committee included Professor John Alby, College of Business Dr. Timothy O'Hare, College of Agriculture and Mr. Dwight Gray, a representative of the Board of Regents.

2. The following cities were nominated for the ninth annual convention of the association Concord, Galveston, Omaha, and Pocatello.

3. If you can write forceful, dynamic, and persuasive letters if you can write routine, favorable, and unfavorable types of memos and if you can prepare clear, concise reports you are needed by the Allen Company.

4. I have noticed that Ms. James arrives at work promptly that she works diligently and that she rarely makes mistakes. _____

5. Harley Brown is an outstanding athlete for example he won gold medals for the discus, marathon, and vaulting exhibitions at the regional meet. _____

_____

_____

6. The study group meets three times a week Monday, Wednesday, and Friday at 8 P.M. _____

7. This policy will pay some of your hospital expenses that is, those named in Clause 19 on page 5. _____

8. I have this theory namely the cost of tuition increases when the salaries of state nonteaching employees increase. _____

9. The following employees have been promoted
   1. Abdul Farrez
   2. Henry Albacorn
   3. Manuel Gutierrez

_____

_____

10. Observe this rule when you enter the restricted area Place all metal items in the door safe. _____

_____

_____

11. This directive explains two requirements The first is related to smoking on the premises. The second involves the use of safety clothing, equipment, and materials in the zones marked "Danger." _____

12. Note A red light will flicker when you are recording; this light simply indicates that your voice is being recorded on the magnetic tape. _____

13. The nurse informed the doctor of the patient's test results the doctor quickly ordered a decreased dosage of 2-4-B. _____

14. A 3 to 1 ratio of assets over liabilities indicates that the assets are not being invested as they should be. _____

15. Operators of diversified farming operations raise small grains e.g., corn, wheat, oats, barley, rye, and soybeans. _____

Lesson 31
Semicolon and Colon

The semicolon and colon are more emphatic marks of punctuation than is the comma; therefore, neither is a substitute for the comma.

Frame 1   Semicolon: Compound Sentences

The semicolon is used in a compound sentence, as discussed previously; in a series already containing commas; and before an expression that introduces an example, enumeration, or explanation.

Explanation

A semicolon is used in these positions within a compound sentence:

1. Before a conjunctive adverb (transitional expression) that joins two independent clauses
2. Between two independent clauses that are not joined by a conjunction
3. Before a coordinate conjunction that connects two independent clauses when:
   a. Confusion would result if only a comma were used
   b. The writer wishes to emphasize each clause

You will remember that a comma is used before the coordinate conjunction that connects two independent clauses.

Example

1. Use a semicolon before a conjunctive adverb (transitional expression) that joins two independent clauses.

> We did not receive the sales figures on time; <u>consequently</u>, we could not bid on the contract.

Note

A comma is used after a transitional expression when it occurs at the beginning of the second clause unless the expression is a one-syllable word: *hence, yet, still,* and *so.*

> We waited until 10 o'clock; <u>yet</u> the mail had not come.

2. Use a semicolon between two closely related independent clauses that are not joined by a conjunction.

> We are quite pleased with Mr. Sampson's work; he is a diligent employee.

   a. Using a comma in the position where a semicolon should be used is an error. The comma causes the reader to believe that the following element is a part of the preceding element and not a separate independent clause. Grammarians call this incorrect usage a "comma splice."

Incorrect   We are quite pleased with Mr. Sampson's work, he is a diligent employee.

   b. A sentence lacks continuity if a semicolon is used between two clauses that are not closely related; a period is a better mark of punctuation in this construction.

499

Incorrect   Thank you for your order; your camera equipment will be delivered by the Seaside Express Company on August 1.

Revised   Thank you for your order. Your camera equipment will be delivered by the Seaside Express Company on August 1.

3. Use a semicolon before a coordinate conjunction that connects two independent clauses if:
   a. The clauses would be confusing with only a comma before the coordinate conjunction, or
   b. Each clause is to be emphasized.

> We ordered accident, W–2, and Workmen's Compensation forms; and W–4, maternity leave, and travel forms were delivered instead.

Note

A comma is acceptable in the next sentence because confusion is not likely to result. If the writer wishes to emphasize each clause, a semicolon may be used preceding the coordinate conjunction.

> Fortunately, all items on Order No. 4721 are available, but on the other hand, we may need to search the local market to obtain a sufficient supply.

Exercise

1. If a sentence in the following group requires punctuation, write the word preceding the required punctuation mark and the punctuation mark in the blank to the right. If punctuation is not required, write No.
2. In the second blank, write the letter that corresponds to the reason for your answer in the first blank:
   A Used , preceding coordinate conjunction
   B Used ; preceding conjunctive adverb
   C Used ; because no connecting word exists
   D Used ; because sentence would be confusing with only a comma
   E Used , after conjunctive adverb containing two or more syllables
   F Used . because the two clauses are not closely related
   G None of these reasons

Example

	Correction	*Reason*
The report is due on September 1 consequently you will need to complete the research prior to August 15.	1; consequently,	B, E
1. One-third of the employees in this department were absent during the bus strike therefore we shall need to work overtime to complete the orders under contract.	_____	_____
2. The unit cost of each component in the system must be increased by ten percent without such an increase we will not be able to maintain a favorable profit margin.	_____	_____

	Correction	Reason

3. Ms. Nota, the assistant personnel manager, is now in charge of the department and she has established a training program.

4. The demand for coal has increased hence the price of coal has increased.

5. The jury was unable to reach a decision the defendant's lawyer had made a very strong case for his defense.

6. You will however remember that I wrote a recommendation for you when you applied to the Abbott Company.

7. People seem to be depositing less money in savings accounts still the rate of inflation continues to rise.

8. Because of an error in the memo, the committee met at 4 P.M. but the chairperson was not present.

9. When you come to the conference, please bring the Sampson, Anderson, and Howard files and the Harvey, Wilson, and Jones files will be mailed.

10. We have reserved January 2, February 6, and March 10 for our conferences and have scheduled them in the Ambassador Room of the Northern Hotel.

ANSWERS TO FRAME 1

	Correction	Reason		Correction	Reason
1.	strike; therefore,	B,E	6.	will, however,	G
2.	percent;	C	7.	accounts;	B
3.	department,	A	8.	P.M.,	A
4.	increased;	B	9.	files;	D
5.	decision.	F	10.	No	G

Frame 2   *Series Separated by Semicolons*

Explanation

The semicolon, being a stronger mark of punctuation than the comma, divides series items into units.

Example

1. Use a semicolon to separate the items in a series that already contains commas.
    a. Series containing commas:

    > We were represented at the American Management Association meeting by Jim Watts, Donald Herdt, and James Taylor.

b.   Series containing commas and semicolons:

> We were represented at the American Management Association meeting by Jim Watts, vice president; Donald Herdt, marketing director; and James Taylor, director of finance.

2.   Use a semicolon to separate a series of dependent clauses that contains internal punctuation or are exceptionally long.

> Ms. Harris said that she would perform a product analysis on Products A, B, and C; that she would perform a market analysis on Products B, C, and D; and that she would prepare a sales campaign for radio, television, and professional journals.

a.   Short dependent clauses without internal punctuation are separated with a comma:

> I believe that Ms. Purdy is a good proofreader, that she writes well, and that she would become a fine administrative assistant.

b.   Regardless of the internal punctuation in the introductory dependent clauses, a comma follows the last dependent clause within a series:

> If your home, large or small, is insured; if your life is insured; and if your family investment planning has been completed, then you can feel secure about your family's future protection.

Exercise

On the line below each sentence that follows, write the word preceding each punctuation mark and the punctuation mark.

1.   Regional sales meetings will be held in San Antonio Texas Atlanta Georgia and Tucson, Arizona.

_____

2.   If, despite frustration, stress, and pressure, each trainee makes logical decisions if each trainee creates a good work atmosphere for employees in the section and if each trainee reacts as a potential manager, we shall hire the entire group this fall.

_____

3.   Appearing in the picture will be Alice Meyer, buyer of women's coats Henri Bende, assistant manager of the Tulsa store and Kitty Challis, manager of the Paris fashion house, Garcon.

_____

4.   The committee consists of Joe Adkins Doni Brooks and Mel Brem.

_____

5.   If you have the proper educational background if you are diligent and if you are ambitious, you will succeed in this company.

_____

ANSWERS TO FRAME 2

1.   San Antonio, Texas; Atlanta, Georgia;
2.   decisions; section;
3.   coats; store;
4.   Adkins, Brooks,
5.   background, diligent,

Frame 3 Semicolon Before Transitional Expression

Explanation

A semicolon precedes and a comma follows certain *transitional expressions* that link two independent clauses and that are used to introduce examples, illustrations, lists, and explanations. These words and their Latin abbreviations that are most frequently used in this capacity are *namely, for example (e.g.),* and *that is (i.e.).*

Example

1. Use a semicolon before and a comma after a transitional expression that connects two independent clauses.

> Ms. Gaines is an outstanding student; <u>for example</u>, she has been nominated for a graduate fellowship.

> Ms. Gaines is an outstanding student; <u>e.g.</u>, she has been nominated for a graduate fellowship.

> This policy will provide the funds for your child's college education; <u>that is</u>, it will mature in the year 1998, when your child is ready to attend college.

2. Use a semicolon before and a comma after a transitional expression that introduces a list, example, or illustration at the end of a sentence.

> The requisition includes some paper products; <u>namely</u>, envelopes, bond paper, and note pads.

Exercise

In the blank provided, write the word preceding a punctuation mark and the punctuation mark.

Example

Sow the seeds closely for example one inch apart.   <u>closely; example,</u>

1. In the four-car wreck, many people were injured e.g. burned, cut, bruised, and maimed.   _____
2. The sentence is incomplete that is it lacks a verb.   _____
3. I have one question namely how many people are expected to attend the banquet?   _____
4. Three people did not attend the meeting i.e. they had duties that prevented their leaving their work stations.   _____
5. When the refrigerator truck had a flat tire, some of the perishable groceries were ruined for example the ice cream.   _____

ANSWERS TO FRAME 3
1. injured; e.g.,   3. question; namely,   5. ruined; example,
2. incomplete; is,   4. meeting; i.e.,

Frame 4 Colon with a List

A *colon* is an emphatic mark of punctuation that calls attention to the element preceding or following it. A colon is used in the following positions:

1. After a complete statement and before a list.
2. After a clause introducing the next clause in a compound sentence.
3. After a complete or incomplete lead-in statement that precedes a list.
4. In a salutation, time designation, and ratio.

Colon usage with quotations is discussed in Lesson 33.

Explanation

A colon is used after a complete statement which indicates or implies that a list follows.

Example

1. Use a colon after a complete statement that introduces a list. The word *follow* or a derivative is often the clue that a list follows the statement.

   > The following items were requisitioned: paper clips, letterhead, and bond paper.

2. Use a colon after a complete statement that implies that a list follows:

   > The class meets four times each week: Monday, Wednesday, Thursday, Friday.

3. Do not separate an object from a verb or preposition with a colon:

   > We need typewriters, adding machines, and copy machines for the new office.
   > (A colon after *need* would separate the verb from its object.)

4. Use a colon after a complete lead-in statement preceding a tabulated list.

   > Please use this format for your procedure:
   > 1. Underscore all headings.
   > 2. Enumerate the points under each heading.
   > 3. Use letters to designate subheadings.

5. Use a colon after an incomplete lead-in statement if the items are on separate lines.

   > The sale items include:
   > 3 bedroom sets
   > 11 occasional chairs
   > 21 end tables
   > 30 vanity lamps

Exercise

If a sentence in the following group requires punctuation, write the word preceding each required punctuation mark and the punctuation mark in the blank provided; if none is required, write C in the blank.

Example

Our new machine has many fine features ease of assembly, durability, attractiveness, and an economical price.

features:

1. On Tour Trip 4 you will see many points of historical interest Mesa Verde, Rocky Mountain National Park, Silverton, and Durango.

   _____

2. The people from this department who attended the meeting were Candy Allerton, Bill Do, and J. R. Turnbull.

   _____

3. The following employees have been put on notice
Ellen Winkler
Sarabelle Yeats
Bob Price   _____
4. Following are characteristics of a good employee enthusiasm, ambition, and ability.   _____
5. This class consists of
5 sophomores
40 juniors
10 seniors   _____

ANSWERS TO FRAME 4
1. interest: 2. C 3. notice: 4. employee: 5. of:

Frame 5   *Colon Between Independent Clauses*

Explanation

You have learned that two closely related independent clauses not joined by a connective are separated by a semicolon. The rules in this frame do not contradict previous rules; instead, they add another dimension to the meaning that punctuation can contribute to a sentence.

Example

1. Use a colon between two independent clauses without a connective when the first clause introduces the second clause.

> The employee was confused for this reason: he was required to report to three supervisors.

2. A formal statement of a rule, policy, and directive is preceded by a colon when the first clause introduces the second.

> Our Board of Directors has established this policy regarding the attendance of employees: A maximum of 90 days' sick leave, 26 days' vacation leave, and 3 days' emergency leave per year will be granted to employees who have been with the firm for ten years. Under no circumstances can any leave time be carried over to the succeeding year.

BUT: Use a semicolon when the first clause does not introduce the second clause.

> The division marketing directors will meet on August 1 to discuss the budget for next year; the discussion will cover estimated administrative expenses, as well as those expenses directly related to the marketing function.

Note

Capitalize the first word of the material following a colon when it:

a. Consists of a formal rule, policy statement, or directive (see 2, example)
b. Consists of two or more statements (see 2, example)
c. Is a tabulated list (Frame 4)
d. Consists of a statement preceded by an introductory word, such as caution or note.

> Caution: Never use a hyphen between an -*ly* adverb and the word it modifies.

Exercise

1. If a sentence in the following exercise requires punctuation, write the word preceding each required punctuation mark and the punctuation mark in the blank provided. If punctuation is not required, write C in the blank.
2. If a word should be capitalized, write it in the blank in capitalized form.

Example

This management rule has not been observed when you give a person a job, give that person the authority to carry it out.   observed: When

1. The company attempted to present a good image to the public in two ways music was piped into all offices, and the reception rooms were colorfully decorated.   _____
2. The police officer arrested Ms. Carpenter for speeding she appeared in court Monday at 2:30 P.M.   _____
3. The principal points in the directive are these Employees shall use the established grievance procedure to resolve their conflicts. The union steward shall be consulted at the appropriate step in the procedure.   _____
4. Violation of this rule shall be cause for dismissal: Smoking is not permitted in an area designated as "Hazardous."   _____
5. Caution: this machine is equipped with a magnetic plate.   _____

ANSWERS TO FRAME 5
1. ways: 2. speeding; 3. these: 4. C 5. This

Frame 6   *Colon: Miscellaneous Usages*

Explanation

A colon is used after the salutation of a business letter, in time designations, and in ratios. No space precedes or follows a colon in the last two usages.

Example

1. Use a colon after the salutation of a business letter.

    Dear Mr. Smith: Dear Reader:

2. Use a colon between the hour and minute designations.

    The train will arrive at 8:45 P.M.

3. Use a colon between the numbers in a ratio. (*Note:* The colon stands for the word to.)

    Assets should exceed liabilities by a ratio of 2:1.

Exercise

Copy the underscored expression in the items that follow and insert the colon at the proper place.

1. Dear Sir   _____
2. Flight No. 173 is due to arrive at 817 P.M.   _____
3. The horse on which I bet came in first and paid 5 to 1.   _____

ANSWERS TO FRAME 6
1. Sir: 2. 8:17 3. 5:1

Frame 7   Business Vocabulary: Agriculture

Explanation

The food that appears on your table was probably provided by American farmers and ranchers. They plant the seed, cultivate the soil, harvest the grain, raise the livestock, and so on. Many years ago farming and ranching were considered livelihoods undertaken primarily by those with a traditional background in farming and agriculture. Today, the situation has changed; farming and ranching are closely allied with business, and the successful farmer or rancher is also a successful business person.

Terms

Diversified farming—the raising of small grains, livestock, and poultry on one farm.
Specialized farming (ranching)—refers to one major operation (wheat growing, or livestock raising) on a farm or ranch.
Acres—the land measurement designating a specific farm or ranch; for example, 640 acres is one section of land that is one mile long on each of its four sides. A 160-acre farm is one-fourth of a section.
Agribusiness—the combination of agriculture and business illustrated by such operations as seed corn growing and sales; manufacture and sale of animal feed, medicine, and supplies; manufacture and sale of housing and storage areas for animals and grain; and the manufacture and sale of equipment to sow, till, and harvest the grain.
County agent—a government employee who advises farmers and ranchers about land preservation, disease control, acreage yields, and crop and livestock improvement programs.
United States Department of Agriculture (USDA), Agricultural Stabilization and Conservation Service—a federal agency that implements and supervises programs affecting farmers and ranchers.

Exercise

Complete each sentence with the appropriate term from the preceding vocabulary list.

1. A person who operates a cattle ranch has a _____ operation, while a person who raises small grains, livestock, and so on has a _____ operation.

2. Ranches and farms may contain from one acre to many hundreds of thousands of acres. One section of land contains _____ acres and encompasses _____ square mile(s) of land.

3. Which of the following is an example of an agribusiness activity?
   _____
   a. manufacture and sale of plastic cups
   b. manufacture and sale of a cultivator
   c. manufacture and sale of medicine for hoof disease
   d. manufacture and sale of supplements for livestock food.

4. The government representative who advises farmers regarding grain and livestock raising is a _____.

5. An agency of which department in the federal government implements and supervises federal programs affecting farmers and ranchers?

_____

ANSWERS TO FRAME 7

1. specialized, diversified   3. b, c, d   5. USDA
2. 640, one   4. county agent

Frame 8 *Applying Your Knowledge*

Directions

1. If any sentence in the following newsletter requires punctuation, write the word preceding the required punctuation mark and the punctuation mark on the line below the sentence.
2. If any sentence is punctuated incorrectly, underscore the incorrect punctuation mark; on the line beneath it, write the reason for its being incorrect.

Example

The deadline for certifying the number of acres you have planted in: corn, sorghum, and soybeans is August 31.
Do not separate the object of the preposition from the preposition by a colon.

CASE

The county executive director of the Agricultural Stabilization and Conservation Service prepared this newsletter for the farmers and ranchers in the county. (10 errors)

ASCS NEWSLETTER
OTOE COUNTY ASCS OFFICE, P. O. Box 190
Syracuse, Nebraska 68446
July 30, 19____

This newsletter covers six topics

_____

1. Wheat Disaster Program

_____

2. Crop Certification

_____

3. Grain Reserve Program

_____

4. 1978 Wheat Loans

_____

5. Farm Storage Facility Loans

_____

6. Condition of Grain

Wheat Disaster Program

If you are a wheat producer who has signed up in the set-aside program and agreed not to plant a certain number of acres in wheat who has harvested a yield of less than 60 percent of the established yield for the farm and who has a low yield due to a disaster condition you should file a disaster application within 15 days after the harvest is completed.

Crop Certification

A producer who pays the cost of having the acreage measured may file late acreage certifications for: wheat, oats, barley, and rye.

Grain Reserve Program

The purpose of the program is to isolate crops from the market for future benefit. The program is expected to

1. Strengthen future market prices.

2. Serve as a hedge against inflationary effects of a poor crop in the future.

3. Meet future emergency needs.

1978 Wheat Loans

The government defines loan maturity in this way All loans mature on the last day of the ninth month following the month in which the loan is

_____

granted.

_____

Farm Storage Facility Loans

_____

Loans are available for up to 85 percent of the entire cost of storage

_____

facilities for example, bins, drying and handling equipment, concrete, and

_____

wiring.

_____

Condition of Grain

_____

Check stored grain at regular intervals report to the ASCS office if this

_____

grain is decreasing in value e.g., becoming moldy, damp, or insect-infested.

_____

ANSWERS TO FRAME 8

Body of Newsletter

This newsletter covers six topics
topics:

1. Wheat Disaster Program
2. Crop Certification
3. Grain Reserve Program
4. 1978 Wheat Loans
5. Farm Storage Facility Loans
6. Condition of Grain

Wheat Disaster Program

If you are a wheat producer who has signed up in the set-aside program

and agreed not to plant a certain number of acres in <u>wheat</u> who has
wheat;
harvested a yield of less than 60 percent of the established yield for the

<u>farm</u> and who has a low yield due to a disaster <u>condition</u> you should file a
farm;   condition,
disaster application within 15 days after the harvest is completed.

Crop Certification

A producer who pays the cost of having the acreage measured may file

late acreage certifications for<u>:</u> wheat, oats, barley, and rye.
 Do not separate a preposition from its object(s) with a colon.
Grain Reserve Program

The purpose of the program is to isolate crops from the market for future

benefit. The program is expected <u>to</u>
to:

1. Strengthen future market prices.

2. Serve as a hedge against inflationary effects of a poor crop in the future.

3. Meet future emergency needs.

1978 Wheat Loans

The government defines loan maturity in this <u>way</u> All loans mature on
the last day of the ninth month following the month in which the loan is
way:
granted.

Farm Storage Facility Loans

Loans are available for up to 85 percent of the entire cost of storage

<u>facilities</u> for example, bins, drying and handling equipment, concrete, and
facilities;
wiring.

Condition of Grain

Check stored grain at regular <u>intervals</u> report to the ASCS office if this
intervals;
grain is decreasing in <u>value</u> e.g., becoming moldy, damp, or insect-infested.
value;

Lesson 32
Dash, Ellipsis Marks, Parentheses, Brackets

Pretest

Directions

1. The words in parentheses are your guide in determining the mark(s) of punctuation required by each sentence:

   (emphasis)—use dash   (omission)—use ellipsis marks
   (explanatory)—use parentheses   (insertion)—use brackets

2. If a sentence is labeled *omission* or *emphasis*, write the word preceding each punctuation mark and the punctuation mark(s) in the blank provided.
3. If the sentence requires a parenthesis or a bracket, write the last word in the parenthetical element and the punctuation mark(s) that precedes or follows it. (The left parenthesis and left bracket are inserted in the proper place.)

Example

(emphasis) The students performed especially well on the test Callae received 100 percent!   ___test—___

1. (explanatory) The two largest states (Alaska and Texas have enormous natural resources within their borders.   _____
2. (explanatory) A few federal offices in this building (nine retained a skeleton staff over the holiday.   _____
3. (explanatory) The Southeastern regional office (located in Charleston has a new manager.   _____
4. (explanatory) The Clayburn Company (the president is Gene Rich made the *Fortune 500* list this year.   _____
5. (emphasis) Only one investment can provide you and your family with future security insurance.   _____
6. (explanatory) Charles Harrison (1900-1976 established this company when he was only twenty-one.   _____
7. (omission) In his speech to reporters, the president of Heritage Inns made this comment: "The eighty-seventh Heritage Inn . . . in Mexico City this winter." _____
8. (explanatory) This city is one of the few in the country encircled by a beltway (see map, Appendix B.   _____
9. (explanatory) The graphic aid illustrating the theory of exploitation (p. 72 is incorrect.   _____
10. (insertion) Ms. Santayana wrote, "The Apex Motel can accomodate [sic at least 500 people in each of its three meeting rooms."   _____

11. (explanatory) Simon submitted his report on Monday (September 10 however, it did not include an appendix. _____

12. (explanatory) If you work late (after 4:30 P.M. you are required to sign out with the security guard. _____

13. (emphasis) Cats, dogs, horses, and cattle these animals are treated at the veterinary hospital. _____

14. (explanatory) Some politicians appear to lack an important quality (perhaps the most important quality an individual can possess honesty! _____

15. (explanatory) The inspection team visited the plant in Bogota (they had previously been to Santiago and Buenos Aires and they were pleased with the progress made by the management in Bogota. _____

16. (explanatory) Bob made his itinerary for the trip (does it include Juneau _____

17. (emphasis) If you are selected for the fall training program and I believe that you will be the company will send you to the home office. _____

18. (explanatory) Have you seen our latest D&B report (we received it a week ago _____

19. (explanatory) Our contractual obligation was completed a month ago (were you aware of that _____

20. (explanatory) The torrential rains destroyed the crops in the Southwest. (The rains occurred at the beginning of August The President may declare this section a disaster area. _____

Lesson 32
Dash, Ellipsis Marks, Parentheses, Brackets

Some marks of punctuation—the dash, ellipses, parentheses, and brackets—are used less frequently in business writing than are the marks previously studied. Each of these marks has a specific function that is recognized by experienced writers and readers.

Frame 1   The Dash as an Alternative Mark

The *dash* may be used to set off important or unimportant information. It is an emphatic, but informal, mark of punctuation; therefore, it should be used in moderation; otherwise, the information set off loses its impact. The dash consists of two hyphens typed without a space preceding, between, or following. Its primary usages are as an alternative mark of punctuation, and in miscellaneous positions. The punctuation mark used with an opening and closing dash must be properly placed to provide continuity in a sentence.

The type of business correspondence in which the dash is most frequently used is direct mail letters. Here the dash serves to call attention to selling points and other words, phrases, or clauses that tend to be persuasive in nature. Because direct mail letters are usually somewhat unorthodox in structure, the punctuation may also be slightly different in presentation; for example, in such a letter the dash may be shown with a space before and after. In this lesson, however, conventional spacing is used with the dash.

Explanation

The dash may be used as an alternative punctuation mark to a comma, semicolon, and parentheses.

Example

1. Use a dash in place of a comma to:
   a. Set off an element that already contains commas.

      Each of the six largest cities in the survey—New York, Philadelphia, Houston, Los Angeles, Detroit, and Chicago—employs over 450,000 workers in administrative, uniformed, and institutional services.

   b. Give more emphasis to the second independent clause in a compound sentence.

      The students performed especially well on the test—Callae received 100 percent!

2. Use a dash in place of a semicolon to achieve a more emphatic but less formal break between the two closely related independent clauses.

      She always gets committee assignments that are interesting—this is one of them.

3. Use a dash in place of a colon to achieve a more emphatic but less formal break before explanatory words, phrases, or clauses.

      He has one weakness—procrastination.

      The study group meets three times a week—Monday at 7:30, Tuesday at 8:15, and Thursday at 6:30.

4. Use dashes in place of parentheses if the parenthetical element requires emphasis rather than deemphasis.

> Hall & Co.—the largest brokerage firm in the country—is handling the sale of this 500,000-acre ranch.

Exercise

If a sentence contains an emphatic element that can be set off by a dash(es) instead of the mark of punctuation shown, use the blank provided to write the word before the dash and the dash.

Example

One person Joey Clary won $10,000 in the Queen City Grocery Store's bingo lottery last week. (The name can be emphasized.)   person— Clary

1. These five people are eligible for promotion: Sandra King, Elroy Hawkins, Molly Murchison, Hank Allen, and George Alvarez.   _____
2. Only one car in the race attained 47 miles per gallon; that was the Dragon!   _____
3. Our four best cereal sellers, Crunchy Oats, Snappy Wheat, Rockin' Rye, and Buckin' Barley, grossed over $1 million last year.   _____
4. Every factor of management but one is available: money!   _____
5. We borrowed the capital ($2 million) from only one bank.   _____

ANSWERS TO FRAME 1
1. promotion—
2. gallon—
3. sellers—   Barley—
4. available—
5. capital—   million—

Frame 2   *The Dash: Miscellaneous Usages*

Explanation

A dash may be used to set off an afterthought, an abrupt break in thought, and summarizing words that follow a list.

Example

1. Use a dash to set off an afterthought.

> Fred spent some time in the service—the Navy, I believe.

2. Use a dash to set off an abrupt break in thought.

> This car will outperform any other—at a more economical cost to you, too!

3. Use a dash to set off words that summarize and follow a list.

> Lettuce, beans, carrots, and onions—these are cold-weather crops.

Exercise

1. Three of the following sentences require a dash to set off an afterthought, an abrupt break in thought, or summarizing words.
2. If the sentence requires a dash in lieu of the punctuation shown, or for emphasis, write the word preceding the dash and the dash.
3. If the sentence does not require a dash, write No in the blank provided.

Example

Lettuce, beans, carrots and onions are cold-weather crops.

    <u> No </u>

1. Lee bought his motorcycle at Grant's Cycle Shop.   <u>   </u>
2. Ivy, lilies, ferns, and violets: all these plants will be on sale by the Student Horticultural Association from April 1 to April 15.   <u>   </u>
3. Bill bought the Tretter property; he bought the Lesser farm too, I believe.   <u>   </u>
4. For less than $1, only 98 cents a day, you can insure the future for yourself and your family!   <u>   </u>
5. Chip Hermes coaches Little League Baseball.   <u>   </u>

ANSWERS TO FRAME 2
1. No   2. violets—   3. property—   4. $1—   day—   5. No

Frame 3   *Ellipsis Marks*

Explanation

The *ellipsis marks* consist of three spaced periods. These marks are used primarily to set off and call attention to a word, phrase, or clause in direct mail communications and to indicate omissions in quoted material.

Example

1. Use three spaced periods to emphasize or call attention to a word, phrase, or clause.

    > Mama Pasta's . . . located at 1112 Fifth Avenue . . . has been owned by the same family for 153 years!

    > By shopping at the Imperial Mall, you can take advantage of these conveniences:

    > . . . 450 parking spaces
    > . . . a free nursery for preschoolers
    > . . . 9 rest areas surrounded by exotic shrubbery
    > . . . a free shuttle service inside and outside the mall

2. Use three ellipsis marks to show an omission at the beginning of a quotation or within a quotation.

    > According to Mr. Stewart's article, ". . . outlay for microfilm equipment and supplies will almost double during the 1980s."

    > "The United States' outlay for microfilm . . . will almost double during the 1980s."

3. To show an omission at the end of a sentence, use the end-of-sentence period plus three spaced periods.

    > "The United States' outlay for microfilm equipment and supplies will almost double. . . ."

Note

No internal punctuation, with the exception of a quotation mark, is used at the point where the ellipsis marks begin.

Exercise

Complete each of the following sentences with the correct word.

1. An omission at the beginning or within a sentence containing quoted material is indicated by _____ spaced periods.
    (number)

2. An omission that occurs at the end of a sentence in quoted material is indicated by the appropriate end-of-sentence punctuation plus _____ spaced periods.
    (number)

3. Ellipsis marks are used in direct mail communications to call attention to or _____ a word, phrase, or clause.

4. _____ other punctuation with the exception of a quotation mark is used at the point where the ellipsis marks begin.

5. Write a sentence explaining how the ellipsis marks are presented in typewritten format when they represent an omission within a sentence.

    _____

    _____

ANSWERS TO FRAME 3

1. three   3. emphasize
2. three   4. No
5. The ellipsis marks consist of three periods with a space before the first period, between each period, and after the last period.

Frame 4   *Parentheses: Common Usages*

Parentheses are used to set off explanatory items (words, phrases, clauses, dates, directions, and enumerations). In many instances either a dash or a parenthesis may be used; however, dashes emphasize and parentheses deemphasize the material that is set off. The writer makes the distinction as to the importance of the material and the emphasis to be placed upon it.

If a parenthesis mark occurs with another punctuation mark, the writer must choose the appropriate mark or combination according to its position in the sentence.

Explanation

Parentheses are used to enclose explanatory material, dates, directions, and enumerations.

Example

1. Use parentheses to enclose an explanatory word, phrase, or clause.

    > A few employees (eleven) chose not to take the health insurance provided by the company.

    > Mrs. Lee Rigdon (née Gladys Parton of Los Angeles) took over the presidency of the company upon her husband's death.

    > Mr. Ashley (he is a partner in the firm of Ashley and Wyatt) believes that we have a good chance to win the suit.

2. Use parentheses in lieu of commas if the parenthetical element already contains commas and if a dash would emphasize the material more than is necessary.

> The water-damaged appliances in your kitchen (stove, dishwasher, and refrigerator) are insured under this policy and can be replaced immediately.

3. Use parentheses to set off dates that are used as reference points.

> Claude Monet (1840-1926) is well known for his paintings of water lilies near his home in France.

> Since the company received its charter to operate in this state (1957), it has been located at 1117 Spring Street.

4. Use parentheses to set off reference sources and directions, particularly in reports.

> Responses were received from 89 personnel directors (see Appendix A).

> Responses were received from 89 personnel directors. (See Appendix A.)

Note that the direction may be placed within or after the sentence to which it pertains.

> Staples' theory (pp. 125-131) will be included in the examination.

5. Use parentheses to enclose numbers or letters that identify listed items in a sentence.

> Despite her handicap, Ms. Abeyta has accomplished these goals: (1) increased the production of her team by 10 percent, (2) converted the team into a cohesive work group, and (3) been nominated as the Employee of the Month.

Note

If a paragraph is numbered, letters may be enclosed within parentheses to eliminate confusion among the identifying elements.

Exercise

In the blank provided, write the word preceding the opening parenthesis and the parenthesis; then write the word preceding the closing parenthesis and this parenthesis. Include any adjoining punctuation.

Example

A few employees eleven chose not to take the health insurance.　　employees (eleven)

1. Humphrey obtained the capital in this way: 1 by selling the Montana Ranch, 2 by selling his first mortgage on the Wyoming property, and 3 by borrowing $50,000 from the local bank. _____
2. The rate of return on this stock increased more rapidly during the last five years than did the rate of return on the other stock see Chart 2, p. 17. _____
3. He was apprehended July 31, 1979, at 3:30 P.M. when he arrived at the Seattle-Tacoma International Airport. _____
4. The clinic therapists counsel employees who show symptoms of stress anger, anxiety, alcoholism, and absenteeism that affect their work. _____
5. File the papers in the order in which they were originated the summons would appear on top in Division 2 of this court. _____

ANSWERS TO FRAME 4

1. way: (1)   Ranch, (2)   and (3)
2. stock (17).
3. apprehended (P.M.)
4. stress (absenteeism)
5. originated (top)

Frame 5   Parentheses: With Other Punctuation

Explanation

No mark of punctuation ever precedes a left (opening) parenthesis; however, the order of punctuation, if any, used with the right (closing) parenthesis has an influence on the meaning of the sentence.

Example

1. Parenthetical element within a sentence:
   a. Any *sentence* punctuation required in conjunction with the right parenthesis follows this parenthesis. The sentence could require a comma, semicolon, colon, or dash at this point.

      If you leave early (before 4:30 P.M.), obtain permission from your immediate supervisor.

      Riley was absent one day (Monday); however, he said that he was ill.

      We appear to lack a vital ingredient for expansion (perhaps the most important one): money!

      Harvey's request for a transfer was turned down by the vice president of finance (see the attached memo)—and he has worked here for 16 years.

   b. Do not use a period before the right parenthesis except for that following an abbreviation.

      The Shreveport plant (it has been operating at capacity) cannot accommodate any more orders this month.

      Bill Evans (he arrived at 3:30 A.M.) will meet with the analysts this afternoon. (period following abbreviation)

Note

The first word within the parenthetical element is not capitalized unless it is a proper noun or adjective.

   c. Use a question mark or exclamation point to punctuate the material within parentheses when appropriate only if the end-of-sentence punctuation is different.

      Harvey spoke at one seminar this year (was it February 1?), and the students enjoyed his presentation. (parenthetical punctuation and end-of-sentence punctuation are different)

      Will the office be open on Labor Day (and will it be open on the Friday before), or are we operating on a different schedule this year? (parenthetical punctuation and end-of-sentence punctuation are the same)

2. Parenthetical element at the end of a sentence:
   a. Place the end-of-sentence punctuation outside the right parenthesis.

   > He will arrive on September 3 (Tuesday).

   > Do you know Emory Borge (he spoke at the sales meeting in Boise)?

   b. Use a question mark or exclamation point before the right parenthesis when it applies only to the material within parentheses and the end-of-sentence punctuation is different.

   > I completed the report last month (haven't you seen it?).

   > Are you going to the meeting (did you attend the last one)?

3. Parenthetical element in a separate sentence: Observe these rules—
   a. Begin the parenthetical element with a capital letter.
   b. Place the end-of-sentence punctuation before the right parenthesis.
   c. Do not place any punctuation after the closing parenthesis.

   > The participants wrote scathing comments about Mr. Wed's presentation. (Why did they resent him so much?) We must be careful not to include him in future lecture series.

Exercise

The left punctuation mark is inserted within each of the following sentences. In the blank provided, write the last word in the parenthetical element, followed by any required punctuation. The word *emphasis* in sentence 7 indicates that you are to use a dash.

Example

Riley was absent one day (Monday however, he said that he was ill.   <u>Monday);</u>

1. Ms. Mandich was hired last year. (She formerly taught at OSU Her teaching assignments have been heavy, but her performance has been outstanding.   _____
2. I told Mr. Sema you would call him (did you   _____
3. Why didn't the president attend the banquet (or why didn't he send a representative or does he consider protocol important?   _____
4. The promissory note is due on October 13 (October 12 is a holiday   _____
5. The last feasibility study shows that we should microfilm invoices (how far back should we microfilm them and the previous study showed that filming invoices would require an extensive change in procedures.   _____
6. He has an outstanding personal quality (at least it is important in our business loyalty.   _____
7. (emphasis) Dr. Dell was sued for malpractice (I don't recall the circumstances and this is his second suit for the same violation.   _____
8. The night shift begins at 4:30 P.M. (6:30 on Saturdays and Sundays and it lasts until 12:30 A.M.   _____
9. Professor Ridge (he was formerly with NASA will teach the course on jet propulsion.   _____
10. Are you familiar with Parkinson's theory (work fills the time allotted to it   _____

ANSWERS TO FRAME 5

1.	OSU.)	5.	them?),	8.	Sundays),
2.	you?).	6.	business):	9.	NASA)
3.	representative),	7.	circumstances)—	10.	it)?
4.	holiday).				

Frame 6   Brackets

Explanation

Brackets are used to make an insertion in quoted material, to make a correction in quoted material, and to enclose material that is already enclosed within parentheses.

Example

1. Use brackets to make an insertion in quoted material.

    > Ms. Adler remarked, "Joe Smith made the lowest bid [$11,500] on the contract to remodel the lobby."

2. Use brackets to enclose sic, meaning that the quotation contains an error as did the original statement. The error may be in spelling, grammar, punctuation, or content.

    > T. C. Sony made this comment in his recent article: "Their [sic] cannot possibly be a company that doesn't plan to some extent how it will meet its payroll."

3. Use brackets to enclose material that is already enclosed within parentheses.

    > Four cities involved in the study (Denver, Des Moines, Portland [Maine], and Tulsa) have increased their tax base.

Exercise

Fill in the blanks in the following sentences with the correct answers.

1. Brackets, like parentheses, consist of _____ marks.

(number)
2. Brackets are used for the following purposes:

    a. _____

    b. _____

    c. _____

3. A punctuation mark used in conjunction with a closing bracket _____ it.

(precedes or follows)
4. The word sic enclosed within quoted material indicates that _____.

ANSWERS TO FRAME 6
1. two
2. a. to enclose sic in quoted material
   b. to enclose an insertion in quoted material
   c. to enclose an element that is already enclosed within parentheses
3. follows
4. The quotation is presented exactly as it was stated originally, even with the error in grammar, punctuation, spelling, or content.

Frame 7   Business Vocabulary: Analytical Report

Explanation

A business report presents facts; these facts may serve as information or may be the basis for making a decision. An analytical report is a formal communication in which the writer not only presents facts but also interprets them and draws conclusions. It may or may not include a recommendation. This type of report is usually assigned by a superior to a subordinate who has the research and writing ability necessary to present a useful report. An analytical report has certain necessary prefatory and supplementary pages.

Terms

Prefatory pages—those pages preceding the body of the report: title page, table of contents, list of illustrations, letter of transmittal, letter of acceptance, synopsis.

Supplementary pages—those pages following the body: appendix and bibliography (or sources consulted).

Synopsis—a condensation of the report. A paragraph is devoted to each division of the report as well as to the introduction, conclusions, and recommendations.

Appendix—a supplementary section containing graphic aids (charts, tables, illustrations, lists, or maps) that are used to support the information within the report.

Bibliography—the list of books, periodicals, and other reading materials that have been referenced in the report.

Sources consulted—the list of reading material and other sources (lectures, interviews, filmed material, television or radio comments) that have been referenced in the report.

Exercise

Complete each of the following sentences with the appropriate term from the preceding vocabulary list.

1. Prefatory pages _____ the body of the report.

2. Supplementary pages _____ the body of the report.

3. A synopsis is a _____ of the report, showing a paragraph for each division of the report body.

4. The supplementary section that contains supporting information such as graphic aids is called the _____.

5. The broader of two terms that show the sources which the writer has referenced in the report is _____.

ANSWERS TO FRAME 7
1. precede   3. condensation   5. sources consulted
2. follow   4. appendix

Frame 8   *Applying Your Knowledge*

Directions

Underscore each error or omission of punctuation in the following synopsis. Write the correction in the space below the error.

CASE

Following is a synopsis of an analytical report entitled "HOW A MICRO-FILM SYSTEM WOULD SAVE MONEY, INCREASE EFFICIENCY, AND SAVE TIME FOR THE DREW COMPANY. (10 errors)

SYNOPSIS

Based upon the report criteria (cost, efficiency, and convenience the Drew Company should install a microfiche system immediately. This recommendation is made by the Hegle Casualty Company after a thorough study of the current and proposed systems.

Initial costs (front-end costs, equipment cost, and supply costs total $39,720. Last year 26 percent, approximately $19,000, of the total proposal budget was spent on reproduction of proposals. (These proposals were on paper media Mr. O'Connor, head of our Proposal Reproduction Unit, said: "Converting to microfiche would involve. . . . and an equipment cost of approximately $20,000." Supplies constitute about 50 percent of office expenses (film, index files, and so on hence they are an important consideration in the initial cost. The remaining 50 percent of office expenses is absorbed by labor (training time costs and repair time costs Duplication, the contact printing of microfiche from a master fiche, is cheaper than paper-to-paper reproduction. Mailing is a distinct plus for a microfiche system; for the price of a single postage stamp, several hundred pages in microfiche form can be mailed first class!

Improving file integrity, eliminating filing errors, decreasing storage space, and insuring against disaster these advantages accrue to the user of a microfiche system. Moreover, these advantages reflect an important criterion (perhaps the most important one efficiency.

The speed of reproducing microfiche is obvious: 420 pages of a proposal on fiche can be duplicated in 48 minutes (an offset machine would require 148 minutes to duplicate the same number of pages

The conclusions favor microfiche as a medium on which to retain proposals for these reasons: (1) after the initial cost, a microfiche system is less costly than a paper system; (2) it provides greater efficiency than does a paper system; and (3) the reproduction capabilities are almost three times greater than those for a paper system.

"A fast, efficient sistem [sic is not a costly system," as Mr. Splitt, a systems analyst, wrote in his article.

ANSWERS TO FRAME 8
SYNOPSIS

Based upon the report criteria (cost, efficiency, and <u>convenience</u> the Drew Company
convenience),
should install a microfiche system immediately. This recommendation is made by the

Hegle Casualty Company after a thorough study of the current and proposed systems.

Initial costs (front-end costs, equipment cost, and supply <u>costs</u> total $39,720. Last
costs)

year 26 percent, approximately $19,000, of the total proposal budget was spent on

reproduction of proposals. (These proposals were on paper <u>media</u>
media.)

Mr. O'Connor, head of our Proposal Reproduction Unit, said: "Converting to

microfiche would <u>involve . . . .</u> and an equipment cost of approximately $20,000."
involve . . .

Supplies constitute about 50 percent of office expenses (film, index files, <u>and so on</u>
and so on);

hence they are an important consideration in the initial cost. The remaining 50

percent of office expenses is absorbed by labor (training time costs and repair time

<u>costs</u> Duplication, the contact printing of microfiche from a master fiche, is cheaper
costs).

than paper-to-paper reproduction. Mailing is a distinct plus for a microfiche system;

for the price of a single postage stamp, several hundred pages in microfiche form can

be mailed first class!

Improving file integrity, eliminating filing errors, decreasing storage space, and

insuring against <u>disaster</u> these advantages accrue to the user of a microfiche system.
disaster—

Moreover, these advantages reflect an important criterion (perhaps the most

important <u>one</u> efficiency.
one):

The speed of reproducing microfiche is obvious: 420 pages of a proposal on fiche

can be duplicated in 48 minutes (an offset machine would require 148 minutes to

duplicate the same number of <u>pages</u>
pages).

The conclusions favor microfiche as a medium on which to retain proposals for

these reasons: (1) after the initial cost, a microfiche system is less costly than a

paper system; (2) it provides greater efficiency than does a paper system; and (3) the

reproduction capabilities are almost three times greater than those for a paper system.

"A fast, efficient sistem [sic is not a costly system," as Mr. Splitt, a systems analyst,
[sic]

wrote in his article.

Lesson 33
Quotation Marks

Pretest

Punctuation

Directions

Insert the omitted punctuation in each of the following sentences that require punctuation and underscore your correction.

Example

Mr. James said, I agree with your evaluation
Mr. James said, <u>"</u>I agree with your evaluation.<u>"</u>

1. "Please send your response immediately the manager said in his memo.
2. "Where can I find a deposit slip the customer asked.
3. Mr. Flynn, the consultant, said that the new system will be operational on October 1
4. Ms. Kilpatrick remarked, "I paid my account last month then she flounced out of the Credit Department.
5. If we hold the meeting in Manchester the sales manager said we should get a good turnout
6. Printed below the transactions shown on the bank statement is this comment "If no difference is reported within 10 days, this account will be considered correct
7. Place these documents in the file marked "Vital Records the company charter, the Articles of Incorporation, and the designs for our primary products
8. Ms. Battalion said, When shall I report for work
9. The customer asked me where she could find out how to obtain a variance so that she could water her new lawn without respect to the restrictions
10. Did the clerk say, "I will report this incident to the floor manager
11. The president said, "No employee is permitted to enter this consumer motivation contest under any circumstances (Student: Consider the quoted material an exclamation after a statement.)
12. The Christian Science Monitor is an outstanding newspaper and covers news events without bias.
13. His article, How to Establish a Judicial Administration Curriculum appeared in The Law Digest, a professional periodical.
14. Melissa Conway, the congressman's wife, broadcasts a five-minute radio program, Melissa's Washington every day.
15. Brown's manuscript, The Escalating Cost of Oil, has been sent to several publishers.
16. He spelled the word receive incorrectly 16 times in 11 pages.
17. The professor asked, "Have you read Ray's article, Toward a Liberally Educated Executive
18. The word rigor mortis comes from the Latin and means "a stiffening of the muscles after death
19. The vice president for finance said, "Let's buy all the shares in the two electronics companies and go for broke
20. Mr. Benz wrote, "Please credit my account for the amount of the purchase

Lesson 33
Quotation Marks

Quotation marks are used to enclose the exact words of a speaker or writer, segments within a published source, and words to be emphasized.

Quotation marks, like parentheses and brackets, are used in pairs. Determining which words should be placed within quotation marks is a simple decision; the purpose of this lesson, therefore, is to illustrate the placement of the quotation marks in relation to other sentence punctuation.

Frame 1   Direct Quotation: Definition

Explanation

A *direct quotation* consists of the exact words of a speaker or writer. The sentence usually includes introductory descriptive material telling who made the remark. The first letter of the first word of a direct quotation is capitalized.

Example

1. Set off a direct quotation with quotation marks.

   > Mr. James said, "I disagree with you."
   > The introductory descriptive material is <u>Mr. James said</u>.
   > The quotation is set off by quotation marks.

2. Do not set off an indirect quotation.

   > <u>Mr. James said</u> <u>that he disagreed with you</u>.
   > (introductory) (not logical for a direct quotation)

Note

If you are in doubt about the words which you believe might be a direct quotation, repeat these words to yourself. If a person would not logically phrase a statement in that manner, you are not dealing with a direct quotation.

Exercise

Quotation marks have been omitted in this exercise.

Directions

In the blank to the right of each sentence, write D if the sentence contains a direct quotation and underscore the direct quotation. If the sentence does not contain a direct quotation, write No in the blank.

Example

Ms. Lucero said to me, <u>I shall recommend you for the supervisory position as soon as you complete your training period.</u>   ___D___

1. Mr. Dober, the manager, said in his recent memo, I shall expect all employees to attend the film shown at noon on March 26.   _____
2. Mr. Dober, the new manager, said in his recent memo that he expected all employees to attend the film shown at noon on March 26.   _____
3. The clerk asked how the paychecks were to be distributed.   _____
4. Many people said that they enjoyed the performance held from noon till nine in the bank lobby.   _____

5. We need the program immediately, wrote Efrim Garge, who is systems manager at the Gallop Company. _____

ANSWERS TO FRAME 1

1. <u>I shall expect all employees to attend the film shown at noon on March 26.</u>   D
2. No
3. No
4. No
5. <u>We need the program immediately</u>   D

Frame 2   Direct Quotation: With the Period and Comma

Explanation

A direct quotation may occur at the beginning, in the middle, or at the end of a sentence. Except under certain circumstances (discussed later), the introductory descriptive material is set off from the direct quotation by a comma. Certain marks of punctuation are placed inside the last quotation mark and others are placed outside. This and succeeding frames illustrate the placement of punctuation marks in relation to the last quotation mark.

Example

1. Place a period within the final quotation mark:

   > Mr. Hall remarked, "Rewrite the letter so that it gives the impression that we are making the refund gladly."

2. Place a comma within the final quotation mark.

   > "I collected the balance from Mr. Bane on October 20," the credit manager said.

3. If the direct quotation is interrupted by such expressions as *he said, she replied,* or other descriptive words, it is called a split quotation. Compare the lettered explanations with the example sentence that follows them.
   a. An opening quotation mark precedes the first word of the quote.
   b. A comma and closing quotation mark follow the first part of the quote.
   c. A comma follows the interrupting expression.
   d. A quotation mark precedes the remainder of the quote.
   e. A period and closing quotation mark follow the quote.

   > "If we can agree on a date," the sales manager wrote,
   > a.   b.   c.
   > "we will hold the meeting in Atlantic City."
   > d.   e.

Exercise

1. Insert punctuation marks in the following sentences.
2. If a word should be capitalized, underscore the first letter of the word.
3. If a sentence does not require punctuation, write No in the blank provided.

Example

In our telephone conversation of April 14, you replied I realize that garnishment proceedings will be instituted immediately.
In our telephone conversation of April 14, you replied, "I realize that garnishment proceedings will be instituted immediately."

1. You may take your vacation the manager's memo read if a skeleton force remains in the office during that time.
2. In our recent telephone conversation, you said that we should review our credit policy.
3. We shall make arrangements to send you a sample he said after we receive your reply on the enclosed card.
4. The instructor said please do not write example problems on the inside cover of your textbook.
5. I read in the contract that we had nine paid holidays.

ANSWERS TO FRAME 2
1. "You may take your vacation," the manager's memo read, "if a skeleton force remains in the office during that time."
2. No
3. "We shall make arrangements to send you a sample," he said, "after we receive your reply on the enclosed card."
4. The instructor said, "Please do not write example problems on the inside cover of your textbook."
5. No

Frame 3   Direct Quotation: With the Colon and Semicolon

Explanation

A semicolon and colon are placed outside the closing quotation mark.

Example

1. Place a semicolon outside the last quotation mark. Use a colon after a complete statement that introduces a quotation.

   > Page 2 of the contract read as follows: "In case of negligence, the party of the first part agrees to pay the party of the second part the sum of $4,500"; however, our oral agreement was on a $4,000 reparation settlement.

2. Use a colon after the introductory statement if the quotation that follows is long.

   > The Chamber of Commerce president said: "New industry will come to a city only if that city provides an adequate labor force. It must also have sufficient transportation facilities and establish an equitable tax base."

3. Place a colon outside a closing quotation mark.

   > File these items in the drawer marked "Territories": sale reports, accounting reports, and discrepancy reports.

Note

Isolated words may be emphasized by quotation marks.

Exercise

1. Insert any required punctuation marks in the appropriate places in each of the following sentences. Write No in the blank provided if none are required.
2. If a word should be capitalized, underscore the first letter of that word.

Example

Our Chairman of the Board of Directors made this statement we have established three branches, hired 150 more employees, and increased sales 10 percent.
Our Chairman of the Board of Directors made this statement: "We have established three branches, hired 150 more employees, and increased sales 10 percent."

1. Senator Iverson made this statement in the telecast the seven companies involved in the price fixing charge will be investigated by the Justice Department. _____

2. Page 7 of the booklet reads as follows select the gasoline tax rate that is applicable for your state however, two rates are shown for Colorado. _____

3. Place only these items in an envelope marked confidential application letter, résumé, and correspondence with the applicant. _____

4. Our chairman of the board said during the past year, our company has made excellent progress. We have established three branches, hired 150 more employees, and increased sales 10 percent. _____

5. Your secretary said that she wrote the letter last week however, it has not arrived. _____

ANSWERS TO FRAME 3

1. Senator Iverson made this statement in the telecast: "The seven companies involved in the price fixing charge will be investigated by the Justice Department."
2. Page 7 of the booklet reads as follows: "Select the gasoline tax rate that is applicable for your state"; however, two rates are shown for Colorado.
3. Place only these items in the envelope marked "Confidential": application letter, résumé, and correspondence with the applicant.
4. Our chairman of the board said: "During the past year, our company has made excellent progress. We have established three branches, hired 150 more employees, and increased sales 10 percent."
5. Your secretary said that she wrote the letter last week; however, it has not yet arrived.

Frame 4   Direct Quotation: With the Question Mark and Exclamation Point

Explanation

A question mark or exclamation point is placed inside the closing quotation mark when the quoted material calls for it. However, when either of these two marks applies to the sentence as a whole, it is placed outside the closing quotation mark. When either of two punctuation marks can be used at the end of a sentence, choose the stronger of the two: (in order) exclamation point, question mark, period.

Example

1. Place a question mark inside the closing quotation mark if it applies only to the quoted material.

    > Mrs. Jones said, "When will I receive my free copy of *Business Forecast*?" (question at the end of a statement)

    > "When is payday?" the new employee asked.

2. Place a question mark outside the closing quotation mark if it applies to the entire sentence. In this case the entire sentence is a direct question and requires an answer.

    > Did Mrs. Jones say in her letter, "I expect to receive my free copy of *Business Forecast* this month"? (statement at the end of a question)

3. Place an exclamation mark inside the closing quotation mark if it applies only to the quoted material.

Note

The writer makes the decision about the placement of the exclamation point depending upon the idea to be conveyed to the reader.

> She said, "The temperature in this room must be 95 degrees!" (exclamation at the end of a statement)

4. Place an exclamation point outside the closing quotation mark if it applies to the entire sentence.

> She sobbed, "I didn't get the promotion"!

Exercise

Insert the omitted punctuation in the following sentences. If a word should be capitalized, underscore the first letter. Sentences requiring an exclamation point are identified.

Example

(exclamation at the end of a statement) Harvey said, I resign.
Harvey said, "I resign!"

1. The memo from the home office included this question: what are you doing to improve the image of the Jax Company in the Dallas area
2. When will I be reimbursed the sales representative asked
3. (exclamation at the end of a statement) The transcriber said you made the error, and I corrected it
4. Did the customer write exactly these words: even following your manual, I am unable to operate this machine properly
5. The seminar participant asked why are classes held at night
6. Why did the teller say, the electronic deposit system isn't working
7. To whom shall I send the complimentary copy asked the clerk

ANSWERS TO FRAME 4
For your convenience in checking, the inserted punctuation is underscored.
1. The memo from the home office included this question: "What are you doing to improve the image of the Jax Company in the Dallas area?"
2. "When will I be reimbursed?" the sales representative asked.
3. The transcriber said, "You made the error, and I corrected it!"
4. Did the customer write exactly these words: "Even following your manual, I am unable to operate this machine properly"?
5. The seminar participant asked, "Why are classes held at night?"
6. Why did the teller say, "The electronic deposit system isn't working"?
7. "To whom shall I send the complimentary copy?" asked the clerk.

Frame 5   Titles: Quotation Marks and Underscore

Explanation

In business correspondence, the title of a complete published work is underscored. However, when the writer wants to emphasize the title (for example, in a direct mail letter), it may be presented in capital letters. The title of a part of a published work is enclosed in quotation marks.

Example

1. Underscore the title of complete published works: books, magazines, newspapers, brochures, manuals, pamphlets, and so on. Also underscore the titles of operas, musicals, movies, and plays.

Note

Underscore the spaces within a title, but do not underscore the punctuation at the end of a title unless it is part of the title itself.

> We plan to use <u>Machine Transcription for Modern Business</u> during the fall semester. (book)
>
> I read the stock quotations in <u>The Wall Street Journal</u>. (newspaper)
>
> <u>Business Week</u> is required reading in some business classes. (magazine)

2. Enclose in quotation marks the parts of complete published works: chapters, articles, and features. Also include in quotation marks lectures, sermons, songs, essays, short poems, and radio and television programs.

> We have a copy of your last article, "The Pros and Cons of High Financial Leverage."
>
> In addition to the assignment, please read Chapter VII, "Adjusting Entries."

3. Enclose within quotation marks the titles of these unpublished works: dissertations, manuscripts, and long reports.

> Perhaps you would be interested in our Research Department's report, "The Declining Economy."

Exercise

Insert the omitted punctuation: quotation marks, underscores, and related punctuation marks.

Example

The August issue of Personnel Journal contains an article that may be of interest to you.
The August issue of <u>Personnel Journal</u> contains an article that may be of interest to you.

1. The article about your new business venture was published in The Denver Post.
2. Chapter III, Business Reports explains and illustrates ten reports.
3. My article, Why Johnny Can't Write Either, was published in the May issue of the American Business Communication Association Bulletin.
4. Have you read Packard's book, The Image Makers
5. A copy of the manual, How to Care for Your Electric Typewriter should be kept at each work station.
6. He played in the movie, The Man in the Gray Flannel Suit
7. Who wrote the song, There's No Business Like Show Business
8. Professor Stevens and Professor Wood coauthored the book, Labor Relations.
9. Audrey Rich's dissertation, Women in the Labor Movement may be published in book form.
10. The program 60 Minutes received the highest rating of all shows televised during the preceding month.

ANSWERS TO FRAME 5
1. The Denver Post
2. "Business Reports,"
3. "Why Johnny Can't Write Either," American Business Communication Association Bulletin
4. The Image Makers?
5. How to Care for Your Electric Typewriter,
6. The Man in the Gray Flannel Suit.
7. "There's No Business Like Show Business"?
8. Labor Relations
9. "Women in the Labor Movement,"
10. "60 Minutes"

Frame 6   Special Usages of Quotation Marks

Explanation

Quotation marks may be used to enclose a word that the reader wishes to emphasize—unless that word is used as a word.

A pair of single quotation marks is used to enclose a quote within a quote.

Example

1. Enclose an emphasized word(s) in quotation marks (or underscore it if it is used as a word).

     The word check has many meanings. (used as a word)

     See the "Prof" about your assignment. (slang)

     The refrigerator crates were clearly stenciled "This side up." (introduced by a word that indicates the following words should be emphasized)

     The term Caveat Emptor is from Latin, and it means "Let the buyer beware." (Underscore a foreign word or phrase and enclose its definition in quotation marks.)

2. Use a pair of single quotation marks to set off a quote within a quote.

     He asked, "Have you read the article, 'The Young Entrepreneurs'?"

     Mrs. Songa said, "Please send the file marked 'Rejects.' "

Note

Like double quotation marks, the single quotation marks are placed OUTSIDE periods and commas and INSIDE semicolons and colons. Their relationship to question marks and exclamation points is dependent upon whether they belong to the material within the single quote or to that within the double quote.

Exercise

Insert the omitted punctuation marks in the appropriate places in the following sentences.

Example

The word check has many meanings.
The word check has many meanings.

1. A Marine is often referred to—in slang, of course—as a gyrene
2. The mailroom supervisor said, "Please mark this package 'Registered
3. The administrator said, "Please requisition these items from the catalog labeled 'Spring 4 boxes of bond paper, 11 reams of typing paper, and 15 boxes of paper clips.
4. Ms. Zentz asked, "Was the letter postmarked 'April 15
5. Why did Bernie say, "Your letter was returned, and it was marked 'Insufficient Postage
6. The word accommodate is frequently misspelled.
7. The word ergo is from Latin, and it means therefore.

ANSWERS TO FRAME 6

1. A Marine is often referred to—in slang, of course—as a <u>"gyrene."</u>
2. The mailroom supervisor said, "Please mark this package 'Registered<u>.'</u>"
3. The administrator said, "Please requisition these items from the catalog labeled 'Spring<u>':</u> 4 boxes of bond paper, 11 reams of typing paper, and 15 boxes of paper clips<u>."</u>
4. Ms. Zentz asked, "Was the letter postmarked 'April 15<u>'?"</u>
5. Why did Bernie say, "Your letter was returned, and it was marked 'Insufficient Postage' "?
6. The word <u>accommodate</u> is frequently misspelled.
7. The word <u>ergo</u> is from Latin, and it means <u>"therefore."</u>

Frame 7   Business Vocabulary: Employee Development

Explanation

The theory accepted by most enlightened managers is that the employee is in the organization not only to perform a job but also to be developed to his or her potential. This development takes place through many facets explained in the terms that follow.

Terms

Performance evaluation—an assessment (usually written) of an employee's performance in relation to a specific job description.

Evaluation interview—a discussion between the evaluated employee and the immediate supervisor concerning the employee's strengths and weaknesses.

Management by objective—a theory requiring that the company's goals and the employees' goals coincide to achieve the maximum production with the minimum cost.

Development programs—carefully designed programs for executives or for employees to improve a specific weakness that a category of employees may have.

Employee counseling—a fairly new development on the business scene. The organization provides psychiatrists, mental health experts, and others to counsel the employees who exhibit signs of stress (tension, anger, alcoholism, dependence upon drugs, for example), helping them to remain productive and satisfied with themselves and their jobs.

Exercise

Fill in each blank in the following sentences with the appropriate term from the preceding vocabulary list.

1. The theory that requires an organization's goals and the employee's goals to
   coincide and thus helps the organization to achieve maximum production with
   minimum cost is _____.

2. Programs that are designed to help a category of employees improve a weakness are _____ .

3. A superior's assessment of an employee's performance in relation to a specific job description is a _____ .

4. A discussion between a superior and an employee that follows an employee's evaluation is an _____ .

5. A professional who counsels employees that exhibit signs of stress is a new type of _____ .

ANSWERS TO FRAME 7

1. management by objective
2. development programs
3. performance evaluation
4. evaluation interview
5. employee counselor

Frame 8   Applying Your Knowledge

Directions

Insert and underscore the missing punctuation marks in the following evaluation report.

CASE

The department head of the Information Systems Department has concluded an evaluation interview and prepared this report to be placed in the employee's file. (10 errors)

EVALUATION REPORT

	Floy Perkins 507-68-7188
Date: September 15	Title: Programmer
Interview No. 3 (six-month basis)	Employment: 18 months

When Ms. Perkins entered the office, I greeted her and said, "Please sit down she immediately turned to the door and said, "I don't feel like having an interview today   At that point, I asked her to reconsider and mentioned that the sooner we had the interview, the sooner we would both understand what her problem is. She reluctantly sat down and said, "I've got so many problems that even my problems are having problems [Student: Treat the preceding material as an exclamation at the end of a sentence; place the punctuation after *problems.*] She continued, "I 'freaked out during the last six months due to a variety of pressures." Then she hesitantly told me about her problems. She said, "My programs have errors because Joe (the assistant supervisor) assigns me the longest, most difficult programs to write, and he expects me to complete them in a minimum amount of time. I've been working at least two hours overtime each night, and I don't get home until approximately 7:30 P.M.

Knowing that Ms. Perkins has a small child, I asked her about the care of the child during her absence. Benjamin, whom she calls "Butch is four years old; he stays at a nursery school until she arrives to pick him up. (Her

fluctuating schedule has made the child fearful that she won't come, particularly if she is later than usual.)

I said to Ms. I kins, "Why didn't you mention this to me before She
responded, "I've been trying so hard to get my job done that I didn't even
think about doing that; now my job is in jeopardy, and my child is ill." I said
to Ms. Perkins, "If I had your problems, I'd be upset too; now that you have
told me about them, I can help you, though." I made this commitment to
Ms. Perkins: "First, I'll discuss your problem with Dr. Accia, who is one of
our counselors. Second, I'll speak to Joe, and we will redefine your workload
(make it more equitable

She said with relief, "I'd appreciate that very much [Student: Consider
this entire sentence to be an exclamation; place the punctuation after *much*.]

I dictated a memo to Dr. Accia with this notation: "Please expedite this
case and include 'Butch' in the counseling

ANSWERS TO FRAME 8

When Ms. Perkins entered the office, I greeted her and said, "Please sit down"; she
immediately turned to the door and said, "I don't feel like having an interview today."

At that point, I asked her to reconsider and mentioned that the sooner we had the
interview, the sooner we would both understand what her problem is. She reluctantly sat
down and said, "I've got so many problems that even my problems are having problems!"
She continued, "I 'freaked out' during the last six months due to a variety of pressures."
Then she hesitantly told me about her problems. She said, "My programs have errors
because Joe (the assistant supervisor) assigns me the longest, most difficult programs to
write, and he expects me to complete them in a minimum amount of time. I've been
working at least two hours overtime each night, and I don't get home until approximately
7:30 P.M."

Knowing that Ms. Perkins has a small child, I asked her about the care of the child
during her absence. Benjamin, whom she calls "Butch," is four years old; he stays at a
nursery school until she arrives to pick him up. (Her fluctuating schedule has made the
child fearful that she won't come, particularly if she is later than usual.)

I said to Ms. Perkins, "Why didn't you mention this to me before?" She responded,
"I've been trying so hard to get my job done that I didn't even think about doing that;
now my job is in jeopardy, and my child is ill." I said to Ms. Perkins, "If I had your
problems, I'd be upset too; now that you have told me about them, I can help you,
though." I made this commitment to Ms. Perkins: "First, I'll discuss your problem with
Dr. Accia, who is one of our counselors. Second, I'll speak to Joe, and we will redefine
your workload (make it more equitable)."

She said with relief, "I'd appreciate that very much"!

I dictated a memo to Dr. Accia with this notation: "Please expedite this case and
include 'Butch' in the counseling."

Lesson 34
Frequently Misused Words

Pretest

The pretest which follows and posttest for this lesson are presented in the form of an Applying Your Knowledge section. The presentation of the tests in this form permits you to determine if certain words are part of your writing vocabulary. The following frequently misused words are covered in this lesson:

1. Foreword, forward
2. instants, instance
3. residents, residence
4. ordnance, ordinance
5. incident, incidence
6. present, presence
7. discreet, discrete
8. any way, anyway
9. every day, everyday
10. compliment, complement, complimentary
11. liable, libel
12. lesson, lessen
13. assistants, assistance
14. correspondents, correspondence
15. precedents, precedence

Directions

1. Draw a line through each misused word in the following letter.
2. Write the correct word in the space below the error.
3. After you have proofread the letter, write five sentences, each correctly using one of the words which you crossed out in the original letter.

CASE

As deputy city clerk, you have written this letter to a land developer. (5 errors)

Mr. Harley Blue, President
Blue Construction and Development Company
2734 Paquin Street, N.W.
Spokane, Washington 99203

Dear Mr. Blue:

In response to the request made in your April 1 letter, I have checked the zoning ordinance for the Brookville addition. The ordnance requires that the developer arrange for water and utility hook-ups no later than one month after the correspondence on the subject property has been approved by the city council. The enclosed map shows that the addition is zoned for multi-family dwellings and light commercial units.

Residence in the Balmoral addition (see green area) are petitioning the council to rezone the Brookville addition. These homeowners believe the value of their property will decrease substantially. I suggest that you not move forward with your plans without contacting the city's legal counsel.

Although the submitting of petitions to stop developments is an every day occurrence, in this instance the homeowners are prepared to wage a long, hard struggle to stop the development. The term "light commercial" is normally used to define retail stores, not light industry as you interpreted. No precedents exist to guide us in the interpretation of the ordinance.

If work is started on this property before an interpretation is made, you would be libel for damages. I realize that as an out-of-state developer you are concerned about the costs and restrictions of entering a distant market; therefore, I sincerely complement you for your patience and your effort to comply with the numerous requirements and restrictions.

Yours truly,

Peter Fuller
Deputy City Clerk

Sentences

1. _____
_____
2. _____
_____
3. _____
_____
4. _____
_____
5. _____
_____

Lesson 34
Frequently Misused Words

Explanation

Because the meanings of the three pairs of words in this frame are often misunderstood, the words are spelled incorrectly. These words are *assistant, assistance; correspondent, correspondence; precedent, precedence.*

Example

1. ASSISTANT/ASSISTANCE
   a. ASSISTANTS (n)—those who assist or help.

      My ASSISTANTS will prepare the schedule for the meeting.

   b. ASSISTANCE (n)—the act of assisting or the help provided.

      I shall need ASSISTANCE to complete this form.

2. CORRESPONDENTS/CORRESPONDENCE
   a. CORRESPONDENTS (n)—people who communicate with each other; employees who contribute news or comments to a publication.

      Three CORRESPONDENTS were hired to cover the Middle East.

   b. CORRESPONDENCE (n)—communication by letters.

      We have had a great deal of CORRESPONDENCE with this customer.

3. PRECEDENT/PRECEDENCE
   a. PRECEDENT (n)—something done or said at an earlier time that may serve as an example or rule for a similar situation.

      No PRECEDENT is available to serve as a guide in this case.

   b. PRECEDENCE (n)—priority of importance.

      The January regulation takes PRECEDENCE over the December regulation.

Exercise

Select the correct word from the parentheses in each sentence and write it in the blank provided.

1. President Roosevelt set a (precedent, precedence) by being elected to the presidency four times in succession.   _____
2. Many people provided (assistants, assistance) by offering their homes to the victims of the flood.   _____
3. Much of our (correspondents, correspondence) has included friendly remarks.   _____
4. Sections 17 and 21 of this law take (precedents, precedence) over the same clauses in the preceding law.   _____
5. The newspaper's (correspondents, correspondence) in Europe have been dispatched to the scene of the violence.   _____
6. The chief executive officer of a corporation has many (assistants, assistance) who function in a staff capacity.   _____

7. In the seating arrangement at the graduation ceremony, a person with the rank of professor takes (precedents, precedence) over one with the rank of assistant professor.

8. Because of the low prices and recent drought, farmers are seeking (assistants, assistance) from the federal government.

9. Much (correspondents, correspondence) can be handled by an administrative assistant who understands the organization and the executive's job.

10. The naming of a woman to the presidency of the bank established a (precedent, precedence) that will pave the way for other women to enter top management in large financial institutions.

ANSWERS TO FRAME 1

1. precedent	5. correspondents	8. assistance
2. assistance	6. assistants	9. correspondence
3. correspondence	7. precedence	10. precedent
4. precedence		

Frame 2

Explanation

The words explained and illustrated in this frame are *forward, Foreword; instants, instance; ordinance, ordnance;* and *residence, residents.*

Example

1. FORWARD/FOREWORD
   a. FORWARD (adj)—brash; precocious; moving ahead; advocating an advanced policy.

   > He is a FORWARD young man.

   b. FORWARD (adv)—toward what is ahead.

   > The driver inched slowly FORWARD toward the intersection.

   c. FORWARD (vt)—to transmit.

   > FORWARD my mail to my new address.

   d. FORWARD (n)—a player in a front offensive position.

   > Mike is a FORWARD on the basketball team.

   e. FOREWORD (n)—a front page in a book, usually the preface.

   > This book does not have a FOREWORD. (usually capitalized)

2. INSTANTS/INSTANCE
   a. INSTANT (adj)—immediate; direct; easy to use.

   > The cafeteria serves INSTANT coffee.

   b. INSTANTS (n)—brief spans of time.

   > In a few INSTANTS he found the right page.

   c. INSTANCE (n)—case; illustration; example; specimen; sample.

   > The rule does not apply in this INSTANCE.

3. ORDNANCE/ORDINANCE
   a. ORDINANCE (n)—a law, usually enacted by a municipality.

   The zoning ORDINANCE will become effective on September 1.

   b. ORDNANCE (n & adj)—arms, weapons, maintenance equipment, and combat vehicles, a unit of the army required to keep, maintain, and distribute ordnance.

   Captain Hawley is in charge of ORDNANCE.

4. RESIDENTS/RESIDENCE
   a. RESIDENTS (n)—people who live in a certain place.

   The RESIDENTS of this city are opposed to the watering restrictions.

   b. RESIDENCE (n)—a dwelling place (house; condominium; apartment).

   Is this your current RESIDENCE?

Exercise

Select the correct word from the parentheses in each of the following sentences and write it in the blank provided.

1. The insurance on your (residents, residence) has been increased to keep pace with the rapidly increasing inflation.
2. A city (ordnance, ordinance) requires that you have a window in your utility room.
3. Many (instants, instance) passed before the defendant spoke.
4. The (Foreword, forward) of the book is on page iii.
5. He maintains a (residents, residence) in Chicago.
6. The foreman moved the gear to the (forward, foreword) position and stopped the machines.
7. Clause 8a does not apply in the (instants, instance) where the owner's property is vacant for six months or longer.
8. Because of poor logistical planning, much of the (ordinance, ordnance) equipment arrived late during the maneuvers.
9. All (residents, residence) have been warned that the electricity will be cut off from 8:15 P.M. to 4:15 A.M.
10. A business elective, for (instants, instance), international marketing, is required by the accreditation committee.

ANSWERS TO FRAME 2

1.	residence	5.	residence	8.	ordnance
2.	ordinance	6.	forward	9.	residents
3.	instants	7.	instance	10.	instance
4.	Foreword				

Frame 3

Explanation

The following words are presented and illustrated in this frame: *incident, incidence; present, presence; discrete, discreet; anyway, any way; everyday, every day.*

Example

1. INCIDENT/INCIDENCE
   a. INCIDENT (n)—an action or occurrence that is a separate unit of experience.

      The border INCIDENT was not considered serious at the time.

   b. INCIDENCE (n)—occurrence; rate of occurrence or influence.

      The doctor noticed a high INCIDENCE of toxic material when he performed the autopsy.

2. PRESENT/PRESENCE
   a. PRESENT (n)—gift; present time.

      The employees collected sufficient money to purchase a PRESENT for Ms. Ano.

   b. PRESENT (vt)—to introduce; to bring before the public; to give; to show.

      The ballet company PRESENTED *Swan Lake* to a capacity audience.

   c. PRESENCE (n)—being present; having a stately bearing.

      The officer's sudden PRESENCE silenced the angry crowd.

3. DISCRETE/DISCREET
   a. DISCREET (adj)—in prudent silence; unpretentious; modest.

      Ms. Sanders reprimanded the clerk DISCREETLY.

   b. DISCRETE (adj)—a distinct, separate entity.

      Whole numbers are DISCRETE, but a number like 2.47 is not DISCRETE.

4. ANYWAY/ANY WAY
   a. ANYWAY (adv)—regardless; in any case.

      Even though you will not cooperate in this project, I plan to go ahead with it ANYWAY.

   b. ANY WAY (way—n)—by whatever means.

      I cannot reach the sales representative in ANY WAY.

5. EVERYDAY/EVERY DAY
   a. EVERYDAY (adj)—daily, routine.

      His not being present when needed is an EVERYDAY occurrence.

   b. EVERY DAY (day—n)—daily.

      I read my mail EVERY DAY.

Exercise

Select the correct word from the parentheses in each of the following sentences and write it in the blank provided.

1. Open the container in (anyway, any way) that you can.   _____
2. A decimal is not a (discrete, discreet) number.   _____
3. The previous schedule showed that the job order would enter production on August 2; the (present, presence) order shows that it will enter on September 2.   _____

4. The cheating (incidents, incidence) occurred after I had warned the class.
5. Despite the fact that employees were told they could not take a leave this month, John asked for one (anyway, any way).
6. The officer of the company (discretely, discreetly) transferred his stock to his wife.
7. The employees purchased many (presence, presents) for the orphanage.
8. Some doctors say that the high (incidents, incidence) of cholera in newborn babies is the result of the mothers' ingesting certain foods.
9. The fatigue uniform is worn only at prescribed times and for prescribed duties, not (everyday, every day).
10. The shooting (incidence, incidents) were not mentioned in the newspaper.

ANSWERS TO FRAME 3

1. any way
2. discrete
3. present
4. incidents
5. anyway
6. discreetly
7. presents
8. incidence
9. every day
10. incidents

Frame 4

Explanation

The words for consideration in this frame are *compliment, complement; liable, libel;* and *lesson, lessen.*

1. COMPLIMENT/COMPLEMENT/COMPLIMENTARY
   a. COMPLIMENT (n)—a flattering remark; respectful recognition.

      The vice president COMPLIMENTED me on the report I prepared.

   b. COMPLIMENTARY (adj)—given free as a courtesy.

      I received a COMPLIMENTARY copy of the book.

   c. COMPLEMENT (vt)—to complete, fill up, or make perfect.

      This handbag will COMPLEMENT your outfit.

   d. COMPLEMENT (n)—something that completes, fills up, or makes perfect; the whole force or personnel of a military unit.

      The squadron now has a full COMPLEMENT of personnel.

2. LIABLE/LIBEL
   a. LIABLE (adj)—obligated according to law; responsible.

      You will be LIABLE for the damage your heavy equipment operators caused to our landscaped areas.

   b. LIBEL (n)—a written or oral defamatory statement that conveys an unjust or unfavorable impression.

      The commentator was sued for LIBEL.

3. LESSON/LESSEN
   a. LESSON (n)—a reading or exercise to be studied by a pupil; something learned by study or experience.

      He learned a valuable LESSON by working his way up in this company.

b.   LESSEN (vt)—to reduce in size, number, or degree; to decrease.

The doctor suggested LESSENING the dosage of this medicine.

Exercise

Select the correct word from the parentheses in each of the following sentences and write it in the blank provided.

1.   When the rain (lessons, lessens), the crops can be planted.
2.   You are (liable, libel) to lose your insurance if you receive any more points.
3.   The president made many (complimentary, complementary) remarks about our department's reaching its goal.
4.   With ten additional airmen, the squadron will have a full (compliment, complement).
5.   A (lesson, lessen) learned through experience may be long remembered.
6.   The statement on the front page of this newspaper is sufficient reason for the company to institute a suit for (liable, libel).
7.   I have two (complementary, complimentary) tickets to the Rose Bowl game.
8.   Almost anyone can be (complimented, complemented) about something.
9.   When the flow of water through the soaker (lessons, lessens), move the soaker to other rose bushes in the area.
10.   The police officer stated that the person making a right turn from a left lane is (liable, libel) for the damages.

ANSWERS TO FRAME 4

1.   lessens
2.   liable
3.   complimentary
4.   complement
5.   lesson
6.   libel
7.   complimentary
8.   complimented
9.   lessens
10.   liable

Answers
to Pretests

Lesson 2

1. living (Frame 3)
2. management (Frame 3)
3. noticeable (Frame 4)
4. truly (Frame 5)
5. mileage (Frame 5)
6. training (Frame 6)
7. conferred (Frame 7)
8. reference (Frame 8)
9. benefited (Frame 7)
10. receipt (Frame 9)
11. relieve (Frame 9)
12. receive (Frame 9)
13. height (Frame 10)
14. admitted (Frame 7)
15. effectively (Frame 3)

Lesson 3

1. NOUN: The <u>United States</u> is called a <u>republic</u> because a <u>president</u> is elected to govern the <u>population</u>. (Frame 1)
2. NOUN: Because the <u>citizens</u> elect <u>people</u> to represent them, this <u>country</u> is also called a <u>democracy</u>. (Frame 1)
3. PRONOUN: A president is elected every four years; <u>he</u> may succeed <u>himself</u> in the presidency once. (Frame 2)
4. PRONOUN: Congressmen and senators represent <u>their</u> constituents and try to satisfy <u>them</u>. (Frame 2)
5. VERB: Many presidents <u>have been educated</u> as lawyers. (Frame 5)
6. VERB: A president <u>can veto</u> a piece of legislation, but it <u>may be passed</u> over his veto. (Frame 5)
7. ADJECTIVE: This <u>large industrial</u> nation has a <u>high unemployment</u> rate. (Frame 6)
8. ADJECTIVE: <u>Young</u> people, <u>eager</u> and well <u>trained</u>, want to work in <u>business</u> organizations or <u>government</u> agencies that pay <u>high</u> salaries. (Frame 6)
9. ADVERB: A <u>highly</u> paid person can <u>usually</u> speak and write <u>well</u>. (Frame 7)
10. ADVERB: Young people who are looking for jobs should <u>very carefully</u> select as a role model someone who represents what they want to become. (Frame 7)
11. PREPOSITION: <u>In</u> preparing <u>for</u> a career, one should read vocational material <u>in</u> the library and elsewhere. (Frame 8)
12. PREPOSITION: Guidance specialists say that a person who begins work today may change jobs seven times <u>during</u> his or her lifetime. (Frame 8)
13. CONJUNCTION: To find out more about the world in which you live, you should read books, newspapers, <u>and</u> professional journals. (Frame 9)
14. CONJUNCTION: Many young people waste their spare time; <u>therefore</u>, they have little knowledge of history <u>and</u> current events. (Frame 9)
15. INTERJECTION: <u>Cheers</u>! I will be graduated in three years. (Frame 10)

Lesson 4

1. True (Frame 1)
2. False (Frame 1)
3. False (Frame 2)
4. False (Frame 4)
5. False (Frame 3)
6. True (Frame 2)
7. False (Frame 6)
8. True (Frame 7)
9. True (Frame 7)
10. True (Frame 7)

Lesson 5

1. False (Frame 1)
2. False (Frame 3)
3. False (Frame 5)
4. False (Frame 6)
5. True (Frame 9)
6. True (Frame 10)
7. False (Frame 7)
8. False (Frame 8)
9. False (Frame 8)
10. False (Frame 8)

Lesson 6

Pretest Part I

1. semiannually or biannually (Frame 4)
2. amoral (Frame 7)
3. anthropology (Frame 7)
4. precedes (Frame 6)
5. pentagon (Frame 9)
6. collectible (Frames 3 and 5)
7. procrastinate (Frame 8)
8. translucent (Frame 6)
9. atypical, nontypical, untypical (Frames 7 and 1)
10. interoffice (Frame 8)

Lesson 7

Pretest Part I

1. b (Frame 3)
2. b (Frame 3)
3. b (Frame 4)
4. a (Frame 4)
5. b (Frame 4)
6. b (Frame 5)
7. b (Frame 4)
8. b (Frame 4)
9. b (Frame 2)
10. c (Frame 2)
11. b (Frame 2)
12. b (Frame 2)
13. c (Frame 2)
14. a (Frame 2)
15. b (Frame 2)
16. a (Frame 4)
17. b (Frame 4)
18. a (Frame 4)
19. a (Frame 4)
20. c (Frames 4 and 3)
21. a (Frame 5)
22. b (Frame 6)
23. a (Frame 5)
24. c (Frame 4)
25. a (Frames 3 and 4)

Pretest Part II

1. True (Frame 1)
2. True (Frame 1)
3. False (Frame 1)
4. True (Frame 2)
5. False (Frame 2)

Lesson 8

January 27, 19____

Dear Businessperson:

As publicity director of the student council at Delaware Junior College, I have been requested to solicit capital for the initiation and publication of a new college journal, Historic Delaware.

The principal purpose of this journal, a ~~biennial~~ biannual publication, to be distributed every fall and spring semester, is to make residents aware of the historical events that have occurred in this state. Our sponsor, Professor Bremer, especially wants us to show the ~~affect~~ effect that people who ~~immigraated~~ immigrated from other countries had on this state and how they influenced its course.

The stories will be written by students in English composition courses; these students have been given access to the archives at the capitol building in Wilmington. The campus Reproduction and Graphics Department has assented to devise the format of the magazine and provide ~~advise~~ advice in layout.

We don't plan to sell advertisements; instead, we hope that initial and succeeding contributions will provide the necessary funding. Each issue will be sold for an amount not in excess of a dollar, and this income will assist us to pay for postage and to

purchase paper, stationery, ~~envelops~~, and other supplies.
           envelopes

Would you like to read about historic Delaware? Your contribution to our capital is

welcomed and will provide you and other citizens with an awareness of our state's past.

Sincerely,

Joseph Azzolita
Publicity Director

Sentences

1. Voting in the local elections is each citizen's <u>biennial</u> duty.
2. The harsh winter weather may <u>affect</u> the price of gas and oil throughout the nation.
3. Dr. Li, who <u>immigrated</u> to the United States two months ago, is the first physician to reside in Georgetown since 1904.
4. Dean Carter will be happy to <u>advise</u> you on your future research plans.
5. Gloom <u>envelops</u> our office whenever someone mentions the possibility of wage-price controls.

Lesson 9

Pretest Part I

1. <u>restaurant</u>, <u>floor</u> (Frame 1)
2. <u>American Management Association</u>, <u>Friday</u>, <u>May</u> (Frame 1)
3. <u>harmony</u> (Frame 1)
4. <u>book</u>, <u>graphs</u>, <u>pictures</u>, <u>forms</u> (Frame 1)
5. <u>matter</u> (Frame 1)
6. <u>recommendation</u> (Frame 1)
7. <u>committee</u> (Frame 1)
8. <u>Writing</u> (Frame 1)

Pretest Part II

1. C (Frame 2)
2. <u>Father</u> (Frame 2)
3. <u>Statistics</u> (Frame 3)
4. C (Frame 3)
5. C (Frame 3)
6. <u>Department</u>, <u>Defense</u> (Frame 4)
7. C (Frame 4)
8. C (Frame 4)
9. <u>Professor</u> (Frame 4)
10. <u>Judge</u> (Frame 4)
11. C (Frame 4)
12. <u>Long's Peak Room</u>, <u>Morgan Student Center</u> (Frame 7)
13. <u>Flight No.</u> (Frame 7)
14. C (Frame 7)
15. C (Frame 5)
16. <u>The Economy Is Looking Up</u> (Frame 8)
17. <u>Stone Age</u> (Frame 6)

Lesson 10

1. branches (Frame 2)
2. secretaries (Frame 3)
3. Kelleys (Frame 3)
4. wives (Frame 4)
5. calves (Frame 4)
6. cellos (Frame 5)
7. cargos or cargoes (Frame 5)
8. Phonetics (Frame 6)
9. printouts (Frame 7)
10. accounts receivable (Frame 7)
11. follow-ups (Frame 7)
12. attorneys-at-law (Frame 7)
13. 3 Rs (Frame 8)
14. AMAs (Frame 8)
15. ands (Frame 8)
16. depts. (Frame 8)
17. parentheses (Frame 10)
18. curricula or curriculums (Frame 10)
19. alumnae (Frame 10)
20. criteria (Frame 10)

Lesson 11

1. P (Frame 1)	11. mile's (Frame 2)
2. N (Frame 1)	12. C (Frame 3)
3. O (Frame 1)	13. nurses' (Frame 3)
4. O (Frame 1)	14. C (Frame 4)
5. O (Frame 1)	15. C (Frame 4)
6. N (Frame 1)	16. Pete's (Frame 2)
7. years' (Frame 3)	17. holders' (Frame 5)
8. secretaries' (Frame 3)	18. C (Frame 5)
9. Doss's (Frame 2)	19. CPAs' (Frame 6)
10. C (Frame 2)	20. Co.'s (Frame 6)

Lesson 12

1. Subject; N; I (Frame 1)
2. Subject; N; he (Frame 1)
3. Apposition with object of preposition us; O; me (Frames 2 & 6)
4. Object of preposition; O; him (Frames 2 & 6)
5. Ownership; P; their (Frame 3)
6. Ownership; P; its (Frame 5)
7. Ownership; P; his (calculator understood) (Frames 3 & 5)
8. Object of preposition; O; me (Frames 2 & 6)
9. Pronoun preceding gerund; P; your (Frame 3)
10. Subject; N; I (Frames 1 & 6)
11. Direct object of verb; O; me (Frames 2 & 6)
12. Subject; N; it's (Frame 5)
13. Ownership; P; hers (Frames 3 & 5)
14. Apposition with subject; N; I (Frames 1 & 6)
15. Apposition with object groups; O; them (Frame 2)
16. Ownership; P; their (Frame 3)
17. Subject; N; It's (Frame 5)
18. Object of preposition; O; us (Frames 2 & 6)
19. Subjective complement; N; I (Frames 1 & 6)
20. Object of preposition; O; her (Frame 2)

Lesson 13

Pretest Part I

1. *its* (3) (Frame 1)   3. *their* (3), *them* (3) (Frame 1)
2. *she* (3) (Frame 1)   4. *They* (3), *me* (1), *they* (3), *I* (1), *it* (3) (Frame 1)

Pretest Part II

5. Al and Tom disagreed with the recommendation, but Tom did not have an alternative suggestion. (Frame 1)

Pretest Part III

6. *Mr. Jones,* (Frame 3) his	9. *patient,* (Frame 3) his (or) her
7. *states,* (Frame 2) their	10. *building,* (Frame 3) it
8. *Mrs. Fenlon,* (Frame 3) her	

Pretest Part IV

11. his or her (Frame 3)	15. his or her (Frame 3)	18. his or her (Frame 3)
12. their (Frame 2)	16. their (Frame 2)	19. its (Frame 2)
13. they (Frame 2)	17. its (Frame 2)	20. his (Frame 2)
14. its (Frame 2)		

21. his or her (Frame 3)
22. Unlicensed real estate associates must submit their credentials to the district board before they can sell in this agency. (Frame 3)
23. Insurance agents are expected to sell their annual quota of policies before they can be named to the Executive Sales Club. (Frame 3)
24. its (Frame 2)
25. she, her (Frame 3)

Lesson 14

1. Who's (Frame 1)
2. who (Frame 2)
3. that (Frame 1)
4. whom (Frame 2)
5. whose (Frame 1)
6. whom (Frame 2)
7. Whoever (Frame 3)
8. who (Frame 2)
9. whom (Frame 2)
10. whomever (Frame 3)
11. whom (Frame 2)
12. These (Frame 4)
13. This (Frame 4)
14. This theory (Frame 4)
15. Any one (Frame 5)
16. Somebody's (Frame 5)
17. is (Frame 5)
18. has (Frame 5)
19. has (Frame 5)
20. whoever (Frame 3)

Lesson 15

PERFORMANCE EVALUATION

I recommend that Mary Cupolat, Secretary B, be given permanent employment with the John F. Folger Publishing Enterprises.

Mary's typing speed (80 wpm) exceeds that of my former secretary, and her ability to proofread is almost perfect. She has <u>all ready</u> [already] learned how to prepare the payroll for computer processing and has begun typing the new edition of the advertising personnel assignment sheet.

Because Mary <u>formally</u> [formerly] worked for another publishing company, at first she was <u>some time</u> [sometimes] too eager to tell us how she did a similar job there. However, she is rapidly learning and accepting our procedures. The department personnel are all together in <u>there</u> [their] desire to welcome Mary as a permanent employee. Her attitude, efficiency, and personality, in addition to her secretarial ability, indicate that she will have an important <u>roll</u> [role] in this department.

Sentences

1. The pages of the manuscript are <u>all ready</u> to be photocopied.
2. Although she had been performing such duties for months, Ms. Hopkins wasn't <u>formally</u> promoted to production manager until last week.
3. Jeff has been studying his calculus for <u>some time</u>; I hope he passes his final examination.
4. Mr. Larson left his briefcase over <u>there</u> by the coffeepot.
5. The chairman checked the <u>roll</u> before he called the meeting to order.

Lesson 16

1. *refrigerator,* is (Frame 1)
2. *Neither,* is (Frame 2)
3. *Some,* have (Frame 2)
4. *architecture,* is (Frame 1)
5. *price,* is (Frame 1)
6. *committee,* have (Frame 1)
7. *Most,* is (Frame 2)
8. *editor,* seems (Frame 1)
9. *class,* was (Frame 1)
10. *He,* doesn't (Frame 1)
11. *company,* has (Frame 1)
12. *furnace, gas heater* were (Frame 2)
13. *dealer, salesperson,* quotes (Frame 3)
14. *combination,* sells (Frame 1)
15. *supplies, equipment, shelving,* are (Frame 3)
16. *nursery, company,* has (Frame 3)
17. *George,* plans (Frame 1)
18. *agency,* complies (Frame 1)
19. *One,* boasts (Frame 2)
20. *chairman, parliamentarian,* consider (Frame 3)
21. *One,* has (Frame 2)
22. *Professor Tate, students,* see (Frame 3)
23. *foreman,* doesn't (Frame 1)
24. *this,* were (Frame 4)
25. *president, founder,* hopes (Frame 3)

Lesson 17

Pretest Part 1

1. Passive: Your order was shipped by the Dudley Company on June 1. (Frame 1)
2. Active: The Quality Control Department has inspected this merchandise. (Frame 1)

Pretest Part II

		Transitive	Intransitive
1.			X (Frame 2)
2.	store	X	(Frame 2)
3.			X (Frame 2)
4.			X (Frame 2)
5.	(passive)	X	(Frame 2)
6.	merchandise	X	(Frame 2)
7.	(passive)	X	(Frame 2)
8.	(passive)	X	(Frame 2)
9.			X (Frame 2)
10.	assistance	X	(Frame 2)
11.	store	X	(Frame 2)
12.	departments	X	(Frame 2)
13.			X (Frame 2)
14.			X (Frame 2)
15.	(passive)	X	(Frame 2)
16.	employees	X	(Frame 2)
17.	(passive)	X	(Frame 2)
18.	devices	X	(Frame 2)

Pretest Part III

1. teaches (Frame 4)
2. reported (Frame 3)
3. done (Frame 4)
4. cost (Frame 4)
5. plans (Frame 3)
6. ridden (Frame 4)
7. paid (Frame 4)
8. stricken (Frame 4)
9. hung (Frame 4)
10. been (Frame 4)

Lesson 18

Pretest Part I

1. insulted (Frame 2)
2. was evaluating (Frame 2)
3. does work (Frame 1)
4. will issue (Frame 3)
5. purchased (Frame 2)
6. will be entering (Frame 3)
7. discharged (Frame 2)
8. will test (Frame 3)
9. will be reproducing (Frame 3)
10. check (Frame 1)

Pretest Part II

1. had paid (Frame 6)
2. will have established (Frame 7)
3. has won (Frame 5)
4. had sent (Frame 6)
5. will have visited (Frame 7)

6. will have flown (Frame 7)
7. had been misappropriating (Frame 6)
8. has been representing (Frame 5)
9. will have analyzed (Frame 7)
10. had assigned (Frame 6)

Lesson 19

Pretest Part I

1. <u>Working in the excavated area;</u> S (Frame 2)
2. <u>embezzling money;</u> OP (Frame 2)
3. <u>teaching day school for children of working mothers;</u> A (Frame 2)
4. <u>swimming;</u> SC (Frame 1)
5. <u>watching the quotations appear on the screen;</u> OV (Frame 2)
6. <u>hauling household goods from coast to coast;</u> SC (Frame 2)
7. No (Frames 1 & 2)
8. <u>hiring clerical and professional personnel;</u> OP (Frame 2)
9. <u>Safeguarding the company's records;</u> S (Frame 2)
10. <u>rezoning this residential area;</u> OV (Frame 2)

Pretest Part II

1. <u>Attending school in Paris for a year;</u> Monte (Frames 3 & 4)
2. <u>having explained the tuition requirements to out-of-state students;</u> registrar (Frames 3 & 4)
3. <u>hunting for specific financial records;</u> accountant (Frames 3 & 4)
4. <u>having filmed the records;</u> technician (Frames 3 & 4)
5. <u>filmed;</u> records (Frames 3 & 4)
6. <u>having been warned about the faulty brake system;</u> driver (Frames 3 & 4)
7. <u>being unaware of the defendant's sudden movement;</u> judge (Frames 3 & 4)
8. <u>having been evicted from his apartment;</u> Paco (Frames 3 & 4)
9. No (Frames 3 & 4)
10. <u>Having lost the election;</u> senator (Frames 3 & 4)

Pretest Part III

1. <u>To be named to the post;</u> noun (subject) (Frame 6)
2. <u>To be accepted for admission;</u> adjective (modifies <u>you</u>) (Frame 6)
3. <u>to find out about the position;</u> adverb (modifies <u>wrote</u>) (Frame 6)
4. <u>to be located on this property;</u> adjective (modifies <u>building</u>) (Frame 6)
5. <u>to become a career diplomat;</u> noun (subjective complement) (Frame 6)
6. <u>To be hired by this company;</u> adjective (modifies <u>applicant</u>) (Frame 6)
7. <u>To have been named to the committee;</u> noun (subject) (Frame 6)
8. <u>to be sent to the California office;</u> noun (object of <u>wanted</u>) (Frame 6)
9. No (<u>to the staff</u> is a prepositional phrase) (Frame 5)
10. <u>to be represented on the community board;</u> adjective (modifies <u>subdivision</u>) (Frame 6)

Pretest Part IV

1. C (Frame 8)
2. To have rearranged the office properly, the office consultant should have placed the furniture in groupings to facilitate communication among the functions. (Frame 8)
3. C (Frame 8)
4. To enter the training program, the employee must have a Class IV or higher classification. (Frame 8)
5. Alexander, having been embarrassed by losing an important advertising account, quit his job. (Frame 8) (or place phrase before <u>Alexander</u>)

Lesson 20

Pretest Part I

Any three of the following:
1. discourteous   3. dishonest   5. inefficient (Frame 1)
2. disorganized   4. inattentive

Pretest Part II

1. This (Frame 2)   5. C (Frame 2)   8. C (Frame 2)
2. a (Frame 2)   6. An (Frame 2)   9. a (Frame 2)
3. a (Frame 2)   7. C (Frame 2)   10. C (Frame 2)
4. C (Frame 2)

Pretest Part III

1. a (Frame 4)   5. b (Frame 4)   8. a (Frame 4)
2. b (Frame 4)   6. a (Frame 4)   9. b (Frame 4)
3. a (Frame 4)   7. a (Frame 4)   10. a (Frame 4)
4. a (Frame 4)

Pretest Part IV

1. a (Frame 5)   5. a (Frame 5)   8. a (Frame 5)
2. b (Frame 5)   6. a (Frame 5)   9. a (Frame 5)
3. a (Frame 5)   7. a (Frame 5)   10. a (Frame 5)
4. a (Frame 5)

Pretest Part V

1. which I just graded   assignment (Frame 6)
2. whose car was stolen   employee (Frame 6)
3. who had the payment   anyone (Frame 6)
4. whom you recommended for a   clerk (Frame 6)
   promotion
5. whom I met at the meeting   professor (Frame 6)

Lesson 21

Pretest Part I

	Adverb	Modified Word	Part of Speech	
1.	early	will bloom	verb	(Frame 2)
	very	early	adverb	(Frame 2)
2.	quite	exhausting	adjective	(Frame 2)
3.	too	long	adjective	(Frame 2)
	entirely	too	adverb	(Frame 2)
4.	today	closed	verb	(Frame 2)
5.	competently	worked	verb	(Frame 2)
	swiftly	worked	verb	(Frame 2)

Pretest Part II

1. bad (Frame 3)   4. well (Frame 3)
2. cautiously (Frame 3) 5. disinterested (Frame 3)
3. well (Frame 3)

Pretest Part III

1. faster (Frame 4)
2. more quickly (Frame 4)
3. the least (Frame 4)
4. more easily (Frame 4)
5. more frequently (Frame 4)

Pretest Part IV

1. <u>cannot</u>, <u>hardly</u>   <u>cannot—can</u> (Frame 6)
2. <u>not</u>, <u>no</u>   <u>no—any</u> (Frame 6)
3. <u>not</u>, <u>neither/nor</u>   <u>neither/nor—either/or</u> (Frame 6)
4. <u>don't</u>, <u>nobody</u>   <u>nobody—anybody</u> (Frame 6)
5. <u>not</u>, <u>nonalcoholic</u>   C (Frame 6)

Pretest Part V

Phrase or Clause	Modified Word	Part of Speech	
1. P	increased	verb	(Frame 7)
2. C	late	adjective	(Frame 8)
3. C	will sell	verb	(Frame 8)
4. C	Read	verb	(Frame 8)
5. C	sign	verb	(Frame 8)

Lesson 22

Body of Letter

Dear Ms. Charlton:

Co-op Student—Joe Burns

Joe's efforts in the Cost Accounting Department are to be commended. He performed his assigned tasks ~~real~~ <u>very</u> well. As a messenger, he learned the route more quickly than did the other new messengers; in addition, he had a ~~more perfect~~ <u>nearly perfect</u> record for accurate deliveries. His pleasant attitude and cheerful manner made everyone's day very pleasant.

After completing his mail delivery, Joe worked in the department copy center. His attention to detail, ability to grasp the procedures quickly, and initiative in handling problems were commendable. Before Joe's arrival, the copy center had been noted for its chaotic operation. Joe ~~lay~~ <u>laid</u> all the reams of paper in labeled locations on the shelves and set the machines in different positions to improve the workflow. More employees are pleased with the center now because they can expect to pick up their reproduction orders on time.

In the afternoons Joe has helped my assistants check inventory cards and prepare the computer input. He worked faster than the others and made ~~less~~ <u>fewer</u> errors—only one per 500 cards compared! Even though Joe's efforts were outstanding, he could improve his performance in two ways.

1. He should be more modest about his accomplishments.
2. He might <u>of</u> made a better impression by not flirting with the women

have
   employees.

I have appreciated and benefited from Joe's contribution to this department and will

be pleased to participate in the program again next year.

Sentences

1. Although Ralph is an excellent computer programmer, his <u>real</u> talents lie in the fields of advertising and public relations.
2. Georgia treated herself to a gourmet dinner after she received a <u>perfect</u> score—800 correct answers to 800 questions—on her entrance exam.
3. Mr. Sienicki <u>lay</u> on the couch in the lounge after suffering a sudden dizzy spell.
4. Because of inflation, $100 buys <u>less</u> food today than it did one year ago.
5. Joe's incidents <u>of</u> flirting with the women employees made a negative impression on his supervisor.

Lesson 23

Pretest Part I

1. <u>in</u>, <u>drawer</u>　　C (Frame 1)
2. <u>On behalf of</u>, <u>club</u>　C (Frame 1)
3. <u>to</u>, <u>Ben</u>, <u>I</u>　　I—me (Frame 1)
4. <u>to</u>, <u>family</u>, <u>her</u>　C (Frame 1)
5. <u>by</u>, <u>Jim</u>, <u>she</u>　she—her (Frame 1)

Pretest Part II

1. Omit (Frame 2)
2. C (Frame 2)
3. C (Frame 2)
4. Omit (Frame 2)
5. Omit (Frame 2)

Pretest Part III

	Modified Word	Part of Speech
1.	error	noun (Frame 3)
2.	adequately	adverb (Frame 3)
3.	Anyone	pronoun (Frame 3)
4.	works	verb (Frame 3)
5.	slow	adjective (Frame 3)

Pretest Part IV

1. with (Frame 4)
2. with (Frame 4)
3. with (Frame 4)
4. with (Frame 4)
5. to (Frame 4)

Pretest Part V

1. among (Frame 5)
2. as (Frame 5)
3. in (Frame 5)
4. Besides (Frame 5)
5. as (Frame 5)

Lesson 24

Pretest Part I

1. <u>When</u>—SC (Frame 4)
2. <u>but</u>—CO (Frame 1)
3. <u>Not only/but also</u>—CR (Frame 3)
4. <u>consequently</u>—CA (Frame 2)
5. <u>Both/and</u>—CR (Frame 3)
6. No (Frame 1)
7. <u>either/or</u>—CR (Frame 3)
8. <u>however</u>—CA (Frame 2)
9. <u>if</u>—SC (Frame 4)
10. <u>for</u>—CO (Frame 1)

Pretest Part II

1.	b (Frame 2)	5.	b (Frame 3)	8.	a (Frame 3)
2.	a (Frame 2)	6.	b (Frame 3)	9.	b (Frame 3)
3.	b (Frame 2)	7.	b (Frame 3)	10.	b (Frame 3)
4.	b (Frame 2)				

Pretest Part III

1.	CC (Frame 8)	5.	CO (Frame 6)	8.	CX (Frame 7)
2.	S (Frame 5)	6.	CO (Frame 6)	9.	CC (Frame 8)
3.	S (Frame 5)	7.	CX (Frame 7)	10.	CO (Frame 6)
4.	CO (Frame 6)				

Lesson 25

Pretest Part I

1. Please return this contract in the enclosed envelope before September 20.
2. Having completed the report in the morning, John was free to attend the meeting in the afternoon.
3. The realtor sold a million dollars' worth of real estate this year; among the transactions was the sale of the Bascom ranch.
4. The retailer, having announced a sale of used stereos, anticipated that a mob would be waiting when the doors opened.

Pretest Part II

1. I believe that she formerly worked either as a teacher or as an editor.   <u> P </u>
2. I will write the report, and Carrie will proofread it.   <u> T </u>
3. Before using the calculator, you should test the battery.   <u> MM </u>
4. He wrote the policy, and a lawyer checked it.   <u> V </u>

Pretest Part III

1. a   2. b   3. b   4. a

Pretest Part IV

1.	the hour of	3.	the year of
2.	I wish to take this opportunity to say that	4.	due to the fact that. Use *because* instead.
		5.	Please be assured that

Pretest Part V

1. <u>which are outdated</u>—The county clerk's outdated records have been sent to the state archives.
2. <u>belonging to the Barret family</u>—The Barret family's house is in the condemned area.
3. <u>in classes in accounting</u>—Students enrolled in accounting classes are encouraged to attend the speech by Ms. Agra, a CPA.
4. <u>are easy to plant and</u>—The easy-to-plant bulbs do not need to be taken up before winter.

Lesson 26

1.	C (Frame 1)	14.	Third (Frame 8)	
2.	10 (Frame 1)	15.	39 (Frame 8)	
3.	ten (Frame 1)	16.	2 (Frame 9)	
4.	C (Frame 2)	17.	C (Frame 10)	
5.	15 10 (Frame 6)	18.	omit *dollar* (Frame 10)	
6.	2 (Frame 2)	19.	135 (Frame 10)	
7.	4 (Frame 3)	20.	$.07 (Frame 10)	
8.	fifteen (Frames 4 and 12)	21.	eighteen (Frame 12)	
9.	C (Frame 5)	22.	C (Frame 12)	
10.	Second (Frame 8)	23.	C (Frame 10, Frame 12)	
11.	C (Frame 6)	24.	C (Frame 1)	
12.	0.3 (Frame 6)	25.	C (Frame 2)	
13.	C (Frame 7)			

Lesson 27

1. . (Frame 1)
2. . (Frame 1)
3. C (Frame 4)
4. . (Frame 1)
5. C (Frame 2)
6. Sr. (Frame 2)
7. M.A. (Frame 2)
8. AMA (Frame 2)
9. Professor (Frame 2)
10. Inc. (Frame 2)
11. ! (Frame 5)
12. Thirty-four (Frame 6)
13. Three-fourths (Frame 6)
14. C (Frame 6)
15. selfish (Frame 6)
16. re-covered (Frame 6)
17. One's (Frame 7)
18. i's (Frame 7)
19. companies' (Frame 7)
20. PTAs' (Frame 7)

Lesson 28

Body of Letter

Alice Alder has been working under my supervision on the Green Lake ~~cite~~ for eight
                                                                    site
weeks. Except for a minor detail, her work has been excellent. She follows a crew

chief's orders precisely and learns procedures rapidly. Moreover, she has not been

requested to alter any carpentry work or ~~try and~~ correct a deviation because of
                                          try to
improper planning. In fact, Alice is especially adept at reading blueprints; she often

detects potential problems and informs her crew chief of their existence.

Alice is an ~~anxious~~, enthusiastic carpenter trainee. Completing the framing on the
             eager
houses at this site before the scheduled date is creditable to Alice because she worked

overtime on several occasions. In addition, her appreciation of the experience and her

enthusiasm for the work contribute to the ~~morals~~ of any crew to which she has been
                                           morale
assigned. Occasionally, Alice implies to her crew chief or me that someone is "goofing

off." These instances have caused some hard feelings between Alice and the regular

workers. I discussed this situation with her, and she now understands that she was

wrong.

I sincerely recommend that Alice be allowed to continue her on-the-job training

with us; the crew chiefs and I will continue to ~~learn~~ her the methods and techniques
                                                 teach
of good craftsmanship.

Sentences

1. When John said, "A little learning is a dangerous thing," he didn't realize that he was <u>citing</u> Alexander Pope.
2. Don't be discouraged if you <u>try and</u> then fail; few worthwhile goals can be attained easily.
3. Glancing at his pale, drawn face, I could see that Andy was <u>anxious</u> about his sister's health.
4. Many of us first learned <u>morals</u> from hearing children's stories like Aesop's <u>Fables</u>.
5. Because Bob never <u>learned</u> algebra, he failed his calculus exam last month.

Lesson 29

Pretest Part I

	Construction	Correction		Construction	Correction
1.	D	Disgusted, (Frame 4)	9.	F	No (Frame 2)
2.	F	No (Frame 4)	10.	D	loan, (Frame 5)
3.	A	Students, (Frame 1)	11.	C	etc., (Frame 3)
4.	B	affable, (Frame 2)	12.	E	calls, (Frame 6)
5.	F	No (Frame 4)	13.	D	apartment, (Frame 5)
6.	F	No (Frame 5)	14.	E	acceptable, (Frame 6)
7.	F	way, (Frame 5)	15.	D	No (Frame 5)
8.	C	No (Frame 3)			

Pretest Part II

1. C (Frame 2)
2. Sorting, indexing, and filing, correspondence is the job of Clerk A. (Frame 3)
   Use a comma to separate elements in a series, but do not separate the last element from the word which the series modifies.
3. C (Frame 4)
4. In the middle of the lobby, will be a giant gazebo containing cut flowers and seating capacity for ten. (Frame 5)
   Do not set off a long prepositional phrase if it is essential to the meaning of the sentence.
5. C (Frame 2)
6. C (Frame 5)
7. C (Frame 6)
8. Whichever paper is the best, will be sent to the state competition. (Frame 5)
   Do not separate the subject (Whichever paper is the best) from the verb (will be sent).
9. C (Frame 1)
10. Before the first session, of the semester, each student must have purchased the following items: three-ring binder, graph paper, calculator, etc. (Frame 3)
    Use a comma after consecutive prepositional phrases, not between them.

Lesson 30

	Correction	Construction
1.	C	NR (Frame 5)
2.	C	O (Frame 4)
3.	Friday,	O (Frame 6)
4.	building,	C (Frame 1)
5.	C	O (Frame 5)
6.	procedure, implement,	NR (Frame 5)
7.	P.M.,	O (Frame 6)
8.	C	O (Frame 1)
9.	month,	O (Frame 6)
10.	purchase,	O (Frame 6)
11.	Pennsylvania,	O (Frame 6)
12.	believe, hand,	P (Frame 2)
13.	mother, 82,	NR (Frame 5)
14.	C	O (Frame 5)
15.	Bonney, way,	P (Frame 2)
16.	steward, elected,	NR (Frame 5)
17.	C	O (Frame 6)
18.	July,	C (Frame 1)
19.	Inflation, say,	P (Frame 2)
20.	corporation, year,	NR (Frame 5)
21.	Symonds, branch,	NR (Frame 4)
22.	C	O (Frame 5)

23.	equipment, old,	NR (Frame 5)
24.	firm, Brown,	O (Frame 3)
25.	C	O (Frame 2)
26.	Southern, mine,	NR (Frame 4)
27.	C	O (Frame 5)
28.	computer,	C (Frame 1)
29.	percent, percent,	O (Frame 6)
30.	C	O (Frame 3)

Lesson 31

Pretest Part I

	Correction	Reason			Correction	Reason
1.	successful; moreover,	B, E		6.	note, however,	G
2.	percent;	C		7.	interested;	B
3.	books,	A		8.	Company,	A
4.	increased;	B		9.	Streets;	D
5.	analyst.	F		10.	No.	G

(In item 9, a semicolon would be used by the writer who believes the sentence would be confusing with only a comma. If you believe otherwise and use a comma in this position, consider your answer acceptable.)

Pretest Part II

1. Business; Agriculture; (Frame 2)
   Use semicolons to set off items in a series that contains commas.
2. association: (Frame 4)
   Use a colon after a complete statement and before a list.
3. letters; memos; reports, (Frame 2)
   Use semicolons to set off long dependent clauses that contain internal punctuation. Use a comma after the last introductory dependent clause.
4. promptly, diligently, (Frame 2)
5. athlete; example, (Frame 3)
   Set off a transitional expression that introduces a list, example, or illustration.
6. week: (Frame 5)
7. expenses; (Frame 3)
8. theory; namely, (Frame 3)
9. promoted: (Frame 4)
   Use a colon after a complete (or incomplete) lead-in statement preceding a tabulated list.
10. area: (Frame 5)
    Use a colon after an introductory clause that precedes a rule, policy, or directive.
11. requirements: (Frame 5)
12. Note: (Frame 6)
13. results; (Frame 1)
14. 3:1 (Frame 6)
15. grains; (Frame 3)

Lesson 32

1.	Texas) (Frame 4)	11.	10); (Frame 5)
2.	nine) (Frame 4)	12.	P.M.), (Frame 5)
3.	Charleston) (Frame 4)	13.	cattle— (Frame 1)
4.	Rich) (Frame 4)	14.	possess): (Frame 5)
5.	security— (Frame 1)	15.	Aires), (Frame 5)
6.	1976) (Frame 4)	16.	Juneau?). (Frame 5)
7.	Inn . . . (Frame 3)	17.	program— be— (Frame 1)
8.	B). (Frame 5)	18.	ago)? (Frame 5)
9.	72) (Frame 4)	19.	that?). (Frame 5)
10.	sic] (Frame 6)	20.	August.) (Frame 5)

Lesson 33

1. immediately,” (Frame 2)
2. slip?” (Frame 4)
3. 1. (Frame 1)
4. month”; (Frame 3)
5. “If Manchester,” said, “we   turnout.” (Frame 2)
6. comment: correct.” (Frame 3)
7. Records”:   products. (Frame 3)
8. “When   work?” (Frame 4)
9. restrictions. (Frame 1)
10. manager”? (Frame 4)
11. circumstances!” (Frame 4)
12. The Christian Science Monitor (Frame 5)
13. “How to Establish a Judicial Administration Curriculum,” (Frame 5) The Law Digest (Frame 5)
14. “Melissa’s Washington,” (Frame 5)
15. “The Escalating Cost of Oil,” (Frame 5)
16. receive (Frame 6)
17. ‘Toward a Liberally Educated Executive’?” (Frame 5)
18. rigor mortis death.” (Frame 6)
19. ‘go for broke.’ ” (Frame 6)
20. purchase.” (Frame 2)

Lesson 34

Mr. Harley Blue, President
Blue Construction and Development Company
2734 Paquin Street, N.W.
Spokane, Washington 99203

Dear Mr. Blue:

In response to the request made in your April 1 letter, I have checked the zoning

ordinance for the Brookville addition.

The ~~ordnance~~ requires that the developer arrange for water and utility hook-ups no
    ordinance
later than one month after the correspondence on the subject property has been

approved by the city council. The enclosed map shows that the addition is zoned for

multi-family dwellings and light commercial units.

~~Residence~~ in the Balmoral addition (see green area) are petitioning the council to
  Residents
rezone the Brookville addition. These homeowners believe the value of their property

will decrease substantially. I suggest that you not move forward with your plans

without contacting the city’s legal counsel.

Although the submitting of petitions to stop developments is an ~~every day~~ occurrence,
                                        everyday
in this instance the homeowners are prepared to wage a long, hard struggle to stop the

development. The term “light commercial” is normally used to define retail stores, not

light industry as you interpreted. No precedents exist to guide us in the interpretation

of the ordinance.

If work is started on this property before an interpretation is made, you would be

~~libel~~ for damages. I realize that as an out-of-state developer you are concerned
liable
about the costs and restrictions of entering a distant market; therefore, I sincerely

~~complement~~ you for your patience and your effort to comply with the numerous
 compliment
requirements and restrictions.

Yours truly,

Peter Fuller
Deputy City Clerk

Sentences

1. Jack served as an <u>ordnance</u> supply clerk in the Army.
2. Because of its warm, dry climate, many people select Arizona as their place of <u>residence</u>.
3. Mr. Jenkins eats Krispy Krackles for breakfast <u>every day</u>.
4. The film actor sued the newspaper for <u>libel</u> when it reported that he had undergone a face-lift three times.
5. A good interior decorator will advise you on which furniture will <u>complement</u> your new carpeting.

INDEX